American Voices

American Voices

CULTURE AND COMMUNITY

FIFTH EDITION

Dolores laGuardia
University of San Francisco

Hans P. Guth
Santa Clara University

Boston   Burr Ridge, IL   Dubuque, IA   Madison, WI   New York
San Francisco   St. Louis   Bangkok   Bogotá   Caracas   Kuala Lumpur
Lisbon   London   Madrid   Mexico City   Milan   Montreal   New Delhi
Santiago   Seoul   Singapore   Sydney   Taipei   Toronto

McGraw-Hill Higher Education 🕸

A Division of The **McGraw-Hill** Companies

Copyright © 2003, 2000, 1998, 1996, 1993

Library of Congress Cataloging-in-Publication Data
LaGuardia, Dolores.
    American voices : culture and community / Dolores laGuardia, Hans P.
Guth.—5th ed.
        p.   cm.
    Includes index.
    ISBN 0-07-255600-5
    1. Readers—United States. 2. Pluralism (Social sciences)—Problems,
exercises, etc. 3. Ethnology—United States—Problems, exercises, etc.
4. Ethnic groups—Problems, exercises, etc. 5. Culture—Problems,
exercises, etc. 6. English language—Rhetoric. 7. Critical thinking.
8. College readers. I. Guth, Hans Paul. II. Title.
PE1127.H5L25 2002
808′.0427—dc21   2002071808

Sponsoring Editor, Renée Deljon; Production Editor, Roger Geissler; Manuscript
Editor, Elizabeth Nickerson; Designer and Cover Designer, Sharon Spurlock; Art
Director, Jeanne Schreiber; Manufacturing Manager, Pam Augspurger. The text
was set in 11/12 Bembo by G & S Typesetters, Inc., and printed on 45# New Era
Matte by R R Donnelly.

Text credits continue at the back of the book on pages 765–771, which constitute an extension of the copyright page.

To our children

TO THE INSTRUCTOR

American Voices is a textbook for the courses in writing and critical thinking that are at the core of a college education. With this text, we aim at helping students to become more alert readers, more purposeful and effective writers, and more committed thinking members of the larger community. This is a book for today's diverse student population—students coming to our classrooms from diverse backgrounds and with varying levels of preparation and motivation. Throughout the text, we aim to help instructors turn reluctant readers into motivated, purposeful readers, introducing them to a range of informed opinion, expert information, careful argument, and authentic personal testimony.

- instructors prepare students to join the public dialogue on various issues, making their voices heard and holding their own in the marketplace of ideas.

- students see the power of writing to record, interpret, and change the social and cultural reality in which we live.

- We stress the continuity between the honest exploration of personal experience and the discussion of public issues that matter in people's lives.

- students become efficient and responsible users of the full range of research materials.

- Finally, throughout the text, we keep in mind the large numbers of writing students whose first language is not English.

PROVEN FEATURES

Exploring Today's Issues. Many readings in this book engage students in the exploration of issues that constitute the unfinished agenda of our society. These issues include the redefining of gender roles and the search for role models for both men and women; the unheard voices of those marginalized in our winner-takes-all society; the proliferation of the prison culture in the Land of the Free; the escalation of violence in our violence-prone country; the way the media shape and transform our perception of reality; safeguarding the endangered natural heritage; and the trauma of terrorism in our post–September 11th world.

Diversity and Community. This book tries to encourage students to share in the true multicultural diversity of the American experience. Many of the selections honor diversity while searching for common ground and constructive change. The range of authorship reflects the multifaceted richness of American culture, both ethnically and socially.

Writing Workshops. The writing workshops following each chapter offer supportive, nonformulaic guidance to student writers. The workshops are sequenced to provide the vital bridge from experience-based writing to public discourse. We help student writers move from writing from experience, through writing from their reading as well as oral sources, to structured papers employing major writing/thinking strategies. We stress the informal research that goes into all writing, preparing students to move from informal to formal research and the documented research-based paper. A rich selection of model student papers helps instructors encourage their student writers.

Forums. To help foster interaction and collaboration, each chapter includes a set of three to four selections that explore a range of perspectives on a topic related to the chapter's larger theme. These selections are grouped under the heading "Forum," and address issues such as freedom of religion, disparity of wealth, same-sex marriage, and Internet censorship.

Motivating Questions and Assignments. Headnotes accompanying selections go beyond routine biography to dramatize issues or highlight an author's experience and perspective. Thought Starters focus students' attention and prompt them to recall the experience and knowledge they bring to a selection. Responsive Reader questions direct students' attention to key points, walking student readers through a structured discussion or argument. Talking, Listening, Writing questions validate the range of reader responses, encouraging students to formulate their own personal reactions and to engage in dialogue with their classmates.

Emphasis on Electronic Communication and Resources. Increasingly, our work with students includes helping them build the electronic communication skills essential for success in today's world. The writing workshops in *American Voices* provide guidelines for navigating the Internet and evaluating and documenting online sources. Additionally, Find It on the Web activities (see below), appear after selected readings.

Flexibility. The organization of *American Voices* suggests a course outline that many instructors have found teachable, with an integration of thematic and rhetorical concerns. However, an alternative table of contents organized by rhetorical strategy helps instructors develop courses focused primarily on rhetorical topics. Chapters, reading selections, and writing workshops are self-contained and may be taught in the order that best suits the needs of individual instructors and different programs.

Substantial Instructor Resources. Please see *Teaching American Voices* under the heading "Additional Print and Electronic Resources" below.

NEW TO THE FIFTH EDITION

Nearly 50% New Readings. In addition to the new selections associated with the text's new theme and forum topic (see below), this edition of *American Voices* presents almost 50% new readings, appearing in chapters throughout the books.

New Theme and Forum. A new theme, *Learning: School and Life,* is explored in Chapter Two. A new Forum, *Terror Invades America,* appears in Chapter 12, *Tomorrows.*

Updated and Expanded Research Coverage. The writing workshops in chapters two, eleven, and twelve have been revised to reflect the ongoing changes in electronic research and documentation.

"Find it on the Web" activities. Concluding the set of post-selection apparatus for selected readings, these activities guide and encourage students in their use of Internet resources.

Chapter-opening Photos. Each chapter now opens with a provocative image related to the chapter's theme. Discussion questions and writing prompts for each photo appear in the instructor's manual.

Web site to accompany *American Voices*, Fifth Edition. Offering abundant links relevant to the authors and issues presented in the book, and organized to follow the book's order, the site provides online resources for student projects, including research papers. The Web site's URL is <www.mhhe.com/laguardia>.

ADDITIONAL PRINT AND ELECTRONIC RESOURCES

Teaching American Voices. This substantial instructor's resource manual is available both in print and online. *Teaching American Voices* provides questions and writing prompts for each chapter-opening photo, overviews of each reading along with helpful teaching notes, and sample answers to the questions asked in the text. The manual also supplies background for the public dialogue surrounding current issues addressed in the book, including historical perspective on key issues in the nation's past.

Teaching Composition Faculty Listserv at <www.mhhe.com/ tcomp>. Moderated by Chris Anson at the University of North Carolina–Raleigh and offered by McGraw-Hill as a service to the composition community, this listserv brings together senior members of the college composition community with newer members—junior faculty, adjuncts, and teaching assistants—in an online newsletter and accompanying discussion group to address issues of pedagogy, both in theory and in practice.

PageOut. McGraw-Hill's own PageOut service is available to help you get your course up and running online in a matter of hours—at no cost. Additional information about the service is available online at <http://www.pageout.net>.

AllWrite! Available online or on CD-ROM, *AllWrite* offers over 3,000 exercises for practice in basic grammar, usage, punctuation, spelling, and techniques for effective writing. The popular program is richly illustrated with graphics, animations, video, and Help screens.

ACKNOWLEDGEMENTS

This book owes much to the publishing professionals at the former Mayfield company and now at McGraw-Hill Higher Education. We owe a special debt to the many committed teachers who have shared with us their concerns and enthusiasms in professional meetings and workshops around the country. We have again taken to heart helpful detailed feedback from professional and dedicated reviewers: Elizabeth Flores, College of Lake County; Judy Glueckstein, University of Wisconsin–Greenbay; Tim Gustafson, University of Minnesota–Minneapolis; Kathleen Herndon, Weber State University; Peggy Jolly, University of Alabama at Birmingham; Scott Leonard, Youngstown State University; Carolyn Mitchell, Foothill College; Cindy Moore, St. Cloud State University; Janice Neuleib, Illinois State University; Erica Scott, Slippery Rock University; Nancy Taylor, California State University–Northridge. Above all, we continue to learn from our students. Often, struggling against odds, they maintain their faith in American education. Their candor, intelligence, and idealism are a marvelous antidote to cynicism and an inspiration for the uncharted future.

Dolores laGuardia
Hans P. Guth

TO THE STUDENT

When you take a course focused on language and written communication, what value will it have for you as a student? How will it make you a more confident and more effective reader and writer?

Language is the medium in which we think—it allows us to put our ideas and feeling into words. It is the medium we use to organize our thinking—to make sense of what we observe. It is the medium we use to communicate with others—sharing data, observations, and ideas. We use language to promote our private and public agendas.

Written language is more permanent and more carefully thought out than spoken language. If something is important enough, we put it in writing. For many, the computer has made writing easier and more natural—it has shortened the distance between the way we speak and the way we write. It has made writing more informal and spontaneous but also more widespread.

What is the common thread in the following examples of language in action? What do they show about the uses and the power of the written word?

- In a paper title "Looking for Boy," a fellow student writes about her brother, who was left behind in the Philippines when part of his family emigrated to the United States. Her brother never made his peace with his father even after he joined the others, and after bitter quarrels he left home and joined the army of the homeless. On Thanksgiving Day, his sister would make the rounds of places that fed the homeless, searching the grizzled faces, looking for her brother.

- An instructor who teaches résumé writing asks you to search the Internet for samples of résumés in your area of interest. For example, you may be searching for entries under key words like "accounting (or accountant) and résumé," "CPA and résumé," or "income tax and résumé." You select several hits and share them with classmates, who critique them for effectiveness.

- In a magazine article, a descendant of Thomas Jefferson argues with fellow members of the Monticello Society, which brings together the president's offspring for social functions. In the wake of DNA tests that show Jefferson to have fathered a child with one of his slaves, the author of the article urges the Monticello Society to welcome the Jeffersons from the other side of the racial divide.

- Countless newspaper and magazine articles and e-mail exchanges debate the pros and cons of antitrust proceedings against Microsoft which has been accused of undermining competitors through mergers and intimidation.

What is the shared element in these examples? Everywhere around us people are using language for a variety of purposes. We use language to make sense of the world around us. We use it to define our place in the world. We use it to address others, to turn to them for agreement and support. We try to make others see a different point of view or persuade them to do something.

This book is designed to give you many opportunities to read, think, and write. The authors reprinted in this book are writing about subjects that really matter to them and that concern all of us. This book gives you a chance to join in the dialogue, in the conversation. Here are some key questions writers raise in this book:

- How do we honor diversity while searching for community? What common future is emerging from the meeting of cultures in a multicultural society? How do Americans from different cultural backgrounds today define their identity and shape their own destiny?

- Was America ever a classless society? How fatalistic or how activist are we today about the invisible walls that divide people from different layers of society? What jobs and educational opportunities are open to Americans with different family backgrounds or social status? Will the widening gulf between the rich and the poor make us "two nations"?

- Is gender destiny? Or is it opportunity? How much is biology, and how much is training, education, or age-old custom? What barriers have women had to overcome, and which are still facing them? How is the self-image of young males today different from that of their fathers? How far has society moved toward accepting people with a different sexual orientation or an alternative lifestyle?

- Do we live in a racist society? What progress has the country made in the area of race relations? Are we moving towad a color-blind society, or will racial strife divide the nation into hostile camps?

Traditionally, Americans have prided themselves on being independent individuals and on making their own choices. We each have the right to be our "own person"—not just a cog in the machine or a number in the computer. We have the right to make our voices heard. We have the right to talk back to government officials, elders in the family, or peer groups at school or college. We have the right to weigh the words of teachers, preachers, advocates of causes, or whoever wants to tell us what we should think and do. Nevertheless, the choices we make are shaped by the culture in which we live. We have the option of conforming or not to the traditional lifestyles of our families—urban or rural, strict or permissive, politically liberal or conservative. We choose to adopt or reject our native or immigrant heritage, staying close to or distancing ourselves from a Southern or Puerto Rican or Irish or Italian past. We each in our own way come to terms with inherited religious faiths—Catholic, Muslim, Baptist, Mormon, Jewish, Buddhist, or other.

This book is a resource that will help you become a better informed and more effective reader and writer. Working with this book will give you a chance to study and reexamine your roots and your assumptions. It will allow you to explain to yourself and to others who you are and what kind of world you want to live in. It will help you make your voice heard when defending your interests or working for a good cause. It will help you learn how to get others to listen as you work for change or defend the status quo. Let this book help you build up your confidence and effectiveness as a reader and writer.

Dolores laGuardia
Hans P. Guth

CONTENTS

ALTERNATIVE RHETORICAL TABLE OF CONTENTS

CONTENTS IN BRIEF

OVERVIEW OF WRITING WORKSHOPS

ABOUT THE EDITORS

Dolores laGuardia teaches at University of San Francisco, where she developed a humanities sequence titled "American Voices: Ourselves and Each Other," with courses focused on African Americans, Asian Americans, Latinos, Native Americans, religious minorities, and alternative lifestyles. She served as the writing specialist for a large Federal grant designed to improve writing instruction at the community college level and does curriculum work for a number of Bay Area institutions. She has TESOL certification and has extensive experience working with students using English as a second language. She has conducted workshops on computer education for the Russian Ministry of Education. She is co-author with Hans Guth of *American Visions: Multicultural Literature for Writers* (1995) and of *Issues across the Curriculum* (1997). She has participated in a number of mentoring programs and is a diversity management consultant for Bay Area universities and senior communities.

Hans P. Guth (Santa Clara University) has worked with writing teachers in most of the fifty states. He has served on national committees and commissions, and he has spoken at many national and regional professional meetings on subjects ranging from redefining the canon to improved professional status for writing faculties. He is co-author with Gabriele Rico of *Discovering Literature* (Third Edition, Prentice Hall, 2003). He is the author or coauthor of numerous composition texts, with close to three million copies in print. He was co-director and program chair of the annual Young Rhetorician's Conference in Monterey from 1984 to 1994, and he has participated in institutes or has organized workshops at institutions including Stanford, Oxford, and Heidelberg Universities. He organized the annual Humor Night at the CCCC national convention from 1986 to 1998.

ORIENTATION
Reading, Writing, Thinking, Internet Searches

What is this book designed to do for you? What needs and expectations will you bring to your reading and writing?

- *This book should make you a better reader.* Is it true that a current generation grew up on sound bites, has a short attention span, and needs images rather than chunks of prose? To be successful in this society, you have to learn to pay close attention. You need to know how to pick out the key points in a presentation. You need to follow pages of closely printed instructions. In reading contracts, you need to notice important points in the fine print. In your writing, you need to draw on data from your reading. You need to know when to quote insiders and experts for support.

- *This book should make you a better writer.* How good are you at putting your ideas into words? How good are you at sizing up an audience? How good are you at laying out information so that your readers can find their way? How good are you at joining an ongoing discussion and making your voice heard? As you become a more effective and confident writer, you learn to draw on your own experience and observation when writing about current topics. You know where to turn for supporting evidence and first-hand testimony. Writing about trends in the job market, you know where to turn for data and for testimony of people who have undergone downsizing and restructuring. When arguments get heated, you become better at presenting an informed opinion that people of goodwill should be willing to consider.

- *This book should help you organize your thinking.* The computer has shortened the distance between how we think and how we write. Writing on the computer, you see your thinking take shape on the screen in front of you. How good are you at sizing up an issue, checking out relevant facts, and bringing together rough notes? How good are you at making sense of

them and pulling them into shape? How good are you at thinking critically—going beyond hearsay or "what everybody says," weighing alternative views?

■ *This book should help you make full use of the resources of the Internet.*
Today's writers and researchers have instant access to a vast range of background, informed opinion, authoritative data, and argument. They develop
techniques that help them navigate the Internet, familiarizing themselves
with search engines, databases, indexes and directories, and websites most
relevant to their field of interest. They develop ways of sifting through
and evaluating material from electronic sources, applying such criteria as
known authorship, authentic texts, and mature level of interest. They consider permanence—the probability that material will remain accessible for
a time or will be archived in the electronic archives of major publications.

THE HABIT OF CLOSE READING

Good readers take in what the writer is trying to say. They are not
satisfied with the "general idea." They look early for a hint or a preview of
the writer's purpose. What is the agenda here? They look for the writer's
main points and follow the train of thought. Where are we headed? They
check out how the writer supports key points—they weigh supporting evidence or expert testimony. They pay attention to important details,
significant ifs and buts.

A Reader's Checklist: Making the Most of Your Reading

What do experienced readers look for when they read? How do they
make the most of their reading? The minds of experienced readers are pro-
grammed to take in answers to questions like the following:

✓ **How or where does the introduction raise the issue?** How does
the writer bring the subject into focus? How does the writer get the
reader's attention, create reader expectations, stir up or defuse controversy? Is there any tie-in with current media coverage or special relevance to current issues?

✓ **Do title and introduction suggest a prevailing attitude or perspective?** How or where does the author's agenda begin to come clear?
What preview is there or early hint of overall point or points? Is there a
strong thesis or thesis statement, or does a key question remain open?

✓ **Where does the organizing strategy become clear?** Is there a clear
overall plan? Are there clear stages in an explanation or steps in an argu-

ment? Is there an itinerary that the reader can follow? Does the reader get a sense of direction?

✓ **Who is the intended audience?** What does the author expect of the reader—background, openness, shared values? Who would be the ideal reader? (Are you?) Who would be the worst possible reader? What are possible sources of reader resistance or confusion?

✓ **Does the argument hinge on a key term?** How well does the author introduce and explain terms like *overachiever, new economy,* or *ergonomics?* Do terms like *issue fatigue* or *third wave feminism* become meaningful and instructive?

✓ **Does the author take the reader along from point to point?** Are turning points clearly marked? Are there helpful strong or subtle transitions? Is the reader going to know where the argument is headed?

✓ **What key examples stand out or are especially revealing?** What telling details or striking images is the reader likely to remember? Are there especially useful supporting examples or others that distract or might throw off the reader? Are there places where examples or stronger support might be needed? Does the writer use convincing evidence? Does the evidence seem slanted or representative?

✓ **What is the tone or level of formality?** Is the writing too flippant or disrespectful? Is anything offensive (who might be offended and why?)? Is the writing too impersonal or roundabout?

✓ **How does the author deal with differing opinions?** Does the author play down or play up controversial issues? Does the author recognize disagreement? Does the writer anticipate and take on or brush off or ignore possible objections? Is the author condescending or too aggressive or too bland?

✓ **What does the conclusion add?** Does it include a key example saved for the last or a strong clincher quotation? Is there any branching out to put the essay in a larger context? Does the writer circle back to an initial question or image? Does the writer provide any concrete, helpful suggestions for action or exploration?

✓ **Does the writing invite a personal response on your part?** Do you agree or disagree with key points? Do you agree or disagree with fellow students when discussing the selection? Would you want to write a letter or an e-mail to the author (especially when the author gives an e-mail address)? Would you want to write a letter to the editor of a newspaper or journal on the subject? Would you want to raise the issue in a chat room or other Internet forum?

Good readers make a receptive audience—they take in what an author has to say. They try to see what need or commitment made the writer write. At the same time, good readers make what they read their own. They interact with what they read. They do not accept everything the writer says at face value. As you read, there should be questions like the following in your mind:

- Am I learning something here? What is new here, and what is familiar?

- What assumptions do I bring to this topic, and which seem to be shared by the writer?

- How does my own experience compare with that of the author? What do I know that perhaps the writer did not know? How does this relate to my previous reading and viewing?

- How much of this article is fact or hard data, and how much is one person's opinion? When the author cites authorities and insiders, do I accept them as authoritative sources?

- Where do *I* stand on this issue? What would I say if I were asked to testify on this topic?

How well do you read? Use the following classic essay by a widely admired star columnist for the *Boston Globe* to test your capacity for close reading. The questions that precede the text ask you to pinpoint the ideas and the features that give the essay shape and direction. How well do you follow the author's trend of thought? How quick are you to take in key points and key examples? Keep questions like the following in mind as you work your way through the essay:

- What does the *title* make you expect?

- What is the common pattern in the examples Goodman uses for her *introduction?* What word provides the common thread? (What meanings or associations does it have for you?)

- How does the introduction lead up to the central idea, or *thesis?* How does the thesis serve as a preview of the basic contrast that shapes much of the essay?

- What kind of *support* does Goodman offer to clarify and develop the basic contrast? How does she use material from personal experience or observation? How does she go beyond it?

- Where does Goodman offer a *concession*—anticipating possible objections, admitting that there are exceptions to her claims?

- What does the *conclusion* add to the essay? Does it merely summarize, or does it go beyond what the author has already said? (How does the last sentence circle back to the title of the essay?)

- Can you relate Goodman's points in any way to your personal experience or observation? Can you make a *personal connection?*
- Do you agree with the author wholeheartedly, or do you want to take issue with any of her points? What would you say if you were asked to respond to her or talk back?

WE ARE WHAT WE DO

Ellen Goodman

I have a friend who is a member of the medical community. It does   *1* not say that, of course, on the stationery that bears her home address. This membership comes from her hospital work. I have another friend who is a member of the computer community. This is a fairly new subdivision of our economy, and yet he finds his sense of place in it. Other friends and acquaintances of mine are members of the academic community, or the business community, or the journalistic community. Though you cannot find these on any map, we know where we belong.

None of us, mind you, was born into these communities. Nor did we move into them, U-Hauling our possessions along with us. None has papers to prove we are card-carrying members of one such group or another. Yet it seems that more and more of us are identified by work these days, rather than by street.

In the past, most Americans lived in neighborhoods. We were members of precincts or parishes or school districts. My dictionary still defines community first of all in geographic terms, as "a body of people who live in one place." But today fewer of us do our living in that one place; more of us just use it for sleeping. Now we call our towns "bedroom suburbs," and many of us, without small children as icebreakers, would have trouble naming all the people on our street.

It's not that we are more isolated today. It's that many of us have transferred a chunk of our friendships, a major portion of our every day social lives, from home to office. As more of our neighbors work away from home, the work place becomes our neighborhood. . . . We may be strangers at the supermarket that replaced the corner grocer, but we are known at the coffee shop in the lobby. We share with each other a cast of characters from the boss in the corner office to the crazy lady in Shipping, to the lovers in Marketing.

It's not surprising that when researchers ask Americans what they like   *5* best about work, they say it is "the shmooze (chatter) factor." When they ask young mothers at home what they miss most about work, it is the people. Not all the neighborhoods are empty, nor is every work place a friendly playground. Most of us have had mixed experiences in these environments. Yet as one woman told me recently, she knows more about the people she passes on the way to her desk than on her way around the block. . . .

It's not unlike the experience of our immigrant grandparents. Many who came to this country still identified themselves as members of the Italian community, the Irish community, the Polish community. They sought out and assumed connections with people from the old country. Many of us have updated that experience. We have replaced ethnic identity with professional identity, the way we replaced neighborhoods with the work place.

I don't think that there is anything massively disruptive about this shifting sense of community. The continuing search for connection and shared enterprise is very human. But I do feel uncomfortable with our shifting identity. The balance has tipped and we seem increasingly dependent on work for our sense of self. If our offices are our new neighborhoods, if our professional titles are our new ethnic tags, then how do we separate ourselves from our jobs? Self-worth isn't just something to measure in the marketplace. But in these new communities, it becomes harder and harder to tell who we are without saying what we do.

BECOMING A BETTER WRITER

How do you produce a finished piece of writing? Writing a paper worth reading is a creative process. You go through phases: focusing on a topic, sizing up the audience, gathering material, shaping a rough draft, revising and rethinking, and final editing. These phases intermesh. For instance, you may readjust your working outline after you finish sorting out your material. Promising leads may not work out, and you may have to look for additional support. Nevertheless, successful writers do justice to the following dimensions of the writing process in one way or another:

TRIGGERING   What is your purpose? What triggers writing—what makes writers write? You may simply be responding to an assignment or to an immediate practical need. You write a résumé because you need a job. Your neighbors write to a planning commission to head off a decision that would adversely affect the neighborhood. Soon such practical writing shades over into other kinds. A woman complaining about job discrimination is likely to find herself writing about not just her own case but other cases as well. The writing moves from one personal story to an issue of concern to a larger audience.

Here are some of the motives that may trigger your writing:

■ *Writers write to explain.* After studying a troubling question, they share their answers with a larger audience. They write about the problems caused by spamming or electronic junk mail. They try to explain why youngsters join youth gangs in local schools. They try to explain why safeguarding the remaining habitats of the monarch butterfly will save the species from extinction. They turn to their readers to say: "Listen! It's important! I want to explain it to you."

■ *Writers write to set the record straight.* You may be reading about how young people suffer from "issue fatigue" or how their lack of "impulse control" explains school shootings. Or you may be reading about the antagonism young Americans allegedly feel about the other sex. You find yourself saying: "That's not the way it is! I know something about this from firsthand experience! Let me set you straight."

■ *Writers write to air a grievance.* They appeal to their readers' sense of fairness. They write to register their solidarity with people trying to make ends meet on a minimum wage or to keep their children healthy without health insurance. They write about being passed over for a job because of a minority background or because they are white males.

GATHERING To write a convincing paper, you have to immerse yourself in the subject. You may start by calling up from the memory bank of past experience the events, buzzwords, and arguments that cluster around your topic. You do a quick search on the Internet. You read up on the issue. You discuss it with friends and roommates, or you interview people who might have the inside story. Here are some **prewriting** techniques that can help you work up a rich fund of material for a paper:

■ **Brainstorming** roams freely over a topic. It dredges up any memories, images, events, or associations that might prove useful. Exploring the ideas related to the word *macho,* for instance, you jot down anything that the word brings to mind. The following brainstorming exercise has already brought together much promising material. What major points for a paper are beginning to come into focus?

BRAINSTORMING

The Weaknesses of Macho

Macho: Big, muscular, unfeeling, rough—harsh, moves to kill. (Sylvester Stallone: I hate what he promotes.) Negative impression. Hard craggy faces with mean eyes that bore holes in you.

Men who have to prove themselves through acts of violence. The man who is disconnected from his feelings, insensitive to women's needs—cannot express himself in a feeling manner.

The word seems to have negative connotations for me because I work part-time in a bar. I am forever seeing these perfectly tanned types who come on to a woman.

When I was a child, macho meant a strong male type who would take care of me—paternal, warmth in eyes. John Wayne: gruff, yet you feel secure knowing someone like this is around.

Crude, huge—the body, not the heart—tendency to violence always seems close to the surface. Looks are very important. Craggy face. Bloodshed excites them. Arnold Schwarzenegger muscles, gross.

Tend to dominate in relationships—desire for control. "Me Tarzan—you Jane."

• **Clustering** is an alternative method of letting your mind bring memories and associations to the surface. Instead of letting the items that come to mind march down the page, clustering makes them branch out from a central core. You pursue different chains of association started by a key word or stimulus word. A pattern already takes shape. You begin to see connections; different items begin to fall into place. Here is a cluster exploring the associations of the word *tradition*. It is followed by a write-up of the material generated by the cluster:

CLUSTERING

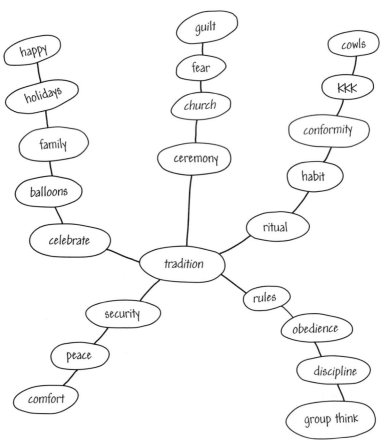

■ **Discovery frames** are sets of questions that can guide you in exploring a topic. Suppose you are working on an updated definition of *feminism*. Is there a "second wave" or a "third wave" of the women's movement? The following discovery frame provides a model that you may want to adapt for other current topics. What materials could you fill in under the tentative headings?

DISCOVERY FRAME

Feminism: The Second Wave

PERSONAL CONNECTION What role have feminist concerns played in your own experience? Where have you encountered ideas associated with the women's movement?

HISTORICAL BACKGROUND What do you know about the history of feminism? What have been outstanding leaders, role models, and key events? (What do you know about Sojourner Truth, Elizabeth Cady Stanton, or Margaret Mead?)

RELATED TERMS How is the word related to similar terms—*emancipation, women's liberation, the suffragist movement, the women's movement?*

MEDIA COVERAGE What is current media coverage of the movement? What images of women are projected in the news, in movies, in advertising? Do earlier stereotypes survive? Are there positive images of "strong women" or "independent women"?

SECOND THOUGHTS Has there been a backlash against the women's movement? What countertrends do books like Susan Faludi's *Backlash* document?

COMMON MEANING What seems to be the core meaning of *feminism*? What is the common thread in your various examples?

LOOKING AHEAD What does the future hold? Were many feminists well-educated middle-class women? Are more working-class women joining the movement?

SHAPING How do you turn a rich collection of material into a coherent paper? Successful writers again and again employ basic organizing strategies:

■ *Bring a central issue into focus.* A focused paper zeroes in on an issue or a limited area and does it justice. Early in a paper, raise the issue. What is this all about? Dramatize the issue with a key example or with a key quotation that brings the issue to life.

STARTER QUOTE: While teenage girls are enrolling in science classes in record numbers, a news study claims that "an alarming new gap" between the genders is taking shape in the computer classes that lead to the highest-paying jobs.

▪ *Push toward a thesis.* What is your paper as a whole going to say? What is it going to prove? After exploring the topic, reading and talking about the issue, you move toward a summing up. What is going to be your main point? What is going to be your **thesis**—your central idea, your unifying message? Remember that in the early stages of your paper your thesis will be a **trial thesis,** or a working thesis. You stake out a claim or make an assertion. You adjust it as necessary as you look at further examples, evidence, statistics, or expert testimony.

> TRIAL THESIS: Dropout rates as high as 42 percent show that affirmative action programs bringing minority students into the nation's colleges have not worked.

As you read more about the record of affirmative action for minority students, you may decide to make the dropout rate part of a larger picture:

> ADJUSTED THESIS: Although many affirmative action students dropped out, those who graduated often had successful professional careers and served as role models for other minority students.

In your finished paper, try summing up the central message of your paper in a sentence that will serve as your **thesis statement** early in your paper. Use the next few sentences to spell out the full meaning of what you claim or assert:

> THESIS: *Vocational education is forever trying to catch up with the real world.* The educational system is preparing people for jobs that have already been automated, taken by robots, or shipped overseas.

> THESIS: *American business is downsizing, causing a rapid decline in employee loyalty.* Executives improve a company's balance sheet by slashing payrolls, leaving insecure workers alienated from a company and a system that has no regard for their interests.

▪ *Work out a meaningful overall plan.* How are you going to lay out your material? If you are to take your readers with you, they need to feel that you have a planned itinerary. What is your program? In the early stage of a writing project, start jotting down a scratch outline, or **working outline.** A working outline helps you visualize your tentative plan—a plan that is subject to revision. The following is a student's working outline for a paper defending affirmative action programs that have been under attack or have been reversed in recent years:

WORKING OUTLINE

Righting Past Injustice

1 injustices of the past

movies like *Beloved* and *Amistad* dramatize the evils of slavery

anniversary revival of the *Roots* television series revisits the nation's contested history

2 continued de facto segregation

inner-city schools remain segregated after "white flight"

courts are retreating from busing and mandatory integration

cancellation of affirmative action programs has reduced minority enrollment at prestige universities

3 lack of minority role models

lack of minority teachers

scarcity of minority doctors and other professionals

slow progress toward minority representation on the police force

Your readers need to know where you are headed. Try to give them early hints of what lies ahead. Often an effective thesis statement already gives a preview of the overall plan:

THESIS: Race relations in this country have moved from legally sanctioned discrimination, through the legal outlawing of discrimination, to the struggle to change ingrained personal attitudes about race.

■ *Line up your supporting material.* Follow up or follow through. Remember that any point worth making is worth backing up. Support any points you make with key examples, authoritative data, or relevant evidence. Bring in material from interviews, quotable quotations. Bring in insider's insights or expert testimony. In a discussion of preserving our remaining wildlife, you may want to stress that safeguards and controls are needed to limit damage caused by wildlife to crops, humans, and property:

SUPPORTING DATA

More than a million collisions between cars and deer occur each year, resulting in an average of 200 human fatalities.

According to the General Accounting Office, 8,000 people a year are bitten by snakes, and on the average 15 of them die.

Raccoons, pigeons, and even starlings spread health threats ranging from rabies to salmonella.

In September 1995, the U.S. Air Force lost 24 aviators and a $190 million AWACS aircraft in a collision with a flock of Canada geese.

REVISING Writing courses today stress the value of revision and re-thinking. In the world of work and of real-world publishing, much written work goes through rewrites in response to feedback from peers, collaborators, or superiors. Whenever possible, allow time before you go back to an early draft. When you come back to a paper for a fresh look, you may see where evidence is weak or missing. You may conclude that your thesis does not yet take into account important facts you discovered late in your investigation. You may become aware of missing links, overstated claims, or detours and backtrackings.

Guidelines for Revision

Every paper is different. Every writing project has its own challenges and rewards. However, in revising a paper about a current issue or drawing on your personal experience, keep in mind points that come up again and again in feedback from writing instructors and editors.

1 **Pointed Title** *Make your title both informative and inviting.* Use it to bring the issue into focus. What is this paper about? What is going to be the main point? What is going to be the prevailing tone or attitude? Strengthen generic titles—very general interchangeable titles that give no real hint of your agenda or point of view.

GENERIC: Immigration Today

(*What about* today's immigration?)

REVISED: **Immigrants Take the Blame**
The New Immigrants: Seeking the Better Life
Illegals: Closing the Gates

2 **Raising the Issue** *Use your introduction to raise the issue.* Bring the issue to life. For instance, dramatize the issue by starting with an eye-opening example, a strong thought-provoking quotation, or a strong opening sentence pointing up a revealing contradiction. Do not just repeat the assignment in your introduction or in your title.

DRAMATIC OPENING EXAMPLE:

KIDNAP BREAKTHROUGH—NEW EVIDENCE LINKS MOM TO RANSOM NOTE!!!! This headline from the *National Enquirer* illustrates the kind of tabloid journalism that catches the attention of over 15 million readers.

STARTER QUOTE:

Is there still a difference between mainstream journalism and tabloid journalism? **"Instead of beating their entertainment and propaganda com-**

Guidelines for Revision

petitors, many journalists are joining them," says Ellen Hume, former professor of journalism at Harvard. "**Substance doesn't sell.**"

POINTED OPENING SENTENCE:

> **Today the sex lives of public figures are front-page news, crowding out news about peace and war.**

3 **Pushing toward a Thesis** *Let your readers know early in your paper where you stand.* What is the point or the message of your paper as a whole? What answer does your paper as a whole give to the question or questions you raise? For instance, don't just say there are issues. What are they? What is the most important one? Work with a trial thesis—to be adjusted as your paper as a whole takes final shape.

TRIAL THESIS: America has long welcomed newcomers with open arms.

> (But historically haven't there been periods of hostility toward the newcomers?)

REVISED THESIS: This country has experienced cycles of anti-immigrant sentiment. There has been anti-Irish feeling, anti-German resentment, and anti-Asian prejudice. Even so, **millions of newcomers became an organic part of American society in the span of one or two generations.**

4 **Strengthening Your Outline** *Make sure your readers understand your overall plan.* Have you laid out the main points in a proposal or the steps in an argument as a three-point or perhaps a five-point program? Highlight the key points that your paper covers. Add or strengthen the transitions that serve as thought links to take the reader from one point to the next.

STRENGTHENED OUTLINE:

The Culture of Violence

1 escalating violence

   children's toys

   video games

   mafia movies and action movies

2 violence defended as fantasy or entertainment

3 peer culture overrules parents' influence

4 need to teach nonaggressive and cooperative values

Guidelines for Revision

5 **Supporting Your Points** *Follow up your points with strong supporting detail.* Back them up with striking examples, revealing facts, thought-provoking statistics, or firsthand observation. Move in for a closer look. Quote expert opinion or insider's testimony. You are entitled to your own opinion, but your reader is entitled to see what made you think so.

UNDEVELOPED: I spent a year in Mexico as an exchange student and admired the Mexican culture.

(*What* did you come to admire about the Mexican culture?)

FOLLOWED UP: I spent a year in Mexico and came to admire the Mexican culture. **The University of Mexico is the oldest university in the Western Hemisphere and older than Harvard. The Mexicans threw off European colonialism a few decades after the American colonies and have a fierce pride in their revolutionary history. The great Mexican painters and muralists—Diego Rivera, Frida Kahlo, David Siqueiros—are known around the world.**

6 **Strong Conclusion** *Conclude your paper on a strong note.* Is there a strong send-off, or is your conclusion a weak repetition of what you already said? Give your readers something to quote or to remember. Try to finish with a strong punchline, save a striking recent example for the end, or wind up with a clincher quotation.

CLINCHER QUOTE: In the words of Lester Crystal, executive producer at NBC and four-time Emmy Award winner, **"Despite the success of 'tabloid TV' news programs, no one can deny that quality broadcast news accounts for a considerable share of high ratings. The ranks of television news overflow with internationally recognized, widely respected journalists."**

EDITING In final editing, you take care of damaging misspellings, misused words, missing or confusing punctuation, and awkward or garbled sentences. Remember that text on a computer screen looks deceptively finished. Professionals recommend that you proofread twice, checking your text line by line first onscreen and then again as hard copy.

A Minimum Checklist for Final Editing

The following are high-priority items for final editing:

1 *Check for familiar spelling demons.* Make sure you have not misspelled the unforgivables: *receive, definite, believe, similar, separate, used to, a lot* (two words). Let your spellcheck catch common problem words: *accommodate, government, predominant, environment, occurred.* Watch for confusing pairs: *accept* (take in) but *except* (take out); *affect* (change in part) but *effect* (the whole result).

2 *Avoid the* it's *trap.* Save yourself grief by changing any *it's* to *it is*—if *it is* is what you mean. Otherwise use *its*—a possessive showing where something belongs: the band and *its* vocalist.

3 *Check for apostrophes with possessives.* (What belongs with what?) Distinguish between singular (one *person's* problems) and plural (both my *parents'* attitude).

4 *Hook up sentence fragments.* Look for sentence fragments that should be linked to a preceding sentence from which they have been split off. (*To fight disease. Living in the city. Which proved untrue.*)

Chimpanzees were bred for experiments **to fight disease.**

5 *Use a semicolon between two closely related statements.* Use a semicolon instead of a comma when there is no other link between the two points.

SEMICOLON: Speed kills**;** caution saves lives.

6 *Use a comma with* and *or* but; *use a semicolon with* however *and* therefore. Use a comma when two statements are joined by *and, but, for, so, yet, or, nor* (coordinators, or coordinating conjunctions). Use a semicolon when two statements are joined by *however, therefore, nevertheless, besides, moreover* (adverbial connectives). Note the optional commas with adverbial connectives.

COMMA: Violent crimes have decreased**, but** juvenile crime has gone up.

SEMICOLON: Inflation has slowed down**; however** tuition is going up.
Inflation has slowed down**;** tuition **however** is going up.
Inflation has slowed down**;** tuition is going up **however.**

ADDED COMMA: Inflation has slowed down**; however,** tuition is going up.
Inflation has slowed down**;** tuition**, however,** is going up.

7 *Make a verb agree with its true subject.* Use matching forms for singular (one of a kind) and plural (several).

SINGULAR: The **genetic makeup** of chimpanzees **is** 97 percent identical with ours. (not *are*)

A Minimum Checklist for Final Editing

PLURAL: Researchers claim there **are genes** predisposing us to diseases. (not *is*)

8 *Deal with the pronoun dilemma.* "Every student turned in **his** exam" used to be grammatically correct. "Every student turned in **his or her** exam"is politically correct because it avoids sexist implications. "All of the students turned in **their** exams" (changing the whole sentence to plural forms) is gender-neutral and the least awkward and the safest choice.

9 *Use correct forms for pronouns and adverbs.* Use the subject form of pronouns to tell us who: *I, he, she, we, they.* Use the object forms to tell us at whom an action aims or for whom it is intended (*me, him, her, us, them*).

SUBJECT FORM: **My classmates and I** did volunteer work.
She and her mother never got along.

OBJECT FORM: The manager never liked **my coworkers and me.**
The news came as a surprise **for her and her mother.**

When you have a choice, use the distinctive adverb form to tell us how (badly, rapidly, immediately).

ADVERB FORM: The city had changed **considerably.** (not *considerable*)
Her family spoke English **really well.** (not *real good*)

10 *Deal with dangling modifiers.* They are left dangling because they point to something that is missing from the sentence:

DANGLING: *Losing a job,* feelings of self-doubt are natural.

(*Who* lost the job?)

EDITED: **Losing a job, we** naturally experience self-doubt.

FEEDBACK AND PEER REVIEW How do you react to comments on your writing? **Feedback** is an important stage of the writing process. Much business writing is reworked in response to comments from coworkers, superiors, or consultants. Much professional writing is revised in response to criticism from editors or reviewers. Many writing classes today adopt a workshop format, with students rewriting early drafts in response to comments from instructors and peers.

When you participate in **peer review** (oral or written) in class, try to combine the two basic functions of a good editor: First, recognize and reinforce what a writer does well. Second, offer constructive suggestions for improving what is weak or has gone wrong. Pay attention to larger questions of purpose, audience, and organization as well as to spelling and punctuation.

Guidelines for Peer Review

Use the following questions as a guide for your participation in peer review.

1 What is the writer trying to do?
2 Does the writer bring a limited topic into focus? How well does the writer bring the topic or the issue to life?
3 Is there a central idea, or thesis? Does the introduction effectively lead up to it? Should it be spelled out more clearly or forcefully?
4 Is there a preview or overview of the plan? Do readers get a sense of the writer's strategy? Does the plan seem to work?
5 How solid is the writer's follow-up or backup of major points? What is the quality of examples, evidence, or support from authorities? Which examples are strong? Which are weak?
6 Are there effective transitions—does the writer take the reader along from point to point? Are turning points or major stages in the argument signaled clearly enough?
7 What is confusing, and what is especially clear? Which sentences seem muddy? What problems are there with spelling or punctuation?
8 Who is the intended audience? Who might be the ideal reader for this paper? Who is ignored or left out?
9 Where do you agree? Where do you disagree, and why?
10 What would you say or write if you had a chance to respond to the writer?

Prepare a peer review of the following paper and compare your responses with those of others.

No Heroes

In todays society young people find few worthy objects for loyalty or outlets for devotion. They join groups ranging from neighborhood gangs to Neo-nazi groups because they need something to be loyal to or to believe in. To better understand this assessment we must look at the past and try to determine what worthy objects used to be available for young people to pledge their support.

The traditional symbols for hero worship fall into three categories: political, military, and sports figures. These seem to reflect well the more popular forms of hero worship in our society—unless we count such idols as rock musicians, movie stars, or outlaws (Jesse James, Bonnie and Clyde).

In the past young adults had political figures to look up to and respect. Respect is the important word here. Today the offices and titles are still there, but much of the dignity attached to them has been lost. Political leaders like Franklin Roosevelt and Harry Truman were admired by millions. John Kennedy still lives on in people's memories as a symbol of idealism and a new Camelot. Nixon ("I am not a crook") did much to cheapen the office of the president with the Watergate scandal. Recently we have had fund-raising scandals with politicians routinely getting tax breaks for rich constituents or accepting donations from foreign sources. *Politician* has become a dirty word for many voters.

The decline in loyalty towards the military was due largely to unpopular wars like those fought in Korea and Vietnam. People were no longer rallying around the flag as they had done for World War I and World War II. People blamed the Cold War for drawing funds away from domestic programs into a huge arms buildup. Many people object to money spent on foreign aid. Why should we help others when our own country has unsolved problems?

It has also become increasingly difficult to hero-worship athletes in todays society. In baseball, we no longer have athletes like Babe Ruth, Lou Gehrig, Willie Mays, Stan Musial, or Mickey Mantle. Players who played the game with respect for the sport and a love of simply playing. Today we have players who hold out for million-dollar salaries with no concern for the fans. We have players who are in trouble with the law and perform below the standards their million-dollar contracts seem to call for.

With all these problems in our society today, one can understand why young people seach for new outlets for their loyalties. Instead of Little League baseball, they get involved in neighborhood gangs. They make heroes of rap singers who glorify violence against women. Young people have lost faith in the values of the establishment and are finding it hard to find worthy alternatives.

WRITING AND THINKING

The computer has shortened the distance between the way we think and the way we write. Much writing at the computer is the electronic equivalent of thinking out loud. What kind of thinking goes into a well-thought-out paper? What thinking strategies do we see at work again and again when people face a problem or try to think through a subject?

REACHING GENERAL CONCLUSIONS Much productive thinking goes from the specific to the general. This generalizing, or **inductive,** model is a discovery mode. It starts from careful observation or data gathering and tries to find the common pattern, the connecting thread. The generalizing, or inductive, model puts input first: We do not launch unsupported opinions but *earn* the right to have an opinion. Before we generalize, we take a close look at our experience, our observation, our data.

The strength of the generalizing model is that it stays close to firsthand experience or close to the facts. A standard application brings together several related incidents or several similar case histories to show the common thread. The classic pattern for an inductive paper is to present the general conclusion first as the thesis. It then presents the detailed examples that led to it. It will often make allowance for exceptions, modifying the general statement accordingly.

THESIS (general pattern)←EXAMPLE 1←EXAMPLE 2←
EXAMPLE 3

A Tale of Three Cities

THESIS: **We treat the homeless not as fellow human beings but as an embarrassment; we hide them for appearance's sake.**

Example 1: One of the major parties holds its national convention in a big city. The city authorities busily clean up the litter. They pick up the homeless and put them in shelters.

Example 2: The other major party holds its convention in a big city. The city authorities spruce up the city. Filth is picked up; beggars and homeless people are made to move on or are moved to temporary shelters.

Example 3: An important foreign visitor—the Pope, the Queen of England—arrives. The city authorities spruce up the city; they make beggars and the homeless less visible, as above.

In practice, writers do not start out toward general conclusions from a totally clean slate. They will often start with tentative ideas. They try out working hypotheses or follow hunches. However, to do an honest job of thinking the matter through, you need to be willing to revise tentative generalizations as the evidence accumulates.

WEIGHING PRO AND CON Much thinking does not proceed in a straight line from evidence to conclusion. We often lean first one way and then another. The play of **pro and con** makes us explore both sides of an issue. To arrive at a balanced conclusion, we line up arguments in favor and arguments against. We can then weigh their respective merits. Often a convincing piece of writing moves from point to counterpoint and from there to a balanced conclusion. The play of pro and con allows us to weigh the evidence and balance conflicting claims. It makes us listen to the other side. It is a safeguard against narrow, one-sided views.

The classic scheme for a pro-and-con argument goes from statement to counterstatement and on to a broader, more balanced view:

THESIS (point)→ANTITHESIS (counterpoint)→SYNTHESIS (balanced view)

The following might be a student writer's notes for a pro-and-con topic: Should motorcycle riders have to wear safety helmets?

The Lure of the Open Road

CON—arguments against helmets:

    freedom of the open road, sense of liberation, free spirits

    outdoor types: exhilaration of being exposed to the elements vs. isolation

    excessively cushioned metal cage

    cost and inconvenience in dragging/storing the clumsy helmets

    principle of choice vs. state interference

PRO—arguments in favor of helmets:

    severe nature of injuries, often more severe than in car accidents

    strain on hospitals, rehabilitation services, horrendous cost to community

    trauma to the other motorist (who knows he/she is implicated in the death or maiming of another human being)

BALANCED CONCLUSION: The need to protect the public and fellow motorists should overrule the individual's desire for freedom.

The pro-and-con approach is especially appropriate to hotly debated issues: affirmative action, English Only, bilingual education, censorship. The commitment to listen to the other side counteracts our tendency to raise our voices and shout people down.

ARGUING FROM PRINCIPLE Much argument does not start from a patient gathering of the facts. It starts from what we already know or think we know. The **deductive** model starts with a general principle and applies it to a specific situation. This model reverses the thinking strategy of the inductive model: Instead of going from the specific to the general, it goes from the general to the specific. Writers who argue from principle appeal to shared values. They apply established guidelines or legal rulings to individual cases. Much depends on the reader accepting the basic assumptions, or **premises.**

RULE OR ASSUMPTION (basic premise)→INDIVIDUAL APPLICATION(S)

You can model such arguments as follows:

IF: Federal guidelines bar colleges from discriminating against students on the basis of gender.
AND IF: The local women's college still excludes male students.
THEN: The college is in violation of federal guidelines.

IF: Justice requires the justice system to be willing to correct its mistakes—to reverse judicial error (as in the case of new DNA evidence).
AND IF: Capital punishment makes the reversal of a wrongful verdict impossible.
THEN: Capital punishment is inherently unjust.

When we argue from principle, we start from basic assumptions and apply them to specific cases. Students of logic have paid much attention to how such arguments work and how they go wrong. A classic example of a deductive argument gone wrong reads as follows:

FIRST PREMISE: All human beings are mortal.
SECOND PREMISE: My dog is mortal.
CONCLUSION: Therefore, my dog is a human being.

Here, we are misreading the first premise. It is not exclusive; it does not say: "All human beings *and no other kinds of living beings* are mortal." We should really read it to mean: "All human beings (and perhaps also many other beings) are mortal."

WRITING AND COMPUTERS

The way we write and think is changing as we do more of our reading, research, and writing on the computer.

FINDING ELECTRONIC SOURCES On the Internet, background and follow-up on any major issue are at your fingertips.

■ A few keystrokes will call up on your computer screen a stream of information and commentary about efforts to reintroduce captive condors and other big birds into the wild or about breakthroughs in high-tech help for people with disabilities.

■ You can read major newspapers, from the *New York Times* to *USA Today,* online. Internet users can go to the online archive of *Harper's* magazine, and browse through essays and fiction representing "150 years of American culture."

- You can call up detailed information on the abolitionist movement from an encyclopedia like *Encarta* online or on CD-ROM, following links to major figures and events in the antislavery movement.

Starting an Internet search on a current issue will often set off an avalanche of related articles and other material. Most users of the Net have selected their own favorite search engine, such as Yahoo! or the more recent Google. They develop their own search techniques. Let's say you want to know if it's true that AIDS education has been a failure, with many teenagers practicing unprotected sex. An unrestricted key word like AIDS is likely to call up several thousand unsorted listings. So you start with something narrower and more selective, like AIDS EDUCATION (or AIDS and EDUCATION). People writing on this topic will not all use this exact term, so you ask yourself: "How else would people talk about this topic?" You try SAFE SEX EDUCATION or TEENAGERS AND AIDS or UNPROTECTED SEX.

To have the computer search not only for titles and descriptions with the exact word *education* but also with related words like *educating,* type only the root of your key word, followed by an asterisk. If you type *educat**, the computer will search for all versions of the word with different endings, such as *educate, education,* and *educational.*

EVALUATING INTERNET MATERIAL How do you sift through and evaluate the results of your search? When materials are first published elsewhere and then put on the Net, the Internet serves as an **electronic library**—an instant-access library. You can often retrieve and check the original print publication. If necessary, you can go back to sources more complete or more carefully checked and verified. Increasingly, however, much material is published *only* on the Net. The Net then serves as a worldwide **electronic publisher**—without the editors, critics, and reviewers that have traditionally sorted and channeled print materials. As in other areas, the computer increasingly allows you to bypass the middleman—the mediator or facilitator.

Since much material on the Net is unedited and unsorted, you will often have to use your judgment about what you have found. Your instructor or your handbook is likely to give you advice like the following:

Guidelines for Evaluating Electronic Sources

When you draw on electronic sources, keep the following criteria in mind:

1 AUTHORSHIP Who wrote or assembled the material? Is the author clearly identified, or is the material anonymous or quasi-anonymous, like much material on the Net? Who sponsors and maintains a website?

2 CREDENTIALS Is there any indication of the credentials or credibility of the authors? Where do they work or write? Are the authors affiliated with a business organization or an academic institution? What is their academic or professional status? Are they recognized authorities or experts in their field?

3 AUTHENTICITY Who put this material on the Net? Was it copied, recycled, or pirated from somewhere? Can you trace it to the original source? Is there any indication of copyright? Who has the rights to this material?

4 COMPLETENESS How reliable and complete is the current version? Has it been excerpted, and by whom? Has it been adapted or updated, and by whom? Is anyone responsible for accuracy and completeness of the current version? Can you trace a more complete original version?

5 BIAS How objective or reliable does the material seem? Are opinions carefully presented and supported by credible evidence or data? Are opposing arguments discussed and refuted, or are they ridiculed and dismissed?

6 PERMANENCE How long will this material be accessible? Will other people be able to retrieve and verify it at a later date?

WRITING ON THE COMPUTER While the computer has changed the way we read and do research, it is also changing the way we write:

- *Writing has become a more natural everyday activity.* It has become less formidable; it has moved closer to talking. Writing on the computer screen can be easily deleted, changed, or done over. Writers are less likely to suffer from writer's block.

- *Taking notes and using notes have become less of a chore.* It has become easy to build a file of promising material, copy key passages, and download key sources. You can paste in material as you transfer files. Efficient, reliable scanners allow you to transfer printed texts to your computer files.

- *Revision has become a more natural part of writing.* You can easily adjust a text to accommodate second thoughts and new information. You are less likely today to think of a piece of writing as finished and done with. You are likely to be more attuned to the opportunities for ongoing revision and for adapting material to different uses.

- *Writing has become more interactive.* Writers are more prepared than they used to be for the instant reply. Participating in the electronic conversation is likely to make you more audience conscious. You become more aware of your readers and what is going on in their minds, even if they are merely lurking rather than actively sharing in the give-and-take.

Culture critics and media watchers today weigh both the promise and the possible downside of electronic reading and writing. They see unprecedented instant access to information and knowledge, but they worry that one general effect of publication on the Web may be to reduce print content. Instructions for creating websites that tout products and services encourage the authors to cut back on plain prose. They show how to concentrate on attractive layouts and liven up the page with graphics. We see a spillover of worries about the reader's attention span in the bits of news and gossip in the opening pages of glossy newsmagazines.

Are we becoming too used to sound bites? Are we getting used to bit facts and "off-the-top-of-your-head" opinions? With so many bite-size pieces of information, you have to make a special effort to establish the connections. You have to put bit facts in context—to see the larger picture. You have to learn to feed a wealth of unsorted information and ideas into a structured argument supported by solid evidence.

Starting a Journal

How do you make writing a habit? How do you make writing a natural, familiar activity—without writing anxiety or writer's block? One big step is to start a **journal,** or writer's log. Write in your journal maybe twice a week—entries ranging from half a single-spaced page to a page or more. Your first entries might be about yourself. You may want to talk about your roots, your family background, your church, or other influences that made you what you are. You may decide to write about your memories (happy or unhappy) of school or about your major interests.

Gradually, you will be branching out: Use your journal to record a running commentary on what you observe, view, and read. Write about incidents that make you think—what happened? Why did it shake you up or change your mind about something? Write about people who matter to you. React to news stories that make you angry or glad. Write about instances of gay-bashing or immigrant-bashing that touched a nerve. Write about a movie that made you think or that made you cry. Write about visits to the theater or to a museum.

In your journal, you will be writing spontaneously and informally. Your instructor may ask to read all or a sampling of it—but mainly as an interested reader, without a red pencil in hand. You may share entries with your classmates. You will be able to be more candid or unguarded than in formal papers. You will be able to put down first impressions as well as second thoughts, puzzling questions as well as tentative answers.

In addition to giving you practice in verbalizing your thoughts and feelings, your journal will serve you as a source of material for more structured papers. Often an entry will already contain the germ of an idea for a paper. For instance, in developing the paper, you might use what you already have but look for related similar incidents, fill in background for something that happened, tell your reader more about the people involved, or bring the story up to date.

Use the first few entries of your journal for a **personal résumé.** Write entries under headings like the following:

- ROOTS—family background, ethnic or racial identity, the meeting of cultures

- SCHOOLING—teachers and classmates, goals and obstacles, successes and failures
- FLASHLIGHT MEMORIES—vividly remembered incidents that have a special meaning for you
- JOBS—part-time jobs, experiences as counselor or mentor, initiation to the workplace
- PERSONAL ISSUES—personal goals and commitments, causes you support, unresolved problems in your life

Study the following sample journal entries. What might each writer do to expand the entry into a fully developed paper?

Schooling

I am a product of the public school system. When I started school at the age of five, I did not speak English, and the fact that I was enrolled in an all-English kindergarten class made my first experience with school extremely frightful. But once I became comfortable with this new environment, I became very outgoing in school. In elementary school I participated in the district spelling bees, winning one of them, and in junior high I became involved in the school band. High school was the climax of my participation in nonacademic things. I was an officer in clubs such as Interact and Speech and Debate. While in high school I occasionally played the piano at weddings, funerals, and quinceaneras, and I did community service. I was always involved in fundraisers, canned-food drives, and serving dinner to the homeless through Interact. I learned how to work with others and earn their respect. More than anything I learned to have a lot of patience. I learned that often adults can be very difficult to work with.

Personal Issues

There are ways of talking about a group with which I identify that offend me. As a woman, terms that offend me include *babe* and *baby*. Women are not infants, and when they are called these names, the implication is that women are childish, immature, and unable to take care of themselves. *Chick* and *fox:* Women are not feathered or furry animals. If these terms are used to "compliment a female's appearance," why not compliment her intelligence? her sense of humor? her ability in sports? Even the word *lady* can connote a submissive, subservient, "polite" woman. Granted, words are "just words." However, they are often a fairly accurate indicator of how a person might act. Unfortunately, I was able to see the connection between words and feelings at first hand. I had grown close to my cousin Ben, who was funny and pleasant to be around. My first warning flag went up when he referred to a movie as a "chick flick." I was working in his father's store, and one day when I asked a customer if

I could help him, he said: "I don't want no goddamn woman waiting on me!"
As I stood there agape, my uncle helped him and laughed at the "joke." Needless to say I was upset and later voiced my concern. That night I received a
phone call from Ben. He told me that I really ought to toughen up if I wanted
to make it in the business world. He proceeded to say that women should
"know their place." I lost all respect for him that night.

Is a picture worth a thousand words? What do these photographs say that the printed word cannot convey?

1
INITIATION
Growing Up American

I never write about anything I have not experienced myself.

—*Shelby Steele*

One writes out of one thing only—one's own experience. Everything depends on how relentlessly one forces from this experience the last drop, sweet or bitter, it can possibly give.

—*James Baldwin*

There are so many young brothers and sisters coming to the forefront, writers who have decided that we can tell our stories any way we damn well please.

—*Terry McMillan*

Much powerful and effective writing is anchored in the writer's own firsthand experience. We all have a story to tell that reveals who we are and how we became who we are. When we trust the listener or reader enough, we may tell that story. Many such stories are stories of growing up, of initiation. We move from an earlier stage to a new stage that requires us to learn. We face a challenge that may seem new and overwhelming to us. However, we may discover later that many others before us had to face it in their own way. We find ourselves reliving an archetypal experience—reliving a pattern that has been played out by many earlier generations.

One such archetypal experience is the move from a protected childhood to an adult world. We begin to face new problems and responsibilities. We may slowly discover that a person we trusted has serious flaws. (The idol has feet of clay.) We may discover that we are outgrowing an institution or a set of ideas that at one time seemed to serve all our intellectual or spiritual needs. We discover what it means to make our own decisions and make our own choices and mistakes.

For many young Americans, an archetypal experience of growing up has meant moving from one environment to another—from country to city, or from the Old Country ways of immigrant parents to the American world of school and profession. Often that move is a time of confusion, with people trying to find their bearings. It is a time of breaking away and searching for a new identity. People may find their loyalties divided between different ways of life and often different languages. They may be trying to bridge different cultures—"straddling two cultures," as Caroline Hwang says in one of the selections in this chapter. Sometimes the initiation or awakening centers on the rediscovery of a culture or a language that was part of the family's past—but that was left behind in the attempt to assimilate, to become part of the mainstream of American life.

Many of the following selections tell the story of such a journey in quest of the writer's identity.

A PLACE WHERE WE BELONG

Ana Veciana-Suarez

For millions of Americans, life in this country has been a new beginning. They were immigrants or the children of immigrants. They were refugees from poverty, failed revolutions, or lost wars. They were refugees from religious persecution or political oppression. Many traveled the classic route from being strangers in an alien country to slowly learning to move in a new language and a new environment. They saw their children slowly becoming American-ized—until memories of the Old Country became nostalgic reminiscences to be cherished with old-timers or with young people setting out to rediscover their roots. Ana Veciana-Suarez is a columnist and novelist who has reached large audiences with her tales of the odyssey of Cuban Americans who settled in Florida after the Cuban revolution. At first isolated by language and culture, they slowly established a prosperous influential Cuban American society in which Latin and North American influences meet. Veciana-Suarez's husband, David, was Jewish, and their children early lived with the multicultural richness of the American experience. Veciana-Suarez collected many of the columns she wrote for the Miami Herald *in her book* Birthday Parties in Heaven. *Her novel* The Chin Kiss King *(1997) has been praised for its "fierce tenderness, bits of magic up her sleeve, and lusty humor"* (Raleigh News & Observer).

Thought Starters: What do you think of when you hear the word *home?* Is there one place that you will always think of as home, or are there several places or environments to which you were especially attached?

The Bible's book of Jeremiah traces the fall of Jerusalem, the destruction of the city and the Temple, and the exile to Babylonia of Judah's king and many of his people. At the end, it precisely tallies the numbers: 3,023 people in the seventh year, 832 in the eighteenth year, 745 in the twenty-third year—in all, 4,600 exiles. You would think that the people of Judah would have gotten the hang of exile by then. After all, their ancestors had wandered in the wilderness for forty years, after they had left Egypt and before homesteading in the Promised Land. Yet, an entire book, Lamentations, is devoted to the aftermath of ruin and exile that followed the destruction of Jerusalem in 586 B.C.

> The old people no longer sit at
> the city gate,
> and the young people no
> longer make music.

1

> Happiness has gone out of our
> lives;
> grief has taken the place of
> our dances.

When the Jewish exiles fled to the Chebar River in Babylonia, and when Moses' Israelites trudged through Moab and Kadesh Barnea, when they crossed the Jordan and camped near the Gulf of Suez, how did they think of home? In what way did they make desert and riverland a familiar, if not welcoming, domicile? Did they carry a potted houseplant from one encampment to the next? Was the carved chair, a family heirloom, given prominent display under the tent? Did they cook food in the same way with the same pots and the same tools? How did they realize they had arrived where they belonged? Was it the certainty of knowing where everything is? The feelings of welcome and repose? Or was it simply arbitrary boundaries drawn from here to there by an alternately loving and wrathful God?

My parents have been exiles for an almost biblical forty years, and though they have not wandered in the physical wilderness like the Israelites, they have known, at least in the beginning, a spiritual wasteland of sorts: the isolation of not belonging, the harshness of the unfamiliar. Their Jerusalem floated one-hundred-and-forty miles from where they live today. It was a paradise of halcyon nights and glorious days, an island where the ocean was bluer, the sand whiter, the palms taller. It never existed, of course. Nostalgia rewrites history. Yet my parents would have given anything over the years to return to Cuba, to live again in Havana's La Vibora neighborhood, in their little tiled house with the wrought-iron, gated porch; to walk the little narrow streets that weren't always clean; and to shop in their little bodegas that weren't always well stocked but where everybody knew their names. (Nineteenth-century American playwright John Howard Payne hit the nail on the head when he wrote in "Home Sweet Home," from the opera *Clari, the Maid of Milan:* "An exile from home splendor dazzles in vain, / Oh give me my lowly thatched cottage again. . . .") Instead of the tiny home in La Vibora, it was *el exilio*—a state of limbo when you are where you don't expect to be—that defined the final years of my parents' youth and all of their middle age. It marked my childhood, too.

We did not celebrate Thanksgiving, the most American of holidays, until my last years in elementary school. I have no early memories of pumpkin pie and sweet potato casseroles, of family gathered around the bounty of a table. Unless it was Christmas Eve. And even then, Christmas was a subdued affair, with none of the overwrought glitz of today. We did not get a Christmas tree until I was in fourth or fifth grade, a fake silver beauty that I watched for hours on end when the revolving colors of a reflector light shone on it. This penury during the holidays, I now believe, had little to do with money but plenty to do with hope—hope that life in these United States would be temporary, hope that next Christmas would be celebrated in Havana, hope that one day they would look back at this period of their lives as something sad but brief, and altogether finished. Celebrating would have been to admit a hopelessness. This is how exile translates into marginality, a living on the sidelines without knowing when to jump into the game.

Yet, little by little, first in word then by action, whether they knew it or not, their lives evolved into a search for rootedness. My parents bought a house when they had saved up enough money and explained it this way: Very few people would rent out to foreigners with young children, even if these renters were clean, modestly dressed, well-mannered, and professionals in another country. Eventually they fixed up this house, added a bathroom and bedroom for the in-laws, put up a fence, remodeled the kitchen, planted a mango tree in the back and red ixora bushes in the front. As their children grew older, as their children birthed children in exile, they spoke less of a return to Cuba—"When we go back home . . ."—and more of the horrible possibility that, in their old age, they would be put in a nursing home in much the same way that *los americanos* sent their old folk away. My mother talked about retiring to a condo in Miami Beach; my father spoke of expanding the business.

When did exile become home? After they planted the mango? When the grandchildren were born? Now, as they approach retirement?

I have grown interested in answers as I see David wandering about my house, or collapsing in his old bed in his old house in the grove. No matter what he says, I know he doesn't feel at home in either place. He is where my parents were about twenty years ago—in between, not there but not quite here either.

My family has lived in three different countries and spoken three different languages in the span of three generations. My grandparents, Catalonians on both sides, fled their homeland because of poverty and civil war. Their foods and their language, that rich guttural Catalan I heard in my childhood, eventually melded with the new customs of their new island home. Their children, in turn, later scrambled across the Florida Straits to another exile, also because of political upheaval. What, I sometimes wonder, might be in store for me? As a woman listening to stories of my ancestors' comings and goings, as a Catholic married to a Jew who has never seen his people's Promised Land, the concept of home is important to me. But not only to me—actually to most everybody I know. We all need a place where we belong, a place to return to, where the contours of the bed are well-known and the light switches are just where they're supposed to be: a place where we can listen quietly, comfortably, to the stirrings of the heart and whispers of the soul.

The Responsive Reader

1. Where in the essay does Veciana-Suarez begin to talk about her family's experiences with exile? Why do you think she begins the essay

with two paragraphs about exiled peoples in the Bible? How does the introduction prepare you for the rest of the essay?

2. What examples does Veciana-Suarez use to convey her parents' feelings about Cuba and the life of exile? How did these feelings change over time? What caused their feelings to change?

3. The way we celebrate holidays is often a strong indicator of ties or lack of ties with a cultural tradition. What role do holidays play in this selection?

4. Although most of Veciana-Suarez's essay concerns her parents' exile, she concludes by describing other members of her family and by observing that "the concept of home is important" to most people she knows. Why do you think she ends the essay this way? Does the information about her grandparents and her husband contribute to your understanding of her reasons for saying that we "all need a place where we belong"?

5. What experiences have you or others in your family had of leaving a home or a homeland behind? How were those experiences similar to and different from those that Veciana-Suarez describes?

6. Veciana-Suarez's parents explained that they bought a house in the United States because few Americans wanted to rent to foreigners with young children. Do you or people you know think of other people as foreigners? What encounters or experiences does the term bring to mind?

Talking, Listening, Writing

7. In a different part of her book, Veciana-Suarez gives a loving account of how her children were taught to celebrate Passover in the traditional manner, with the appropriate foods, ritual, and prayer. Give an account of this or another cherished ethnic holiday observance that you know well or can research.

8. Is it possible for people to feel that more than one country is home? Have you known people who remained "wanderers between two worlds"?

9. Judging from your experience or observation, do members of ethnic groups or immigrant groups still tend to live in sections of town where they cluster "with their own kind," or do most Americans live in ethnically mixed neighborhoods?

Collaborative Projects

10. Working with a group, use library research and personal interviews to collect first-person accounts by immigrants to the United States from an area of the world to which you have special ties or in which you have a special interest. Is there a common thread? Are there shared experiences that become part of the collective memory of a group? You may want to share your findings with your classmates as part of a multiethnic festival with readings from immigrants' stories.

BORN AMONG THE BORN-AGAIN
Garrison Keillor

Garrison Keillor became legendary in the Midwest as the host of A Prairie
Home Companion, *a live radio show originating in St. Paul, Minnesota, and
giving audiences a nostalgic mix of old-style storytelling, savvy appeals to local
pride, the sentimental songs of barbershop quintets and crooners, and homespun
humor delighting in the quirks and foibles of family and neighbors. Keillor is
a master at creating a nostalgic vision of a small-town American past removed
from the upheavals and paranoias of the twentieth century. He collected many
of the stories he told on his show in* Lake Wobegon Days *(1985), explaining that many were "true stories from my childhood, dressed . . . up as fiction."
He said in an interview in* Time *that he looked to the stories he heard in his
family as a child "as giving a person some sense of place," reassuring us "that
we were not just chips floating on the waves, that in some way we were meant
to be here, and had a history. That we had standing." In recent years, Keillor
has taken his show on the road, showing an uncanny knack for relating to the
local subculture—its history, its folk music, its in-jokes—in places as far apart
as San Jose, California, and Fairbanks, Alaska, or New York City, New
York. In the selection that follows, Keillor replays a classic story of growing up:
A youngster growing up in a family with strong religious views (or other strong
beliefs) starts to rebel against having to be "different" from his peers. How
much in this story shows Keillor's homespun sense of humor? How much is serious or thought-provoking?*

Thought Starters: What has shaped your impressions of small-town or
back-country American life? Do you share the nostalgia for a simpler small-
town life?

. . . In a town where everyone was either Lutheran or Catholic, we   *1*
were neither one. We were Sanctified Brethren, a sect so tiny that nobody
but us and God knew about it, so when kids asked what I was, I just said
Protestant. It was too much to explain, like having six toes. You would
rather keep your shoes on.

Grandpa Cotten was once tempted toward Lutheranism by a preacher
who gave a rousing sermon on grace that Grandpa heard as a young man
while taking Aunt Esther's dog home who had chased a Model T across
town. He sat down on the church steps and listened to the voice boom out
the open windows until he made up his mind to go in and unite with the
truth, but he took one look from the vestibule and left. "He was dressed up
like the Pope of Rome," said Grandpa, "and the altar and paintings and the

gold candlesticks—my gosh, it was just a big show. And he was reading the whole darn thing off a page, like an actor."

Jesus said, "Where two or three are gathered together in my name, there am I in the midst of them," and the Brethren believed that was enough. We met in Uncle Al and Aunt Flo's bare living room, with plain folding chairs arranged facing in toward the middle. No clergyman in a black smock. No organ or piano, for that would make one person too prominent. No upholstery—it would lead to complacence. No picture of Jesus—He was in our Hearts. The faithful sat down at the appointed hour and waited for the Spirit to move one of them to speak or to pray or to give out a hymn from our Little Flock hymnal. No musical notation, for music must come from the heart and not off a page. We sang the texts to a tune that fit the meter, of the many tunes we all knew. The idea of reading a prayer was sacrilege to us—"If a man can't remember what he wants to say to God, let him sit down and think a little harder," Grandpa said.

"There's the Lord's Prayer," said Aunt Esther meekly. We were sitting on the porch after Sunday dinner. Esther and Harvey were visiting from Minneapolis and had attended Lake Wobegon Lutheran, she having turned Lutheran when she married him, a subject that was never brought up in our family.

"You call that prayer? Sitting and reciting like a bunch of school-children?"   5

Harvey cleared his throat and turned to me and smiled, "Speaking of school, how are you doing?" he asked.

There was a lovely silence in the Brethren assembled on Sunday morning as we waited for the Spirit. Either the Spirit was moving someone to speak who was taking his sweet time or else the Spirit was playing a wonderful joke on us and letting us sit, or perhaps silence was the point of it. We sat listening to rain on the roof, distant traffic, a radio playing from across the street, kids whizzing by on bikes, dogs barking, as we waited for the Spirit to inspire us. It was like sitting on the porch with your family, when nobody feels that they have to make talk. So quiet in church. Minutes drifted by in silence that was sweet to us. The old Regulator clock ticked, the rain stopped, and the room changed light as the sun broke through—shafts of brilliant sun through the windows and motes of dust falling through it—the smell of clean clothes and floor wax and wine and the fresh bread of Aunt Flo, which was Christ's body given for us. Jesus in our midst, who loved us. So peaceful; and we loved each other, too. I thought perhaps the Spirit was leading me to say that, but I was just a boy, and children were supposed to keep still.

And my affections were not pure. They were tainted with a sneaking admiration of Catholics—Catholic Christmas, Easter, the Living Rosary, and the Blessing of the Animals, all magnificent. Everything we did was plain, but they were regal—especially the Feast Day of Saint Francis, which they did right out in the open, a feast for the eyes. Cows, horses, some pets, right on the church lawn. The turmoil, animals bellowing and barking and clucking and a cat scheming how to escape and suddenly leaping out of the girl's arms who was holding on tight, the cat dashing through the crowd, dogs straining at the leash, and the ocarina band of third graders playing a song, and the great calm of the sisters, and the flags, and the Knights of Columbus decked out in their handsome black suits—the whole thing was gorgeous. I stared at it until my eyes almost fell out, and then I wished it would go on much longer.

"Christians," my Uncle Al used to say, "do not go in for show," referring to the Catholics. We were sanctified by the blood of the Lord; therefore we were saints, like Saint Francis, but we didn't go in for feasts or ceremonies, involving animals or not. We went in for sitting, all nineteen of us, in Uncle Al and Aunt Flo's living room on Sunday morning and having a plain meeting and singing hymns in our poor thin voices, while not far away the Catholics were whooping it up. I wasn't allowed inside Our Lady, of course, but if the Blessing of the Animals on the Feast Day of Saint Francis was any indication, Lord, I didn't know but what they had elephants in there and acrobats. I sat in our little group and envied them for the splendor and gorgeousness, as we tried to sing without even so much as a harmonica to give us the pitch. Hymns, Uncle Al said, didn't have to be sung perfect, because God looks on the heart, and if you are In The Spirit, then all praise is good.

The Brethren, also known as The Saints Gathered in the Name of   *10* Christ Jesus, who met in the living room were all related to each other and raised in the Faith from infancy except Brother Mel, who was rescued from a life of drunkenness, saved as a brand from the burning, a drowning sailor, a sheep on the hillside, whose immense red nose testified to his previous condition. I envied his amazing story of how he came to be with us. Born to godly parents, Mel left home at fifteen and joined the Navy. He sailed to distant lands in a submarine and had exciting experiences while traveling the downward path, which led him finally to the Union Gospel Mission in Minneapolis, where he heard God's voice "as clear as my voice speaking to you." He was twenty-six, he slept under bridges and in abandoned buildings, he drank two quarts of white muscatel every day, and then God told him that he must be born again, and so he was, and became the new Mel, except for his nose.

Except for his nose, Mel Burgess looked like any forty-year-old Brethren man: sober, preferring dark suits, soft-spoken, tending toward girth. His nose was what made you look twice: battered, swollen, very red with tiny purplish lines, it looked ancient and dead on his otherwise fairly handsome face, the souvenir of what he had been saved from, the "Before" of his "Before . . . and After" advertisement for being born again.

For me, there was nothing before. I was born among the born-again. This living room so hushed, the Brethren in their customary places on folding chairs (the comfortable ones were put away on Sunday morning) around the end table draped with a white cloth and the glass of wine and loaf of bread (unsliced), was as familiar to me as my mother and father, before whom there was nobody. I had always been here.

. . . So one Sunday our family traipsed over to a restaurant . . . that a friend of Dad's had recommended, Phil's House of Good Food. The waitress pushed two tables together and we sat down and studied the menu. My mother blanched at the prices. A chicken dinner went for $2.50, the roast beef for $3.75. "It's a nice place," Dad said, multiplying the five of us times $2.50. "I'm not so hungry, I guess," he said. "Maybe I'll just have soup." We weren't restaurantgoers—"Why pay good money for food you could make better at home?" was Mother's philosophy—so we weren't at all sure about restaurant customs. For example, could a person who had been seated in a restaurant simply get up and walk out? Would it be proper? Would it be *legal?*

The waitress came and stood by Dad. "Can I get you something from the bar?" she said. Dad blushed a deep red. The question seemed to imply that he looked like a drinker.

"No," he whispered, as if she had offered to take off her clothes and dance on the table.   15

Then another waitress brought a tray of glasses to a table of four couples next to us. "Martini," she said, setting the drink down, "whiskey sour, whiskey sour, Manhattan, whiskey sour, gin and tonic, martini, whiskey sour."

"Ma'am? Something from the bar?" Mother looked at her in disbelief.

Suddenly the room changed for us. Our waitress looked hardened, rough, cheap; across the room a woman laughed obscenely, "Haw, haw, haw"; the man with her lit a cigarette and blew a cloud of smoke; a swearword drifted out from the kitchen like a whiff of urine; even the soft lighting seemed suggestive, diabolical. To be seen in such a place on the Lord's Day—*what had we done?*

My mother rose from her chair.

"We can't stay. I'm sorry," Dad told the waitress. We all got up and   20 put on our coats. Everyone in the restaurant had a good long look at us. A bald little man in a filthy white shirt emerged from the kitchen, wiping his hands. "Folks? Something wrong?" he said.

"We're in the wrong place," Mother told him. Mother always told the truth, or something close to it.

"This is *humiliating,*" I said out on the sidewalk. "I feel like a *leper* or something. Why do we always have to make such a big production out of everything? Why can't we be like regular people?"

She put her hand on my shoulder. "Be not conformed to this world," she said. I knew the rest by heart ". . . but be ye transformed by the renewing of your mind, that ye may prove what is that good and acceptable and perfect will of God."

"Where we gonna eat?" Phyllis asked.

"We'll find someplace reasonable," said Mother, and we walked six   *25*
blocks across the river and found a lunch counter and ate sloppy joes (called
Maid-Rites) for fifteen cents apiece. They did not agree with us, and we were
aware of them all afternoon through prayer meeting and Young People's.

The Responsive Reader

1. How does Keillor take you into the Brethren's world of attitudes and beliefs? What would you stress in trying to initiate an unsympathetic listener into their lifestyle, their way of thinking and feeling? (What role
   does Brother Mel play in this story? What does he contribute to your
   understanding of the family's religion?)
2. For the author, what was the appeal of the strange and different Catholic
   tradition?
3. The story leads up to a high point—to a climactic incident that dramatizes the boy's feelings about his background, about his family. What *are*
   the boy's feelings? Where do you first become aware of them? Do you
   sympathize with him?

Talking, Listening, Writing

4. Religion often seems a taboo subject in our society. Why? Courts ban
   displays of the Christmas scene on public property as well as prayers in
   public schools or at commencement ceremonies. Why? Where do you
   stand?
5. Have you ever felt the urge to speak up on behalf of a group considered
   different or alien or undesirable in our society? Speak or write in defense
   of the group.
6. Has the awareness of being "different" played a role in your life or in the
   life of someone you know well? (Or have you ever worried about being
   too much the *same* as everyone else?)

Collaborative Projects

7. Is there a "religious revival" among the young? What kind of religious
   ideas or religious affiliations appeal to young people today? Help organize an informal poll of your classmates that would shed light on these
   questions.

MY FATHER'S OTHER LIFE

Susan J. Miller

When writers tell their life stories, one of the oldest topics is the conflict between parent and child. In personal memoirs and in play and story, writers have played out the tension between the generations. They may focus on the struggle of the restless young against the stifling influence of parents. They may chronicle the rebellion of the defiant son against the authoritarian father or the daughter's rejection of the role model provided by the mother. In our society today, bad parenting has become a buzzword heard in articles and books and therapy sessions where people trace their psychological difficulties to childhood traumas. The dysfunctional family has for many become the focus for their explanations of personal and social ills. In the following piece, Susan J. Miller tells an archetypal story of disillusionment with the father who was at one time at the center of happier childhood days. She grew up in an impoverished, dysfunctional household in the New York area. Her grandmother still spoke Yiddish. New York was then a mecca of jazz aficionados; her father was on the fringe of a jazz scene that featured greats like Charlie Parker, known to his admirers as Bird, and Dizzy Gillespie, the father of bebop.

Thought Starters: What stories or images do terms like *bad parenting* and *dysfunctional families* bring to mind? What chains of association do they start?

One night, at an hour that was normally my bedtime, I got all dressed up, and my mother and father and I drove into New York, down to the Half Note, the jazz club on Hudson Street. I was thirteen, maybe fourteen, just beginning teenagehood, and had never gone anywhere that was "nightlife." I had heard jazz all my life, on records or the radio, my father beating out time on the kitchen table, the steering wheel, letting out a breathy "Yeah" when the music soared and flew. When they were cooking, when they really swung, it transported him; he was gone, inside the music. I couldn't go on this trip with him, but I thought I could understand it. It seemed to me that anyone could, hearing that music. Bird, Diz, Pres, Sweets, Al, Zoot. It was my father's music, though he himself never played a note.

I knew the players, for about the only friends my parents had were musicians and their wives. They fascinated me: their pants with black satin stripes, their battered horn cases. When I was a little kid, I'd lie in bed listening to them talk their hip talk in the next room. I knew I was the only kid in our white neighborhood to be overhearing words like "man" and "cat" and "groove," and jokes that were this irreverent and black. I knew they were cool and I loved it.

At the Half Note that night, the three of us walked through the door, and the owner appeared, all excited to see my father, and in the middle of this smoky nightlife room, he kissed my hand. This was real life, the center of something. We sat down. In front of us, on a little stage, were Jimmy Rushing, a powerful singer, and two sax players, Al Cohn and Zoot Sims, whom I'd known all my life. And there was a whole roomful of people slapping the tables, beating out time, breathing "Yeah" at the great moments, shaking their heads, sometimes snapping their fingers, now and then bursting out with "Play it, man," or "Sing it." When the break came, Zoot sat down with us and ate a plate of lasagna or something and didn't say much except for these dry asides that were so funny I couldn't bear it. And there was my dad: these men were his friends, his buddies. They liked the things about my father that I could like—how funny he was, uncorny, how unsentimental, how unafraid to be different from everyone else in the world.

As a child, I didn't know that my father and many of the musicians who sat with their wives in our living room, eating nuts and raisins out of cut-glass candy dishes, were junkies. It wasn't until I was twenty-one, a college senior, that my father told me he had been a heroin addict, casually slipping it into some otherwise unremarkable conversation. The next day, my mother filled in the story. My father had begun shooting up in 1946, when my mother was pregnant with my brother, who is nineteen months older than me. He stopped when I was around thirteen and my brother was fifteen.

I never suspected a thing. Neither did my brother. We never saw any   5
drug paraphernalia. There was a mysterious purplish spot in the crook of my father's elbow, which he said had something to do with the army. His vague explanation was unsatisfactory, but even in my wildest imaginings I never came near the truth. In the Fifties, in the white, middle- and working-class communities where we lived, no one discussed drugs, which were synonymous with the utmost degradation and depravity. My parents succeeded in hiding my father's addiction from us, but as a result, we could never make sense of the strained atmosphere, our lack of money, our many moves. The addiction was the thread that tied everything together, but we didn't know that such a thread existed, and so decisions seemed insanely arbitrary, my mother's emotions frighteningly hysterical. She was terribly depressed, sometimes desperate. I regularly found her sitting, eyes unfocused, collapsed amid the disorder of a household she was too overwhelmed to manage.

My father was from Brighton Beach, Brooklyn, and earned his living dressing windows in women's clothing stores in and around New York City. Being a window dresser was a touch creative, but most importantly it meant he didn't have to fit in; all he had to do was get the job done. He was a man of socially unacceptable habits. He was fat, he picked his teeth, he burped, he farted, he bit his nails until he had no nails and then he chewed his fingers, eating himself up. He was a high-octane monologuer, a self-taught high-school dropout who constantly read, thought, and talked politics and culture, gobbling up ideas, stuffing himself as fast as he could—with everything.

By the time I was in college my father was taking amphetamines, LSD, mescaline, peyote, whatever he could get. I would receive long letters from him, written when he was coming down from an acid or mescaline trip. Often he tripped alone in the living room of our New Jersey apartment, awake all night, listening to records, writing and thinking while my mother slept. I read pages of his blocky, slanted printing, about how the world is a boat and we are all sinking. Usually I threw them away without finishing them, scanning his stoned raps in front of the big, green metal trash can in the college mail room, picturing him in the living room with the sun rising, wired up, hunched over the paper, filling up the page, wanting me to know all the exciting things he had discovered. Part of me wanted to hear them and love him—and indeed did love him for taking the acid, for taking the chance. But another part shut down, unable to care.

He would not have been a good father even if he hadn't been an addict. By his own admission, he came to parenthood ignorant of love and acquainted only with hate.

My mother told me about my grandmother Esther, the wicked witch of Brighton Beach. According to my mother, my grandmother despised men. She lavished attention on her daughter, my father's only sibling. She dealt in machinations, lies, and deceptions, feeding the fires of hate between father and son, sister and brother. When my father did well in school, his mother scorned him. She tore up a citation he'd won—and then spat on it. She never kissed him, except on the day he went off to boot camp. His mother and my mother, then his young wife, were standing on the platform, saying good-bye. Seeing the other mothers tearfully embracing their sons, his mother was shamed into touching hers: she pecked his cheek.

My father only once told me a story about himself and his mother. I 10 was in college at the time. The two of us were driving on the highway on a beautiful, clear, cold winter day. My father was behind the wheel. Fourteen years earlier, in 1956, his father had died in the hospital while my father and his mother, Esther, were visiting him. My father took Esther home to Brooklyn, where she asked him for a favor. There were some terms in her will she wanted to review. Would he read it out loud to her? (Even in Yiddish my grandmother was illiterate.) My father was tired and upset and somewhat puzzled that his mother wished to go over her will on the night of her husband's death, but he agreed. The will turned out to be simple: Esther's house and savings were to go to Sarah, her daughter. Then he heard himself, the fly in the web, reading: And to my son, Sidney, I leave nothing, because he is no good.

My father stared at the road ahead.

Why, I cried, would she have you read that to her? What did you do?

My father's voice was tired and bitter. She wanted to see what I would do, he said; she wanted to watch my reaction. Ma, I said, I gotta go home now. I'm tired and it's late. I didn't want to show her how bad I felt, I didn't want to give her the satisfaction. I didn't care about the money. Let my fucking sister have the money. But why did she have to write that sentence? Why did she have me read it?

My father started to cry. He had never cried in front of me. His hands loosened their grip on the wheel. The car began to drift into the opposite lane, across the white unbroken line.

Look out, I yelled. He grabbed the wheel and turned us toward   *15* safety. Look out, I yelled, and he did. Look out, I yelled, for what else could I have said?

In August 1988, my father was diagnosed with liver cancer, the result of chronic hepatitis, a disease associated with heroin addiction. The doctors predicted he would live for five months. He tried chemotherapy, ate a macrobiotic diet, enrolled in an experimental holistic treatment program. When I visited him in November, it was clear that things would not turn around.

My mother, who had stuck by him through everything, was still by his side. He was eager to share his latest revelation. A social worker in the treatment program had asked him what he would miss most when he died. He said: I told her that, yeah, sure, I'll miss my wife and my kids, but what I'll miss most is the music. The music is the only thing that's never let me down.

That the revelation would hurt us—my mother especially—never occurred to him. He never kept his thoughts to himself, even if it was cruel to express them. Neither my mother nor I said a word. The statement was the truth of him—not only what he said but also the fact that he would say it to us, and say it without guilt, without apology, without regret.

The Responsive Reader

1. What images or associations do you connect with the jazz scene to which Miller's account takes you? How are your expectations confirmed or disappointed in the opening paragraphs of the essay? What details bring the scene to life for you?
2. Where is the turning point in this essay that introduces you to the other side of the father's life and personality? What is your initial reaction?
3. What was the impact of addiction on the everyday life of the family? What was the impact on the daughter's outlook or personality?
4. What do you learn about the father's childhood or his relationship to his mother as a possible key to the father's personality? Does what you learn change your feelings about the father? Does it excuse him in his daughter's eyes—or in yours?

5. At the end, the author circles back to the father's love of music. How and with what effect?

Talking, Listening, Writing

6. In your judgment, is the author too hard on her father?
7. Have you ever experienced disillusionment with someone you admired? Have you ever had mixed feelings or been torn between contradictory emotions about someone important to you?
8. Where in this essay does Miller give a one-paragraph capsule portrait of her father? What is the keynote? Write a similar capsule portrait of someone who has been important in your life.

Find It on the Web

You may want to explore bad parenting or the dysfunctional family as a recurrent theme in newspaper or magazine articles on the changing American family. Much has been written on alternative families or extended families as new forms of family life. Hara Estroff Marano in "A New Focus on Family Values" (*Psychology Today* November/December 1997) is an example of a writer trying to refocus the discussion on positive advice to what keeps the family together as an institution "committed to love and caring as its primary function." You may want to do a "first search" on the Internet to find recent material on extended families or alternative families.

LAKOTA WOMAN
Mary Crow Dog

Lakota Woman (written with Richard Erdoes) is the story of Mary Crow Dog, who grew up on a reservation in South Dakota in a one-room cabin, without a father in the house and without running water or electricity. Her publisher said about her, "Rebelling against the aimless drinking, punishing missionary school, narrow strictures for women, and violence and hopelessness of reservation life, she joined the new movement of tribal pride sweeping Native American communities in the sixties and seventies and eventually married Leonard Crow Dog, the movement's chief medicine man, who revived the outlawed Ghost Dance." William Kunstler has called the book the "moving story of a Native American woman who fought her way out of bitterness and despair to find the righteous ways of her ancestors." When she was a child on the reservation, Mary Crow Dog says, "Indian religion was forbidden. Children were punished for praying Indian, men were jailed for taking a sweat bath. Our sacred pipes were broken, our medicine bundles burned or given to museums." For a time, before she set out in search of the native traditions of her people, she conformed to the image of the Christian convert. She remembers being confirmed in a white dress, with veil and candle—"white outside and red inside, the opposite of an apple." What in her story fits in with what you know about the indigenous peoples of North America? What changes your mind about the experience of Native Americans?

Thought Starters: What shaped your early impressions of Native Americans? Have recent readings, movies, or television shows changed the way you think about them?

It is not the big, dramatic things so much that get us down, but just being Indian, trying to hang on to our way of life, language, and values while being surrounded by an alien, more powerful culture. It is being an iyeska, a half-blood, being looked down upon by whites and full-bloods alike. It is being a backwoods girl living in a city, having to rip off stores in order to survive. Most of all it is being a woman. Among Plains tribes, some men think that all a woman is good for is to crawl into the sack with them and mind the children. It compensates for what white society has done to them. They were famous warriors and hunters once, but the buffalo is gone and there is not much rep in putting a can of spam or an occasional rabbit on the table.

As for being warriors, the only way some men can count coup nowadays is knocking out another skin's teeth during a barroom fight. In the old

1

days a man made a name for himself by being generous and wise, but now he has nothing to be generous with, no jobs, no money; and as far as our traditional wisdom is concerned, our men are being told by the white missionaries, teachers, and employers that it is merely savage superstition they should get rid of if they want to make it in this world. Men are forced to live away from their children, so that the family can get ADC—Aid to Dependent Children. So some warriors come home drunk and beat up their old ladies in order to work off their frustration. I know where they are coming from. I feel sorry for them, but I feel even sorrier for their women.

To start from the beginning, I am a Sioux from the Rosebud Reservation in South Dakota. I belong to the "Burned Thigh," the Brule Tribe, the Sicangu in our language. Long ago, so the legend goes, a small band of Sioux was surrounded by enemies who set fire to their tipis and the grass around them. They fought their way out of the trap but got their legs burned and in this way acquired their name. The Brules are part of the Seven Sacred Campfires, the seven tribes of the Western Sioux known collectively as Lakota. The Eastern Sioux are called Dakota. The difference between them is their language. It is the same except that where we Lakota pronounce an *L,* the Dakota pronounce a *D.* They cannot pronounce an *L* at all. In our tribe we have this joke: "What is a flat tire in Dakota?" Answer: "A b*d*owout."

The Brule, like all Sioux, were a horse people, fierce riders and raiders, great warriors. Between 1870 and 1880 all Sioux were driven into reservations, fenced in and forced to give up everything that had given meaning to their life—their horses, their hunting, their arms, everything. But under the long snows of despair the little spark of our ancient beliefs and pride kept glowing, just barely sometimes, waiting for a warm wind to blow that spark into a flame again.

My family was settled on the reservation in a small place called He-Dog, after a famous chief. There are still some He-Dogs living. One, an old lady I knew, lived to be over a hundred years old. Nobody knew when she had been born. She herself had no idea, except that when she came into the world there was no census yet, and Indians had not yet been given Christian first names. Her name was just He-Dog, nothing else. She always told me, "You should have seen me eighty years ago when I was pretty." I have never forgotten her face—nothing but deep cracks and gullies, but beautiful in its own way. At any rate very impressive.

On the Indian side my family was related to the Brave Birds and Fool Bulls. Old Grandpa Fool Bull was the last man to make flutes and play them, the old-style flutes in the shape of a bird's head which had the elk power, the power to lure a young girl into a man's blanket. Fool Bull lived a whole long century, dying in 1976, whittling his flutes almost until his last day. He took me to my first peyote meeting while I was still a kid.

He still remembered the first Wounded Knee, the massacre. He was a young boy at that time, traveling with his father, a well-known medicine

5

man. They had gone to a place near Wounded Knee to take part in a Ghost Dance. They had on their painted ghost shirts which were supposed to make them bulletproof. When they got near Pine Ridge they were stopped by white soldiers, some of them from the Seventh Cavalry, George Custer's old regiment, who were hoping to kill themselves some Indians. The Fool Bull band had to give up their few old muzzle-loaders, bows, arrows, and even knives. They had to put up their tipis in a tight circle, all bunched up, with the wagons on the outside and the soldiers surrounding their camp, watching them closely. It was cold, so cold that the trees were crackling with a loud noise as the frost was splitting their trunks. The people made a fire the following morning to warm themselves and make some coffee and then they noticed a sound beyond the crackling of the trees: rifle fire, salvos making a noise like the ripping apart of a giant blanket; the boom of cannon and the rattling of quick-firing Hotchkiss guns. Fool Bull remembered the grown-ups bursting into tears, the women keening: "They are killing our people, they are butchering them!" It was only two miles or so from where Grandfather Fool Bull stood that almost three hundred Sioux men, women, and children were slaughtered. Later grandpa saw the bodies of the slain, all frozen in ghostly attitudes, thrown into a ditch like dogs. And he saw a tiny baby sucking at his dead mother's breast.

I wish I could tell about the big deeds of some ancestors of mine who fought at the Little Big Horn, or the Rosebud, counting coup during the Grattan or Fetterman battle, but little is known of my family's history before 1880. I hope some of my great-grandfathers counted coup on Custer's men, I like to imagine it, but I just do not know. Our Rosebud people did not play a big part in the battles against generals Crook or Custer. This was due to the policy of Spotted Tail, the all-powerful chief at the time. Spotted Tail had earned his eagle feathers as a warrior, but had been taken East as a prisoner and put in jail. Coming back years later, he said that he had seen the cities of the whites and that a single one of them contained more people than could be found in all the Plains tribes put together, and that every one of the wasičuns' factories could turn out more rifles and bullets in one day than were owned by all the Indians in the country. It was useless, he said, to try to resist the wasičuns. During the critical year of 1876 he had his Indian police keep most of the young men on the reservation, preventing them from joining Sitting Bull, Gall, and Crazy Horse. Some of the young bucks, a few Brave Birds among them, managed to sneak out trying to get to Montana, but nothing much is known. After having been forced into reservations, it was not thought wise to recall such things. It might mean no rations, or worse. For the same reason many in my family turned Christian, letting themselves be "whitemanized." It took many years to reverse this process.

My sister Barbara, who is four years older than me, says she remembers the day when I was born. It was late at night and raining hard amid thunder and lightning. We had no electricity then, just the old-style kerosene lamps with the big reflectors. No bathroom, no tap water, no car. Only a few white teachers had cars. There was one phone in He-Dog, at the trading post. This was not so very long ago, come to think of it. Like most Sioux at that time my mother was supposed to give birth at home, I think, but something went wrong, I was pointing the wrong way, feet first or stuck sideways. My mother was in great pain, laboring for hours, until finally somebody ran to the trading post and called the ambulance. They took her—us—to Rosebud, but the hospital there was not yet equipped to handle a complicated birth, I don't think they had surgery then, so they had to drive mother all the way to Pine Ridge, some ninety miles distant, because there the tribal hospital was bigger. So it happened that I was born among Crazy Horse's people. After my sister Sandra was born the doctors there performed a hysterectomy on my mother, in fact sterilizing her without her permission, which was common at the time, and up to just a few years ago, so that it is hardly worth mentioning. In the opinion of some people, the fewer Indians there are, the better. As Colonel Chivington said to his soldiers: "Kill 'em all, big and small, nits make lice!"

I don't know whether I am a louse under the white man's skin. I hope 10 I am. At any rate I survived the long hours of my mother's labor, the stormy drive to Pine Ridge, and the neglect of the doctors. I am an iyeska, a breed, that's what the white kids used to call me. When I grew bigger they stopped calling me that, because it would get them a bloody nose. I am a small woman, not much over five feet tall, but I can hold my own in a fight, and in a free-for-all with honkies I can become rather ornery and do real damage. I have white blood in me. Often I have wished to be able to purge it out of me. As a young girl I used to look at myself in the mirror, trying to find a clue as to who and what I was. My face is very Indian, and so are my eyes and my hair, but my skin is very light. Always I waited for the summer, for the prairie sun, the Badlands sun, to tan me and make me into a real skin.

The Crow Dogs, the members of my husband's family, have no such problems of identity. They don't need the sun to tan them, they are full-bloods—the Sioux of the Sioux. Some Crow Dog men have faces which make the portrait on the buffalo Indian nickel look like a washed-out white man. They have no shortage of legends. Every Crow Dog seems to be a legend in himself, including the women. They became outcasts in their stronghold at Grass Mountain rather than being whitemanized. They could not be tamed, made to wear a necktie or go to a Christian church. All during the long years when practicing Indian beliefs was forbidden and could be punished with jail, they went right on having their ceremonies, their sweat baths and sacred dances. Whenever a Crow Dog got together with some relatives, such as those equally untamed, unregenerated Iron Shells, Good Lances, Two Strikes, Picket Pins, or Hollow Horn Bears, then you could hear the sound of the can gleska, the drum, telling all the world that a Sioux ceremony was in the making. It took courage and suffering to keep the flame alive, the little spark under the snow.

The first Crow Dog was a well-known chief. On his shield was the design of two circles and two arrowheads for wounds received in battle—two white man's bullets and two Pawnee arrow points. When this first Crow Dog was lying wounded in the snow, a coyote came to warm him and a crow flew ahead of him to show him the way home. His name should be Crow Coyote, but the white interpreter misunderstood it and so they became Crow Dogs. This Crow Dog of old became famous for killing a rival chief, the result of a feud over tribal politics, then driving voluntarily over a hundred miles to get himself hanged at Deadwood, his wife sitting beside him in his buggy; famous also for finding on his arrival that the Supreme Court had ordered him to be freed because the federal government had no jurisdiction over Indian reservations and also because it was no crime for one Indian to kill another. Later, Crow Dog became a leader of the Ghost Dancers, holding out for months in the frozen caves and ravines of the Badlands. So, if my own family lacks history, that of my husband more than makes up for it.

Our land itself is a legend, especially the area around Grass Mountain where I am living now. The fight for our land is at the core of our existence, as it has been for the last two hundred years. Once the land is gone, then we are gone too. The Sioux used to keep winter counts, picture writings on buffalo skin, which told our people's story from year to year. Well, the whole country is one vast winter count. You can't walk a mile without coming to some family's sacred vision hill, to an ancient Sun Dance circle, an old battleground, a place where something worth remembering happened. Mostly a death, a proud death or a drunken death. We are a great people for dying. "It's a good day to die!" that's our old battle cry. But the land with its tar paper shacks and outdoor privies, not one of them straight, but all leaning this way or that way, is also a land to live on, a land for good times and telling jokes and talking of great deeds done in the past. But you can't live forever off the deeds of Sitting Bull or Crazy Horse. You can't wear their eagle feathers, freeload off their legends. You have to make your own legends now. It isn't easy.

The Responsive Reader

1. Mary Crow Dog says, "As a young girl I used to look at myself in the mirror, trying to find a clue as to who and what I was." Who is she? What are key elements in her sense of self?

2. What is her attitude toward Native American men? How does she describe and explain their behavior? How does she contrast their past and their present?

3. What do you learn here about the buried or half-forgotten past that, the author says, was for many years "not thought wise to recall"? What is the author's relation to "our people's story"? What do you learn about customs, traditions, beliefs?

Talking, Listening, Writing

4. Some writers speak for themselves as individuals; others give voice to the experience of many. They speak for a group, for a region, or for a generation. Would you consider Mary Crow Dog an effective and representative spokesperson for Native Americans? Why or why not?
5. Do you think white Americans today should feel guilty about the treatment of Native Americans now and in the past? Why or why not?
6. Are you in favor of people like Mary Crow Dog restoring the forgotten or formerly banned culture and religion of their group?
7. Mary Crow Dog says, "You have to make your own legends now. It isn't easy." What does she mean?

Collaborative Projects

8. How much do you know about the American Indian Movement or other organizations dedicated to recovering the cultural heritage of a group in American society? Are there comparable organizations for Spanish-speaking Americans (Chicanos, Latinos), for blacks or African Americans, or for Asian Americans? Pool your knowledge or relevant background with that of other students in your class.

MERICANS

Sandra Cisneros

> *Millions of Americans come from a Spanish-speaking background. Their families may have had ties with the culture of Mexico or Puerto Rico or Cuba. They may have grown up speaking or hearing Spanish and learned English as a second language. Sandra Cisneros was born of a Mexican father and a Mexican American mother in Chicago. She became one of the country's best-known* Chicana—*short for* Mexicana—*authors. For her many readers, the stories in her collection* The House on Mango Street *bring to life the Spanish-speaking neighborhoods that are enclaves in many American cities. The following story is from a later collection,* Woman Hollering Creek *(1991). The story focuses on Mexican American children visiting their grandmother in Mexico. How American are they? How Mexican are they? La Virgen de Guadalupe is the Virgin Mary of Guadalupe, at whose church the grandmother prays. The PRI is the traditional Mexican ruling party, often criticized by progressives for having abandoned the original ideals of the Mexican revolution.*

Thought Starters: What do you know about Hispanic or Latino Americans from sources other than TV or movies? Does your community have a barrio? Does it have Spanish-language stations or publications?

We're waiting for the awful grandmother who is inside dropping pesos   *1*
into *la ofrenda* box before the altar to La Divina Providencia. Lighting votive candles and genuflecting. Blessing herself and kissing her thumb. Running a crystal rosary between her fingers. Mumbling, mumbling, mumbling.

There are so many prayers and promises and thanks-be-to-God to be given in the name of the husband and the sons and the only daughter who never attend mass. It doesn't matter. Like La Virgen de Guadalupe, the awful grandmother intercedes on their behalf. For the grandfather who hasn't believed in anything since the first PRI elections. For my father, El Periquín, so skinny he needs his sleep. For Auntie Light-skin, who only a few hours before was breakfasting on brain and goat tacos after dancing all night in the pink zone. For Uncle Fat-face, the blackest of the black sheep—*Always remember your Uncle Fat-face in your prayers.* And Uncle Baby—*You go for me, Mamá*— *God listens to you.*

The awful grandmother has been gone a long time. She disappeared behind the heavy leather outer curtain and the dusty velvet inner. We must stay near the church entrance. We must not wander over to the balloon and punch-ball vendors. We cannot spend our allowance on fried cookies or

Familia Burrón comic books or those clear cone-shaped suckers that make everything look like a rainbow when you look through them. We cannot run off and have our picture taken on the wooden ponies. We must not climb the steps up the hill behind the church and chase each other through the cemetery. We have promised to stay right where the awful grandmother left us until she returns.

There are those walking to church on their knees. Some with fat rags tied around their legs and others with pillows, one to kneel on, and one to flop ahead. There are women with black shawls crossing and uncrossing themselves. There are armies of penitents carrying banners and flowered arches while musicians play tinny trumpets and tinny drums.

La Virgen de Guadalupe is waiting inside behind a plate of thick glass.   5
There's also a gold crucifix bent crooked as a mesquite tree when someone once threw a bomb. La Virgen de Guadalupe on the main altar because she's a big miracle, the crooked crucifix on a side altar because that's a little miracle.

But we're outside in the sun. My big brother Junior hunkered against the wall with his eyes shut. My little brother Keeks running around in circles.

Maybe and most probably my little brother is imagining he's a flying feather dancer, like the ones we saw swinging high up from a pole on the Virgin's birthday. I want to be a flying feather dancer too, but when he circles past me he shouts, "I'm a B-Fifty-two bomber, you're a German," and shoots me with an invisible machine gun. I'd rather play flying feather dancers, but if I tell my brother this, he might not play with me at all.

"*Girl*. We can't play with a *girl*." Girl. It's my brothers' favorite insult now instead of "sissy." "You *girl*," they yell at each other. "You throw that ball like a *girl*."

I've already made up my mind to be a German when Keeks swoops past again, this time yelling "I'm Flash Gordon. You're Ming the Merciless and the Mud People." I don't mind being Ming the Merciless, but I don't like being the Mud People. Something wants to come out of the corners of my eyes, but I don't let it. Crying is what *girls* do.

I leave Keeks running around in circles—"I'm the Lone Ranger,   10
you're Tonto." I leave Junior squatting on his ankles and go look for the awful grandmother.

Why do churches smell like the inside of an ear? Like incense and the dark and candles in blue glass? And why does holy water smell of tears? The awful grandmother makes me kneel and fold my hands. The ceiling high and everyone's prayers bumping up there like balloons.

If I stare at the eyes of the saints long enough, they move and wink at me, which makes me a sort of saint too. When I get tired of winking saints, I count the awful grandmother's mustache hairs while she prays for Uncle Old, sick from the worm, and Auntie Cuca, suffering from a life of troubles that left half her face crooked and the other half sad.

There must be a long, long list of relatives who haven't gone to church. The awful grandmother knits the names of the dead and the living into one long prayer fringed with the grandchildren born in that barbaric country with its barbarian ways.

I put my weight on one knee, then the other, and when they both grow fat as a mattress of pins, I slap them each awake. *Micaela, you may wait outside with Alfredito and Enrique.* The awful grandmother says it all in Spanish, which I understand when I'm paying attention. "What?" I say, though it's neither proper nor polite. "What?" which the awful grandmother hears as "¿Guat?" But she only gives me a look and shoves me toward the door.

After all that dust and dark, the light from the plaza makes me squinch   *15*
my eyes like if I just came out of the movies. My brother Keeks is drawing squiggly lines on the concrete with a wedge of glass and the heel of his shoe. My brother Junior squatting against the entrance, talking to a lady and man.

They're not from here. Ladies don't come to church dressed in pants. And everybody knows men aren't supposed to wear shorts.

"¿*Quieres chicle?*" the lady asks in a Spanish too big for her mouth.

"*Gracias.*" The lady gives him a whole handful of gum for free, little cellophane cubes of Chiclets, cinnamon and aqua and the white ones that don't taste like anything but are good for pretend buck teeth.

"*Por favor,*" says the lady. "¿*Un foto?*" pointing to her camera.

"*Sí.*"   *20*

She's so busy taking Junior's picture, she doesn't notice me and Keeks.

"Hey Michele, Keeks. You guys want gum?"

"But you speak English!"

"Yeah," my brother says, "we're Mericans."

We're Mericans, we're Mericans, and inside the awful grandmother   *25*
prays.

The Responsive Reader

1. What makes the "awful grandmother" in the story the representative of the Old Country culture and Old Country ways? What do you learn about her religion—about the church where she worships, about saints and miracles, and about her prayers? Why are there so many "don'ts" in what she tells her grandchildren? Why does she think of Americans as barbarians?

2. Does Cisneros intend the American tourists at the end of the story to be stereotypically American? How does Micaela see them? Is she making fun of them—if so, why? (Does the tourist lady get any credit for having studied Spanish?)

3. Like many young Americans, Micaela and her brothers are somewhere on the spectrum that runs from the Old Country culture to

stereotypically all-American ways. Where on the spectrum would you place them? How "Merican" are they? What is revealing about the names they call each other, their play, their fantasy world, their manners?

Talking, Listening, Writing

4. Students with a Hispanic or Latino background point out that part of the traditional culture is the requirement to be respectful toward your elders. Do you think Micaela, the girl telling the story, is too disrespectful or negative about the grandmother? How far has Micaela gone toward being alienated from the traditional culture?
5. Have you ever felt like one of the "in-between" people—unable to identify fully with what was expected of you as a member of a family or group?

REFUGEE SHIP

Lorna Dee Cervantes

Lorna Dee Cervantes was born in San Francisco of Mexican descent and was a student at San Jose State University. She said in a poem addressed to her brother, "We were so poor . . . We were brilliant at wishing." Her poems often play on the contrast between an older generation with strong ties to an ethnic past and a younger generation living in the Americanized present. Cervantes published Emplumada, *her first collection of poems, in 1981. She founded Mango Publications, a small press publishing books and a literary magazine.*

Thought Starters: What do you know about refugees? What do you know about boat people?

Like wet cornstarch, I slide   1
past my grandmother's eyes. Bible
at her side, she removes her glasses.
The pudding thickens.
Mama raised me without language,   5

I'm orphaned from my Spanish name.
The words are foreign, stumbling
on my tongue. I see in the mirror
My reflection: bronzed skin, black hair.

I feel I am a captive   10
aboard the refugee ship.
The ship that will never dock.
El barco que nunca atraca.

The Responsive Reader

1. In her poems, Cervantes casually shifts to Spanish words she heard in her childhood when she talks about the scenes and people of her youth. So then why does the speaker in the poem say that her mother raised her "without language"? Why do you think the mother did what she did? Why does the speaker feel "orphaned" from her Spanish name? (How can you be orphaned from a name?)
2. Why, right after talking about language, does the person speaking in the poem look at herself in the mirror? What's the point of what she sees?

3. Why does the poet feel trapped like a captive on a refugee ship? Why will the ship never dock? What do you know about refugees and refugee ships that would explain how the ship became a central symbol in this poem?
4. The last line of the poem repeats in Spanish the preceding line about the ship that will never dock. Why is it fitting that this idea is stated in both English and Spanish?

Talking, Listening, Writing

5. This poem spans three generations. What happened in the passage from one generation to another? Do you think this poet is alienated from her Hispanic or Latina heritage?
6. Linguists use the term *code-switching* for people shifting from one language to another. Have you observed people doing this? Is there any pattern to how and when they shift from one language to another?
7. Have you ever become estranged or alienated from a group to which you once belonged?

FORUM: *Bridging the Cultures*

I identify with Americans, but Americans do not identify with me.
Caroline Hwang

For many young Americans, growing up with diverse cultural influences is as American as pizza. America may no longer be a nation of immigrants, but for many it is still a nation of the children of immigrants. For many others, it has been a nation of working-class families trying to ensure a better education and a better life for their sons and daughters. For still others, it has been a nation where parents try to preserve their traditional values while their offspring feel the pull of the lifestyles of a new generation.

Many American life stories chronicle the move from one world to another. A typical life story may record the mental journey from the world of a traditional immigrant home to the American world of school—with baseball, proms, cheerleaders, dating, junk food, and diet cola. The book *Fifth Chinese Daughter* tells the story of moving on from a home where elders were revered, where boys had many privileges while girls did the chores, and where dating was considered sinful. It tells the story of trying to become part of a new world where girls were told to speak up!—to form their own opinions and make their own decisions.

Does the diversity of the American experience have to lead to a clash of cultures, or can it lead to a meeting of cultures? What is likely to be more common—confrontation or fruitful interaction and change? Is growing up in a diverse society likely to produce a new blend and a rich mix—or a lack of orientation and unresolved issues?

THE GOOD DAUGHTER

Caroline Hwang

> *Caroline Hwang is an editor for* Redbook; *she is a former English major and an aspiring novelist. Her parents came to this country from Korea, and she is part of the Asian American minority that is becoming increasingly visible in American life. Hwang is one of millions of young Americans who "straddle two cultures"—and who at times feel like foreigners in their own land. Hwang says, "I feel displaced in the only country I know." Like many first-generation Americans, she found she was torn between the need to shape her own life on the one hand and filial duty on the other—the attitude of a dutiful son or daughter trying to please the parents.*

Thought Starters: Can you tell when classmates or newcomers are the children of immigrants? How can you tell? Do you think of them as "all American" or as immigrants?

The moment I walked into the dry-cleaning store, I knew the woman behind the counter was from Korea, like my parents. To show her that we shared a heritage, and possibly get a fellow countryman's discount, I tilted my head forward, in shy imitation of a traditional bow.

"Name?" she asked, not noticing my attempted obeisance.

"Hwang," I answered.

"Hwang? Are you Chinese?"

Her question caught me off-guard. I was used to hearing such queries from non-Asians who think Asians all look alike, but never from one of my own people. Of course, the only Koreans I knew were my parents and their friends, people who've never asked me where I came from, since they knew better than I.

I ransacked my mind for the Korean words that would tell her who I was. It's always struck me as funny (in a mirthless sort of way) that I can more readily say "I am Korean" in Spanish, German and even Latin than I can in the language of my ancestry. In the end, I told her in English.

The dry-cleaning woman squinted as though trying to see past the glare of my strangeness, repeating my surname under her breath. "Oh, *Fxuang*," she said, doubling over with laughter. "You don't know how to speak your name."

I flinched. Perhaps I was particularly sensitive at the time, having just dropped out of graduate school. I had torn up my map for the future, the one that said not only where I was going but who I was. My sense of identity was already disintegrating.

When I got home, I called my parents to ask why they had never bothered to correct me. "Big deal," my mother said, sounding more flippant than I knew she intended. (Like many people who learn English in a classroom, she uses idioms that don't always fit the occasion.) "So what if you can't pronounce your name? You are American," she said.

Though I didn't challenge her explanation, it left me unsatisfied. The *10* fact is, my cultural identity is hardly that clear-cut.

My parents immigrated to this country 30 years ago, two years before I was born. They told me often, while I was growing up, that, if I wanted to, I could be president someday, that here my grasp would be as long as my reach.

To ensure that I reaped all the advantages of this country, my parents saw to it that I became fully assimilated. So, like any American of my generation, I whiled away my youth strolling malls and talking on the phone, rhapsodizing over Andrew McCarthy's blue eyes or analyzing the meaning of a certain upperclassman's offer of a ride to the Homecoming football game.

To my parents, I am all American, and the sacrifices they made in leaving Korea—including my mispronounced name—pale in comparison to the opportunities those sacrifices gave me. They do not see that I straddle two cultures, nor that I feel displaced in the only country I know. I identify with Americans, but Americans do not identify with me. I've never known what it's like to belong to a community—neither one at large, nor of an extended family. I know more about Europe than the continent my ancestors unmistakably come from. I sometimes wonder, as I did that day in the dry cleaner's, if I would be a happier person had my parents stayed in Korea.

I first began to consider this thought around the time I decided to go to graduate school. It had been a compromise: my parents wanted me to go to law school; I wanted to skip the starched-collar track and be a writer— the hungrier the better. But after 20-some years of following their wishes and meeting all of their expectations, I couldn't bring myself to disobey or disappoint. A writing career is riskier than law, I remember thinking. If I'm a failure and my life is a washout, then what does that make my parents' lives?

I know that many of my friends had to choose between pleasing their *15* parents and being true to themselves. But for the children of immigrants, the choice seems more complicated, a happy outcome impossible. By making the biggest move of their lives for me, my parents indentured me to the largest debt imaginable—I owe them the fulfillment of their hopes for me.

It tore me up inside to suppress my dream, but I went to school for a Ph.D. in English literature, thinking I had found the perfect compromise. I would be able to write at least about books while pursuing a graduate degree. Predictably, it didn't work out. How could I labor for five years in a program I had no passion for? When I finally left school, my parents were disappointed, but since it wasn't what they wanted me to do, they weren't devastated. I, on the other hand, felt I was staring at the bottom of the abyss. I had seen the flaw in my life of halfwayness, in my planned life of compromises.

I hadn't thought about my love life, but I had a vague plan to make concessions there, too. Though they raised me as an American, my parents expect me to marry someone Korean and give them grandchildren who look like them. This didn't seem like such a huge request when I was 14, but now I don't know what I'm going to do. I've never been in love with someone I dated, or dated someone I loved. (Since I can't bring myself even to entertain the thought of marrying the non-Korean men I'm attracted to, I've been dating only those I know I can stay clearheaded about.) And as I near that age when the question of marriage stalks every relationship, I can't help but wonder if my parents' expectations are responsible for the lack of passion in my life.

My parents didn't want their daughter to be Korean, but they don't want her fully American, either. Children of immigrants are living paradoxes. We are the first generation and the last. We are in this country for its opportunities, yet filial duty binds us. When my parents boarded the plane, they knew they were embarking on a rough trip. I don't think they imagined the rocks in the path of their daughter who can't even pronounce her own name.

The Responsive Reader

1. In what ways did Hwang's parents try to have her become "fully assimilated"—and why? In what ways did she grow up "all American"? How did she discover that at the same time they wanted her to be true to her ethnic heritage?
2. What is a paradox? Why does Hwang consider herself a living paradox? What would you include in a composite portrait of her "cultural identity"? Would you call her life a "life of halfwayness"? Why or why not?

Talking, Listening, Writing

3. Do young people from immigrant families have a special problem trying to "choose between pleasing their parents and being true to themselves"? Do you tend to agree a "happy outcome" is impossible? Have you seen evidence to support this view, or have you seen evidence to the contrary? Can something similar be true for everyone—regardless of ethnic roots?
4. Telling the story of the Korean woman who laughed at the way she pronounced her name, Hwang says, "Perhaps I was particularly sensitive at the time." Do you think Hwang is oversensitive about her problems of identity? Do you think Americans from an immigrant or a minority background tend to be oversensitive about how they are seen by others?
5. Hwang says that she knows more about Europe than about the continent her parents came from. Do you think this is still true of most Americans

who came from immigrant backgrounds and received a Eurocentric education? How Eurocentric was your own education?

6. Have you ever tried to get any special favor because of your being part of a group? Have you ever tried to obtain the equivalent of a "fellow countryman's discount"—and with what result?

Collaborative Projects

7. What's in a name? (As a friend or prospective employer, would you have advised Hwang—Fxuang—to change her name to something more American? Why or why not?) Names of media celebrities used to sound like inventions of public relations specialists: Dylan Thomas, Tony Curtis, Marilyn Monroe, John Wayne. (What were their real names?) A reverse trend set in some years ago: Among white ethnics, Judy again became Tschudi, Rusk again became Ruszkiewicz. At the same time, among African Americans, Leroy Jones became Imamu Amiri Baraka, Cassius Clay became Muhammad Ali, and many others followed suit. What additional examples can you track down? What do these name changes tell you about trends in American culture or in "identity politics"?

A DAUGHTER'S STORY

Nguyen Louie

> *Is there a typical American student? Or is it typically American for everyone to have the right to be his or her own person? What is familiar or predictable about the following life story of a fellow student? Is there anything representative about waystations in her life, about her relationship with her parents, or about her thoughts and feelings while growing up? What, if anything, is different or unexpected about Nguyen's story? In what ways is her story different from yours? Can you relate to some of the things that make it different? Nguyen Louie wrote this autobiographical essay when she was a student at Brown University. It was first published in* Ms. *magazine as part of a series of testimonies exploring mother-daughter relationships. In Nguyen's story, her relation to the ethnic history of her parents and to a second culture plays a role—but, as with many other young Americans, it is only part of the story.*

Thought Starters: Has the "generation gap" become a cliché, or is it still a live issue for many young Americans during their growing up?

I was born two days before International Women's Day (IWD). As I *1* was growing up, this was always a hectic time of year because my mother was busy going to meetings and organizing programs for the IWD event. I resented the fact that it seemed to take precedence over my birthday. I always wanted a full-fledged birthday party with a dozen friends, junk food, and presents. Instead, I stayed in day care with other children whose mothers were members of the Third World Women's Alliance. On my eleventh birthday I was allowed to be part of the IWD event; I gave a speech in front of 300 people to raise money for a child care center in Angola. My mother coached me and bought me a purple jumpsuit for the occasion. For the first time, I was doing something that might make a difference on the other side of the world. I think I grew more during that five-minute speech than I had during the previous year. That's when I realized why my mother did what she did and why it was important.

My parents were at Berkeley during the sixties. They agitated for the development of ethnic studies, dropped out of school, and protested against the Vietnam war. They were very liberal. They also gave me a lot of freedom to grow on my own. With that flexibility, I didn't feel the need to rebel. I don't really understand the kinds of relationships my girlfriends have with their mothers. Usually their mothers were overprotective, making my friends want to defy them even more. Although my mom and I are not equals, we are best friends. I can talk to her, confide in her, laugh with her, and cry with her.

We weren't always so close. As a young child, I was resentful that she didn't have much time to spend with me. I felt closer to my father; he did things with me. We watched videos, ate potato chips, played board games, and went for walks together. When my dad brought his paperwork home, I would poke around and ask him what he was doing. My parents were probably gone from home the same amount of time, but I blamed my mother more. I guess it was because I thought my mother was supposed to be around.

When I was six, my mother became pregnant with my brother, Lung San. I was lonely and looked forward to having a sibling to play with, but I didn't expect my parents to spend so much time with him and not with me. Again, I blamed my mother. I tried to run away, but made it only to the corner because I wasn't supposed to cross the street. Consequently I was forced to compromise with my parents and accept my new role as a responsible big sister, one who was too mature to have tantrums and run away. By age 12, I preferred to stay home from the conventions my parents went to and take care of my brother.

Looking back, I realize that my mother always made sure we had quality time together. My father and I were content to bum around the house, but my mother insisted that we go out and do things. We went on excursions to the Berkeley marina, Golden Gate Park, and Chinatown, and we took family vacations in Santa Cruz and Hawaii. Although it may sound cheesy, my family is very trusting, loving and closely knit.

I used to feel pressure to be active in my mother's causes. I felt that I was letting her down if I didn't go to meetings. Being active was the right thing to do, but it wasn't always what I wanted to do. I wanted to be a "normal" teenager, to go to the movies or bowling with my friends. Often it seemed like my parents did not have any fun; they were always gone, and they came home exhausted. I wasn't able to see that their work was interesting or worthwhile. To me, it seemed oppressive. In a lot of ways I am more conservative than my mom. I often fight change. My mom wants me to get out there and be more active, and sometimes I just don't think I have the time or energy for it. I just want to be myself.

When I was 13, my parents sent me to Cuba for a month with an international youth organization. My mother said, "It will open your eyes, and you'll learn so much." I adamantly did not want to go. My body was changing and I had started to menstruate, and I was insecure and anxious about having to deal with guys or compete with girls on this trip. The mere thought of it terrified me. But my parents were firm; they put me on the plane, and I went.

My parents were right. It was an eye-opening experience. Delegations of young people had come to Cuba from all over the world. I learned how impoverished some other kids were and about the struggles they were going through. When I went home I felt I had a responsibility to do something, to use the information I had gained and become more active. I started out with good intentions, but my resolve dwindled when I went to junior high school. There were cliques that required being popular and looking cute, and I wanted to be myself. I didn't want to change myself to fit into any clique. I was often lonely and miserable. I hated junior high.

In high school I discovered it was O.K. to be myself. In fact, it was cool to be an individual. I became secure and comfortable with myself and made a lot of good friends who accepted me for who I was. When I was a sophomore I was a founding member of the Asian Awareness Club. When complaints arose about Asian students getting beaten up and kicked in the hallways, we organized workshops on interracial relationships and Asian stereotypes. Part of what I liked about the club was organizing with my friends and deciding to do it on my own. My parents weren't telling me, "You are going to this meeting and will learn something from it." I planned the meetings and the different issues we discussed.

I decided to go to Brown because of its academic diversity and the fact *10* that it offered the flexibility of creating your own major. Also, being at home with my parents was too comfortable; I needed to get out on my own and be more independent. Breaking away from my parents was the hardest thing for me to do. But my parents made the transition easier by flying out with me to the East Coast and giving me lots of support.

When I got to Brown, I went through a difficult time. I had never been so aware of my socioeconomic background, but at Brown it seems that the majority of the students have been through private East Coast preparatory schools, and I felt they had the upper hand. I also found it strange to meet so many students whose primary goal is to make money. Many students aspire to be doctors not because they want to help people, but in order to have extravagant lifestyles. I was disheartened by this attitude. The first semester was a struggle for me. My parents stressed that although grades are important, they are not matters of life and death. They just said, "Do the best you can." I still feel the need to work, but the pressure is coming from within myself.

I am a feminist by my own interpretation: I believe that men and women are equal physically and intellectually; therefore, they are entitled to equal rights, treatment, and respect. I take this for granted, and I immediately assume people are wrong for thinking otherwise. It's almost instinctive. Yet I would never introduce myself as a feminist; I am a Chinese-Korean-American young woman. Being a feminist is an integral part of who I am, but it is not all that I am.

I can't see myself being as much of an activist as my mother, but activism is definitely a part of me. It's in my blood. I'm not sure whether that's a blessing or a curse. I plan to tap into the activism on campus, but I don't want to devote my life to it. I prefer to deal with things on a personal level. What I want from life is to achieve my maximum potential, to be happy, and to be comfortable. I want to find a balance.

The Responsive Reader

1. What do you learn about the mother's involvement as an organizer or activist? What is the author's attitude toward her mother? How did it develop or change during her growing up? (Does the author consider herself an "activist"?)
2. Has the term *liberal* become a dirty word in our society? In what sense were Louie's parents "liberals"? What do you learn here about traditional liberal causes? Why would ethnic studies be one of them?
3. Phrases like "sibling rivalry," "quality time," and "the desire to be normal" are familiar to students of pop psychology and of talk shows focusing on personal concerns. Are these phrases just buzzwords? What role did they play in Louie's growing up?
4. "Educational experiences" that people might mention in a vita might include travel and contrasting experiences at different stages of their schooling. What was eye-opening about the author's trip to Cuba? What made the difference between her junior high and her high school experience?
5. How did the author become aware of the role of race or ethnicity? What shaped her attitude toward or interest in "diversity"? How did she become aware of the role of class in American society?

6. Louie says, "I am a feminist by my own interpretation." What *is* her own version of feminism? How does it compare with yours or with your definition of the term?

Talking, Listening, Writing

7. Do you think Nguyen Louie could be called a typical or representative young American? Why or why not? Do you think she has had a privileged or sheltered experience while growing up? Do you think she has allowed herself to be steered too much by her parents?
8. Was there a waystation or a turning point in your growing up when you discovered the role of poverty, of race, of class, or of gender in our society?
9. Is there activism on your campus? What form does it take? Who gets involved? Do you?

ON BEING WHITE

Mara Joseph

For decades, the national dialogue about race highlighted demands from underprivileged groups aspiring to their place in the sun. Affirmative action programs took aim at compensating for the results of poverty, residential segregation, segregated, underfunded schools, and widespread discrimination in employment. As affirmative action programs slowly made Americans from minority backgrounds more visible in government employment, higher education, and management jobs, a backlash developed amid charges of reverse discrimination. Whites passed over for college admission, hiring, or promotion began to make their grievances heard. When she wrote the following short essay, Mara Joseph was a cultural anthropology major at the University of California at Davis. She is on the defensive concerning challenges to the status of her privileged class, and she objects to the politicizing of classes that should be devoted to impartial scholarship.

Thought Starters: What was your first experience with prejudice—either as a person experiencing prejudice or as someone realizing that you were prejudiced against others? Did the experience make a lasting impression on you? Why or why not?

I admit it freely. I am a privileged individual. I grew up in a wealthy *1* area outside of Los Angeles, went to a very good public high school and have had all the things I could possibly need or want provided for me by two loving parents.

Until one day last month, I have never felt like I was being discriminated against. That day, while sitting in an anthropology lecture about race, class and gender, I started to feel as though the color of my skin (a rather blinding white at this time of year) was putting me in an unfair position.

And recently, I discovered that I am not the only person to feel this way either.

Just the other day, a friend told me about the cultural English class he had taken, in which he was the only white person. The main assignment in the class? Write about your experience as an immigrant to America who does not speak English.

Needless to say, my blue-eyed and blond friend, who is probably a   5
fifth- or sixth-generation American, didn't do very well in the class.

Another friend had a similar experience in her Asian American studies class, in which she was expected to write about her life as an Asian American (clearly a bit difficult for a person of European descent).

Once again, she did poorly in the class, and so did the few other white people in it.

On a similar note, David Horowitz's article decrying reparations was published recently in my college newspaper, although it was quickly revealed as an oversight by the editor who extended sincere apologies for the mistake.

I never saw the article, but I know the general idea behind reparations: Payment should be given to African Americans to compensate for the atrocities their ancestors endured as slaves.

Of course, I agree that slavery was a horrible tragedy and a scar on our   10
country's history, as it is among many other countries involved in the slave trade during previous centuries. But I don't see how I am in any way responsible for it.

In fact, I don't see how my ancestors are either, because, like many other Americans, I am descended from recent immigrants.

Just years before the civil rights movement began in this country, my relatives were busy dealing with their own problems—namely Hitler and Nazi Germany (they were Austrian Jews).

Even if my relatives were among early British colonizers in this country and owners of slaves, I would hope to not be held responsible for their ignorance and injustice. To punish someone for actions they didn't commit is as unjust as punishing someone for the color of their skin.

But instead of learning from the past and moving on, it seems that many people would rather dwell and seek revenge. Instead of using college courses to teach students what the immigrant or racial experience is like, the classes catered to members of that particular culture.

Because so many of the other comments I have made in my afore-   15
mentioned anthropology class have been shot down or ignored, I am writing this in hopes of reminding others that we are all immigrants in the

United States (with the notable exception of Native Americans), and we all have our own unique stories and valid opinions to share.

I agree with those who say that people should never be judged based on the color of their skin—so why are these same people often the first to judge me for the color of mine?

The Responsive Reader

1. What is provocative or attention-getting about Joseph's title? How do you react to it?
2. What mental picture do you form of the writer after reading her first two paragraphs? Do you tend to identify or sympathize with her, or do you find yourself prejudiced against her? Do you think that from the start her essay will divide her audience along racial lines?
3. Do you agree that today's generation of young white Americans should not feel "in any way responsible" for the atrocities of slavery and the slave trade? Do you agree with her that reparations for the harm done by slavery would punish people "for actions they didn't commit"?
4. What charges does the writer make concerning political and racial bias in her classes? How convincing are her examples?
5. What is Joseph's point in saying that "we are all immigrants"? Do you think it is an important point of valid argument in discussions of inequalities in our society?
6. How do you think Joseph would want us to "learn from the past and move on"?

Talking, Listening, Writing

7. Joseph says that some college courses are catering to students of particular backgrounds rather than "using college courses to teach students what the immigrant or racial experience is like." Have you observed a political or ideological slant in any of your own classes? In what classes is slanting toward one or the other end of the political spectrum likely to be an issue? How do you or your fellow students cope with it?
8. Do you ever feel singled out because of the way you look or because of other features that might identify you as a member of an ethnic or religious group? What reactions do you face from people who are from different racial, ethnic, or religious backgrounds? Why do you think they react as they do? How do you respond? How would you like them to react to you?
9. Are aggrieved whites in general or especially angry white males a factor in your classes or on your campus? What role do they play? How do you relate to them?
10. Should colleges limit enrollment in ethnic studies classes or similar courses specifically to members of the racial or ethnic groups that are the focus of a course?

Drawing on Your Experience

Much powerful writing is rooted in firsthand experience. The life story of Maya Angelou—born in the segregated Old South, overcoming the obstacles in her path, becoming a widely admired performer and poet— has made her a role model for a younger generation. The story of Richard Rodriguez—finding himself the only Mexican kid in an all-white class-room, with only a few words of English—has had a special meaning for readers navigating their own passage from an immigrant past to an Ameri-can future.

However, even when a writer does not focus exclusively on his or her own story, drawing on personal experience gives a special, authentic touch to the discussion of larger issues. When we read about gender roles or the immigrant experience, we assume that the writer knows the subject at first hand. Reading about affirmative action, we want to know if the author can say: "I was there"—as a target, a beneficiary, a witness, or a close, caring observer. We want to see what theories or statistics mean to the lives of people the author has known or observed. Words are just words until we can relate them to the experience of someone who is involved or who cares.

Writing that draws on personal experience has special strengths:

- When you take stock of your own personal experience, you write about what you know best. No one is more of an expert than you are on what matters to you as a person. Nobody knows more about where and how you grew up. Nobody knows better what home or family meant to you or what helped and hindered you in school or on the job.

- Writing from experience sets up a special confidential relationship between writer and reader. As the writer, you show that you trust your readers enough to share with them your personal thoughts and feelings. The basic assumption in writing that takes stock honestly of the author's own experience is that readers will be able to relate—to see the connection with what matters in their own lives.

TRIGGERING Papers based on personal experience often seem better motivated than other kinds. Here are some reasons to do this kind of writing:

- *People want to share what they have experienced.* When they have faced a serious challenge, they need to tell somebody—if only a diary or journal. Have you ever felt uprooted from friends or from familiar surroundings? Have you ever felt like an outsider in your school or your neighborhood? Have you ever had to live with the aftermath of divorce? These are experiences that may make you want to tell your story. Many people find that writing about a family problem, serious illness, or living with disability helps them cope.

- *People need to sort things out in their own minds.* Have you ever felt torn between feuding parents? Have you ever been divided between what your friends expected and what was expected of you in school? Writing gives you a chance to go back over what happened and try to understand. When you have had difficult relationships with family, or when you had to leave behind a tradition or earlier belief, writing gives you a chance to come to terms with the experience.

- *People feel the need to state a grievance.* When people have been wronged, they may feel the need to go on record. Have you ever witnessed a wrongful arrest? Have you ever seen people denied benefits that you felt were rightfully theirs? When people see injustice, they may want to bear witness (rather than "not get involved"). When you have witnessed an incident of police brutality (or citizen brutality) or bureaucratic bungling, you may feel the need to make your voice heard. When you hear well-financed politicians criticize welfare mothers, you may want to testify in their behalf.

- *People feel the need to pay tribute.* They experience pleasure in sharing what is good—discovering the rewards of tutoring or being a mentor, for instance. They pay tribute to someone who served as a role model or helped them in time of need.

GATHERING What will make a paper about your personal experience become real for your reader? The answer is: Work up a rich fund of material. What sights, sounds, or emotions do you remember? What really happened? What do you remember about the people? What were your honest feelings? Preliminary notes like the following, for a paper about the writer's first experiences in the world of work, have the ring of authentic personal testimony:

> The summer before the sixth grade, my mother decided it was time to send me out into the berry fields. I hated it. I made barely any money for the time I was out there. My back ached from bending and picking strawberries,

and my hands were forever purple. All my friends were frolicking in the sun while I was stuck in the fields. However, after a few summers of picking, the owners moved me up to the supervising/truck working position. I now got paid by the hour and achieved a status my older brothers had never achieved. This past summer was probably the last summer I will ever work in the fields. I came to love associating with the pickers. The migrant workers are some of the best people I know. Because of working outside, I got a great tan. I know how to drive tractors or tie down trucks, and I was the only girl at my position. However, the time had come to move on. Berry picking was a great experience, but there are other places out there for me too.

Honest writing about personal experience faces up to the good and the bad. Check out the real-life material in the following notes for a student's paper on her and her friends' "health-threatening" struggle to live up to the stereotype of the "ideal woman." She says, "No matter how skinny we became, we never thought we were thin or perfect enough." This is the kind of material that speaks for itself even before you start spelling out for your readers what you learned from the experience:

When I was fifteen, two of my girlfriends taught me to throw up. We thought we were terribly clever; we could gorge with impunity and not gain weight. It was a lark and a clever act of rebellion against the constant punitive dieting we subjected ourselves to and that our girlfriends, mothers, and older sisters continued to endure. Within three years, bingeing and purging had become an essential rhythm of my life. For my friend, throwing up was her solution to being thin and not having to diet. To her, it was her rebellion against a system that required women to look skinny and starved. She and her friends would eat vast quantities of food: an entire roast chicken; leftover pasta with salmon in heavy cream sauce; salad with walnuts, Roquefort cheese, and homemade croutons; key lime and apple pies; and peach cobbler with ice cream. By the time she graduated from high school, she was bingeing and purging almost every day. This way she was able to appear "fragile, helpless, and weak—all the qualities so admired in females." Trying to stop, my friend went to therapists, doctors, meetings, and Overeaters Anonymous. A woman running one meeting asked, "Would you be willing to stop if it meant gaining ten pounds?" No one in the group could say yes.

Remember that *telling* your readers about your experiences and feelings is not enough. You need to make them real for your reader. Anchor them to concrete incidents and situations. Re-create the people and situations that inspired your feelings and shaped your thoughts. Re-create the people, the places, the events, so that words will not just remain words. Bring to life incidents that served as an eye-opener for you or for your family or friends.

SHAPING   To turn your memories into a structured paper, you focus on what matters. You lay out the material in an order that makes sense. Unsorted experience tends to be miscellaneous. One thing happens after another. Avoid papers that fall into the "and–then" pattern: This happened, and then this happened, and then this happened. An effective paper brings a key issue or concern into focus. It focuses on something that really mattered to you. It may highlight a major strand in your life, leaving much else aside.

In a successful paper about personal experience, different incidents have added up. They have become part of a pattern. The author has pushed toward a **thesis**, or unifying central idea. The following passage by a student of Japanese descent sums up his strong personal feelings. This paragraph could be the key passage of a paper about the experiences that helped make the question of identity a major issue in the student writer's mind:

"What are you?" I have often been at a loss for words as to how to answer this question. Should I answer, Japanese? American? Japanese American? I do not consider myself fully Japanese, since I have not been brought up with the language and the strict traditional culture. I am not an ordinary American because of obvious visible differences. Trying to answer this question has often left me in an awkward position and has sometimes led me to regret my existence.

Often you can organize a personal experience paper by focusing on the key issue in a series of events. Maybe you will be telling the story of your attempt—successful or not—to make peace with a stepmother who you felt was always watching you "with evil eyes." However, here are some other ways to organize your paper:

- You may write a paper about a major *turning point*—a crucial turn in the road toward your becoming your own person.

- You may want to use a strong *then-and-now* pattern to organize your paper. What were assumptions about gender roles when you grew up, and what are they now? How did your own thinking change?

- You might trace the tension between two strong conflicting influences in your growing up. Perhaps your allegiance was divided between two parents very different in their personalities and commitments, or perhaps you experienced a strong pull between the traditional culture of the home and the peer culture of the neighborhood or school.

A PAPER FOR PEER REVIEW What makes the following personal-experience paper a strong paper? What is the connecting thread or unifying idea? What are striking details that a reader might remember? What suggestions would you make for revision? Where do you think the writer might need to work in real-life examples or striking details?

Life on the East Side

I grew up on the east side of my town. Until I moved into the college dorms, the east side was the only environment I really knew. It is not a "Leave it to Beaver" neighborhood. There are no white picket fences, nor do children roam the neighborhood freely. In my neighborhood and in my old high school, drugs and gangs are serious problems. There are few traditional families left. Most kids do not come home from school to parents waiting with milk and cookies but to babysitters or empty houses. While students in other parts of town go to band practice or hang out at the mall with their friends, kids on the east side hang out with their fellow gang members spraypainting the local park.

Living in an environment such as this limits a person's freedom. Growing up, I was denied the luxuries that people from "better" neighborhoods take for granted. In my neighborhood, my friends could not go to the local bowling alley, mall, or miniature golf course without running into gang members. There aren't many places to go for someone without a driver's license because the local hangouts just aren't safe. Driving was especially important to my friends and me because it meant we were not limited to places near our homes and could go to places where we felt more secure. It is sad that fear of violence prevents parents from letting their children go to the local rollerskating rink, but on the east side this is just a reality one accepts.

My family is typical of the east side in that we never had much money. It hasn't been easy coming from a family that lives from paycheck to paycheck. There is always a sense of tension in the house that comes from the uncertainty of not knowing if there is going to be enough money to pay the bills or where the money for unexpected expenses like car repairs will come from. It is hard to watch my parents struggle. Neither of my parents attended college, and they thus had limited options for work. My dad works long hours at a job he doesn't like and consequently usually comes home overtired and in a bad mood. My sister and I have had all our physical and emotional needs met, however. My parents always found the money for things like braces for our teeth, prom dresses, and class trips. Obviously, I have never had a brand new car or taken a trip to Europe, but I have never felt deprived either.

Life on the east side gives one a different perspective. It has taught me realities that I might not otherwise have learned. I do not live in the worst part of town. In high school, I had friends who hated walking down the street to their own houses because they were afraid. At least I can walk through my own neighborhood during the day and feel fairly secure. That I consider a luxury. I have learned not to take anything for granted. I believe people spend too much time obsessed with what they don't have. My house is tiny, and all four of us have to share one bathroom. This used to be a problem for me, and I was jealous of friends who lived in large houses with their own bathrooms. Then I volunteered for work in homeless shelters. Now I am thankful that I have a house.

I learned much during my four years at my east side high school, and much of this learning occurred outside the classroom. With more than four thousand students, the school is a model of cultural and economic diversity. I was lucky to have friends from many different backgrounds. I am comfortable with all races and religions. The school has its problems, but it also has many strengths that outsiders overlook.

Being in college I get to live out a dream. However, the new environment also presents me with new obstacles. While I am not ashamed of my past, I still feel as though I have to prove that I belong here. I have made friends and am treated no differently than anyone else. Yet coming from a school with a bad reputation I feel I have to do everything twice as well as other people. I know that no person is inferior to another person, but there is still a small part of me that can't help feeling tainted by negative images of the east side. However, there are few things I would change about my past. My environment has had much to do with who I am today.

REVISING Always make time for revision. Revising gives you a chance to look at your own writing with the reader's eye. Check a first draft to see what needs work:

- *Move in for the closer look.* Build up concrete detail. Add detail to make your readers visualize the setting. Add physical details, revealing gestures, or favorite sayings to make us see and hear a favorite uncle or cranky neighbor. Act out key events in more striking detail.

- *Look for places where you have fallen back on clichés.* Ready-made phrases are handy: "finding oneself," "breakdown in communication," "the fear of commitment." However, make sure such phrases do not sound second-hand. Try your own way of saying what you feel—which may be partly similar to but also in part different from what others have felt before you.

- *Check for overgeneralizing.* It is easy to read too much into a single incident. A key incident may dramatize a pattern, but it may also have resulted from an unusual combination of circumstances. (A teacher or a police officer may have had a bad day—just as a heart-warming, generous gesture may have been a once-in-a-lifetime event.)

- *Try not to sound too one-sided or self-righteous.* Readers get wary when everything that went wrong in your life was someone else's fault.

- *Try not to make everything sound zany, hectic, or funny.* Readers tire of a strained facetious tone. A good tone to aim for may be seriousness with an occasional lighter touch.

Topics for Experience Papers (A Sampling)

1. Have you ever rebelled against tradition, or have you ever returned to a tradition that you had left behind? What led to your change of heart? Was there a turning point? What was the outcome?
2. Have you ever been torn between competing influences on your life or your thinking? Have you ever experienced divided loyalties? How did you sort them out?

3. Have you experienced a change in your religious outlook? For instance, have you or people close to you become or considered becoming "reborn Christians"? Or have you had the experience of leaving a childhood faith behind?

4. Have you encountered special obstacles—or special opportunities—because of who or what you are? What has been your personal experience with discrimination or prejudice? (Or, what is your experience with favoritism or having the "inside track"?)

5. Have you felt defensive about your identity? Have you ever felt ashamed or embarrassed about your background? Do you feel resentful or uncomfortable when people pry into where you came from or what you are? How do you cope?

6. In your growing up, have you encountered a challenge to your sense of self-worth? Has a problem in your family or personal life affected your outlook or helped shape your personality?

7. Where and how did you become aware of race? Where or when did you become aware of the role of ethnicity or varying national origins? What difference has race or ethnicity made in your life?

8. Have you ever discovered a new lifestyle or rediscovered a cultural identity? What difference has it made in your life?

9. Have you ever changed your mind on a major issue? Have you ever had a change of heart on a subject like marriage, having children, abortion, or divorce?

10. What shaped your views on what it means to be a man or a woman? Did you have any role models who influenced or changed your views of gender roles? Have you had occasion to reexamine or revise your views?

11. What has been your initiation into the world of work? What jobs—good or bad—made an impression on you? Do you believe in the "work ethic"?

2
LEARNING
School and the World

Education is much in the news. The widespread perception is that the nation's schools are failing. Employers complain about job applicants lacking basic skills. In the high-tech sector, employers bring in employees from India and Pakistan with the necessary grounding in math and computer science. There is much talk about education reform, much of it centered on increased standardized testing.

Journal Writing: Education in the News

Here is a sampling of news items on the currents and crosscurrents that impinge on the successes and failures of the nation's schools. Write a journal entry commenting on items that seem to show a pattern or that you can relate to your own experience with the world of education, or track similar recent news items and comment on them in your journal.

A new federal initiative mandates testing every year, with financial rewards and penalties for high-performance and underperforming schools.

"High-stakes" testing will deny many unqualified students a high school diploma.

Justices overturn a voucher plan to use tax money to pay parents of pupils in private schools. Supporters vow to try again.

Corporations spent $1.3 billion sponsoring last year's Olympic Games, and "they worry about the continuing failure of the nation's schools." (Lewis Lapham)

The new cabinet had only one Ph.D., Secretary of Education Rod Paige—and his doctorate was in physical education.

A teacher says that support personnel and teacher's assistants disappeared, but "every social problem in our society walks through the schoolroom door."

A student who was told he could not enter a classroom to say good-bye to a girl returns with a gun and kills the teacher, shooting him point-blank in the face.

Teacher salaries in Texas, one of the richest states in the Union, are $6000 below the national average.

A state legislature mandates a period of "silent meditation" at the beginning of the schoolday, then changes the wording to "silent meditation and prayer," and finally allows audible prayer.

A troubled student commits suicide, using a gun he found under a friend's parents' bed.

In a big-city school without winter heat, students sit at their desks huddled in heavy coats till the mayor prods maintenance personnel to secure a missing boiler part for the centralized heating system.

The poorest schools with the most urgent student needs have the highest proportion of underqualified or uncredentialed teachers.

Teachers buy pencils and paper with their own money because of budget cuts.

A parent sues a school district for $1.5 million because the son was cut from the varsity team, thus damaging his chances to go on to a career as a highly paid professional athlete.

College football coaches earn million-dollar salaries.

The following reading selections feature testimonies from teachers and students, whose voices are often not heard in the clamor over educational reform. Writing in a professional journal for educators, a teacher reported that in the planning of a major statewide new testing program the input from teachers had been "minuscule."

NO REST FOR THE OVERACHIEVER

Thessaly La Force

The story of American education often seems to be a story of two nations. Some students, like the high school student who wrote the following brief article, live in a high-pressure world. They participate in honors classes, advanced placement classes for college credit, and mentoring or coaching programs for important tests. In addition, they accumulate plus points for theater, music recitals, and participation in student government. Many other students attend schools that do not have honors classes or advanced placement classes. Art and music programs may have been cut. The self-advertised overachiever who wrote the following article was seventeen at the time. She was a student at Marin Academy High School in San Rafael, California. She was a commentator and reporter for Youth Radio, an award-winning journalism training program.

Thought Starters: In your own schooling, have you observed a growing emphasis on academic achievement? Have you experienced increasing pressure or stress in your schoolwork? What form did it take? How did you respond?

This summer is looking more like school than ever before. While ¹ friends are scattered across the globe this summer, they're not backpacking across Europe. They're checking in for college. That's right, college. High school students are signing up for school, just for fun.

Mind you, this isn't day camp.

These aren't simple classes you can blow off. They have homework, grades, papers and finals crammed into a couple of weeks. If you're lucky, you'll get credit for the next school year.

I'm taking a class in ethnic studies at the University of California at Berkeley. I decided as early as December that I wanted to sign up for a college course. And don't think the pressure was coming from my parents. They had no idea about it until I asked for a check.

In my ethnic studies class, a lot of the students are still in high school ⁵ like I am. Some of them are as young as 16. One girl proudly introduced herself as a student body class president. And that's when it hit me: Most of the high school students who are taking these college classes are overachievers—just like me.

But why are high school students signing their summer away for school? Are we crazy?

My friend taking classes said to me, "It's so strange we're having a stressful summer."

Summer isn't supposed to be like that. Part of me suspects that in a couple of years, when I'm well into college, I'll regret pushing myself so hard. Am I really furthering my education? Or am I just so used to being stressed that I can't shut it off?

See, it's getting harder and harder to take things easy as a teenager. High school choices—even in the summer—are all part of your career path these days.

Last spring, I was juggling five honors classes, two Advanced Place- 10 ment classes, a theater production and student body elections. When a music recital was scheduled on top of all that, I almost cracked.

I called my music teacher in tears, begging her to postpone it. She refused, insisting I had cold feet. A week after the recital, she approached me to apologize. She's been teaching students for a long time and admitted she's never seen stress like this before.

But don't blame adults and administrators for our obsessions. We're the ones giving ourselves the stress. We want the stress. We willingly sign up for these summer courses. The work just never stops. We finish the school year and dive back into books and grades before we notice we were stressed out in the first place.

I think the reason why we program year-round sessions of stress in our lives is because we are overly mindful of our future. Everything I do, every opportunity I take, is for my future. And now stress is so ingrained in my life that it seems normal.

But when did my future become more important than my present?

The Responsive Reader

1. Based on her account, what would you include in an Overachiever's Résumé for Thessaly? Are any of the items predictable? Are any surprising?
2. If you had to name one central motive or driving force behind Thessaly's academic life, what would it be? How would you explain or define it?
3. How would you describe La Force as a person? Does she remind you of students you know or have known? Do you find her likable or admirable? Why or why not?
4. Where does she show that she has moments of doubt or second thoughts about her high-pressure academic life? How serious or how sincere do they seem to you?

Talking, Listening, Writing

5. Who or what accounts for the relentless emphasis on achievement on the part of Thessaly and her friends? Is it the parents? (What role do the parents play in this account?) Is it pressure from the school or the teachers? Does the pressure come from the larger culture?

6. What advice would you give to La Force and students like her? Is she right to place so much emphasis on the future, even at the expense of the present?

Collaborative Projects

7. Working with a group, you may want to research current trends in criteria for college admission. Is it true that extracurricular activities and contributions to the community are increasingly being weighted in addition to test scores and grades?

GOING TO SCHOOL IN EAST LA

Mike Rose

Mike Rose is a university teacher whose reports from the front lines of our educational system have inspired other teachers and students. Himself the son of poor Italian immigrants, Rose has devoted his career to helping students from minority or low-income backgrounds succeed in our system of education. He believes in the untapped potential — the native intelligence and ability to learn of students shortchanged by traditional educational assumptions and procedures. Rose first reached a wide audience with his Lives on the Boundary *(1989). He wrote this book to explore how his own early experiences were "reflected in other working-class lives I have encountered: the isolation of neighborhoods, information poverty, the limited means of protecting children from family disaster" and also "the resilience of imagination, the intellectual curiosity and literate enticements that remain hidden from the schools, the feeling of scholastic inadequacy, the dislocations that come from crossing educational boundaries." The following selection is from* Possible Lives, *the book Mike Rose published as a sequel or companion volume to* Lives on the Boundary.

Thought Starters: Mike Rose has been fascinated by the way American education helps define and perpetuate the class structure of this country. Did you go to school, or are you going to school, mostly with students of your own class or social level? Or did or do you study and associate with students from a cross section of American society?

It was early in the morning, the sky beginning to lighten, when   *1*
Carlos Jiménez and I passed East Los Angeles Community College on our way to Garfield High School, close to the eastern boundary of East Los Angeles. The sun was coming up, breaking through the clouds, light gray and pearl, shining on beige stucco houses, small Spanish arches. Carlos's mother had taught at Garfield, and he's taught there for eleven years. The school was built in 1925, originally serving a predominantly Anglo and immigrant Jewish, Armenian, and Japanese population, but since World War II the surrounding community has become more Mexican in character and has been relatively stable; it is not uncommon for families to remain in the area for two generations, unusual in highly mobile Los Angeles. As the demographers would put it, it is a blue-collar community with a low transiency rate. One indicator of this residential stability is that Garfield, whose constituency is overwhelmingly Latino, needs to provide English-as-a-second-language instruction for only about 15 percent of its student body. Many schools outside of East LA have a higher Latino immigrant population.

Garfield High School was the location for the movie *Stand and Deliver,* the tribute to calculus teacher Jaime Escalante, but though Carlos respected Escalante's work (Escalante is no longer there), he bristled at the film's portrayal of the school as a place that did not believe in the potential of its students. There was a time when the school was in terrible shape, had one of the highest drop-out rates in the city, but student and community activism in the late 1960s contributed to change in general conditions. And during the mid-seventies, before Escalante's tenure, a core of dedicated teachers (John Bennett, Dennis Campagna, Tom Woessner) began building a rigorous advanced placement program, made up of courses, like those depicted in *Stand and Deliver,* which prepare students for tests that secure college credit. For some time, John Bennett has been preparing successful teams for the city's Academic Decathlon competition. "It's a decent school, and the kids are so damned nice," Carlos said en route. "There are the problems that come with poverty—kids are absent, some run away from home, and there is some gang activity—but by and large we don't have too many problems. Some LA schools have it a lot harder." One thing going for Garfield is that it is connected to its community. The annual football game with crosstown rival Roosevelt (another famous East LA school, but farther west, closer to the LA River and the downtown Civic Center) draws twenty-five thousand people. As one young local explained to me, "You look at the band and the parade—you can see that Garfield is real together. The people there are united."

Carlos would get to Garfield about seven—the time we arrived—and that would give him an hour to arrange his day. He taught U.S. history, two sections of advanced placement history, a course in Mexican-American history, and he coached field events and sprints for the track team. Because there had been so few materials available, he wrote the book he uses for the Mexican-American history course, sitting at his kitchen table, a pile of library books before him, typing units on Cortés or the Mexican Revolution or the Zoot Suit Riots onto duplicating stencils and distributing them to this class the next day. The materials have been revised and published as a textbook. His interest in athletics went back to his own career as a high school and college sprinter and triple-jumper, and he has developed his coaching skills in a series of sports clinics. He was a methodical teacher, relying on detailed notes, working from an outline of events displayed via an overhead projector, giving frequent quizzes, and assigning lots of writing. He would leave school about five, except on those days when there was a track meet; then it would be closer to seven-thirty or eight.

Along the entire south wall of Carlos's classroom was a series of pictures and texts that represented the sweep of Mexican and Mexican-American history: from a drawing of three Aztec warriors looking at an eagle with a snake in its beak to Hernán Cortés to Miguel Hildalgo and the Grito de Dolores, calling for "freedom and justice for the common man."

Then came a picture-list of the Mexican presidents, drawings of Benito Juaréz and Emiliano Zapata, a poster for Luis Valdez's *Zoot Suit,* another poster of Cesar Chávez, the cover from Richard Vasquez's novel *Chicano,* a photograph of one of the murals that decorate the walls in East LA—a strong female figure in the style of Diego Rivera harvesting the fields: brown, orange, gold, and blue. At the very end of the pictorial time line was a poster for the Garfield-Roosevelt football game, the two team captains shaking hands, "a winning tradition."

Following Carlos through his day, I got to hear lectures on the Texas Revolt and the short-lived Lone Star Republic, on the Spanish-American War and the debates within the United States between the Internationalists and the Anti-Imperialism League, on the major battles of World War II— Guadalcanal, Anzio, Iwo Jima—watching an old film, watching the faces of the students as the camera focused on the young faces of dead soldiers, listening to a girl beside me, her hand to her mouth, whisper "No." I sat through homeroom ("Good morning, Bulldogs . . ." the public address system blared) and a conference period during which Carlos dealt with a boy who had been kicked out of his house. I sat in as Carlos and another advanced placement teacher brought their classes together for an academic decathlon-style competition. I watched Carlos coach his pole vaulters. And through the day, I got to talk with his students. Here are [. . .] interviews with Ana Gaytan—a junior who was in Carlos's homeroom, had elected one of his sections of advanced placement history, and ran the two-mile for the track team—and Eddie Torres, a senior in Carlos's Mexican-American history class who was in the process of sending out applications for college.

5

Ana was about five foot two, slim, stood with her back straight, held her books to her chest. She talked about the way Carlos's room made her feel: "comfortable" and "at home." "Spanish was the first language I spoke and wrote," she explained, "and it feels good to see it reflected here. Sometimes during homeroom I'll turn around and just start reading the things on the wall—you know, about the Aztecs or about Father Hidalgo—and it makes me want to know more about it." Eddie—hint of a mustache, neat in T-shirt and jeans, opening a big binder he carried instead of a book bag—explained further as he looked for his homework. "If you grow up in East LA, all you hear are negative things. The movies, negative. The news, negative. The newspapers, negative. But, you know, this room is something *positive.* As you walk around the room, you say, 'Hey, we're somebody!' So that's why I took the Mexican-American history course. I wanted to know who we are."

Ana was interested in working with children—she volunteered at a nearby center for handicapped children—and hoped someday to be a pe-diatrician. Her days were very full, helping at home, attending a church group, school, homework, track practice. Her father was a lithographer and was going to night school to improve his English, but the family always tried to have dinner together. After dinner, she would clean up, then take a shower to jolt herself awake for her homework. When we spoke, she had just finished a paper for her English class on the emptiness of the character Daisy in *The Great Gatsby.* "Over the years," she said, "you just learn to set a schedule for yourself."

Eddie had more recently found his way. "Many of my friends have dropped out." He shrugged. "The hope, the self-esteem, was not there." He used to take general courses, and according to Carlos, his writing was not up to par. But he got tired of the "worksheets and busy work" and wanted classes where "you could give your own opinion—discuss and debate"—courses that "would help me in the future." He wanted to go away to college, to see new things. "Sometimes we Mexicans stay too tied to the family, but I think we need to gain new experience also." So he elected Carlos's Mexican-American history and advanced placement courses in history and Spanish. "I wanted to feel the pressure of the tough courses," he explained. "I wanted to know what that was like."

The Responsive Reader

1. Many people spend a large part of their lives in a school setting. Rose starts with a brief description of the school that is the setting for the students in his account. What would you include in your own capsule portrait of the school? What features or details seem most important as "indicators" of what the school is like? Is anything different from what you might have expected?
2. Do the students in Rose's account become real to you? What kind of people are they? Do you think of them as strangers, or do you come to know and like or dislike them? What are you likely to remember about them?
3. Richard Rodriguez, author of *Hunger of Memory,* once said that Mexican American students used to learn more about the wars of distant British warlords than about the work of their own parents and grandparents in the fields. In recent years, schools have started to honor the history of students from diverse backgrounds. What role does the concern with Mexican American history play in this account?
4. Rose has long promoted and paid tribute to the work of dedicated teachers working against odds. What role do such teachers play in this account? What motivates them? What are their methods and attitudes? What obstacles do they encounter, and how do they deal with them?
5. Rose stresses the vital connection between the school and the community as a key to the success of a school. How does he show this connection in this account?

Talking, Listening, Writing

6. In Rose's piece, Carlos Jiménez creates his own textbook to teach Mexican American history. Have you observed similar initiatives to put students in touch with their roots or their heritage? Supporters say that such initiatives promote self-esteem and help students overcome negative attitudes toward school. Critics claim that such initiatives may prove divisive, with other students feeling left out. What is your own estimate of the challenges and results?

7. What would you tell interested outsiders about your high school or college? What would you include beyond dry facts to give them a sense of what it is like to go to school there? What would you say about facilities, atmosphere, teachers, students, or community support?

Collaborative Projects

8. Carlos Jiménez decorated his classroom wall with "a series of pictures and texts that represented the sweep of Mexican and Mexican-American history." Suppose you were working on a class project to create an introduction to an ethnic, racial, or religious group to which you belong or in which you have a special interest. What would you include? What themes or key ideas would you stress? What assumptions or stereotypes that readers and viewers might bring to your project would you try to address?

MARKETERS ARE STORMING
THE SCHOOLHOUSE

Michael J. Sandel

> *In recent years, aggressive advertisers have moved into new areas in the search for ways to get commercial messages to the consumer. Fans shrug when sports arenas with time-honored names like Candlestick Park or Texas Stadium turn into 3-Com Park or Coca-Cola Arena. College athletes are becoming used to being walking advertisements, carrying a corporate logo on their uniforms and running shoes. School districts sign exclusive contracts with manufacturers of soft drinks to supplement tight budgets. Are critics of the growing "commercialization of schools" waging a losing battle? Michael J. Sandel wrote the following article for the "Hard Questions" column of the* New Republic, *a journal of commentary and informed opinion offering readers a range of views.*

Thought Starters: Americans are used to being surrounded by advertising. Keep a log of the commercial messages you encounter during a single day. Which of them did you really notice? Which of them might have an impact on your behavior as a consumer?

When the Boston Red Sox installed a display of giant Coke bottles   *1*
above the left field wall this season, local sportswriters protested that such tacky commercialism tainted the sanctity of Fenway Park. But ballparks have long been littered with billboards and ads. Today, teams even sell corporations the right to name the stadium: the Colorado Rockies, for example, play in Coors Field. However distasteful, such commercialism does not seem to corrupt the game or diminish the play.

The same cannot be said of the newest commercial frontier—the public schools. The corporate invasion of the classroom threatens to turn schools into havens for hucksterism. Eager to cash in on a captive audience of consumers-in-training, companies have flooded teachers with free videos, posters and "learning kits" designed to sanitize corporate images and emblazon brand names in the minds of children. Students can now learn about nutrition from curricular materials supplied by Hershey's Chocolate or McDonald's, or study the effects of the Alaska oil spill in a video made by Exxon. According to *Giving Kids the Business,* by Alex Molnar, a Monsanto video teaches the merits of bovine growth hormone in milk production, while Proctor & Gamble's environmental curriculum teaches that disposable diapers are good for the earth.

Not all corporate-sponsored educational freebies promote ideological agendas; some simply plug the brand name. A few years ago, the Campbell

Soup Company offered a science kit that showed students how to prove that Campbell's Prego spaghetti sauce is thicker than Ragu. General Mills distributed science kits containing free samples of its Gusher fruit snacks, with soft centers that "gush" when bitten. The teacher's guide suggested that students bite into the Gushers and compare the effect to geothermal eruptions. A Tootsie Roll kit on counting and writing recommends that, for homework, children interview family members about their memories of Tootsie Rolls.

While some marketers seek to insinuate brand names into the curriculum, others take a more direct approach: buying advertisements in schools. When the Seattle School Board faced a budget crisis last fall, it voted to solicit corporate advertising. School officials hoped to raise $1 million a year with sponsorships like "the cheerleaders, brought to you by Reebok" and "the McDonald's gym." Protests from parents and teachers forced the Seattle schools to suspend the policy this year, but such marketing is a growing presence in schools across the country.

Corporate logos now clamor for student attention from school buses   5
to book covers. In Colorado Springs, advertisements for Mountain Dew adorn school hallways, and ads for Burger King decorate the sides of school buses. A Massachusetts firm distributes free book covers hawking Nike, Gatorade and Calvin Klein to almost 25 million students nationwide. A Minnesota broadcasting company pipes music into school corridors and cafeterias in fifteen states, with twelve minutes of commercials every hour. Forty percent of the ad revenue goes to the schools.

The most egregious example of the commercialization in schools is Channel One, a twelve-minute television news program seen by 8 million students in 12,000 schools. Introduced in 1990 by Whittle Communications, Channel One offers schools a television set for each classroom, two VCRs and a satellite link in exchange for an agreement to show the program every day, including the two minutes of commercials it contains. Since Channel One reaches over 40 percent of the nation's teenagers, it is able to charge advertisers a hefty $200,000 per thirty-second spot. In its pitch to advertisers, the company promises access to the largest teen audience in history in a setting free of "the usual distractions of telephones, stereos, remote controls, etc." The Whittle program shattered the taboo against outright advertising in the classroom. Despite controversy in many states, only New York has banned Channel One from its schools.

Unlike the case of baseball, the rampant commercialization of schools is corrupting in two ways. First, most corporate-sponsored learning supplements are ridden with bias, distortion and superficial fare. A recent study by Consumers Union found that nearly 80 percent of classroom freebies are slanted toward the sponsor's product. An independent study of Channel One released earlier this year found that its news programs contributed little to students' grasp of public affairs. Only 20 percent of its airtime covers current political, economic or cultural events. The rest is devoted to advertising, sports, weather and natural disasters.

But, even if corporate sponsors supplied objective teaching tools of impeccable quality, commercial advertising would still be a pernicious presence in the classroom because it undermines the purposes for which schools exist. Advertising encourages people to want things and to satisfy their desires: education encourages people to reflect on their desires, to restrain or to elevate them. The purpose of advertising is to recruit consumers; the purpose of public schools is to cultivate citizens.

It is not easy to teach students to be citizens, capable of thinking critically about the world around them, when so much of childhood consists of basic training for a commercial society. At a time when children come to school as walking billboards of logos and labels and licensed apparel, it is all the more difficult—and all the more important—for schools to create some distance from a popular culture drenched in consumerism.

But advertising abhors distance. It blurs the boundaries between places, and makes every setting a site for selling. "Discover your own river of revenue at the schoolhouse gates!" proclaims the brochure for the 4th Annual Kid Power Marketing Conference, held last May in New Orleans. "Whether it's first-graders learning to read or teenagers shopping for their first car, we can guarantee an introduction of your product and your company to these students in the traditional setting of the classroom!" Marketers are storming the schoolhouse gates for the same reason that Willie Sutton robbed banks—because that's where the money is. Counting the amount they spend and the amount they influence their parents to spend, 6- to 19-year-old consumers now account for $485 billion in spending per year. 10

The growing financial clout of kids is itself a lamentable symptom of parents abdicating their role as mediators between children and the market. Meanwhile, faced with property tax caps, budget cuts and rising enrollments, cash-strapped schools are more vulnerable to the siren song of corporate sponsors. Rather than raise the public funds we need to pay the full cost of educating our schoolchildren, we choose instead to sell their time and rent their minds to Burger King and Mountain Dew.

The Responsive Reader

1. What is the "bottom line" underlying the controversy? How does Sandel size up the buying power of young Americans and the corporate respect for it?

2. What is Sandel's analysis of "news programs" distributed by corporate sponsors. What are his objections? How justified or well-founded do they seem to you?

3. Sandel and other critics of corporate dealings with the schools claim that gifts of equipment or products to the schools are often not really public-spirited and beneficial to learning and students' growth. They are "freebies"—offered with ulterior motives. What are Sandel's examples, and how convincing are they?

4. A major public relations strategy of corporate advertisers is the effort to co-opt the concerns of public-spirited citizens—for instance, to stress the environmental or health benefits of corporate products or practices. What are Sandel's examples? Why does he find them objectionable?

5. Sandel employs the traditional strategy of satire—holding up the most outlandish examples of a trend or phenomenon to ridicule. What to you are the most ridiculous or outlandish examples Sandel cites?

Talking, Listening, Writing

6. Have you, or has someone you know well, been exposed to advertising in the classroom or on campus? What form did it take? What was your or the other person's reaction? Was the advertising effective? Was it objectionable?

7. Do you agree with Sandel's basic assumption that there is an essential difference between advertising to adults and the commercial exploitation of the young? Why or why not?

8. How would you define *consumerism?* What are its key features? How essential is it to the functioning of American society or the American way of life?

9. Developments like those criticized by Sandel in this essay often precipitate vigorous debate in the concerned communities. Would you get involved? Choose from one of the following letter-writing assignments or take on another similar writing task:

   • Write a letter or e-mail as a corporate public relations person to respond to Sandel's argument.

   • Write a letter or e-mail from a school administrator to concerned parents.

   • Write a letter or e-mail from a college athlete objecting to or defending the use of a corporate logo on athletic uniforms and equipment.

   • Write a letter or e-mail to the editor of *New Republic* to accuse its columnist of being anti-business or to defend him against the charge.

ELECTRONIC COMMUNICATION
MAY AID SOCIAL INTERACTION

Stanford Report

Supporters of the computer revolution aim at providing computer access for every student. Enthusiastic advocates made computer literacy the fast lane to the age of the information highway and the knowledge explosion. The "information resources specialist" featured in the following report from a campus newsletter was an early leader in the movement to help teachers and students become computer literate and make full use of the resources of the Internet. At the same time, promoters of the cyberspace revolution heard from critical observers and cyberskeptics warning against inflated expectations and negative side effects.

Thought Starters: When did you first start to become computer literate? Who or what initiated you? What early obstacles or problems did you encounter? How would you rate your computer literacy now?

Consider Zachary,[*] made to order for isolation by computer. A self-described loner, he asked for a single room when he arrived as a freshman in 1995. His room, like most at Stanford, was wired directly to the university's computer network. Critics of this "plug-per-pillow" arrangement said it would lead students to hide in their electronic caves, avoiding face-to-face interaction, not to mention ruining the chance to develop the proper wrist action for Frisbee. Zachary was poised to be their poster boy.

His dorm, Rinconada House in Wilbur Hall, was the first college dorm in the world with its own web page and one of the first to use "list-serv" software that permitted all 96 residents to send and read e-mail messages circulated to the entire group. Zachary soon plugged in to these on-line discussions and became one of the list's most frequent correspondents.

Isolation city? Au contraire. At meals, other students sought him out to comment about his online musings. People dropped by his room to talk. Over the year, resident fellows Rich and Roni Holeton watched Zachary gradually become gregarious and adopt his dormmates as extended family. "Without his e-mail postings, this might never have happened," Rich Holeton says. "We might never have learned what a thoughtful guy he is."

Holeton (A.B. '75) found a number of surprises that jolt conventional wisdom about computer communication in research he conducted of Rinconada's e-mail discussions for the 1995-96 academic year. Instead of being an "either-or" situation, where time spent on computers takes away from time spent with others, e-mail extended and added to personal conversations, drawing in new members of the community, he found.

*All student names are pseudonyms.

1

5

"The computers became a tool for building, rather than destroying, social relations," he said.

Residents used the e-mail discussion list, along with meetings, hallway conversations, phone calls and notices posted on the walls, to organize and publicize events, find lost keys, trade jokes and call out players for that quick game of Frisbee. They used this computer grapevine, along with conversations and dorm meetings, to hammer out community issues like how much noise is too much during study hours. They added e-mail to the traditional bull session when they wanted to talk about social and political issues ranging from a grape boycott to date rape. When a dormmate died suddenly, the e-mail list was one of the ways they shared their grief.

Several studies have been made of computer-mediated communication in virtual communities linked by work or common interest, but Holeton said to his knowledge, Rinconada is the first real community to be studied—the first place where e-mail list correspondents live together and see each other day and night.

He analyzed all the messages posted to the Rinconada list for a year, and compared his findings with the results of a survey in which the students rated the usefulness of e-mail as a form of communication.

Except as a means of discussing academics, e-mail was considered by the students to be as useful or more useful than other means of dorm communication. (Holeton's study results—including data, analyses and samples of online discussions on topics from free speech to planning a dorm dance—can be viewed at http://www-leland.stanford.edu/-holeton/ wired-pages/wired-main.html). 10

Holeton is an information resources specialist, teaching language and literature professors new ways to use electronic media in the classroom. He spent 10 years as a Stanford writing instructor; his third anthology for writing classes, *Composing Cyberspace,* has just been published. In his writing classes, he used computer discussion groups as a way to expand the usual classroom dynamic, where a few gregarious people usually dominate the conversation. He found that online, he could get everyone involved.

Students in a dorm are not subject to a teacher's prodding, however. As he expected, Holeton found that a small core of a dozen students dominated Rinconada's e-mail discussions. But even shy students who seldom posted messages were using the list to keep themselves cued in to the community.

"Most students rated themselves as occasional writers but frequent readers of the list," Holeton says. Those so-called lurkers used the list mostly for housekeeping purposes, that is, to find out about events or ask if anyone had seen a chemistry book left in the lounge. But in dialogues about social and political issues, some of the most thoughtful commentary came from lurkers who clearly felt comfortable jumping into a conversation that they had been following in silence.

Holeton says one thing his study couldn't find out was whether shy students used e-mail to avoid face-to-face conversations. His personal observations showed that for some, like Zachary, e-mail was an icebreaker that helped open up personal contact.

Men traditionally dominate discussions in dorm meetings as well as in the classroom, and Holeton says he was troubled to find that the same dynamic continues online. One woman. Hillary, posted more messages to the list than anyone else, but she and Bertha were the only two in the core group who participated often. Men also dominated the discussions that Holeton labeled "critical dialogue," the sort of social and political debate that an academic setting is designed to promote; women joined in more often in discussions about the dorm community. "Men may participate more because they are more comfortable with the traditional combative debate style of critical dialogue," Holeton says.   15

When he looked more closely, however, he found some of the most interesting debates were initiated and joined by women. One thread of conversation that went on for several months began when Mona passed on a letter from another college, a cautionary tale about date rape. A thoughtful debate continued among several men about responsibility for consent in sex and for violence against women. Betty was the one to add, "It's fine to analyze all the little points of the law and of ethics on a theoretical level, but it seems to me that the real issue here is . . . about respect and communication."

The particularity of the Rinconada online study is that the participants see each other every day at dinner or in the dormitory hall. Instead of igniting "flame wars" that sometimes turn computer discussion groups into a mess of personal insults, Rinconadans composed thoughtful, reasonable disagreements, often with a phrase like, "I attack your arguments, but not your character."

Says Holeton, "They were a special community, and they knew it. Their intellectual exchange on the e-mail list was enhanced by their feelings for each other, and their friendships and group feeling were enhanced by their written exchanges. At their best, they modeled an intellectual community in a new, fuller sense."

The Responsive Reader

1. What are the criticisms or negative expectations that this report sets out to defuse or counteract? How does Zachary, poised to be "poster boy" for negative criticism, become the hero of this account?
2. What are the findings of the various studies this report cites? What did they show about "computer-mediated communication" and "virtual communities"? How solid or authoritative do these studies seem to you? According to the researchers, what questions did they leave unanswered?
3. What light did Holeton's studies shed on the gender gap in the world of computers? What gave males the edge in online discussion? Have you made similar or different observations?
4. Do you think that Rinconada House is a special case, or can computers enhance social interaction in other, less enclosed, settings? Why or why not?

Talking, Listening, Writing

5. Have you ever thought that you might be interacting with the computer at the expense of interacting with real people? Are you a member of any e-mail groups or listservs? How much do you feel a part of those "communities"? How well do you know the other respondents and lurkers?
6. Luddites are critics of the worship of technology in modern society. They think that we were better off when we walked to work, ate home-grown food, and found inspiration not in movie multiplexes but in the great outdoors. Have you seen evidence of the attitude of cyberskeptics who feel that the promise or benefits of the computer revolution have been overrated? Do you personally see computers as "a tool for building [. . .] social relations" or as an obstacle to normal social interaction?

Collaborative Projects

7. Working with a group, conduct an informal survey to explore a question like the following: Is there a gender gap in computer literacy and utilization of the Internet? (Is it true that women students spend relatively less time at the computer and rely less on electronic sources than males? Is gender a factor in decisions to participate or not to participate in online discussions?) How does social background or economic status affect students' access to computers and electronic resources? (How significant is the disparity in the availability and utilization of resources?)

Find It on the Web

Pioneering educators who have kept teachers and students up-to-date on developments in computer use and Internet resources include Richard Holeton, Cynthia Selfe, and Christine Hult. Institutions that have played leading roles in supporting research and programs include Michigan Technical University and Colorado State. Check these or similar sources for recent publications on current challenges and issues.

The following are sample titles from one student's search:

Dawson, Jerry. "The Future of Educational Technology." 15 Jan. 2002. <http://horizon.unc.edu/projects/monograph/CD/Instructional_Technology/Dawson.asp>

Holeton, Richard. "The Semi-Virtual Composition Classroom: A Model for Techno-Amphibians." 14 Jan. 2002. <http://horizon.unc.edu/projects/monograph/CD/Language_Music/Holeton.asp>

Pacheco, Maria. "Use of Computers and Computer Networks in the Physical Chemistry Laboratory and Lecture." 15 Jan. 2002. <http://horizon.unc.edu/projects/monograph/CD/Science_Mathematics/Pacheco.asp>

LEARNING TO LOVE

Nell Bernstein

> *Young Americans grow up in a society sending them mixed signals about love and sex. On the one hand, the media seem obsessed with sex and titillation. On the other hand, church groups and conservative politicians deplore moral laxness and preach abstinence. What guidance should parents and teachers provide for the sex lives and emotional lives of the young in their charge? Educators are caught in the crossfire between those who claim that sex education is badly needed to combat AIDS and other health risks of unprotected sex and those who claim that sex education hastens the onset of sexual activity. Nell Bernstein is the editor of* YO! (Youth Outlook), *a regional newspaper produced by Pacific News Service. Her article was part of an issue of* Mother Jones *magazine designed to show the value of sex education in spite of past mistakes and tremendous obstacles to dealing with a taboo-ridden subject. At the same time, the magazine's editors quoted with approval an educator who said "parents are the primary sex educators" and "all institutions—families, schools, churches, and social service agencies—should help teenagers become loving, caring, responsible adults."*

Thought Starters: Media critics deplore the emphasis on sex and violence in the media. Do you encounter programs or movies that give young people positive and believable images of "loving" and "caring"?

When the University of Chicago released a comprehensive sex survey   *1*
detailing what Americans are doing in private, one bedroom door remained firmly shut—the one at the end of the hall with the Pearl Jam poster and the "Keep Out" sign.

It's public knowledge that federal funding for the sex survey (which looked at Americans age 18 to 59) had been scratched and that private foundations ended up footing the bill. What's gone unreported, however, is that a comprehensive study of adolescent sexual behavior was also in the works, and it was not revived after the federal funding cut.

The adolescent survey was even more politically unpalatable than its adult counterpart. Dr. Richard Udry, a social scientist at the University of North Carolina, is one of the researchers who planned the five-year, 24,000-teen survey. He recalls that Louis Sullivan, then secretary of Health and Human Services, "said the study might give the wrong message to adolescents, when the official policy of the administration was to encourage abstinence." The researchers talked to a few foundations but concluded that they would not be able to raise enough money to do the study properly.

The final nail in the American Teenage Study's coffin came when the Senate approved a Jesse Helms–sponsored bill and subsequent amendment: the first transferred the original funding for both the adult and adolescent surveys to the abstinence-only Adolescent Family Life program, and the second prohibited the government from ever funding either study in the future. Helms argued that the Senate faced "a clear choice—between support for sexual restraint among our young people, or, on the other hand, support for homosexuality and sexual decadence."

The death of the American Teenage Study is right in line with the country's unofficial policy on teen sex, which might be described as "Don't Ask, Tell." As panic over teen pregnancy and AIDS escalates, adults have defined their role as dispensing warnings and imperatives, rather than examining the complexities of young people's lives. 5

Teen sex, like teen violence, has come to be seen as a national crisis, both symptom and symbol of a "generation out of control." But even as it reaches a near-hysterical pitch, the national dialogue on adolescent sexuality remains painfully abstract. Sex is to the '90s what drugs were to the '80s: the locus of adult anxiety over what the kids are doing when we're not around (which is more and more of the time); something we want desperately to stop but not necessarily to understand.

Efforts to manage the "crisis" of adolescent sexual activity consistently focus on consequences rather than motivations, and are driven in great part by political enmities. The left accuses the right of imposing its own repressive mores on defenseless teens, of driving young girls to back-alley abortions and lives of shame. The right charges the left with fostering legions of junior Murphy Browns, who drain the public coffers with their babies and diseases. This ideological battle is reflected back to teenagers in lectures about "values" and "choices"—sex education buzzwords that are also, not coincidentally, the rallying cries of political movements.

As the chasm widens between the rhetoric of their elders and the word on the street, young people are left alone with their deepest questions about relationships, pleasure, and risk. In North Carolina, educators are training junior high school girls to counsel friends whose boyfriends assault them, having found that most battered girls do not discuss it with an adult. A recent study showed that half of all 15-year-old girls have never discussed birth control or STDs with a parent, and one-third have never discussed how pregnancy occurs.

Another study indicates that growing numbers of teenagers are having sex at home in the afternoon, while their parents are out of the house—a far cry from the era of backseats and drive-ins, of sneaking out from under the watchful parental eye. And what are we offering those kids left all by themselves in the downstairs bedroom? A "True Love Waits" button, or a condom and a map of their genitals—neither of which addresses the underlying loneliness of a generation raised in empty houses.

Most of the research on adolescent sexual behavior focuses on declining virginity rates and growing social costs. We know, for example, that 10 more than half of American women and three-quarters of American men have had intercourse by their 18th birthday, compared to a quarter of women in the mid-1950s (they didn't count men then). We know that 3 million teens acquire a sexually transmitted disease each year, and that 1 million become pregnant, a third of whom have abortions. And although the number of reported AIDS cases among teenagers is still very small, we know that 20 percent of AIDS cases are among people in their 20s, many of whom probably contracted HIV as teenagers.

What we don't know is why young people do what they do, and how it makes them feel. "There's a tremendous amount of information about a truly small number of questions," says Mindy Thompson Fullilove, associate professor of clinical psychology and public health at Columbia University. "Anything that is not about contraception is missing. We tend to be very obsessed with counting things. We don't value asking, 'What do you mean?'"

While teen sexual activity is increasing, condom use among teenagers is also on the rise: among urban adolescent males, it nearly doubled between 1979 and 1988. Teenage girls are no more likely than older unmarried women to have multiple partners, and are actually less likely to have an unwanted pregnancy. But if advocates across the political spectrum agree on one thing, it's that teen sex is fraught with danger—and they tailor their messages accordingly. "It's always 'Don't get AIDS,'" points out Dr. Lynn Ponton, a professor of psychiatry at the University of California at San Francisco, "never 'Have a good time.'"

A study of state guidelines for sexuality education done by the Sexuality Information and Education Council of the United States found that HIV and other STDs were among the most widely covered topics; "shared sexual behavior" and "human sexual response," among the least. In other words, young people are learning in school that sex can hurt or kill them without learning that it can also bring them pleasure or give them a connection to another person.

"Fear messages never persuade anybody to do anything except for a very short period of time," says John Gagnon, a sociologist at the State University of New York at Stony Brook and co-author of the Chicago sex study. He notes that adults lose credibility when they feed young people oversimplified warnings instead of trusting them to understand ambiguous realities. "It's absolutely irresponsible not to give kids sex ed, including information on condoms, and the possibility of not having sex. But it's also irresponsible not to mention that many people find sex a great source of pleasure."

Also lost in the "Just Say No" frenzy are ways for young people to say 15 yes—not just to sex, but to love, family, each other. All around them, adults are rewriting the social script: bearing children out of wedlock; introducing kids to stepfathers, ex-wives, casual girlfriends, and other "options"; publicly venting fury at each other in vicious divorce and custody battles.

As we struggle to sort things out for ourselves, we are offering fewer and fewer coherent models for conducting and sustaining intimate relationships. Lifelong marriage, whether or not the desirable norm for sexual relationships, at least had the advantage of being imitable.

With our relentless focus on disease and pregnancy, we leave our children without much explicit guidance when it comes to high-risk activities of the heart. We talk to young people as if their genitals were a matter of public concern, while their souls were none of our business. "People say 'Use a condom,'" says Stephanie Brown, who manages the teen clinic at a Planned Parenthood in Northern California, "but not 'Why are you having sex with this person?'"

Those who do ask that question say they often hear surprisingly sentimental answers. "The degree to which adolescents believe in being in love is absolutely extraordinary," says Gagnon. Surveys show that the vast majority of young people want to marry and raise children with a spouse. Unlike the children of the '60s—for whom the fear of ending up like their parents manifested itself as a terror of being old, married, and bored—today's teens fear ending up old and alone.

One of the better-kept secrets about teen pregnancy is that many of the babies born to adolescents are anything but "unwanted." Ask a 15-year-old why she got pregnant and she's more likely to tell you that she wanted company than that she didn't know how to use a condom. One pregnant 18-year-old I know—a girl who spent last Christmas alone in her apartment, while her mother and stepfather went on vacation together—told me she'd always planned to have a baby right after high school, to make a person all her own, who would love her and not leave. Like most of her friends, she had no illusions that the young man she made the baby with—or any man—would fill that role. "Do you think I'm selfish?" she wanted to know.

With responsible adults focusing mainly on the pitfalls of sexual activity, the task of showing young people what sex and love have to offer is left to that trusted family friend, the television. And television—along with movies, music, and advertising—offers up a sexual universe that has little room for either "values" or "choices." In this universe, sex is everything—and the beautiful people, the glamorous people, the people who *matter,* are having it all the time.

"Abstinence makes the heart grow fonder," promise the advocates. 20 Meanwhile the media map out a very different route to love and fulfillment, hammering home the message that—as Woody Allen put it when called upon to explain his own sexual involvement with a teenager—"the heart wants what it wants."

Perhaps most dangerously for teenagers, points out Sexuality Information and Education Council of the United States director Debra Haffner, the media reinforce the idea that good sex means being swept away: "It just happens. There's almost no sexual negotiation, no portrayal of sexual communication, no limit setting, very little condom and contraceptive use. What we see on TV is that people kiss and then they have intercourse."

The Chicago study painted a picture of sex in America that was much more moderate and restrained. But when Baltimore-based sex educator Deborah Roffman asked her students what they *thought* the study would find, she says, "They predicted the image of sexual behavior that is presented in the media—that there was a lot of intercourse, that married people were less happy with their sex lives than single people, that Americans are sex bunnies." The effect of the dissonance between the official teachings on sex and what the media dish up, says Roffman, is clear: "Any teacher knows that when students get mixed messages from adults, they test."

Gagnon is even more explicit about the role of adults in convincing young people that they are "ready" for sex. "The 'raging hormones' argument is nonsense," he says. "Society *elicits* sexual behavior in kids." But—as with so many problems that plague our children—we rarely acknowledge our own complicity. We prefer to define adolescent sexuality as a crisis of self-control that we, the responsible (but not culpable) adults, must find ways to manage.

Bombarded with messages telling them both that sex is the ticket to love, glamour, and adulthood—and that it is bad and will kill them, adolescents in America are ultimately left with few models and little guidance in the area where they need it most: human relationships. Busy with their battles over propaganda and prophylactics, adults aren't addressing young people's yearning for intimacy, for contact, for connections that prove they matter. "Adults are so evasive, so unwilling to confront the reality of young people's lives," says Gagnon. "It's a maelstrom. And we've abandoned kids to it."

The Responsive Reader

1. Is sex still a taboo subject? What evidence does Bernstein provide that surveys of adolescent sexual behavior are "politically unpalatable" in our society? How does adolescent sexual activity become an issue in the political struggles between the right and the left?
2. Is there a breakdown of communication between young people and their parents on the subject of sex? What evidence does Bernstein give of the widening "chasm" between young people and the older generation on questions related to sex and sexual relations?
3. According to this article, what do current studies and statistics show about teenage sexuality? What, according to Bernstein, are the limitations of current research?
4. Why does Bernstein criticize current efforts at sex education? What's wrong with emphasis on the "pitfalls of sexual activity"? What are some of the well-kept "secrets" about teenagers' attitudes that current debates fail to take into account?

5. What's wrong with the "sexual universe" offered up by the media? For Bernstein, what is the result of the discrepancy between "the official teachings on sex and what the media dish up"?

Talking, Listening, Writing

6. Do you think Bernstein is right about the sense of isolation and confusion experienced by many young people? In your experience, is it true that young people "are left alone with their deepest questions about relationships, pleasure, and risk"?
7. As a parent, would you take sides in the ideological battles over sex education? How would you explain or defend the stand you take to people on the other side?

Collaborative Projects

8. Is sex education too limited to make any difference? Is it true that sex education amounts to maybe half a dozen hours during a school year— while young Americans are constantly exposed to sexual messages outside school? Working with a group, you may want to explore what goes on in sex education classes in your area or community.

BLACK COLLEGE IN (WHITE) AMERICA

Kenyatta Matthews

> *The fight against segregated schools was long a major focus of the civil rights movement. Long drawn-out court battles and outbreaks of violence marked the effort to open the doors of white schools and colleges to African American students and offer equal educational opportunity. At the same time, the nation had traditional predominantly black institutions like Howard University in Washington D.C., with a proud tradition of training leaders in the African American community. The author of the following article attended Howard and says, "the experience gave me the strength I needed to really accept who I was." She became a copy editor at* Ms. *magazine, which for many years has been a leading influential voice for the women's movement.*

Thought Starters: Have you or your family ever had to make choices about what school to attend? What were the factors influencing the decision? In retrospect, was the decision made the right decision?

Entering Howard in 1994, I had two beliefs: there were no black people in Denver or Delaware, and sisterhood was best achieved through a sorority. [1]

My relatives, high school teachers, guidance counselors, and some friends had another belief: you won't be successful in the real (read: white) world with a degree from a historically black college or university (HBCU). I worried that they were right. Let's face it—if college prepares you for the real world, then time at an HBCU is like being schizophrenic. Spending four years or more isolated in a predominantly black environment while the rest of the world moves along to the drum of a powerful white majority seems to be a bit detached from reality—not to mention a waste of money. When you graduate, you're going to most likely deal with a white boss and work with white colleagues. And because you were off in a black world, you'll be out of the all-important networks essential for getting ahead in your field.

Well, Howard proved us wrong on all counts. I found that black people lived everywhere, from Bridgeport, Connecticut (another place that I was sketchy about) to Belize. I learned how to do headwraps from some New Jersey women, developed a taste for tart tamarind balls thanks to a Trini student, and learned firsthand how critical the situation is for women in Kenya when a student shared her story of how hard she had to fight to come to Howard instead of marry.

In an environment with people who looked just like me, I garnered the strength I needed to really accept who I was. Sisterhood became less about sororities and surface similarities and more about seeking diversity in the company I kept. My five girls and I were the Benetton of Howard; all different skin tones, hair textures, sizes. We overcame the anxieties of good versus bad hair, light versus dark skin. However, other insecurities surfaced. Class caused conflict when we searched for apartments that each of us could afford.

With the freedom to accept who I was came awareness. I became a   5
feminist in my own way, although I never called it that in college. Wearing my hair natural, championing abortion and reproductive rights, and reading feminist literature amounted to anything but the "f" word in my mind. I had seen how feminists were received. A young woman who called herself one was booed during a class discussion and asked if she was a lesbian. Students, both men and women, complained because my favorite English professor added feminist works to the American Literature syllabus. There were no major marches to protest the two known rapes in my dorm freshman year. (They were finally acknowledged a few years later by candidates for the student association, to show that they were sensitive to safety issues.) My most enlightened girl called herself a womanist.

My feminist leanings came to the fore sophomore year when my friends and I decided to forgo the "official" female vigil on campus in support of the Million Man March and attend the real thing—despite warnings to stay away. Bounding down the Mall amid a sea of black men, some of whom told us to go home and called us disrespectful, is, to this day, one of the most vivid and explicit ways I have claimed space as a black woman. So, when it came to applying for internships my last years in college, I had no fear about my ability to compete. I had chosen to watch history in person instead of from the sidelines; I had competed with male colleagues in my classes (which were usually headed by a white professor—another myth debunked, that Howard professors were all people of color). I boldly walked into interviews, pouf of afro atop my head, and articulated my goals and why I was qualified with a clear strong voice, because I felt as if I belonged in this world—me with round hips and butt, chubby brown cheeks, nappy hair, and wealth of intelligence. I never worried that my natural hair would cost me my first editorial internship; that my African name would stop an employer from reading the rest of my resume; or that Howard University was a signpost for incompetence.

Being at an HBCU gave me a chance to make the rest of the world's problems with me secondary, and allowed me to make my problems with myself a priority. It was worth every minute.

The Responsive Reader

1. Matthews was well aware of familiar arguments against attending a traditionally all-black school. What were these arguments—what were her doubts and worries?

2. How did her experience at Howard University change her assumptions or help her overcome her doubts? What were key experiences and observations that convinced her she had made the right choice?
3. What in this essay shows that the Howard experience turned out more "diverse" than the "historically black" label would imply?
4. Matthews says that at one time she thought "sisterhood was best achieved through a sorority." During her college experience, Matthews became a "feminist in my own way"—and without using the "f" word. What were key beliefs and commitments in her new feminist outlook? How did the college fail to encourage or support her feminist commitment?
5. What do you know, or what can you find out, about the Million Man March? How did the event become a turning point in Matthew's intellectual and spiritual growth? How did she go counter to what was expected of her as a young black woman?

Talking, Listening, Writing

6. Educators some years ago started to stress the importance of students developing self-esteem. What experience in your life was especially significant in developing or challenging your self-confidence? How might your life have been different had you not had this experience? What are the key factors building or impairing your self-esteem?
7. Matthews says that she was reluctant to call herself a feminist because she "had seen how feminists were received." Have you seen or do you remember evidence of how feminists and feminism have been stigmatized? What does feminism mean to you today? Young women today talk about "third wave feminism." What do they mean?

Collaborative Projects

8. Spike Lee is a provocative and highly successful African American director whose movies challenge familiar assumptions and conventional wisdom about the black community. His *School Daze* takes viewers to a Howard University setting. You may want to arrange viewing the movie with a group and plan for a follow-up group discussion of the issues raised in the film.

DONALD DUK AND
THE WHITE MONSTERS

Frank Chin

Frank Chin was one of the first Asian American writers to become known to a wide audience. He attended the University of California at Berkeley in the sixties; in the seventies, he was the first Chinese American to have a play produced on the New York stage. His plays Chickencoop Chinaman *and* Year of the Dragon *attacked the familiar stereotype of Asian males as sinister villains in the Fu Manchu mode. Maxine Hong Kingston, probably the best-known Chinese writer in America, has said of him that "the main energy that goes through his work is anger." He has been angry at publishers for publishing four female Asian writers for every Asian male; he has criticized other Chinese American writers for misrepresenting and putting down the traditional culture. His spiritual roots are in Chinese myth and in the martial ideal of strong masculine archetypes—independent of state and bureaucracy and trusting "no one." His novel* Donald Duk *(1991) shows another side of his gift for inspiring controversy and mixed reviews. It has been called a "devilishly wild and wacky tale by a word-and-sword slinger of wit, audacity, and intelligence" (Michi Weglyn). The following excerpt—the opening pages of the novel—shows his talent for seeing the humor in issues of ethnic identity that are usually treated in a more solemn fashion. As you read the following pages, what kind of humor do you encounter? Do you consider it demeaning or offensive? Why or why not?*

Thought Starters: Writers acknowledging the humorous side of minority experience may be secure enough in their pride to acknowledge the sad and funny side of the rich collective experience of their group. But they may also be accused of perpetuating the self-contempt that makes members of minorities play the clown for a white audience. Is there such a thing as nonoffensive ethnic humor? Where have you encountered it?

Who would believe anyone named Donald Duk dances like Fred   *1*
Astaire? Donald Duk does not like his name. Donald Duk never liked his name. He hates his name. He is not a duck. He is not a cartoon character. He does not go home to sleep in Disneyland every night. The kids that laugh at him are very smart. Everyone at his private school is smart. Donald Duk is smart. He is a gifted one, they say.

No one in school knows he takes tap dance lessons from a man who calls himself "The Chinese Fred Astaire." Mom talks Dad into paying for the lessons and tap shoes.

Fred Astaire. Everybody everywhere likes Fred Astaire in the old black-and-white movies. Late at night on TV, even Dad smiles when Fred Astaire dances. Mom hums along. Donald Duk wants to live the late night life in old black-and-white movies and talk with his feet like Fred Astaire, and smile Fred Astaire's sweet lemonade smile.

The music teacher and English teacher in school go dreamy eyed when they talk about seeing Fred Astaire and Ginger Rogers on the late-night TV. "Remember when he danced with Barbara Stanwyck? What was the name of that movie . . . ?"

"Barbara Stanwyck?"   5

"Did you see the one where he dances with Rita Hayworth?"

"Oooh, Rita Hayworth!"

Donald Duk enjoys the books he reads in school. The math is a curious game. He is not the only Chinese in the private school. But he is the only Donald Duk. He avoids the other Chinese here. And the Chinese seem to avoid him. This school is a place where the Chinese are comfortable hating Chinese. "Only the Chinese are stupid enough to give a kid a stupid name like Donald Duk," Donald Duk says to himself. "And if the Chinese were that smart, why didn't they invent tap dancing?"

Donald Duk's father's name is King. King Duk. Donald hates his father's name. He hates being introduced with his father. "This is King Duk, and his son Donald Duk." Mom's name is Daisy. "That's Daisy Duk, and her son Donald." Venus Duk and Penny Duk are Donald's sisters. The girls are twins and a couple of years older than Donald.

His own name is driving him crazy! Looking Chinese is driving him   10
crazy! All his teachers are making a big deal about Chinese stuff in their classes because of Chinese New Year coming on soon. The teacher of California History is so happy to be reading about the Chinese. "The man I studied history under at Berkeley authored this book. He was a spellbinding lecturer," the teacher throbs. Then he reads, "The Chinese in America were made passive and nonassertive by centuries of Confucian thought and Zen mysticism. They were totally unprepared for the violently individualistic and democratic Americans. From their first step on American soil to the middle of the twentieth century, the timid, introverted Chinese have been helpless against the relentless victimization by aggressive, highly competitive Americans.

"One of the Confucian concepts that makes the Chinese vulnerable to the assertive ways of the West is 'the mandate of heaven.' As the European kings of old ruled by divine right, so the emperors of China ruled by the mandate of heaven." The teacher takes a breath and looks over his spellbound class. Donald wants to barf pink and green stuff all over the teacher's book.

"What's he saying?" Donald Duk's pal Arnold Azalea asks in a whisper.

"Same thing as everybody—Chinese are artsy, cutesy and chicken-dick." Donald whispers back.

Oh, no! Here comes Chinese New Year again! It is Donald Duk's worst time of year. Here come the stupid questions about the funny things Chinese believe in. The funny things Chinese do. The funny things Chinese eat. And, "Where can I buy some Chinese firecrackers?"

And in Chinatown it's *Goong hay fot choy* everywhere. And some gang   15
kids do sell firecrackers. And some gang kids rob other kids looking for firecrackers. He doesn't like the gang kids. He doesn't like speaking their Chinese. He doesn't have to—this is America. He doesn't like Chinatown. But he lives here.

The gang kids know him. They call him by name. One day the Frog Twins wobble onto the scene with their load of full shopping bags. There is Donald Duk. And there are five gang boys and two girlfriends chewing gum, swearing and smirking. The gang kids wear black tanker jackets, white tee shirts and baggy black denim jeans. It is the alley in front of the Chinese Historical Society Museum. There are fish markets on each side of the Chinatown end of the alley. Lawrence Ferlinghetti's famous City Lights Bookstore is at the end that opens on Columbus Street. Suddenly there are the Frog Twins in their heavy black overcoats. They seem to be wearing all the clothes they own under their coats. Their coats bulge. Under their skirts they wear several pairs of trousers and slacks. They wear one knit cap over the other. They wear scarves tied over their heads and shawls over their shoulders.

That night, after he is asleep, Dad comes home from the restaurant and wakes him up. "You walk like a sad softie," Dad says. "You look like you want everyone to beat you up."

"I do not!" Donald Duk says.

"You look at yourself in the mirror," Dad says, and Donald Duk looks at himself in his full-length dressing mirror. "Look at those slouching shoulders, that pouty face. Look at those hands holding onto each other. You look scared!" Dad's voice booms and Donald hears everyone's feet hit the floor. Mom and the twins are out in the hall looking into his open door.

"I am scared!" Donald Duk says.   20

"I don't care if you are scared," Dad says. His eyes sizzle into Donald Duk's frightened pie-eyed stare. "Be as scared as you want to be, but don't look scared. Especially when you walk through Chinatown."

"How do I look like I'm not scared if I *am* scared?" Donald Duk asks.

"You walk with your back straight. You keep your hands out of your pockets. Don't hunch your shoulders. Think of them as being down. Keep your head up. Look like you know where you're going. Walk like you know where you're going. And you say, 'Don't mess with me, horsepuckie! Don't mess with me!' But you don't say it with your mouth. You say it with your eyes. You say it with your hands where everybody can see them. Anybody get two steps in front of you, you zap them with your eyes, and they had better nod at you or look away. When they nod, you nod. When you walk like nobody better mess with you, nobody will mess with you. When you walk around like you're walking now, all rolled up in a little ball and hiding out from everything, they'll get you for sure."

Donald does not like his dad waking him up like that and yelling at him. But what the old man says works. Outside among the cold San Francisco shadows and the early morning shoppers, Donald Duk hears his father's voice and straightens his back, takes his hands out of his pockets, says "Don't mess with me!" with his eyes and every move of his body. And, yes, he's talking with his body the way Fred Astaire talks, and shoots every gang kid who walks toward him in the eye with a look that says, "Don't mess with me." And no one messes with him. Dad never talks about it again.

Later, gang kids laugh at his name and try to pick fights with him during the afternoon rush hour, Dad's busy time in the kitchen. Donald is smarter than these lowbrow beady-eyed goons. He has to beat them without fighting them because he doesn't know how to fight. Donald Duk gets the twins to talk about it with Dad while they are all at the dining room table working on their model airplanes.   *25*

Dad laughs. "So he has a choice. He does not like people laughing at his name. He does not want the gangsters laughing at his name to beat him up. He mostly does not want to look like a sissy in front of them, so what can he do?"

"He can pay them to leave him alone," Venus says.

"He can not! That is so chicken it's disgusting!" Penelope says.

"So, our little brother is doomed."

"He can agree with them and laugh at his name," Dad says. "He can tell them lots of Donald Duk jokes. Maybe he can learn to talk that quack-quack Donald Duck talk."   *30*

"Whaaat?" the twins ask in one voice.

"If he keeps them laughing," Dad says, "even if he can just keep them listening, they are not beating him up, right? And they are not calling him a sissy. He does not want to fight? He does not have to fight. He has to use his smarts, okay? If he's smart enough, he makes up some Donald Duck jokes to surprise them and make them laugh. They laugh three times, he can walk away. Leave them there laughing, thinking Donald Duk is one terrific fella."

"So says King Duk," Venus Duk flips. The twins often talk as if everything they hear everybody say and see everybody do is dialog in a memoir they're writing or action in a play they're directing. This makes Mom feel like she's on stage and drives Donald Duk crazy.

"Is that Chinese psychology, dear?" Daisy Duk asks.

"Daisy Duk inquires," says Penelope Duk.   *35*

"And little Donnie Duk says, *Oh, Mom!* and sighs."

"I do not!" Donald Duk yelps at the twins.

"Well, then, say it," Penelope Duk says. "It's a good line. So *you, you know.*"

"Thank you," Venus says.

"Oh goshes, you all, your sympathy is so . . . so . . . so literary. So dra-   *40*
matic," Donald Duk says. "It is truly depressing."

"I thought it was narrative," Venus says.

"Listen up for some Chinese psychology, girls and boys," Daisy Duk says.

"No, that's not psychology, that's Bugs Bunny," Dad says.

"You don't mean, Bugs Bunny, dear. You always make that mistake."

"Br'er Rabbit!" Dad says.   *45*

"What does that mean?" Donald Duk asks the twins. They shrug their shoulders. Nobody knows what Br'er Rabbit has to do with Dad's way of avoiding a fight and not being a fool, but it works.

One bright and sunny afternoon, a gang boy stops Donald and talks to him in the quacking voice of Walt Disney's Donald Duck. The voice breaks Donald Duk's mind for a flash, and he is afraid to turn on his own Donald Duck voice. He tries telling a joke about Donald Duck not wearing trousers or shoes, when the gangster—in black jeans, black tee shirt, black jacket, black shades—says in a perfect Donald Duck voice, "Let's take the pants off Donald Duk!"

"Oh oh! I stepped in it now!" Donald Duk says in his Donald Duck voice and stuns the gangster and his two gangster friends and their three girlfriends. Everything is seen and understood very fast. Without missing a beat, his own perfect Donald Duck voice cries for help in perfect Cantonese *Gow meng ahhhh!* and they all laugh. Old women pulling little wire shopping carts full of fresh vegetables stop and stare at him. Passing children recognize the voice and say Donald Duck talks Chinese.

"Don't let these monsters take off my pants. I may be Donald Duk, but I am as human as you," he says in Chinese, in his Donald Duck voice, "I know how to use chopsticks. I use flush toilets. Why shouldn't I wear pants on Grant Street in Chinatown?" They all laugh more than three times. Their laughter roars three times on the corner of Grant and Jackson, and Donald Duk walks away, leaving them laughing, just the way Dad says he can. He feels great. Just great!

Donald Duk does not want to laugh about his name forever. There   *50*
has to be an end to this. There is an end to all kidstuff for a kid. An end to diapers. An end to nursery rhymes and fairy tales. There has to be an end to laughing about his name to get out of a fight. Chinese New Year. Everyone will be laughing. He is twelve years old. Twelve years old is special to the Chinese. There are twelve years in the Asian lunar zodiac. For each year there is an animal. This year Donald will complete his first twelve-year cycle of his life. To celebrate, Donald Duk's father's old opera mentor, Uncle Donald Duk, is coming to San Francisco to perform a Cantonese opera. Donald Duk does not want Chinese New Year. He does not want his uncle Donald Duk to tell him again how Daddy was a terrible man to name his little boy Donald Duk, because all the *bok gwai,* the white monsters, will think he is named after that barebutt cartoon duck in the top half of a sailor suit and no shoes.

The Responsive Reader

1. What is a stereotype, and what is the role or power of ethnic stereotypes in our society? Why and where is Donald critical of stereotypes and official textbook descriptions of his group? Does this account modify or confirm stereotypes in your own mind?
2. What is Donald's relation to his Chinese background and to other Chinese?
3. How much in Donald's story stems from his being Chinese American? How much could be part of the story of many other adolescents?

Talking, Listening, Writing

4. Humor is very personal; much of what is funny to one person or group is not a laughing matter to others. How do you relate to the author's sense of humor?
5. A dual or divided cultural heritage may be considered a liability—a source of self-doubt, divided loyalties, or a lacking sense of belonging. It may be considered an asset—a chance for a richer, fuller identity, drawing on two different ways of realizing one's human potential. Have you encountered the clash or the merging of two different traditions, two different lifestyles, two different cultures? Do you think of a dual heritage as a liability or an asset?

Collaborative Projects

6. What recognition do some of today's most successful Asian American writers enjoy? Working alone or as a member of a group, look for sources that shed light on the reputation of one of the following: Frank Chin; Amy Tan, author of *The Joy Luck Club* and *The Kitchen God's Wife;* David Henry Hwang, whose *M. Butterfly* won him a Tony Award in 1989; Hawaiian poet Garrett Hongo; Bharati Mukherjee, from India, author of *The Middleman and Other Stories* and the novel *Jasmine.*

INDIAN BOARDING SCHOOL: THE RUNAWAYS

Louise Erdrich

> *Louise Erdrich, of Chippewa and German American descent, grew up in North Dakota and later went to live in New Hampshire. Her best-selling novel,* Love Medicine *(1984), won the National Book Critics Circle Award; among her other books are* The Beet Queen *(1986),* Tracks *(1988), and* The Bingo Palace *(1994). Her poem is a vivid expression of rebellion against schooling that becomes forced conversion to a different way of life.*

Thought Starters: What are your thoughts about "Americanizing" cultural minorities?

Home's the place we head for in our sleep.   1
Boxcars stumbling north in dreams
don't wait for us. We catch them on the run.
The rails, old lacerations that we love,
shoot parallel across the face and break   5
just under Turtle Mountains. Riding scars
you can't get lost. Home is the place they cross.

The lame guard strikes a match and makes the dark
less tolerant. We watch through cracks in boards
as the land starts rolling, rolling till it hurts   10
to be here, cold in regulation clothes.
We know the sheriff's waiting at midrun
to take us back. His car is dumb and warm.
The highway doesn't rock, it only hums
like a wing of long insults. The worn-down welts   15
of ancient punishments lead back and forth.

All runaways wear dresses, long green ones,
the color you would think shame was. We scrub
the sidewalks down because it's shameful work.
Our brushes cut the stone in watered arcs   20
and in the soak frail outlines shiver clear
a moment, things us kids pressed on the dark
face before it hardened, pale, remembering
delicate old injuries, the spines of names and leaves.

The Responsive Reader

1. What were the runaways running away from? What do you learn about their past history? What do you learn about the system against which they are rebelling? What is in store for them?
2. Much of what we observe in this poem has symbolic meanings and overtones. What vivid details in the runaways' surroundings mirror their thoughts and feelings?
3. One editor said that "the language of hurt and injury pervades this poem." What examples can you find? What role does each play in the poem?

Talking, Listening, Writing

4. Does the intense sense of grievance in this poem take you by surprise?
5. In your own experience, has schooling been a means of liberation, widening perspectives and extending opportunities? Or has it been an instrument of oppression—aiming at forced changes in attitudes, narrowing your outlook, or trying to make you over into something you did not want to be?
6. Is there something to be said in defense of policies of enforced Americanization?

Collaborative Projects

7. In the school district(s) in which you live, what is the policy regarding cultural diversity? If you can, talk to teachers or administrators in a position to know.

FORUM: *Free to Worship*

Many immigrants came to this country in search of religious freedom. They ranged from Puritans who had been persecuted as dissenters in England to Jews who had been the victims of pogroms in czarist Russia. The separation of church and state, enshrined in the American Constitution, promised freedom of worship and liberty of conscience. America would not have an established religion that would become a center of power and privilege and whose adherents would exclude outsiders from public office or a university education.

Although the religious beliefs and practices of Native Americans were suppressed, America presented a spectrum of beliefs and rituals astonishing by Old World standards. In New England, where Puritans had at first persecuted backsliders and killed fellow citizens as witches, Quakers and Unitarians became part of the social mix. Mormons became an influential and prosperous minority after the initial years of persecution. Americans in the heavily Baptist South gradually overcame traditional prejudices against Catholics. In the Midwest, a rainbow of denominations and sects built their own chapels and preached and worshiped as the spirit moved them. Recent times saw the establishment of Buddhist congregations and a new American form of Islam.

Today, many observers see in our society a movement toward a "new spirituality." People are looking for spiritual significance in their lives, drawing on a wide range of sources. They are looking for an antidote to fashionable cynicism, for an answer to pessimism or despair. At the same time, powerful forces are pushing the nation toward a common center of religious belief. Is this country a "Christian nation"? Are there religious beliefs that we must all share?

PRAYER ISN'T ALWAYS ALLOWED

Loretta Johnson

> *Much has been written about the role of the religious revival in recent American politics. Americans with strong religious convictions have become increasingly politically active, organizing support for candidates invoking traditional religious values in situations ranging from school board elections to statewide or national contests. A test issue often is the candidate's stand for or against school prayer. Opponents say that the Constitution forbids making students in public schools join in prayers or other religious observances that do not represent their parents' religious convictions or their own. Advocates of school prayer claim that the founders never intended this nation to be a godless society. The following article was written by the religion editor of the local newspaper in Minot, a farming town in North Dakota, close to the Canadian border.*

Thought Starters: For many Americans, religion is a private matter and a matter of individual choice. Where do you encounter religion in the public sphere? Where have you seen it play a role in American politics?

I love to travel. And my family and friends know that. They also know *1*
that when I travel, it's often by car and never alone. There are always four
of us in the car: me, myself, God and I.

I am at the wheel; God is in the passenger seat to my right; me and
myself are relegated to the rear seat.

In June, I traveled to Oroville, Calif., a small town about an hour and
a half north of Sacramento, to attend a friend's graduation from high school.
An incident occurred there that still bothers me.

The graduation ceremony of Las Plumas High School took place
June 4 at Harrison Stadium. It included an invocation, speeches by the valedictorian and the salutatorian and a benediction.

The invocation began, "Dear Heavenly Father. . . . We thank you for *5*
all our family and teachers and for all those who have an impact on our
lives" and ended, "We ask this in the name of Jesus Christ. Amen."

Attention getter

A certain part of the valedictorian's address definitely got my attention. It was, "One person cannot dictate what another should be, but one
cabinet (body) can have a positive influence on the lives of another by
supporting and accepting his progressive character. The people around

you should not be the mold for your character. You must be what you want to be."

During the benediction, the graduating senior said, "Tonight we thank you for the many accomplishments we have made. We thank you for the preparation we have been given for the future."

He closed with, "Thank you for sending your Son, Jesus Christ, as the living example to set the standard by which we may live our lives to further succeed. Thank you most of all for sacrificing him onto death on a cross that we may have eternal life by believing in him. I ask you for your blessing on each graduate here as we take this critical step forward in our lives, and I pray he will continually inspire us as we continue on in life, in Jesus' precious and holy name. Amen."

After the Las Plumas graduation ceremony, many of the attendees gathered on the field for congratulatory hugs and handshakes.

Different ceremony

The following evening, Oroville High School, another public school   10
in the same school district, conducted its graduation ceremonies in the same stadium. But things were much different.

The invocation was skipped over. The first co-valedictorian spoke. But, when the second co-valedictorian, Chris Niemeyer, approached the podium, he and the principal exchanged words. Niemeyer was asked to leave the stage.

Some people in the stands shouted, "We want Chris," and stomped their feet. Others held small signs supporting the students in their right to free speech.

Niemeyer left the stage with tears streaming down his face. He paused at the end of the walkway where two of his classmates joined him in a hug. Soon the entire class joined the group in a purple mass of graduation robes, arms and square caps.

Oroville High School Principal Larry Payne called for order about a half dozen times and then finally announced, "If we cannot have proper decorum we will cancel the ceremony." Order then resumed. Two students then sang, "It's All Over Now, Baby Blue." At the end of the song one of the students grabbed the principal's microphone and said, "God bless."

Niemeyer was not allowed to give his address, and a classmate was not   15
allowed to deliver the invocation because they included references to God and Jesus.

Payne had reviewed the talks and rejected them because of their strong religious content. U.S. District Court Judge Lawrence Karlton rejected an emergency, last-ditch plea by the two students asking for the right to make religious references in their addresses.

After Oroville High graduation ceremony, many of the students, their parents and friends gathered for a prayer rally off the field.

The *Enterprise-Record*, a newspaper published in Chico, Calif., which is near Oroville, published the text of the talks in its June 6 edition.

Yes, there were references to God and Jesus in the invocation and valedictory address for the Oroville High graduation.

The invocation began, "Dear Heavenly Father, we humbly come be-   20
fore you this evening to thank you for all that we have accomplished through you. Father God, these last four years have not been easy for us, but we know that you were there with us the whole time, and we thank you for that."

It closed with, "We ask these things in the precious holy name of Jesus Christ. Amen."

Key to success

The co-valedictorian extended his gratitude to the high school staff for the great learning experience he had had. He then went on to say, "Along with the great instruction, I have also been introduced to ideas and philosophies that have not corresponded with my own personal beliefs. I now have the opportunity to speak from my heart and share what I know is the key to success."

He went on to say, "I believe that God has a plan for each of our lives—a plan to prosper us and give us a hope for the future. As individuals, we have a choice of whether to choose his perfect will in our lives or our own futile plans."

Both schools are public and yet the graduation ceremonies were dramatically different. Is there a happy medium possible?

Times certainly have changed. Included in the 10 original amend-   25
ments of the Bill of Rights of the Constitution of the United States, Article I states: *"Congress shall make no law respecting an establishment of religion, or prohibiting the free exercise thereof; or abridging the freedom of speech, or of the press, or the right of the people peaceably to assemble, and to petition the Government for a redress of grievances."*

The Supreme Court ruled in a 6-1 decision June 25, 1962, that the recitation of an official prayer in the public schools of New York State was unconstitutional.

And, on June 4, the same day as the Las Plumas graduation, the House failed to ratify a constitutional amendment that would have returned official prayer to public schools and permitted the government to fund religious schools and organizations.

I'm certain the issue of prayer or no prayer in schools will continue as will the issue of guns, knives and drugs in schools.

But, for today, I'm thankful I have the right to exercise my beliefs and not be discouraged by others in what I say, write or do.

Looking back

Back in the '60s, I graduated from a small high school in the Minot area, 30
and to the best of my recollection, all the graduating seniors were present
for baccalaureate the Sunday before the actual graduation ceremony. So
were their parents. There was no shame in being there.

Prayer was a part of my growing up. I attended church and said evening prayers with my family. Prayer is still a part of my life and has been a
mainstay through good times and bad.

Which school was right?

To me, it's the one that allowed the references to God during the
graduation ceremonies. So, just as I take God on my journeys, may the
graduating seniors have God with them as they start their journeys down a
new path.

I'd rather have freedom of prayer in school than the weapons that
are being brought there for purposes other than guidance, direction and
protection.

Praise be to God. When we hit a deer on the return trip, I used my 35
freedom of speech and said, "Thank God we aren't hurt."

The Responsive Reader

1. What is the issue that was dramatized for Johnson by her trip to California? What were the key differences between the two situations she
   describes?
2. Johnson repeatedly speaks for "the students"—students who share her
   views. What would you include in a composite portrait of them? To
   judge from your own high school experience, how many students share
   their views?

Talking, Listening, Writing

3. The American Civil Liberties Union (ACLU) has often carried the torch
   in lawsuits accusing public officials of breaching the wall separating
   church and state. One ACLU advertising campaign used the headline
   "Whose Prayer?" If the courts approved a form of prayer in public
   schools, who would choose the prayer? What kind of prayer with what
   kind of wording would be acceptable?
4. After the religious wars devastating Europe in the seventeenth century,
   the British writer Jonathan Swift (author of *Gulliver's Travels*) said: "We
   have just enough religion to hate but not to love one another." Do you
   think this charge would be fair or unfair if leveled at Johnson?

MY 60-SECOND PROTEST
FROM THE HALLWAY

Emily Lesk

> *American tradition and folklore have long honored the maverick—the non-conformist who marches "to a different drummer." Many Americans came to this country in search of freedom of religion as refugees from societies where religious conformity was required. The founders broke with tradition by refusing to establish a state religion and by keeping church and state separate. Americans have long prided themselves on freedom of choice in matters of religious thought and observance. At the same time, pressures toward religious conformity developed in the new nation. The high school senior who wrote the following prize-winning essay for a* Newsweek *student contest resisted what she felt was interference in her right to make her own decisions in matters of worship and belief.*

Thought Starters: What has been your experience with religious instruction or religious observance in a school setting? What has been your contact with students from religious backgrounds different from yours? Has difference of religious outlook or of attitudes toward religion ever been an issue for you?

It's 8.32 A.M. School began two minutes ago. My bulging book bag is inside my first-period classroom saving my favorite seat. I am standing in the near-empty hallway, leaning against a locker right outside the classroom. I should be in class, yet my teacher has never objected to my minute-long absence, which has become a daily routine. I trace around the edges of the floor tiles with the toe of my running shoe, pausing several times to glance up at the second hand of the standard-issue clock mounted across the hall.

Although I have casually checked this clock countless times during my high-school career, this year looking at it has made me think about how significant 60 seconds can be. Last spring, the Commonwealth of Virginia passed a law that requires every public school in the state to set aside one minute at the beginning of each day during which students must remain seated while they "meditate, pray, or engage in any other silent activity." Every morning, at around 8:31, a resonant voice echoes over the school intercom, "Please rise for the Pledge of Allegiance." I stand up straight and salute the flag. After the pledge the voice commands me to "pause for a minute of silence." I push my chair under my desk and stride out of the classroom.

My objection to Virginia's Minute of Silence law is very simple. I see the policy as an attempt to bring organized prayer into the public schools, thus violating the United States Constitution. Last June at a statewide student-government convention, I spoke with state lawmakers, who confirmed my suspicion that the minute of silence is religiously motivated. One delegate proudly told me that she supported the law because reciting the Lord's Prayer had been a part of her own public-school education.

I agree with the law's strongest critics, who argue that it promotes religious discrimination because many faiths do not pray in the seated position mandated by the legislation. How would a Muslim third grader react to those students (and maybe a teacher) who might fold their hands and bow their heads to pray? Would she feel pressured to join in just to avoid criticism?

My opposition to this law is ironic because I consider myself religious and patriotic. I recite the Pledge of Allegiance daily (including the "one nation under God" part, which to me has historical, not religious, implications). As a Reform Jew, I get peace and self-assurance from religious worship and meditation, both at my synagogue and in my home. But my religious education also taught me the importance of standing up against discrimination and persecution.

In a school of 1,600 students, fewer than two dozen have joined me in protest. I usually walk out of class with one or two kids, sometimes none. Most days, when I glance back into the classroom, I see several students praying, heads bowed or eyes closed, while others do homework or daydream. Although I have not encountered any outright opposition, I often overhear classmates making sarcastic comments or dismissing the protest as futile. When I see that so many of my peers and teachers find no reason to question something I feel so strongly about, I wonder if my objection is justified. What do my 30 extra daily paces accomplish?

In contemplating that question, I've come to realize that taking a stand is about knowing why I believe what I do and refusing to give in despite the lack of support. My decision to protest was largely personal. Though I stayed in class the first morning the law was implemented—because I was caught off guard and because I was curious to see how others would respond—sitting there felt like a betrayal of my values. I also felt an obligation to act on behalf of the students all over Virginia who found their own beliefs violated but don't attend schools that allow them to express their opinions.

Deep down, I know this issue will be decided in a courtroom, not in my corridor. On May 8, the Fourth U.S. Circuit Court of Appeals heard oral arguments from ACLU lawyers representing seven families who are challenging the law, and will probably reach a decision over the summer. But for now I'll walk out of class each day to show my school community that an easy alternative to complacency does exist. This year I will have spent approximately three hours standing in the hallway in protest, watching the second hand make its 360-degree journey. As a senior about to graduate, I've thought a lot about the impact I've had on my school. I hope that my protest inspired other kids to use the time to think, not about a beckoning test, but about their views—even if those views differ from my own.

The Responsive Reader

1. Many discussions of the school prayer issue move on the level of constitutional principle and legal precedent. What details in Lesk's opening paragraphs help her take the reader to the actual everyday world of school? Have you been a clock watcher? How does Lesk use the time ticking off on the clock to make both the setting and the issue real for her readers?

2. How does Lesk support her suspicion that the new state law mandating the minute of silence was "religiously motivated"? Do you think her suspicion is justified? Do you think the new policy was an attempt to "bring organized prayer into the public schools"?

3. According to Lesk, how or why do the instructions for the minute of silence cause a problem for students of other faiths, like the Muslim third-grader she mentions? What is Lesk's own religious orientation or commitment? How does she use it to explain her taking a stand on the school prayer issue?

4. Lesk describes in some detail the thoughts and feelings before and after her decision. Do you understand how she felt? What were the reactions of other students? Do you think the reactions would have been similar at a school you attended or know well? Would you have been one of the students "dismissing the protest as futile"?

Talking, Listening, Writing

5. Are you surprised that Lesk has no problem with the Pledge of Allegiance? Why or why not? Do you think there is a difference between requiring students to salute the flag or recite the Pledge of Allegiance and requiring them to participate in a moment of meditation or prayer? What is the difference? Or how are they similar or the same?

6. Many people are reluctant to take a stand—to "make waves" or become identified as troublemakers or malcontents. How serious would a problem have to be before you joined in a formal protest? What policy or situation would you be willing to protest?

7. Lesk says that she hopes her example will inspire other students to think about their views and to exercise their right to express their opinions. After thinking about what you believe and what you are willing to stand up for, what would you include in a "This I Believe" statement presenting your views to others? What stance would you adopt toward others with different views?

8. Can religious issues be avoided in school? Where or how have you encountered them? How did people deal with them?

Collaborative Projects

9. How diverse or how homogeneous is the religious background of students at your school or a school you know well? Working with a group, conduct an informal survey or interviews to find out where your fellow students stand in matters of religious outlook or spiritual commitment. Do students identify with different denominations, and do these differ in outlook? Do Mormons, Jews, Muslims, Buddhists, or Hindus feel they are generally accepted, or do they think they stand out because of their religious affiliation? How do students with no specific religious allegiance identify themselves?

MY ONLINE SYNAGOGUE

Niles Elliot Goldstein

Goldstein and his cybersynagogue give new meaning to the idea of "old wine in new bottles." He developed his style of online Judaism after serving as the rabbi of conventional congregations. He shares the view that many Americans are "nonobservant" or only nominally members of an organized religion. However, they are nevertheless looking for something "that will enrich their lives and root them in a spiritual community." Like many Americans, Goldstein thinks of himself as "ecumenical"—willing to reach out beyond the traditional "boundaries and parameters" that divide one religious group from another. How viable does his new kind of "virtual religious community" seem? Do you think it has a future?

Thought Starters: Where and when do you see religion playing a role in American life? Where do you encounter it?

I am the rabbi of a cybersynagogue. In many ways what I do on the   *1*
Internet is starkly different from the work I did when I was a pulpit rabbi.
For one thing, this congregation is open 24 hours a day. If anyone has a
pressing concern or question, all he has to do is leave it on "Ask the Rabbi"
(forums.msn.com/Religion), and he'll get a response from me long before
most of my colleagues would even receive the message. While you can't
perform a bris or conduct a funeral over the Internet, for many people that

lack of focus on ritual is itself an enticement. Those turned off by organized religion but open to spiritual issues often find themselves drawn to our section of cyberspace. And because there is no control over who joins our community, not all of our members are Jews. As Abraham welcomed the three strangers into his tent, I welcome our visitors (even the occasional evangelist who tries to convert me) as honored guests. We're as ecumenical as a religious entity can be.

In other ways my work is surprisingly similar to that of a conventional cleric. My "lectern" may be made of wires instead of wood, but I still use it to preach my sermons. I might not teach adult-education classes to congregants while they're seated around a table, but I talk about the Jewish tradition with Internet users every day (and intermittently conduct live discussions on various topics in our Judaism chat room, also at the address above). I may not have an actual office for private counseling or confidential conversation, but I do have an e-mail address for those situations where discretion or personal, one-on-one communication is required. I've led some people through the mourning process and helped others trace their religious genealogies. And though I didn't do the matchmaking at a congregational picnic, three of our married assistants met their spouses online.

When I began serving the Judaism Community a couple of years ago— only one of many faith communities on the Internet, including Christianity, Islam, Buddhism, even paganism—I asked the subscribers what kind of a rabbi they were looking for. Asking a question like this in a conventional congregation would have been difficult, if not impossible. There are so many factors that go into the relationship between spiritual leaders and their congregations—managerial, financial and psychological, to name just a few—that even minor issues can get complicated. Touching a subject as large as the role of a rabbi in a particular religious community is a recipe for conflict.

At one of my former "real" synagogues, when a particularly wealthy member thought his opinion wasn't carrying the weight it deserved, he threatened to leave the temple. Another member who hated public speaking refused, despite my urging, to make known her view on a controversial issue at an important meeting. But in a virtual congregation, where distinctions between congregants don't exist and where boundaries between clergy and laity are more relaxed and less intimidating, I received a great deal of feedback and have been able to adjust my rabbinate accordingly. With no building to maintain or budget to balance, our cybersynagogue allows democracy to flourish. No congregant can withdraw his support for the capital campaign. No clique can monopolize power. No rabbi can dictate policy.

Like many Americans, most of the users I encounter in the newsgroup 5 have problems with religious practice. They are often nonobservant and find little meaning in ancient rituals or indecipherable liturgies. But just the fact that they are in the newsgroup is spiritually significant. They, like many of the rest of us in American society, are yearning for something more, something that will enrich their lives and root them in a spiritual community. Historically, religion has been defined by boundaries and parameters, distinctions in beliefs, holy books, practices, calendars. The Internet has no boundaries. I once asked our users what they thought about the notion of creating new rituals, ones that speak more to our own experiences. One woman suggested a liturgy to mark menopause. A father wanted to construct a ceremony for sending his daughter off to college. A teenager argued for a new blessing to be recited at the time of a boy's first wet dream. I didn't like all the ideas, but I loved the free, uncensored exchange of views, an exchange that would have been extremely difficult outside the Internet.

Yet on the Internet, a single individual can cause great damage. With few control mechanisms, anybody can say almost anything to anyone. One of our Jewish participants has been so intolerant, disrespectful and offensive toward those of other faiths—as well as toward fellow Jews—that I have tried to have him banned from the newsgroup. I have not succeeded. He has continued to insult and alienate our members and has interfered with my ability to properly do my job. Flesh-and-blood members of a real congregation would not tolerate this situation. Free speech is and should be a cherished American value, but when it is abused (as it sometimes is on the Internet) it can be destructive to a community.

In an age when religion has been deconstructed and decentralized, few media reach as many potential "congregants" as the Internet. We never have to look for extra chairs to accommodate overflow crowds. Millions of believers can join us from anywhere in the world. The anonymity that a virtual religious community confers encourages people to speak more candidly. But in the absence of face-to-face encounters, relationships between members of our community will always be limited. Nothing will ever be able to replace the embrace of another human being or the feeling of families at prayer. Contact is not communication. We may all be created in the image of God, but only the shadows of those images will be visible online. The Internet is a mixed blessing. It draws people together at the same time that it distances them. It expands the horizons of religion while collapsing its moorings and traditions. Contemporary faith stands at the cutting edge of technology. It may have also reached its final frontier.

The Responsive Reader

1. In practical terms, how does Goldstein's "online synagogue" operate? How does it use the opportunities of cyberspace? How close does it bring religion to "the cutting edge of technology"?
2. When Goldstein ceased being a "pulpit rabbi," what happened to the conventional duties of a rabbi or other leader of a congregation? How are his current functions similar; how are they different?

3. How does Goldstein support his claim that his cyberspace synagogue is more open and democratic than much conventional religion?

4. Is Goldstein candid about the drawbacks and abuses of his kind of cyberspace religion? Does he show it to be a "mixed blessing"? Where or how?

Talking, Listening, Writing

5. Are you one of those who find little meaning "in ancient rituals or indecipherable liturgies"? Or would you defend ritual and religious observance as an essential part of religion?

6. Do you think that Goldstein succeeds in bringing religion closer to the actual thoughts and feelings of people today—closer to our everyday experience? (Do you think some of the topics or suggestions he mentions are too irreverent or too vulgar?)

Exploring Internet and Nonprint Sources

Informal research goes into most writing that aims at the educated reader. On issues from the push for gender parity in college athletics to vouchers making tax money available to religious schools, you will want to go beyond what you already know. Much effective student writing today draws on a mix of conventional print sources, online sources, and live community or campus input.

TRIGGERING Your interest in a current local or national issue may send you to a range of sources. Who has checked out the facts? Who has listened to witnesses, experts, or insiders? Who cares enough to make a strong plea for support or for a course of action?

- On issues like school shootings or juvenile violence, you are likely to draw from current media coverage—ranging from daily newspapers and the glossy newsmagazines to television news and documentaries.

- On questions about money and politics, you may want to turn to magazines of opinion, from the traditional *Harper's* and *Atlantic* to more political periodicals, ranging from the *National Review* to the *New Republic* or the *Nation*.

- On an issue like juveniles being tried as adults, you may want to read what the experts have to say or try to get some detailed statistics from a reliable nonpartisan source.

- On local issues like preserving one of the remaining habitats of the monarch butterfly or the nesting grounds of a regional bird species, you may want to listen to environmentalists, local officials, and spokespersons for developers.

- On a current campus issue, you may want to conduct an informal survey of fellow students.

GATHERING: QUICK-SEARCHING THE INTERNET For the informal research that goes into most writing, many writers today do a quick-search on the Internet. On the Internet, hard data, background information, informed commentary, and expert testimony are at your fingertips for many current issues. Major national newspapers and newsmagazines are available online, and back issues are available in the online archives of the publications. Many articles on current medical advances and science issues published in health or science magazines for the general reader are available online. Increasingly, technical and scholarly journals will be available to you not only in the periodical room or on the periodical shelves of your library but also online.

Find It on the Web
The Range of Online Sources

The following are partial results of one student's "first search" on the topic of political correctness.

Language Stereotypes, "Put-downs" and "Politically-Correct" Reference Index. Department of Translation Studies. University of Tampere. 15 Nov. 2001. 28 Jan. 2002. <http://www.uta.fi/FAST/US8/PC/>

This website, maintained by the University of Tampere, Finland, is a list of links to discussions of and research into politically correct language. It guides users to research into the origins of the term *politically correct* and discussions of the political correctness of certain words, as well as issues and events relating to political correctness. The sources include material such as Purdue University's *Purdue Writing Lab Guide to Non-Sexist Language.* Codgill, Sharon. *Being Politically Correct.* 28 Oct. 1999, 28 Jan. 2002.

<http://www.stcloudstate.edu/~scogdill/339/polcor.html>

This website, by an English professor at St. Cloud State, provides her list of politically correct terms and expressions for use by students. It contains sections on pronoun use and salutations, and an extensive vocabulary of politically correct terms.

O'Riordian, Michael. "Politically Correct Journalism." *Thunderbird Magazine* 1 Mar. 2000, 28 Jan. 2002. <http://www.journalism.ubc.ca/thunderbird/2000/march/correct.html>

This article, from the official magazine of the Sing Tao School of Journalism at the University of British Columbia, summarizes a presentation by journalist Chris Wood, attacking political correctness as an instrument of censorship.

Ross, Kelley L. "Against the Theory of 'Sexist Language.'" 1996. 28 Jan. 2002. <http://www.triesian.com/language.htm>

This article examines the theory that gender differences in language correlate with the status of women in society. There is also an extensive discussion on whether "femaleness" in language is regarded as more or less valuable than "maleness."

Fujita, Mariko. "Writing Politically Correct Japanese Fairy Tales." *The Language Teacher Online.* 16 Sept. 1998, 28 Jan. 2002. <http://langue .hyper.chubu.ac.jp/jalt/pub/tlt/98/may/sh_fujita.html>
The activity described by Fujita Mariko of Keio Shonan Fujisawa Junior and Senior High School in a professional journal for teachers is aimed at teaching Japanese high school students to be more politically correct and aware. It includes an example written by the author's students. It shows that political correctness is now a global phenomenon.

Experienced users of the Internet pride themselves on being up-to-date on the latest or most sophisticated **search engines,** helping them sift the mass of material on the Internet and guiding them to the most relevant material for their project. Remember familiar advice from editors and instructors:

- *Become familiar with how your search engine functions.* Some search engines will search for different versions of a key word like *educat** with the asterisk: *education, educator, educators, educating.* Other search engines, like Google, will search only for complete words you actually type in.

- *Become familiar with online resources available by subscription or through your college library.* Cost and availability become factors when you want to use reference sources like the *Encarta* encyclopedia or specialized databases.

- *Be wary of anonymous or near-anonymous material on the Internet.* Who wrote or assembled the material? Is the author or sponsoring institution clearly identified? Who sponsors and maintains a website? Whose agenda does it serve?

- *Check authenticity or integrity of the material.* How reliable and complete is the current version? Has it been shortened or excerpted, and by whom? Was it copied, recycled, or pirated from somewhere? Can you trace it to the original source?

- *Check for permanence or continued availability.* How long will this material be accessible? Has it been archived? Will other people be able to retrieve and verify it at a later date?

Suppose you are writing about Lady Diana, who rose from obscurity through a storybook marriage to the heir to the British throne, as an example of the cult of celebrity. Is she going to remain an icon of our media culture, like Elvis Presley and Marilyn Monroe before her, or is the out-pouring of interest and sympathy focused on her divorce, her troubled later years, and her violent death going to fade from public memory?

Finding an astonishing range of online sources, you will start recording notes like the following:

THE CULT OF DIANA

People around the world were devastated when Diana Spencer, former Princess of Wales, was killed in a terrible accident on August 31, 1997. The author of one of many articles on the first anniversary of her death, found in the online archives of a major publication, said that Lady Diana "was an obsession for Britons in her lifetime and has been raised to the status of demigod."

THE CULT OF DIANA

In an online article by Renora Licata for a website called *Death of a Princess,* Princess Diana is described as "beloved by the public for her warmth and humanity."

> Her warmth and kindness found many outlets, particularly in regard to those struck down with the HIV virus. She was spontaneous in manner, happily ignoring royal protocol to bestow a kiss on a child in a crowd, and writing letters to members of the public signed "love Diana."

THE CULT OF DIANA

In a magazine article titled "A Tribute to Princess Diana" in *The Natural Child Project Magazine,* written by Jane Hunt, her devotion to her children was definitely recognized: "Diana was also a devoted mother, who had to raise her children in extraordinary circumstances. She took on all of these challenges, raising her children with as much love, warmth, and compassion as anyone could manage in these circumstances." These circumstances included the continuous harassment by the media and the fact that her children were almost always off to boarding school.

SHAPING In sorting out a range of promising material, you will be attending to two key steps in the writing process.

- You start looking for the connecting thread. Overall, what does the story of Lady Di show? What may be your overarching thesis? What does her story show about the cult of celebrity? Or what does it show about today's popular culture?

- As you develop and support your overall point, how are you going to lay out the material that led you to your conclusion? Each of the following trial theses already sets up an organizing strategy for the paper as a whole. The first one promises a paper that would first focus on the idealized image of Lady Diana that attracted her many fans and admirers. However, it would then go on to the "darker side." It would look at the scandals that attracted the tabloids, the sensation-mongering press, and the paparazzi—the celebrity-hounding "journalists from hell":

TRIAL THESIS: Lady Diana attracted an abundance of fans with her charm and charisma; however, like other icons of popular culture she had a dark side that was long kept hidden from the public.

The following trial thesis also already sets up a program for the rest of the paper. Media watchers have often focused on the role the media play in first lionizing and building up celebrities. However, often the constant pressure of unrelenting media scrutiny then makes it impossible for people to lead anything like a normal life:

TRIAL THESIS: Perhaps one of the greatest lessons that can be learned from the life and death of Diana is that the media's constant presence in her life contributed to many of her personal problems and even her untimely death.

A major step in a writing project often is to push ahead from an open-ended and noncommittal early trial thesis to a thesis that makes a more definite and a more focused claim:

WEAK: Lady Diana provides an important example of the role the celebrity title entails in today's popular culture.
(So what is that role? How do you see it? Sum it up here?)

REVISED: **An amazing combination of contradictory qualities coexisting within the same individual helped create the media image of Lady Diana.** She was a natural beauty, much photographed like a classic fashion model. At the same time, her admirers sympathized with her role as a victimized mother and her struggle with eating disorders and divorce. Her humanitarian work took her to encounters with starving children and with AIDS patients.

The revised thesis sets up a possible three-point program for the rest of the paper. The thesis and the sentences that follow it provide a preview creating expectations that the rest of the paper will fulfill.

REVISING Make the most of opportunities for revising and rethinking. Welcome feedback from instructor's comments and peer reviews. Each paper and each writing project is different. Nevertheless, readers will again and again ask you to attend to predictable revision needs: Sharpen your thesis, adjusting it to what your investigation as a whole has really shown. Do more to highlight your overall plan: Fill in missing links, signaling turning points in the argument. If necessary, shuffle major parts of the paper for a better flow—from the more easily understandable to the more challenging, or from safe areas of agreement to the more controversial.

Here are other common suggestions for improvement:

- *Sharpen the title.* Aim at a title that is both informative and inviting. The following titles range from promising in a fairly formal style to the more provocative and beckoning:

> The Legacy of Princess Diana
>
> Lady Di: The Unquenchable Thirst
>
> Diana Lives!

- *Bring the issue to life.* Capture the reader's attention with a live or dramatic introduction. Start with a striking incident or attention-getting quotation:

> Elton John sang, "And your footsteps will always fall here, along England's greatest Hills; your candle burned out long before your legend ever will" at the funeral of Princess Diana on September 6, 1997.

- *Strengthen supporting material.* Fill in striking real-life examples. Give your readers concrete details that will help them visualize a scene or get into the spirit of an occasion:

> The cult of Diana may have found its shrine comparable to Elvis Presley's Graceland. Writing about her burial site at Althorp, her childhood home, T. R. Reid writes, "If there is a cult of 'Diana' this is its cathedral. On top, the Temple has a large cross and a single word: DIANA. Inside, where the altar would be is a marble silhouette of the late princess and a stone slab etched with a quotation of hers that reads like something from the New Testament: 'Whoever is in distress call on me.'"

EDITING What questions about format and mechanics do you face when you draw on printed or oral sources? In editing your paper, make it clear who says what.

- You will often use **direct quotation**—material quoted verbatim, word for word. Make sure you are copying each quotation exactly. Put all material quoted verbatim in quotation marks. (Remember to *close* the quotation marks when your direct quotation ends.) Your readers will appreciate your adding a short **credit tag** giving the credentials of the person you quoted:

DIRECT: Julio Sanchez, **legal scholar specializing in immigration law,** says, **"Any coyote in Tijuana can tell you that illegal immigration is inevitable as long as the gap between rich and poor countries continues to grow."**

(A **colon** may replace the comma before a formal or especially important quotation.)

- When you **paraphrase** what someone said, you put someone else's ideas into your own words. Such **indirect quotation** appears in your paper *without* quotation marks:

INDIRECT: According to Julio Sanchez, legal scholar specializing in immigration law, any guide helping Mexicans cross the border would tell us **that illegal immigrants will keep coming as long as the gap between poverty at home and wealth beyond the border continues to grow.**

- At times, you will use a **block quotation** for a substantial block of material—four lines or more. Indent a block quotation about an inch or *ten* spaces (no additional indent even if your quote starts at the beginning of a paragraph). *Don't* use quotation marks—the double indenting already signals direct quotation. However, use regular quotation marks for anything quoted *within* the block quotation.

BLOCK QUOTATION: As one vocal critic of the jargon of Washington insiders has said,

In the language of today's spin doctors and practitioners of double-speak, the "bottom line" is that the "window of opportunity" that enabled us to "push the envelope" has developed a "downside" that will "negatively impact" the "parameters" of future growth.

- Use block quotations sparingly—at strategic places. For the smooth flow of a paper, rely mainly on shorter quotations and **partial quotations** worked organically into your own text.

PARTIAL QUOTATION: **"Equestrian sports are ideally suited to become a leading women's sport,"** Coach Hiernan claims. Women have an **"intuitive understanding"** with the animals they train, and they have the patience often lacking in male riders, who **"tend to force the issue."**

A SAMPLE PAPER   Study the following student paper as an example of student writing that has profited from a search of the Internet. How does the introduction raise the key issue explored in this paper? Where does the author best state or sum up the unifying thesis? What are the major waystations in this tribute to a popular culture idol? What is the range of sources?

Do you think this paper is too uncritical or worshipful in its attitude toward its subject, or do you think it is a generous and much-needed defense of its subject against the predatory exploitative media?

Princess Diana: The Media Killed Her but Now Keep Her Alive

"I don't think she ever understood why her genuinely good intentions were sneered at by the media, why there appeared to be a permanent quest on their behalf to bring her down. It is baffling," Princess Diana's brother stated in his eulogy, posted on the CNN News website. Testimonies like these have been coming forward ever since the tragic death of Princess Diana in an effort to tell Princess Diana's real story.

Since the day Diana Spencer became Princess Diana by marrying Prince Charles, she was hounded and pestered by the media and was unable to live a normal life. The media and the paparazzi followed her wherever she went and dug up whatever damaging materials they could. What the media failed to tell the public while she was alive was that she was an extremely generous woman, a dedicated mother, and a woman beloved by the people of her country. Princess Diana's life was portrayed as a life full of lies, deception, and problems. However, ever since the paparazzi caused or contributed to Princess Diana's death, the media have finally understood that she was human, and had to deal with problems just like everybody else. Those flaws that haunted Princess Diana for her entire life have been finally put in perspective, and now people throughout the world have begun to see why people admire her.

Online newsletters and news services are popular types of Internet source bringing out the side of Princess Diana that was obscured by the media. These newsletters offer detailed information about her life, including the various charities she funded. During her life, the British tabloids portrayed Princess Diana as materialistic and vain by displaying pictures of her wearing twenty thousand-dollar gowns. It is true that she did wear expensive clothes, such as the outfits displayed on a website called "Princess Diana Costumes" maintained by Penny Ladinier. What the media did not stress was all the time she spent working with her charities and the money she donated to them. In a CNN News article titled "Diana fund gives charities $21.3 million," her generosity is evident as she donated a large amount of money to six different charities, including a charity benefiting landmine victims. Not only did the money say something about her character, but also the fact that she actually visited a minefield in Angola is mind-blowing. Vivienne Perry finds Princess Diana's contributions to be very unselfish as well in an interview concerning the donations posted on the CNN News site: "I think the fund will become the most important grant-giving body in the country, and a lifeline to an enormous number of charities."

Donations to numerous charities were only one side of Princess Diana that was hidden by the media while Princess Diana was alive. A great deal of information about her dedication to her children was concealed or played down while she was alive, and more information about her devotion as a mother is now revealed in many magazine articles online. In a magazine article titled "A Tribute to Princess Diana" in *The Natural Child Project Magazine,* written by

Jane Hunt, her devotion to her children was definitely recognized: "Diana was also a devoted mother, who had to raise her children in extraordinary circumstances. She took on all of these challenges, raising her children with as much love, warmth, and compassion as anyone could manage in these circumstances." These circumstances included the continuous harassment by the media and the fact that her children were almost always off to boarding school. Despite her children's absence, Princess Diana made every effort to show affection towards her children, and according to Michael Johnston, the creator of the website called "Prince William," she defied the royal establishment to do so: "Princess Diana broke royal protocol by hugging the boys in public and taking them to amusement parks and McDonald's."

This caring side of hers didn't end with her donations to charities or the love she demonstrated toward her children. In an online article by Renora Licata for a website called *Death of a Princess,* Princess Diana is described as "beloved by the public for her warmth and humanity."

> Her warmth and kindness found many outlets, particularly in regard to those struck down with the HIV virus. She was spontaneous in manner, happily ignoring royal protocol to bestow a kiss on a child in a crowd, and writing letters to members of the public signed "love Diana."

The media portrayed this act, according to Mike Person, the creator of the *Death of a Princess* website, as "ignorant and defiant of royal protocol." Princess Diana was unable to get the respect from the press that she deserved and was forced to live on the run, which in the end was a deciding factor in her death. Her death was due to the persistence on the part of the media to reveal all of Princess Diana's secrets—her marriage problems, her self-esteem problems, and her being disliked by the royal family. Jane Hunt writes in "A Tribute to Princess Diana":

> At times, she faltered, responding with all-too-human anger, jealousy, and despair. But then she would somehow recover her poise, and her generosity. She would—in the manner of a true princess—perform a magical alchemy, turning her own private sorrows into compassion and hope for others.

DRAWING ON ORAL SOURCES Good writers are often good listeners. Before they speak up themselves, they take in what other people have to say. When official pronouncements or statistics leave key questions unanswered, they talk to people who have relevant information. Before they jump into the fray, they listen and get their bearings. They may listen during the course of informal conversations, or they may set up formal interviews, leading the interviewee through a series of pointed questions (sometimes submitted in advance).

You will often want to talk to someone in the know when you wonder: What's the human meaning of these statistics? What's behind this public relations announcement? What's behind official denials or alibis? When someone has been accused of wrongdoing, what is that person's side of the story? Here are some sample questions on which a productive interview (or interviews) might shed light:

- What's behind the faceless current immigration statistics? What brought recent immigrants here from a country like Cambodia, Somalia, or the former Soviet Union?
- Do students from diverse ethnic, racial, or cultural backgrounds feel accepted on your campus?
- How do charges of police brutality look from the other side of the desk—from the point of view of police officers or their superiors?

When you write a paper on a subject of public interest, you may get helpful ideas from talking with a roommate, a family member, a teacher, a coworker, or a friend. At times your paper may profit from informal conversations with strangers or an exchange overheard on a bus. However, often the most productive source of information and opinion for a paper may be a formal interview or a series of interviews.

When you first approach people to set up an interview, you may find a natural reluctance to set aside time to talk to a stranger. However, once you explain why you value their input, you may find that people love to be consulted as an authority.

You will typically prepare a *set of questions* designed to give focus and direction to an interview. (You should, however, be flexible enough to adapt your prepared questions as promising areas of talk open up.) If you are investigating life after retirement, you might come to an interview with a tentative set of questions like the following:

- Is it true that the elderly are a privileged group in our society?
- What did you do before you retired?
- Were you ready for retirement?
- How or why did you retire?
- What do you think about mandatory retirement?
- What about retirement was least like what you expected or the hardest to handle?
- What was best about retirement?
- What advice would you give people starting to plan for retirement?
- If you could turn the clock back thirty years, what would you do differently?

The following is part of a fact-finding interview. The interviewer asked businesslike, open questions. The student interviewer had heard about the superior academic performance of Asian students, and he went to a math teacher to get an insider's point of view. What kind of questions did the interviewer ask? What is the flow of the questions—does one naturally lead to another? How informative and how straightforward are the answers?

QUESTION: On the average, what percentage of your classes is made up of Asian students?
ANSWER: Well, the lower-level courses have very few, but the higher-level courses have many. Of all the students I've taught during the last five years, maybe forty percent have been Asian.

QUESTION: When you say higher-level courses, what classes are you referring to?
ANSWER: Calculus, trigonometry, differential equations.

QUESTION: As for the students in these higher-level math classes, are most of them American-born Asian students, or were they born in other countries?
ANSWER: Many of my students are immigrants, born in Asia. Many of them have come to this country within the last two to ten years.

QUESTION: Do your Asian students tend to score higher on tests and get better grades than other groups of students?
ANSWER: All of us teachers say the same thing to ourselves and to each other. There are more good grades going to Asians than to any other ethnic, racial, or cultural group.

QUESTION: Do you discuss this trend with your peers on an informal or formal basis, say, in staff or departmental meetings?
ANSWER: We discuss it informally. It's hard to discuss it formally with a chairperson sitting in because it seems almost racist to discuss the subject in those terms. We talk informally about what we have noticed and how we feel.

QUESTION: Have you talked to the students about why they do well?
ANSWER: I get various answers, but it boils down to that they learn to use their minds earlier. I don't think that they are necessarily born with higher intelligence, but they are pushed hard from the earliest years. In their home countries, they had to cram and memorize their books. Their curriculum moved faster, so that by the seventh grade they were doing algebra and by the ninth grade they were doing calculus.

QUESTION: What is the driving force or incentive for their success?
ANSWER: They work a lot harder, although we have to remember that others have dropped out along the way, and we see only the hardest workers or better students. The ones that do reach us do better than their American counterparts. Why? I think culturally they have a great respect for learning and for teachers. At home their parents would never think of saying something critical about a teacher.

A reporter from *Rolling Stone* visited a school after a violent incident. As part of his investigation, the reporter interviewed a teacher who had taught at the school for many years. Here is how the reporter used extensive selections from the interview. You may want to visit an area high school or return to your own high school to interview one or more teachers, asking for their reactions. Do they think conditions at their school are deteriorating or improving? Are they concerned about violence or about discipline? Do they think in terms of "good kids" and "bad kids"? Do they have thoughts about who is a "good influence" and who is a "bad influence"?

Back in the days when he was a student at South Eugene High, Kessinger said, "probably ninety to ninety-five percent of the kids were 'good kids.' They went to class and believed in trying to treat people and institutions with respect. Maybe two percent were the ones who hung out, skipped school, got in trouble.

"Today, sixty to sixty-five percent of the kids are in trouble, and maybe forty percent at most are 'good kids.' And they're good only because they are real careful about who they hang out with. Seeing how careful these kids have to be to stay out of trouble really gets to you.

"In my day, it was hard to find a bad influence. Today, it's hard to find a good influence, and the good influences that are out there, they're very careful to protect themselves. It's not just that we seem to be getting worse and worse, it's that there doesn't seem to be any end to it."

"By the time your kids are fifteen or sixteen," Kessinger said, "the percentage of good kids could be down to five or ten percent. Sorry to be so discouraging, but I really believe that." —*from Randall Sullivan, "A Boy's Life,"* Rolling Stone

The following student paper draws on both Internet sources and oral sources. How would you sum up the overall message or central thesis of the paper? How and how soon does it become clear? What is the plan or organizing strategy for the paper implied in the opening paragraph, and how well or successfully is it carried out? What is the range of Internet sources? How well are they identified? How effectively are they used? How well is the student survey set up? How informative are the results? Overall, where does the student writer draw the line between what is unnecessary and necessary concern about speech. Do you think the distinction the writer makes could be implemented in practice?

Censorship with a Halo?

Political correctness is a touchy topic. While the term has taken on a very negative connotation in modern usage, no one will deny that some measure of control of language must be enforced. The proliferation of hate groups, particularly on the Internet, calls us to enforce some sort of restraint in our speech and writing. On the other hand, some conventions laid down in the name of political correctness have been simply laughable, and others have been decried by the very groups they aim to protect.

Many people feel that censorship in the name of political correctness has gone too far. Chris Wood, guest lecturer at the Sing Tao School of Journalism at the University of British Columbia, said, "Political correctness has become censorship with a halo." The use of political correctness as a reason to justify censorship, he said, robbed journalists of their ability to observe and report truthfully, regardless of the consequences. Kelley L. Ross, PhD, wrote an extensive and well-researched essay attacking the theory that gender conventions in the English language are sexist, using examples of other languages to show that sexual equality in a culture and the sexual neutrality of its language are not meaningfully correlated. She draws on examples from English, Greek, Spanish, French, and old Persian to show how apparently sexist language may be more benign than it is portrayed to be, and how the achievement of perfect gender equality in language is no guarantee of gender equality in society

An excellent example of why many people feel political correctness has gone too far is the conventions that a number of branches of the government wanted to adopt for referring to the blind. The National Federation of the Blind drafted a resolution condemning the terms that were being chosen to refer to the blind. It distinguishes politically correct terms into three distinct categories. First, terms such as "visually impaired" or "hard of seeing," which it objects to on the grounds that such terms should only be used to distinguish between people with limited sight and those with none. It goes on to speak against those terms, such as "sightless," which are awkward and serve no real purpose. Finally, it objects to using a phrase such as "person who is blind" instead of "blind person," if the reason for that use is motivated by political correctness and is meant to emphasize that a blind person is first and foremost a person. They make these objections on the grounds that this kind of special treatment achieves the opposite of its purported goal, portraying blindness as something shameful that requires special treatment and portraying the blind as "touchy and belligerent."

However, many people who object to censorship and complain about the spread of political correctness fail to understand the reasons behind it. The continued existence of racism, sexism, and hate in our culture requires that some measure of control be present. The following quote, from "On Tactics and Strategy for USENET" by Milton John Kleim, Jr., shows us what exists when speech is not policed enough:

> USENET offers enormous opportunity for the Aryan Resistance to disseminate our message to the unaware and the ignorant. It is the only relatively uncensored (so far) free-forum mass medium which we have available. The State cannot yet stop us from "advertising" our ideas and organizations on USENET . . . NOW is the time to grasp the WEAPON which is the Net, and wield it skillfully and wisely while you may still do so freely.

Radicals such as Kleim, a Holocaust denier, racist, and member of White Power organizations, are allowed to convey whatever message they choose. Calling the universally accepted historical fact of the Nazi genocide of the Jews the "legend of the Holocaust," Kleim says:

> The Holocaust Myth is peddled by both professional liars, and well-meaning but misguided historians. Enormous amounts of material have been produced and hundreds of millions of dollars have been

expended in this campaign to disseminate the "acceptable" version of the plight of the Jews under the Third Reich.

While our constitution protects our right to free speech, what political correctness ideally aims at is not the denial of free speech but the restraint of individuals such as Kleim, whose words perpetuate the hate and tension in our society.

A survey of fellow students on a number of topics related to political correctness yielded interesting results. When asked if they agreed with revising the Bible to remove sexist language, 80% said it should remain unchanged, 13.3% said it could be revised, and 6.7% were undecided. On the topic of whether using ethnic slurs such as the N word in re-creations to create a greater sense of realism was appropriate, 93.3% said that it was appropriate, while 6.7% said that it was inappropriate. On the question of whether having a Native American as a team mascot was demeaning to Native Americans, 73.3% said it was not demeaning, while 26.7% said that it was. The question that evoked the most different responses, however, was whether political correctness has gone too far, and whether people should be allowed greater freedom of expression even if it means allowing people to air offensive views. 60% said that political correctness has gone too far, and that people should be allowed to air more extreme views. 13.3% said that political correctness had not gone too far, and that it was appropriate in the context of the tension and hate that certain kinds of language can evoke. Finally, 26.7% did not respond or had mixed feelings on the issue.

There is no simple solution to the issue of political correctness. There are too many people, with too many different views, for any single plan to satisfy them all. The best we can hope for is a compromise that pleases most people most of the time. While there must be a degree of restraint in language, the general impression is that political correctness has gone beyond its mandate. Despite this there is a large, and still growing, amount of hate rhetoric circulating, particularly on the Internet. A plan to combat hateful and discriminatory language should focus on restraining these fonts of race rhetoric and hate speech, rather than going after relatively minor issues.

Topics for Papers Using Internet or Oral Sources (A Sampling)

1. Do today's immigrants tend to be slower to assimilate than previous generations? Do they tend to stay separate from the mainstream?
2. What is the current state of arguments about the minimum wage? Who supports raising the minimum wage? Who opposes raising the minimum wage and why?
3. What has been the experience of people who have moved from welfare to workfare? Are there reliable statistics? Can you draw on personal testimonies from online sources or personal interviews?
4. Is there a true mixing of students in today's schools, or do students tend to divide along ethnic, racial, or cultural lines?
5. How many young Americans grow up in single-parent homes? Do they face special challenges? How do they cope?

6. What is the visibility of women in today's professional sports? How do men's sports and women's sports compare in attendance, publicity, earnings, or influence on the lives of young people?
7. What is the self-image of police officers today? How do they cope with the dangers and traumas of police work? How do they respond to charges of police brutality?
8. What is it like to grow up in an orthodox Jewish family? in the Mormon church? in a devout Catholic family? in an atheist family?
9. What is it like to marry someone from a different cultural, ethnic, or racial background? What is it like to be in a "cross-cultural" marriage?
10. What is it like to live as an American in a foreign country? What stereotypes about Americans is an American likely to encounter? What attitudes or reactions should an American expect?

3
NEW WORLD
Diversity and Community

We are a people in search of a national community.

—Barbara Jordan

*It's that same old, same old story. We all have an immigrant ancestor,
one who believed in America; one who, daring or duped, took sail.*

—Fae Myenne Ng

*I am giving you a version of America, your America, that you may
not have chosen to see or may have missed. I used to travel on the
train going out to my job in Queens from the Upper West Side. After
a certain subway stop, the entire train is filled with nonwhites. And
those people are the people I am writing about, saying they have huge
interesting lives.*

—Bharati Mukherjee

For many years, the unofficial ideology of the United States was that
of the melting pot. People would come to this country from across the seas
to make a new start—in the words of one refugee from the persecutions
and massacres of the Old World, to "start all over again." The promise of
America was the promise of equal opportunity—regardless of class, religion, or ethnic origin. Arriving on these shores, the immigrants would
leave old allegiances and old hatreds behind to form a new "nation of
nations."

The American historian Arthur Schlesinger stated a widely held belief when he said,

> America has been in the best sense of the term a melting pot, every
> element adding its particular element of strength. The constant infu-
> sion of new blood has enriched our cultural life, speeded our material
> growth, and produced some of our ablest statesmen. Over 17 million
> immigrants arrived in the single period from the Civil War to World
> War I . . . the very nationalities which had habitually warred with one
> another in the Old World have lived together in harmony in the New.
> America has demonstrated for everyone with eyes to see that those
> things which unite peoples are greater than those which divide them,
> that war is not the inevitable fate of mankind.

The policy implementing this belief was assimilation. The goal was to
Americanize new immigrants as quickly as possible, making them share in
a common language and a common culture. Their children would already
be new Americans, growing up in a world of baseball, hot dogs, chewing
gum, and Coca-Cola.

In the years since Schlesinger wrote, the melting-pot metaphor and
the policy of assimilation have come in for much reexamination and revision. The melting-pot theory had not worked, or not worked well, for large

segments of American society. Native Americans had been shunted off to reservations in areas where no white people could make a living. African Americans leaving the segregated South found themselves living in segregated inner cities in the North. Many Mexicans, Puerto Ricans, and Cubans were living in Spanish-speaking neighborhoods with strong ties to their own culture. A large new Asian immigration transformed parts of cities into new Chinatowns or Little Saigons.

Confronted with the limits of assimilation, minority leaders and teachers started to teach a return to the roots. They promoted black pride, pride in the Chicano heritage, or *la raza,* or the preservation of Native American traditions. Sociologists and political leaders called for a new recognition of diversity, of pluralism. They asked for recognition of the side-by-side of different languages and cultural strands in a new American "mosaic"—with many different particles fitted together in a rich larger pattern, a larger whole.

Conservative columnists like George Will talked about the "cult of diversity" as a threat to mainstream American culture. *Multiculturalism*—the recognition of a rich web of cultural influences in American life—became a fighting word. How will tomorrow's Americans think of diversity and community? How much diversity will our society welcome or accommodate? Will a multicultural society have a common center?

THE MOSAIC VS. THE MYTH

Anna Quindlen

Anna Quindlen became known as a widely syndicated columnist for the New York Times, *winning a Pulitzer Prize for commentary in 1992. Like other columnists, she writes about the issues of the day not as an expert—a political scientist, sociologist, or psychologist. She writes as a shrewd, informed observer who helps her readers make sense of the news. Like other columnists, Quindlen is a trend watcher who sizes up and explains the changes in aware-ness and public consciousness that slowly become part of the way we think about the world in which we live. Like other journalists with liberal or femi-nist leanings, she has come in for her share of hate mail from angry letter writ-ers. Recently, she has decided to devote more of her time to fiction, her first love. She published her second novel,* One True Thing, *in 1994. In the follow-ing column, she comments on the gradual change from the melting-pot ideal of American society to a new outlook more tolerant or accepting of diversity.*

Thought Starters: How is American society like a melting pot? How is it like a mosaic? How is it like a "tossed salad"?

There is some disagreement over which wordsmith first substituted *1* "mosaic" for "melting pot" as a way of describing America, but it is un-doubtedly a more apt description. And it undoubtedly applies in Ms. Miller's third-grade class and elsewhere in the Lower East Side's Public School 20.

The neighborhood where the school is located is to the immigrant ex-perience what Broadway is to actors. Past Blevitzky Bros. Monuments ("at this place since 1914"), past Katz's Delicatessen with its fan mail hung in the window, past the tenement buildings where fire escapes climb graceful as cat burglars, P.S. 20 holds the corner of Essex and Houston.

Its current student body comes from the Dominican Republic, Cam-bodia, Bangladesh, Puerto Rico, Colombia, mainland China, Vietnam and El Salvador. In Ms. Miller's third-grade class these various faces somehow look the same, upturned and open, as though they were cups waiting for the water to be poured.

There's a spirit in the nation now that's in opposition to these chil-dren. It is not interested in your tired, your poor, your huddled masses. In recent days it has been best personified by a candidate for governor and the suggestion in his campaign that there is a kind of authentic American. That authentic American is white and Christian (but not Catholic), ethnic ori-gins lost in the mists of an amorphous past, not visible in accent, appearance or allegiance.

This is not a new idea, this resilient form of xenophobia. "It is but too   5
common a remark of late, that the American character has within a short
time been sadly degraded by numerous instances of riot and lawless violence," Samuel F. B. Morse wrote in an 1835 treatise called "Imminent
Dangers to the Free Institutions of the United States through Foreign Immigration," decrying such riffraff as Jesuits.

Times are bad, and we blame the newcomers, whether it's 1835 or
1991. Had Morse had his way, half of me would still be in Italy; if some conservatives had their way today, most of the children at P.S. 20 would be, in
that ugly phrase, back where they came from. So much for lifting a lamp
beside the golden door.

They don't want to learn the language, we complain, as though the
old neighborhoods were not full of Poles and Italians who kept to their
mother tongue. They don't want to become American, we say, as though
there are not plenty of us who believe we lost something when we re-
nounced ethnicity. "Dagos," my mother said the American kids called
them, American being those not Italian. "Wops." How quickly we forget
as we use pejoratives for the newest newcomers.

Our greatest monument to immigration, the restored Ellis Island,
seems to suggest by its display cases that coming to America is a thing nostalgic, something grandparents did. On the Lower East Side it has never
been past tense, struggling with English and poverty, sharing apartments
with the bathroom in the hall and the bathtub in the kitchen.

They send their children to school with hopes for a miracle, or a
job, which is almost the same thing. This past week the School Volunteer
Program, which fields almost 6,000 volunteer tutors, sponsored the first
citywide Read Aloud: 400 grown-ups reading to thousands of kids in 90
schools. In P.S. 20, as so many have done before, the kids clutched their
books like visas.

It is foolish to forget where you come from, which, in the case of the   10
United States, is almost always somewhere else. The true authentic American is a pilgrim with a small "p," armed with little more than the phrase "I
wish. . . ." New ones are being minted in Ms. Miller's class, bits of a mosaic far from complete.

The Responsive Reader

1. Why is the term *mosaic* "a more apt description" for what Quindlen saw
   on the Lower East Side than *melting pot?* (Or is it?)
2. What does Quindlen say about the nature and history of xenophobia—
   the fear of foreigners—in this country? (Is it alive in your own community or in society at large?)
3. How does Quindlen forge links between the present wave of immigration and America's past? What is her idea of the "true authentic
   American"?

Talking, Listening, Writing

4. Do you consider yourself a "true authentic American" in Quindlen's terms? Or are you one of those whose ethnic origins are "lost in the mists of an amorphous"—shapeless, indistinct—past?

Collaborative Projects

5. Quindlen says, "It is foolish to forget where you come from." You may want to work on a family history, with special attention to ethnic or regional origins. Your class may decide to bring these family histories together as a class publication.

JEFFERSON, HEMINGS AFFAIR CAN'T BE DENIED

Cynthia Tucker

Thomas Jefferson symbolizes for many both the promise and the contradictions of America's historical heritage. He was a plantation owner from Virginia who helped formulate the rallying cries of the American Revolution and became the third president of the new country. He wrote the Declaration of Independence when a revolutionary ideology was calling the "divine right" of kings into question. A new egalitarian philosophy was challenging the privileges of a hereditary aristocracy. Jefferson's manifesto asserted that God had not created masters and servants, aristocrats and commoners. All had been "created equal." All were entitled to human dignity. Jefferson wrote the first draft of the Declaration with the assistance of Benjamin Franklin and John Adams. It was edited by Congress and published as the unanimous declaration of the thirteen original United States of America on July 4, 1776.

Until recently, traditionalist or mainstream historians angrily denied Jefferson's relationship with a female slave. Other biographers and historians, however, had come to accept it. In a book about Jefferson, Fawn M. Brodie accepted the liaison with Hemings as fact and described it as a "serious passion that brought Jefferson and the slave woman much private happiness over a period lasting over thirty-eight years." In 1998, an article in the prestigious science magazine Nature *claimed that DNA tests proved that at least one of Sally Hemings's children was Jefferson's. Responses to the new findings have ranged from indictments of the hypocrisy of men of Jefferson's generation to feminist commentary on Sally Hemings's story as an example of the patriarchal exploitation of women. Cynthia Tucker of the* Atlanta Constitution *was one of many columnists and commentators who discussed what the new research meant for the "historical record" and the self-image of Americans as a nation.*

Thought Starters: Have you seen evidence that race and sex are often an explosive mixture in this country?

The strangest thing about the Jefferson–Sally Hemings controversy   *1*
has always been just that: the controversy. It has been downright surreal to hear historian after mainstream historian vehemently deny even the possibility of a sexual relationship between a founding father and one of his slaves.

Any black American could have told you that that sort of relationship was part and parcel of the experience of slavery. Countless blacks have among their genetic forebears some slavemaster(s).

That story is as common as dirt. How else do you account for the millions of black Americans with light skin and straightish hair, some with blue or green eyes? The existence of these light-skinned blacks was evident well before the Civil War, when most black Americans were still bound in slavery.

Backed by reams of circumstantial evidence, a handful of writers and historians, including Barbara Chase-Riboud and law professor Annette Gordon-Reed, have insisted that Jefferson engaged in a long-term affair with Hemings. They note that Hemings was the half-sister of Jefferson's dead wife and bore a striking resemblance to her.

Jefferson never remarried, and was presumably lonely after his wife *5* died. Still, the denials of a Jefferson-Hemings affair from the majority of modern-day historians were furious, almost as savage as the tongue-lashings unleashed upon 19th-century Richmond journalist James Thomson Callender, who first reported the affair in 1802. And the denials came from highly regarded sources. Just last year, Joseph J. Ellis won the National Book Award for a Jefferson biography, "American Sphinx: The Character of Thomas Jefferson," that rejects the notion of a Jefferson-Hemings affair.

But in a plot worthy of William Faulkner, the truth of the Jefferson-Hemings relationship has come crashing into the front parlor, where it can no longer be denied. Newly revealed DNA evidence strongly suggests that Jefferson fathered at least one of Hemings' children. And that brings us back to the more interesting part of this story: What were those historians thinking?

The defenders of Jefferson's image as a paragon of principle and virtue claimed that his noble character would have prevented such a liaison. What a strange moral hierarchy those historians must hold. It ought to be clear that once a man's basic character has permitted him to own other human beings, sexual exploitation of those human beings is no stretch.

Jeffersonites insist, however, that it is unfair to judge a founder of American democracy by modern moral standards, which hold slavery reprehensible. In Jefferson's world, they point out, slavery was commonplace.

While they are right, that hardly disentangles Jefferson from Hemings. Judging Jefferson by the standards of his time, when women (of all colors) of lesser social status were often sexually exploited by more powerful men, the likelihood of an affair should have been obvious.

So another truth has been revealed: Some rather commonplace prej- *10* udices kept prominent historians from seeing what should have been obvious even before science intervened. How many other history texts have been written inaccurately and how many other historic episodes wrongly interpreted because of those same prejudices?

This overdue acknowledgment of the truth about Thomas Jefferson ought to hurry the long-delayed business of setting the rest of the historical record straight: Black Americans are not only integral to the American experience, we are also in the family.

The Responsive Reader

1. According to Tucker, what is the history of the controversy about Jefferson and Sally Hemings? Who were major players? How does she describe the role of "mainstream" historians? How does she explain their attitude? What for Tucker is "surreal" about the controversy?
2. What is a sphinx? Why did one biographer call Jefferson an "American sphinx"?
3. What for Tucker is the "truth about Thomas Jefferson"? How does she want you to go about "setting the rest of the historical record straight"?

Talking, Listening, Writing

4. Should we apply today's standards of sexual morality to the leaders of the past? Is it fair "to judge a founder of American democracy by modern moral standards" regarding slavery and the exploitation of women?
5. Many American liberals believe in the principles of Jeffersonian democracy: universal public education, an educated citizenry as the cornerstone of democracy, respect for the individual, equal opportunity for all, and tolerance for dissent. For you, would the revelations about Jefferson undermine his role as a moral authority and as a source of guidance and inspiration?

Find It on the Web

After the publication of the DNA evidence in *Nature,* pundits and columnists across the ideological spectrum weighed in. Commentaries ranged from Ellen Goodman's "Tom and Sally" (*Boston Globe* 5 November 1998) to Patricia J. Williams's "What's Love Got to Do with It" (*Nation* 23 November 1998). Newsmagazines published accounts of reunions of the white and the African American branches of the Jeffersonian family tree. You may want to search Internet archives of major newspapers or magazines to study the range of reactions on the nation's op-ed (editorial opinion) pages.

DIVERSITY AND ITS DISCONTENTS
Arturo Madrid

> *Arturo Madrid is a native of New Mexico who studied at the University of New Mexico and at UCLA. His first teaching assignment was at Dartmouth; he later became president of the Thomas Rivera Center at the Claremont Graduate School in California. He represents Spanish-speaking Americans of the Southwest who live in lands that were once part of Mexico and for whom the Anglos, or* americanos, *were the "immigrants," or new arrivals. The following article is excerpted from a speech he gave at the National Conference of the American Association of Higher Education. He urged his audience of educators to recognize excellence in workers as well as managers, in people who are not glib or superficially sophisticated, and in people regardless of class, gender, race, or national origin. What do you learn from this article about the feeling of being the "other"?*

Thought Starters: What does it mean to be "different"? How does it shape a person's outlook and personality?

My name is Arturo Madrid. I am a citizen of the United States, as are   *1*
my parents and as were my grandparents and my great-grandparents. My ancestors' presence in what is now the United States antedates Plymouth Rock, even without taking into account any American Indian heritage I might have.

I do not, however, fit those mental sets that define America and Americans. My physical appearance, my speech patterns, my name, my profession (a professor of Spanish) create a text that confuses the reader. My normal experience is to be asked, "And where are *you* from?" My response depends on my mood. Passive-aggressive, I answer, "From here." Aggressive-passive, I ask, "Do you mean where I am originally from?" But ultimately my answer to those follow-up questions that will ask about origins will be that we have always been from here.

Overcoming my resentment I try to educate, knowing that nine times out of ten my words fall on inattentive ears. I have spent most of my adult life explaining who I am not. I am exotic, but—as Richard Rodriguez of *Hunger of Memory* fame so painfully found out—not exotic enough . . . not Peruvian, or Pakistani, or whatever. I am, however, very clearly the *other,* if only your everyday, garden-variety, domestic *other.* I will share with you another phenomenon that I have been a part of, that of being a missing person, and how I came late to that awareness. But I've always known that I was the *other,* even before I knew the vocabulary or understood the significance of otherness.

I grew up in an isolated and historically marginal part of the United States, a small mountain village in the state of New Mexico, the eldest child of parents native to that region, whose ancestors had always lived there. In those vast and empty spaces people who look like me, speak as I do, and have names like mine predominate. But the *americanos* lived among us: the descendants of those nineteenth-century immigrants who dispossessed us of our lands; missionaries who came to convert us and stayed to live among us; artists who became enchanted with our land and humanscape and went native; refugees from unhealthy climes, crowded spaces, unpleasant circumstances; and, of course, the inhabitants of Los Alamos, whose sociocultural distance from us was accentuated by the fact that they occupied a space removed from and proscribed to us. More importantly, however, they—*los americanos*—were omnipresent (and almost exclusively so) in newspapers, newsmagazines, books, on radio, in movies, and, ultimately, on television.

Despite the operating myth of the day, school did not erase my otherness. It did try to deny it, and in doing so only accentuated it. To this day what takes place in schools is more socialization than education, but when I was in elementary school—and given where I was—socialization was everything. School was where one became an American, because there was a pervasive and systematic denial by the society that surrounded us that we were Americans. That denial was both explicit and implicit. 5

Quite beyond saluting the flag and pledging allegiance to it (a very intense and meaningful action, given that the United States was involved in a war and our brothers, cousins, uncles, and fathers were on the frontlines), becoming American was learning English, and its corollary: not speaking Spanish. Until very recently ours was a proscribed language, either *de jure*—by rule, by policy, by law—or *de facto*—by practice, implicitly if not explicitly, through social and political and economic pressure. I do not argue that learning English was not appropriate. On the contrary. Like it or not, and we had no basis to make any judgments on that matter, we were Americans by virtue of having been born Americans and English was the common language of Americans. And there was a myth, a pervasive myth, to the effect that if only we learned to speak English well—and particularly without an accent—we would be welcomed into the American fellowship.

Sam Hayakawa and the official English movement folks notwithstanding, the true text was not our speech, but rather our names and our appearance, for we would always have an accent, however perfect our pronunciation, however excellent our enunciation, however divine our diction. That accent would be heard in our pigmentation, our physiognomy, our names. We were, in short, the *other*.

Being the *other* involves contradictory phenomena. On the one hand being the *other* frequently means being invisible. Ralph Ellison wrote eloquently about that experience in his magisterial novel, *Invisible Man*. On the other hand, being the *other* sometimes involves sticking out like a sore thumb. What is she/he doing here?

For some of us being the *other* is only annoying; for others it is debilitating; for still others it is damning. Many try to flee otherness by taking on protective colorations that provide invisibility, whether of dress or speech or manner or name. Only a fortunate few succeed. For the majority of us otherness is permanently sealed by physical appearance. For the rest, otherness is betrayed by ways of being, speaking, or doing.

The first half of my life I spent downplaying the significance and consequences of otherness. The second half has seen me wrestling to understand its complex and deeply ingrained realities; striving to fathom why otherness denies us a voice or visibility or validity in American society and its institutions; struggling to make otherness familiar, reasonable, even normal to my fellow Americans. 10

I spoke earlier of another phenomenon that I am a part of: that of being a missing person. Growing up in northern New Mexico I had only a slight sense of us being missing persons. *Hispanos,* as we called (and call) ourselves in New Mexico, were very much a part of the fabric of the society, and there were *hispano* professionals everywhere about me: doctors, lawyers, schoolteachers, and administrators. My people owned businesses, ran organizations, and were both appointed and elected public officials.

My awareness of our absence from the larger institutional life of the society became sharper when I went off to college, but even then it was attenuated by the circumstances of history and geography. The demography of Albuquerque still strongly reflected its historical and cultural origins, despite the influx of Midwesterners and Easterners. Moreover, many of my classmates at the University of New Mexico were *hispanos,* and even some of my professors. I thought that would obtain at UCLA, where I began graduate studies in 1960. Los Angeles had a very large Mexican population and that population was visible even in and around Westwood and on the campus. Many of the groundskeepers and food-service personnel at UCLA were Mexican. But Mexican-American students were few and mostly invisible, and I do not recall seeing or knowing a single Mexican-American (or, for that matter, African-American, Asian, or American Indian) professional on the staff or faculty of that institution during the five years I was there. Needless to say, people like me were not present in any capacity at Dartmouth College, the site of my first teaching appointment, and of course were not even part of the institutional or individual mind-set. I knew then that we—a we that had come to encompass American Indians, Asian-Americans, African-Americans, Puerto Ricans, and women—were truly missing persons in American institutional life.

Over the past three decades the *de jure* and *de facto* types of segregation that have historically characterized American institutions have been under assault. As a consequence, minorities and women have become part of American institutional life. Although there are still many areas where we are not to be found, the missing persons phenomenon is not as pervasive as it once was. However, the presence of the *other,* particularly minorities, in institutions and in institutional life resembles what we call in Spanish a *flor de tierra* (a surface phenomenon): we are spare plants whose roots do not go deep, vulnerable to inclemencies of an economic, or political, or social, nature.

Our entrance into and our status in institutional life are not unlike a scenario set forth by my grandmother's pastor when she informed him that she and her family were leaving their mountain village to relocate to the Rio Grande Valley. When he asked her to promise that she would remain true to the faith and continue to involve herself in it, she asked why he thought she would do otherwise. "Doña Trinidad," he told her, "in the Valley there is no Spanish church. There is only an American church." "But," she protested, "I read and speak English and would be able to worship there." The pastor responded, "It is possible that they will not admit you, and even if they do, they might not accept you. And that is why I want you to promise me that you are going to go to church. Because if they don't let you in through the front door, I want you to go in through the back door. And if you can't get in through the back door, go in the side door. And if you are unable to enter through the side door I want you to go in through the window. What is important is that you enter and stay."

Some of us entered institutional life through the front door; others through the back door; and still others through side doors. Many, if not most of us, came in through windows, and continue to come in through windows. Of those who entered through the front door, some never made it past the lobby; others were ushered into corners and niches. Those who entered through back and side doors inevitably have remained in back and side rooms. And those who entered through windows found enclosures built around them. For, despite the lip service given to the goal of the integration of minorities into institutional life, what has frequently occurred instead is ghettoization, marginalization, isolation.

Not only have the entry points been limited, but in addition the dynamics have been singularly conflictive. Gaining entry and its corollary, gaining space, have frequently come as a consequence of demands made on institutions and institutional officers. Rather than entering institutions more or less passively, minorities have of necessity entered them actively, even aggressively. Rather than waiting to receive, they have demanded. Institutional relations have thus been adversarial, infused with specific and generalized tensions.

The nature of the entrance and the nature of the space occupied have greatly influenced the view and attitude of the majority population within those institutions. All of us are put into the same box; that is, no matter what the individual reality, the assessment of the individual is inevitably conditioned by a perception that is held of the class. Whatever our history, whatever our record, whatever our validations, whatever our accomplishments, by and large we are perceived unidimensionally and dealt with accordingly. I remember an experience I had in this regard, atypical only in its explicitness. A few years ago I allowed myself to be persuaded to seek the presidency of a well-known state university. I was invited for an interview and presented myself before the selection committee, which included members of the board of trustees. The opening question of that brief but memorable interview was directed at me by a member of that august body. "Dr. Madrid," he asked, "why does a one-dimensional person like you think he can be the president of a multidimensional institution like ours?"

Over the past four decades America's demography has undergone significant changes. Since 1965 the principal demographic growth we have experienced in the United States has been of peoples whose national origins are non-European. This population growth has occurred both through birth and through immigration. A few years ago discussion of the national birthrate had a scare dimension: the high—"inordinately high"—birthrate of the Hispanic population. The popular discourse was informed by words such as "breeding." Several years later, as a consequence of careful tracking by government agencies, we now know that what has happened is that the birthrate of the majority population has decreased. When viewed historically and comparatively, the minority populations (for the most part) have also had a decline in birthrate, but not one as great as that of the majority.

There are additional demographic changes that should give us something to think about. African-Americans are now to be found in significant numbers in every major urban center in the nation. Hispanic-Americans now number over 15 million people, and although they are a regionally concentrated (and highly urbanized) population, there is a Hispanic community in almost every major urban center of the United States. American Indians, heretofore a small and rural population, are increasingly more numerous and urban. The Asian-American population, which has historically consisted of small and concentrated communities of Chinese-, Filipino-, and Japanese-Americans, has doubled over the past decade, its complexion changed by the addition of Cambodians, Koreans, Hmongs, Vietnamese, et al.

Prior to the Immigration Act of 1965, 69 percent of immigration was   *20* from Europe. By far the largest number of immigrants to the United States since 1965 have been from the Americas and from Asia: 34 percent are from Asia; another 34 percent are from Central and South America; 16 percent are from Europe; 10 percent are from the Caribbean; the remaining 6 percent are from other continents and Canada. As was the case with previous immigration waves, the current one consists principally of young people: 60 percent are between the ages of 16 and 44. Thus, for the next few decades, we will continue to see a growth in the percentage of non-European-origin Americans as compared to European-Americans.

To sum up, we now live in one of the most demographically diverse nations in the world, and one that is increasingly more so.

During the same period social and economic change seems to have accelerated. Who would have imagined at mid-century that the prototypical middle-class family (working husband, wife as homemaker, two children) would for all intents and purposes disappear? Who could have anticipated the rise in teenage pregnancies, children in poverty, drug use? Who among us understood the implications of an aging population?

We live in an age of continuous and intense change, a world in which what held true yesterday does not today, and certainly will not tomorrow. What change does, moreover, is bring about even more change. The only constant we have at this point in our national development is change. And change is threatening. The older we get the more likely we are to be anxious about change, and the greater our desire to maintain the status quo.

Evident in our public life is a fear of change, whether economic or moral. Some who fear change are responsive to the call of economic protectionism, others to the message of moral protectionism. Parenthetically, I have referred to the movement to require more of students without in turn giving them more as academic protectionism. And the pronouncements of E. D. Hirsch and Allan Bloom are, I believe, informed by intellectual protectionism. Much more serious, however, is the dark side of the populism which underlies this evergoing protectionism—the resentment of the *other*. An excellent and fascinating example of that aspect of populism is the cry for linguistic protectionism—for making English the official language of the United States. And who among us is unaware of the tensions that underlie immigration reform, of the underside of demographic protectionism?

A matter of increasing concern is whether this new protectionism, and *25* the mistrust of the *other* which accompanies it, is not making more significant inroads than we have supposed in higher education. Specifically, I wish to discuss the question of whether a goal (quality) and a reality (demographic diversity) have been erroneously placed in conflict, and, if so, what problems this perception of conflict might present.

As part of my scholarship I turn to dictionaries for both origins and meanings of words. Quality, according to the *Oxford English Dictionary,* has multiple meanings. One set defines quality as being an essential character, a distinctive and inherent feature. A second describes it as a degree of excellence, of conformity to standards, as superiority in kind. A third makes reference to social status, particularly to persons of high social status. A fourth talks about quality as being a special or distinguishing attribute, as being a desirable trait. Quality is highly desirable in both principle and practice. We all aspire to it in our own person, in our experiences, in our acquisitions and products, and of course we all want to be associated with people and operations of quality.

But let us move away from the various dictionary meanings of the word and to our own sense of what it represents and of how we feel about it. First of all we consider quality to be finite; that is, it is limited with respect to quantity; it has very few manifestations; it is not widely distributed. I have it and you have it, but they don't. We associate quality with homogeneity, with uniformity, with standardization, with order, regularity, neatness. All too often we equate it with smoothness, glibness, slickness, elegance. Certainly it is always expensive. We tend to identify it with those who lead, with the rich and famous. And, when you come right down to it, it's inherent. Either you've got it or you ain't.

Diversity, from the Latin *divertere,* meaning to turn aside, to go different ways, to differ, is the condition of being different or having differences, is an instance of being different. Its companion word, diverse, means differing, unlike, distinct; having or capable of having various forms; composed of unlike or distinct elements. Diversity is lack of standardization, of regularity, of orderliness, homogeneity, conformity, uniformity. Diversity introduces complications, is difficult to organize, is troublesome to manage, is problematical. Diversity is irregular, disorderly, uneven, rough. The way we use the word diversity gives us away. Something is too diverse, is extremely diverse. We want a little diversity.

When we talk about diversity, we are talking about the *other,* whatever that other might be: someone of a different gender, race, class, national origin; somebody at a greater or lesser distance from the norm; someone outside the set; someone who possesses a different set of characteristics, features, or attributes; someone who does not fall within the taxonomies we use daily and with which we are comfortable; someone who does not fit into the mental configurations that give our lives order and meaning.

In short, diversity is desirable only in principle, not in practice. Long   *30* live diversity . . . as long as it conforms to my standards, my mind set, my view of life, my sense of order. We desire, we like, we admire diversity, not unlike the way the French (and others) appreciate women; that is, *Vive la différence!*—as long as it stays in its place.

What I find paradoxical about and lacking in this debate is that diversity is the natural order of things. Evolution produces diversity. Margaret Visser, writing about food in her latest book, *Much Depends on Dinner,* makes an eloquent statement in this regard:

> Machines like, demand, and produce uniformity. But nature loathes it: her strength lies in multiplicity and in differences. Sameness in biology means fewer possibilities and therefore weakness.

The United States, by its very nature, by its very development, is the essence of diversity. It is diverse in its geography, population, institutions, technology; its social, cultural, and intellectual modes. It is a society that at its best does not consider quality to be monolithic in form or finite in quantity, or to be inherent in class. Quality in our society proceeds in large measure out of the stimulus of diverse modes of thinking and acting; out of the creativity made possible by the different ways in which we approach things; out of diversion from paths or modes hallowed by tradition.

One of the principal strengths of our society is its ability to address, on a continuing and substantive basis, the real economic, political, and social problems that have faced and continue to face us. What makes the United States so attractive to immigrants is the protections and opportunities it offers; what keeps our society together is tolerance for cultural, religious, social, political, and even linguistic difference; what makes us a unique, dynamic, and extraordinary nation is the power and creativity of our diversity.

The true history of the United States is one of struggle against intolerance, against oppression, against xenophobia, against those forces that have prohibited persons from participating in the larger life of the society on the basis of their race, their gender, their religion, their national origin, their linguistic and cultural background. These phenomena are not consigned to the past. They remain with us and frequently take on virulent dimensions.

If you believe, as I do, that the well-being of a society is directly related to the degree and extent to which all of its citizens participate in its institutions, then you will have to agree that we have a challenge before us. In view of the extraordinary changes that are taking place in our society we need to take up the struggle again, irritating, grating, troublesome, unfashionable, unpleasant as it is. As educated and educator members of this society we have a special responsibility for ensuring that all American institutions, not just our elementary and secondary schools, our juvenile halls, or our jails, reflect the diversity of our society. Not to do so is to risk greater alienation on the part of a growing segment of our society; is to risk increased social tension in an already conflictive world; and, ultimately, is to risk the survival of a range of institutions that, for all their defects and deficiencies, provide us the opportunity and the freedom to improve our individual and collective lot. 35

Let me urge you to reflect on these two words—quality and diversity—and on the mental sets and behaviors that flow out of them. And let me urge you further to struggle against the notion that quality is finite in quantity, limited in its manifestations, or is restricted by considerations of class, gender, race, or national origin; or that quality manifests itself only in leaders and not in followers, in managers and not in workers, in breeders and not in drones; or that it has to be associated with verbal agility or elegance of personal style; or that it cannot be seeded, nurtured, or developed.

Because diversity—the *other*—is among us, will define and determine our lives in ways that we still do not fully appreciate, whether that other is women (no longer bound by tradition, house, and family); or Asians, African-Americans, Indians, and Hispanics (no longer invisible, regional, or marginal); or our newest immigrants (no longer distant, exotic, alien). Given the changing profile of America, will we come to terms with diversity in our personal and professional lives? Will we begin to recognize the diverse forms that quality can take? If so, we will thus initiate the process of making quality limitless in its manifestations, infinite in quantity, un-restricted with respect to its origins, and more importantly, virulently contagious.

I hope we will. And that we will further join together to expand—not to close—the circle.

The Responsive Reader

1. What does it mean to Madrid to be the "other"? What is or was the role of such factors as history, genealogy, appearance (or "physiognomy"), and language in his sense of being different?
2. What was Madrid's experience with or perception of the *americanos?*
3. What was Madrid's experience with the school as the institution most directly representing American society? What was its goal? What was its governing myth? Did it fail or succeed?
4. What are different ways of dealing with minority identity or minority status? How did (and does) Madrid react or cope? Did his attitude or awareness change at different stages in his life?
5. What is Madrid's account of the changes as American colleges and universities try to deal with the issue of diversity? Have the changes been for the better?
6. What is Madrid's last word on the role of diversity in American society?

Talking, Listening, Writing

7. On balance, what do you think predominates in this essay—the "discontents" of the past or the challenges of the future?
8. Have you ever tried to put yourself in the shoes of someone with a history or with grievances and aspirations very different from your own? Tell the story of an experience that opened up for you a new perspective or opened a new window on the world. What did you learn from the experience?
9. Have you ever had difficulty answering the question "Who are you?" or "What are you?"

Collaborative Projects

10. Have the hiring and retention of minority faculty been an issue at your own institution? You and classmates may want to arrange interviews with people who are in a position to know.

MORMONS: WALKING A MILE IN THEIR SHOES

Walter Kirn

The American "nation of nations" has also been a nation of grassroots religious and political movements commanding the loyalty of large numbers looking for meaning and direction in their lives. One of the most successful and prominent of these homegrown American movements is the Mormon church— the Church of Jesus Christ of Latter-day Saints. Starting as a persecuted religious minority, it has been called "the most numerically successful creed born on American soil and one of the fastest growing anywhere"—with close to five million members in the United States alone, with more than $30 billion in assets, and with a worldwide missionary effort bringing millions overseas into the fold. Mormons believe that Joseph Smith, the founder, received Scriptures from an angel in 1823, which were added to the Christian Bible. Smith was murdered by a mob, and 30,000 followers were driven from their dream city of Nauvoo in Illinois in 1846. Brigham Young led them on a thousand-mile trek to Salt Lake City, there to found the "new Zion." The author of the following article grew up as a Mormon and joined large numbers of the faithful in a reenactment of the trek.

Thought Starters: What encounters have you had with missionaries—Mormon missionaries or other? What was their mission? What motivates them or people like them? How receptive or how reluctant an audience are you for them?

The best way to reach the Garden of Eden, I found, was to fly into *1* Kansas City, Mo., rent a car and drive north on Interstate 35 for two hours, exiting at a town named Cameron and following the signs to Adam-ondi-Ahman. The place was marked on my atlas merely as a "Mormon shrine," but having grown up as a Mormon, I knew better. According to Joseph Smith, the farm-boy prophet who at 14 felt his first heavenly inklings and by 30 had attracted thousands of followers, this was where God created humankind and where Christ would return to rule the earth.

I parked in a lot beside two other cars, both of which had Utah plates, and followed a path to a posted overlook. I had been here before, as a devout 14-year-old on a church-led bus tour. Now, a more skeptical adult, I wanted to follow the Mormon trail again, traveling (in the order of settlement) from Missouri, Joseph Smith's abortive Zion, back east to Nauvoo, Ill., the first true Mormon city, then west along the route of exile to Salt

Lake City, Utah. Preserving and highlighting the past is a Mormon prior-ity—witness the re-enactment of the wagon train. Leaders of the church seem to understand that its vivid history, as much as its sometimes cloudy theology, is what attracts the potential convert.

Standing beside a clean-cut young couple dressed rather formally for the summer weather, I looked out over Adam's home, a broad green valley that is currently planted in corn. Smith planned a town here that never took hold, just one among several Mormon promised lands, from Kirtland, Ohio, to Independence, Mo., that he and his flock were violently driven from. The public did not like Mormons in those days (segments of it still don't) and charged them with a host of crimes ranging from fraternizing with native "savages" to advocating the abolition of slavery. Smith's early church was a radical institution. It preached communitarian economics, the brotherhood of man and polygamy. But perhaps Smith's deepest break from orthodoxy had to do with geography, not theology: he taught that the New Jerusalem was here, smack dab in the middle of America.

I drove east out of Eden across the Mississippi, reflecting that perhaps Smith's prophecies were not so wacky after all. Even Mark Twain (a noto-rious Mormon mocker who famously dissed the *Book of Mormon* as "chlo-roform in print") set his own idyllic fables along the riverway. Indeed, if God *had* planted Eden in America, he could not have found better soil or growing weather. Even the air smells fertile in northern Missouri—humid, rich and fertile—almost malted.

In Nauvoo I stopped at the church-run visitors center, up the hill   5
from the restored historic district. The place had changed since I had seen it as a kid. Installed below a towering statue of a decidedly muscular Christ were several video monitors equipped with touch screens. Each screen had a menu of philosophical questions. I selected "What is the purpose of life?" although I was tempted to cut to the chase by touching "Is there life after death?" Instantly a robotic male voice answered, "To see if we will follow the plan of our Heavenly Father, each of us is given two great gifts. One is time, the other freedom of choice . . . Every day, every hour, every minute of our span of mortal years must sometime be accounted for." The screen showed a high school boy inside his car, a lurid, seductive neon sign reflected in its windshield. The pensive young man looked as though he had suddenly realized he had been wasting precious mortal minutes and had better drive home while there was still time.

I spent another half an hour at the screen, taking advantage of its forthright answers to a veritable maze of cosmic quandaries. As a teenager I had appreciated such certainties; as an adult I was tempted to make fun of them. My secular college professors had insisted that truth is always com-plicated, relative, but I still felt the tug of religious absolutism. Watching a woman in a wheelchair beside me earnestly punching up answers on her screen, I concluded I was not alone.

I toured what was left of old Nauvoo and learned that Smith had run his growing church from an office above his family's general store. I liked this detail. It brought the man alive for me. Unlike Brigham Young, the stern puritan who succeeded him, Smith was an improviser, a boyish mystic, brimming with charismatic, homegrown visions. In the fields beyond his store, he liked to dress up as a general and drill his personal army, the Nauvoo Legion. In 1844, the year he was murdered, he announced a candidacy for the U.S. presidency.

The frontier jail where Smith was killed lies southeast of Nauvoo, in Carthage, Ill. I arrived in the middle of a guided tour: 30 or 40 Mormon teens sat on the floor of a second-story room and listened to a husky, white-haired elder narrate the tragedy of Smith's last hours. The elder, using a walking stick to imitate the rifles of the mob, enacted the death scene with stagey gusto, but when the bloody climax came—Smith's disastrous fall from the building—he grew somber. "I personally think that when Joseph fell out that window, the Savior was right there to catch him." There were tears in his eyes now and more tears on the cheeks of the girl with corn-silk blond hair sitting beside him.

The elder went on to point out two bullet holes in a nearby door, which led to several questions from the kids about the circumstances of the assassination. Did Joseph speak any last words? Wasn't there once a blood-stain on the floor? These kids had seen too many action movies, I sensed, but I could not fault them for their curiosity. Like early Christians eager to handle pieces of the Cross, the kids desired a physical connection with this obscure Midwestern passion play, which was not unlike a 19th century Waco. I felt the same curiosity at their age—intrigued by an American faith that served up not only abstract precepts but also the chance to walk in the footsteps of its heroes.

After Smith's death and Young's rise to power, those footsteps led due   10
west. Mormons like to compare themselves to Jews; they too had a strenuous exodus: across the Mississippi, into Iowa, through Nebraska and Wyoming, into Utah. For the past two years, a few hundred hardy souls have been retracing this journey on horseback and on foot. Many of the pilgrims are blood descendants of the pioneers, and although their re-creation of the procession includes a few dozen motorized support vehicles, the trek is not for the tenderfoot.

I joined up with the march in western Wyoming, near the ghost town of Piedmont. The wind blew gales of dust into people's faces. Some children were limping. The sun was high and hot. At the head of the party were scores of clattering wagons; to the rear, a long line of pedestrians pulling handcarts. Between the groups, a solitary woman, dressed in a bonnet and a long print dress, strode briskly along with her eyes on her tennis shoes.

Karen Hill had trudged almost a thousand miles since spring and had a hundred more to go. The wife of the trek's organizer, Brian Hill, Karen converted to Mormonism when she was 25. "Everyone has a different reason to be here," she said. Karen's was to support her husband. "What I didn't expect," she said, "was the exhaustion, physical and emotional. I think it was the same for the first saints." She recalled a song she had written miles back: "There are angels among us, there are angels about . . . The veil is getting thinner now."

I dropped back a mile and joined the handcart company. Gordon Beharrell, an elderly Englishman, was carrying a fluttering Union Jack in tribute to his 19th century countrymen who had converted to Mormonism by the thousands and walked this route before him. "I intended to re-enact their adventure, but for me this hasn't been a re-enactment. I've experienced real hardship and real pain." Beharrell told an inspiring story then. Before setting out, he was found to have colon cancer and underwent major surgery. Then, as he neared Scott's Bluff, Neb., he fell ill from complications and was hospitalized again. "When I was released, I could barely walk five yards. I had to be loaded on a cart and pulled. Then two elders gave me a healing blessing. The next Wednesday I managed to walk two miles, then six the next day, then 11 the next. Soon I was making 25 miles a day, and I've been going steady ever since. I attribute all this to a certain British grit, but mostly to the power of that blessing."

There were other sojourners with tales to tell. Earl Gillmore, sunbaked, middle-aged and wearing a guitar across his back, had been homeless and unemployed when he set out. "I didn't have the money to do this, but somehow I knew I was supposed to be here. My whole walk has been on faith." Along the way, Gillmore was hired as camp cook and promised a job in Salt Lake City. "I finally know what it means," he said, "to endure to the end." Ted Moore, a Missouri gold miner, gave a more humorous testament of faith. He dug through the pots and pans in his handcart and pulled out a dusty "Pioneer" Barbie doll. "She's going the whole way with me," Moore said. "Every step that I take, Barbie takes."

A few hours before sundown, the wagon train made camp. I had   15
walked only a few miles that day, but I was parched and exhausted. A meal was served. I sat in the dirt and devoured a plate of meat loaf, while around me devout believers watered horses, repaired bent wagon wheels, fed bottles to crying infants. In just a few days, to quote their ancestors, they would cross the mountains and be "safe in Zion." I could not help wishing them well. In their epic trek across Smith's American Eden, they have lost more paradises than they've found.

The Responsive Reader

1. The Mormon church has in recent years reacted strongly to negative criticism. What facts and sidelights emerge from Kirn's article for a reader mainly interested in the actual history and teachings of the movement—regardless of the observer's attitude?

2. Kirn describes himself as "more skeptical" as an adult than he had been as a devout teenager. What appreciation of positive elements in the Mormon faith emerges nevertheless from his article? What made the founder of the faith likable and interesting for him? (And how does Brigham Young, Smith's successor, represent for Kirn another side of the faith?) How does the earnestness and dedication many observers see come through in this account—in what incidents or details?

3. What evidence of Kirn's skepticism do you find in this piece? What aspects of Mormonism does he seem skeptical about? How did his college experience change his view of religious truth? (In this context, what is the difference between relativism and absolutism?) How would you sum up his attitude overall?

Talking, Listening, Writing

4. Have you ever participated in an event or had an experience that became a lesson in living history? How did it bring historical facts or familiar ideas to life?

5. The word *cult* has in recent years become a fighting word. What is the objection to it? Are there "cults" in today's America that are outgrouped or marginalized? Why or how?

Collaborative Projects

6. Kirn calls the death of Joseph Smith an "obscure Midwestern passion play" and refers to it as "a 19th century Waco." The story of Waco, a religious compound destroyed during an assault by federal agents, has been the subject of bitter controversy and recrimination. Working with a group, you may want to research early and recent media coverage. What triggered the confrontation and resulting tragedy? What are the major points of contention?

Find It on the Web

Much of the early persecution of the Mormons was caused by their support and defense of the practice of polygamy. (Brigham Young is said to have had twenty-seven wives.) Is polygamy still an issue today? Can you find evidence of recent media coverage on the Internet?

THE SPIRITUALLY DIVERSE SOCIETY

Jeremiah Creedon

> *The author of the following account focuses on today's search for spiritual meaning outside organized religion. He sees increased immigration, especially from Asia, bringing many Americans face to face with religious philosophies from other parts of the world. Spiritual teachers or gurus from other cultures extend their influence beyond their original followers to American popular culture, and the information explosion has brought religious and spiritual texts from around the world into the nation's bookstores. Ministers report that outsiders not committed to the basic beliefs of the congregation attend because they like its work with AIDS or the homeless or because they love its tradition of church music. The result, the author claims, is a "robust spiritual marketplace" and a rise in "do-it-yourself spirituality."*

Thought Starters: Have you been exposed to religious teachings or sacred art from other parts of the world?

We're living in what observers call an age of extreme "religious pluralism." The same cultural forces that have driven many to leave their inherited faiths have also affected others who have stayed. Almost all the major denominations now contain internal movements that are trying to transform them. Many traditionalists, of course, are fighting to block reforms. Syncretism, the formal term for the blending of rituals and beliefs from different faiths, is a dirty word to conservative worshipers, dreaded like a plague of locusts—and maybe as hard to stop. New hybrid modes of worship are constantly appearing, from the new Christian megachurches, whose mammoth services can resemble arena rock, to tiny garage religions hardly bigger than the average band.

The latest edition of the *Encyclopedia of American Religions* lists more than 2,100 religious groups, a figure that has almost doubled in 20 years. They range from the most straitlaced forms of Judaism and Christianity to UFO cults awaiting deliverance by flying saucer. The influx of Asian religions is clearly mirrored in the *Encyclopedia,* and so is the recent rapid rise of Islam, which other sources put at about 3.5 million adherents. With about 750,000 believers, including 100,000 American converts, Buddhism is said to be the country's fastest-growing faith.

The statistics ultimately yield a portrait full of contradictions. One certainty is that we live in a very religious country—in fact, the United States is generally considered to be the most religious country in the Western industrial world. Though nine out of ten American adults believe that God exists, there's growing disagreement about how God should be described. God is Michelangelo's bearded old man in the Sistine Chapel. God is pure intelligence. God is cosmic energy. God is a Goddess. At least eight out of ten American adults consider themselves to be Christians, but most are hazy about the basic tenets of their faith. The pollsters say that Americans pray more often than they have sex, but no one knows how many consider sex and prayer to be the same thing.

The undeniable reality, concludes George Barna in *The Index of Leading Spiritual Indicators* (Word Publishing, 1996), "is that America is transitioning from a Christian nation to a spiritually diverse society." One result of this spiritual upheaval is a "new perception of religion: a personalized, customized form of faith views which meet personal needs, minimize rules and absolutes, and bear little resemblance to the 'pure' form of any of the world's major religions."

John H. Berthrong, associate dean at Boston University's School of Theology and director of the Institute for Dialogue Among Religious Traditions, has seen this trend unfold in his classroom. "When I talk to students about their own sense of religious identity, I find that more and more of them have been brought up in homes that are post-Christian," he says. "So to say that they are reacting against Christianity is wrong; they've never been Christians. Even some of the ones who are Christian will say. 'But I really like Taoism and Buddhism too, and my meditation is Vipassana, but I also do a lot of work at my local church because I like the choir.'" 5

A Christian theologian and scholar of Confucianism, Berthrong has spent 20 years fostering communication among different religions. His observations on the modern fluidity of belief are the basis of a new book he's writing called *The Divine Deli,* to be published by Orbis. "I think a lot of traditional boundaries for many people are simply dissolving," he says. Berthrong sees a trend toward "multiple citizenship" in a number of separate faiths—and no complete allegiance to any one. In terms of basic issues like child rearing and church fund-raising, the trend's potential impact is profound. And that's before anyone raises the touchy matter of doctrine. "Many of the more conservative Christian theologians don't find any of this either amusing or profitable," he adds. "It's one of the areas that really defines the difference between liberal theology and conservative theology."

Chenyang Li, associate professor of philosophy and religious studies at Monmouth College, and author of the forthcoming book, *The Tao Encounters the West,* looks to his native China for an example of how multiple religious participation can work. In China, he explains, an individual's religious life may be a harmonious interplay among Confucianism, Taoism, and Buddhism. Even though their basic value systems may not always be perfectly aligned, aspects of each faith can be useful in different areas of life, or even in the same area. Confucianism and Buddhism, for example, may be at odds about worldly success, says Li, but this play of opposites can be used to achieve breadth (a kind of enlightened tolerance) and balance, which are important Chinese cultural ideals.

The Responsive Reader

1. Have you had personal contact with current trends in religious life the author mentions—such as the "new Christian megachurches" with "mammoth services"? "tiny garage religions"? the rise of Islam? How was the experience different from your experience with more traditional forms of worship?
2. What for you is striking or new about the author's statistics? Do you agree that the picture they paint is "full of contradictions"?

Talking, Listening, Writing

3. Do you think "we live in a very religious country"?
4. The founding teacher of a meditation center said, "Wide experimentation in spiritual life is symptomatic of the growing recognition that the things we thought would make us happy aren't working, and there is a deep need to connect to what is sacred in our lives." Have you seen evidence of "wide experimentation in spiritual life"? When and where?

Collaborative Projects

5. Scholars from nineteenth-century anthropologists to today's feminists have explored the possibility of a religious stage before patriarchy—before the rule of male gods. They have examined evidence of a prehistoric cycle where worship centered on earth goddesses or mother goddesses—with some still surviving into historic times, like the Babylonian Ishtar or the Greek Demeter, goddess of the harvest. You may want to team up with classmates to report on current research on this subject.

WHY I AM OPTIMISTIC ABOUT AMERICA

Daniel J. Boorstin

Daniel J. Boorstin is one of this country's best-known historians, who served as Librarian of Congress, a position that one editor has called "the highest intellectual honor the U.S. government can bestow." Boorstin grew up in the 1920s in Tulsa, Oklahoma, which he says called itself "The Oil Capital of the World." He became the Pulitzer Prize–winning author of books including The Americans, The Discoverers, *and* The Creators. *At a time when many American historians have focused on the darker side of American history, he has looked in our common past for "lessons in national idealism and political realism." For instance, he has celebrated the Lewis and Clark expedition of 1804–06 into the uncharted territories beyond the Mississippi as an example of the spirit of discovery "that has built our nation"—a "triumph for science and natural history" at the same time that it served the cause of trade and of territorial expansion. In this century, he sees the spirit of exploration and bold leadership exemplified in the 1969 Apollo mission to the moon, but he also sees it threatened by the obsession with "cost-effectiveness," a term that he says "did not enter our language until about 1964." In the article that follows, Boorstin tries to explain the roots of his American brand of optimism at a time when he sees pessimism and negativism prevailing in much of American life.*

Thought Starters: Is America different from other countries? Is it unique among nations? How or why?

You ask what is the basis for my optimism. With a Europe in disarray   1
in a century plagued by two murderous World Wars, by genocides without precedent—the German-Nazi massacre of six million and the Stalin-Soviet massacre of 30 million—how can I speak so hopefully about the American future?

One answer is very personal. I was raised and went to public school in the 1920s in Tulsa, Okla., which then called itself "The Oil Capital of the World," but could perhaps have been called "The Optimism Capital of the World." Only 10 years before my family came to Oklahoma, the Indian Territory had been admitted to the Union as the 46th state.

The city thrived on "booster" pride, and before I graduated from Central High School, it boasted two daily newspapers, three skyscrapers, houses designed by Frank Lloyd Wright and a public-school system superintended by the former U.S. Commissioner of Education. The Kiwanis, Rotary, and Chamber of Commerce competed furiously in projects of civic improvement. For our high school English classes, we memorized and declaimed patriotic orations—from Patrick Henry's "Give Me Liberty or Give Me Death" and Lincoln's "Gettysburg Address" to Henry Grady's "The New South" and Emile Zola's "Plea for Dreyfus." We wrote speeches on the virtues of the federal Constitution for a national contest, which held its finals before the Supreme Court in Washington.

Of course there were dark shadows—like the relentless racial segregation, the brutal race riots of the 1920s, and the Ku Klux Klan. But these were not visible or prominent in my life. The city burgeoned, proudly built a grand new railroad depot, a university, an elegant public library and a city hall—and soon it was embellished by art museums of national rank.

My father was one of the most enthusiastic "boosters," and the grow-   5
ing city seemed to justify his extravagant optimism. I came to sympathize with that American frontier newspaperman who was attacked for reporting as facts the mythic marvels of his upstart pioneer village—including its impressive hotel and prosperous Main Street. In America, he said, it was not fair to object to the rosy reports of community boosters simply because they had "not yet gone through the formality of taking place." I suppose I have never been cured of my distinctively American Oklahoma optimism, bred in the bone and confirmed by the real history of Tulsa.

Another reason for my optimism is in American history. The exhilarating features of our history and culture have in the past been captured in the idea of "American Exceptionalism." This is a long word for a simple idea: the traditional belief that the United States is a very special place, unique in crucial ways. American Exceptionalism is a name too for a cosmopolitan, optimistic and humanistic view of history—that the modern world, while profiting from the European inheritance, need not be imprisoned in Old World molds. And, therefore, that the future of the United States and of its people need not be governed by the same expectations or plagued by the same problems that had afflicted people elsewhere.

How have we lost sight of this beacon?

We have been seduced by the rise of our country as a "superpower." For while power is quantitative, the uniqueness of the United States is not merely quantitative. We have suffered, too, from the consequences of our freedom. Totalitarian societies exaggerate their virtues. But free societies like ours somehow seize the temptation to exaggerate their vices. The negativism of our press and television reporting are, of course, the best evidence of our freedom to scrutinize ourselves. Far better this than the chauvinism of self-righteousness which has been the death of totalitarian empires in our time.

Yet we must never forget that, while to the Old World we were the Unexpected Land, we have ever since been the Land of the Unexpected. The main features of the culture of our United States are just what the wise men of Europe, looking at their own past, could not have conjured up. A short list of the American surprises includes what we have done here with four basic elements of culture—religion, language, law, and wealth.

Religion. By the time of the European settlement of North America, *10* the history of the rising nations of Western Europe had been punctuated by torture and massacre in the name of religion. There was the notorious Spanish Inquisition of the 15th century (1478), the bloody Massacre of St. Bartholomew (1572) in France and, in Germany during the very years of the Puritan settlements in New England, the Thirty Years War (1618– 1648), which spread into a general conflict between Protestant and Catholic Europe. In that war alone, some 10 percent of the German population was slaughtered in the name of religious orthodoxy.

This seemed not to augur well for a nation like ours, whose Pilgrims were obsessed with religion and had fled England to fulfill their passionate dream. Their religious faith gave them courage to brave the ocean-crossing, the hardships of an unknown land and the risks of hostile natives, despite their lonely remoteness from ancestral homes.

Who could have predicted that the United States, unlike the nations from which our people came, would never suffer a religious war? That the Protestants and Catholics who had tortured and massacred each other in Europe would establish peaceful neighboring communities from New England to Maryland and Virginia? That Jews would here find asylum from ghettos and pogroms? That—though the U.S. would remain conspicuously a nation of churchgoers—the separation of Church and State would become a cornerstone of civic life? Or that public-school principals in the 20th century would be challenged by how to promote a holiday spirit without seeming to favor or neglect Christmas, Hanukkah or Kwanzaa?

Language. In Europe, languages had made nations. Spanish, Portuguese, English, French, German and Italian had produced their own literatures—even before there was a Spain, a Portugal, an England, a France, a Germany or an Italy. But the United States was the first great modern nation without its own language. Our country has been uniquely created by people willing and able to borrow a language.

Oddly enough, the English language has helped make us a congenitally multicultural nation, since most Americans have not come from the land of Shakespeare. So we have learned here that people do not lose their civic dignity by speaking the language of a new community. The English language has been invigorated and Americanized by countless importations of words from German, Italian, French, Spanish, Yiddish and American Indian tongues, among others.

The surprising result is that, without a unique national language, our *15* community has developed a language wonderfully expressive of the vitality and variety of our people. Perhaps we should really call Broken English our distinctive American language, for it bears the mark of our immigrant history.

Law. Nowadays, we can be puzzled at the spectacle of peoples from Russia to South Africa contending over how, whether, and when to adopt a "constitution." They seem to have the odd notion that a "constitution" can be created instantly by vote of a legislature or by a popular election. All this offers a sharp contrast to our Anglo-American experience.

The tradition of a fundamental law—a "constitution"—that we inherited from England reached back to at least the 13th century. The by-product of a nation's whole history, the unwritten English constitution was a pillar of government and of the people's rights. No one could have foreseen that such a tradition would find a transatlantic written reincarnation in the deliberations of 55 colonials meeting in Independence Hall in Philadelphia in 1787. So our United States was created by a constitution. With another surprising result—that our parvenu nation at the end of the 20th century now lives by the most venerable (and probably most venerated) written constitution in the world. And that the constitution would survive by its very power to be amended (with difficulty).

Yet who could have predicted that a nation whose birth certificate bore the declaration that "all men are created equal" should have been one of the last to abolish slavery? Slavery was abolished in the British Empire in 1833. Still, three decades passed before Lincoln's Emancipation Proclamation of 1863 freed slaves in the Southern secessionist states, followed by the Thirteenth Amendment to the Constitution outlawing slavery in all the United States (1865). The slave trade survived only in certain Muslim states and in parts of Africa.

On the other side, we must note that our only Civil War was fought in a struggle to free a subject people. For this, too, it is hard to find a precedent. And a legacy of the history of slavery in the United States has been the equally unprecedented phenomenon of a conscience-wracked nation. This has led us to create a host of novel institutions—"equal opportunity" laws, "affirmative action," among others—in our strenuous effort to compensate for past injustices.

We should not be surprised that Russians are obsessively suspicious of foreigners coming to their country—after their long domination by the Mongols, their invasion by Napoleon and his forces of "liberation" who burned Moscow, and by the Germans in World War II who left 20 million casualties. No wonder the Russians see the foreigner as the invader or the agent of invaders. *20*

In the United States, we have been luckily free of this stereotype. Instead, our vision of the newcomer has been refracted in the experience of our own recent immigrant ancestors. "Strangers are welcome," Benjamin Franklin explained in his *Information to those Who Would Remove to America* (1782), "because there is room enough for them all, and therefore the old inhabitants are not jealous of them." This has been the mainstream of our history: welcoming the newcomer as worker, customer, community-builder, fellow-citizen-in-the-making. The uniquely American notion of a Nation of Nations was never more vivid than today.

Wealth. We are told that the United States is a *rich* nation. But what really distinguishes us is less our wealth than our radically novel way of measuring a society's material well-being.

Wealth—which was at the center of English mercantilist thinking before the American Revolution—was a static notion. The wealth of the world, measured primarily in gold and silver treasure, was supposed to be a fixed quantity, a pie that could be sliced one way or another. But the size of the pie could not be substantially increased. A bigger slice for Great Britain meant a smaller slice for France or Spain or somebody else, and one nation's gain was another's loss.

Our New World changed that way of thinking. People have come here not for wealth but for a better "way of life." America blurred the boundary between the material and the spiritual. All this was reinforced by the spectacular progress of our technology, exploiting the resources of a rich, little-known and sparsely populated continent.

The American Revolution then was, among other things, a struggle   25 between the time-honored idea of "wealth" and a New World idea of "standard of living." This characteristically American idea appears to have entered our language only at the beginning of this century. It could hardly have been conceived in an Old World burdened with the legacy of feudal "rights," landed aristocracies, royal courts, sacrosanct guild monopolies and ancestral cemeteries. Wealth is what someone possesses, but a standard of living is what people *share*. Wealth can be secretly hoarded, but a standard of living can only be publicly enjoyed. For it is the level of goods, housing, services, health, comfort and education agreed to be appropriate.

All these remarkable transformations of the culture of the Older World add up to American Exceptionalism.

Recently, we have heard apologies for expressions of belief in American uniqueness—as if it were somehow provincial or chauvinist. But our ex-Colonial nation in this post-Colonial age would do well to see what the prescient French man of letters André Malraux observed on his visit to President Kennedy in the White House in 1962: "The United States is today the country that assumes the destiny of man . . . For the first time, a country has become the world's leader without achieving this through conquest, and it is strange to think that for thousands of years one single country has found power while seeking only justice."

And, he might have added, while seeking community. We must see the unique power of the United States, then, not as the power of power, but as the power of example. Another name for history.

The depressing spectacle today of a Europe at war with itself has offered us a melodrama of those same ghosts of ethnic, racial, and religious hate that generations of immigrants have come to America to escape. Now, more than ever, we must inoculate ourselves against these latent perils. Luckily, the states of our federal union are not ethnic, racial, or religious enclaves. Luckily, we have remained a wonderfully mobile people. There is no better antidote to these perils abroad than a frank and vivid recognition of the uniqueness of our history—of the special opportunities offered us. Nor could there be greater folly than refusing to enjoy the happy accidents of our history.

The uniqueness that Jefferson and Lincoln claimed for us, we must re-   30 member, was for the sake of *all* mankind. Our Declaration of Independence takes its cue from "the course of human events." The Great Seal of the United States on our dollar bill still proclaims "Novus Ordo Seclorum"— a new order of the centuries. When before had people put so much faith in the unexpected?

The Responsive Reader

1. What do you learn in Boorstin's opening paragraphs about the American tradition of boosterism? How did it influence his upbringing and education? How is it reflected in his current outlook?

2. Nations have often considered themselves special in the sight of God or favored by destiny. What, according to Boorstin, is the essence of "American Exceptionalism"? In what sense is it a "cosmopolitan, optimistic and humanistic view of history"?

3. What do you know about the history of religious strife and persecution in the Old World? Which of Boorstin's historical references or allusions do you recognize? How and why was the American experience different?

4. What does Boorstin mean when he says that the United States "was the first great modern nation without its own language"? What evidence can you cite that the English language has been "invigorated and Americanized" by borrowings from many sources? Why should we perhaps call Broken English "our distinctive American language"?

5. How, according to Boorstin, did our "parvenu," or Johnny-come-lately, nation come to live by "the most venerable (and probably most venerated) written constitution in the world"? What is unique about the American attitude toward foreigners or other nations? What other features of the American tradition are "unprecedented" in the legal and political sphere?

6. Americans are often criticized for their materialism. How, according to Boorstin, was the American attitude toward wealth different from that of Old World countries?

7. How, according to this author, is America's power in the world different from that exercised by earlier superpowers?

Talking, Listening, Writing

8. *Pollyanna*—describing a bubbly optimist always ignoring the grim facts—is one of the most American words in the English language. Would you call Boorstin a Pollyanna? Does he recognize the role of evil in the world and in American history? What role does evil play in his essay?

9. What "latent perils" does Boorstin see that may endanger America's future?

10. Is the American tradition of welcoming the newcomer dead?

Collaborative Projects

11. Are religious divisions and animosities a thing of the past? Working with a group, you may want to interview students and others, trying to determine whether or not they see strong religious feelings as a danger to national harmony.

Find It on the Web

Commentators on the political right accuse the left of exaggerating America's social ills. Commentators on the left accuse conservatives of harping on the decline of moral values in order to attack liberal permissiveness. Are both sides too negative about life in present-day America? Voices like Gregg Easterbrook's in "America the O.K." (*New Republic* 4 & 11 January 1999) accuse both sides of negativism. Easterbrook documents positive trends in areas including employment, crime prevention, family life, minority education, and the environment. Among sources cited by Easterbrook are David Whitman's book *The Optimism Gap* and publications by Harvard sociologist Orlando Patterson. Doing a first search on the Internet on one of the topics above, can you sort out sources that seem to promise an encouraging or a discouraging treatment of present-day America?

THE INGRATE

Paul Laurence Dunbar

> *During the time of slavery, it was illegal to teach slaves to read and write. Deep down the slaveholders must have sensed that education in the long run liberates people from the chains of ignorance and oppression. Paul Laurence Dunbar was one of the first African American writers to reach large white audiences after Emancipation. As his colleague Charles Chesnutt said, Dunbar wrote at a time when "a literary work by an American of acknowledged color was a doubtful experiment, both for the writer and for the publisher." Dunbar became famous for his Br'er Rabbit stories, handing on the folklore of the rural South. Both his dialect poems and his short stories have been criticized for perpetuating stereotypes—for showing black people "as folksy, not-too-bright souls, all of whose concerns are minor" (Saunders Redding). Other critics have classified Dunbar with contemporaries like Booker Washington, whose aim was to show whites how "civilized" the Negro had become and to prove that black people could become responsible and respectable. However, Dunbar also wrote stories that challenged racism with both solemn indignation and wry humor. A familiar figure in African American folklore is the trickster, depending for survival on his wits. In the following story, Dunbar turns the tables by having a literate slave outwit his skinflint master.*

Thought Starters: Where in your schooling or independent reading did you first encounter outstanding African American writers from the nation's past? For instance, were you exposed to Frederick Douglass, W. E. B. Du Bois, Langston Hughes, or Richard Wright? What did you read? What did you learn?

I

Mr. Leckler was a man of high principle. Indeed, he himself had admitted it at times to Mrs. Leckler. She was often called into counsel with him. He was one of those large-souled creatures with a hunger for unlimited advice, upon which he never acted. Mrs. Leckler knew this, but like the good, patient little wife that she was, she went on paying her poor tribute of advice and admiration. Today her husband's mind was particularly troubled—as usual, too, over a matter of principle. Mrs. Leckler came at his call.

"Mrs. Leckler," he said, "I am troubled in my mind. I—in fact, I am puzzled over a matter that involves either the maintaining or relinquishing of a principle."

"Well, Mr. Leckler?" said his wife interrogatively.

1

"If I had been a scheming, calculating Yankee, I should have been rich now; but all my life I have been too generous and confiding. I have always let principle stand between me and my interests." Mr. Leckler took himself all too seriously to be conscious of his pun, and went on: "Now this is a matter in which my duty and my principles seem to conflict. It stands thus: Josh has been doing a piece of plastering for Mr. Eckley over in Lexington, and from what he says, I think that city rascal has misrepresented the amount of work to me and so cut down the pay for it. Now, of course, I should not care, the matter of a dollar or two being nothing to me; but it is a very different matter when we consider poor Josh." There was deep pathos in Mr. Leckler's tone. "You know Josh is anxious to buy his freedom, and I allow him a part of whatever he makes; so you see it's he that's affected. Every dollar that he is cheated out of cuts off just so much from his earnings, and puts further away his hope of emancipation."

If the thought occurred to Mrs. Leckler that, since Josh received only   *5* about one tenth of what he earned, the advantage of just wages would be quite as much her husband's as the slave's, she did not betray it, but met the naive reasoning with the question, "But where does the conflict come in, Mr. Leckler?"

"Just here. If Josh knew how to read and write and cipher—"

"Mr. Leckler, are you crazy!"

"Listen to me, my dear, and give me the benefit of your judgment. This is a very momentous question. As I was about to say, if Josh knew these things, he could protect himself from cheating when his work is at too great a distance for me to look after it for him."

"But teaching a slave—"

"Yes, that's just what is against my principles. I know how public   *10* opinion and the law look at it. But my conscience rises up in rebellion every time I think of that poor black man being cheated out of his earnings. Really, Mrs. Leckler, I think I may trust to Josh's discretion and secretly give him such instructions as will permit him to protect himself."

"Well, of course, it's just as you think best," said his wife.

"I knew you would agree with me," he returned. "It's such a comfort to take counsel with you, my dear!" And the generous man walked out onto the veranda, very well satisfied with himself and his wife, and prospectively pleased with Josh. Once he murmured to himself, "I'll lay for Eckley next time."

Josh, the subject of Mr. Leckler's charitable solicitations, was the plantation plasterer. His master had given him his trade, in order that he might do whatever such work was needed about the place; but he became so proficient in his duties, having also no competition among the poor whites, that he had grown to be in great demand in the country thereabout. So Mr. Leckler found it profitable, instead of letting him do chores and field work in his idle time, to hire him out to neighboring farms and planters. Josh was a man of more than ordinary intelligence; and when he asked to be allowed to pay for himself by working overtime, his master readily agreed—for it promised more work to be done, for which he could allow the slave just what he pleased. Of course, he knew now that when the black man began to cipher this state of affairs would be changed; but it would mean such an increase of profit from the outside that he could afford to give up his own little peculations. Anyway, it would be many years before the slave could pay the two thousand dollars, which price he had set upon him. Should he approach that figure, Mr. Leckler felt it just possible that the market in slaves would take a sudden rise.

When Josh was told of his master's intention, his eyes gleamed with pleasure, and he went to his work with the zest of long hunger. He proved a remarkably apt pupil. He was indefatigable in doing the tasks assigned him. Even Mr. Leckler, who had great faith in his plasterer's ability, marveled at the speed with which he had acquired the three R's. He did not know that on one of his many trips a free negro had given Josh the rudimentary tools of learning, and that ever since the slave had been adding to his store of learning by poring over signs and every bit of print that he could spell out. Neither was Josh so indiscreet as to intimate to his benefactor that he had been anticipated in his good intentions.

It was in this way, working and learning, that a year passed away, and Mr. Leckler thought that his object had been accomplished. He could safely trust Josh to protect his own interests, and so he thought that it was quite time that his servant's education should cease.   *15*

"You know, Josh," he said, "I have already gone against my principles and against the law for your sake, and of course a man can't stretch his conscience too far, even to help another who's being cheated; but I reckon you can take care of yourself now."

"Oh, yes, suh, I reckon I kin," said Josh.

"And it wouldn't do for you to be seen with any books about you now."

"Oh, no, suh, su't'n'y not." He didn't intend to be seen with any books about him.

It was just now that Mr. Leckler saw the good results of all he had done, and his heart was full of a great joy, for Eckley had been building some additions to his house and sent for Josh to do the plastering for him. The owner admonished his slave, took him over a few examples to freshen his memory, and sent him forth with glee. When the job was done, there was a discrepancy of two dollars in what Mr. Eckley offered for it and the price which accrued from Josh's measurements. To the employer's surprise, the black man went over the figures with him and convinced him of the incorrectness of the payment—and the additional two dollars were turned over.   *20*

"Some o' Leckler's work," said Eckley, "teaching a nigger to cipher! Close-fisted old reprobate—I've a mind to have the law on him."

Mr. Leckler heard the story with great glee. "I laid for him that time—the old fox." But to Mrs. Leckler he said, "You see, my dear wife, my rashness in teaching Josh to figure for himself is vindicated. See what he has saved for himself."

"What did he save?" asked the little woman indiscreetly.

Her husband blushed and stammered for a moment, and then replied, "Well, of course, it was only twenty cents saved to him, but to a man buying his freedom every cent counts; and after all, it is not the amount, Mrs. Leckler, it's the principle of the thing."

"Yes," said the lady meekly.   25

II

Unto the body it is easy for the master to say, "Thus far shalt thou go, and no farther." Gyves, chains, and fetters will enforce that command. But what master shall say unto the mind, "Here do I set the limit of your acquisition. Pass it not"? Who shall put gyves upon the intellect, or fetter the movement of thought? Joshua Leckler, as custom denominated him, had tasted of the forbidden fruit, and his appetite had grown by what it fed on. Night after night he crouched in his lonely cabin, by the blaze of a fat pine brand, poring over the few books that he had been able to secure and smuggle in. His fellow servants alternately laughed at him and wondered why he did not take a wife. But Joshua went on his way. He had no time for marrying or for love; other thoughts had taken possession of him. He was being swayed by ambitions other than the mere fathering of slaves for his master. To him his slavery was deep night. What wonder, then, that he should dream, and that through the ivory gate should come to him the forbidden vision of freedom? To own himself, to be master of his hands, feet, of his whole body—something would clutch at his heart as he thought of it, and the breath would come hard between his lips. But he met his master with an impassive face, always silent, always docile; and Mr. Leckler congratulated himself that so valuable and intelligent a slave should be at the same time so tractable. Usually intelligence in a slave meant discontent; but not so with Josh. Who more content than he? He remarked to his wife: "You see, my dear, this is what comes of treating even a nigger right."

Meanwhile the white hills of the North were beckoning to the chattel, and the north winds were whispering to him to be a chattel no longer. Often the eyes that looked away to where freedom lay were filled with a wistful longing that was tragic in its intensity, for they saw the hardships and the difficulties between the slave and his goal and, worst of all, an iniquitous law—liberty's compromise with bondage, that rose like a stone wall between him and hope—a law that degraded every free-thinking man to the level of a slave catcher. There it loomed up before him, formidable, impregnable, insurmountable. He measured it in all its terribleness, and paused. But on the other side there was liberty; and one day when he was away at work, a voice came out of the woods and whispered to him "Courage!"—and on that night the shadows beckoned him as the white hills had done, and the forest called to him, "Follow."

"It seems to me that Josh might have been able to get home tonight," said Mr. Leckler, walking up and down his veranda, "but I reckon it's just possible that he got through too late to catch a train." In the morning he said, "Well, he's not here yet; he must have had to do some extra work. If he doesn't get here by evening, I'll run up there."

In the evening, he did take the train for Joshua's place of employment, where he learned that his slave had left the night before. But where could he have gone? That no one knew, and for the first time it dawned upon his master that Josh had run away. He raged; he fumed; but nothing could be done until morning, and all the time Leckler knew that the most valuable slave on his plantation was working his way toward the North and freedom. He did not go back home, but paced the floor all night long. In the early dawn he hurried out, and the hounds were put on the fugitive's track. After some nosing around they set off toward a stretch of woods. In a few minutes they came yelping back, pawing their noses and rubbing their heads against the ground. They had found the trail, but Josh had played the old slave trick of filling his tracks with cayenne pepper. The dogs were soothed and taken deeper into the wood to find the trail. They soon took it up again, and dashed away with low bays. The scent led them directly to a little wayside station about six miles distant. Here it stopped. Burning with the chase, Mr. Leckler hastened to the station agent. Had he seen such a negro? Yes, he had taken the northbound train two nights before.

"But why did you let him go without a pass?" almost screamed the   *30* owner.

"I didn't," replied the agent. "He had a written pass, signed James Leckler, and I let him go on it."

"Forged, forged!" yelled the master. "He wrote it himself."

"Humph!" said the agent. "How was I to know that? Our niggers round here don't know how to write."

Mr. Leckler suddenly bethought him to hold his peace. Josh was probably now in the arms of some northern abolitionist, and there was nothing to be done now but advertise; and the disgusted master spread his notices broadcast before starting for home. As soon as he arrived at his house, he sought his wife and poured out his griefs to her.

"You see, Mrs. Leckler, this is what comes of my goodness of heart. I   *35* taught that nigger to read and write, so that he could protect himself—and look how he uses his knowledge. Oh, the ingrate, the ingrate! The very weapon which I give him to defend himself against others he turns upon me. Oh, it's awful—awful! I've always been too confiding. Here's the most valuable nigger on my plantation gone—gone, I tell you—and through my own kindness. It isn't his value, though, I'm thinking so much about. I could stand his loss, if it wasn't for the principle of the thing, the base in-gratitude he has shown me. Oh, if I ever lay hands on him again!" Mr. Leckler closed his lips and clenched his fist with an eloquence that laughed at words.

Just at this time, in one of the underground railway stations, six miles north of the Ohio, an old Quaker was saying to Josh, "Lie still—thee'll be perfectly safe there. Here comes John Trader, our local slave catcher, but I will parley with him and send him away. Thee need not fear. None of thy brethren who have come to us have ever been taken back to bondage.—Good evening, Friend Trader!" and Josh heard the old Quaker's smooth voice roll on, while he lay back half smothering in a bag, among other bags of corn and potatoes.

It was after ten o'clock that night when he was thrown carelessly into a wagon and driven away to the next station, twenty-five miles to the northward. And by such stages, hiding by day and traveling by night, helped by a few of his own people who were blessed with freedom, and always by the good Quakers wherever found, he made his way into Canada. And on one never-to-be-forgotten morning he stood up, straightened himself, breathed God's blessed air, and knew himself free!

III

To Joshua Leckler this life in Canada was all new and strange. It was a new thing for him to feel himself a man and to have his manhood recognized by the whites with whom he came into free contact. It was new, too, this receiving the full measure of his worth in work. He went to his labor with a zest that he had never known before, and he took a pleasure in the very weariness it brought him. Ever and anon there came to his ears the cries of his brethren in the South. Frequently he met fugitives who, like himself, had escaped from bondage; and the harrowing tales that they told him made him burn to do something for those whom he had left behind him. But these fugitives and the papers he read told him other things. They said that the spirit of freedom was working in the United States, and already men were speaking out boldly in behalf of the manumission of the slaves; already there was a growing army behind that noble vanguard, Sumner, Phillips, Douglass, Garrison. He heard the names of Lucretia Mott and Harriet Beecher Stowe, and his heart swelled, for on the dim horizon he saw the first faint streaks of dawn.

So the years passed. Then from the surcharged clouds a flash of lightning broke, and there was the thunder of cannon and the rain of lead over the land. From his home in the North he watched the storm as it raged and wavered, now threatening the North with its awful power, now hanging dire and dreadful over the South. Then suddenly from out the fray came a voice like the trumpet tone of God to him: "Thou and thy brothers are free!" Free, free, with the freedom not cherished by the few alone, but for all that had been bound. Free, with the freedom not torn from the secret night, but open to the light of heaven.

When the first call for colored soldiers came, Joshua Leckler hastened   *40*
down to Boston, and enrolled himself among those who were willing to fight to maintain their freedom. On account of his ability to read and write and his general intelligence, he was soon made an orderly sergeant. His regiment had already taken part in an engagement before the public roster of this band of Uncle Sam's niggers, as they were called, fell into Mr. Leckler's hands. He ran his eye down the column of names. It stopped at that of Joshua Leckler, Sergeant, Company F. He handed the paper to Mrs. Leckler with his finger on the place.

"Mrs. Leckler," he said, "this is nothing less than a judgment on me for teaching a nigger to read and write. I disobeyed the law of my state and, as a result, not only lost my nigger, but furnished the Yankees with a smart officer to help them fight the South. Mrs. Leckler, I have sinned—and been punished. But I am content, Mrs. Leckler; it all came through my kindness of heart—and your mistaken advice. But, oh, that ingrate, that ingrate!"

The Responsive Reader

1. Does this story make a good trickster story? Much of the literature of Dunbar's time was didactic—spelling out and preaching the values of the author. How would you spell out the moral of the tale? Do you think the story is still effective, or does it get too preachy for you?
2. What did you know about the "underground railroad"? What do you learn about it from this story?
3. According to historians of the post–Civil War period, the new black educated middle class advanced its cause in alliance with liberal whites. How does the story and its treatment of whites reflect this tendency?

Talking, Listening, Writing

4. The oppressed have often acted outwardly submissive while resenting or plotting against their masters. They have tried to maintain their pride while outwardly acting in a humble manner. How does this story mirror this pattern? Has this strategy outlived its usefulness—is it obsolete?

Collaborative Projects

5. You may want to team up with your classmates to organize an African American Literature Week, with readings ranging from fiction by writers like Paul Laurence Dunbar and Richard Wright to poetry by writers like Langston Hughes and Gwendolyn Brooks.

FOR MY FATHER

Janice Mirikitani

> And they commanded we dwell in the desert
> Our children be spawn of barbed wire and barracks
>
> Janice Mirikitani

Janice Mirikitani is a West Coast poet who coedited Third World Women *(1973), looking for what was "universal, freeing, connective" in Third World literature. She also edited* Ayumi *(1980), an anthology of Japanese American writing. Her poems have ranged in topic from the terrors of Vietnam to the internment of Japanese Americans during World War II. She pays tribute to anonymous poor immigrants from Asia who filled "the sweatshops/the laundries." She writes about Japanese Americans who, like her father, were taken from their homes and businesses to relocation camps like Tule Lake. She expresses her solidarity with Asian women pursued as a mysterious and exotic novelty by blue-eyed men whispering "doubtful words of love."*

Thought Starters: What do you know about the relocation camps of World War II? What do you know about current attempts at reparation or restitution?

He came over the ocean   1
carrying Mt. Fuji on
his back/ Tule Lake on his chest
hacked through the brush
of deserts   5
and made them grow
strawberries

      we stole berries
      from the stem
      we could not afford them   10
      for breakfast

his eyes held
nothing
as he whipped us
for stealing.   15
the desert had dried
his soul.

wordless
he sold
the rich,   *20*
full berries
to hakujin
whose children
pointed at our eyes

    they ate fresh   *25*
    strawberries
    on corn flakes.

Father,
i wanted to scream
at your silence.   *30*
Your strength
was a stranger
i could never touch.

iron
in your eyes   *35*
to shield
the pain
to shield desert-like wind
from patches
of strawberries   *40*
grown
from
tears.

The Responsive Reader

1. How did the father's experience affect his personality? What kind of person had he become? (Is there a key line or passage in the poem that for you sums up what the poet says about him?)
2. What is the daughter's attitude toward the father? Is she judging him?
3. Would it have made a difference to the poem if the father had grown some crop other than strawberries? Are the strawberries a symbol in the poem? Of what? Does the desert become a symbol?
4. What glimpses do you get in this poem of the "hakujin" (or white people's) society surrounding this Japanese family?

Talking, Listening, Writing

5. Have you had an opportunity to observe the effect poverty or persecution had on someone's character?

6. Do you think there are some character traits that poor people tend to share? Are there some that rich people share? Are there some that middle-class people share?
7. Do you know any people (or do you know of any people) who spent time in the camps—internment camps, prison camps, concentration camps—that were a major feature of twentieth-century history? What did you learn about their story? Have you heard anyone talk about the camp experience?

Making Connections

Writers like Crow Dog, Chin, and Mirikitani offer different perspectives on the experience of young Americans from minority backgrounds. Do you see a common theme or common themes? Do you see significant differences?

FORUM: *Redeeming Past Injustice*

From the point of view of many immigrants, the story of America has always been the story of the distant golden shore. In America, things would be different. People living in wretched conditions, exploited by greedy landlords or brutalized by repressive governments, dreamed of a country where people could be free and equal. People persecuted because they dissented on minor points of doctrine dreamed of a New Jerusalem where they could worship according to the dictates of their conscience.

Much current rewriting of American history has moved beyond both the traditional patriotism of "America-first" historians and the myth of America as the land of promise. Much current writing takes into account the point of view of the conquered, the dispossessed, the enslaved. The tide of white invaders that swept over the Americas did not fill an empty space—"virgin land." In the Caribbean islands, the native population, doomed to extinction by the arrival of Columbus and the Spaniards, is variously estimated to have numbered as much as ten million. Millions of people were brought to the land of the free in chains to work as slaves. California and the Southwest were Mexican before they were annexed to the United States.

In recent years, much discussion has focused on injustices in the nation's past. Should a current generation feel guilty for past abuses? Should white Americans feel obligated to compensate members of minorities for lands stolen or treaties broken by their ancestors? Should American society today indemnify descendants of slaves? Should we apologize to Japanese Americans whose parents or grandparents were stripped of their property and confined in relocation camps in World War II?

Today courts are reexamining ancient treaty rights that a tribe may be trying to recover. Powerful television series and movies have retold the story of slavery and of the aftermath of slavery from the point of view of the victims. Activist lawyers are working to rehabilitate Americans who were the victims of a racially biased justice system. At the same time, influential voices are saying that excessive preoccupation with the injustices of the past is divisive. Is it true that dwelling on their history as victims keeps people from shaping their own destiny?

THE DAY THE SLAVES GOT THEIR WAY

Matthew Kauffman

> *Slavery has been the great trauma of America's experience as a nation. An estimated half a million African slaves were in the country at the time of the American Revolution in 1776. The slave trade revived after the War of Independence, with an estimated 80,000 people a year carried out of Africa as slaves, many of them in American ships. Slavers mixed prisoners coming from different ethnic groups and speaking different languages so that organized group resistance could not materialize. Nevertheless, a number of slave mutinies or slave rebellions are on record, rediscovered by modern writers and historians as forgotten pages from American history. The following selection focuses on the legal aftermath of a slave rebellion that is also treated in Robert Hayden's poem "Middle Passage" and in a book that Howard Jones wrote in 1987. The article was first published in Hartford, Connecticut, in the* Hartford Courant. *It appeared on the occasion of the 150th anniversary of the court case that lined up American abolitionists in support of Africans who had staged a successful mutiny on a slave ship bound for Cuba. In 1998, the* Amistad *movie powerfully dramatized the story of the rebels.*

Thought Starters: What shaped your own views of slavery and abolition? What was the role of teachers, books, the media?

For weeks in the summer of 1839, seafarers along the East Coast had   *1*
spotted a sleek, black schooner with no national flag waving above its tattered sails. The ship moved slowly, seemingly with no destination, and those who approached the mysterious vessel reported that the crew was composed almost entirely of half-naked black men.

When the crew of a Coast Guard cutter boarded the vessel near Montauk Point, N.Y., on Long Island, they found that the men were slaves who had overpowered their captors at sea, killed four white men and commandeered the schooner. The captain ordered the ship towed to New London, Conn., where, he expected, the slaves would be tried as murderers and mutineers.

But the seizure of the Amistad, as the schooner was called, touched off a two-year legal battle that pitted the governments of two nations against a small group of feisty abolitionists determined to prove that the Africans were enslaved illegally and should be freed.

A celebration of the 150th anniversary of that legal struggle has been planned in New Haven, where the Africans were jailed for much of the time their fate was argued in the courts. The city has scheduled lectures, exhibits, school essay contests, artistic performances, outdoor events and a community dinner.

The case will be celebrated as the first major court victory for the   5
anti-slavery forces and as an early example of the involvement of blacks on the frontline of the battle against slavery.

Americans were riveted by the case, but the fate of the Africans is less well-known today. In the early 1970s, Amistad House opened in Hartford as a group home for troubled teenage girls, but the house closed in 1983. One of the men who kidnapped Patricia Hearst 15 years ago called himself Cinque after Joseph Cinque, the leader of the rebellion.

Organizers hope the celebration will revive interest in the saga.

"What I would love to see is that it become an integral part of Connecticut history," said Alfred Marder, a New Haven peace worker and a member of the 100-member committee planning the celebration.

The 52 slaves aboard the schooner undoubtedly had little concern for their place in history when they rose up against their Cuban captors. They wanted to go home, so they spared the lives of two men and ordered them to sail east toward Africa. But during the night, the Cubans secretly turned the ship around, and spent nearly two months zig-zagging north along the East Coast, hoping to be rescued.

The Cubans had documents indicating that the Africans were ladinos,   10
Africans taken to Cuba before the importation of slaves to the island was outlawed in 1817, but abolitionists suspected that the papers were fraudulent. If the blacks had been illegally imported from Africa, the abolitionists argued in court, then they were not slaves guilty of murder, but kidnap victims who acted reasonably to regain their liberty.

The case became a lightning rod for those who opposed slavery, including Roger Sherman Baldwin, who later became governor of Connecticut and a U.S. senator, and former President John Quincy Adams, who argued the case before the U.S. Supreme Court. A leading abolitionist declared the Amistad case a "providential occurrence" delivered to force a nationwide hearing on the evils of slavery.

Abolitionists, who were determined to keep the Africans, and the issue of slavery, on the minds of Americans, embarked on a tremendous public relations drive, inviting people to visit the Africans in jail, delivering lectures across the country and arranging to have life-size wax dummies made of Cinque and others.

Hundreds and sometimes thousands of people visited the Africans in jail each day. In Hartford, an especially entrepreneurial jailer charged visitors 12½ cents each for a peek at the captives.

Despite the excitement, lawyers for the Africans knew they had an uphill battle. The administration of President Martin Van Buren, bowing to pressure from the Spanish government and pro-slavery forces in America, worked against the Africans.

Despite Van Buren's inclinations, the Africans won in the lower court. *15*
But the case was appealed to the Supreme Court, and lawyers for the
Africans knew that only two of the nine men on the court opposed slavery.
Nevertheless, in March 1841, the court granted the Africans the wish ex-
pressed by Cinque, who knew only enough English to utter in court the
simple plea, "Give me free."

The Africans, the court ruled, were not slaves and were not criminals.

The Africans from the Amistad returned to their homeland 10 months
later, but before leaving, the prominent New Haven lawyers who had arranged their defense sought to turn the Africans into Christian missionaries.
Cinque and the others took up residence in Farmington, Conn., and spent
six hours a day in a classroom. They also cultivated a 15-acre farm and participated in a nationwide tour to help raise money for their voyage home.

The Amistad rebellion rates only a few paragraphs in most encyclopedias and is rarely taught in schools or included in textbooks, said Howard
Jones, a University of Alabama history professor who wrote a 1987 book
on the case.

New Haven schools, however, are ordering 2,000 booklets on the
Amistad affair, and an effort is under way to have the Amistad rebellion fea-
tured on a U.S. postage stamp during the sesquicentennial of the Supreme
Court decision.

New Haven also hopes to raise $100,000 for a statue of Cinque, which *20*
would be erected on the street where the town jail stood.

The Responsive Reader

1. How much do you learn from this article about the Amistad rebellion
and its legal aftermath? (What are some of the "hard facts"?)
2. How much knowledge of slavery and the abolitionist movement does
the writer assume? How much does he add to your understanding of
slavery and of the antislavery forces? (One hundred fifty years later, can
you get into the spirit of the abolitionist movement?)

Talking, Listening, Writing

3. Prepare a defense (or an indictment) of the accused "murderers and
mutineers."
4. As a member of a school board or similar body, would you vote in favor
of commemorating the Amistad affair or similar historical episodes?
Why or why not?

Collaborative Projects

5. You may want to team up with classmates to stage a mock trial of the
Amistad group. (You may want to turn to the Hayden poem and the
Jones book or to other sources—history books, encyclopedias—for ad-
ditional information.)

I WON'T BE CELEBRATING COLUMBUS DAY

Suzan Shown Harjo

Suzan Shown Harjo is of Cheyenne and Muskogee ancestry. She wrote the following guest column for Newsweek *as the coordinator of a coalition of Native American groups. Plans for celebrating the 500th anniversary, or quincentenary, of Columbus's first voyage to America brought into collision radically different visions of America's past. To those organizing the celebrations, Columbus Day meant an occasion to commemorate the discovery of a new continent, leading eventually to the birth of a new nation. Harjo writes from a very different point of view. She sets out to commemorate the native inhabitants of the "New World," who were subjugated, driven from their lands, stripped of their culture and religion, and decimated by wholesale extermination and the white man's diseases. As you read the following article, do you find yourself taking sides between the "Columbus-bashers" and the organizers of "Columbus hoopla"?*

Thought Starters: Are you aware of controversies surrounding Columbus Day, Martin Luther King Day, Presidents' Day, or similar commemorative occasions? What is at issue?

Columbus Day, never on Native America's list of favorite holidays, *1* became somewhat tolerable as its significance diminished to little more than a good shopping day. But this long year of Columbus hoopla will be tough to take amid the spending sprees and horn blowing to tout a five-century feeding frenzy that has left Native people and this red quarter of Mother Earth in a state of emergency. For Native people, this half millennium of land grabs and one-cent treaty sales has been no bargain.

An obscene amount of money will be lavished on parades, statues and festivals. The Christopher Columbus Quincentenary Jubilee Commission will spend megabucks to stage what it delicately calls "maritime activities" in Boston, San Francisco and other cities with no connection to the original rub-a-dub-dub lurch across the sea in search of India and gold. Funny hats will be worn and new myths born. Little kids will be told big lies in the name of education.

The pressure is on for Native people to be window dressing for Quincentennial events, to celebrate the evangelization of the Americas and to denounce the "Columbus-bashers." We will be asked to buy into the thinking that we cannot change history, and that genocide and ecocide are offset by the benefits of horses, cut-glass beads, pickup trucks and microwave ovens.

The participation of some Native people will be its own best evidence of the effectiveness of 500 years of colonization, and should surprise no one. But at the same time, neither should anyone be surprised by Native people who mark the occasion by splashing blood-red paint on a Columbus statue here or there. Columbus will be hanged in effigy as a symbol of the European invasion, and tried in planned tribunals.

The United Nations has declared 1993 the "Year of the Indigenous *5* People." Perhaps then we can begin to tell our own stories outside the context of confrontation—begin to celebrate the miracle of survival of those remaining Native people, religions, cultures, languages, legal systems, medicine and values. In the meantime, it should be understood that, even in polite society, voices will be raised just to be heard at all over the din of the celebrators.

Native people will continue marking the 500th anniversary of 1491, the good old days in our old countries. There was life here before 1492—although that period of our history is called "pre-history" in the European and American educational systems.

We would like to turn our attention to making the next 500 years different from the past ones; to enter into a time of grace and healing. In order to do so, we must first involve ourselves in educating the colonizing nations, which are investing a lot not only in silly plans but in serious efforts to further revise history, to justify the bloodshed and destruction, to deny that genocide was committed here and to revive failed policies of assimilation as the answer to progress.

These societies must come to grips with the past, acknowledge responsibility for the present and do something about the future. It does no good to gloss over the history of the excesses of Western civilization, especially when those excesses are the root cause of deplorable conditions today. Both church and state would do well to commit some small pots of gold, gained in ways the world knows, to bringing some relief to the suffering and some measure of justice to all.

The United States could start by upholding its treaty promises—as it is bound to do by the Constitution that calls treaties the "Supreme law of the Land." Churches could start by dedicating money to the eradication of those diseases that Native people still die from in such disproportionately high numbers—hepatitis, influenza, pneumonia, tuberculosis.

Church and state could start defending our religious freedom and stop *10* further destruction of our holy places. The general society could help more of our children grow into healthy adults just by eliminating dehumanizing images of Native people in popular culture. Stereotypes of us as sports mascots or names on leisure vans cannot be worth the low self-esteem they cause.

Native people are few in number—under 2 million in the United States, where there are, even with recent law changes, more dead Indians in museums and educational institutions than there are live ones today.

Most of us are in economic survival mode on a daily basis, and many of us are bobbing about in the middle of the mainstream just treading water. This leaves precious few against great odds to do our part to change the world.

It is necessary and well past time for others to amplify our voices and find their own to tell their neighbors and institutions that 500 years of this history is more than enough and must come to an end.

Native people will memorialize those who did not survive the invasion of 1492. It is fitting for others to join us to begin an era of respect and rediscovery.

The Responsive Reader

1. How does Harjo employ the rhetoric of protest, the language of dissent? How are the terms she uses to describe this nation's early history different from what you remember from your schooling or early reading? What grievances does she stress? What are major points in her indictment?
2. For you, is there any part of the article that is particularly telling or thought-provoking? Is there any part that you think is particularly unfair?
3. Which of Harjo's charges and arguments are familiar, and which are new to you?

Talking, Listening, Writing

4. What has been your experience with the current rewriting of American history? Have you encountered examples of history revised to reflect the point of view of the exploited, the dispossessed? Explore the contrast between what you might have been taught earlier and the changes now seen in many courses and textbooks.
5. Would you vote to rename "Columbus Day" and call it "Indigenous People's Day"?

Collaborative Projects

6. The current rethinking of the nation's early history has produced reevaluations of figures like Christopher Columbus, Thomas Jefferson, and Father Junípero Serra. For use in a future research project, you may want to look for a recent book or article on one of these or a similar figure. How do current attitudes compare with earlier, more worshipful, ones? (Your class may want to organize a panel discussion to pool findings on one or several of these figures.)

HOLLYWOOD FORSAKES HISTORY FOR EVENTS

James P. Pinkerton

In the following movie review, James Pinkerton reviews Beloved *(1998), a widely discussed movie based on the spectacularly successful 1987 novel by Toni Morrison, winner of the Nobel Prize for literature and the first American woman to be so honored in fifty-five years. One critic called Morrison the essential black American writer—holding a prestigious professorship at Princeton University, acclaimed by critics, and holding a high place on college reading lists while at the same time reaching a large popular audience in this country and around the world. Morrison became a major voice for the experience of African Americans in books ranging from* The Bluest Eye *(1970) and* Sula *(1973) to* Song of Solomon *(1977) and* Jazz *(1992). In the movie based on* Beloved, *Oprah Winfrey played the role of the African American woman who would rather kill her child than be recaptured and have the child grow up in slavery. Dissenting from critical praise of the movie, Pinkerton describes it as "yet another salvo in the continuing culture war" that conservative white males like him are fighting against minorities, women, and gays whom they see as a threat to their values.*

Thought Starters: Can you describe a movie or television program that for you was a true history lesson—a true "work of historical memory"? What did you learn from it? What made it stand out?

Oprah Winfrey calls "Beloved" the black equivalent of "Schindler's   *1*
List." To be sure, every ethnic group has a right, and perhaps even a duty, to project its painful history onto the silver screen. If white southerners of generations past were entitled to "Birth of a Nation" and "Gone With the Wind," then surely the black experience in the South can be told in film, too, from "Cabin in the Sky" to "Rosewood."

Once upon a time, Hollywood recreated history with regularity; wizened character actor George Arliss made a career in anachronistic costume, playing everyone from Benjamin Disraeli to Cardinal Richelieu to Baron Rothschild. But, today, studio-nomics cuts against routinized Hollywood historicism. So instead filmgoers get "event" histories, from "Titanic" to "Saving Private Ryan." The blitz for "Beloved," which opened Friday, includes Oprah on a dozen magazine covers.

The tagline of the film, "The past has a life of its own," is a southern Gothicism that echoes the grand master of that genre, William Faulkner, who famously observed, "The past is not over and done, it is not even past."

"Beloved" is based on the true story of a black woman who tried to kill her children rather than see them returned to slavery. And while the film, drawn from Toni Morrison's novel, strives toward what the historian Thomas Carlyle called "the inner fact of things," its magical-realist Anne Riceish dimension undercuts its moral impact.

But the bigger problem "Beloved" will face is its emphasis on victim-   5
ization. And, while every tragedy is worth telling, perhaps, if the tale is tragic and only that, its audience will be limited. Indeed, sometimes bleak sadness is crowded out by even bleaker sadness, leaving some genocides little noted, as in Armenia, Cambodia and, today, Rwanda.

Closer to home, the recent murder of Matthew Shepard, a gay college student in Laramie, Wyo., reminds us that new tragedies are always in the making.

If brutality is the norm in human history, then what's most dramatically compelling are chronicles of men and women who rise above the iniquity around them. Which explains why the 1989 movie "Glory," in which Denzel Washington won an Oscar for his portrayal of a black soldier fighting for Union and Emancipation in the Civil War, has achieved such resonance.

Of course, one might conclude from the movie that Morrison's real target is not so much slavery as it is masculinity. The men in the film, black and white, are either irrelevant or irredeemably evil, so infamous that they would suck the milk out of a woman's breasts to deprive her children of sustenance. When a male character tells Winfrey, "I never mistreated a woman in my life," she snaps back: "Well, that makes [one] of you."

As a group, women deserve their place in the cinematic sun, but the unmistakable message of "Beloved"—and for that matter, Morrison's other work—is not the promise of harmony, but rather the persistence, even the permanence, of male-female inequality. And so "Beloved" may not be a work of historical memory at all, but rather yet another salvo in the continuing culture war that rages today.

The Responsive Reader

1. Pinkerton echoes a familiar complaint about current treatments of American history when he objects to the "emphasis on victimization." What is his objection? Have you heard other complaints about "victimology"—where or in what context?
2. Like other traditionalists, Pinkerton calls for more positive or more affirmative media treatments of American history. What is his prime example? Are you a good audience for movies or programs about people "who rise above [. . .] iniquity"—who triumph in some way over injustice?
3. How does Pinkerton describe the attack on "masculinity" that he sees as the real target of the movie? Have you seen evidence that male-female antagonism is a major front in the current culture wars? Have you seen

evidence that African American women writers and artists are at times very negative about African American males?

Talking, Listening, Writing

4. Do you believe there is too much emphasis on victimization? Is there too much or too little focus on the victims of injustice in the American media or American society?
5. Why does Pinkerton mention the genocides in Armenia, Cambodia, and Rwanda? (Can you pool resources with your classmates to fill in fellow students on why the historical events there became infamous in the annals of human brutality?) What do these events have to do with racism in America, or how are they relevant to Pinkerton's argument?
6. Do you believe that "brutality is the norm in human history"?

Collaborative Projects

7. Some of the great movie classics—from *Birth of a Nation* and *Gone with the Wind* mentioned here by Pinkerton to *Citizen Kane*—became the center of political controversy. How or why? You may want to team up with classmates to investigate these controversies for a presentation on the Politics of the Cinema.

Drawing On Your Reading

Good writers are good readers. When they take a break from working at the keyboard, they pick up a magazine or a book. They browse, or they look something up. They take notes. They are compulsive underliners and collectors of clippings from newspapers. Increasingly, they click on the "top of the news" from major news sources on their computer screens to keep up to date on current issues. They may surf the Internet to look for research into how to retard aging or into the status of "morning after" pharmaceutical abortion.

Effective writers know how to draw on their reading. At the right point in a paper, they refer to an event currently in the news. To clinch an argument, they cite authoritative statistics. For a punchline, they bring in a quotable quote from a media guru like Ellen Goodman or George Will.

TRIGGERING   Writers interact with their reading in a number of ways.

- *Reading helps us firm up tentative ideas.* We write to show that what was at first only a hunch was confirmed by our reading. A tentative theory was validated by the testimony of experts or insiders. When we quote what we have read, we show that our ideas are more than superficial impressions. What we say about overcrowding in prisons or about dysfunctional schools has the backing of qualified observers.

- *Reading motivates us to talk back.* Much writing is triggered when we say: "Just a minute! That is simply not so" or "That is badly oversimplified!" We then write to set the record straight. We write to show where we agree with other writers and where we think they go wrong. We might be reading a reassuring discussion of slaves' living conditions in the Old South (since slaves were valuable property, owners were not likely to jeopardize their health). We might agree up to a point but soon say: "Yes, but! Look at what has been left out here!"

■ *Reading raises questions in our minds.* An author who supports reintroducing wolves into northern states may bring an important question into focus: How far are we going to go to protect endangered wildlife? At the same time, we may start asking: Are we going to be able to protect tourists in national parks or the livestock of farmers?

GATHERING   Good writers do not just read quickly to get "the general idea." Early in an article or in a book, they get the drift of the argument. They size up the agenda of the writer. They follow an argument point by point, noting the supporting evidence. They underline or highlight key points; they put question marks or exclamation marks in the margin. They take notes, making sure not to pounce on some minor point or to misrepresent the intention of the author.

The following might be your **running commentary** on a passage about the struggle between "evolutionists" and "creationists" over the origin of life. Why do many parents object when students in biology classes study Darwin's account of evolution but not the biblical account of creation? When you track an author's key reasons for the "fear of science," this is how you might highlight or underscore key points and spear them in marginal annotation:

Keynote: fear of science

. . . there is a pervasive <u>uneasiness—even an actual fear</u>—of science that will drive even those who care little for Fundamentalism into the arms of the Creationists. . . .

shifting scientific theories

For one thing, science is <u>uncertain</u>. Theories are <u>subject to revision</u>; observations are open to a <u>variety of interpretations</u>, and scientists quarrel among themselves . . .

"cold" scientific universe

Second, science is complex and chilling. The mathematical language of science is understood by very few. The vistas it presents are <u>scary</u>— an enormous universe ruled by chance and impersonal rules, empty and uncaring . . .

destructive potential

Third, science is dangerous. There is no question but that <u>poison gas,</u> genetic engineering and nuclear weapons and power stations are terrifying. . . .
—From Isaac Asimov, *"The 'Threat' of Creationism,"* New York Times

SHAPING   How are you going to organize your material? What is going to be your overall plan? When you interpret a **single source** or argue with it, a basic "Yes, but" pattern often works well. For perhaps two-thirds of the paper, you might present, explain, and illustrate in turn each of the author's major points. However, your paper then might reach a turning point: You start saying "Yes, but." For instance, you might want to point out that many young Americans today are exposed to science fact and fiction—about dinosaurs, about space travel—from a very young age. Are they going to have the same "fear of science" as an older generation?

In papers using material from **several sources**, you need to integrate or correlate the material in your notes. You show the connections—perhaps concentrating on where several authors agree and where they disagree. You need to guard against presenting undigested chunks of material. In an effective paper, the materials you have brought in mesh—without the seams showing.

Here is an example of how a student reader pulled relevant material from several different sources and then worked it into a smoothly flowing paragraph. The student had taken notes on the promise of a major medical breakthrough—and then on the doubts and second thoughts that followed. The following is a sampling of the student's notes:

from "Man-Made Hearts: A Grim Prognosis," *U.S. News & World Report:*
The future looked good for permanent artificial hearts. Supporters said the devices might someday become as much of a long-term life-saver as plastic valves and pacemakers . . .

from Robert Bazell, "Hearts of Gold," *New Republic:*
Exotic medical procedures certainly make compelling news stories. . . . The trouble is that they are indeed experimental, and often they do not work.

from Kathleen Deremy and Alan Hall, "Should Profit Drive Artificial Hearts?" *Business Week:*
If the use of artificial hearts becomes widespread, it could add up to $3 billion a year to U.S. health care costs. And that will raise some onerous questions, says Henry Aaron, an economist at Brookings Institution. . . . "The dilemma is: Does everybody get it? If not, who does?"

from Beth Vaughan-Cole and Helen Lee, "A Heart Decision," *American Journal of Nursing:*
Finally, life-extending technology raises the "right to die" issue. . . . If the recipient should be crippled physically or psychologically, the extension of life might be more of a curse than a blessing . . .

In the finished paragraph, the student has used the input from these notes to support a central point: Doubts and second thoughts replaced the initial euphoria about the artificial heart.

People have long had false teeth, artificial limbs, and pacemakers—why not an artificial heart? For a while, the future looked bright for another "breakthrough" or a "medical miracle." However, after the death of the first artificial heart recipient, many observers had second thoughts about the outlook for the permanent artificial heart as "a long-term lifesaver." Doubts and reservations multiplied. As Robert Bazell said in the *New Republic*, "Exotic medical procedures certainly make compelling news stories," but the "trouble is that they are indeed experimental, and often they do not work." The costs are horrendous: In an article in *Business Week*, Kathleen Deremy and Alan Hall estimated that the widespread use of artificial hearts could add up to $3 billion a year to the nation's health care costs. And the procedure raises thorny questions of medical ethics: Who decides who gets the artificial heart and who is left out? What stand do we take on the "right-to-die" issue—does the patient have the right to suicide?

REVISING Reworking a first draft of a paper drawing on your reading, pay special attention to how you have introduced and identified quoted material. Who said this and where? What makes this author an authority or a reliable source? What are the quoted author's credentials? What is the point of the quotation—why are you using it here?

Here is a sampling of informative **credit tags** (brief lead-ins to a quotation):

> SOURCE: In his article "Race and Personal Identity in America," Glenn C. Loury talks about the "process of becoming free of the need to have my choices validated by 'the brothers.'"

> CREDENTIALS: Ellen Berkowitz, a psychiatrist with the Florida State University program in medical sciences, summed up the current view when she said, "Mental illnesses are just like any other illness, and for the most part they are treatable."

> POINT: Lester C. Thurow, in a review of Greider's *One World, Ready or Not*, belittles the fears of those who predict that the speculative excesses of today's financial markets will lead to another great collapse and another Great Depression: "Not even spectacular crashes change the economic system appreciably—much less bring it down."

A PAPER FOR PEER REVIEW Read the following sample paper. What is the central issue it raises? Does it have a thesis, or central idea? What is the overall plan, or what are major sections of the paper? How does the paper use the student's reading to support major points? What kind of reader would make an ideal audience for this paper? How do you yourself react to it?

Pink Collar Workers

Many women, like myself, when hearing the word "feminist" try to stay as far away as possible. Images of protests, marching libbers on the war path, and loud radical women come to mind. I held many misconceptions about the Women's Movement. (I thought that as many as 80% of these women hated men.) However, after having a Women's Studies class, I feel I understand much more about what the movement is trying to accomplish. After reading about the injustices that women are faced with, I can say without a doubt that I, too, am a feminist.

A conference at Seneca Falls in 1848 represented the first wave of feminism in the U.S. A small assembly affirmed their belief in equality of men and women and wanted to pursue the struggle for sex equality. The first wave of feminism was led by women activists of the antislavery movement. Some extremely outspoken feminists were Susan B. Anthony, Elizabeth Cady Stanton, Lucretia Mott, and Matilda Joslyn Gage. They all agreed that the women's right to vote was the first priority. This was not achieved until 1920, after some seventy-two years of struggle. There was only one single woman of those who had attended the Seneca Falls Convention who was still alive to cast her first vote. The following quote is from Elizabeth Cady Stanton, writing to Lucretia Mott:

> The more I think on the present condition of woman, the more I am oppressed with the reality of her degradation. The laws of our country, how unjust they are! Our customs, how vicious! What God has made sinful, both in man and woman, custom has made sinful in woman alone.

The next quote is from Susan B. Anthony from a letter she wrote to her sister, urging her to join the movement:

> We need not wait for one more generation to pass away in order to find a race of women worthy to assert the humanity of women; and that is all we claim to do.

I grew up with a best friend whose parents, especially her mother, would tell her that as long as she found a "good" man, she wouldn't have to worry about college or a good job. At school, my friend took classes like sewing and cooking. I always felt really bad for her because my parents were exactly the opposite. They always encouraged me to take pre-college classes and to first finish college before settling down. Their philosophy was that I should first be strong in myself and have a good job, then think about marriage. That way, if something was to end the marriage (divorce, death), I could take care of myself. While we were growing up, I was in after-school sports, but my friend wasn't allowed to so she'd go home and wait for me.

Everywhere we look, magazines and movies convey a message of how a woman should look and should be. I once saw an ad selling perfume where there was a beautiful woman's head attached to a snake's body with hands open toward a man. The caption read, "Dare to be tempted." This ad implied that women are like the snake in the garden trying to tempt and deceive men. If people keep seeing ads and movies like that, they will eventually begin to believe them.

Today's women of the second wave of feminism are asking how long before the struggle for equal rights—which has been pursued by feminists every year since 1920—is won. While women have won important rights during the past, some of these rights are still under challenge (e.g., abortion). Statistics show that men's incomes have increased by about 5% over women's during the same period in which women supposedly have been making more marked advances toward equality than before. So, are women more liberated now than before? Until men and women promote support toward women's issues, there will not be any advances. Even if an issue doesn't affect you directly, feminists need to be supportive of each other if any advancements are to be made.

Topics for Papers Based on Reading (A Sampling)

1. Much current historical writing is revisionist history. How do you react to current rewriting or revision of the American past? Choose a selection like Harjo's "I Won't Be Celebrating Columbus Day" or Crow Dog's "Lakota Woman." You may want to structure your paper as a "Yes, but" paper. You may first sketch common ground you share with the author and then go on to present and defend your disagreements. Or you may choose to defend the author against possible objections.

2. Parents have come in for much criticism by people concerned about bad parenting. The selections by Miller, Chin, and Mirikitani talk about a father's role in the family or the relationship between father and child. Other selections in this book deal more generally with the writer's family background. Focus on the father's role or the parents' role in one or more of the selections.

3. The Native American past has often been seen through the lens of prejudice, but it has also often been viewed in an idealized or romanticized light. Do selections like Mary Crow Dog's "Lakota Woman" and Louise Erdrich's "Indian Boarding School: The Runaways" help you go beyond traditional stereotypes or Hollywood images? What do you think young Americans should learn from these and similar sources about the true nature of the Native American experience?

4. Right-wing pundits complain about current negative attitudes toward America. You may want to focus on positive or affirmative attitudes in selections like Daniel J. Boorstin's "Why I Am Optimistic about America." Do these writers share common attitudes or perspectives?

5. Terms like multiculturalism and diversity have become fighting words in the culture wars of recent years. You may decide to write a "Yes, but" paper showing where you agree or disagree with Arturo Madrid on diversity or with Anna Quindlen on the American mosaic. Or compare and contrast their views.

6. Asian Americans have become a highly visible minority in recent years. Do you see common themes or recurrent topics in readings by or about young Asian Americans? You may want to read or reread selections like those by Frank Chin and Janice Mirikitani.

7. There has been much discussion in recent years of different directions in the women's movement, of a backlash against feminism, and of

"second wave" or "third wave" feminists. Which of the writers in this book would you choose to help you do a composite portrait of a "true" feminist?

8. History has often been the record of wars, revolutions, invasions, and great ideological confrontations. What dimension of history is represented by the writing of Garrison Keillor and of Walter Kirn in this volume? What do they remind us of that in conventional political and military history is left out?

9. Have you read about controversies regarding the preservation of Native American remains in museums and the preservation of Native American burial grounds or religious sites? Find several articles, and write a paper that brings the issues into focus for your readers.

10. How fatalistic are we going to be about living in a violent society? Look for selections in this book that shed light on the causes of violence. Bring together material from several of the readings to focus attention on a key factor or several related key factors.

4
OUTSIDERS
Unheard Voices

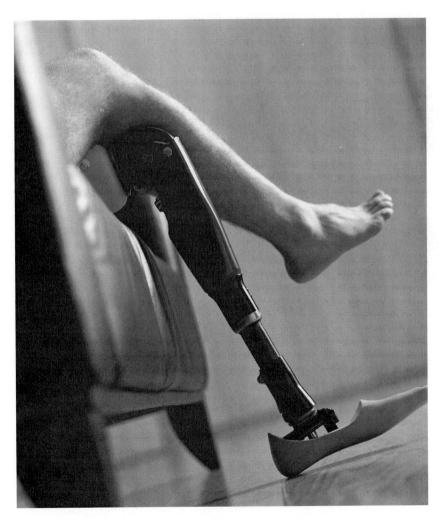

> *I feel I am of them—*
> *I feel I belong to those convicts and prostitutes myself,*
> *And henceforth I will not deny them—*
> *For how can I deny myself?*
>
> —*Walt Whitman*

The promise of America to successive waves of immigrants was that it had created a new classless society. No longer would society be run for the benefit of a small privileged elite. The blessings of liberty would be available to all. No longer would the many toil so that the few could squander the fruits of honest labor. In some of the great movements of our history, the unfree and disenfranchised reminded American society of its unkept promise. Abolition, the civil rights movement, and the women's movement aimed to make the promise of equal rights come true.

Today, however, observers find much evidence of inequality and the failure of human hopes. The gap between the rich and the poor is widening, with millions of American children growing up in poverty. The United States has a larger percentage of its population in jail than any other country. The gulf that separates a homeless encampment from the high-tech digs of a billionaire like Bill Gates is as wide as the one that separated the hut of the French peasant from the Sun King's palace at Versailles. The dropout rates for minority students in high school and college are an unanswered challenge to the Jeffersonian ideal of an educated citizenry, of free universal education. Sections of some American cities have turned into war zones, with guns and drugs out of control.

At the same time, affluent American society seems to be turning its back on its poor and sick. The social safety net, the war on poverty, and food stamps for the needy have been made to seem part of a discredited vocabulary of "tax-and-spend" liberalism. Americans with untreated illnesses sleep under highway overpasses and eat out of garbage cans.

Is our society going to heed those who ask us to listen to the unheard voices of the disenfranchised and the dispossessed, or are the affluent going to insulate themselves from the marginalized, the outsiders? Are we again, as in Victorian England, going to be one state but "two nations"—the privileged and those society has written off? Are buzzwords like *workfare* (instead of welfare), *compassionate conservative,* and *empowerment* the talk of spinmeisters and political consultants, or do they speak to the social conscience of Americans?

IS THERE LIFE AFTER WELFARE?

Annie Downey

In the nineties, a push toward welfare reform aimed at "ending welfare as we know it" and moving welfare recipients from welfare to workfare. Political leaders and media voices talked about ending welfare dependency and the "cycle of poverty." Federal legislation set the maximum amount of time welfare mothers and their children could receive welfare support at five years. Articles from authors in think tanks like the Hoover Institute argued against raising the minimum wage. The author of the following article tells the story of welfare not from the point of view of the affluent well-fed and well-insured but from the point of view of the recipient. With few outlets for her kind of story, she first published her account in a zine (Hip Mama)—zines being the marginal underground cousins and poor relations of America's glossy commercialized magazine culture. Her story was reprinted in the Utne Reader *and in* Harper's *magazine.*

Thought Starters: In recent years there has been much discussion of "profiling"—drawing up composite portraits of types or groups of people as an aid to law enforcement, social workers, and others. If before reading the following article you were asked to prepare a profile of a welfare mother, what would you include in your composite portrait? Compare your own welfare-mother profile with those prepared by fellow students.

I am a single mother of two children, each with a different father. I am a hussy, a welfare rider—burden to everyone and everything. I am anything you want me to be—a faceless number who has no story.

My daughter's father has a job and makes over two grand a month; my son's father owns blue-chip stock in AT&T, Disney, and Campbell's. I call the welfare office, gather old bills, look for day care, write for my degree project, graduate with my son slung on my hip, breast-feeding.

At the welfare office they tell me to follow one of the caseworkers into a small room without windows. The caseworker hands me a packet and a pencil. There is an older woman with graying hair and polyester pants with the same pencil and packet. I glance at her, she looks at me, we are both ashamed. I try hard to fill out the packet correctly, answering all the questions. I am nervous. There are so many questions that near the end I start to get careless. I just want to leave. I hand the caseworker the packet in an envelope; she asks for my pencil, does not look at me. I exit unnoticed. For five years I've exited unnoticed. I can't imagine how to get a job. I ride the bus home.

After a few weeks a letter arrives assigning me to "Group 3." I don't even finish reading it. I put my son in his stroller and walk to the food shelf.

My grandmother calls later to tell me that I confuse sex with love. I tell her that I am getting a job. She asks what kind. I say, "Any job."

"Oh, Annie," she says. "Don't do that. You have a degree. Wait."

I say, "I can't, Gram, I've got to feed my kids, I have no one to fall back on." She is silent. I grasp the cord. I know I cannot ask for help.

It is 5 a.m. My alarm wakes up my kids. I try nursing my son back to sleep, but my daughter keeps him up with her questions: "Don't go out without telling me. Who's going to take care of us when you leave? What time is it?" I want to cry. It is still dark and I am exhausted. I've had three hours of sleep. I get ready for work, put some laundry in the washer, make breakfast, set out clothes for the kids, make lunches. I carry my son; my daughter follows. They cling to me. They cry when I leave. I see their faces pressed against the porch window and the sitter trying to get them inside.

I slice meat for $5.50 an hour for nine hours five days a week. I barely feed my kids, I barely pay the bills.

I struggle against welfare. I struggle against this faceless number I have become. I want my story. I want my life. But without welfare I would have nothing. On welfare I went from teen mom to woman with an education. I published two magazines, became an editor, a teacher. Welfare, along with Section 8 housing grants and Reach Up, gave my children a life. My daughter loves and does well in school. My son is round, and at 20 months speaks wondrous sentences about the moon and stars. Welfare gave me what was necessary to be a mother.

Still, I cannot claim it. There is too much shame in me. The disgusted looks in the grocery lines, the angry voices of *Oprah* panelists, the unmitigated rage of the blue and white collar. I never buy expensive ice cream in pints. I don't do drugs. I don't own a hot tub. But the voices won't be stilled.

I am one of 12 million who are 1 percent of the federal budget. I am one of the 26 percent of AFDC recipients who are mothers and the 36.6 percent who are white. I am one of the 68 percent of teen mothers who were sexually abused. I am $600 a month below the poverty level for a family of three. I am a hot political issue. I am 145-65-8563. Group 3.

I have brown hair and eyes. I write prose. My mother has been married and divorced twice. I have never been married. I love Pablo Neruda's poetry, Louise Gluck's essays. I love my stepfather but not my real father. My favorite book is *Love in the Time of Cholera* by Gabriel García Márquez. My favorite movie, *The Color Purple*.

I miss my son's father. I love jazz. I've always wanted to learn how to ballroom dance. I am not a number. I have a story, I have a life, I have a face.

The Responsive Reader

1. If you were a social worker investigating Downey's case, what key facts in her personal history and family background would you note? Which to you would seem most relevant or important? Why? Which to you seem familiar or predictable? Which seem unusual and why?
2. What is Downey's history as a welfare recipient and job seeker? What stages and what details would you include in a résumé of her record as a single mother below the poverty line?
3. As early as the days of the Great Depression, Americans struggling against poverty have rebelled against the paperwork, the obscure classifications, the bureaucratic language, and the failure to deal with applicants as human beings. According to Downey, what is it like to be a faceless number in the welfare bureaucracy? How does it make her feel or react?
4. What light does Downey shed on how society shames welfare recipients? What evidence have you personally seen of strong negative feelings toward welfare recipients? How are they shown or expressed? Do you share them? Why or why not?
5. At the end, Downey does another verbal self-portrait that seems to have nothing to do with her economic situation or welfare status. What does she include there and why? What kind of send-off does her conclusion provide for her article?

Talking, Listening, Writing

6. Drawing on input from Downey's essay, prepare a journal entry titled "A Day in the Life of a Welfare Mother."
7. Have you ever been on welfare or accepted charity? If so, what is the most important lesson you learned from the experience? Would you accept welfare if you were unable to make ends meet?
8. Have you ever felt that people viewed you as "a faceless number who has no story"?
9. What was the worst job you ever held? Why did you take the job? How long did you keep it? What made it the worst job you ever held? For you, what would be the best possible job?

Collaborative Projects

10. Working with a group, investigate how welfare-to-work programs are faring in your area or community. What is required of former welfare recipients? What problems have the programs encountered? How successful are they? If possible, talk to former welfare recipients, social workers, employers.

MOTHER'S DAY IN FEDERAL PRISON

Amanda Coyne

> *Do you tend to feel that prison, like a serious accident or catastrophic illness, is something that happens to others—to people who are different from you and from people you care for? Amanda Coyne is a writer who tries to put a human face on the mind-numbing numbers of America's growing prison industry. Americans have grown used to staggering statistics about an exploding prison population. Coyne takes you to a visiting room at a women's prison to make you look at the faces of real people—both the women incarcerated there and the families they left behind. Coyne was a graduate student at the University of Iowa when she wrote this article for* Harper's *magazine.*

Thought Starters: Do you ever visit a jail, a hospital, a juvenile home, a homeless shelter, or a similar institution? What is the routine? What goes through the visitor's mind? How does the visitor behave—or how should the visitor behave?

You can spot the convict-moms here in the visiting room by the way they hold and touch their children and by the single flower that is perched in front of them—a rose, a tulip, a daffodil. Many of these mothers have untied the bow that attaches the flower to its silver-and-red cellophane wrapper and are using one of the many empty soda cans at hand as a vase. They sit proudly before their flower-in-a-Coke-can, amid Hershey bar wrappers, half-eaten Ding Dongs, and empty paper coffee cups. Occasionally, a mother will pick up her present and bring it to her nose when one of the bearers of the single flower—her child—asks if she likes it. And the mother will respond the way that mothers always have and always will respond when presented with a gift on this day. "Oh, I just love it. It's perfect. I'll put it in the middle of my Bible." Or, "I'll put it on my desk, right next to your school picture." And always: "It's the best one here."

But most of what is being smelled today is the children themselves. While the other adults are plunking coins into the vending machines, the mothers take deep whiffs from the backs of their children's necks, or kiss and smell the backs of their knees, or take off their shoes and tickle their feet and then pull them close to their noses. They hold them tight and take in their own second scent—the scent assuring them that these are still their children and that they still belong to them.

The visitors are allowed to bring in pockets full of coins, and today that Mother's Day flower, and I know from previous visits to my older sister here at the Federal Prison Camp for women in Pekin, Illinois, that there is always an aberrant urge to gather immediately around the vending machines. The sandwiches are stale, the coffee weak, the candy bars the ones we always pass up in a convenience store. But after we hand the children over to their mothers, we gravitate toward those machines. Like milling in the kitchen at a party. We all do it, and nobody knows why. Polite conversation ensues around the microwave while the popcorn is popping and the processed-chicken sandwiches are being heated. We ask one another where we are from, how long a drive we had. An occasional whistle through the teeth, a shake of the head. "My, my, long way from home, huh?" "Staying at the Super 8 right up the road. Not a bad place." "Stayed at the Econo Lodge last time. Wasn't a good place at all." Never asking the questions we really want to ask: "What's she in for?" "How much time's she got left?" You never ask in the waiting room of a doctor's office either. Eventually, all of us—fathers, mothers, sisters, brothers, a few boyfriends, and very few husbands—return to the queen of the day, sitting at a fold-out table loaded with snacks, prepared for five or so hours of attempted normal conversation.

Most of the inmates are elaborately dressed, many in prison-crafted dresses and sweaters in bright blues and pinks. They wear meticulously applied makeup in corresponding hues, and their hair is replete with loops and curls—hair that only women with the time have the time for. Some of the better seamstresses have crocheted vests and purses to match their outfits. Although the world outside would never accuse these women of making haute-couture fashion statements, the fathers and the sons and the boyfriends and the very few husbands think they look beautiful, and they tell them so repeatedly. And I can imagine the hours spent preparing for this visit—hours of needles and hooks clicking over brightly colored yards of yarn. The hours of discussing, dissecting, and bragging about these visitors—especially the men. Hours spent in the other world behind the door where we're not allowed, sharing lipsticks and mascaras, and unraveling the occasional hair-tangled hot roller, and the brushing out and lifting and teasing . . . and the giggles that abruptly change into tears without warning—things that define any female-only world. Even, or especially, if that world is a female federal prison camp.

While my sister Jennifer is with her son in the playroom, an inmate's mother comes over to introduce herself to my younger sister, Charity, my brother, John, and me. She tells us about visiting her daughter in a higher-security prison before she was transferred here. The woman looks old and tired, and her shoulders sag under the weight of her recently acquired bitterness.

"Pit of fire," she says, shaking her head. "Like a pit of fire straight from hell. Never seen anything like it. Like something out of an old movie about prisons." Her voice is getting louder and she looks at each of us with pleading eyes. "My *daughter* was there. Don't even get me started on that place. Women die there."

John and Charity and I silently exchange glances.

"My daughter would come to the visiting room with a black eye and I'd think, 'All she did was sit in the car while her boyfriend ran into the house.' She didn't even touch the stuff. Never even handled it."

She continues to stare at us, each in turn. "Ten years. That boyfriend talked and he got three years. She didn't know anything. Had nothing to tell them. They gave her ten years. They called it conspiracy. Conspiracy? Aren't there real criminals out there?" She asks this with hands outstretched, waiting for an answer that none of us can give her.

The woman's daughter, the conspirator, is chasing her son through the maze of chairs and tables and through the other children. She's a twenty-four-year-old blonde, whom I'll call Stephanie, with Dorothy Hamill hair and matching dimples. She looks like any girl you might see in any shopping mall in middle America. She catches her chocolate-brown son and tickles him, and they laugh and trip and fall together onto the floor and laugh harder.

Had it not been for that wait in the car, this scene would be taking place at home, in a duplex Stephanie would rent while trying to finish her two-year degree in dental hygiene or respiratory therapy at the local community college. The duplex would be spotless, with a blown-up picture of her and her son over the couch and ceramic unicorns and horses occupying the shelves of the entertainment center. She would make sure that her son went to school every day with stylishly floppy pants, scrubbed teeth, and a good breakfast in his belly. Because of their difference in skin color, there would be occasional tension—caused by the strange looks from strangers, teachers, other mothers, and the bullies on the playground, who would chant after they knocked him down, "Your Momma's white, your Momma's white." But if she were home, their weekends and evenings would be spent together transcending those looks and healing those bruises. Now, however, their time is spent eating visiting-room junk food and his school days are spent fighting the boys in the playground who chant, "Your Momma's in prison, your Momma's in prison."

He will be ten when his mother is released, the same age my nephew will be when his mother is let out. But Jennifer, my sister, was able to spend the first five years of Toby's life with him. Stephanie had Ellie after she was incarcerated. They let her hold him for eighteen hours, then sent her back to prison. She has done the "tour," and her son is a well-traveled six-year-old. He has spent weekends visiting his mother in prisons in Kentucky, Texas, Connecticut (the Pit of Fire), and now at last here, the camp—minimum security, Pekin, Illinois.

Ellie looks older than his age. But his shoulders do not droop like his grandmother's. On the contrary, his bitterness lifts them and his chin higher than a child's should be, and the childlike, wide-eyed curiosity has been replaced by defiance. You can see his emerging hostility as he and his mother play together. She tells him to pick up the toy that he threw, say, or to put the deck of cards away. His face turns sullen, but she persists. She takes him by the shoulders and looks him in the eye, and he uses one of his hands to swat at her. She grabs the hand and he swats with the other. Eventually, she pulls him toward her and smells the top of his head, and she picks up the cards or the toy herself. After all, it is Mother's Day and she sees him so rarely. But her acquiescence makes him angrier, and he stalks out of the playroom with his shoulders thrown back.

Toby, my brother and sister and I assure one another, will not have these resentments. He is better taken care of than most. He is living with relatives in Wisconsin. Good, solid, middle-class, churchgoing relatives. And when he visits us, his aunts and his uncle, we take him out for adventures where we walk down the alley of a city and pretend that we are being chased by the "bad guys." We buy him fast food, and his uncle, John, keeps him up well past his bedtime enthralling him with stories of the monkeys he met in India. A perfect mix, we try to convince one another. Until we take him to see his mother and on the drive back he asks the question that most confuses him, and no doubt all the other children who spend much of their lives in prison visiting rooms: "Is my Mommy a bad guy?" It is the question that most seriously disorders his five-year-old need to clearly separate right from wrong. And because our own need is perhaps just as great, it is the question that haunts us as well.

Now, however, the answer is relatively simple. In a few years, it won't *15* be. In a few years we will have to explain mandatory minimums, and the war on drugs, and the murky conspiracy laws, and the enormous amount of money and time that federal agents pump into imprisoning low-level drug dealers and those who happen to be their friends and their lovers. In a few years he might have the reasoning skills to ask why so many armed robbers and rapists and child-molesters and, indeed, murderers are punished less severely than his mother. When he is older, we will somehow have to explain to him the difference between federal crimes, which don't allow for parole, and state crimes, which do. We will have to explain that his mother was taken from him for five years not because she was a drug dealer but because she made four phone calls for someone she loved.

But we also know it is vitally important that we explain all this without betraying our bitterness. We understand the danger of abstract anger, of being disillusioned with your country, and, most of all, we do not want him to inherit that legacy. We would still like him to be raised as we were, with the idea that we live in the best country in the world with the best legal system in the world—a legal system carefully designed to be immune to political mood swings and public hysteria; a system that promises to fit the punishment to the crime. We want him to be a good citizen. We want him to have absolute faith that he lives in a fair country, a country that watches over and protects its most vulnerable citizens: its women and children.

So for now we simply say, "Toby, your mother isn't bad, she just did a bad thing. Like when you put rocks in the lawn mower's gas tank. You weren't bad then, you just did a bad thing."

Once, after being given this weak explanation, he said, "I wish I could have done something really bad, like my Mommy. So I could go to prison too and be with her."

We notice a circle forming on one side of the visiting room. A little boy stands in its center. He is perhaps nine years old, sporting a burnt-orange three-piece suit and pompadour hair. He stands with his legs slightly apart, eyes half-shut, and sways back and forth, flashing his cuffs and snapping his fingers while singing:

> . . . Doesn't like crap games with barons and earls.
> Won't go to Harlem in ermine and pearls.
> Won't dish the dirt with the rest of the girls.
> That's why the lady is a tramp.

He has a beautiful voice and it sounds vaguely familiar. One of the visitors informs me excitedly that the boy is the youngest Frank Sinatra impersonator and that he has been on television even. The boy finishes his performance and the room breaks into applause. He takes a sweeping bow, claps his miniature hands together, and points both little index fingers at the audience. "More. Later. Folks." He spins on his heels and returns to the table where his mother awaits him, proudly glowing. "Don't mess with the hair, Mom," we overhear. "That little boy's slick," my brother says with true admiration.

Sitting a few tables down from the youngest Frank Sinatra is a table of Mexican-Americans. The young ones are in white dresses or button-down oxfords with matching ties. They form a strange formal contrast to the rest of the rowdy group. They sit silently, solemnly listening to the white-haired woman, who holds one of the table's two roses. I walk past and listen to the grandmother lecture her family. She speaks of values, of getting up early every day, of going to work. She looks at one of the young boys and points a finger at him. "School is the most important thing. *Nada mas importante.* You get up and you go to school and you study, and you can make lots of money. You can be big. You can be huge. Study, study, study."

The young boy nods his head. "Yes, *abuelita.* Yes, *abuelita,*" he says.

The owner of the other flower is holding one of the group's three infants. She has him spread before her. She coos and kisses his toes and nuzzles his stomach.

When I ask Jennifer about them, she tells me that it is a "mother and daughter combo." There are a few of them here, these combos, and I notice that they have the largest number of visitors and that the older inmate, the grandmother, inevitably sits at the head of the table. Even here, it seems, the hierarchical family structure remains intact. One could take a picture,

20

replace the fast-food wrappers with chicken and potatoes, and these families could be at any restaurant in the country, could be sitting at any dining room table, paying homage on this day to the one who brought them into the world.

Back at our table, a black-haired, Middle Eastern woman dressed in   25
loose cottons and cloth shoes is whispering to my brother with a sense of urgency that makes me look toward my sister Charity with questioning eyes and a tilt of my head. Charity simply shrugs and resumes her conversation with a nineteen-year-old ex–New York University student—another conspirator. Eight years.

Prison, it seems, has done little to squelch the teenager's rebellious nature. She has recently been released from solitary confinement. She wears new retro-bellbottom jeans and black shoes with big clunky heels. Her hair is short, clipped perfectly ragged and dyed white—all except the roots, which are a stylish black. She has beautiful pale skin and beautiful red lips. She looks like any midwestern coed trying to escape her origins by claiming New York's East Village as home. She steals the bleach from the laundry room, I learn later, in order to maintain that fashionable white hue. But stealing the bleach is not what landed her in the hole. She committed the inexcusable act of defacing federal property. She took one of her government-issue T-shirts and wrote in permanent black magic marker, "I have been in your system. I have examined your system." And when she turned around it read, "I find it very much in need of repair."

The Responsive Reader

1. What would you include in capsule portraits or thumbnail sketches of the women inmates Coyne describes in her article? What kind of people are they? (You and your classmates may want to stage a miniproduction in which you and your fellow students assume the identity of the inmates, with each telling her story.)
2. Is there a common element or common denominator in the histories of the inmates? Is there anything to be learned from their stories?
3. In what ways is the jail Coyne visited a woman's world? Which of the scenes or details Coyne records do you think would be missing or different in the visiting room of a prison for men?
4. Do you tend to think that imprisonment, like a serious accident, is something that happens to others—not to people like you and those you care for? Or do you recognize yourself or people close to you in any of the inmates you see in this article?

Talking, Listening, Writing

5. Do you believe it is possible in our justice system for the main offender to get off with three years in prison while a friend or lover serves ten? When it happens, is it a fluke? What makes it possible?

6. People who go into prisons to teach or befriend inmates or who agitate for prisoners' rights are sometimes called "do-gooders" or "bleeding hearts" by self-styled "hard-nosed" individuals. Temperamentally, are you inclined to be "hard-nosed" or to be a "bleeding heart"? How and where does the difference show in how you act and talk? What do you think accounts for the difference?

Collaborative Projects

7. Growing numbers of women are involved with the justice system or go to jail. You may want to team up with classmates to investigate current trends in your area or your state. Your group may try setting up interviews with insiders in law enforcement or the court system whose jobs bring them into close contact with female offenders. Will Hermes's article "Jailhouse Lawyer" (*Utne Reader* January/February 1999), about a woman who won a MacArthur Foundation award for her work as an advocate for women in prison, may help your group identify current issues and initiatives.

TIME

Nathan McCall

During the decade spanning the Reagan and first Bush presidencies, the population of America's prison Gulag archipelago tripled from half a million to an estimated million and a half human beings. In some communities, prison construction was one of the few growth industries left. Three-strike laws were projected to swell prisons to the point where money spent on jails would out-strip the money the nation spends on schools. Nathan McCall is an African American journalist who went to hell and back in the American prison system and told his story in Makes Me Wanna Holler *(1994). Growing up in a black working-class neighborhood in Portsmouth, Virginia, he had a stepfather who brooked "no hustling, gambling in the streets, or carrying on" and who believed in "work, work, work." McCall says he and his brothers "saw my old man working hard, and he had nothing." Like many young black males, McCall was carrying a gun by the time he was fifteen and was in jail by the time he was twenty. After serving three years for armed robbery, he studied journalism at Norfolk State University. He became a reporter for the* Virginia Pilot–Ledger Star *and the* Atlanta Journal and Constitution *and joined the prestigious* Washington Post *in 1989.*

Thought Starters: Is America's large prison population invisible in the American media?

I was standing in my cell doorway, checking out the scene on the floor below, when a white convict appeared in the doorway across from mine. He stood stark still and looked straight ahead. Without saying a word, he lifted a razor blade in one hand and began slashing the wrist of the other, squirting blood everywhere. He kept slashing, rapid-fire, until finally he dropped the razor and slumped to the floor, knocking his head against the bars as he went down.

Other inmates standing in their doorways spotted him and yelled, "Guard! Guard! Guard!" Guards came running, rushed the unconscious inmate to the dispensary, and ordered a hallboy to clean up the pool of blood oozing down the walkway. Later, when I asked the hallboy why the dude had tried to take himself out, he said, "That *time* came down on him and he couldn't take the pressure. You know them white boys can't handle time like us brothers. They weak."

It was a macho thing for a guy to be able to handle his time. Still, every once in a while, time got to everybody, no matter how tough they were. Hard time came in seasonal waves that wiped out whole groups of cats, like a monsoon. Winter was easiest on everybody. There was the sense that you really weren't missing anything on the streets because everyone was indoors. Spring and summer were hell. The Dear John letters started flowing in, sending heartbroken dudes to the fence for a clean, fast break over and into the countryside. Fall was a wash. The weather was nice enough to make you think of home, but winter was just ahead, giving you something to look forward to. Time.

I saw the lifers go through some serious changes about time. Some days, those cats carried theirs as good as anybody else, but other days, they didn't. You could look in their eyes sometimes and tell they had run across a calendar, one of those calendars that let you know what day of the week your birthday will fall on ten years from now. Or you could see in the wild way they started acting and talking that they were on the edge. Then it was time to get away from them, go to the other side of the prison yard, and watch the fireworks. They went *off*. Especially the brothers. They were determined not to go down kicking and screaming and slashing their wrists like the white boys. The brothers considered themselves too hard for that. When the time got to be too much for them, they'd go fuck with somebody and get themselves in a situation where there was no win. It was their way of saying, "Go on, kill me. Gimme a glorious way to get outta this shit."

My time started coming down on me when I realized I'd reached the one-year mark and had at least two to go. I tried to cling tighter to Liz, but that didn't work. After I was transferred from the jail to Southampton, it seemed we both backed out on the marriage plans. She didn't bring it up, and neither did I. Liz's visits and letters slacked off, and I felt myself slipping out of touch with the outside world. When Liz did visit, she seemed distant and nervous, like there was something she wanted to tell me but couldn't get out. That drove me crazy, along with about a hundred thousand other irritations that constantly fucked with my head.

I thought a lot about the irony of the year 1976: It was the year Alex Haley published the slave epic *Roots* and the country was celebrating the two hundredth year of its freedom from tyranny. It seemed that every time I opened a magazine or walked past a TV set, there was talk about the year-long bicentennial celebration. I'd heard white people brag about being free, white, and twenty-one. There I was, black, twenty-one, and in the penitentiary. It seemed I'd gotten it all wrong.

It's a weird feeling being on the edge and knowing that there's not much you can do about it but hang on. You can't get help for prison depression. You can't go to a counselor and say, "Look, I need a weekend pass. This punishment thing is taking more out of me than I think it was intended to take."

I didn't want to admit to myself that the time was getting to me that much, let alone admit it to anybody else. So I determined to do the macho thing: suffer quietly. Sometimes it got so bad I had to whisper to myself, "Hold on, Nate. Hold on."

Frustrated and depressed, I went to the prison and bought a green spiral-bound tablet and started a journal, partly out of a need to capture my fears and feelings, and partly to practice using the new words I learned. I adopted a journal theme—a quote I ran across by the writer Oliver Wendell Holmes—as encouragement to keep me pushing ahead and holding on:

> I find the great thing in this world is not so much where we stand as in what direction we are moving. To reach the port of heaven, we must sail, sometimes with the wind and sometimes against it—but we must sail, and not drift, nor lie at anchor.

It made me feel better sometimes to get something down on paper just like I felt it. It brought a kind of relief to be able to describe my pain. It was like, if I could describe it, it lost some of its power over me. I jotted down innermost thoughts I couldn't verbalize to anyone else, recorded what I saw around me, and expressed feelings inspired by things I read. Often, the thoughts I wrote down reflected my struggle with time. 10

> *Each day I inspire myself with the hope that by some miracle of God or act of legislature I will soon regain my freedom. However, from occasional conversations, I find that many other inmates have entertained the same hope— for years.*
> *May 21, 1976*

Even the guys doing less than life had a hard time. Anything in the double digits—ten years to serve, twenty, forty, sixty—could be a back-breaker. I had a buddy, Cincinnati. Real outgoing cat. Every time you saw him, he was talking beaucoup trash. But Cincinnati was doing a hard forty, and it drove him up a wall at least twice a week. He fought it by trying to keep super-busy. With a white towel hung loosely over his shoulder and several cartons of cigarettes tucked under his arm, Cincinnati (we called him that because that's where he was from) would bop briskly across the yard, intent on his missions. He'd stop and jawbone with a group of guys hanging out near the canteen, then hand a carton of cigarettes to one of them and hurry off to the next meeting.

Cincinnati was one of several major dealers at Southampton who used the drug-peddling skills they'd learned on the streets to exploit the crude prison economy. In that economy, cigarettes replaced money as the medium of exchange. Favors and merchandise were negotiated in terms of their worth in packs of cigarettes. For twelve cartons of cigarettes, a guy could take out a contract to have somebody set up on a drug bust, or get them double-banked or shanked. Eight packs could get you a snappy pair of prison brogans from one of the brothers on the shoe-shop crew. For three packs each week, laundry workers would see to it your shirts and pants were crisply starched. Cincinnati liked to get his gray prison shirts starched so that he could turn up the collar and look real cool.

The really swift dealers found ways to convert a portion of their goods to forbidden cash, which they used to bribe guards to get them reefer and liquor, or saved for their eventual return to the streets.

Cincinnati, who was about two years older than me and had logged a lot more street time, was penitentiary-rich. He decorated his cell with plush blue towels and stockpiled so much stuff that the rear wall of his cell looked like a convenience store. It was stacked from floor to ceiling with boxes of cookies, cigarettes, and other stuff he sold, "two for one," to inmates seeking credit until payday.

Watching cats like him, I often thought about Mo Battle and his theory about pawns. Cincinnati handled time and played chess like he lived: He failed to think far ahead and he chased pawns all over the board. In his free time off from the kitchen, where he worked, he busied himself zigzagging across the prison yard, collecting outstanding debts and treating his petty "bidness" matters like they were major business deals. 15

Cincinnati was playful and cheery most of the time. He was as dark as night and had a shiny gold tooth that gleamed like a coin when he smiled. Short and squat, he had a massive upper body and a low center of gravity, like Mike Tyson. In fact, his voice, high-pitched and squeaky, sounded a lot like Tyson's, too. It was the kind of voice that sounded like it belonged to a child. But nobody mistook Cincinnati for a child. He was a tank, and could turn from nice guy to cold killer in a split second.

He addressed everybody as "bro'." I'd see him on the yard and say, "Yo, Cincinnati, what's happ'nin'?" And if he was in a good mood, he'd say, "Bro' Nate, life ain't nothin' but a meatball."

But time came down on Cincinnati, like it did on everybody else. He had to do at least ten of his forty years before going up for parole. I could tell when he was thinking about it. I'd run into him on the yard and say, "What's happ'nin', Cincinnati?" He'd shake his head sadly and say, "Bro' Nate, I'm busted, disgusted, and *can't* be trusted."

Cincinnati was so far away from home that he never got visits. On visiting days, he usually went out to the main sidewalk on the yard and looked through the fence as people visiting other inmates pulled into the parking lot.

Other times, I could tell how depressed he was by the way he handled defeat on the chessboard. I beat him all the time and taunted him, but sometimes he didn't take it well. Just before I put him in checkmate, he'd get frustrated and knock one of his big arms against the board, sending the pieces crashing to the floor. Then he'd look up with a straight face and say, "Oh, I'm sorry, Bro' Nate. I didn't mean to do that." 20

We were playing chess one day when Cincinnati stared at the board a long time without making a move. I got impatient. "Go on and move, man! You gonna lose anyway!"

Ignoring me, Cincinnati kept his eyes glued to the board and didn't speak for a long time. After a while, he said, "Bro' Nate, I'm gonna make a break for the fence. I been thinking about it a long time. I got a lotta money saved up. I can get outta state. You wanna come?"

Any inmate who says he's never thought about escaping is either lying or telling the sad truth. The sad truth is, the only dudes who don't think about making a break are those who are either so institutionalized that their thoughts seldom go beyond the prison gates, or who were so poor in the streets that they had been rescued and are glad to be someplace where they are guaranteed three hots and a cot.

There were a few desperate, fleeting moments when I thought half-seriously about making a run. Southampton is ringed by a tall barbed-wire fence with electrical current running through it, but everybody knew the heat was turned off much of the time. Sometimes, I'd stare at that fence and think about how to scale it. I pictured myself tossing my thick winter coat on top of the barbed wire to test the heat and protect my hands, climbing quickly to the top, and leaping to the other side to make my dash before tower guards could get off a good shot. I'd mapped an escape route based on what I'd seen of the area while traveling with the gun gang. I'd thought it through like a chess match, move for move. That's why I didn't try. When I thought it through, I always saw a great chance of getting busted or leading such a miserable life on the run that it would be another form of imprisonment.

Looking at Cincinnati, I jokingly turned down his offer to run. "Naw, *25* brother-man. I'm gonna squat here. I'm expecting a visit from my lady this weekend. I'd hate for her to come and find me gone. Besides, I can handle my bid. You do the crime, you gotta do the time, Jack!"

I forgot about our conversation until a week or two later, when the big whistle at the guard tower sounded, signaling all inmates to go to their cells to be counted. The whistle blew at certain times every day, but on this day, it sounded at an odd hour, meaning there was something wrong. After we went to our cells, the word spread that Cincinnati had made a break. He'd hidden in the attic of the school building, then scrambled over the fence after a posse left the compound to hunt for him.

Following the count, guys in my building (I was in C-3 by then) grew real quiet. Every time someone escaped, I got quiet and privately rooted for him to get away. I sat on my bunk thinking about Cincinnati, trying to picture him out in the pitch dark, his black face sweating, ducking through bushes, hotly pursued by white men with guns and barking dogs. I imagined him low-running across some broad field, dodging lights and listening for suspicious sounds. I imagined the white country folks, alerted to the escape, grabbing their shotguns and joining the hunt.

Some weeks after Cincinnati made his break, he got caught somewhere in the state. It saddened me. He was shipped to a maximum-security prison more confining than Southampton, and he got more time tacked on to the forty years that was already giving him hell.

Prison paranoia is a dangerous thing. It can affect a person to the extent that he becomes distrustful of anyone and everyone. Even though my woman has displayed no signs of infidelity, I find myself scrutinizing her behavior each week (in the visiting room), searching her eyes for the slightest faltering trait. I search in hope that I discover none, but hope even more that if there is, I will detect it before it discovers me and slithers back into some obscure hiding place. June 4, 1976

I walked into the crowded visiting room and took a seat at the table with Liz. My intuition told me that something was up. She'd come alone, without my parents or my son, and her brown eyes, usually bright and cheery, were sad and evasive. In a letter she'd sent to me earlier in the week, she had said there was something she wanted to discuss. I sensed what it was, and I'd come prepared.

We exchanged small talk, then there was this awkward silence. Finally, *30* I spoke, relieving her of a burden I sensed was killing her. "You're seeing someone else, aren't you?"

She nodded. "Yes."

There was a long pause as she waited for my reaction. I looked down at the floor and thought about what I'd just heard. My worst fear had come true. Liz couldn't hang. I'd have to do the time alone. I understood. She'd done the best she could. She'd been a helluva lot more supportive and re- liable than I would have been under the circumstances. The best I could do was be grateful for what she'd done. Take it and grow, as she used to say. I tried to put on a brave face, and I said, "I understand, really. . . . Well, noth- ing I can do about that but wish you the best. I would like you to hang in there with me, but really, I don't know when I'm gettin' outta here."

She listened quietly and nodded as I talked. When I finished, she didn't say much. We sat there, bummed out, looking at each other. Mr. and Miss Manor. Liz wished me well. Her eyes watered. Then she said good- bye, and left.

I practically ran back to my cell that Saturday morning. I wanted to get back there before the tear ducts burst. It was like trying to get to the bathroom before the bladder gives out. I made it, went inside, and flopped down on a stool. I turned on the stereo, slid in one of my favorite gospel tapes, *Amazing Grace,* by Aretha Franklin, and closed my eyes. The tape opened with a song called "Mary, Don't You Weep." The deep strains of a full gospel choir, comforting the sister of Lazarus after his death, sang in a rich harmony that sent shivers through me:

Hush, Mary, don't you weep.
Hush, Mary, don't you weep.

When I heard those words, the floodgate burst and the tears started *35* streaming down my face. Streaming. The pain ran so deep it felt physical, like somebody was pounding on my chest. I'd never been hurt by a woman before. I had never cared enough to be hurt by one. I sat there, leaning on the cell door, listening to Aretha and crying. Inmates walked past and I didn't even lift my head. I didn't care who saw me or what they thought. I was crushed. Wasted. I cried until tears blurred my vision. Then I got up, picked up my washcloth, rinsed it in the sink, held it to my face, and cried some more. Liz was gone. I remembered that she had once told me, "I'll follow you into a ditch if you lead me there." Well, I had led her there, but she'd never promised to stay.

Sometimes I'd get grinding migraines that lasted for hours on end. I figured it was caused by the pain of losing Liz, and the stress and tension hounding me. When the frequency of the headaches increased, I came up with ways to relieve the stress. I'd leave the place. I'd stretch out on my bunk, block out all light by putting a cloth over my eyes, and go into deep meditation or prayer. Starting with my toes, I'd concentrate hard and command every one of my body parts to chill. Often, by the time I reached my head the tension was gone.

Then I'd take my imagination and soar away from the prison yard. I'd travel to Portsmouth or some faraway, fictional place. Or I'd venture beyond the earth and wander through the galaxy, pondering the vastness of what God has done. I developed a hell of an imagination by doing those mental workouts, and it put me in touch with my spirit in wondrous ways. When the concentration was really good, I'd lose all feeling in my body, and my spirit would come through, making me feel at one with the universe. It was like being high: It felt so good, but I couldn't figure out a way to make it last.

> *I just witnessed a brutal fight in the cafeteria. The atmosphere was certainly conducive to violence: hot, odorous air filled with noise and flies. The two combatants went at each other's throats as if their lives meant nothing to them. After being confined for an extended period of time, life does tend to lose its value. I pray that I can remember my self-worth and remain cool.*
> *July 27, 1976*

A group of us from Tidewater were sitting around, sharing funny tales from the streets and telling war stories about crazy things we'd done. When my turn came, I told a story about a near stickup on Church Street in Norfolk. "Yeah, man, we ran across a dude who had nothing but chump change on him. We got mad 'cause the dude was broke, so we took his change and started to take his pants. He had on some yellow, flimsy-looking pants, so we made him walk with us under a streetlamp so we could get a better look at them. When we got under the streetlamp, we could see the pants were cheap. And they were dirty. So we let the dude slide, and keep his pants . . ."

Everybody was laughing. Everybody but a guy from Norfolk named Tony. Squinting his eyes, he leaned over and interrupted, "Did you say the guy had on yellow pants?"

"Yeah." 40

"Goddammit, that was *me* y'all stuck up that night!" he said, pointing a finger at me.

Everything got quiet. The guys looked at me, then at Tony, then back at me. Somebody snickered, and everybody else joined in. I laughed, too, until I looked at Tony and realized he still wasn't laughing. He was hot. He looked embarrassed and mad as hell.

To lighten the mood, I extended my hand playfully and said, "Wow, man, I'm sorry 'bout that. You know I didn't know you then."

Tony looked at my hand like he wanted to spit on it. "Naw, man. That shit ain't funny." The way he said it, I knew he wasn't going to let the thing drop. I knew that stupid macho pride had him by the throat and was choking the shit out of him.

A week or two after the exchange, he came into the library, where I 45 was working, sat in a corner, and started tearing pages out of magazines. The library was filled with inmates. I walked over to the table and said, "Yo, Tony, you can't tear the pages outta the magazines, man. Other people have to read 'em."

He looked up, smiled an evil smile, then ripped out another page and said. "What you gonna do 'bout it? You ain't no killer." The room grew quiet. I felt like all eyes were on me, waiting to see what I would do. I started thinking fast. Tony was stout and muscular and I figured he'd probably do the moonwalk on me if he got his hands on me. He was sitting down and I was standing. I glanced at an empty chair near him. I thought, *I could sneak him right off the bat, grab that chair, and wrap it around his head.* Then I thought about the potential consequences of fighting at work. I could lose my job, get kicked out of the library. I thought, *I gotta let it slide. I have to.* I looked at Tony, shrugged my shoulders, and said, "I ain't gonna do nothin', man. The magazines don't belong to *me.*"

Tony sat there, staring at me, and tore more pages out of magazines. I walked away.

Later that night, I thought about it some more. I thought about how he'd come off. I thought, *He disrespected me.* I was too scared to let that man get away with disrespecting me. I felt I had faith that God would take care of me, but whenever I got that scared about something, I relied on what I knew best—faith in self. So I prayed, then set God aside for the time being and put together a shank like I'd learned to make while in the Norfolk jail. I melded a razor blade into a toothbrush handle, leaving the sharp edges sticking out, like a miniature tomahawk. I told one of my buddies what I intended to do. "I gotta get that niggah, man. He disrespected me and tried to chump me down."

The next day, we went looking for Tony on the yard. We spotted him leaving the dispensary with a partner. While my friend kept a lookout for guards, I approached Tony. Without saying anything, I pulled the razor blade and swung it at his throat. He jumped back. I lunged at him again and he flung his arms in front of his face, blocking the blow. The razor slashed his coat. He held up his hands and said, "Hold it, hold it, hold it, man! Be cool. Everything's cool. We all right, man. I ain't got no beef with you."

I pointed the razor at him. "Niggah, don't you *never* take me to be no   50
chump!"

"All right, bro', I was just playing with you yesterday."

I turned and walked away, relieved that he'd backed down and grateful that none of the guards standing on the yard had seen what went down.

My parents came to see me that afternoon. I went into the visiting room still hyper from the scene with Tony. As we talked, I looked at them and wondered what they'd say if they knew I had just risked everything I'd worked for to prove a manhood point. I wondered if Tony was going to try to get some get-back or pay somebody to try to shank me when my back was turned. I wondered if the time was coming down on me so badly that I was losing my grip.

At chow time that evening, my homie Pearly Blue came to the table and sat next to me. There was a slight smirk on his face. I sensed he was feeling a certain delight in knowing he'd warned me to hang tight with my homies to keep hassles away. "Yo, man, I heard you had a run-in with Tony."

"Yeah, a small beef."   55

"I told you these old rooty-poot niggahs will try you if they think you walk alone. . . . You know if you need to make another move on him, the homies can take care of it."

I kept looking straight ahead as I ate. "Naw, man. I got it under control."

I had no problems from Tony the remainder of the time I was at Southampton.

The one thing that seemed to soothe everybody in the joint was music. The loudest, most fucked-up brothers in the place chilled out when they had on a set of headphones. Some white inmates had musical instruments—guitars, saxophones, flutes—and they practiced in their cells at night. Most of the brothers didn't like hearing white music. The brothers would holler through the cell bars, "Cut that hillbilly shit out!"

But one white guy, from some rural Virginia town, was exempt from   60
the hassles. He was a fairly good guitar player, and an even better singer. Every night, before the lights went out, he calmed the building with music. He sang the same song, and it reverberated throughout the place. He strummed his guitar and sang the John Denver tune "Take Me Home,

Country Roads." He sang it in a voice so clean it sounded like he was standing on a mountain crooning down into one of those luscious green valleys he was singing about:

> Country rooaads,
> Take me hoomme,
> To the plaaace
> Where I beloooonng . . .

When those lyrics floated into my cell, I'd sit quietly, lean my head against the concrete wall, and listen. That song reminded me of how lonely I was and made me think of home. It made me think of Liz. It made me think of my son, my family, my neighborhood, my life. Sometimes, when he sang that song, tears welled in my eyes and I'd wipe them away, get into bed, and think some more.

That song seemed to calm everybody in the building, even the baad-asses who were prone to yell through their cells. It had the soothing effect of a lullaby sung by a parent to a bunch of children.

The Responsive Reader

1. Can you empathize with the author of this account of prison life? Why or why not? What kind of person is he? How did the prison experience affect him? How did it shape his attitude toward life?
2. How do the different inmates McCall remembers deal with "doing time"? How do they cope? What strategies do they develop, and how successful are these?
3. Many stories of prison life focus on trying to survive in a brutally violent environment. For the author, what is the point of the story he tells about his confrontation with Tony? What is the point or the lesson of the story for you?
4. How do white people look as seen through the eyes of black inmates? Does McCall think whites and blacks deal differently with the prison experience? Is race a major segregating factor or dividing line in McCall's prison?
5. What is the role of music in McCall's story?

Talking, Listening, Writing

6. Do you tend to think people in jail are a different breed from ordinary law-abiding citizens? Do you know anyone who is doing or has done time? What is the person's story?
7. Critics of the American justice system claim that in our society poor people go to jail. People of color go to jail. Poor people of color go to jail. To judge from McCall's account, are the critics right?

8. What is the racial or ethnic mix and social status of defendants in your local courts?

Collaborative Projects

9. The cost of prison construction and of housing ever-growing numbers of inmates has soared in recent years. What is the bottom line? What statistics are available on the actual and projected costs of the prison industry? How does the cost of confining a young person for most of his or her life compare, say, with the cost of supporting a welfare family or with the average funds spent in poor neighborhoods on educating a child?

WHY THE ABLE-BODIED
STILL DON'T GET IT

Andre Dubus

> *Society has come a long way in its treatment of and attitudes toward people with disabilities. Ramps and special elevators facilitate wheelchair access to schools, public buildings, and restaurants. Public transit provides special lifts or alternative transportation. Employers are finding new ways of allowing people with disabilities to use their skills. The media tout breakthroughs in space-age technologies that promise to help physically impaired people to see, to hear, or to walk. Nevertheless, the author of the following article and other voices speaking for the disabled express their rage and frustration at deep-seated engrained attitudes and unresolved issues. Why?*

Thought Starters: Like other spokespersons for people with physical or mental impairments, the author of the following article assumes the existence of two worlds: the world of the fully enabled and the world of the impaired. What has been your own experience with that second universe? Where do you come into contact with or confront disability? What attitudes, expectations, or obligations does it bring into play?

In my sixth year as a cripple, I read a newspaper story about a 34-year-old man who, while he was playing rugby, received an injury that changed his body, and so his life, forever—he is a quadriplegic. The newspaper story focused on the good effect he had on his friends and other people in the city where he lived. They raised money for him; they visited him in the hospital; they said they drew strength from his courage. The injured man said he had regained the use of his hands and that someday he would walk again and play golf. He was still in the hospital.

I was hit by a car on the highway, and lost my left leg above the knee; my right leg was too damaged to use. On the night of my injury I was 49 years old and my sixth child was in her mother's womb. Friends visited me, phoned, wrote letters. Eight writers raised money for me with readings; I didn't even know five of them till we met at the readings. The quadriplegic was talking about playing a game on grass in summer, and his injury was far worse than mine. As he lay on the ground after being hurt, he said *I'm still single*.

So why, as I ate cereal and read this story, did I feel rage instead of gratitude? I wanted to yell at someone, wanted above all to put someone in a wheelchair for one long pushing, pulling, muscle-aching, mind-absorbing day. But who? The reporter and his editor? That newspaper gives

1

favorable reviews to restaurants that the quadriplegic cannot go into, and it doesn't tell you whether or not the restaurant is accessible to people in wheelchairs. This means the reviewers and editors don't think of us as people. They wouldn't review a restaurant that was accessible only to Caucasians or only to men.

Who will carry the quadriplegic up even one step to a restaurant? And why would he want to be carried, when his helplessness, his very meatness, slaps his soul? Chairs with motors cost around $8,000, and if you plan to leave your home you need a van with a lift, and someone to drive it. The quadriplegic will not walk. He will forever be dependent on someone. He cannot sit on a toilet, he cannot wipe himself, or shave, shower, make his bed, dress. He will use a catheter. He cannot cook. He will not feel the heat of a woman, except with his face.

When I was a graduate student at the University of Iowa Writers' Workshop, I had a friend in a wheelchair. I met him in late afternoon on a cold winter day. There was snow on the ground and the sidewalks, and he was pushing his chair up a long steep hill. I was walking at the bottom of the hill when I heard his voice. I stopped and saw him looking over his shoulder at me, calling, "Can you give me a push?"

He couldn't make it any farther up the hill. I felt the embarrassment of being whole while he was not, and went up to him and pushed. In this way we introduced ourselves: I spoke to the back of his head, and he spoke into the cold air in front of him. The hill led to a street that was flat, and he told me I could stop pushing. Across the street was a bar, and we went in. I don't remember how he got down to the street, over the sidewalk's curb, and back up again on the other side. He did it alone. His crippling, he said, came from polio, while he was in the army. In rehabilitation he had learned to lean his chair backward, bring the small front wheels down on the curb, and push and lift the big rear wheels onto it.

He had broad shoulders and a deep voice that I loved hearing. I do not remember how much of his lower body was paralyzed. He had a girlfriend and, one evening in a bar, he said to me *I can have intercourse*. I don't remember pulling him up the steps to our house when he came for dinner or a party, but we had more than one step and my wife and I must have helped him. He told me of learning to use a wheelchair, how the instructors took the men on wheels out of the hospital and raced to a nearby bar. *You had to keep up and get over the curbs* he said. *If you fell on your back, tough shit.* He laughed and I laughed with him, and that's how I thought of people in wheelchairs until I became one: stout-hearted folk wheeling fast on sidewalks, climbing curbs, and of course sometimes falling backward, but that seemed to me like slipping and falling on the outfield grass while you're chasing a fly ball. That is, until over 20 years later, when I fell backward in my chair, and slammed my head against the floor, and I lay helpless and hurt. It was summer and the windows were open and my neighbor, in his house 30 yards away, heard my head striking wood.

5

My friend was very skillful in his wheelchair, and I lacked imagination. Or I lacked the compassion and courage to imagine someone else's suffering. I never thought of my friend making his bed, sitting on a toilet, sitting in a shower, dressing himself, preparing breakfast and washing its dishes, just to leave his house, to go out into the freezing Iowa air.

In my freshman year of college in Louisiana, I studied journalism. If I had become a reporter, and if one day I had walked into a hospital and interviewed a quadriplegic, I would have written the same kind of story I read in the newspaper that morning. It's a good story. The human spirit is strong, and the heart is capable of such hope that, even when we know the truth and it's not the truth we want, we still persevere. I would have celebrated this, as a reporter; and that night, after writing my story about the brave and hopeful quadriplegic, I would have climbed four steps to a restaurant.

And I wouldn't have imagined sitting in a 250-pound wheelchair staring at those few steps leading to the restaurant's door; or looking into a woman's eyes and, in my chest, feeling passion my body could no longer release.

A friend of mine who was a Marine lieutenant in Vietnam was blown into the air by a mine and lost his left leg below the knee. He had been a quarterback in school. When he came home to his small town, limping on an artificial leg, he saw his coach. The coach asked what happened to his leg, and my friend said, "I twisted my knee."

I met him nearly 20 years later, and less than a month before I was injured. We were at a writers' conference, and he didn't limp. When he told me about his leg, I said I never would have known. A long time after my injury, when I was still working with a physical therapist, I talked with this friend on the phone and reminded him of what I had said that summer. "You pissed me off," he said. "People don't know how tiring it is, and how much it hurts."

We were talking on the phone again when he told me about his coach. "You didn't tell him you were in the war?" I asked.

"I was afraid of his reaction."

I sing of those who cannot. To view human suffering as an abstraction, as a statement about how plucky we all are, is to blow air through brass while the boys and girls march in parade off to war. Seeing the flesh as only a challenge to the spirit is as false as seeing the spirit as only a challenge to the flesh. On the planet are people with whole and strong bodies, whose wounded spirits need the constant help that the quadriplegic needs for his body. What we need is not the sound of horns rising to the sky but the steady beat of the bass drum. When you march to a bass drum, your left foot touches the earth with each beat, and you can feel the drum in your body: *boom* and *boom* and *boom* and *pity people pity people pity people.*

The Responsive Reader

1. One of the first words Dubus uses is the word *cripple*. Media people, teachers, and politicians years ago learned not to use this word, because it is demeaning, abusive, outgrouping, or insensitive. Why does Dubus use it?
2. Dubus is a writer who uses a powerful personal narrative to make his points. In the opening paragraphs, he tells the story of the rugby player and his own story. What in both of these stories would make readers experience positive feelings or make them expect gratitude? Why does the author instead feel a growing rage?
3. In the flashback to his graduate student days, Dubus reverses the perspective: He looks at a disabled person from the point of view of the enabled person. How does he make you see and come to know the other person as a fellow human being? Why does he nevertheless feel that he failed or fell short in befriending the other person?
4. What does the story of the Vietnam veteran add to Dubus's essay? What added dimension or broader perspective does it bring to the essay? Would you feel differently about a disabled veteran than you would about other people with disabilities? Why or why not?
5. Dubus is a writer who lets authentic personal experience speak for itself before he strongly makes his points. How does his conclusion sum up his central message? How does it go beyond what he has already said?

Talking, Listening, Writing

6. Do you think Dubus's article would keep media people from creating "brave and hopeful" articles or programs about disability? Would you defend the positive slant the media often give to reporting about disability? What would you say?
7. When Dubus describes his encounters with people with disabilities before he himself became disabled, he says, "I lacked imagination. Or I lacked the compassion and courage to imagine someone else's suffering." How do you think we could show that imagination, that compassion, or that courage? What does Dubus want from able-bodied readers?
8. After reading and discussing Dubus's article, write a letter to the editor, a chat room posting, or a communication asking your readers to rethink their attitudes toward people with disabilities.

Find It on the Web

What promising leads can you identify for an investigation of technological advances designed to help disabled or impaired people see, hear, or walk? Which seem to raise realistic hopes for future progress? Pool your findings with coworkers' in preparation for a possible class presentation or written report.

The following are sample entries from one student's annotated search report:

Dellio, Michael. "A Wheelchair for the World." *Wired News*. 27 July 2000. 10 Jan. 2002. <http://www.wired.com/news/technology/0,1282, 37795-2,00.html>

This website is a review of a technologically advanced wheelchair, designed to help those with disabilities move around in a more normal fashion. It is controlled by an array of small computers that automatically adjust to allow it to cross uneven ground, remain upright in almost any circumstances, and even climb stairs as quickly as a nondisabled person.

Johansen, Anders S. "ALS Computer Solutions FAQ." 9 Jan. 2002. <http://www.secondguess.dk/techfaq.html>

This FAQ (frequently asked questions) provides a discussion of the symptoms of ALS (amyotrophic lateral sclerosis), the problems experienced by those affected by it, and a list of technological devices designed to mitigate those problems. It lists common types of technological aids, along with pros and cons for most solutions.

Gerrey, William, and William Crandall. "Presentation to the U.S. Architectural and Transportation Barriers Compliance Board." 21 Feb. 1991. 9 Jan. 2002. <http://www.ski.org/rehab/WCrandall/General/PRES. HTM>

This presentation, while somewhat dated, is an example of the sort of technological solutions proposed to aid the disabled. It responds to specific questions relating to how technology can aid the visually and aurally impaired and provides specific solutions to these issues.

Hammett, Corinne F. "Quietly Making Life Better with One-of-a-Kind Inventions for Persons with Disabilities." *Tapping Technology*. May 2000. 9 Jan. 2002. <http://www.mdtap.org/tt/2000.05/art_2.html>

This article describes the efforts of Gordon Herald, a retired electrical engineer, and of other members of the VME (Volunteers for Mechanical Engineering) to make life better for the disabled. The VME is a group of individuals who work on a volunteer basis to provide free, individualized solutions to meet the needs of disabled individuals. It provides solutions when mainstream equipment is overly expensive or simply not available.

Solomon, Karen. "Smart Biz: Enabling the Disabled." *Wired News.* 3 Nov. 2000. 9 Jan. 2002. <http://www.wired.com/news/print/ 0,1294,39563,00.html>

This article focuses on the business reasons and new legislation pushing companies to become accessible to the disabled. Using examples, statistics, and legal precedents, the author outlines both the current lack of accessibility and the many compelling reasons for companies to become accessible to the disabled.

THE OTHER BODY: DISABILITY AND IDENTITY POLITICS

Ynestra King

> *Ynestra King is an outspoken political activist whose books include* Ecofeminism and the Reenchantment of Nature *(1993). In the following article, first published in* Ms. *magazine, she reminds us that "of all the ways of becoming 'other' in our society, disability is the only one that can happen to anyone, in an instant, transforming that person's life and identity forever." In the dark ages of attitudes toward people with disabilities, physically impaired students like King were shunted off to special classes and special buildings, segregated from "normal" children. In the meantime, society has come a long way. New laws require schools to mainstream children with disabilities. Ramps, elevators, and enlarged facilities provide improved access to classrooms, libraries, and restrooms. Why, then, does King, like Andre Dubus in "Why the Able-Bodied Still Don't Get It," feel an "underlying rage at the system"?*

Thought Starters: Have disabled people become more visible in the media, in the schools, and in public life? What images do current movies or television programs present of people with disabilities?

Disabled people rarely appear in popular culture. When they do, their   1
disability must be a continuous preoccupation overshadowing all other areas of their character. Disabled people are disabled. That is what they "do." That is what they "are."

My own experience with a mobility impairment that is only minorly disfiguring is that one must either be a creature of the disability, or have transcended it entirely. For me, like most disabled people (and this of course depends on relative severity), neither extreme is true. It is an organic, literally embodied fact that will not change—like being a woman. While it may be possible to "do gender," one does not "do disability." But there is an organic base to both conditions that extends far into culture, and the meaning that "nature" has. Unlike being a woman, being disabled is not a socially constructed condition. It is a tragedy of nature, of a kind that will always exist. The very condition of disability provides a vantage point of a certain lived experience in the body, a lifetime of opportunity for the observation of reaction to bodily deviance, a testing ground for reactions to persons who are readily perceived as having something wrong or being different. It is fascinating, maddening, and disorienting. It defies categories of "sickness" and "health," "broken" and "whole." It is in between.

Meeting people has an overlay: I know what they notice first is that I am different. And there is the experience of the difference in another person's reaction who meets me sitting down (when the disability is not apparent), and standing up and walking (when the infirmity is obvious). It is especially noticeable when another individual is flirting and flattering, and has an abrupt change in affect when I stand up. I always make sure that I walk around in front of someone before I accept a date, just to save face for both of us. Once the other person perceives the disability, the switch on the sexual circuit breaker often pops off—the connection is broken. "Chemistry" is over. I have a lifetime of such experiences, and so does every other disabled woman I know.

White middle-class people—especially white men—in the so-called First World have the most negative reactions. And I always recognize studied politeness, the attempt to pretend that there's nothing to notice (this is the liberal response—Oh, you're black? I hadn't noticed). Then there's the do-gooder response, where the person falls all over her/himself, insisting on doing everything for you; later they hate you; it's a form of objectification. It conveys to you that that is all they see, rather like a man who can't quit talking with a woman about sex.

In the era of identity politics in feminism, disability has not only been an added cross to bear, but an added "identity" to take on—with politically correct positions, presumed instant alliances, caucuses to join, and closets to come out of. For example, I was once dragged across a room to meet someone. My friend, a very politically correct lesbian feminist, said, "She's disabled, too. I thought you'd like to meet her." Rather than argue—what would I say? "I'm not interested in other disabled people," or "This is my night off"? (The truth in that moment was like the truth of this experience in every other moment, complicated and difficult to explain)—I went along to find myself standing before someone strapped in a wheelchair she propels by blowing into a tube with a respirator permanently fastened to the back of the chair. To suggest that our relative experience of disability is something we could casually compare (as other people stand by!) demonstrates the crudity of perception about the complex nature of bodily experience.

My infirmity is partial leg paralysis. I can walk anywhere, climb stairs, drive a car, ride a horse, swim, hang-glide, fly a plane, hike in the wilderness, go to jail for my political convictions, travel alone, and operate heavy equipment. I can earn a living, shop, cook, eat as I please, dress myself, wash and iron my own clothes, clean my house. The woman in that wheelchair can do none of these fundamental things, much less the more exotic ones. On a more basic human level I can spontaneously get my clothes off if I decide to make love. Once in bed my lover and I can forget my disability. None of this is true of the woman in the wheelchair. There is no bodily human activity that does not have to be specially negotiated, none in which

5

she is not absolutely "different." It would take a very long time, and a highly nuanced conversation, for us to be able to share experiences as if they were common. The experience of disability for the two of us was more different than my experience is from the daily experience of people who are not considered disabled. So much for disability solidarity.

With disability, one is somewhere on a continuum between total bodily dysfunction—or death—and complete physical wholeness. In some way, this probably applies to every living person. So when is it that we call a person "disabled"? When do they become "other"? There are "minor" disabilities that are nonetheless significant for a person's life. Color blindness is one example. But in our culture, color blindness is considered an inconvenience rather than a disability.

The ostracization, marginalization, and distortion response to disability are not simply issues of prejudice and denial of civil rights. They reflect attitudes toward bodily life, an unease in the human skin, and an inability to cope with contingency, ambiguity, flux, finitude, and death.

Visibly disabled people (like women) in this culture are the scapegoats for resentments of the limitations of organic life. I had polio when I was seven, finishing second grade. I had excelled in everything, and rarely missed school. I had one bad conduct notation—for stomping on the boys' blocks when they wouldn't let me play with them. Although I had leg braces and crutches when I was ready to start school the next year, I wanted desperately to go back and resume as much of the same life as I could. What I was not prepared for was the response of the school system. They insisted that I was now "handicapped" and should go into what they called "special education." This was a program aimed primarily at multiply disabled children, virtually all of whom were mentally retarded as well as physically disabled. It was in a separate wing of another school, and the children were completely segregated from the "normal" children in every aspect of the school day, including lunch and recreational activities. I was fortunate enough to have educated, articulate parents and an especially aggressive mother; she went to the school board and waged a tireless campaign to allow me to come back to my old school on a trial basis—the understanding being that the school could send me to special education if things "didn't work out" in the regular classroom.

And so began my career as an "exceptional" disabled person, not like the *other* "others." And I was glad. I didn't want to be associated with those others either. Apart from the objective limitations caused by the polio, the transformation in identity—the difference in worldly reception—was terrifying and embarrassing, and it went far beyond the necessary considerations my limitations required.

My experience as "other" is much greater and more painful as a disabled person than as a woman. Maybe the most telling dimension of this knowledge is my observation of the reactions of others over the years, of how deeply afraid people are of being outside the normative appearance

We are finite, contingent, dependent creatures by our very nature; we will all eventually die. We will all experience compromises to our physical integrity. The aspiration to human wholeness is an oppressive idealism. Socially, it is deeply infantilizing.

It promotes a simplistic view of the human person, a static notion of human life that prevents the maturity and social wisdom that might allow human beings to more fully apprehend the human condition. It marginalizes the "different," those perceived as hopelessly wedded to organic existence—women and the disabled. The New Age "human potential movement"—in the name of maximizing human growth—is one of the worst offenders in obscuring the kind of human growth I am suggesting.

I too believe that the potential for human growth and creativity is infinite—but it is not groundless. The common ground for the person—the human body—is a place of shifting sand that can fail us at any time. It can change shape and properties without warning; this is an essential truth of embodied existence.

Of all the ways of becoming "other" in our society, disability is the only one that can happen to anyone, in an instant, transforming that person's life and identity forever.   *25*

The Responsive Reader

1. Why does King find the way we respond to people with disabilities "fascinating, maddening, and disorienting"? Why does she object to society expecting that for people like her disability "must be a continuous preoccupation"? Why are first meetings a special problem? Why are encounters with the other sex a special problem? What is wrong with the way "liberals" or "do-gooders" respond to the disabled?
2. Like other spokespersons for the disabled, King is severely critical of "special education" for the students with disabilities. What is the central objection to it?
3. What is wrong with public policies for assisting the disabled? What is wrong with "hire the handicapped" campaigns?
4. King says, "It's a dreadful business, this needing help." What makes it so dreadful? Why would it be more dreadful in the United States than in any other place? Does King make you understand why disabled people prefer assistance from equipment to assistance from people?

Talking, Listening, Writing

5. What is the exact nature of King's disability? What is her history? Where or how in this article do you find out? Why doesn't she tell you "up front"?
6. Many observers of our culture have criticized the American beauty myth, youth worship, and fitness cult. Why does King see our norms and ideals as imposing a special burden on people like her?

7. What evidence have you seen of increased attention to the needs of people with disabilities? Do you think our society gives too little thought to the needs of the disabled? too much? just about the right amount?

8. In 1997, *Time* reported that "disabled protesters" were denouncing a projected monument commemorating President Franklin Delano Roosevelt—because it showed him, as newsreels had during his presidency, without the wheelchair he was using as the result of being disabled by polio. What principle do you think is at stake here? Would you take sides in the controversy one way or the other?

Collaborative Projects

9. Does your college have policies or programs addressing the needs of students with disabilities? How are they implemented? How meaningful or successful are they?

THE LESSON
Toni Cade Bambara

*Toni Cade Bambara has been described as a "dancer, teacher, critic, editor, activist, and writer." She was born and educated in New York City, with degrees from Queens and City College. She started writing in the politically active sixties and has published two volumes of short stories—*Gorilla, My Love *(1972) and* The Sea Birds Are Still Alive *(1977)—and a novel,* The Salt Eaters *(1980). Critics commenting on her work have focused on her blend of politics and sexual politics; on the role of gender, family, and community in her stories; and on her awareness of the subjective, personal quality of the world we construct for ourselves. The following story, about black kids from a poor neighborhood coming downtown, makes us see affluent white society through their eyes. It thus turns the tables on the affluent majority, whose spokespersons endlessly study and analyze and report on the children of the poor. A major part of the contrast between the two worlds is set up by the tough street language of the young people, with the story told in what one editor has called "uncondescending, witty, poetic Black English."*

Thought Starters: How often do you cross over from an affluent part of town to a poor part of town or vice versa? What is your business there? What do you observe? What are your feelings?

Back in the days when everyone was old and stupid or young and foolish and me and Sugar were the only ones just right, this lady moved on our block with nappy hair and proper speech and no makeup. And quite naturally we laughed at her, laughed the way we did at the junk man who went about his business like he was some big-time president and his sorry-ass horse his secretary. And we kinda hated her too, hated the way we did the winos who cluttered up our parks and pissed on our handball walls and stank up our hallways and stairs so you couldn't halfway play hide-and-seek without a goddamn gas mask. Miss Moore was her name. The only woman on the block with no first name. And she was black as hell, cept for her feet, which were fish-white and spooky. And she was always planning these boring-ass things for us to do, us being my cousin, mostly, who lived on the block cause we all moved North the same time and to the same apartment then spread out gradual to breathe. And our parents would yank our heads into some kinda shape and crisp up our clothes so we'd be presentable for travel with Miss Moore, who always looked like she was going to church, though she never did. Which is just one of the things the grownups talked about when they talked behind her back like a dog. But when she came calling with some sachet she'd sewed up or some gingerbread she'd made or some book, why then they'd all be too embarrassed to turn her down and we'd get handed over all spruced up. She'd been to college and said it was only right that she should take responsibility for the young ones' education, and she not even related by marriage or blood. So they'd go for it. Specially Aunt Gretchen. She was the main gofer in the family. You got some ole dumb shit foolishness you want somebody to go for, you send for Aunt Gretchen. She been screwed into the go-along for so long, it's a blood-deep natural thing with her. Which is how she got saddled with me and Sugar and Junior in the first place while our mothers were in a la-de-da apartment up the block having a good ole time.

So this one day Miss Moore rounds us all up at the mailbox and it's pure-dee hot and she's knockin herself out about arithmetic. And school suppose to let up in summer I heard, but she don't never let up. And the starch in my pinafore scratching the shit outta me and I'm really hating this nappy-head bitch and her goddamn college degree. I'd much rather go to the pool or to the show where it's cool. So me and Sugar leaning on the mailbox being surly, which is a Miss Moore word. And Flyboy checking out what everybody brought for lunch. And Fat Butt already wasting his peanut-butter-and-jelly sandwich like the pig he is. And Junebug punchin on Q.T.'s arm for potato chips. And Rosie Giraffe shifting from one hip to the other waiting for somebody to step on her foot or ask her if she from Georgia so she can kick ass, preferably Mercedes'. And Miss Moore asking us do we know what money is, like we a bunch of retards. I mean real money, she say, like it's only poker chips or monopoly papers we lay on the grocer. So right away I'm tired of this and say so. And would much rather snatch Sugar and go to the Sunset and terrorize the West Indian kids and take their hair ribbons and their money too. And Miss Moore files that remark away for next week's lesson on brotherhood. I can tell. And finally I say we oughta get to the subway cause it's cooler and besides we might meet some cute boys. Sugar done swiped her mama's lipstick, so we ready.

So we heading down the street and she's boring us silly about what things cost and what our parents make and how much goes for rent and how money ain't divided up right in this country. And then she gets to the part about we all poor and live in the slums, which I don't feature. And I'm ready to speak on that, but she steps out in the street and hails two cabs just like that. Then she hustles half the crew in with her and hands me a five-dollar bill and tells me to calculate 10 percent tip for the driver. And we're off. Me and Sugar and Junebug and Flyboy hangin out the window and hollering to everybody, putting lipstick on each other cause Flyboy a faggot anyway, and making farts with our sweaty armpits. But I'm mostly trying to figure how to spend this money. But they all fascinated with the meter ticking and Junebug starts laying bets as to how much it'll read when Flyboy can't hold his breath no more. Then Sugar lays bets as to how much it'll be when we get there. So I'm stuck. Don't nobody want to go for my plan, which is to jump out at the next light and run off to the first bar-b-que we can find. Then the driver tells us to get the hell out cause we there already. And the meter reads eighty-five cents. And I'm stalling to figure out the tip and Sugar say give him a dime. And I decide he don't need it bad as I do, so later for him. But then he tries to take off with Junebug foot still in the door so we talk about his mama something ferocious. Then we check out that we on Fifth Avenue and everybody dressed up in stockings. One lady in a fur coat, hot as it is. White folks crazy.

"This is the place," Miss Moore say, presenting it to us in the voice she uses at the museum. "Let's look in the windows before we go in."

"Can we steal?" Sugar asks very serious like she's getting the ground rules squared away before she plays. "I beg your pardon," say Miss Moore, and we fall out. So she leads us around the windows of the toy store and me and Sugar screamin, "This is mine, that's mine, I gotta have that, that was made for me, I was born for that," till Big Butt drowns us out.

"Hey, I'm goin to buy that there."

"That there? You don't even know what it is, stupid."

"I do so," he say punchin on Rosie Giraffe. "It's a microscope."

"Whatcha gonna do with a microscope, fool?"

"Look at things."

"Like what, Ronald?" ask Miss Moore. And Big Butt ain't got the first notion. So here go Miss Moore gabbing about the thousands of bacteria in a drop of water and the somethinorother in a speck of blood and the million and one living things in the air around us is invisible to the naked eye. And what she say that for? Junebug go to town on that "naked" and we rolling. Then Miss Moore ask what it cost. So we all jam into the window smudgin it up and the price tag say $300. So then she ask how long'd take for Big Butt and Junebug to save up their allowances. "Too long," I say. "Yeh," adds Sugar, "outgrown it by that time." And Miss Moore say no, you never outgrow learning instruments. "Why, even medical students and interns and," blah, blah, blah. And we ready to choke Big Butt for bringing it up in the first damn place.

"This here costs four hundred eighty dollars," says Rosie Giraffe. So we pile up all over her to see what she pointin out. My eyes tell me it's a chunk of glass cracked with something heavy, and different-color inks dripped into the splits, then the whole thing put into a oven or something. But for $480 it don't make sense.

"That's a paperweight made of semi-precious stones fused together under tremendous pressure," she explains slowly, with her hands doing the mining and all the factory work.

"So what's a paperweight?" asks Rosie Giraffe.

"To weigh paper with, dumbbell," say Flyboy, the wise man from the East.

"Not exactly," say Miss Moore, which is what she say when you warm or way off too. "It's to weigh paper down so it won't scatter and make your desk untidy." So right away me and Sugar curtsy to each other and then to Mercedes who is more the tidy type.

"We don't keep paper on top of the desk in my class," say Junebug, figuring Miss Moore crazy or lyin one.

"At home, then," she say. "Don't you have a calendar and pencil case and a blotter and a letter-opener on your desk at home where you do your homework?" And she know damn well what our homes look like cause she nosys around in them every chance she gets.

"I don't even have a desk," say Junebug. "Do we?"

"No. And I don't get no homework neither," says Big Butt.   20

"And I don't even have a home," say Flyboy like he do at school to keep the white folks off his back and sorry for him. Send this poor kid to camp posters, is his specialty.

"I do," says Mercedes. "I have a box of stationery on my desk and a picture of my cat. My godmother bought the stationery and the desk. There's a big rose on each sheet and the envelopes smell like roses."

"Who wants to know about your smelly-ass stationery," say Rosie Giraffe fore I can get my two cents in.

"It's important to have a work area all your own so that . . ."

"Will you look at this sailboat, please," say Flyboy, cuttin her off and   25
pointin to the thing like it was his. So once again we tumble all over each other to gaze at this magnificent thing in the toy store which is just big enough to maybe sail two kittens across the pond if you strap them to the posts tight. We all start reciting the price tag like we in assembly. "Handcrafted sailboat of fiberglass at one thousand one hundred ninety-five dollars."

"Unbelievable," I hear myself say and am really stunned. I read it again for myself just in case the group recitation put me in a trance. Same thing. For some reason this pisses me off. We look at Miss Moore and she lookin at us, waiting for I dunno what.

"Who'd pay all that when you can buy a sailboat set for a quarter at Pop's, a tube of glue for a dime, and a ball of string for eight cents? It must have a motor and a whole lot else besides," I say. "My sailboat cost me about fifty cents."

"But will it take water?" say Mercedes with her smart ass.

"Took mine to Alley Pond Park once," say Flyboy. "String broke. Lost it. Pity."

"Sailed mine in Central Park and it keeled over and sank. Had to ask   30
my father for another dollar."

"And you got the strap," laugh Big Butt. "The jerk didn't even have a string on it. My old man wailed on his behind."

Little Q.T. was staring hard at the sailboat and you could see he wanted it bad. But he too little and somebody'd just take it from him. So what the hell. "This boat for kids, Miss Moore?"

"Parents silly to buy something like that just to get all broke up," say Rosie Giraffe.

"That much money it should last forever," I figure.

"My father'd buy it for me if I wanted it."   *35*

"Your father, my ass," say Rosie Giraffe getting a chance to finally push Mercedes.

"Must be rich people shop here," say Q.T.

"You are a very bright boy," say Flyboy. "What was your first clue?" And he rap him on the head with the back of his knuckles, since Q.T. the only one he could get away with. Though Q.T. liable to come up behind you years later and get his licks in when you half expect it.

"What I want to know is," I says to Miss Moore though I never talk to her, I wouldn't give the bitch that satisfaction, "is how much a real boat costs? I figure a thousand'd get you a yacht any day."

"Why don't you check that out," she says, "and report back to the   *40* group?" Which really pains my ass. If you gonna mess up a perfectly good swim day least you could do is have some answers. "Let's go in," she say like she got something up her sleeve. Only she don't lead the way. So me and Sugar turn the corner to where the entrance is, but when we get there I kinda hang back. Not that I'm scared, what's there to be afraid of, just a toy store. But I feel funny, shame. But what I got to be shamed about? Got as much right to go in as anybody. But somehow I can't seem to get hold of the door, so I step away from Sugar to lead. But she hangs back too. And I look at her and she looks at me and this is ridiculous. I mean, damn, I have never ever been shy about doing nothing or going nowhere. But when Mercedes steps up and then Rosie Giraffe and Big Butt crowd in behind and shove, and next thing we all stuffed into the doorway with only Mercedes squeezing past us, smoothing out her jumper and walking right down the aisle. Then the rest of us tumble in like a glued-together jigsaw done all wrong. And people lookin at us. And it's like the time me and Sugar crashed into the Catholic church on a dare. But once we got in there and every-thing so hushed and holy and the candles and the bowin and the handker-chiefs on all the drooping heads, I just couldn't go through with the plan. Which was for me to run up to the altar and do a tap dance while Sugar played the nose flute and messed around in the holy water. And Sugar kept givin me the elbow. Then later teased me so bad I tied her up in the shower and turned it on and locked her in. And she'd be there till this day if Aunt Gretchen hadn't finally figured I was lyin about the boarder takin a shower.

Same thing in the store. We all walkin on tiptoe and hardly touchin the games and puzzles and things. And I watched Miss Moore who is steady watchin us like she waitin for a sign. Like Mama Drewery watches the sky and sniffs the air and takes note of just how much slant is in the bird for-mation. Then me and Sugar bump smack into each other, so busy gazing at the toys, specially the sailboat. But we don't laugh and go into our fat-lady bump-stomach routine. We just stare at that price tag. Then Sugar run a finger over the whole boat. And I'm jealous and want to hit her. Maybe not her, but I sure want to punch somebody in the mouth.

"Watcha bring us here for, Miss Moore?"

"You sound angry, Sylvia. Are you mad about something?" Givin me one of them grins like she tellin a grown-up joke that never turns out to be funny. And she's lookin very closely at me like maybe she planning to do my portrait from memory. I'm mad, but I won't give her that satisfaction. So I slouch around the store bein very bored and say, "Let's go."

Me and Sugar at the back of the train watchin the tracks whizzin by large then small then getting gobbled up in the dark. I'm thinkin about this tricky toy I saw in the store. A clown that somersaults on a bar then does chin-ups just cause you yank lightly at his leg. Cost $35. I could see me askin my mother for a $35 birthday clown. "You wanna who that costs what?" she'd say, cocking her head to the side to get a better view of the hole in my head. Thirty-five dollars could buy new bunk beds for Junior and Gretchen's boy. Thirty-five dollars and the whole household could go visit Granddaddy Nelson in the country. Thirty-five dollars would pay for the rent and the piano bill too. Who are these people that spend that much for performing clowns and $1000 for toy sailboats? What kinda work they do and how they live and how come we ain't in on it? Where we are is who we are, Miss Moore always pointin out. But it don't necessarily have to be that way, she always adds then waits for somebody to say that poor people have to wake up and demand their share of the pie and don't none of us know what kind of pie she talking about in the first damn place. But she ain't so smart cause I still got her four dollars from the taxi and she sure ain't gettin it. Messin up my day with this shit. Sugar nudges me in my pocket and winks.

Miss Moore lines us up in front of the mailbox where we started from, seem like years ago, and I got a headache for thinkin so hard. And we lean all over each other so we can hold up under the draggy-ass lecture she always finishes us off with at the end before we thank her for borin us to tears. But she just looks at us like she readin tea leaves. Finally she say, "Well, what did you think of F. A. O. Schwarz?"

Rosie Giraffe mumbles, "White folks crazy."

"I'd like to go there again when I get my birthday money," says Mercedes, and we shove her out the pack so she has to lean on the mailbox by herself.

"I'd like a shower. Tiring day," say Flyboy.

Then Sugar surprises me by sayin, "You know, Miss Moore, I don't think all of us here put together eat in a year what that sailboat costs." And Miss Moore lights up like somebody goosed her. "And?" she say, urging Sugar on. Only I'm standin on her foot so she don't continue.

"Imagine for a minute what kind of society it is in which some people can spend on a toy what it would cost to feed a family of six or seven. What do you think?"

"I think," say Sugar pushing me off her feet like she never done before, cause I whip her ass in a minute, "that this is not much of a democracy if you ask me. Equal chance to pursue happiness means an equal crack at the dough, don't it?" Miss Moore is besides herself and I am disgusted with Sugar's treachery. So I stand on her foot one more time to see if she'll shove me. She shuts up, and Miss Moore looks at me, sorrowfully I'm thinkin. And somethin weird is goin on, I can feel it in my chest.

"Anybody else learn anything today?" lookin dead at me. I walk away and Sugar has to run to catch up and don't even seem to notice when I shrug her arm off my shoulder.

"Well, we got four dollars anyway," she says.

"Uh hunh."

"We could go to Hascombs and get half a chocolate layer and then   55
go to the Sunset and still have plenty money for potato chips and ice cream sodas."

"Uh hunh."

"Race you to Hascombs," she say.

We start down the block and she gets ahead which is O.K. by me cause I'm going to the West End and then over to the Drive to think this day through. She can run if she want to and even run faster. But ain't nobody gonna beat me at nuthin.

The Responsive Reader

1. How would you describe the world of the tough street kids in this story? Are poor kids different from rich kids? Are the kids in this story different from other poor kids? How?
2. What is the "lesson" the young people in the group learn when they come to the toy store?
3. What role does Miss Moore play in the story? How do her students relate to their teacher? How do you?
4. What are key features of the tough street language used in this story? Do you find the profanity offensive? Why or why not?

Talking, Listening, Writing

5. Where are you in this story? Or does this story have nothing to do with you?
6. Do you think this story is too preachy or the moral too obvious?
7. Why do people talk tough? How "tough" are the kids in this story?
8. Would you describe your own community as divided along lines of class or of poverty and wealth? How are the lines drawn?
9. You may want to tell your classmates a personal story or write a paper from your personal experience leading up to "Ain't nobody gonna beat me at nuthin" or a similar punchline.

STAMPS

Bethlyn Madison Webster

> *Bethlyn Madison Webster was working as a part-time teacher when she published the following poem. Like many modern poets, she focuses on what she observes and lets it largely speak for itself. She finds meaning in what a more casual observer might have considered just a very ordinary event—a routine transaction in the checkout line at the grocery store. The poem tells a story with a point. However, the reader has to do any overt editorializing or spell out more fully the message that is implied in the poem.*

Thought Starters: Have you ever had to accept charity? Have you ever had to ask others for support? What were your feelings? What went through your mind? In retrospect, how do you feel about the experience?

I'm watching the woman   *1*
who is watching my groceries
rolling along the conveyor belt.
She stands Cheerio-mouthed
in a pink and white dress   *5*
sporting a crisp, curled hairdo
and staring as much as she pleases
while I stand behind my husband,
hiding behind him and the baby.
She has seen him produce   *10*
a book of foodstamps
from his pocket, and I think she wants
to see how her tax dollars
are being wasted today.
Eggs, milk, peanut butter, bread   *15*
root beer and a bag of store brand
chocolate chips. She looks
at those the longest.
I want to tell her that we work
for ten cents above minimum.   *20*
I want to explain
that it's Friday, we're tired,
and our chocolate is none of her business.
Somehow, we're on display
along with the tabloids and gum.   *25*

With long pink-nailed fingertips,
she puts her stuff up now:
a big red rib-eye steak
a head of green lettuce,
the leafy kind, and a bottle of merlot.   *30*
Our total is rung
and my husband pays.
The checker lays the coupons upside-down,
like a blackjack hand,
and pounds them with a rubber stamp.   *35*

The Responsive Reader

1. People complaining about dull reading often say that it is as dull as a grocery list or a laundry list. How can you tell that the poet did not intend
   the grocery lists in this poem to be dull or irrelevant? For you, what are
   the most telling or the most striking details in this poem?
2. Who are you in this poem—the food stamp recipient, the affluent customer, or the checker? Or do you see yourself as an outside observer
   who is not "involved"? Why do you identify the way you do?

Talking, Listening, Writing

3. Poets often focus on something that has a larger symbolic meaning. Are
   the food stamps a symbol in this poem? How would you spell out their
   possible symbolic meaning?

Collaborative Projects

4. Much welfare reform has meant the loss of benefits to large numbers of
   Americans. The food stamp programs that for many years helped feed
   poor families were severely cut back. *Time* magazine reported that 40
   percent or more of disabled children stood to lose the supplementary social security payments that helped their families. You may want to team
   up with classmates to investigate the history, the politics, and the impact
   of cutbacks in one major area of the "welfare state" or the "social safety
   net" in our society.

FORUM: *Disparity of Wealth*

> *At Colonel Sanders' Kentucky Fried Chicken restaurant, there used to be 10 to 15 people, including myself, looking for food in the garbage every night.*
>
> *Former homeless person now working at a Catholic soup kitchen*

What became of the promise of equal opportunity? Is anyone still talking about the "level playing field"? In the words of one observer, "a drop that looks more and more like one wall of the Grand Canyon separates the top economic tenth from the rest of the population."

In 1848, the great conservative British politician Benjamin Disraeli published a book warning that England was becoming "two nations." New technologies and expanding trade had created a newly rich upper crust living in magnificent mansions. Increasingly, an impoverished industrial working class lived in crowded, disease-ridden slums. Today, in a new era of free-for-all capitalism, many observers again see a widening gulf between the rich and the poor. They see the CEO of a large bank taking successive ten-million-dollar bonuses after reducing his tellers to part-time jobs, taking away their pension rights and health benefits, thwarting their hopes of owning a home or helping their children share in the American Dream. They see ballplayers signed to multimillion-dollar contracts while food stamps are taken away from America's poorest families.

After the spectacular bankruptcy of a major energy-producing company, chief executives walked away with hundreds of millions of dollars in last-minute bonuses and insiders' stock sales while loyal employees—who had invested their lives and their savings in the company—found that their stock was worth nothing and that their retirement plans were worth less than five cents on the dollar. A high-government official who had repeatedly consulted with top executives of the now-defunct company on government energy policy had earned a reported $58 million during his last year in private industry. At the same time, a scholar in a conservative think tank funded from industry sources published an article on the adverse results of raising the minimum wage.

A student researching the gap between the rich and the poor in our "winner-takes-all" society reported numbers like the following:

In 1975 about 20 percent of the nation's net worth was held by the top 1 percent of households; today 36 percent is. (*U.S. News & World Report*)

A 24-year-old basketball star signed a contract for six years for $120 million.

By the middle-nineties, U.S. executives were paid $224 for every dollar earned by a worker. (*Chronicle of Higher Education*)

CNN doubled the salary of talk-show host Larry King by signing him to a five-year, $7 million contract while at the same time laying off 70 employees in a cost-cutting move.

Are we accepting the huge disparity of wealth as simply an economic fact of life in a democratic society?

CLASS STRUGGLE ON THE REFRIGERATOR

Adair Lara

Adair Lara is a columnist who writes in an amusing, informal way about the challenges of everyday life—family, school, work, relatives. In this column, she looks at indicators of social status—telltale signs revealing the underlying class structure of a society that prides itself on not having rigid social barriers. She makes us think about distinctions for which Americans may not always have sociological labels or official categories, but that people sense nevertheless and that shape their behavior and channel their aspirations.

Thought Starters: Do you think of some people as "low class"? Do you think there is an "upper class" in this country? Do you think of yourself and your friends as "middle class"? Why or why not? If not, do you want to be "middle class"?

I was reading an article [. . .] Steve Rubenstein wrote about a new $6,000 refrigerator that is so fancy it can be told to stop producing ice cubes on the Sabbath. But when Steve pointed out that refrigerator magnets wouldn't stick to its designer wood panels, the salesman sniffed, "We're in a niche. The people who can afford one of our refrigerators may not be the same people who use refrigerator magnets."

I glanced over at our fridge. We bought it new about a year ago for $600. It's white, I think—I really can't be sure because just about every inch of it is covered with photo magnets. I buy the magnets at Office Depot (they're really designed for business cards) and cut up photos to fit them. Over the magnets are invitations, clippings, New Yorker cartoons, movie listings, poems, report cards.

I sighed. Every time I think I've made a successful escape from the working-class thing, there it is again.

I still collect those Cashmere Bouquet soaps from motel rooms. When I worked at a posh style magazine, my boss circled the words "kitchen table" in the lead of a story I was working on and scrawled in the margin, "Our readers don't have kitchen tables."

And I wondered, where then do they read the paper? When I was little, we had not only a kitchen table in our kitchen—it looked suspiciously like the redwood picnic benches down the road at Samuel Taylor Park—but also a couch. I still miss that couch.

I'm a have with the soul of a have-not.

I shop [. . .] at garage sales, trying on brown leather jackets and point-ing out the boxes of wineglasses to Bill, elbowing aside teenagers to offer 15 cents for a 25-cent pair of used Van sneakers.

It's embarrassing, but it's not my fault. My mother did our shopping at a thrift store called the Bargain Box. She liked bargains. "It was only $75 for the pair of you," she told my twin and me once, referring to the bill for our birth at the public clinic.

So I think nothing of wearing other people's castoffs. I only think, "What a perfectly good pair of black Gap jeans. And only a dollar." Two of my sisters opened secondhand clothing shops when they grew up, just switching the side of the counter they were on.

All of us Daly kids are better off than our parents were when we were   *10* kids, but it hasn't sunk in. We all still stockpile toilet paper as if we might run out. My sister Connie just Fed-Ex'ed me a nicely wrapped box of presents in return for a favor, and I unwrapped them to find a toothbrush holder, a knitted grandma hat, a pair of too-small white slippers and a Dick Francis audiotape.

It looked exactly like the stuff you see left over at the end of the day at a garage sale—probably is.

We still kind of go nuts when anything's free. When another sister and I went wine tasting, I noticed her slipping the free chocolates into her pocket and urging me to load up on the free apples. I ignored her, being preoccupied with getting my share of the thimblefuls of wine they were pouring, the cheapskates.

You can take the girl out of the class, but you can't take the class out of the girl. Or, in this case, get anything resembling class into the girl. A boyfriend who was watching me decorate the house for Christmas once in-formed me that it was very working class of me to hang holiday cards from a string across the mantel.

I saw what he meant, but privately I wondered how else I was supposed to demonstrate to visitors that I had received all of these cards. I didn't have enough magnets to put them all on the fridge.

The Responsive Reader

1. For Lara, what are telltale signs of her working-class origins? How does the refrigerator in the title come to play its role as an indicator of social class? What do garage sales and the kind of presents her sister sends have to do with class status? What other indicators of her social background and class status keep cropping up in her essay?
2. Like many Americans of an earlier generation, Lara became an example of social mobility—being "better off than our parents were." Where in her article do you see her in contact with or moving on a new, higher, social level, and with what result?

3. What behaviors explained by their past have Lara and her sister carried over into their new lives? Are they all just amusing? Or might some become a handicap in a career or in social situations?

Talking, Listening, Writing

4. What telltale indicators of social class or social status would you include in pegging the social status of your family or of friends you know well? What is most important or most revealing—for instance, cars, home furnishings, favorite pastimes, shopping habits, personal habits?

5. Americans have often prided themselves on living in a classless society, without the rigid class barriers of traditional societies. Are Americans becoming more class conscious? Are they becoming more separated according to family background, level of schooling, or job opportunities? What major dividing lines or class barriers have you observed?

6. Are most of your friends from the same class or social background as you? Do you feel uncomfortable in the presence of people whose class is different (whether higher or lower), or do you mix easily with people from different backgrounds?

7. Lara says, "I'm a have with the soul of a have-not." What does she mean? Try your hand at writing a journal entry that starts with a line like the following:

    I'm a commuter with the soul of a cowboy.

    I'm an art student on the outside but a farm girl on the inside.

    I just started to play the guitar, but I imagine myself as a rock star.

Collaborative Projects

8. Is America predominantly a middle-class society? Do most people you know think of themselves as middle class? If not, do they aim at becoming middle class? Working with a group, poll or interview classmates, family, or friends. What ideas or criteria do they associate with the term *middle class?* What for them are middle-class homes, jobs, neighborhoods, and people like?

LOCKOUT!

Peter Rothberg

> *Some observers trace the huge disparity of incomes in our society to a winner-takes-all philosophy. In the electronics industry, managers at the top of the economic food chain became billionaires while their temporaries worked for minimal wages and without health plans. Entertainers with megahits sell*

millions of CDs while local musicians providing live entertainment work at poorly paid day jobs to make ends meet. A small elite of highly paid sports superstars commands fantastic salaries while many college athletes never grad-uate and never make it to the big leagues. The following article from Nation *magazine takes you to the unreal world of superstar athletes, taking readers back to a "labor dispute" between millionaire owners and millionaire employ-ees. The author was also the producer of* RadioNation, *a weekly syndicated radio program.*

Thought Starters: Do you pay attention to reports of multimillion-dollar deals negotiated for outstanding sports figures and their agents? What are some recent examples?

The National Basketball Association is about to lose its distinction as   1
the only major sports league never to lose a game to labor strife. On July 1,
the owners locked out the players and suspended all league business until the
two parties sign a new labor accord.

The key issue is the salary cap, which under the 1995 contract was not
to exceed 51.8 percent of total revenues—said revenues hitting $1.7 billion
last season. The owners say salaries have skyrocketed to 57 percent, and now
insist on eliminating what's known as the Larry Bird Exception. This allows
teams to re-sign their own free agents at any price over and above the cap.
This is how the Chicago Bulls were able to pay Michael Jordan $33 million
last year even though the supposed cap for an entire team of twelve was set
at $26.9 million. The players' union sees any closing of this loophole as an
unacceptable giveback. As Billy Hunter, its executive director, explains,
"Our position is if you don't want to pay it, just don't do it. Just say no."
The owners' position, in effect, is that they can't say no; that with thirteen
of the twenty-nine NBA teams having lost money last season, they need to
be saved from themselves. The union counters that no more than four or
five teams are in the red and that the owners have to be accountable for the
salaries they themselves mete out. Would the owners favor a cap on their
stock options?

Such free-market arguments notwithstanding, it's clear that the current salary structure makes it difficult for small-market teams—with less
TV money, lower ticket prices and smaller shares of merchandising revenue—to compete. It's also true that the NBA's lowest-tier players are being
squeezed by the astronomical salaries commanded by the mega-stars. Last
year about 120 players (more than 20 percent) earned the league minimum
of $272,500, while thirteen earned more than $10 million each. Currently
9 percent of the players earn 82 percent of the approximately $1 billion in
salaries.

The league has proposed forbidding any one player from earning more than 30 percent of his team's available cap. This would make for some pay equity by forcing salaries down at the highest end, but the union opposes it, arguing that stratospheric salaries for stars ultimately mean higher wages for all. Although the union favors a raised minimum wage for veterans, its version of trickle-down economics is as dubious as the one Reagan peddled to the country.

The fortunes of professional athletes were not always thus. As workers they were late in organizing, and just a generation ago they were bound forever to the team that first signed them. The so-called reserve clause, which applied in basketball as well as in baseball, football and hockey, stripped them of any effective bargaining power. Even a legend like Joe DiMaggio was forced to take pay cuts at the peak of his career. Things changed with Curt Flood, a hero of the 1964 and 1967 champion St. Louis Cardinals and a hero for labor. He challenged the reserve clause in court, lost and was blackballed from Major League Baseball. But his loss set the ball rolling, and in 1976 the courts struck down the clause, and free-agency was born.

The irony today is that while a Michael Jordan need never worry about a pay cut, his union's star-driven strategy may engender class division among the players. With its emphasis on maintaining the salaries of stars like union president Patrick Ewing—scheduled to earn $18 million with the Knicks—and few prescriptions to redress income disparities, the union player reps' meetings are sure to become interesting in the months ahead. More ironic is that just three years ago, many of these same stars—urged on by powerful agents like David Falk, who represents Ewing, Jordan and numerous other big-money players—tried to decertify the union when the former leadership supported an agenda deemed insensitive to the needs of the league's top earners. (Jordan himself was openly contemptuous of the union then; now he's all for it.)

But as they battle over how their pie is sliced, both the stars and the owners are making a big mistake in assuming that the NBA will forever have the fan base to sustain the incomes they've all come to expect. The signposts are visible. Nike, Reebok and Fila, whose profits have risen in tandem with the popularity of the NBA, took million-dollar losses in the last quarter and all have started dropping NBA endorsers faster than Allen Iverson drops defenders. The Starter Corporation, maker of NBA apparel, reported a loss of nearly $40 million in sales last year. The NBA regular season is already largely uninspiring, and the economics of the business make it difficult for teams to maintain a core of players that fans can get to know and love. The marketing and packaging of the NBA and, yes, the crazy salaries have led to a glittery product long on flash but short on fundamentals and passion.

Longtime fans have become increasingly alienated by the transformation of their sport into glam entertainment. No one at the top cares, though, as long as the corporate boxes keep selling and ticket prices keep rising (by more than 25 percent since 1995). So what if lifelong fans are leaving their seats in droves. There's still a waiting list for tickets, and the kids priced out of the games can still buy Bulls jackets.

The Responsive Reader

1. What do you learn here about the world of big-league finance? For the benefit of classmates who are not sports fans, can you explain the workings of the salary cap—and the exceptions to the salary cap? What was a reserve clause, and what does *free agency* mean?
2. How do you interpret the mind-boggling statistics about the players' salaries? What for you is the main point? In the contest between owners and players, does the author take sides? Whose?
3. According to Rothberg, what effect has the big-money economics of professional basketball had on the sport? What does he see as the long-range effects on relations between teams and their fan base? What light does he throw on the relations between the teams and their big-money corporate sponsors?

Talking, Listening, Writing

4. Critics sometimes call current sky-high executive salaries obscene. Would you ever call the "stratospheric salaries" of star athletes similar names? Why or why not? How would you justify them, or how would you challenge them?
5. A Catholic university in California was criticized for accepting Nike as a big-money sponsor for its athletic teams. Nike had been the target of widely publicized charges of exploiting women and children working in substandard conditions in Third World countries. Do you think collegiate teams should be held responsible for the business ethics of their corporate sponsors?

Collaborative Projects

6. Publications like *Forbes* magazine and *Business Week* publish statistics on the country's highest-paid executives. *Rolling Stone* and similar publications track data on the highest-paid media stars. Publications like *Sports Illustrated* publish similar numbers on the income of sports celebrities. You may want to team up with classmates to compile income statistics on the newly rich published in *Time* magazine and other establishment publications.

OBSCENELY HIGH PAYOUT TO DEPARTING CHIEF

Ken Garcia

The business pages of the nation's newspapers and the newsletters of brokerage houses celebrate the exploits of a new brand of "tough-guy" executives who earn their million-dollar bonuses by ruthless cost cutting. They bypass labor unions by outsourcing work to low-wage, no-benefits nonunion labor. As the executive who is the subject of the following newspaper column did, they earn multimillion-dollar annual bonuses by reducing thousands of employees to the status of temporaries with "flexible scheduling," taking away their pension rights and the health plans for them and their families. They engineer mergers and takeovers that prove a bonanza for lawyers, accountants, and executives while abolishing thousands of jobs for employees. Only rarely are journalists as openly critical as Ken Garcia of the modern "take-no-prisoners" corporate chieftains. The institution that was "sold down the river" was the Bank of America, founded in 1904 by A. P. Giannini as a bank catering to Italian immigrants. The story goes that Giannini would loan five dollars at a time to help poor women defray the costs of pregnancy and childbirth.

Thought Starters: Banks and bankers have long played a special role as villains in American folklore and American politics. Why? Do any of the traditional stereotypes or resentments survive for the current generation?

David Coulter will probably not even be a footnote in San Francisco   *1*
history. He has no real claim to fame. Five years from now most people
won't remember his name.

But they should. For Coulter has left a black mark on San Francisco
that previous mayors and hundreds of other elected officials couldn't begin
to touch. And for his disloyalty to the city, he's about to walk away with a
severance package of as much as $100 million.

Coulter, until Tuesday, was the CEO of a formerly proud San Francisco institution known as Bank of America. It was the bank that helped
rebuild the city after the 1906 earthquake, and the corporation that has probably employed more city residents than any other local business this century.

BofA in many respects was San Francisco, a great financial institution
that took pride and interest in its home by the bay. It withstood global economic surges and the era of hostile takeovers—at least until Coulter came
into town and decided to sell the bank for so many shares of silver.

To Coulter it was an investment thing—bigger was better. Sure,   *5*
8,000 or 10,000 people would have to lose their jobs, but that's business
in the modern age. It's about stock, and market share and compensation
packages.

And people? Well, there are sacrifices to be made.

"The potential exists for efficiencies in the combined expense base," was the bank's original way of explaining why so many workers needed to lose their jobs in a merger that will create a $600 billion bank. And then, more recently, Coulter announced that BofA would no longer refer to its workers as employees, but rather as associates—so much easier to end an association than to terminate an employee.

After Coulter sold Bank of America to NationsBank of Charlotte, N.C., this year, it was reported that his employment agreement was worth between $50 million and $100 million, whether he stayed or left.

It was called one of the biggest compensation packages in the history of American business. And according to one compensation consultant, if Coulter decided to stay on to help run the new mega-bank "he should be fired for stupidity."

That won't be a problem now, since Coulter resigned this week rather 10
than wait to be pushed from his corporate sky rise after leading the bank to a 50 percent plunge in earnings, one of the biggest slumps in its history. And Coulter's punishment for selling BofA down the river and shortchanging millions of customers? Riches beyond avarice and no looking back.

The Chronicle reported . . . that when Coulter brokered the deal to sell Bank [of] America to NationsBank in April, it was widely assumed that he might succeed Hugh McColl as CEO of the combined bank. But since Coulter's employment agreement gave him the same whether he stayed or left, the only incentive he had to stay on was to oversee the final sellout of one of the city's oldest institutions.

That will now fall to other executives, most of whom are based in Charlotte, which is now the real headquarters for the bank A.P. Giannini started in North Beach. Many of BofA's top executives have jumped ship, raking in tens of millions in return for their resignations.

McColl said in a press release that it was "painful" to have to accept Coulter's resignation—apparently so difficult that he had stopped taking Coulter's telephone calls.

Nothing personal, mind you. Strictly business.

Now that Coulter is gone, about the only thing remaining from the 15
old BofA is its name and its gleaming corporate tower on California Street.

Coulter tried to deal with the criticism that McColl stole San Francisco's premier bank by suggesting it was a pre-emptive strike to deal with the merger mania then gripping the world's investment centers. But since customer service has already taken a dive and the bank's earnings dropped, it would appear that the real benefit went to those who sold, not to those who stayed.

After almost every mega–bank merger, fees have increased and the level of personal interaction has diminished. A few financial gurus originally touted the BofA-NationsBank merger, saying it would increase the number of services available to patrons. So far, though, the greatest asset in the merger appears to be the ability of bank customers to use their ATM cards at 15,000 machines in 22 states—which at one point meant that customers from each bank could be billed by the other for using their machines.

So BofA is now being run by a Southern shark who likens himself to General George S. Patton, and NationsBank's control over a San Francisco institution is almost complete. The bank's earnings are in a nose-dive and the mood in BofA's executive suites is said to be close to shock.

And all Coulter has to show for it is a lousy $100 million. What a painful way to end an association.

Now you know why the black granite sculpture outside BofA's for- *20* mer headquarters is often referred to as the "banker's heart." It might be appropriate soon to begin engraving it with names.

The Responsive Reader

1. What does Garcia consider the crucial facts in Coulter's story? How would you sum up his estimate of the impact on the community? How would you sum up Garcia's attitude toward the business executives involved? Would you call him "antibusiness"?
2. Do you know of businesses that are a source of local pride or are part of local or regional history? Do you or people you know feel loyal to local merchants or institutions? Does it matter to you whether the profits from businesses you support stay in the community or whether they go to people outside your community or your state?

Talking, Listening, Writing

3. Do you think community spirit and loyalty to employees should play a role in business decisions? Or should they be overruled by the bottom line and the obligation to increase "shareholder value"?
4. When you have a choice as a consumer, do you support small local business or big outside corporations? When buying a book or a cup of coffee, would you rather turn to an independent business or to an outlet that is part of a large chain?
5. Like other journalists, Ken Garcia invites readers to respond by e-mail to his column. At the time he wrote this column, his e-mail address was garciak@sfgate.com. What would you say if you wrote him a note in response?

Find It on the Web

Establishment publications like *Forbes* magazine print annual lists of the top 100 richest people in America. Gadfly publications print lists like the *Mother Jones* list of "The Top 400 Rich White Guys, and the way their multimillion-dollar campaign contributions influence political elections. You may want to do a quick-search on the Internet for recent updates of these or similar lists.

YOU CAN'T GET BY ON NICKELS AND DIMES

Molly Ivins

> *Molly Ivins is a sharp-tongued Texas columnist who has been a sharp-eyed critic of the good-ole-boy Texas legislature. A favorite target of her biting sense of humor is what she sees as a basic issue in America—the way we rely on Big Money to finance elections. In her view, what's wrong with American government is the extent to which rich people and their paid operatives run the country. In the following book review, Ivins pays tribute to a fellow social critic and kindred spirit. Barbara Ehrenreich has published widely in opinion makers' publications from* Ms. *and* Mother Jones *to the* New York Times, *the* New Republic, *the* Atlantic Monthly, *and the* Nation. *She has long been an effective voice of the women's movement, chronicling the progression from the image of an independent woman as a "disheveled radical" to the new stereotype of the career woman, carrying an attaché case and "skilled in discussing market shares and leveraged buyouts." In one of the two books recommended in this review, Ehrenreich reports on her experience trying to live on the wages of America's pink-collar workers.*

Thought Starters: Have you or people you know well ever been part of the "service industries"? What is it like to work as a server, maid, gardener, house cleaner, or other kind of helper or attendant? What do you think would be the best and the worst of the job?

What a glorious year for the summer reading list! Enough gems to   *1*
stock any list—fiction and non-, funny and tragic, sometimes both simultaneously; plus a perfect plethora of peppy public policy books.

But there are two books I especially want to recommend, both by women I admire and know slightly: "Nickel and Dimed" by Barbara Ehrenreich and "Washington" by the late Meg Greenfield of the Washington Post. If you read them in conjunction, it more than doubles the strength of each.

Ehrenreich's book, it seems to me, is the stronger of the two. She did what reporters used to do before they became so unbearably self-important: She reports what the society actually looks like from the bottom. Starting in 1998, she went out and got successive and sometimes simultaneous no-skills, close-to-minimum wage jobs and tried to make it from one month to the next. She couldn't do it. As she so painfully shows, the joker in the deck for low-wage workers is the cost of housing.

The reason you don't hear much about it is that the official poverty rate has remained, as Ehrenreich puts it, "at a soothingly low 13 percent" for several years. Trouble is, the official poverty rate is calculated by the cost of food, which is relatively inflation-proof. The living-wage movement— to establish a minimum wage based on the true cost of living—puts the true minimum at about $14 an hour. Ehrenreich was working for between $6 and $7, living in everything from trailer parks (an upscale option), to not-so-low-rent apartments, to a dorm.

This is where the system is seriously gamed against low-income work-   5
ers. Ehrenreich observes: "It did not escape my attention, as a temporarily low-income person, that the housing subsidy I normally receive in my real life—over $20,000 a year in the form of a mortgage-interest deduction— would have allowed a truly low-income family to live in relative splendor. . . . If rents are exquisitely sensitive to market forces, wages clearly are not."

She points out that when the rich and poor compete for housing in the same market, the rich always win—thus we get fancy downtown con-dos, McMansions in the suburbs and golf courses galore, but nowhere for low-income workers to live, especially since they are clumped in inner cities and the new jobs are in the "edge cities."

The increase in the cost of housing has been neatly matched by a si-multaneous drop in government support. Expenditures on public housing have fallen since the 1980s, when that prince of social services Ronald Rea-gan was president.

Working more than 40 hours a week at $6-to-$7 an hour in variously priced markets (including a faintly hilarious stint with the Merry Maids housecleaning service in Maine), Ehrenreich found she could not make a no-frills living. She thinks she might have done so in Minneapolis had things fallen out so that she could work weekends as well.

In theory, the working poor have some weapons in what is in fact class warfare in this country: They can organize, and they can vote. Why, in re-ality, they A, can't, and B, don't, is part of the degeneration of democracy.

For a fascinating read on how this works at the other end of the power   10
scale, try Meg Greenfield's posthumous book, "Washington." Greenfield had a great b.s. detector. Her central metaphor for the Capital of the World's Only Remaining Superpower is high school, and it is eerily apt— the same cliques, rivalries, obsession with popularity, peer pressure and eternal presidents of the student council.

The Responsive Reader

1. As summarized by Ivins, what are the basic economics and statistics of the "no-skills, close-to-minium wage" jobs that Ehrenreich researched? Why is the cost of housing "the joker in the deck"? How do the reali-ties of the housing market work against the poor?

2. Have you seen any evidence of the "working poor" trying to organize or of the difficulties they encounter? Do you think it is true that the poor

are the least likely to vote? Who do you think are the people most likely to vote? Do you and your friends vote? Why or why not?

3. Meg Greenfield was a respected senior nationally syndicated columnist. Do you think it is disrespectful to say that she had "a great b.s. detector"? From what you see of Washington politics in the media, can you see any parallels between the world of high school and the world of national politics? Can you cite some recent examples or cases in point?

Talking, Listening, Writing

4. In your area, does much construction activity produce luxury apartments, upscale custom homes, and posh fitness clubs or golf clubs? Is there any evidence of a push toward affordable or low-cost housing?

5. Terms like *class warfare* and *the working poor* date back to an earlier period of social conflict, but they have recently come back into use. The term *class warfare,* once a slogan of the political left, is today also used by the political right. How or why? You may want to do a quick-search on the Internet to track current or recent uses of these terms.

Collaborative Projects

6. Working with a group, try to draw up a hypothetical budget for a single mother—with or without child—trying to make it by working forty hours or more at $6 to $7 an hour in your area or community. If you can, draw on the help of accounting or business majors to help you figure deductions from the paycheck and job expenses. Try to be specific about the housing you would try to rent and the food you would be able to buy.

Find It on the Web

Congressional, statewide, or citywide initiatives to raise the minimum wage or to establish a "living wage" trigger heated debates. Who are the advocates, and what are their arguments? Who are the opponents, and what are their arguments?

The following are sample entries from one student's preliminary source list:

Kuttner, Robert. "Boston's Living Wage Law Highlights New Grassroots Efforts to Fight Poverty." *The American Prospect.* 1997. 14 Jan. 2002. <http://www.prospect.org/columns/kuttner/bk970818.html>

Berg, John. Rev. of *A Living Wage: American Workers and the Making of Consumer Society.* John Berg's Book Reviews. 2000. 15 Jan. 2002. <http://world.std.com/~jberg/living wage.html>

"Cost of Living." *The Columbia Encyclopedia.* 6th ed. July 2001. 15 Jan. 2002. <http://www.bartleby.com/65/co/costlivi.html>

Pushing toward a Thesis

What kind of thinking shapes an effective paper? One familiar and productive think scheme finds the common thread in a number of related events. It finds a pattern where at first there was a confusing collection of data. If you get violently ill every time you eat shrimp, you will sooner or later tag shellfish and your allergy to it as the likely culprit. If Asian American students consistently do better than Anglos on a math teacher's tests, she will start looking for some common element in the Asian Americans' backgrounds as the clue to their superior performance.

This kind of thinking is one basic way of moving from fact to **inference**—moving from raw data to what we think they mean. The technical term for thinking that looks for the common element in a set of observations is **induction,** or inductive thinking. If it weren't for inductive thinking, a person allergic to shellfish would keep eating it, and getting sick as a result, forever. Many solidly argued papers line up the examples, the evidence, that all point in the same direction. If it is an effective paper, the reader is likely to say: "Yes, I agree. Looking at the facts or the data, I would have drawn the same conclusion." Typically, the paper presents the general point *early,* as the writer's **thesis**—and then goes on to provide the examples, data, or evidence that led to the general conclusion.

Suppose you ask yourself: "We frequently hear charges of racism—against employers, against the police, against educational institutions. Is racism on the rise?" You look at potentially relevant evidence: the videotape, played over and over on national TV, of a brutal beating of a black motorist by Los Angeles police. You study reports of a multimillion-dollar verdict against a restaurant chain for discriminating against African American customers. If you proceed inductively, you may learn something here that you did not realize before. One student exploring this topic found testimony—by an emergency room physician, by the daughter of an old-style police officer—to the effect that beatings of members of minority groups by police are more common than we like to think. He concluded that what is on the rise is not so much racism as such but our heightened *awareness* of it. Alleged racist behavior and racist incidents, he decided, are "under more intense scrutiny" in our society today than they have been in the past. This conclusion became the thesis of his paper.

Obviously, we never approach an issue with a completely open mind. We have preconceptions—opinions to which we are already more or less firmly committed. We may have jumped to conclusions on the basis of limited firsthand experience. We may have accepted without question what we heard in the family or were taught in school. We may be going along with what is widely believed in a group with which we identify. Inductive thinking kicks in when you are ready to say: "What I think about this issue may be based on hearsay, limited evidence, or groupthink. Let me check this out." The conclusion you reach will still be your opinion—but it will be an *informed* opinion. Your readers may find it worthwhile to think about it, argue with it, or make it their own.

TRIGGERING The need to make sense of a rich array of data is one of the most basic human needs. Here are some situations that may trigger a search for general conclusions:

- *Much writing charts current trends.* When people find that many available jobs are for temporaries or part-timers, without a pension plan or health benefits, they start checking around to see if this is a widespread pattern. Is it true that many steady and well-paid middle-management positions are gone for good? Is it true that many high-wage manufacturing jobs have been replaced by low-wage jobs in Korea or Taiwan?

- *Much writing tests stereotypes or clichés.* For instance, is it true that Americans are incorrigible optimists? (What makes American Peace Corps volunteers go into distant villages thinking they will be able to change age-old patterns of behavior? Was it the experience of getting out from under the stifling tutelage of kings and aristocrats? Was it the experience of being able to start all over somewhere in the wide open spaces of the West? Is the tradition of American optimism wearing thin?)

- *Much writing searches for answers to nagging questions.* For instance, who are the homeless? Assuming that the homeless come from many different backgrounds, what are common factors in their histories? (If we could agree on some conclusions about how they got there, we might be able to agree on ways to keep others from traveling the same route.)

GATHERING When we first explore a topic, we may stumble onto related facts that all seem to point roughly in the same direction. Testing or following up our first hunches, we may soon be able to gather relevant information in a more systematic fashion. If you ask, "What is different about the Japanese?" data like the following may soon begin to tell their own story:

Students graduating from twelfth grade:	Japan	90%
	United States	77%
Average daily hours of homework during high school:	Japan	2.0
	United States	.5
Daily absentee rate:	Japan	very low
	United States	9%
Years required of high school mathematics:	Japan	3
	United States (typical)	1
Years required of foreign language (grades 7–12):	Japan	6
	United States	0–2
Engineering majors in undergraduate population:	Japan	20%
	United States	5%

SHAPING A focused paper or a coherent paragraph often results when the writer has funneled related observations into a general conclusion. In a paragraph like the following, the writer has laid related observations end to end. Her general point provides the **topic sentence** that starts the paragraph:

> *I am often treated as a stereotypical blonde.* I have a soft musical voice. I have always had high grades, and I have worked as a tutor to help other students improve theirs. Still, some people do not take me seriously because of the way I look and sound. I have been told to put up my hair in a bun, wear glasses, quit wearing make-up, and work to lower the pitch of my voice. Men are not the only ones doing the stereotyping. I had a female instructor criticize my voice as unprofessional after an oral report. I had a female student tell me during a group project that my "Barbie doll" voice would make the wrong impression on the audience.

The difference between the thinking that produced this passage and the actual paragraph printed here is a question of what comes first. During the thinking process, we start with the data and then draw a conclusion. However, in most of the writing that presents our findings, we state the general point first and then marshal the evidence that led up to it. When we put the general point first in a paragraph, we call it the topic sentence. When we put the more inclusive or overarching generalization early in a paper, we call it the **thesis**. (Sometimes, you may want to lead your readers up to the general point, simulating the actual process of sorting the data and discovering the common thread.)

Often an effective paper is modeled on the inverted upside-down funnel. What came *out of* the funnel comes first; what went *into* the funnel comes later. The thesis comes first, and then the writer lays out the observations that were funneled into the general conclusion that the thesis sums up. The claim the writer makes comes first; the evidence comes second. The following might be the thesis of a paper about the lack of political involvement among students:

THESIS: A pervasive apathy about political issues marks today's generation of students.

The rest of the paper would then present the evidence that led to this conclusion. Successive paragraphs might focus on points like the following:

- Turnouts for controversial speakers invited to your campus have been small.
- Turnout for elections for student government has been dismal.
- Debates scheduled on topics like AIDS and safe sex have fizzled.
- Few students turned out for special events scheduled to honor minority authors or to recognize outstanding women on campus.

REVISING Whenever you claim to have found a general pattern, you have to guard against jumping to conclusions. Revision is a chance to rethink what your evidence really shows. It is a chance to reword sweeping generalizations. Keep in mind advice like the following:

- *Spell out your thesis.* What exactly are you claiming? It is a weak beginning to start by saying that "certain factors" play a role in prejudice or homelessness. What are they? Which are the most important?

- *Limit your generalizations.* Obviously, readers will question claims that people of one nationality or religion are marvelously more gifted and generous than those from another. Neither will educated readers listen patiently to claims that members of any one group are inherently lazy or violence prone. But less provocative generalizations—about voter apathy, about immigrants on welfare—may also have to be worded more cautiously, with due consideration for exceptions and countertrends. Above all, they will have to be checked against the evidence you are actually able to present.

- *Build your case on representative examples.* Try to present a cross section of relevant instances. Try to listen to a cross section of witnesses, pro and con. Do not build your case on one outstanding case that might turn out to be a freak example.

What general conclusions does the author of the following sample paper present to her readers? What data did she funnel into her paper? How real or convincing are the observations on which she based her findings?

Bodies Betrayed by the Mind

I would do anything to look like a skinny model or a Barbie doll. I used to starve myself for days at a time. I lost a lot of weight, but when I started getting sick and my hair fell out, I started eating and gained it all back. Honestly, if I could, I would stop eating again to be thin, but I physically can't—I get sick instantly. I also have a friend who has severe kidney and mental problems because of anorexia.

The anonymous seventeen-year-old who made this comment represents a feeling and experience common to many young women in the United States.

There are two predominant causes of anorexia and bulimia in young women in particular. Both are a form of social pressure that gives young ladies a standard of beauty to which they feel they need to aspire. "Specialists in eating disorders have concluded that social factors are largely responsible for the rising incidence of eating disorders suffered almost exclusively by young women," claims Larry Percy, a media consultant. The feeling of being pressured is best represented in a health pamphlet on eating disorders that says "guilt about gaining too much weight may develop into fear." At this point the problem has become severe. The causes are not related to food; they are related to how a child has learned to perceive herself and the incessant advertisement of images portraying unnaturally thin women. Thus, many women grow up with a fear of gaining weight and being criticized or belittled by society.

As kids mature they experience waves of competition that either are forgotten or ingrained in them. Parents might be surprised to know that some simple gifts are psychologically harmful to children, like Barbie dolls. Little girls may compare their own bodies with those of the dolls and even begin to compete. Studies have been performed to translate the size of a Barbie doll into a real woman. While the doll's figure varies slightly in size, her waist measurement would not exceed twenty-three inches if human, and would, on average, be closer to seventeen. Her long legs would give her a height ranging from six feet, two inches to seven feet, five inches. A seven foot, five inch Barbie woman would have a bust measurement of thirty-six inches.

When a twelve-year-old compares her body to this popular standard, she is going to be very disappointed and may feel inadequate at a very young age. According to observers of the Barbie phenomenon, not only does Barbie influence women's perceptions of the ideal figure but there are living Barbie fashion models and performers. Laurie Lang of my university's Health Center says, "minority women feel better because they are less visible—I mean, how many black Barbie dolls do you see?"

As young women mature, they are affected more by the media and by images that "define what forms of femininity are acceptable and desirable," according to Larry Percy. Women are faced with models that symbolize how women should look, how they should behave, and how women can expect to be seen by others. Perfection is the ultimate goal. In a Chanel No. 5 perfume ad, there is a picture of French movie idol Catherine Deneuve beside an enlarged bottle of the perfume. She is an ageless, skinny woman with high cheek bones, beautiful eyes, a sexy smile, and gold-colored hair. She also looks very elegant.

"What Catherine Deneuve's face means to us in the world of magazines and films, Chanel No. 5 seeks to mean and comes to mean in the world of consumer goods. It signifies flawless French beauty, which makes it useful as a piece of linguistic currency to sell Chanel," notes Judith Williamson in her piece on decoding advertisements.

As we delve further into the media's images of perfect beauty, we realize that the images are hardly perfect at all. Various studies (including my own) have concluded that the ideal figure of a woman is slimmer than her own; this is also the figure that is most appealing to men. The models in the media often have a hard time portraying the supreme female image because there has been an "image-slimming effect" of over fifty percent since the turn of the century. Freedman quotes one fashion model as saying it took a crew of people to get her into a pair of size three designer jeans and to carry her into position to be photographed: "To look as I did in that ad, you would have to fast for two months and hold your breath for twenty minutes." Using an illustration of ten different female body types numbered from one to ten in size (excluding height), I asked ten women between the ages of sixteen and twenty to show me how they perceive their own body and how they would like to look. Eight out of ten said they would like to have the second to skinniest figure on the chart and the other two, already that skinny, said they would like to remain the same. The eight identified themselves as being three or more body sizes bigger when often that was not the case. Although the interviewees recognized the fact that the "Twiggy" look is an unhealthy look, the common attitude as captured by one woman seems to be, "They aren't healthy yet they're the ideal. I would love to be the ideal; who wouldn't?"

The university has had trouble getting pamphlets on anorexia and bulimia because of the widespread demand from campuses that have a real problem with eating disorders among their students. A little over ten percent of college women have "a pattern of bingeing and purging," while only two percent of men experience this problem. Many young women are known to take unsafe diuretics and "fat burning" pills. Anorexia and bulimia are associated with numerous health problems that can be life-threatening. It is recognized that certain personality types make certain people more susceptible to eating disorders; however, every person is a candidate. As long as women continue to be bombarded with unhealthy standards of nearly unattainable slimness, the number of victims of eating disorders will steadily increase. Sadly, the media seem to persist in imposing these standards of beauty on an impressionable young society.

"When I watch a commercial or a news broadcast and I see a normal-looking spokeswoman, it's shocking!" said a student. The point is valid. Not only have the media caused major health problems and sentiments of insufficiency on the part of women, but they have also begun to measure success, in part, in terms of beauty. Women have to learn to resist this media lure. Women are naturally fatter than men so that they can have babies. Female hormones naturally bind fat cells, giving women breasts and other associated female "swells." If a woman does not interfere with her body's true chemistry is she neither successful nor beautiful? No. She is an individual who recognizes that beauty comes in all forms, shapes, and sizes, and she was probably raised by conscientious parents.

Topics for Papers Drawing Conclusions (A Sampling)

1. What makes "angry white males" angry? Commentators have written much about the political weight carried by angry white males. From what you have seen or heard, what are their most important grievances?
2. To judge from your own observation, is there such a thing as "recreational drug use"—by people who can take it or leave it?
3. What gets young people into trouble with the law? Have you observed common traits or recurrent patterns?
4. Did your high school or does your college have cliques? Is there a common pattern in the behavior of cliques or of the people who belong to them?
5. We hear much talk about dysfunctional families. What do you know about them? What makes them dysfunctional? What are key elements such families seem to share?
6. To judge from your own observation of our society, how large is the gap between the rich and the poor? Is it widening, as many observers say?
7. Do people "stay with their own kind"? On your campus, do people of the same racial or ethnic background flock together? How much mingling is there of people from diverse backgrounds?
8. Is "immigrant-bashing" a sign of the times? How serious or how widespread is anti-immigration sentiment in our society? Is it a factor in your community?
9. What newcomers do well in America? To judge from your own observation, which immigrant groups have the least (or the most) difficulty in adjusting to their new environment?
10. Are good manners dead? Is mean-spirited or loutish behavior part of our culture? For instance, is "road rage" just part of a general decay of good manners?

5

IDENTITY
Rethinking Race

I think that between the Negroes of the South and the women at the North all talking about rights, the white men will be in a fix pretty soon.

—*Sojourner Truth*

Every one of us could write a book about race. The text is already imprinted in our minds and evokes our moral character.

—*Andrew Hacker*

Throughout American history, the promise of equality before the law and in the eyes of God has been invoked by groups denied their place in the sun. Harriet Beecher Stowe's novel *Uncle Tom's Cabin,* which was read by millions around the world, asserted that the African captives who were brought to this country in chains were our sisters and brothers. Therefore, slavery was an abomination in the sight of God.

For anthropologists, the concept of race has no scientific standing. All human beings are members of the same species, capable of intermarrying. In that basic sense, all human beings are "created equal." Skin color varies from very dark in some tropical climates to very pale in some countries of the frozen North. Members of some ethnic groups in Africa tend to be very short; members of other ethnic groups tend to be very tall (and may be sought after by basketball teams).

Nevertheless, the *perception* of race has often played a crucial and at times murderous role in human history. It has been a powerful divisive influence in the history of this country. Slavery was built on the assumption that some races were created inferior. In the minds of many, the bloodiest war in American history was fought to abolish the institution. Whether and how racism survives in contemporary American society is the subject of much debate and of charges and countercharges. A Jewish student reports that in high school she was called "every name that anti-Semites have created: cheap, smart, rich, stuck up, big-nosed, and JAP."

Race is one of the factors, and in recent history perhaps the most deadly one, that keep us from being judged by the "content of our character." Being identified as a member of a group, we encounter expectations, pressures, or barriers visible and invisible. Sometimes, these barriers are crudely obvious, as when a country club does not accept Jews. Sometimes, they are more subtle, as when a prominent journal of opinion consistently devalues or undercuts the black leadership. Many feel that race continues to be the great unresolved challenge to traditional American values.

MIXED LIKE ME

David Bernstein

David Bernstein was a twenty-six-year-old magazine editor in Washington, D.C., when he wrote the following essay. He was one of the "Generation X," or "twenty-something," group of writers included in a collection called Next: Young American Writers on the New Generation *(1994). These writers were born after the great events that had shaped the outlook of an earlier generation: the traumas and divisions of the lost Vietnam War; the struggles and triumphs of the civil rights movement; the militant early years of the women's movement. Living in a post–Cold War world, many of these authors write about outgrowing the think schemes and stereotypes of the past. As Bernstein says, the opening statement of his essay might have sounded provocative thirty years ago; readers today may find it only mildly interesting and "move along." Because of his mixed ethnic parentage, Bernstein is in a unique position to reexamine this country's "way of thinking about race." What is his perspective on the future of race relations in America?*

Thought Starters: What do you think and know about "mixed marriages"? Has intermarriage been an issue in your family or among people you know? Are you aware of changing social attitudes on this topic?

I am a twenty-six-year-old man, half black and half Jewish, who founded and edits a conservative magazine that deals with race relations and culture. Such a statement would have been extraordinary thirty years ago; today we treat it with mild interest and move along. No one would argue that my life has been typical—typical of the "black experience," of the "Jewish experience," or of any other dubious paradigm associated with a particular race or ethnicity. I have not overcome racism or poverty, and people become visibly disappointed when I tell them that my mixed background has not been a cause of distress, or any other difficulty for that matter.

However, my story may be of some interest. For better or worse, America is going to look more and more like me in the next century—that is to say, individuals are going to be walking embodiments of the melting pot. The argument over whether America is more like cheese dip or the multiculturalist "tossed salad" (Are you getting hungry yet?) will be made moot by the increasing incidence of mixed marriage and of the growing class of mutts like me who have more ethnicities than the former Yugoslavia.

My parents married in 1965, in Washington, D.C. If they had lived then in the comfortable suburb where they now reside, they would have been breaking the law—miscegenation, as marriage between blacks and whites was known in those days, was still illegal in Maryland. My mother was a native Washingtonian who, until her teen years, felt sorry for the few white people who lived near her, her mother, and two siblings; she thought they were albinos. Her parents—both of whom had moved from the country to Washington when they were teenagers—were separated when my mother was just a toddler. She was raised, along with an older sister and brother, in a small brownstone apartment in downtown D.C. Her brother, the oldest child, went off to fight in the Korean War, one of the first black airmen to participate in the integrated armed forces. While in Korea, he fell in love with and married a Korean girl. Meanwhile, my mother attended segregated public schools until senior high school, when she was in the first class that integrated Eastern Senior High School in the wake of the Supreme Court's *Brown* decision. After graduation, she opted not to attend college, because she didn't know what she wanted to do—and "didn't want to waste" my grandmother's money.

My father grew up in North Philadelphia, one of those old working-class neighborhoods where there were Jewish blocks, Italian blocks, Irish blocks, and so on. His parents were second-generation Americans: Grandpa Bernstein's family was from Poland; my grandmother's family from Leeds, England. (I understand the Blasky family still lives there, apparently running a successful wallpaper-hanging business.) My grandfather and my father's two brothers fought in World War II; my father, who was too young to go, became a paratrooper soon after the war ended. After leaving the Army in the early 1950s, he moved to Washington, where he and my mother eventually ended up working at the same furniture-rental place.

Despite the rich possibilities for mischief making presented by their union, my parents did not marry to make a political statement. While their contemporaries marched for civil rights and held sit-ins, they hung out with a mixed-race group of cool cats at various jazz nightclubs in downtown D.C. Most of these establishments were burned to the ground after Martin Luther King's assassination in 1968, bringing to an end that unique era of naive integration. Since those riots, race relations in this country have been tinged with guilt, fear, and lies.

In 1970, my father's company transferred him to the redneck mill town of Reading, Pennsylvania. My mother hated it; my father tolerated it; and I went about the business of growing up. I went to a mostly white private school and Monday afternoons attended Hebrew school with the children of Reading's prosperous and assimilated Jewish community. My Cub Scout group and summer camp were at the local Jewish community center, which had been bombed recently by Reading's prominent community of neo-Nazis.

It was also at the center that I was first called a "nigger." My mother had been preparing me my entire life for that to happen, but when it did, I was hardly bothered at all. I actually felt sorry for the kid who shouted it at me during a softball game; he genuinely felt bad afterward and apologized about six times. (Even though it's out of sequence in our little narrative, I should recount the only other time I have been called a "nigger." A couple of years ago, I was riding on D.C.'s Metro with two white liberal friends when a white homeless person approached me and stated, "You niggers get all the jobs." My friends were horrified and silent. I laughed and told the bum that he was right; that was how it should be.)

We moved back to Washington in 1977. Again, I attended private school, this time at Georgetown Day School, a place founded in the 1940s as Washington's first integrated school. Despite the forty-year tradition, there were still not many blacks at GDS. The students were largely from well-to-do, secular Jewish families with traditions of liberal political activism. My family, though secular, was not well-to-do or politically active. My parents were somewhat liberal, but it was a liberalism of function rather than form; in other words, they might be considered budding neoconservatives. I inherited from my parents a healthy suspicion of conventional wisdom—which, in the case of my teachers and peers, was overwhelmingly on the left. By 1980, I was one of six kids in my junior-high class to vote for Ronald Reagan in our mock election.

My "political awakening" was just beginning. In high school I co-wrote a piece in the school newspaper on what it meant to be conservative, an awfully crafted piece of literature that nearly caused a riot, despite its (by my standards today) extremely mushy conservatism. I started to realize that you could make liberals mad just by saying the "c" word. On election day 1984, I wore a jacket and tie to school to celebrate President Reagan's impending victory. One friend didn't talk to me for a week.

It never dawned on me that, as a "person of color," I ought to be "mortally" opposed to this Reagan guy. All I ever heard come out of his mouth just sounded like good sense to me. I heard over and over again on TV that the man was a racist and that he was bad for black people. But what stuck with me from all this was that the people who repeated this charge were buffoons. Early on, the idea of race was not central to my view of politics. This would change rather sharply later on. 10

My freshman year in college was spent at Allegheny College in lovely Meadville, Pennsylvania. Within weeks, it was apparent to me and several of my friends there that the school was lousy. A group of us dedicated our lives to the idea of transferring out of that freezing mud hole of a campus. In one of our brainstorming sessions on how to make our transfer applications look beefier, we locked onto the idea of starting a "Conservative Club," which would be a forum for discussing ideas on the right. It sounded like fun, and more importantly, we would all be made vice presidents of the club, an ideal way to bolster our extracurricular résumés.

Once again, just using the word *conservative* nearly brought the campus down around our ears. Two of the conspirators in our résumé-building scheme went before the student government in order to get the necessary recognition, supposedly just a formality. Forty-five minutes later, after shrieks of outrage from the so-called student leaders of this $13,000-a-year institution of higher learning, we were told that the student government was afraid to get involved in "neo-Nazi" groups and that we should come back in a month with a detailed statement of just what we stood for. Only one member of the SG stood up for us—a young woman who pointed out that on a campus with absolutely no political activity, people who showed some initiative to do something, anything, ought to be encouraged.

But this was a college where political discourse was typified by this statement from the school's chaplain: "We should divest from South Africa. Harvard and Princeton already have, and if we want to be as good as them, we must do so as well." In this kind of environment, which is now typical at liberal-arts colleges around the country, it should have come as no surprise that conservatism was associated with evil. It wasn't the last time that the supposed characteristics of conservatives like me—that we were narrow-minded, ignorant, and shrill—were to be embodied better by our critics.

I did finally escape from Allegheny College, going back home to the University of Maryland. At UM, I decided to make politics a full-time vocation. I worked in Washington afternoons and evenings at various political jobs, first at the Republican National Committee and later at a small, conservative nonprofit foundation. In between, I took a semester off to work for Senator Bob Dole's ill-fated presidential campaign. Returning to Maryland, I was soon elected president of the campus College Republicans, a position that occasionally put me at the center of campus political attention.

This was not because I was a vocal, articulate (some would say loud-mouthed) conservative but because I was a *black* conservative. Conservatives are a dime a dozen, smart ones are common, but a black one? "Nelly, wake the kids! They have to *see* this!"   15

Other conservatives loved having me around. After all, most of them were presumed to be Nazis from the get-go by the ultrasensitive P.C. crowd; having a black person say you're okay was temporary protection from the scholastic inquisition. Further, as a black conservative, I was thought to have special insight into why more blacks didn't identify with the Republican party. Again and again, I was asked how conservatives could find more blacks (or African-Americans, if the petitioner wanted to be sensitive). After a while, I think I actually began to believe that, somehow, I had special understanding of the souls of black folk, and with increasing confidence I would sound off about the political and social proclivities of African-Americans.

In a perverted way, liberals and left-radicals liked having me around as well—because I helped justify their paranoia. I was living proof that imperialist, racist forces were at work, dividing black people and turning us against one another. How else, they theorized, could a black person so obviously sell out both his race and the "progressive" whites who were the only thing standing between him and a right-wing lynch mob? The ardor (and obvious pleasure) with which they alternatively ignored and condemned me demonstrated their belief that I was more than just the opposition: I was a traitor, a collaborator in my own oppression. Finally, one particularly vitriolic black militant suggested in the school newspaper that black conservatives ought to be "neutralized." I took it personally.

And I got fired up. There comes a time in every conservative activist's life when he gets the heady rush of realization at how much fun (and how easy) it is to annoy liberals. Indeed, it was something I had been doing for years. People on the left, with their self-righteousness, humorless orthodoxies, and ultrasensitivity to their own and everyone else's "oppression" are only fun at parties if you get them pissed off. Naturally, then, it is something that conservatives spend a lot of time doing.

Rush Limbaugh, R. Emmett Tyrell, P. J. O'Rourke, hundreds of editors of conservative college newspapers like the *Dartmouth Review,* and thousands of College Republican activists turned the 1980s into one long laugh for conservatives at the expense of the P.C. crowd. The staleness of liberal beliefs, the inability of the campus activists to move beyond sloganeering to real thought, and the creation of a regime on campus by college professors and administrators that treats open discussion as anathema offered fertile ground for conservative humorists.

But it also allowed many conservatives to dismiss leftism as a political force, and they were unprepared when it was resurrected as such in the person of Bill Clinton—thus in 1992, it was the right that too often degenerated into empty sloganeering. The intellectual stagnation of liberalism contributed to the intellectual sloth of too many conservatives, concerned more with one-liners than actually formulating policy.   20

I was no exception. I slipped easily into the world of leftist haranguing. I was always good for a sound bite in the school newspaper, and as a unique case—a black Jewish conservative—I had opportunities to comment with some built-in authority on a range of issues. Controversy with the Black Student Union? I would have a comment. Someone wants the university to divest from South Africa? I would be there with other conservatives holding a press conference presenting the other side. Controversy between Arab students and Jewish students? The College Republicans would uphold the Reagan tradition of unswerving support for Israel as long as I was in charge.

I tried not to lose sight of why I was doing this; that annoying liberals was just a means, not an end. But like every young right-winger, I'm sure that more than once I've annoyed just for annoyance's sake. There are worse sins, but this is the only one I'll admit to in print.

Since those heady college days, I have become a magazine editor. *Diversity & Division* looks at race relations in America from the perspective of young people, particularly of its black Jewish editor and white male managing editor. Do I still go after liberals? Yeah, sure. But the issues we talk about—those bearing on the future, on how we are all going to get along—are not very funny. And the things that leftists advocate on these issues, from radical multiculturalism to quotas, promise to make it next to impossible for us to survive as a multicultural society.

There are two lessons, I think, that my little autobiography teaches. First is my comfort in moving between worlds of different cultures and colors. The conventional wisdom about us mixed-race types, that we are alienated, never feeling comfortable in either culture, is baloney. I am black. I am Jewish. I am equally comfortable with people who identify themselves as either one, or neither one. Why? Because to me the most defining characteristic of who I am is not my race, ethnicity, religious beliefs, political party, or Tupperware club membership. Rather, I see myself as an individual first, part of the larger "human family," with all the suballegiances reduced to ancillary concerns.

This is obviously a very romantic and idealistic notion. It is also, equally as obviously, the only ideology that will allow us to overcome prejudice and bigotry and enable everyone to get along. In me, the melting pot the idea has become the melting pot the reality, with (I must immodestly say) reasonably positive results. My commonality with other people is not in superficial appeals to ethnic solidarity—it is far more fundamental. 25

That is why I am sickened by people who continue to insist that we must all cling to our ancestors' "cultures" (however arbitrarily defined at that moment) in order to have self-awareness and self-esteem. The notion of "self" should not be wrapped up in externalities like "culture" or "race"—unless you want to re-create the United States as Yugoslavia, Somalia, or any other such place where people's tribal identities make up their whole selves. Indeed, true self-awareness stands opposed to grouping human beings along arbitrary lines like race, gender, religion, weight, or preferred manner of reaching orgasm. Groupthink is primitive. It is not self-awareness; rather it is a refuge for those afraid of differences.

Those who preach about diversity believe that tolerance means not exulting one class of human being over another, by recognizing that every race and culture has made a contribution to modern civilization: a worthy goal, especially if this were true. But this way of thinking ignores a powerful truth, an obvious solution to the bigotry and suspicion that these sensitivity warriors say they are out to eliminate. The reality is that groups aren't equal; individuals are. If it is "self-evident that all men are created equal" isn't it even more self-evident that blacks and whites, men and women, Christians and Jews are created equal?

Granted, we haven't lived up to this absolute ideal. But we are beginning to see the implications of setting our aspirations below what we know to be the best. Here's the second lesson I think my story tells.

Despite my obvious distaste for the entire notion of group politics, I have become wrapped up in it. By editing a magazine that deals primarily with racial issues, I am not doing what I would most like to be doing. But I am doing what is expected. Under our phony system of racial harmony, college-educated blacks are expected to do something that is, well, black. Black academics are concentrated in Afro-American studies, sociology, and other "soft" fields where they can expound at length about the plight of the American Negro. Everyone, it seems, needs an expert on what it means to be black. Corporations need human-relations specialists to tell them about the "special needs" of black employees. Newspapers need "urban beat" reporters. Foundations, political parties, unions, and any other organizations you can name all need black liaisons to put them "in touch with the community." And, of course, conservatives need a magazine that reassures them that many of the ideas that they have about race relations are not evil and fascistic. These jobs are generally somewhat lucrative, fairly easy to do, and carry just one job requirement—you have to be black.

No one is forced to follow this course; there should be no whining   *30* about that. But in life, as in physics, currents flow along the path of least resistance. As long as it is easy to make a living as a professional race man, the best and brightest blacks will be siphoned off into this least-productive field in our service economy. The same is true, of course, of Hispanics, Asians, or whatever minority group is in vogue in a specific region or profession. Our educational system, our country's entire way of thinking about race, is creating a class of professionals whose entire raison d'être is to explore and explain—and thus perpetuate—the current regime. All the preaching of sensitivity, all the Afrocentric education, all the racial and ethnic solidarity in the world will not markedly improve race relations in America. Indeed, the smart money says that this obsession with our differences, however well-meaning, will make things much, much worse.

But this is a point that, blessedly, may well be rendered moot for the next generation. Intermarriage is the great equalizer; it brings people of different races together in a way that forced busing, sensitivity training, and affirmative action could never hope to—as individuals, on equal footing, united by common bonds of humanity. Four hundred years ago Shakespeare wrote of intermarriage:

> Take her, fair son, and from her blood raise up
> Issue to me; that the contending kingdoms . . .
> May cease their hatred; and this dear conjunction
> Plant neighbourhood and Christian-like accord
> In their sweet bosoms . . .

Eventually, if all goes well, America's melting pot will be a physical reality, bringing with it the kind of healing Shakespeare had in mind. Let's just hope we don't file for an ethnic divorce before then.

The Responsive Reader

1. What is Bernstein's perspective on the strife-ridden racial legacy of the past? What glimpses do you get in his essay of racism or race-related violence in the society around him? In his and his family's history, what was the role of miscegenation laws, segregation, and the movement toward integration?
2. Bernstein questions "dubious" paradigms, or theoretical models, associated with race or ethnicity. Where and how does he go counter to the reader's stereotypes and conventional expectations about race?
3. What were major factors in Bernstein's "political awakening"? Does his conservatism seem as wrong-headed to you as it did to many on campus? Why was his role as a black conservative of special interest to both conservatives and liberals?
4. Liberal-bashing has become a favorite conservative pastime in the days of Rush Limbaugh. What do you learn from Bernstein about its motivation or psychological workings? *Political correctness* became a buzzword as a conservative groundswell gained force. What are Bernstein's key criticisms of the "P.C. crowd"?
5. How or why does Bernstein rehabilitate the "melting pot" metaphor that many others have left behind? What does he see as the dangers of multiculturalism? What for him are the shortcomings of "group politics"?

Talking, Listening, Writing

6. On the basis of Bernstein's essay, what would you include in a capsule portrait of a young conservative? What are key positions or telltale features?
7. Have you seen evidence that harping on differences can be a mistake?
8. Do you think it inevitable that members of minority groups will turn politically conservative as they become affluent and move into the middle class?
9. Do you think of yourself as conservative, liberal, radical, or none of the above? Explain and defend your position.

Collaborative Projects

10. What statistics concerning race and ethnicity are kept at your school and in your community? Who collects them? Who uses them, and for what purpose? How are racial or ethnic criteria employed? What are the pitfalls in collecting and interpreting them? Your class may want to parcel out different aspects of this question to small groups.

HOW IT FEELS TO BE COLORED ME

Zora Neale Hurston

Zora Neale Hurston once said about the idea of democracy that she was all for trying it out. In fact, she couldn't wait to do so as soon as the Jim Crow laws that legalized discrimination against African Americans were a thing of the past. Hurston was born in Eatonville, an all-black town in Florida, and was working as a domestic when she managed to attend college. She finally went on to Howard University, which has been called "a center of black scholarship and intellectual ferment." As a scholarship student at Barnard College in New York City, she became an associate of the anthropologist Franz Boas, who asked her to return to the South to collect black folk tales. She had earlier published earthy slice-of-life sketches of black life; her classic collection of African American folklore, Mules and Men, *appeared in 1935. Like other students of black dialect and folk tradition, she was accused by militants of perpetuating damaging stereotypes of African Americans as uneducated and unsophisticated. Like other minority artists and writers dependent on white patronage, she was accused of selling out to the white establishment. Although for a time one of the best-known voices of the Harlem Renaissance of the twenties and thirties, she died in a county welfare home and was buried in an unmarked grave. In recent years, feminists have rediscovered her fiction; her masterpiece, the novel* Their Eyes Were Watching God *(1937), is now widely read in college classes. A recent biographer has called her "the most significant unread author in America."*

Thought Starters: How aware are people you know of their separate racial or ethnic identity? Is it constantly on their minds?

I am colored but I offer nothing in the way of extenuating circumstances except the fact that I am the only Negro in the United States whose grandfather on the mother's side was *not* an Indian chief.

I remember the very day that I became colored. Up to my thirteenth year I lived in the little Negro town of Eatonville, Florida. It is exclusively a colored town. The only white people I knew passed through the town going to or coming from Orlando. The native whites rode dusty horses, the Northern tourists chugged down the sandy village road in automobiles. The town knew the Southerners and never stopped cane chewing when they passed. But the Northerners were something else again. They were peered at cautiously from behind curtains by the timid. The more venturesome would come out on the porch to watch them go past and got just as much pleasure out of the tourists as the tourists got out of the village.

The front porch might seem a daring place for the rest of the town, but it was a gallery seat to me. My favorite place was atop the gate-post. Proscenium box for a born first-nighter. Not only did I enjoy the show, but I didn't mind the actors knowing that I liked it. I usually spoke to them in passing. I'd wave at them and when they returned my salute, I would say something like this: "Howdy-do-well-I-thank-you-where-you-goin'?" Usually the automobile or the horse paused at this, and after a queer exchange of compliments, I would probably "go a piece of the way" with them, as we say in farthest Florida. If one of my family happened to come to the front in time to see me, of course negotiations would be rudely broken off. But even so, it is clear that I was the first "welcome-to-our-state" Floridian, and I hope the Miami Chamber of Commerce will please take notice.

During this period, white people differed from colored to me only in that they rode through town and never lived there. They liked to hear me "speak pieces" and sing and wanted to see me dance the parse-me-la, and gave me generously of their small silver for doing these things, which seemed strange to me for I wanted to do them so much that I needed bribing to stop. Only they didn't know it. The colored people gave no dimes. They deplored any joyful tendencies in me, but I was their Zora nevertheless. I belonged to them, to the nearby hotels, to the county—everybody's Zora.

But changes came in the family when I was thirteen, and I was sent to school in Jacksonville. I left Eatonville, the town of the oleanders, as Zora. When I disembarked from the river-boat at Jacksonville, she was no more. It seemed that I had suffered a sea change. I was not Zora of Orange County any more, I was now a little colored girl. I found it out in certain ways. In my heart as well as in the mirror, I became a fast brown—warranted not to rub nor run.   5

But I am not tragically colored. There is no great sorrow dammed up in my soul, nor lurking behind my eyes. I do not mind at all. I do not belong to the sobbing school of Negrohood who hold that nature somehow has given them a lowdown dirty deal and whose feelings are all hurt about it. Even in the helter-skelter skirmish that is my life, I have seen that the world is to the strong regardless of a little pigmentation more or less. No, I do not weep at the world—I am too busy sharpening my oyster knife.

Someone is always at my elbow reminding me that I am the granddaughter of slaves. It fails to register depression with me. Slavery is sixty years in the past. The operation was successful and the patient is doing well, thank you. The terrible struggle that made me an American out of a potential slave said "On the line!" The Reconstruction said "Get set!"; and the generation before said "Go!" I am off to a flying start and I must not halt in the stretch to look behind and weep. Slavery is the price I paid for civilization, and the choice was not with me. It is a bully adventure and worth all that I have paid through my ancestors for it. No one on earth ever had a greater chance for glory. The world to be won and nothing to be lost. It is thrilling to think—to know that for any act of mine, I shall get twice as much praise or twice as much blame. It is quite exciting to hold the center of the national stage, with the spectators not knowing whether to laugh or to weep.

The position of my white neighbor is much more difficult. No brown specter pulls up a chair beside me when I sit down to eat. No dark ghost thrusts its leg against mine in bed. The game of keeping what one has is never so exciting as the game of getting.

I do not always feel colored. Even now I often achieve the unconscious Zora of Eatonville before the Hegira. I feel most colored when I am thrown against a sharp white background.

For instance at Barnard. "Beside the waters of the Hudson" I feel my race. Among the thousand white persons, I am a dark rock surged upon, overswept by a creamy sea. I am surged upon and overswept, but through it all, I remain myself. When covered by the waters, I am; and the ebb but reveals me again. 10

Sometimes it is the other way around. A white person is set down in our midst, but the contrast is just as sharp for me. For instance, when I sit in the drafty basement that is The New World Cabaret with a white person, my color comes. We enter chatting about any little nothing that we have in common and are seated by the jazz waiters. In the abrupt way that jazz orchestras have, this one plunges into a number. It loses no time in circumlocutions, but gets right down to business. It constricts the thorax and splits the heart with its tempo and narcotic harmonies. This orchestra grows rambunctious, rears on its hind legs and attacks the tonal veil with primitive fury, rending it, clawing it until it breaks through to the jungle beyond. I follow those heathen—follow them exultingly. I dance wildly inside myself; I yell within, I whoop; I shake my assegai above my head, I hurl it true to the mark *yeeeeoouw!* I am in the jungle and living in the jungle way. My face is painted red and yellow and my body is painted blue. My pulse is throbbing like a war drum. I want to slaughter something—give pain, give death to what, I do not know. But the piece ends. The men of the orchestra wipe their lips and rest their fingers. I creep back slowly to the veneer we call civilization with the last tone and find the white friend sitting motionless in his seat, smoking calmly.

"Good music they have here," he remarks, drumming the table with his fingertips.

Music! The great blobs of purple and red emotion have not touched him. He has only heard what I felt. He is far away and I see him but dimly across the ocean and the continent that have fallen between us. He is so pale with his whiteness then and I am *so* colored.

At certain times I have no race, I am *me*. When I set my hat at a certain angle and saunter down Seventh Avenue, Harlem City, feeling as snooty as the lions in front of the Forty-Second Street Library, for instance. So far as my feelings are concerned, Peggy Hopkins Joyce on the Boule Mich with her gorgeous raiment, stately carriage, knees knocking together in a most aristocratic manner, has nothing on me. The cosmic Zora emerges. I belong to no race nor time. I am the eternal feminine with its string of beads.

I have no separate feeling about being an American citizen and colored.   15
I am merely a fragment of the Great Soul that surges within the boundaries. My country, right or wrong.

Sometimes, I feel discriminated against, but it does not make me angry. It merely astonishes me. How *can* any deny themselves the pleasure of my company! It's beyond me.

But in the main, I feel like a brown bag of miscellany propped against a wall. Against a wall in company with other bags, white, red and yellow. Pour out the contents, and there is discovered a jumble of small things priceless and worthless. A first-water diamond, an empty spool, bits of broken glass, lengths of string, a key to a door long since crumbled away, a rusty knifeblade, old shoes saved for a road that never was and never will be, a nail bent under the weight of things too heavy for any nail, a dried flower or two, still a little fragrant. In your hand is the brown bag. On the ground before you is the jumble it held—so much like the jumble in the bags, could they be emptied, that all might be dumped in a single heap and the bags refilled without altering the content of any greatly. A bit of colored glass more or less would not matter. Perhaps that is how the Great Stuffer of Bags filled them in the first place—who knows?

The Responsive Reader

1. There has been much talk about the need for self-esteem—the need for women and minorities to overcome culturally conditioned feelings of inferiority and inadequacy. What is the secret of Hurston's self-esteem?
2. What were major stages in Hurston's awareness of race? (For instance, when was it that she "became" colored? How does she distance herself from other definitions of "Negrohood"? When is she least aware of racial difference?)
3. What is Hurston's last word on the role of race in her life and in the larger society? Do her words seem dated or still valid today?

Talking, Listening, Writing

4. How does Hurston's attitude toward race compare with what you think is predominant in today's generation?
5. What efforts have you observed to restore people's pride in their own racial or ethnic identity? Have you personally participated in such efforts? How successful are they?
6. Have you experienced self-doubt, feelings of inadequacy, or feelings of inferiority? What causes them? How do you cope with them?

Collaborative Projects

7. How much do you know about the art and literature of diverse ethnic or cultural traditions? Your class may want to organize a presentation of poems, tales, songs, or music. (Will you encounter any questions about what is authentic, what is exploitative, or what is offensive or demeaning?)

ON THE JOB

Joe Gutierrez

> *Studs Terkel is known for several best-selling collections of interviews with ordinary Americans. He was born in Chicago in 1912 and grew up there, attending the University of Chicago and the Chicago Law School. He has been a disc jockey, sports commentator, and television emcee; he hosted a popular talk show for thirty-five years. In books like* Working, Hard Times, *and* American Dreams: Lost and Found, *he proved a good listener, getting the people he interviewed to cut through media hype and political slogans and to talk with amazing honesty about their lives, thoughts, and feelings. The following interview with a fifty-year-old steel worker is from Terkel's* Race: How Blacks and Whites Feel about the American Obsession *(1992). A reviewer said about this book, "Studs Terkel has got people to say things in such a way that you know at once they have finally said their truth and said it better than they ever believed they could say it."*
>
> *Joe Gutierrez, the person interviewed in the following selection from* Race, *spent four years in a seminary preparing to be a priest but then quit to work in the steel mills like his father. Gutierrez said about his family:*
>
>> *My father worked at the Ford plant in Detroit when he first came from Mexico. Then he came to Chicago and the steel mill and worked there as far back as I can remember. . . . My mother was a hillbilly from Georgia. She married at fourteen. We're fifteen children. She didn't speak Spanish and he didn't speak English. I didn't know two words of Spanish until I got out into the steel mill.*
>
> *Gutierrez is of Mexican American descent, with a Mexican father and a North American mother. He says of Spanish Americans, or Latinos, "Latins are right in the middle." In how many ways does the person speaking to you in this interview find himself "right in the middle"?*

Thought Starters: Do you listen to what the person speaking in the following interview calls "working people"? What do you learn?

I didn't identify with Mexicans until people started throwing racism around. My name is José but I've always been called Little Joe. The whites didn't know my last name and thought I was Italian or Greek. So they let out their true feelings. *1*

I was not accepted by the Mexicans because I couldn't speak the language: "You look white, so you don't want to be a Mexican." I forced myself to learn the language so at least I could get by.

We were the only Mexican family in the neighborhood. The Mexicans, Puerto Ricans, and blacks lived on the East Chicago side by the mills. Now it's all changed. You've got a neighbor that's black, another Puerto Rican, another something else. All on our street.

We were about eight years old, my brother, Vince, and I when we went to a public swimming pool in a park in East Chicago. We took a black kid with us. This was 1948. As soon as we dove in the pool, everybody got out. The lifeguard got out, too, a female. They shut down the pool. I was never raised to be a racist, so I didn't know what it was all about.

There's a certain amount of racism among Mexicans against blacks,   5
and Mexicans against Puerto Ricans. But I see more racism with the blacks than with the white or Latin.

We went through a union election. We're about thirty percent black. Every time I ran for office, there was a solid black vote for the black, regardless of the person. It made no difference. Over the years, I felt it would change because people would look at the person's qualifications. For the most part, it hasn't changed. That's true among Latins also. They'll vote Latin just because he's Latin. Whites? Yeah, pretty much the same.

A good friend of mine, a white from Kentucky, just got elected griever in the metal-plate department. I said, "The black griever we have is simply unqualified; he's done a terrible job. I don't expect the blacks to vote for him. He won't get over twenty votes." He said, "The guy's gonna get a hundred votes." He was right. For three years, the guy did an awful job. They still came out and backed him. I understand the past injustices, but . . .

The guys who are honest say, "Look, we've been down so long, the first time we get somebody to represent the black community, he projects an image of leadership and we overlook the bad. We just want a black there."

It baffles my mind because I've had an ongoing fight in the mills: I don't care if you're black, brown, or white, we're all workers. I sometimes get chastised by the so-called leaders of the Latin community because I don't stand up and say we should all go for *la raza*. There are some Latins who always vote that way. I voted that way before I got involved with the union. I didn't know people. If I saw a Sánchez or Gonzalez or Rodríguez, I voted for him. I met a Cisneros who couldn't write his own name and didn't give a damn about the union, was a company guy. I said nah, nah, nah. He may be Latin but he doesn't represent the interests of working people. I don't care about image.

With whites, what comes first is my pocketbook. I can work with a   10
black, with a Latin, but as soon as I leave that steel mill, I get on South 41 and go back to my world. Here it's a temporary world for eight hours a day, five days a week. When you park your car and walk into that plant, you walk into another world. All your prejudices, all your hates, you leave in the parking lot.

At the workplace, there's not much tension. You still have people who feel they're treated unfairly because they're black or Latin. When some whites get disciplined, they say, "I'm white, you didn't discipline the black guy." It's a crutch. But in general, it's not there. You're working around heavy equipment and you've got to look out for your buddy. It's very easy to get hurt in a steel mill.

As for whites, there's still a lot of prejudice out there. I know how to erase it. If you give other people a chance—if you give me the opportunity to present my views, maybe you'll get to know me and like me. Look, there's some people you just don't like. It's got nothing to do with color; it's got a lot to do with personality.

Latins are right in the middle. For the longest time, they were classified as blacks. You go to Texas, and Latinos are treated like blacks.

With people losing jobs, there's always got to be somebody to blame. We had nineteen thousand people at Inland Steel. Now we're below ten thousand. For years, whites had all the better jobs. In 1977, the government came in and said you've got to do something about discrimination in the workplace or we'll do it for you. They signed a Memorandum of Understanding that implemented plantwide seniority. It was good for everybody. Now a black or Latino as well as a white could transfer in any department and utilize seniority.

At the time, whites ran the trains, Latins worked on the tracks, and   15
blacks worked in the coke plants. When the changes took place, there was a lot of hatred among whites against minorities in general. "I've worked in this mill for twenty-five years, and here's one of them coming over and bumping me out of a job." It didn't happen that way for the most part, because you still had contract language to go by. You couldn't leapfrog over somebody.

We had an election the other day and won by a landslide. I acted as a watcher. Some voted only for Latins, others only for blacks, and some whites only for whites. Our slate had a president who's white, a Latin who's vicepresident, and two black trustees. It was a mix all around. We voted for the person. We represented the rank-and-file against the old guys. For the most part, we're forty, forty-one years old. You don't have a younger crop because there are no jobs for them.

What's ahead doesn't look good. With a new power plant, a lot of departments will shut down. The coke plants will go. You'll see some of the old hatred coming back. Blacks will say, "You gave us the rotten jobs whites wouldn't take, working on batteries, causing cancer and so forth, and when things get bad, we're the first to go." We're hearing it now. With fewer and fewer jobs, it'll get worse.

I don't like racists—white, black, Latin, anybody. Life's too short for meanness. There was a lot in the army when I was in it. Sometimes it comes out of people you don't expect it from. There's a guy who's decent, a hard worker, a good family man, and he'll say, "That fuckin' nigger." It's like getting hit in the gut. I stop him: "Why do you say that?" He just shrugs. He's Mexican, a deacon in the church. I'm a lector there. I tell this guy, "If a white guy says nigger, the word you use, I bet he calls you spic, taco-bender. Cut out this bullshit."

What's happened is that people were getting tired of the sixties. There was a legitimate grievance among the blacks in this country and a lot of us took part in the marches. But about twelve, fifteen years ago, younger blacks started coming into the steel mills. The older guys found allies among the Latins on the shop floor. But the younger guys came in with one thought in mind: We've been screwed and if we don't keep on their backs, they're gonna screw us again. To them, we're no different than the whites. It started backfiring.

Those of us who were sympathetic are less that way today. I had won   20
over a lot of blacks because I did a good job. But there are some blacks, I swear to God, I don't care what you did, it made no difference. All they saw was black. It's damaging to themselves. What more can a boss wish for?—divide and conquer!

When the government came down with a consent decree, Inland Steel ignored it. Every other company—LTV, Bethlehem, USX—paid minorities monies—two, three thousand dollars apiece—on the basis of years of discrimination at work. Inland Steel paid not a penny. They had a sharp lawyer who said, "Look, people are tired of civil rights, of marches, of busing, of affirmative action. The mood of the country is changing. Let's fight it." The government didn't follow through, and they didn't pay a penny. It's the Reagan years, and Bush is going even further.

I don't think the company is racist. That's too simple. It's the bottom line, the dollar. They don't care about you, no matter what your color is. You're nothing to them. If you're black or Latin or white, if they can set you up against the other workers, they're going to use you. They don't give a damn what color you are. It's the profit.

We have to keep working together, and when we hear the word nigger or spic—or cracker—stand up and say, "I don't appreciate that. Enough of this bullshit!"

The Responsive Reader

1. Like many Americans, Gutierrez does not have a clear-cut racial or ethnic identity. What experiences shaped his sense of who he is or where he belongs?
2. What has shaped his perceptions of the role of race in American life—in the communities in which we live?
3. What are Gutierrez's observations of the role of race on the job? For instance, what does he say about the hierarchy, or pecking order, in the distribution of jobs? What does he say about company policy on the subject of race? (Does he think it is racist?)

4. Readers of Studs Terkel's books marvel at the candor with which the people he interviews seem to talk about subjects on which many people hide their feelings or lie to both themselves and others. Does anything in this interview seem especially honest or candid? Is there anything that might make you question the speaker's sincerity?

Talking, Listening, Writing

5. What in this interview seems familiar; what seems different or new? Have you had experiences similar to those of Gutierrez—or other experiences that contrast with his?
6. Does this interview make you rethink some of your assumptions about ethnicity and race? How?
7. Would you call Gutierrez a typical American? Why or why not?
8. One reviewer said that Terkel's research "runs directly counter to the meanness of spirit so often expressed and exploited by today's politicians." She said that if Terkel's interviewees are representative, there is a far greater degree of "public consensus" and of "yearning for resolution" than one might imagine. What did she mean? Does this sample interview bear out her observations?

AFFIRMATIVE ACTION OR NEGATIVE ACTION

Miriam Schulman

For several decades, affirmative action to correct injustices suffered by minorities and by women was official government policy. In government employment, government contracts, and college admissions especially, programs were instituted to step up the representation of underrepresented groups. In recent political campaigns, however, affirmative action programs have come under attack for giving "special preferences" on the basis of race and gender. A widely publicized initiative campaign in California, inspiring similar efforts elsewhere, aimed at making it illegal for any state institution to take race or gender into account in dealing with its citizens. According to Nicholas Lemann, writing in Time *magazine, the initiative was predicted to "wipe out a host of programs . . . from magnet schools to science tutoring for girls" and to "decrease the minority presence at the University of California's two flagship schools, Berkeley and UCLA." According to some estimates the already minimal admission rate of African American students to be trained as members of the country's educational and professional elite would be cut in half. (Approved by the voters, the initiative was challenged as unconstitutional and got bogged down in the courts.) The following article is from* Issues in Ethics, *the publication of the Markkula Center for Applied Ethics at Santa Clara University. The author is trying to go beyond election-year politics and the anxieties of the proverbial angry white male to the ethical and political issues at the heart of the controversy.*

Thought Starters: Have you or people you know been the beneficiary or the victim of affirmative action?

It was 1986, and I was having a discussion with my freshman composition class at Santa Clara University about racial preference. Several white students were telling me about friends who should have gotten into SCU but didn't because the University was accepting so many "affirmative action students." Others were assuring me that they would have been accepted at Stanford if some minority student had not gotten their slot.

There were no African American students in the class; at that time, the freshman African American population at Santa Clara stood at 24 out of the total 886 freshmen. When I tried to get my students to look at the numbers and explain why they felt so threatened, they regarded me with the half-indulgent look college students used to reserve for '60s children such as myself and shrugged. They knew what they knew.

And me? As much as I liked my students, I found it easy to write off their opinions as racist, or at the least, paranoid.

Ten years later, as the issue of affirmative action threatens to fracture the state of California, I think back on that conversation. It has come to represent for me what is wrong with the public dialogue on this subject: We throw out anecdotal evidence, mixed with a few facts and figures, and then we all retreat into our preconceived ideas without any empathetic consideration of the other side. At least I know I was not really listening to what my students had to say.

I do not mean to suggest that I have changed my mind about affirmative action. I still support it, which may seem a strange admission in the introduction to an article that I hope will be seen as an evenhanded exploration of the ethical issues involved. But I have come to believe that—in the affirmative action debate, at least—we cannot move forward unless we understand the justice of the other side's position.   *5*

At its heart, the controversy over affirmative action is a controversy about justice. When we try to judge the justice of a social policy, we start with the basic premise that everyone should be treated similarly unless there is a morally relevant reason why they should be treated differently. Whatever benefits and burdens the society has to distribute, justice requires them to be allocated on this basis.

For simplicity, I'll confine myself to exploring how this premise applies to race (which, by the way, is how the debate over affirmative action is usually couched, despite the fact that such programs include women and other minorities). Most people agree that the history of slavery and Jim Crow in this country violated the first premise of justice. The color of someone's skin is not a morally justifiable reason for treating people differently.

Ah, but if that's so, say opponents of affirmative action, why is it acceptable to *favor* people because of their skin color? If everyone were treated similarly, wouldn't we have a colorblind society? Indeed, the California Civil Rights Initiative, the ballot proposition that sought to overturn affirmative action, reads like this:

> The state shall not discriminate against, or grant preferential treatment to, any individual or group on the basis of race, sex, color, ethnicity, or national origin in the operation of public employment, public education, or public contracting.

To clarify the values that make us come down on one or the other side in this debate, we must address the justice of preference. In the case of affirmative action, we must decide if there are ever circumstances that make it fair to favor one race over another when it comes to jobs or university admissions.

One answer to that question might be found in the principle of compensatory justice, which states that people who have been treated unjustly ought to be compensated. No reasonable person would argue with the fact   *10* that African Americans have suffered more than their share of injustice over the course of U.S. history. Many proponents of affirmative action defend the programs as a kind of reparation for the terrible wrongs of slavery and segregation. The white majority, in this view, must compensate African Americans for unjustly injuring them in the past.

A related concept brings this argument into the present: Affirmative action, proponents hold, neutralizes the competitive disadvantages that African Americans continue to experience because of past discrimination; segregated neighborhoods served by poor schools would be an example.

President Johnson had this justification for preferential treatment in mind when he signed the 1964 Voting Rights Act and said: "You do not take a person who, for years, has been hobbled by chains and liberate him, bring him up to the starting line of a race, and then say, 'You are free to compete . . .' and still justly believe that you have been completely fair."

While the argument for compensatory justice seems persuasive to me, I find that it often plays differently with the folks who are called upon to do the compensating. First of all, many people are not ready to concede their complicity in the wrongs of the past. It's very hard to persuade a young Asian college applicant, whose parents did not arrive in this country for a century after abolition, that she must take responsibility for slavery. Others cannot see how their race puts them at a competitive advantage. Most Appalachian out-of-work coal miners don't see themselves as the beneficiaries of past favoritism.

Even the average white male—who has weaker grounds for rejecting the compensatory argument—is beginning to rebel against racial preference. While it may fall outside the realm of morality to consider whether an argument is popular or not, those of us who want affirmative action to continue must confront the fact that many Americans believe these programs are asking them to take their punishment like . . . well, like a man. A lot of them are refusing to bend over.

I believe there's an equally valid moral argument for affirmative action that avoids the punitive overtones of the justice approach, focusing instead on why these programs are in everyone's best interest. In resolving the affirmative action question for myself, I find the best guidance in a common-good approach to ethics: The common good consists primarily in "ensuring that the social policies, social systems, institutions, and environments on which we depend are beneficial to all. Appeals to the common good urge us to view ourselves as members of the same community, reflecting on broad questions concerning the kind of society we want to become and how we are to achieve that society." 15

I look around me—at the poverty, crime, and alienation that so disproportionately afflict our minority communities—and I ask myself, Is this the kind of society I want to live in or the world I want my children to grow up in? The answer to that question is much clearer to me than deciding where justice resides in the affirmative action debate.

This is not simply a matter of feeling compassion or guilt, though neither of those responses strikes me as inappropriate. But beyond how I feel, I have a stake in addressing these problems. I know that social blights cannot be confined to a particular neighborhood or community; eventually, I will pay for every angry, jobless, poorly educated person—through the welfare system and through the prison system (the cost of which is fast surpassing schools in California).

However imperfect, affirmative action has made a small dent in the inequities that have characterized the distribution of jobs and educational opportunities in the United States. According to *The New York Times,* "The percentage of blacks in managerial and technical jobs doubled during the affirmative action years. During the same period, as Andrew Hacker pointed out in his book *Two Nations* [Ballantine Books, 1992], the number of black police officers rose from 24,000 to 64,000 and the number of black electricians, from 14,000 to 43,000."

Abolition of affirmative action would clearly reverse these gains. Cities that have dropped minority set-aside programs, for example, have experienced a sharp drop in the percentage of government contracts going to minorities. To say that these programs should be retained is not, however, to ignore the claims of fairness and justice raised by opponents of affirmative action. But I wonder if we need to define these in the competitive manner that has characterized so much of the debate—"You got my spot," as my students might have put it. Wouldn't it be better to create a vision of a society in which my good fortune did not mean your suffering?

Much of the threat my students felt, I now believe, came from the realistic assessment that they faced a dearth of employment and educational prospects. The best way to foster their support for affirmative action would be to address the underlying scarcity.   20

That was the experience in Atlanta, which, in preparation for the Olympic Games, awarded almost a third of $387 million in construction and vending contracts to women- and minority-owned businesses. "Grumbling has been minimal during Olympic preparations, largely because Atlanta's economy is so strong that work has been plentiful," writes Kevin Sack in *The New York Times.*

A common-good argument for affirmative action is part of a broader approach that envisions a society with plentiful work and good education for everyone. I can imagine the eyeballs rolling as I write these lines. Naive. Utopian. But, really, every ethical system is utopian in that it suggests an ideal. Why is my concept any more idealistic than the California Civil Rights Initiative, which is premised on a colorblind society where no one is ever discriminated against on the basis of race?

The Responsive Reader

1. In the introduction to her article, how does Schulman show that she will try to listen to the other side?
2. What is her basic definition of *justice?* (Is it the same as yours?) How does she apply it to the history of the race issue in this country?
3. What is "compensatory justice"? According to Schulman, what are its limitations as an argument for affirmative action? What is "punitive" about it?
4. What is the essence of the author's "common-good" approach to ethics? How does it apply to the current situation in our society and the prospects for its future?
5. What is the author's estimate of the past record or accomplishments of affirmative action? On balance, does she seem to think of it as a success or as a failure?
6. What do you think of Schulman's "Utopian" vision of a future when affirmative action would work without anyone getting hurt?

Talking, Listening, Writing

7. Do you think ethics means a concern with what is good for other people, or can it mean an enlightened concern with what is good for oneself, one's family, or one's group?
8. According to a *Time* article on the history of affirmative action, the idea behind it was that "custom, ethnocentrism, poverty, bad schools, old-boy networking, and a host of other factors would conspire against the new civil rights of African Americans and any real socioeconomic advancement." What is "ethnocentrism"? What is "old-boy networking"? Which of the "factors" listed here are still playing a major role, and which may have become less relevant? How much closer are we to the ideal of a "color-blind" society?

Collaborative Projects

9. Working with a group, you may want to check the current status of affirmative action or anti–affirmative action initiatives or legislation. You may want to focus on one major area, such as college admission, government employment, or government contracts.

WHY THEY EXCEL

Fox Butterfield

> *Fox Butterfield won the National Book Award for his book* China: Alive
> in the Bitter Sea *(1982). He first became intrigued by the motivation and
> academic performance of Asian students when he was a young journalist in
> Taiwan. The young Vietnamese student he interviewed for the following ar-
> ticle had left Vietnam ten years earlier and had not heard from her parents,
> who stayed behind, for three years. However, their admonitions to be a good
> daughter and a good student were still ringing in her ears. One of the sayings
> she remembered from her childhood was "If you don't study, you will never
> become anything. If you study, you will become what you wish." In his article
> about why Asian students excel, Butterfield draws on a mix of personal expe-
> rience, firsthand investigation, and expert opinion. Asians have been called the
> "model minority"—who work hard, study hard, and enter college and grad-
> uate in large numbers. How does this article support and explain the idea of
> the model minority?*

Thought Starters: How much of what you know about Vietnamese or
Chinese or other Asian students is based on personal contact or observation?
How much is hearsay or media stereotype?

Kim-Chi Trinh was just 9 in Vietnam when her father used his sav-   *1*
ings to buy a passage for her on a fishing boat. It was a costly and risky
sacrifice for the family, placing Kim-Chi on the small boat, among strangers, in hopes she would eventually reach the United States, where she
would get a good education and enjoy a better life. Before the boat reached
safety in Malaysia, the supply of food and water ran out.

Still alone, Kim-Chi made it to the United States, coping with a suc-
cession of three foster families. But when she graduated from San Diego's
Patrick Henry High School, she had a straight-A average and scholarship
offers from Stanford and Cornell universities.

"I have to do well—it's not even a question," said the diminutive
19-year-old, now a sophomore at Cornell. "I owe it to my parents in
Vietnam."

Kim-Chi is part of a tidal wave of bright, highly motivated Asian-
Americans who are surging into our best colleges. Although Asian-
Americans make up only 2.4 percent of the nation's population, by 1990
they had come to constitute 17.1 percent of the undergraduates at Harvard,
18 percent at the Massachusetts Institute of Technology and 27.3 percent at
the University of California at Berkeley.

With Asians being the fastest-growing ethnic group in the country—   5
two out of five immigrants are now Asian—these figures will increase. At
the University of California at Irvine, in a recent year, a staggering 35.1 percent of the undergraduates are Asian-American, but the proportion in the
freshman class is even higher: 41 percent.

Why are the Asian-Americans doing so well? Are they grinds, as some
stereotypes suggest? Do they have higher IQs? Or are they actually teaching the rest of us a lesson about values we have long treasured but may have
misplaced—like hard work, the family and education?

Not all Asians are doing equally well. Poorly educated Cambodian
and Hmong refugee youngsters need special help. And Asian-Americans
resent being labeled a "model minority," feeling that is just another form of
prejudice by white Americans, an ironic reversal of the discriminatory laws
that excluded most Asian immigration to America until 1965.

But the academic success of many Asian-Americans has prompted
growing concern among educators, parents and other students. Some universities have what look like unofficial quotas, much as Ivy League colleges
did against Jews in the 1920s and '30s. Berkeley Chancellor Ira Heyman
apologized for an admissions policy that, he said, had "a disproportionately
negative impact on Asian-Americans."

I have wondered about the reason for the Asians' success since I was
a fledgling journalist on Taiwan in 1969. That year, a team of boys from
a poor, isolated mountain village on Taiwan won the annual Little League
World Series at Williamsport, Pa. Their victory was totally unexpected. At
the time, baseball was a largely unknown sport on Taiwan, and the boys had
learned to play with bamboo sticks for bats and rocks for balls. But since
then, teams from Taiwan, Japan or South Korea have won the Little League
championship in 16 out of the 21 years. How could these Asian boys beat
us at our own game?

Fortunately, the young Asians' achievements have led to a series of   10
intriguing studies. "There is something going on here that we as Americans
need to understand," said Sanford M. Dornbusch, a professor of sociology
at Stanford. Dornbusch, in surveys of 7000 students in six San Fran-
cisco−area high schools, found that Asian-Americans consistently get better grades than any other group of students, regardless of their parents' level
of education or their families' social and economic status, the usual predic-
tors of success. In fact, those in homes where English is spoken often, or
whose families have lived longer in the United States, do slightly less well.

"We used to talk about the American melting pot as an advantage,"
Dornbusch said. "But the sad fact is that it has become a melting pot with
low standards."

Other studies have shown similar results. Perhaps the most disturbing have come in a series of studies by a University of Michigan psychologist, Harold W. Stevenson, who has compared more than 7000 students
in kindergarten, first grade, third grade and fifth grade in Chicago and

Minneapolis with counterparts in Beijing; Sendai, Japan; and Taipei, Taiwan. On a battery of math tests, the Americans did worst at all grade levels.

Stevenson found no differences in IQ. But if the differences in performance are showing up in kindergarten, it suggests something is happening in the family, even before the children get to school.

It is here that the various studies converge: Asian parents are able to instill more motivation in their children. "My bottom line is, Asian kids work hard," said Professor Dornbusch.

In his survey of San Francisco–area high schools, for example, he reported that Asian-Americans do an average of 7.03 hours of homework a week. Non-Hispanic whites average 6.12 hours, blacks 4.23 hours and Hispanics 3.98 hours. Asians also score highest on a series of other measures of effort, such as fewer class cuts and paying more attention to the teacher.

Don Lee, 20, is a junior at Berkeley. His parents immigrated to Torrance, Calif., from South Korea when he was 5, so he could get a better education. Lee said his father would warn him about the danger of wasting time at high school dances or football games. "Instead," he added, "for fun on weekends, my friends and I would go to the town library to study."

The real question, then, is how do Asian parents imbue their offspring with this kind of motivation? Stevenson's study suggests a critical answer. When the Asian parents were asked why they think their children do well, they most often said "hard work." By contrast, American parents said "talent."

"From what I can see," said Stevenson, "we've lost our belief in the Horatio Alger myth that anyone can get ahead in life through pluck and hard work. Instead, Americans now believe that some kids have it and some don't, so we begin dividing up classes into fast learners and slow learners, where the Chinese and Japanese believe all children can learn from the same curriculum."

The Asians' belief in hard work also springs from their common heritage of Confucianism, the philosophy of the 5th-century B.C. Chinese sage who taught that man can be perfected through practice. "Confucius is not just some character out of the past—he is an everyday reality to these people," said William Liu, a sociologist who directs the Pacific Asian-American Mental Health Research Center at the University of Illinois in Chicago.

Confucianism provides another important ingredient in the Asians' success. "In the Confucian ethic," Liu continued, "there is a centripetal family, an orientation that makes people work for the honor of the family, not just for themselves." Liu came to the United States from China in 1948. "You can never repay your parents, and there is a strong sense of guilt," he said. "It is a strong force, like the Protestant Ethic in the West."

Liu has found this in his own family. When his son and two daughters were young, he told them to become doctors or lawyers—jobs with the best guaranteed income, he felt. Sure enough, his daughters have gone into law, and his son is a medical student at UCLA, though he really wanted to be an investment banker. Liu asked his son why he picked medicine. The reply: "Ever since I was a little kid, I always heard you tell your friends their kids were a success if they got into med school. So I felt guilty. I didn't have a choice."

Underlying this bond between Asian parents and their children is yet another factor I noticed during 15 years of living in China, Japan, Taiwan and Vietnam. It is simply that Asian parents establish a closer physical tie to their infants than do most parents in the United States. When I let my baby son and daughter crawl on the floor, for example, my Chinese friends were horrified and rushed to pick them up. We think this constant attention is overindulgence and old-fashioned, but for Asians, who still live through the lives of their children, it is highly effective.

Yuen Huo, 22, a senior at Berkeley, recalled growing up in an apartment above the Chinese restaurant her immigrant parents owned and operated in Millbrae, Calif. "They used to tell us how they came from Taiwan to the United States for us, how they sacrificed for us, so I had a strong sense of indebtedness," Huo said. When she did not get all A's her first semester at Berkeley, she recalled, "I felt guilty and worked harder."

Here too is a vital clue about the Asians' success: Asian parents expect a high level of academic performance. In the Stanford study comparing white and Asian students in San Francisco high schools, 82 percent of the Asian parents said they would accept only an A or a B from their children, while just 59 percent of white parents set such a standard. By comparison, only 17 percent of Asian parents were willing to accept a C, against 40 percent of white parents. On the average, parents of black and Hispanic students also had lower expectations for their children's grades than Asian parents.

Can we learn anything from the Asians? "I'm not naïve enough to think   25
everything in Asia can be transplanted," said Harold Stevenson, the University of Michigan psychologist. But he offered three recommendations.

"To start with," he said, "we need to set higher standards for our kids. We wouldn't expect them to become professional athletes without practicing hard."

Second, American parents need to become more committed to their children's education, he declared. "Being understanding when a child doesn't do well isn't enough." Stevenson found that Asian parents spend many more hours really helping their children with homework or writing to their teachers. At Berkeley, the mothers of some Korean-American students move into their sons' apartments for months before graduate school entrance tests to help by cooking and cleaning for them, giving the students more time to study.

And, third, schools could be reorganized to become more effective— without added costs, said Stevenson. One of his most surprising findings is that Asian students, contrary to popular myth, are not just rote learners subjected to intense pressure. Instead, nearly 90 percent of Chinese young-sters said they actually enjoy school, and 60 percent can't wait for school vacations to end. These are vastly higher figures for such attitudes than are found in the United States. One reason may be that students in China and Japan typically have a recess after each class, helping them to relax and to increase their attention spans. Moreover, where American teachers spend almost their entire day in front of classes, their Chinese and Japanese coun-terparts may teach as little as three hours a day, giving them more time to relax and prepare imaginative lessons.

Another study, prepared for the U.S. Department of Education, com-pared the math and science achievements of 24,000 13-year-olds in the United States and five other countries (four provinces of Canada, plus South Korea, Ireland, Great Britain and Spain). One of the findings was that the more time students spent watching television, the poorer their per-formance. The American students watched the most television. They also got the worst scores in math. Only the Irish students and some of the Cana-dians scored lower in science.

"I don't think Asians are any smarter," said Don Lee, the Korean-   30
American at Berkeley. "There are brilliant Americans in my chemistry class. But the Asian students work harder. I see a lot of wasted potential among the Americans."

The Responsive Reader

1. Have you encountered the idea of the "model minority"? Do you remember any evidence, ideas, explanations? (Have you encountered challenges or rebuttals to this idea?)
2. The author dramatizes the issue by using Kim-Chi Trinh as a case in point. What key details and key ideas does the author want you to take in and remember?
3. How does the author use key statistics, expert testimony, and his "in-sider's" knowledge of the Confucian heritage to support his points?
4. What recommendations is Butterfield's article designed to support? Are they surprising or predictable? Which are strongest or most convincing? (Who has the last word in this article?)

Talking, Listening, Writing

5. Does this article change your ideas or preconceptions? Does it make you think? Why and how—or why not?
6. Do you want to take issue with all or part of this article? On what grounds? Where would you turn for supporting evidence?
7. What has shaped your own ideas about success and failure in our system of education? In your experience as a student, what have you learned about learning?

8. Some people support admission quotas to ensure fair representation of minority students in colleges and universities. Do you agree with them? Do you think there should be quotas to prevent *over*representation of groups like the Asian students described in Butterfield's article?

Collaborative Projects

9. Why do model students do well? Why do dropouts fail? How many dropouts are really pushouts—pushed out by educational policies or economic pressures that defeat them? How many dropouts drop back in for a second (or third) chance? You may want to focus on one of these questions. Working with a group, quiz students, teachers, counselors, or others in a position to know. Find some current articles or new reports. What conclusions do your explorations suggest? Is there a consensus among your sources?

EVERYDAY USE

Alice Walker

Alice Walker's novel The Color Purple *(1982) established her as a domi-nant voice in the search for a new black identity and black pride. In her Pulitzer Prize–winning novel, as in some of her short stories, her heroines are black women struggling to emerge from a history of oppression by white society and abuse by black males who "had failed women—and themselves." Walker's women find strength in bonding with other women, and they turn to the Afri-can past in the search for alternatives to our exploitative technological civiliza-tion. Walker's more recent novel,* The Temple of My Familiar *(1989), has been called a book of "amazing, overwhelming" richness, with characters "push-ing one another towards self-knowledge, honesty, engagement" (Ursula K. Le Guin). Born in Eatonton, Georgia, Walker knew poverty and racism as the child of sharecroppers in the Deep South. While a student at Spelman College in Atlanta, she joined in the rallies, sit-ins, and freedom marches of the civil rights movement, which, she said later, "broke the pattern of black servitude in this country." She worked as a social worker for the New York City Welfare Department and as an editor for* Ms. *magazine. In the following story, the older generation holds on to its hard-won pride and independence, while mem-bers of a younger generation assert their break with the past by adopting Mus-lim names and African greetings. What do the quilts symbolize in the story? How do they bring the confrontation between the characters to a head?*

Thought Starters: Stereotyping lumps together diverse members of a group. Have you observed striking contrasts between members of the same ethnic, racial, or religious group?

for your grandmama

I will wait for her in the yard that Maggie and I made so clean and wavy yesterday afternoon. A yard like this is more comfortable than most people know. It is not just a yard. It is like an extended living room. When the hard clay is swept clean as a floor and the fine sand around the edges lined with tiny, irregular grooves, anyone can come and sit and look up into the elm tree and wait for the breezes that never come inside the house.

Maggie will be nervous until after her sister goes: she will stand hope-lessly in corners, homely and ashamed of the burn scars down her arms and legs, eyeing her sister with a mixture of envy and awe. She thinks her sister has held life always in the palm of one hand, that "no" is a word the world never learned to say to her.

You've no doubt seen those TV shows where the child who has "made it" is confronted, as a surprise, by her own mother and father, tottering in weakly from backstage. (A pleasant surprise, of course: What would they do if parent and child came on the show only to curse out and insult each other?) On TV mother and child embrace and smile into each other's faces. Sometimes the mother and father weep, the child wraps them in her arms and leans across the table to tell how she would not have made it without their help. I have seen these programs.

Sometimes I dream a dream in which Dee and I are suddenly brought together on a TV program of this sort. Out of a dark and soft-seated limousine I am ushered into a bright room filled with many people. There I meet a smiling, gray, sporty man like Johnny Carson who shakes my hand and tells me what a fine girl I have. Then we are on the stage and Dee is embracing me with tears in her eyes. She pins on my dress a large orchid, even though she has told me once that she thinks orchids are tacky flowers.

In real life I am a large, big-boned woman with rough, man-working   5 hands. In the winter I wear flannel nightgowns to bed and overalls during the day. I can kill and clean a hog as mercilessly as a man. My fat keeps me hot in zero weather. I can work outside all day, breaking ice to get water for washing; I can eat pork liver cooked over the open fire minutes after it comes steaming from the hog. One winter I knocked a bull calf straight in the brain between the eyes with a sledge hammer and had the meat hung up to chill before nightfall. But of course all this does not show on television. I am the way my daughter would want me to be: a hundred pounds lighter, my skin like an uncooked barley pancake. My hair glistens in the hot bright lights. Johnny Carson has much to do to keep up with my quick and witty tongue.

But that is a mistake. I know even before I wake up. Who ever knew a Johnson with a quick tongue? Who can even imagine me looking a strange white man in the eye? It seems to me I have talked to them always with one foot raised in flight, with my head turned in whichever way is farthest from them. Dee, though. She would always look anyone in the eye. Hesitation was no part of her nature.

"How do I look, Mama?" Maggie says, showing just enough of her thin body enveloped in pink skirt and red blouse for me to know she's there, almost hidden by the door.

"Come out into the yard," I say.

Have you ever seen a lame animal, perhaps a dog run over by some careless person rich enough to own a car, sidle up to someone who is ignorant enough to be kind to him? That is the way my Maggie walks. She has been like this, chin on chest, eyes on ground, feet in shuffle, ever since the fire that burned the other house to the ground.

Dee is lighter than Maggie, with nicer hair and a fuller figure. She's a   10 woman now, though sometimes I forget. How long ago was it that the other house burned? Ten, twelve years? Sometimes I can still hear the flames and feel Maggie's arms sticking to me, her hair smoking and her dress falling off her in little black papery flakes. Her eyes seemed stretched open, blazed open by the flames reflected in them. And Dee. I see her standing off under the sweet gum tree she used to dig gum out of; a look of concentration on her face as she watched the last dingy gray board of the house fall in toward the red-hot brick chimney. Why don't you do a dance around the ashes? I'd wanted to ask her. She had hated the house that much.

I used to think she hated Maggie, too. But that was before we raised the money, the church and me, to send her to Augusta to school. She used to read to us without pity; forcing words, lies, other folks' habits, whole lives upon us two, sitting trapped and ignorant underneath her voice. She washed us in a river of make-believe, burned us with a lot of knowledge we didn't necessarily need to know. Pressed us to her with the serious way she read, to shove us away at just the moment, like dimwits, we seemed about to understand.

Dee wanted nice things. A yellow organdy dress to wear to her graduation from high school; black pumps to match a green suit she'd made from an old suit somebody gave me. She was determined to stare down any disaster in her efforts. Her eyelids would not flicker for minutes at a time. Often I fought off the temptation to shake her. At sixteen she had a style of her own: and knew what style was.

I never had an education myself. After second grade the school was closed down. Don't ask me why: in 1927 colored asked fewer questions than they do now. Sometimes Maggie reads to me. She stumbles along good-naturedly but can't see well. She knows she is not bright. Like good looks and money, quickness passed her by. She will marry John Thomas (who has mossy teeth in an earnest face) and then I'll be free to sit here and I guess just sing church songs to myself. Although I never was a good singer. Never could carry a tune. I was always better at a man's job. I used to love to milk till I was hooked in the side in '49. Cows are soothing and slow and don't bother you, unless you try to milk them the wrong way.

I have deliberately turned my back on the house. It is three rooms, just like the one that burned, except the roof is tin; they don't make shingle roofs any more. There are no real windows, just some holes cut in the sides, like the portholes in a ship, but not round and not square, with rawhide holding the shutters up on the outside. This house is in a pasture, too, like the other one. No doubt when Dee sees it she will want to tear it down. She wrote me once that no matter where we "choose" to live, she will manage to come see us. But she will never bring her friends. Maggie and I thought about this and Maggie asked me, "Mama, when did Dee ever *have* any friends?"

She had a few. Furtive boys in pink shirts hanging about on washday after school. Nervous girls who never laughed. Impressed with her they

15

worshiped the well-turned phrase, the cute shape, the scalding humor that erupted like bubbles in lye. She read to them.

When she was courting Jimmy T she didn't have much time to pay to us, but turned all her faultfinding power on him. He *flew* to marry a cheap city girl from a family of ignorant flashy people. She hardly had time to re-compose herself.

When she comes I will meet—but there they are!

Maggie attempts to make a dash for the house, in her shuffling way, but I stay her with my hand. "Come back here," I say. And she stops and tries to dig a well in the sand with her toe.

It is hard to see them clearly through the strong sun. But even the first glimpse of leg out of the car tells me it is Dee. Her feet were always neat-looking, as if God himself had shaped them with a certain style. From the other side of the car comes a short, stocky man. Hair is all over his head a foot long and hanging from his chin like a kinky mule tail. I hear Maggie suck in her breath. "Uhnnnh," is what it sounds like. Like when you see the wriggling end of a snake just in front of your foot on the road. "Uhnnnh."

Dee next. A dress down to the ground, in this hot weather. A dress so loud it hurts my eyes. There are yellows and oranges enough to throw back the light of the sun. I feel my whole face warming from the heat waves it throws out. Earrings gold, too, and hanging down to her shoulders. Bracelets dangling and making noises when she moves her arm up to shake the folds of the dress out of her armpits. The dress is loose and flows, and as she walks closer, I like it. I hear Maggie go "Uhnnnh" again. It is her sis-ter's hair. It stands straight up like the wool on a sheep. It is black as night and around the edges are two long pigtails that rope about like small lizards disappearing behind her ears.

"Wa-su-zo-Tean-o!" she says, coming on in that gliding way the dress makes her move. The short stocky fellow with the hair to his navel is all grinning and he follows up with "Asalamalakim, my mother and sister!" He moves to hug Maggie but she falls back, right up against the back of my chair. I feel her trembling there and when I look up I see the perspiration falling off her chin.

"Don't get up," says Dee. Since I am stout it takes something of a push. You can see me trying to move a second or two before I make it. She turns, showing white heels through her sandals, and goes back to the car. Out she peeks next with a Polaroid. She stoops down quickly and lines up picture after picture of me sitting there in front of the house with Maggie cowering behind me. She never takes a shot without making sure the house is included. When a cow comes nibbling around the edge of the yard she snaps it and me and Maggie *and* the house. Then she puts the Polaroid in the back seat of the car, and comes up and kisses me on the forehead.

Meanwhile Asalamalakim is going through motions with Maggie's hand. Maggie's hand is as limp as a fish, and probably as cold, despite the sweat, and she keeps trying to pull it back. It looks like Asalamalakim wants to shake hands but wants to do it fancy. Or maybe he don't know how people shake hands. Anyhow, he soon gives up on Maggie.

"Well," I say. "Dee."

"No, Mama," she says. "Not 'Dee,' Wangero Leewanika Kemanjo!"   25

"What happened to 'Dee'?" I wanted to know.

"She's dead," Wangero said. "I couldn't bear it any longer, being named after the people who oppress me."

"You know as well as me you was named after your aunt Dicie," I said. Dicie is my sister. She named Dee. We called her "Big Dee" after Dee was born.

"But who was *she* named after?" asked Wangero.

"I guess after Grandma Dee," I said.   30

"And who was she named after?" asked Wangero.

"Her mother," I said, and saw Wangero was getting tired. "That's about as far back as I can trace it," I said. Though, in fact, I probably could have carried it back beyond the Civil War through the branches.

"Well," said Asalamalakim, "there you are."

"Uhnnnh," I heard Maggie say.

"There I was not," I said, "before 'Dicie' cropped up in our family,   35 so why should I try to trace it that far back?"

He just stood there grinning, looking down on me like somebody inspecting a Model A car. Every once in a while he and Wangero sent eye signals over my head.

"How do you pronounce this name?" I asked.

"You don't have to call me by it if you don't want to," said Wangero.

"Why shouldn't I?" I asked. "If that's what you want us to call you, we'll call you."

"I know it might sound awkward at first," said Wangero.   40

"I'll get used to it," I said. "Ream it out again."

Well, soon we got the name out of the way. Asalamalakim had a name twice as long and three times as hard. After I tripped over it two or three times he told me to just call him Hakim-a-barber. I wanted to ask him was he a barber, but I didn't really think he was, so I didn't ask.

"You must belong to those beef-cattle peoples down the road," I said. They said "Asalamalakim" when they met you, too, but they didn't shake hands. Always too busy: feeding the cattle, fixing the fences, putting up salt-lick shelters, throwing down hay. When the white folks poisoned some of the herd the men stayed up all night with rifles in their hands. I walked a mile and a half just to see the sight.

Hakim-a-barber said, "I accept some of their doctrines, but farming and raising cattle is not my style." (They didn't tell me, and I didn't ask, whether Wangero (Dee) had really gone and married him.)

We sat down to eat and right away he said he didn't eat collards and   *45*
pork was unclean. Wangero, though, went on through the chitlins and corn
bread, the greens and everything else. She talked a blue streak over the
sweet potatoes. Everything delighted her. Even the fact that we still used
the benches her daddy made for the table when we couldn't afford to buy
chairs.

"Oh, Mama!" she cried. Then turned to Hakim-a-barber. "I never
knew how lovely these benches are. You can feel the rump prints," she
said, running her hands underneath her and along the bench. Then she
gave a sigh and her hand closed over Grandma Dee's butter dish. "That's
it!" she said. "I knew there was something I wanted to ask you if I could
have." She jumped up from the table and went over in the corner where
the churn stood, the milk in it clabber by now. She looked at the churn and
looked at it.

"This churn top is what I need," she said. "Didn't Uncle Buddy
whittle it out of a tree you all used to have?"

"Yes," I said.

"Uh huh," she said happily. "And I want the dasher, too."

"Uncle Buddy whittle that, too?" asked the barber.   *50*

Dee (Wangero) looked up at me.

"Aunt Dee's first husband whittled the dash," said Maggie so low you
almost couldn't hear her. "His name was Henry, but they called him Stash."

"Maggie's brain is like an elephant's," Wangero said, laughing. "I can
use the churn top as a centerpiece for the alcove table," she said, sliding a plate
over the churn, "and I'll think of something artistic to do with the dasher."

When she finished wrapping the dasher the handle stuck out. I took
it for a moment in my hands. You didn't even have to look close to see
where hands pushing the dasher up and down to make butter had left a kind
of sink in the wood. In fact, there were a lot of small sinks; you could see
where thumbs and fingers had sunk into the wood. It was beautiful light
yellow wood, from a tree that grew in the yard where Big Dee and Stash
had lived.

After dinner Dee (Wangero) went to the trunk at the foot of my bed   *55*
and started rifling through it. Maggie hung back in the kitchen over the
dishpan. Out came Wangero with two quilts. They had been pieced by
Grandma Dee and then Big Dee and me had hung them on the quilt frames
on the front porch and quilted them. One was in the Lone Star pattern. The
other was Walk Around the Mountain. In both of them were scraps of
dresses Grandma Dee had worn fifty and more years ago. Bits and pieces
of Grandpa Jarrell's Paisley shirts. And one teeny faded blue piece, about the
size of a penny matchbox, that was from Great Grandpa Ezra's uniform that
he wore in the Civil War.

"Mama," Wangero said sweet as a bird. "Can I have these old quilts?"

I heard something fall in the kitchen, and a minute later the kitchen
door slammed.

"Why don't you take one or two of the others?" I asked. "These old things was just done by me and Big Dee from some tops your grandma pieced before she died."

"No," said Wangero. "I don't want those. They are stitched around the borders by machine."

"That'll make them last better," I said.   60

"That's not the point," said Wangero. "These are all pieces of dresses Grandma used to wear. She did all this stitching by hand. Imagine!" She held the quilts securely in her arms, stroking them.

"Some of the pieces, like those lavender ones, come from old clothes her mother handed down to her," I said, moving up to touch the quilts. Dee (Wangero) moved back just enough so that I couldn't reach the quilts. They already belonged to her.

"Imagine!" she breathed again, clutching them closely to her bosom.

"The truth is," I said, "I promised to give them quilts to Maggie, for when she marries John Thomas."

She gasped like a bee had stung her.   65

"Maggie can't appreciate these quilts!" she said. "She'd probably be backward enough to put them to everyday use."

"I reckon she would," I said. "God knows I been saving 'em for long enough with nobody using 'em. I hope she will!" I didn't want to bring up how I had offered Dee (Wangero) a quilt when she went away to college. Then she had told me they were old-fashioned, out of style.

"But they're *priceless!*" she was saying now, furiously; for she has a temper. "Maggie would put them on the bed and in five years they'd be in rags. Less than that!"

"She can always make some more," I said. "Maggie knows how to quilt."

Dee (Wangero) looked at me with hatred. "You just will not under-   70
stand. The point is these quilts, *these* quilts!"

"Well," I said, stumped. "What would *you* do with them?"

"Hang them," she said. As if that was the only thing you *could* do with quilts.

Maggie by now was standing in the door. I could almost hear the sound her feet made as they scraped over each other.

"She can have them, Mama," she said, like somebody used to never winning anything, or having anything reserved for her. "I can 'member Grandma Dee without the quilts."

I looked at her hard. She had filled her bottom lip with checkerberry   75
snuff and it gave her face a kind of dopey, hangdog look. It was Grandma Dee and Big Dee who taught her how to quilt herself. She stood there with her scarred hands hidden in the folds of her skirt. She looked at her sister with something like fear but she wasn't mad at her. This was Maggie's portion. This was the way she knew God to work.

When I looked at her like that something hit me in the top of my head and ran down to the soles of my feet. Just like when I'm in church and the spirit of God touches me and I get happy and shout. I did something I never had done before: hugged Maggie to me, then dragged her on into the room, snatched the quilts out of Miss Wangero's hands and dumped them into Maggie's lap. Maggie just sat there on my bed with her mouth open.

"Take one or two of the others," I said to Dee.

But she turned without a word and went out to Hakim-a-barber.

"You just don't understand," she said, as Maggie and I came out to the car.

"What don't I understand?" I wanted to know.

"Your heritage," she said. And then she turned to Maggie, kissed her, and said, "You ought to try to make something of yourself, too, Maggie. It's really a new day for us. But from the way you and Mama still live you'd never know it."

She put on some sunglasses that hid everything above the tip of her nose and her chin.

Maggie smiled; maybe at the sunglasses. But a real smile, not scared. After we watched the car dust settle I asked Maggie to bring me a dip of snuff. And then the two of us sat there just enjoying, until it was time to go in the house and go to bed.

80

The Responsive Reader

1. What kind of person is the mother? What role do her daydreams play in the story? How does her initial self-portrait as the narrator, or person telling the story, prepare you for what happens later?

2. What is the contrasting history of the two sisters? What is most important in their earlier history?

3. What do Dee and her companion stand for in this story? Do you recognize their attitudes and way of talking?

4. How does the confrontation over the quilts bring things to a head? What is the history of the quilts and their symbolic meaning? How does the climactic ending resolve the conflict in this story?

Talking, Listening, Writing

5. If you had to choose a role model from this story, would you opt for the mother or for Dee? Defend your choice.

Collaborative Projects

6. Do you ever chafe at being a passive reader—who cannot enter into the story to help it steer one way or another? Write a passage in which one daughter or the other tells her side of the story. Or rewrite the ending the way you would have preferred the story to come out. Or write a sequel to the story bringing it up to date. Arrange for members of the class to share their imaginative efforts.

PHENOMENAL WOMAN

Maya Angelou

> *Maya Angelou has had a spectacular career as writer, poet, singer, dancer, actor, and television producer. She early became a leader in the movement toward racial equality and Black Pride, working as the Northern coordinator for the Southern Leadership Conference. She lived for several years in Ghana, editing the* African Review. *Angelou has told her story in a series of autobiographical volumes including* I Know Why the Caged Bird Sings, Gather Together in My Name, Singin', Swingin' and Gettin' Merry like Christmas, *and* The Heart of a Woman. *She was born in 1928 in St. Louis, Missouri; after the breakup of the parents' marriage, she went to live with her grandmother in Arkansas among Southern rural blacks who, she says, valued age more than wealth and religious piety more than beauty. Her story is the story of overcoming poverty, segregated schools, and the fear of violence at the hands of white people and of abuse by her own people as well. Her grandmother ran a country story in Sparks, Arkansas, a small Southern town where many of her contemporaries knew only to "chop cotton, pick cotton, and hoe potatoes," all the while dreaming of being "free, free from this town, and crackers, and farming, and yes-sirring and no-sirring."*

Thought Starters: Women and members of minority groups started to tell themselves that low self-esteem is a self-realizing prophecy: People forever doubting their ability to succeed will not excel. Have you encountered talk about initiatives to raise self-esteem—or skeptical reactions to the self-esteem movement?

Pretty women wonder where my secret lies.   *1*
I'm not cute or built to suit a fashion model's size,
But when I start to tell them,
They think I'm telling lies.
I say,   *5*
It's in the reach of my arms,
The span of my hips,
The stride of my step,
The curl of my lips.
I'm a woman   *10*
Phenomenally.
Phenomenal woman,
That's me.

I walk into a room
Just as cool as you please,   *15*

And to a man,
The fellows stand or
Fall down on their knees.
Then they swarm around me,
A hive of honey bees.   *20*
I say,
It's the fire in my eyes,
And the flash of my teeth,
The swing in my waist,
And the joy in my feet.   *25*
I'm a woman
Phenomenally.
Phenomenal woman,
That's me.

Men themselves have wondered   *30*
What they see in me.
They try so much
But they can't touch
My inner mystery.
When I try to show them   *35*
They say they still can't see.
I say,
It's in the arch of my back,
The sun of my smile,
The ride of my breasts,   *40*
The grace of my style.
I'm a woman
Phenomenally.
Phenomenal woman,
That's me.   *45*

Now you understand
Just why my head's not bowed.
I don't shout or jump about
Or have to talk real loud.
When you see me passing   *50*
It ought to make you proud.
I say,
It's in the click of my heels,
It's the bend of my hair,
The palm of my hand,   *55*
The need for my care.
'Cause I'm a woman
Phenomenally.
Phenomenal woman,
That's me.   *60*

The Responsive Reader

1. Originally, a phenomenon was literally a fact of nature—something our senses could take in. However, the word came to mean something outstanding, impressive, or even startling that we happen to observe. What does Angelou tell us is outstanding about her? Which features are mostly physical—sketching out an impressive physique? Which begin to suggest an attitude—a way of being in the world? How would you sum up that bearing or attitude?

2. Poets are more aware than ordinary people of the overtones of words—the images they call up, the attitudes they carry, the feelings they inspire. What for you are some key words in this poem? What images, attitudes, or feelings do they call up or suggest?

3. What is the role of other people in this poem? What role do they play or should they play in the life of the phenomenal woman? What expectations or stereotypes does the poet think they might bring to this poem—and how does she reject those or turn them back?

4. How should this poem be read? The poet uses many of the features of traditional poetry. Each of the four stanzas or segments follows the same pattern of challenge and response—with the "I say" each time starting the poet's answer to the question or challenge. The three lines at the end of each stanza are a traditional **refrain**—a coming back or echo effect repeating the same key lines. What other uses of repetition or of echo effects can you chart in this poem? What is the effect of the poet's use of patterning and repetition on the reader or listener?

5. What makes the swaying rhythm of much of the poem fitting for its message? How does the sound of the poem echo or mirror the sense?

Talking, Listening, Writing

6. What makes some people self-confident while others are not? What causes high or low self-esteem? Can self-esteem be taught or learned? Can it become too much of a good thing?

7. If you had to choose one word to label your most outstanding character trait, what would it be? Write and prepare to share a journal entry that might start "_____ woman (or man), that's me."

Collaborative Projects

8. Publications from *Time* to *Ms.* magazine have assembled special sections honoring outstanding women. Working with a group, you may want to assemble a collection of texts and images for a presentation honoring phenomenal women. What areas of human life or what kinds of accomplishment will your group want to see represented? Where would you turn for material?

FORUM: *Educating about Race*

Kwame Ture (Stokely Carmichael) was my friend for 40 years. The thing that touched me most about him was that he loved his black people. He was deeply committed to their plight and worked all his 57 years to improve conditions for African Americans. One of his greatest contributions was his 1966 wake-up call to black Americans, saying that they are "a mighty people" who can and must determine and define their own destiny.

Marion Barry, Jr., mayor of Washington, D.C.,
in his eulogy of his former coworker in the
Student Nonviolent Coordinating Committee

The civil rights movement of the sixties and seventies, inspired by the eloquence of the Reverend Martin Luther King, Jr., and fueled by the enthusiasm of countless black activists and white liberal sympathizers, broke the shackles of legalized segregation in America. It established the principle of equal access to education. It helped create a new African American middle class of lawyers, educators, scholars, and public officials. It made crude demeaning racial stereotypes unacceptable on television screens and in boardrooms, if not in locker rooms.

Today, however, there is widespread agreement that the civil rights movement has run its course, leaving many questions about race in America unresolved. Politicians—supported by prominent conservative black Americans—exploit a backlash against affirmative action programs, rechristened as "racial preferences." Pundits pore over income statistics, test results, and surveys, drawing widely differing conclusions.

On the one hand, conservatives marshal statistics showing that the income gap between black and white is narrowing and that we can no longer put the blame on racism in an increasingly "color-blind" society. On the other hand, conservative social scientists have published studies claiming that a low average racial IQ predisposes a racial minority to a life of poverty and crime. Alternatively, conservatives focus on the breakdown of moral values in the black community, blaming black Americans for their own plight.

In the meantime, is it true that more young African Americans are in jail than in college? Is it true that sentences for cocaine use are five times as severe for blacks as they are for whites? In many of America's inner cities, no one—white liberal, black neoconservative, or closet racist—would walk at night. What are we going to tell the next generation about race in America? How are we going to educate them for what lies ahead?

OUR CHILDREN ARE OUR FUTURE— UNFORTUNATELY THEY'RE BIGOTS

Richard Cohen

During the era of the civil rights movement, many Americans believed in progress toward better race relations. They envisioned a future where African Americans and other minorities would emerge from poverty and deprivation to become fully integrated into American life. However, in the nineties, trend watchers like the Washington Post *columnist who wrote the following selection noticed a growing backlash against official policies of tolerance, integration, and affirmative action. "Forced busing" to achieve better racial balance in the schools had proved bitterly divisive and contributed to "white flight" from public education. The media sensationalized racial incidents like the beating by Los Angeles police of the black motorist Rodney King and the killing of a black youth by a white mob in Bensonhurst. Journalists started to give prominent treatment to racial incidents on college campuses. Is the nation backsliding where the fight against racism is concerned?*

Thought Starters: Would you call your campus integrated or divided along ethnic and racial lines? Can you cite incidents that point to racial animosity or racial harmony? Do your friends and acquaintances sound prejudiced to you?

There's hardly a politician in the land who, when children are mentioned, does not say they are our future. That's true, of course—and nothing can be done about it—but the way things are going we should all be worried. A generation of bigots is coming of age.

The evidence for that awful prognostication can be found in a recent public opinion survey conducted for the Anti-Defamation League by the Boston polling firm of Marttila & Kiley—two outfits with considerable credentials in the field of public opinion research. For the first time, a trend has been reversed. Up to now, opinion polls have always found that the more schooling a person has, the more likely he is to be tolerant. For that reason, older people—who by and large have the least education—are the most intolerant age group in the nation.

But no longer. The ADL found a disturbing symmetry: Older and younger white Americans share the same biases. For instance, when white people were asked if blacks prefer to remain on welfare rather than work, 42 percent of the respondents 50 years old and over said the statement was "probably true." Predictably, the figure plummeted to 29 percent for those 30 to 49. But then it jumped to 36 percent for respondents under 30.

Similarly, a majority of younger respondents thought blacks "complain too much about racism" (68 percent) and "stick together more than others" (63 percent). For both statements, the young had a higher percentage of agreement than any other age category. The pattern persisted for the other questions as well—questions designed to ferret out biased attitudes. In the words of Abraham Foxman, the ADL's national director, the generation that's destined to run this country is either racist or disposed to racism to a degree that he characterized as "a crisis." It's hard to disagree with him.

What's going on? The short answer is that no one knows for sure. 5 But some guesses can be ventured and none of them is comforting. The first and most obvious explanation has to do with age itself: The under 30 generation is pathetically ignorant of recent American history. Younger people apparently know little about—and did not see on television—the civil rights struggles of the 1950s and 1960s, everything from the police dogs of Birmingham to the murder of civil rights workers. They apparently do not understand that if blacks tend to see racism everywhere, that's because in the recent past, it *was* everywhere and remains the abiding American sickness.

But historical ignorance is not the only factor accounting for the ADL's findings. Another, apparently, is affirmative action. It has created a category of white victims, either real or perceived, who are more likely than other whites to hold prejudicial views. For instance, the ADL asked, "Do you feel you have ever been a victim of reverse discrimination in hiring or promotion?" Only 21 percent said yes. But the percentage rose to 26 percent for college graduates and 23 percent for people with postgraduate degrees. Since the ADL found that "about one third" of the self-described victims of reverse discrimination fell into the "most prejudiced" category, these numbers are clearly worth worrying about. Too many of the American elite are racially aggrieved—although possibly some of them were bigoted in the first place.

One could argue that not all of the statements represent proof of bigoted attitudes. For instance, white college students who witness voluntary self-segregation on the part of black students—demands for their own dorms, for instance—have some reason to think that blacks "stick together more than others." Nevertheless, the data strongly suggest that progress on racial attitudes is being reversed—with contributions from both races. Worse, this is happening at a time when the economic pie is shrinking and competition for jobs increasing. If the economic trend continues, racial intolerance is likely to grow.

No one I spoke with at either the Anti-Defamation League or at Marttila & Kiley thought their findings were definitive or could offer concrete explanations. But the numbers conform to what you and I know—or think we do—about racial friction on the nation's campuses and a growing uneasiness about affirmative action. After all, most of those programs were instituted during a period of sustained economic growth, a boom time especially for college graduates, when jobs were plentiful. That's no longer the case.

Given the ADL's findings, it's clear that something has to be done. It's nothing less than a calamity that a generation has come of age without a deep appreciation of the recent history of African Americans. At the same time, black leaders who advocate or condone separatism had better appreciate the damage they are doing. And finally, affirmative action programs, as well-intentioned as they may be, need to be re-examined—and without critics automatically being labeled as racist. No doubt these programs have done some good. But there's a growing body of evidence—of which the ADL poll is only the latest—that they also do some bad.

The Responsive Reader

1. According to this columnist, how does the survey he cites reverse traditional assumptions about intolerance?
2. What test questions did the survey use to determine whether young people were "disposed to racism"? Which to you seem most relevant or important? Would you challenge any of them? Does Cohen question any of them?
3. Why and how, as in other, similar, discussions, does affirmative action become a central issue in this column?

Talking, Listening, Writing

4. Cohen concludes that "something has to be done." What? How useful or convincing are his suggestions?
5. Do you agree that racism is on the rise in our society? What evidence can you cite to support your opinion?
6. Do you or institutions or organizations you know have a concrete program for addressing the problem Cohen examines?

Collaborative Projects

7. Working with a group, explore questions like the following: How much attention do people pay to opinion polls? How much confidence do they place in them? What role have opinion polls played in recent elections or policy decisions by officials?

THE TINY, BROWN PROFESSOR

Patricia Smith

Young Americans increasingly have cross-cultural experiences. How do they learn positive or negative attitudes toward children from other ethnic, racial, or religious backgrounds? Some observers claim that parents pass on negative at-

titudes to the next generation. Some studies show that children may be influenced by their peers as much as or more than by their parents. And some psychologists claim that children have spontaneous impulses of rejection toward those perceived as different that they have to unlearn. The following account was written by a woman of color who is a successful journalist and who is committed to ideas of diversity and tolerance widely accepted in the media and by educators. She records some of the conflicting impressions and mixed emotions encountered by those translating their liberal ideas into everyday practice.

Thought Starters: Have you always been part of the in-group? If not, what were your earliest experiences with being treated as an outsider or feeling like an outsider? When were you first part of a group that treated someone else as an outsider? What did you learn from the experience?

I plotted to skip the Purim Carnival this year, even though it meant   *1*
passing up the enticingly interactive reading of the megillah and the crooning of Purim songs by Rabbi David and Cantor Margot. I finally had to admit that I felt acute discomfort at the Jewish temple where my granddaughter attends preschool. Even in the midst of an idyllic crossing of cultures, the real world was bound to intrude.

When we relocated to New York State last summer, our timing couldn't have been worse. Most of the preschools were packed to bursting for the upcoming fall session. The one with space for a four-year-old came highly recommended, boasted an innovative curriculum, and was affiliated with Temple Beth Abraham. And every student in the school was white. This was initially a concern, since we'd just moved from Ridgefield, Connecticut—the home of SUVs, A-line skirts, and the world's whitest women—where the only blacks, browns, reds, and yellows Mikaila encountered were crammed in a box marked "Crayola." I wanted a school that reflected our new community's diversity. Here, I was assured, teaching tolerance was a priority. Well, that took care of the kids. The parents were another story.

To be fair, several of the moms and dads were welcoming from the start. But once the realization set in that I was not one of the West African or Caribbean nannies who deliver and collect their charges, my relationship with many of them was strained, at best. I kept right on speaking to people who kept right on staring past me. At school events, I was marginalized, stuck at the nerd table, an oddity viewed with resentful curiosity and suspicion. What was I doing there? What did I want? Weren't there other places I could go?

Nope, I'm not imagining things. When Mikaila clamors for a play date with a classmate, or vice versa, the kid's mom undergoes an intriguing transformation. Her eyes flutter, she stammers, suddenly there's a very interesting something else at the other end of the hall. Since I am a stickler for personal hygiene and don't drool in conversation, I can only conclude that there's some misunderstanding about playtime at our place. Perhaps it's assumed that the kids will be force-fed a diet of fried pig parts and gangster rap while they make fun with my collection of loaded pistols. Oh, and don't forget the warm malt liquor in the Tigger juice cup. Calms the little buggers right down.

The urge to scoop up my granddaughter and skedaddle to someplace more receptive was tempered by the change in Mikaila. Her world grew.   5

Dressed in a satiny black tutu, my high heels, and a ratty pair of wool leg warmers, she stomps purposefully in circles in the living room, banging a spoon on the bottom of an empty Pringles potato chip can for backbeat. Her chant is insistent, filled with new-found passion: "Shabbat Shalom—HEY! Shabbat Shalom—HEY! Shabbat Shalom—HEY!" Each "HEY!" is punctuated by a dramatic surge in volume.

This is now Mikaila's favorite song, surpassing the "Macarena" by miles. There may be other words besides the three, but she doesn't care to know them. It's got beat. It's got rhythm. It's got the cool "s" sound, every preschooler's favorite. You can boogie to it. It's got that "HEY!" to top things off. And if you're tiny, brown, and sing it in public, you get lots of attention.

At home in the evenings, I am often urged to sit still for my dose of Judaic culture. My miniature professor instructs me in the Hebrew alphabet. She knows how to craft a menorah with marshmallows and pretzels. Her handmade Torah hangs from a special hook in her room. We make a racket with our groggers, and a bright purple dreidel sits atop my computer monitor.

Mikaila is energized by her instructors, but she, too, is a teacher, sharing as much as she learns, barreling her way through any pesky intolerance her playmates may have picked up from their parents. She is brown, not afraid to say so, and an expert at getting everyone in range to see how special her difference is. I believe wholeheartedly in her ability to rock the world.

So am I devastated by this selective snub, this slice of reality? Initially,   10
I was flooded with those ol' colored-girl terrors, those stark slaps of exclusion. In response, I did exactly what I shouldn't do, what never even occurred to Mikaila. I cowered, folded into myself, grew silent. I made myself unapproachable so I had an excuse for not being approached.

I spent a lot of time dealing with only the kids. They're way cooler anyhow, and it will be some time before any of life's perceived badness seeps through. I chatted with them even as their mothers glowered. We winked, giggled, and whispered when no one was listening. They taught me to be much bigger than I am. I may have even pried open their vistas a bit. Little Jared, fascinated from the first by my crinkly braids, finally got up the nerve to reach out and touch. His single flabbergasted word: "Wow."

But living life fully means never letting the inhabitants of the world keep you away from the world. And sometimes clinging to that tenet pays off.

I resolutely planned to skip the Purim bash, but I didn't. We checked it out, and we had a ball. For some reason, parents ventured forth with friendly, if clipped, overtures. A week later, at a birthday party for one of the kids, more adults initiated conversations, and Mikaila's play-date dance card began to fill up. Although my granddaughter had attended the school for eight months, I was just learning many of the parents' names, and they were just learning mine. The picture that kept coming to mind was that of a mountain's resolute stone face being blasted away.

So what happened? Did I "prove" myself in some fashion, maybe simply by always being there, chipping away at that mountain of resistance? Did Mikaila's relentless charm shame our would-be detractors into surrender? If I had to guess, I'd say that my perceptive four-year-old taught me that there's no place I don't belong—and with a shake of her grogger and a little help from her friends, she pulled open yet another door and beckoned me through.

The Responsive Reader

1. What made Smith enroll her granddaughter in the temple preschool? Was she naive in not anticipating the "discomfort" and the problems she encountered? Was this her first experience with being the only person of color in a predominantly white or all-white setting?
2. Smith is torn between her belief in diversity and "those ol' colored-girl terrors, those stark slaps of exclusion." When she felt marginalized by the parents at the preschool, was she feeling too defensive? Do you think she was "imagining things"?
3. Have you had experience with being exposed to the music, folklore, history, or rituals of another culture the way Mikaila is in this account? Do you think such experiences have a lasting influence or result? Why or why not?
4. Was there a breakthrough in Smith's relationship with the parents, or was what happened a natural development? Although the author's tone is lighthearted most of the time, where does she turn most serious in sizing up what took place?

Talking, Listening, Writing

5. Smith describes Mikaila as "barreling her way through any pesky intolerance her playmates may have picked up from their parents." Based on your own experience or your observation of those you know well, do you think parents or peers influence children's views more strongly? Do you think that children are generally more "innocent" and more tolerant than their parents about racial, ethnic, and religious differences?

6. Smith's testimony is what social scientists call **anecdotal**—it is one person's story or one person's observation. It may mean something, and it may not. It may be representative, or it may not be. What in her account seems to you to be part of larger patterns? What do you think people who, like her, believe in diversity and tolerance can learn from her account?

7. As a parent, would you basically wish your children to go to school with others mostly of their own kind, or do you believe in the educational value of children mixing with others of a different background?

HOME TRUTHS ABOUT RACE

Joan Ryan

Joan Ryan is a columnist who represents the "well-meaning white liberal" position in the debate about racism. In preparing for the following column, she had invited readers to comment on how to teach young Americans that "color doesn't matter." At the time, white audiences widely believed that lawyers "playing the race card" had convinced a predominantly black jury to free O. J. Simpson, prominent black athlete accused of abusing and finally murdering his white wife. A statewide initiative aimed at scuttling affirmative action had drastically reduced black enrollment at the prestigious University of California campus at Berkeley and in its law school. In Germany, politicians and opinion makers were feuding over plans for a memorial to commemorate the millions of victims of racism during the Holocaust.

Thought Starters: Suppose a youngster—son or daughter, niece or nephew, kindergarten pupil—asked you what all the talk of race is about or what racism is. Where would you start? What would you say?

Two weeks ago, in [a] special . . . issue on race, I invited readers to share their views on how "to instill in our children the ideal that color doesn't matter."

The response has made me feel frighteningly stupid (an emotion always close to the surface anyway)—but also uplifted. Reading the letters and e-mails was like sitting in on the kind of frank and unvarnished discussion you hear at family dinner tables, where the real-life issues of the world are hashed out.

Of course color matters, readers said. "I get angry with all this talk about our having achieved a color-blind society," wrote one Chinese American man with two children. "I feel that is a lie that really just sets up people of color to work harder at an unachievable goal. . . . Color-blind means we all have to pretend that we can be white . . ."

An African American woman with a 12-year-old son wrote: "You posed the wrong question. I've often thought that this premise . . . is at the core of the problem of race relations. Color matters because, it's who we are."

Another African American, a 32-year-old man in Berkeley, wrote: "Being told (by my parents) that 'People are people' was not helpful when I was consistently receiving the message from others that I was, in fact, different." 5

A Japanese American woman pointed out that kids "have enough brains to look around and see that we live in a white-dominated society." It's important, she says, to "give children the vocabulary for naming what they see, so that racial hurts are not locked away inside them in silence."

Many also felt I gave my son a bad answer when, as we read a book about Abraham Lincoln, he wanted to know why people were slaves. I told him that white Americans used their power and prejudice to enslave blacks for free labor.

"You taught him it's better to be white than to be black. I would have been ashamed to do that to my kids," wrote one.

Others said I should have explained that slavery is not a uniquely American horror. "Tell your son that other people of different skin colors have also been held in slavery over history," one man said.

Another wrote: "Slavery, you might have said, is a bad thing no matter who does it. In this way, you would have put the focus where it belongs: on slavery (rather than race)." 10

One father in Sonoma said I could have broadened the discussion from slavery to oppression. "Kids understand that the powerful take advantage of the less powerful—they see it in the schoolyard and in the playing fields. It was more important for us that our kids understand they should never allow themselves to be oppressors. . . . The virtue we hoped to instill was compassion."

Several parents said they tried to teach their children racial tolerance by moving into racially diverse neighborhoods and sending their children to diverse schools. "Then we raised them with the Golden Rule, simply to treat all people as they would like to be treated," wrote a mother in Berkeley.

A white Oakland mother of two who is married to an African-Caribbean man says the key is to talk. When her daughters asked why flesh-colored Band-aids didn't come in their "cafe au lait" skin color and why the good people on TV were white and the bad people weren't, "we discussed it so that it wouldn't become some kind of shameful secret."

"When our daughters were very young," the mother wrote, "we told them that people are like the flowers in the garden. They all come in different colors, and no color is better than any other."

Thanks for the lessons. 15

The Responsive Reader

1. In the liberal tradition, Ryan believes in the virtues of a "frank and un-varnished discussion." She believes in listening to a range of views. What is the range of views in the comments she reprints? Do any of them seem familiar or predictable to you? Are any of them particularly new or thought-provoking for you? Is there a latent consensus or common center?

Talking, Listening, Writing

2. How do *you* feel about trying to teach young Americans that "color doesn't matter"? Would you call this goal admirable? unrealistic? doomed to failure? the only hope for a better future?
3. What would have been your own response to Ryan's invitation to share views on how to instill the ideal of a "colorless" society in our children? Write a "Letter to the Future" to be read at a future time by a young relative or other young American.

DOUBLE STANDARD ON DRUG SENTENCES

Cynthia Tucker

Cynthia Tucker is a widely syndicated African American journalist from the South who does not expect much from presidential advisory boards, commissions on race relations, or "national conversations on race." She has written about a period of hopeful new beginnings when voters elected a president who counted African Americans among his closest associates and whose childhood in Arkansas had given him "the cross-cultural training to eat and worship and pray with blacks with an ease that was natural." At the same time, a booming economy and widespread prosperity could have made it easier for whites to be generous and less hostile and for minorities to be less resentful. However, a presidency crippled by scandal and lack of backbone squashed her hopes for a real conversation among the races, addressing crime, cultural patterns that contribute to poverty, drug abuse, and "continuing race-consciousness, if not outright racism."

Thought Starters: Do you know Americans who have the "cross-cultural training to eat and worship and pray" with natural ease with Americans of a different racial background or ethnicity?

There are forgotten neighborhoods in America where the holiday sea-   *1*
son imposes a distinct and peculiar ritual: Mom and the kids, or Grandma
and the grandkids, pack up a few goodies in tin plates and paper bags, carefully wrapped in foil. They set out early for a visit preordained to be brief
and circumscribed, its joy limited by the setting. They go to visit a relative
in prison.

The places in America already decimated by poverty and economic
collapse—the black and brown inner-cities—are also places where many
of the young men are out of circulation. They cannot become taxpayers or
decent parents or reasonable prospects for marriage. They will leave prison
with criminal records that guarantee them limited job opportunities.

Lacking decent incomes, they will never marry the mothers of their
children. And that, in turn, will guarantee another generation of children
who have had little contact with their fathers.

America has succeeded in locking up more of its citizens than any
other country on the planet. The state of California alone has more inmates
than France, Britain, Germany, Japan, Singapore and the Netherlands combined, according to a report by Eric Schlosser in the December issue of the
Atlantic Monthly.

We have incarcerated violent, dangerous felons as well as non-violent   *5*
drug abusers. We have created laws designed to keep the streets safe. And
we have designed laws whose only result is to ensure that entire neighborhoods regularly send their young men off to prison.

And we have confused the one with the other.

Let's make some distinctions. Many convicted felons are thugs and
punks. Some of them practiced their violent tendencies on their families
and friends first—beating a girlfriend, robbing a neighbor, abusing a child.
They deserve to be in prison.

But a substantial portion of the 850,000 black Americans behind bars
are there for non-violent drug offenses. Marc Mauer of the Washington,
D.C.–based Sentencing Project estimates the number at 216,000—about
one-fourth. With drug treatment of the sort routinely available to drug-
addicted actors and athletes, or to white-collar employees with good health
insurance, many of them would become tax-paying citizens, able to support
a family, own a home.

To avoid being labeled "soft" on crime, even politicians who know
better have refused to acknowledge a simple truth: We waste money, as well
as lives, when we lock up non-violent drug offenders.

"Among those arrested for violent crimes, the proportion who are   *10*
African-American men has changed little over the past 20 years. Among
those arrested for drug crimes, the proportion who are African-American
men has tripled. Although the prevalence of illegal drug use among
white men is approximately the same as that among black men, black
men are five times as likely to be arrested for a drug offense," Schlosser
wrote.

We ought to be able to talk about alternative sentences for non-violent drug abusers—free drug treatment, with participation a condition of probation, for example.

The streets may be safer because we have succeeded in locking away for good many of the most dangerous predators, the gangbangers and serial killers, the robbers and rapists and car-jackers. But the country is no better off for a shameless double standard that celebrates the privileged athlete, actor or businessman who licks his drug habit in a ritzy sanitarium, while imprisoning the crackhead too broke to afford drug treatment.

That policy guarantees a permanent underclass.

The Responsive Reader

1. Tucker pounds home a familiar thesis: America keeps "locking up more of its citizens than any other country on the planet." Does she bring this central point to life for you? Where and how?
2. In discussing the huge prison population, Tucker emphasizes the price society pays beyond the cost of incarceration. What is the effect on families and on the community? What are the aftereffects for the black community and for society in general?
3. Tucker makes a basic distinction between violent and nonviolent offenders. Do you think politicians could label her "soft" on crime? Why or why not?
4. According to Tucker, what is the "shameless double standard" society applies in the war on drugs?
5. Much of the dialogue on race in this country has been long on analysis of problems or diagnosis of social pathologies. It has been short on workable suggestions or positive advice. Do you find workable suggestions or positive advice in this column?

Talking, Listening, Writing

6. Sentimentality is a warm, self-approving feeling that allows us to feel generous and compassionate at no real cost to our own comfort or established routines. Do you think our tendency to remember the homeless, the poor, or prisoners at holiday times is sentimental? Do you think you are sentimental about the poor and unfortunate?

Find It on the Web

You may want to search for articles on social and political trends in the black community like those published in *The Black Scholar,* a journal by Manning Marable and other African American intellectuals. You may want to check for websites of organizations like the NAACP, the Urban League, the Nation of Islam, or the Black Radical Congress.

Organizing Your Writing

How good are you at organizing your writing? Effective writers know how to lay things out. They present information and ideas in such a way that we say: "Now I see how this works." To organize your material, you may have to sort out a set of data—like statistics on temporary employment or teenage pregnancy. You may have to analyze the stages in a process to show us how to get from point A to point B. You may have to set up categories to show what goes with what. Looking at a problem, you may have to identify major factors that contribute to it and then show us how to deal with them.

These major organizing strategies prove useful again and again as you try to help readers make sense of a confusing situation. In organizing your writing, you will often ask yourself one or more questions like the following: What are the major steps in a process? (What does it take to produce the desired end result?) Do traditional classifications do justice to the current situation—or should we adjust our mental categories? Can we isolate some of the causes of a bad situation and work toward a solution?

TRIGGERING Your ability to sort things out may be put to the test in situations like the following:

- Can you show people who dislike additive-laden supermarket food how to grow their own vegetables or bake their own bread?

- Do you feel that current talk about immigrants tends to lump together many different kinds of people? Can you show that legal status, voting rights, and entitlements vary greatly for different classifications of immigrants?

- Are you skeptical of politicians' claims about job creation and job growth? Can you show why the trend toward "temporary" work, without benefits, is likely to accelerate?

- If the city council is debating different plans for zoning or development, and if you are violently opposed to one of the alternatives, can you show the consequences of adopting plan A and those of adopting plan B?

GATHERING If you want to shed light on a confusing situation, you have to start from a solid base of data. You will need substantial input before you try to explain how things fit together or how things work. For instance, immigration has resurfaced in recent political campaigns as a hot issue. Blue-collar workers are worried about immigrants taking their jobs. Politicians frighten taxpayers with stories about spiraling welfare costs for aliens. At some point, you may ask: Who are these people? Do they all fit the same stereotype? Or are there major kinds of immigrants representing different facets of the "new immigrant" population?

The following might be sample notes you type (or jot down) during your material-gathering stage:

Several small businesses in this community are run by Korean grocers or liquor store owners. Both spouses and maybe older children work in the store. The store is open from early in the morning till late at night.

The local newspaper reports on a new city ordinance concerning day workers who everyone knows line up along a street every morning where employers pick them up for a day's work. Many of these workers are probably illegals. The city council is going to prohibit workers looking for temporary work from lining up along the street.

A pharmacy downtown is now run by a Vietnamese family. The business is a family operation. Little kids run around the store even late in the evening. Come to think of it, what used to be a dead part of town has come back to life with little stores, ethnic restaurants, and colorful shop signs.

I had high school friends whose parents were from Australia and worked in a high-tech company. They never took out citizenship papers and always talked about going back because of the threat of unemployment and poor health insurance.

Newspaper stories crop up about prominent politicians and wealthy Americans employing illegal nannies or gardeners and not paying social security taxes.

The immigration authorities raid sweatshops in New York City.

A visiting professor talks about visiting a migrant camp that is on no map and that the local sheriff said he knew nothing about (!). The people worked for local growers on a seasonal basis, living in shacks.

As you dig in, you may try to remember additional details and check out some of the newspaper stories. At the same time, you may start thinking in terms of three major categories. An early scratch outline might look something like this:

- *established immigrants*—many of these are legal immigrants who came as refugees or as relatives of earlier immigrants and are tax-paying, small-scale entrepreneurs
- *the migrant population*—many of these are illegals employed in sweatshops or by agribusiness as part of a black market economy; many live from day to day and from job to job
- *the in-between people*—many of these are professionals who work here when times are good but have not established permanent ties

When you present your classification of the "new immigrants" in your paper, you will try to flesh out each category with convincing real-life examples. Your readers will not have to agree with you, but you are giving them "a basis for discussion."

SHAPING Among the thinking and writing strategies that help you organize your papers, several prove useful again and again. For instance, you may trace the stages in a process, so you can show what leads to what. What is first, and what is the next step? You may classify, putting things that belong together in the same bin. What goes with what? You may analyze cause and effect: What are the consequences if we do A, and what will happen if we do B?

To get a handle on how something works, we often mark off stages. We trace a **process**—whether to help readers understand evolution or to help them raise chickens. Thinking in terms of major stages enables you to focus on one thing at a time—while yet seeing it as part of a larger whole. You do justice to what seems important during a particular phase without losing sight of the whole. Marie de Santis, in a later chapter of this book, charts the life cycle of the salmon somewhat as follows:

The Last of the Wild Salmon

PHASE ONE: THE SALMON RUN Salmon fight their way upstream, motivated by a powerful instinctual drive. In prodigious leaps, they overcome waterfalls and manmade obstacles.

PHASE TWO: THE SPAWNING GROUNDS Lacerated by their upstream fight, the salmon reach the spawning grounds. They lay and fertilize a myriad eggs.

PHASE THREE: NEW LIFE The parents die, but after an interval fingerlings are in evidence everywhere, which eventually begin their journey downstream.

PHASE FOUR: TRANSITION The young salmon stay in the delta—they live in a sweetwater environment for a time, until they are ready for the saltwater environment of the ocean.

PHASE FIVE: RETURN TO THE OCEAN   The adult salmon live in the ocean for a number of years—until a powerful urge propels them to seek the spawning grounds of their birth, and the cycle begins anew.

Classification—sorting things out into categories—is a basic way of making sense of an array of data. We ask: What goes with what? Schools track students according to IQ, aptitude, or test results. Mortgage companies classify potential home buyers as low-risk, high-risk, and need-not-apply. To place people on a socioeconomic scale, sociologists used to rely on the traditional upper class–middle class–lower class scheme. Today, a sociologist might set up a more realistic scheme of classification, like the following:

Are You Upwardly Mobile?

- upper class (families of large inherited wealth and the corporate elite)
- upper middle class (midlevel managers, professional people, successful businesspeople)
- lower middle class (lower-echelon employees, office workers, teachers, nurses, owners of marginal businesses)
- underclass (dropouts, chronically unemployed, long-term welfare cases)

In trying to understand what goes on in our world, we often focus on **cause and effect.** Once we understand what caused a problem, we may be able to work toward a solution. Once we recognize the causes of a bad situation, we may be able to keep from repeating the same mistakes. For instance, why do both conservatives and feminists seem to have second thoughts about no-fault divorce?

No-fault divorce seemed to promise relief from vindictive court battles traumatizing the family members and enriching lawyers. However, experts found that in reality many women found themselves with insufficient child support, only a few years of hard-to-collect alimony, and a family home that had to be sold so property could be divided. Many divorced women experienced a drastic decline in their standard of living. Why? Lenore J. Weitzman, a professor of sociology at Harvard, identified the causes somewhat as follows:

1 While treating women as theoretical equals, courts ignored the drastically unequal earning power of a man who had built a career and of a homemaker or part-time worker trying to enter the labor force after many years of marriage.

2 The "equal" division of property is in fact unequal if the property is divided between one person (usually the male) and three or four other people (the mother and children).

3 The elimination of misconduct as grounds for divorce eliminated the bargaining power that women used to have when men would make eco-

nomic concessions in order to obtain the "innocent" partner's consent to a divorce.

4 Dividing tangible property such as money and real estate did not, at least at first, take into account such intangible assets as advanced degrees, pension rights, insurance entitlements, or business contacts.

A close look at cause and effect often offers clues on how to remedy a bad situation. If we can identify the most common causes of domestic violence, maybe we can institute educational programs or legal remedies that would help. If we can pinpoint the causes for high dropout rates in local schools, perhaps we can support remedial action.

REVISING In a first draft, you may have concentrated on getting your facts right or on working in different kinds of material. In a revision, you have a chance to ask yourself: Have I done enough to make my readers find their way? Will this paper make them say: "Now I see"? Here are questions you may want to keep in mind while reworking a paper:

▪ *Should you do more to show why your explanations matter?* You might be able to add a quote from an authority on nutrition testifying to the value of baking your own bread or raising free-range chickens. You might be able to show how a realistic estimate of the current immigrant population can help voters make informed decisions about welfare policy.

▪ *Should you do more to make your readers see your overall scheme?* Should you do more to give a preview or overview so that readers know how parts of your paper fit into the larger picture? Make sure they have a sense of what the whole process is as you close in on details. As you develop major categories, make sure readers see how these relate to one another.

▪ *Should you do more to bring in real-life examples or real people?* Categories you set up can easily remain lifeless and theoretical—"academic" in the bad sense.

▪ *Should you aim at more balanced treatment of different parts or stages?* Does any part of your paper seem too skimpy—because you were hurried, or because you did not have the right kind of support ready at the time?

A PAPER FOR PEER REVIEW In the following paper, how effectively has the student writer brought a familiar problem into focus? How clearly does he identify key factors contributing to the situation? How convincing are the answers or the solutions he suggests?

Why AIDS Education Has Failed

I remember walking into a locker room where students were crowding around a radio. "Magic Johnson has AIDS!" In the following months, AIDS awareness peaked all over the country. Magic Johnson's misfortune sparked an interest and a newfound curiosity in the youth of America, who felt they could relate to the basketball star. The media had specials on AIDS and on the HIV virus daily. Misconceptions were being answered about the virus and the disease.

Nevertheless, according to a recent article in the *New York Times,* the number of teenagers with AIDS increased 70 percent in the course of two years, and AIDS was the fifth leading cause of death among people 15 to 24 years old. Although many schools now require AIDS education, many teenagers continue to have unprotected sex. The blame for the failure of AIDS education can be placed on typically adolescent attitudes, on the attitudes of school boards and parents in local communities, and on the generally conservative nature of the political world.

Although studies show that as many as half of sexually active students use condoms, their main motivation is to avoid conception. Vivian Sheer, in an article in *Human Communication Research,* calls teenagers who put themselves at risk "sensation seekers" who like the immediate gratification that unprotected sex provides. Teenagers at this age feel immortal; the attitude is, "It will not happen to me." My own friends and acquaintances see condoms as a hassle; they "ruin an intimate mood, destroy spontaneity, and reduce the partner's sexual pleasure."

Often the community needs as much education as the students. Schools have been slow to address the medical, legal, and ethical issues raised by the presence of an HIV-infected student or even a faculty member. Although experts say that "comprehensive, open discussion about sexuality" is the most effective way of educating people about AIDS, this "open discussion" type of teaching has had to do battle against conservative communities. Parents as well as political leaders preach abstinence and the promotion of moral conduct as the answer. In the words of one school board member, children should be taught what is right and wrong; "they shouldn't be presented with options."

Advocates of sex education find themselves hampered by moralistic restrictions on explicit information about high-risk sexual practices and the effective use of condoms. Often the giving of explicit information is prohibited outright by a politically dominant faction. A surgeon general of the United States was forced from office for her outspoken discussion of adolescent sexuality and advocacy of condom use. Political leaders are more concerned with their image than with saving the lives of young people. I could find no evidence of a coordinated government effort that targets adolescents or collects research data concerning teenagers, a situation that one observer called "a national disgrace."

Nongovernment efforts like the AIDS education project for the National Coalition of Advocates for Students try to make people see the AIDS crisis from a public health perspective. How many lives must be put at risk before another superstar is infected and the media for a short time again keep the AIDS issue in the limelight? In the meantime, students are beginning to develop their own initiatives to protect themselves. In a high school in Massachusetts, students fought and negotiated for a year to make condoms available with counseling. In Connecticut, HIV testing was made available to students without a parent's consent. These battles fought and won show the maturity and capability of teenagers to deal with this topic and their desire to slow the epidemic down.

Topics for Analysis Papers (A Sampling)

1. Have you seen affirmative action at work? How does it work? What are typical issues or typical results?
2. Have you seen the local economy in your hometown or your college town go through major stages? Have you observed different cycles—for better or for worse?
3. Bookstores do a brisk business selling books like *Internet for Dummies.* Write exceptionally clear and foolproof instructions for upgrading a computer, cruising the Internet, or a similar task.
4. Many different kinds of immigrants have come into the country in recent years. How would you sort them out, setting up major categories?
5. In recent decades, alternative living arrangements and lifestyles have come to compete with the traditional nuclear family. What are major current alternatives to the traditional family?
6. What is the ethnic or racial mix at your school? Can you sort out major groups? What sets them apart?
7. Teachers and parents worry about teenagers who seem alienated from what schools have to offer or who see no point in trying hard in school. To judge from your own experience or observation, what makes young people tune out teachers and school?
8. Many Americans seem to accept staggering divorce rates as a fact of life. Is it still worthwhile to look at major causes of divorce and talk about possible answers?
9. From what you have seen, what makes some people bigots? Why are some people more prejudiced or narrow-minded than others? What makes the difference—for instance, family, peers, school, media exposure?
10. What have you seen of programs to fight the spread of drugs among young people? Do they work? Why or why not?

6
CULTURE WARS
Constructing Gender

The legal subordination of one sex to another is wrong in itself and now one of the chief hindrances to human improvement.
—*John Stuart Mill*

Many cultures have had assumptions about what it means to be a man and what it means to be a woman. What parents, counselors, teachers, and employers expect of a young woman may steer her toward options very different from those open to a young man. How much is biology—how true is it that "biology is destiny"? How much is culture—with boys taught from the beginning to be tough and adventurous, and girls taught from the beginning to be dainty and play with dolls? How much is genetic; how much is learned?

In recent decades, there has been a seismic shift in how we think about gender roles and how we define "masculine" and "feminine" traits. Today we no longer take it for granted that the judge will be male and the court clerk female, the physician a man and the nurse a woman, the manager a male and the secretary a female, the college professor a male and the high school teacher someone's wife, and the police officer a male and the meter maid a maid. Medical schools and law schools enroll large numbers of female students, pointing to something closer to parity down the road. All-male businessmen's clubs and military academies survive only in backwaters.

At the same time, while highly visible female CEOs and top managers are today less of a rarity, the top-level executive suites and boardrooms of American business are still largely peopled by males. Congress remains largely a white male preserve. The star athletes in many big-money sports are predominantly male. Women in pink-collar occupations are paid less than construction workers and truck drivers. Public school teachers are far from receiving pay comparable to that of other professionals.

Whether or not women consciously identify with the feminist movement, they are likely to be involved in women's issues: There is growing concern about widespread sexual abuse of women and children, with rape victims and women in battered women's shelters demanding less cavalier treatment by law enforcement and the justice system. The integration of women into the military has led to widespread charges of sexual harassment and exploitation. Abortion rights are everywhere contested by male-dominated legislatures. For feminists, the mantra of "family values" is merely code for the male lords of creation trying to send their women back to baking cookies and chauffeuring their offspring as "soccer moms."

How do we become aware of the limits and opportunities that await us when we are identified according to such factors as gender, race, ethnicity, or sexual orientation? What chance do we have to shape our own destiny, to forge our own identity? In her feminist rereading of Charlotte

Brontë's novel *Jane Eyre,* Adrienne Rich traces one young woman's journey toward self-realization. Young Jane exercises the limited options open to her as a poor young woman in nineteenth-century England. She goes to work as a governess in the mansion of Rochester, the gloomy aristocrat. When she finds he is married to a mentally ill woman, she refuses the temptation of an extramarital romance and leaves his employ. Later, she rejects the option of serving as a platonic helpmate to a high-minded missionary on his way to convert the heathens. She discovers female friends and teachers who think of other women not as rivals but as sisters. She finally marries the widowed Rochester when she can join in the union as a partner, as an equal.

How optimistic or how realistic is the scenario acted out in Brontë's novel? What chance do people in our culture have to transcend the barriers created by gender, ethnicity, or sexual orientation?

FEWER TEEN GIRLS ENROLLING IN TECHNOLOGY CLASSES

Nanette Asimov

In the eighties, a widely quoted book coined the term math anxiety *to describe the tendency of young women to avoid math and science or to do poorly in math and science classes. Here was a clear example of a gender gap that gave male students the edge when planning for careers in the emerging technologies of the modern world. What caused the gap? Did it have something to do with innate ability or inherited feminine traits? Is there a special kind of intelligence needed for calculus and the hard sciences that is more of a masculine than a feminine characteristic? Or was the gap a result of cultural factors? Was it the result of early childhood training, when boys played with gadgets and girls played with dolls? In the following news item, a reporter covers a follow-up study published by the American Association of University Women. What happened to the gender gap? Have changing attitudes and expectations taken care of it, or is it still a factor—something teachers and students have to reckon with or take into account?*

Thought Starters: When you take a class, do you think of students as male or female students—or as just students? Do you expect men and women to talk in class, study, and succeed about the same—or differently?

Teenage girls nationwide are enrolling in calculus, biology and chemistry classes as never before—but an "alarming new gap" is showing up in the physics and computer classes that lead to higher-paying jobs, says a study to be released today.   *1*

"This failure threatens to make women bystanders in the burgeoning technology industry of the 21st century and keep women underrepresented in high-salaried, intellectually challenging careers," says the report by the American Association of University Women.

"Gender Gaps: Where Schools Still Fail Our Children" looks at progress in the six years since a landmark national study revealed the subtle ways that American schools treat boys and girls differently, from calling on girls less often to steering them into nontechnical classes.

Today, the report shows, female students are somewhat better off.

"Girls clearly are improving in math and science enrollment, but there is an alarming new gap that has to do with technology," said Janice Weinman, executive director of the AAUW, which also commissioned the '92 report, "How Schools Shortchange Girls."   *5*

Since then, such groups as the National Council of Teachers of Mathematics have tackled the gender gap in math and science classes and pushed for changes that are beginning to have an effect.

According to the latest report, the national math group has taken a strong role in encouraging schools to pay more attention to girls—who may be more reticent in math class than male peers.

School principals are also tapping more young women for honors classes in calculus, biology and chemistry.

The Responsive Reader

1. To judge from your experience, is it true that the gender gap has narrowed in areas like math and science? What have you seen in classes that you or your friends have taken? What has made the difference, or what problems seem to remain?
2. Do you agree that a new gender gap is developing between young men and women in the computer age? Will women be "bystanders in the burgeoning technology industry of the 21st century"? What evidence have you seen of current trends or countertrends? What causes are at work? What can be done or should be done about them?

Talking, Listening, Writing

3. Have you seen evidence in other areas that "American schools treat boys and girls differently"? How serious or widespread are such differences? In what areas of schooling or education are they most important?

Collaborative Projects

4. According to a traditional male prejudice, women "talk too much." However, studies of classroom behavior show that male students often dominate class discussion. (According to this news report, women may be "more reticent" in math classes than their male peers.) You may want to help organize a study of male and female participation in class discussion in classes attended by you and fellow students. You may want to arrange for observers to track frequency of participation, average length of contribution, relevance or value of contribution, tendency to interrupt others, or other significant behaviors.

Student Voices

The following is a sampling of student reactions to the news item about the gender gap in cyberspace. Do you agree or disagree strongly with one or more of them? Do any of them change your mind? Write a response to one or more of these. Join in the conversation.

1   Sure, I think there is a big gender gap in the computer age. I am a math major and female. The majority of the people in my math classes, science classes, and computer science classes are male (probably 8 out of 10). I don't know what can be done to change these statistics. If women really wanted to do this stuff, they could. For some reason, women are just not as prone to be in technology. Maybe they don't want to be nerds. Maybe they feel intimidated by all the men in the field. I think there will always be some kind of gender gap in these fields. If there isn't, it will probably be because affirmative action is trying to equal things out in an unnatural way.

2   I am well aware that a gender gap exists in the computer age. I personally know six or seven male students that I would consider highly literate in computers and technology and only one female student. I would be lying if I said this phenomenon surprised me. Both men and women view one another as different—not unequal, but different. The one girl I know who is into computers is as knowledgeable as any of the males. I do not doubt the capacity of women to enter and succeed in this field, merely the desire. From my observation, women seem less interested in computers, video games, and huge stereo systems, while many males are obsessed with them.

3   More young men than women have an interest in the "burgeoning technology" of the computer age. As a result, women will hold positions of secretaries and assistants to the high-salaried males in the field, with women's salaries not comparable to those of the technology wizards. Because of their low-pay careers, women will not be treated as equals in the workplace or by society as a whole. If this trend continues, it will eventually reverse all the hard work women have put into closing the gender gap in the workplace. My female friends seem to think uniformly that computer classes would be too hard for them and that computer technology "is a guy thing." They do not give themselves a chance to succeed, and they underestimate their full capacity. Girls should be encouraged from a young age to work with computers and explore the different realms of technology. Their academic capacity should not be prejudged; instead, it should be boosted by self-esteem and a strong academic foundation. Parents should instill the thought that "being anything I want to be is possible if I want to."

4   More of my male friends are computer literate than my female friends, and I have observed the dominance of males in chat rooms. I think a way to change this trend would be to expose more female students to computers and technology by requiring them to take classes in these subjects in high school. Another idea might be to have all-women technology classes to present a nonthreatening, non-male-dominated environment to young girls.

Find It on the Web

At a global technology summit held by Bill Gates, only 2 of the 103 cyber honchos were women. However, it is estimated that actually more than one-third of the world's online users are female. Female college students and interested males may check out websites with names like *Amazon City* or *cybergrrl* or *nerdgrrl* or *chickclick*. They may check out books with titles like *netchick*. You may want to check out any sources with *grrl* or *minx* in the title. You can check out recent issues of *Wired*, a magazine available both as print copy and online.

THE JOY OF WOMEN'S SPORTS
Ruth Conniff

The author of the following article is the Washington editor of the Pro-gressive magazine. She traces the changes in women's collegiate sports since the passing of the 1972 Education Amendments Act, whose Title IX stated: "No person in the United States shall on the basis of sex be excluded from par-ticipating in, be denied the benefits of, or be subjected to discrimination under any educational program or activity receiving Federal financial assistance." Be-fore Title IX, Division I colleges spent two percent of their athletic budgets on women's sports, and there were virtually no athletic scholarships for women. Title IX required colleges to allot an equal or proportionate share of money spent on athletic programs to women's sports—or risk losing all federal fund-ing. In spite of challenges and reverses, and in spite of fitful enforcement, Title IX led to vastly increased participation of women in collegiate sports. The same issue of the Nation *magazine that printed this article included an article by the author of a book on a women's basketball team,* Lauren Kessler's Full Court Press.*

Thought Starters: Do you think women students are less interested in sports than men?

It has been my generation's great good fortune to grow up in the era   *1* of Title IX. Never before has a single law made it possible for so many pre-viously disfranchised people to have so much fun. Since Title IX of the Ed-ucation Amendments Act passed in 1972, requiring publicly funded schools to offer equal opportunities to male and female athletes, the number of American high school girls who play sports has jumped from one in twenty-seven to one in three. The effects are visible everywhere: an explosion of female Olympic stars, college and professional women's teams playing to packed stadiums, new magazines aimed at female athletes. But most of all, the effect of Title IX is evident in the freedom, strength and joy of a whole generation of young women.

In June I went to Buffalo, New York, to watch the NCAA track championships with Kamila Hoyer-Weaver, a young woman I coached when she was a high school runner, and her mother, Joan.

"What must it be like to get this far—to be ready at this level?" Joan mused, as we stood near the starting line before the women's 1,500-meter race. College runners in ponytails and racing flats were doing their warmup strides and nervously shaking out their legs. Behind us, a high jumper made the best attempt of the meet so far, and the stands erupted in cheers.

"For women my age it's a foreign thing to understand this competition," she said. "We weren't even raised to be competitive."

Kamila, a freshman at the University of Wisconsin, has an entirely different point of view. She came to watch her teammates who have made it to this elite level—some of the best athletes in the country. She has been steeped in competition, as a high school runner and basketball player, and now as part of a Division I college program.

I watched Kamila and her friends grow up during the six years I spent coaching runners at nearby Madison East High School—my alma mater. It was a joy to see those saucer-eyed kids on the starting line, pale and sometimes sick with nerves, propel themselves into accomplished, self-assured womanhood. This, it seems to me, is the whole project of adolescence—testing yourself, facing your fears, discovering what you can do. Sports provide the natural arena for it. Instead of turning inward, nurturing the crippling self-consciousness that often afflicts adolescent girls, these female athletes thrust themselves into the world. Along the way, they shed some of their peer group's cloying affectations and picked up an appealing jocky swagger. Kamila blossomed from a shy back-of-the-packer to a consistent varsity scorer in cross-country and track. At the end of her high school career, I traveled with her to the state meet where she ran a lifetime best in the 800, taking eighth place at 2:20.14. Now, she is reaching the next stage.

"She gets to run with the big girls," Kamila said admiringly of Kathy Butler, the NCAA cross-country champion from Wisconsin. The "big girls" are a group of Olympic hopefuls, including the famous Suzy Favor Hamilton, UW graduates who still train full time with their former college coach, Peter Tegen. "It's inspiring to see them on the track with us," Kamila says.

At Wisconsin, Kamila is in the center of women's track history. Coach Tegen, who founded the Wisconsin women's program twenty-five years ago, has nurtured a series of Olympians, beginning with Cindy Bremser, Wisconsin's first female All-American. In a speech at our girls' city banquet one year, Bremser told us how she began jogging for exercise in college and ended up at the Olympics, where she took fourth in the 1,500 meters in 1984.

"The talent that was developed while I was at Wisconsin has had an impact on the rest of my life," she said. "It's opened doors for me that I never would have dreamed of."

In the eighties, when I was running for East, Suzy Favor was starting her career on one of our rival teams, Steven's Point Area High School. She and her teammates would warm up together, a pack of fierce-looking girls with French braids and black-and-red windsuits. At the start of each race their fans chanted "SPASH! SPASH! SPASH!" Their coach blew a horn you could hear for miles as his runners came charging over hills and through the woods. Favor, who was a rocket even then, went on to become the four-time NCAA champion in the 1,500 and the American record-holder in the 1,000 meters.

All this is ancient history to Kamila, who is well beyond the gee-whiz era of women's sports. She takes it for granted that there is a long line of female champions in whose footsteps she can follow. She says her heroes are Amy Wickus, a 1995 graduate of Wisconsin and the indoor collegiate record-holder in the 800 (2:01.65), Hazel Clark of Florida, this year's winner of the outdoor NCAA women's 800 (2:02.16) and Michael Jordan ("but I guess he's everybody's hero").

After the meet, back at the hotel, she talks with ABC track commentators Carol Lewis, the Olympic long jumper, and Dan O'Brien, Olympic gold medalist in the decathlon. It's nice to see how easily she moves among these female and male stars. For much of the weekend, she has been hanging out with Gabe Jennings, her classmate from high school, now a freshman at Stanford. Gabe took second in the men's 1,500 and made the national news. The day before his final race, he was sitting in the stands with Kamila and her mom, watching the men's and women's races, trading track stories.

One of the best things about the rise of women's sports is the friendship and camaraderie it engenders between boys and girls. In track and other individual sports, male and female athletes travel together, support each other and have fun as a team. Because the goal of each athlete is to improve his or her own best performance, and because men and women go through the same workouts and races, there is a feeling of equality.

"It's easier to build friendships with guys who do track," says Avrie Walters, Kamila's teammate, who made it to the 1,500 trials at the nationals. "There's a kind of respect," Stephanie Pesch, another Wisconsin runner, adds. "It's like they understand what you've achieved."

"I like it, even if you're just training at the track and the guys yell for   15
you," says Kamila.

At East High, the boys' and girls' cross-country runners were particularly close. They took turns hosting spaghetti dinners at their houses before meets. They ran along the course to cheer for each other during races. When both teams won the city meet, they did a victory dance together, beating on drums some of the boys had brought along, hopping around the finish chute, forming a crazy, mismatched can-can line and swinging each other by the arms in a spontaneous outburst of celebration.

These moments of coeducational enthusiasm are part of what's precious to me about my own experience in sports. Both in college and in a postcollegiate track club, I made lifelong friends with the men and women I ran with, shared the ups and downs of training and competition, and partied afterward. Hearing the encouraging words of my male track coaches, seeing my male teammates pound each other on the back and yell when my female teammates and I sprinted across the finish line to win, made an indelible impression on me. To the great benefit of us all, sports have changed how men look at women, and how women view themselves.

That's not to say there's no more conflict between the sexes when it comes to sports.

The *Washington Post* ran a story recently about the forty-six-year-old World Series for boys, which the Babe Ruth League is holding this August in Loudoun County, Virginia. In keeping with a musty tradition, tournament organizers have been advertising for local teenage girls to be "hostesses" to escort the players, entertain them and cheer for them during the tournament. Each girl, the *Post* reported, is supposed to wear a kind of modified baseball uniform with a skirt.

This idea went over like a ton of bricks with the female high school   *20*
athletes of Loudoun County.

"You can consider me a feminist . . . when they told me about that, I said 'Nope,'" Brooke Hoeltzel, a junior at Loudoun Valley High School, said. "A lot of my friends are athletes, and they have the same view I did."

Tournament organizers were quoted blaming the culture of Washington, with all its professional women, for the problems their hostess-recruitment effort encountered. "In Kentucky and Arkansas it does fine," said Erik Zimmerman, who heads the Loudoun organizing committee for the boys' World Series.

But girls like Hoeltzel say they don't have time to jump around in a little skirt. They have their own summer-league games to play. After getting a taste of playing, it seems, there's no going back.

"I'm an athlete," Hoeltzel told me. "I'm not a cheerleader, I know that. This would make me a cheerleader."

"What's the big difference?" I ask.   *25*

"With an athlete I think of an equal, a guy and a girl," she says. "And with a cheerleader it's sitting on the sidelines. I'm not one to sit there and watch."

Joy Miller, a Loudoun County mother of two daughters, ages 9 and 12, agrees. Her 9-year-old, who plays fast-pitch ball in a 10-and-under league, has been hitting and catching since she was 4. And both girls are now trying out for a summer travel team. They've been all fired up since they attended a clinic put on by Olympic softball player Dot Richardson.

"My daughters would rather be out swinging a bat than being a hostess for the boys," Miller told me.

When I get hold of Erik Zimmerman on the phone, he sounds weary from the media attention his event has been getting, first from the *Post,* then from the local television stations. "It's interesting, they've all been women interviewing me," he says dryly. He wants to set the record straight: For one thing, the hostess uniforms are not skirts. "We figured out a long time ago that skirts were not appropriate. After all, they're going to a ball game. So what they're wearing are skorts," he says.

Skorts?   *30*

"It's a pair of shorts that look like a skirt."

I try to picture the girl athletes' reaction to this.

Zimmerman seems nice enough. He tells me about his 15-year-old daughter, who played three sports last year. "I'm the last person to denigrate women's sports," he says. But when I ask him if the Babe Ruth League has considered adding a girls' program, he says no. "I don't think girls are interested in playing baseball."

In spite of the boom in women's sports, a backlash is brewing against Title IX. Opponents of the law say it forces schools to cut men's programs in order to give women money and facilities they don't want or need.

Earlier this year, John Stossel of ABC's *20/20* offered one tale of the ravages of what he called "the equality police." At the Merritt Island High School in Florida, he reported, the boys' baseball team had a stadium with lights, bleachers, a concession stand and fancy scoreboard. The girls' softball team had a field just the other side of a locked fence, with patchy grass and no lavatories. Two softball players, Jennifer and Jessica Daniels, sued the school board for discrimination under Title IX.

"So the school board proposed a solution," Stossel intoned. "They would unplug the boys' scoreboard, shut down the concession stand and the press box and rope off the bleachers so no one could sit here. That would make things equal."

This scorched-earth response was not what the girls had in mind, of course. Stossel didn't bother to explain that their lawyer, Lisa Tietig of the ACLU, argued that it was unconstitutional to rope off the bleachers, since this would be discriminating against the boys. A judge agreed, and the boys got to keep their facilities.

I talked to Tietig after the *20/20* show aired, "I was so mad about that," she said. "It really distorted things. And of course everyone would hate the girls after seeing it."

The lawsuit, which has expanded to include all of the public schools in the county, is not scheduled for trial until the year 2000. But already for the girls in Merritt Island, the results of their legal action have been good. The school took down the locked fence between the boys' and girls' fields, so the girls and their fans can use the toilets. (Before the lawsuit, according to Tietig, the school had refused to consider unlocking the fence.) The school board paid for outdoor lights for the girls, and the community arranged to buy the girls a scoreboard and fix the grass. "The kids on the boys' and girls' teams have banded together," says Tietig. "And the parents of both teams helped each other out. They've been down on their hands and knees weeding the girls' field. It's a lot better."

In general, parents no longer accept the idea that their sons deserve a better shot at sports than their daughters. That is the transformative effect of Title IX.

Still, according to Billie Jean King, who started the Women's Sports Foundation when she retired from tennis, after twenty-five years schools

35

40

have come only about halfway to compliance with Title IX. Overall, boys still have almost twice as many opportunities to play in school athletic programs as girls do.

"The Office of Civil Rights has been incredibly ineffective in executing its responsibility" to enforce the law, King writes in a foundation report. "Moms and dads are being forced to go to court and suffer the expense and animosity generated by such judicial solutions. While they have won their cases, it is clear that the promises of Title IX will not be realized in my lifetime if each school not in compliance must be taken to court to force them to 'do the right thing.'"

Lately, opponents of Title IX have been trying to persuade people that you can be in favor of girls' sports and still be against Title IX. Leo Kocher, a wrestling coach who heads the National Coalition for Athletics Equity, argued this case on *20/20.* "We're just perpetrating an awful thing against the men," he said. "We're saying we're punishing you because you have more interest in sports than women."

It's true that Division I colleges across the country have been eliminating men's minor sports, from wrestling to gymnastics to baseball. And many coaches blame Title IX. But budget figures from the colleges don't support the argument that women's teams are the cause. The NCAA's latest gender-equity study shows that budget increases over the past five years for Division I-A men's sports was more than three times larger than the increase for women. More important, at the same time that Division I-A colleges have been cutting minor men's teams, spending on the big programs— mainly football—has increased dramatically.

Sixty-three percent of the $1.7 million increase in funding for Division I-A men's sports over the past five years went to football. Just that extra money for football exceeded the total operating budget for *all* Division I-A women's sports combined.

"The real problem is that schools are refusing to hold the line on men's football and basketball budgets," says Donna Lopiano, executive director of the Women's Sports Foundation.

Football is the Pentagon of athletic department budgets. Big schools continue to pour the bulk of their money into it, leaving the other, small-budget sports to fight it out over the scraps.

Interestingly, the smaller Division II and III schools have actually added men's teams over the same period that Division I schools have been cutting them. As a result, men's participation in college sports is at an all-time high. When you count all men's teams in all divisions, men have seen a net increase of seventy-four teams since the advent of Title IX. "The poor schools are adding sports for men," Lopiano says. "The richest schools are dropping sports. Why? Because they're fueling the football monster."

Schools have a lot of control over how they allocate their sports budgets. And, contrary to popular belief, Title IX does not require that girls get

45

the exact number of slots on a team as boys, nor the same amount of funding. Instead, it gives schools three options for meeting the requirements of the law. They can show (1) that female athletes are getting an opportunity to play sports proportional to their representation in the student population; or (2) that, even if female athletes are underrepresented, the school is making progress by gradually expanding the female sports program; or (3) that, even if female athletes are underrepresented, women and girls are getting as much opportunity to play as their interests demand.

It's a shame to see men's and women's minor sports pitted against each *50* other, because they have a lot in common. They are less about entertainment for sedentary fans than about participation. They are more inclusive than the big-time, quasi-professional programs. And they are subversive in a way, because they are driven by something other than the values of the market. You often hear the word "pure" bandied about to describe college women's teams. It's part of their charm that, as in minor men's programs, the athletes are playing for the love of it, not because they're raising revenue or planning on a multimillion-dollar professional career.

"Sports are the laboratory of the human spirit," says Anson Dorrance, the coach of one of the winningest teams in women's soccer, the University of North Carolina Tar Heels. He says he's learned to enjoy his sport more by coaching the women's game. In his book, *Training Soccer Champions,* he talks about how his coaching style has evolved. As a men's coach at UNC for thirteen years, Dorrance says, he used a lot of negative techniques, yelling at and bullying his athletes, waging a constant battle of egos with his players. "You basically have to drive men, but you can lead women," he writes. "And, in my opinion, the way you coach women is a more civilized mode of leadership."

Dorrance's female athletes responded badly to bullying, which forced him to become a more reasonable coach. On the flip side, he had to teach his players to overcome their training as girls to be sweet and passive. "They have this internal war going on between wanting to prove they are great soccer players and the social agenda of wanting to be accepted by the group," Dorrance writes of his younger players. "So when they go into direct confrontation with a veteran, it's almost like they feel they have to acquiesce."

To drill this out of his players, Dorrance throws them into what he calls a "competitive cauldron" at practice: "They sort of beat it into each other that it's okay to compete."

Clearly his athletes have got the message, winning national championship after national championship. Some have gone on to the world-champion US women's team, including April Heinrichs, the US team's assistant coach in 1996.

"I think women bring something incredibly positive to athletics," *55* Dorrance told me. "They are wonderfully coachable and so appreciative of anything you give them. If men could draw something from the women's model, their image would improve."

Out of the interaction of male and female athletes and coaches arises the prospect of a better approach to sports, and to life. That's good news not just for women but also for men. My colleague at East High, Ty Prosa, who switched from being a boys' coach to coaching the girls' track team, says this about his experience: "With boys, the old-fashioned idea is that coaches give orders, and the athletes are supposed to accept it. You're like a drill sergeant in the Marines. Girls have more questions. I was unprepared to deal with this questioning at first. It took me a lot of effort to overcome my feeling that it was a challenge to my authority. But now I really enjoy coaching girls. I'm more invested in their success, because they give me more feedback, and I've become a better coach."

Sports bring out the most fundamental parts of human nature. There's the potential for cruelty, cowardice and unethical behavior, as in any other social sphere. But sports can also put us in touch with the greatest parts of being human—our own courage, compassion and capacity for the sheer physical enjoyment of life.

The happiness and freedom sports bring us, as participants, is a radical notion in consumer culture. There's all that pleasure to be had, from ourselves and each other, without buying anything. That potential slips away when, instead of participants, we become only spectators. We let professional athletes become stand-ins for ourselves.

The Responsive Reader

1. For Conniff, what are dramatic outward signs of the "explosion" of women's sports? How does she dramatize the contrast between today's expectations and those of an earlier generation? What are some outstanding success stories she includes in her article?

2. According to Conniff, what role do sports play in helping adolescent women deal with the challenges and obstacles of growing up? How does the vastly expanded participation of young women in athletic programs help them move toward "self-assured womanhood"?

3. Does Conniff see the growth of women's sports as driving a wedge between the boys and girls she observes?

4. From the beginning, supporters of Title IX attracted much hostile attention from the defenders of traditional men's sports, in particular football and basketball. What kind of backlash does Conniff describe? What examples does she give of the initiatives or maneuvers of the opposition? On what grounds does she criticize the spin and methods of hostile media coverage?

5. How does Conniff counter charges that the growth in women's sports is a danger to traditional male sports? What figures does she use to support her position? What misconceptions does she try to counter?

6. In Conniff's view, why and how should supporters of men's and women's collegiate sports be natural allies against the influence of professional sports and the role of heavily commercialized programs? How is the growing influence of women having a positive influence on men's sports? What new ideal vision of the role of sports does Conniff sketch when she talks about "the prospect of a better approach to sports, and to life"?

Talking, Listening, Writing

7. Have you seen evidence that a commitment to women's sports can "transform" women's lives? What evidence have you seen that the increased visibility of women athletes is changing the way we think about sports?
8. Do you know people who see the push toward women's sports by the "equality police" as a threat to traditional male sports? What are their arguments or concerns? Do most people you know accept or support growing support for women's athletics?
9. One supporter of women's sports said, "There are too many magazines out there that tell us how to do our hair, what to wear." In the treatment of women's sports, have you seen a shift in emphasis from looking good or "aesthetically pleasing" to performing well? (Are cheerleaders passé?)

Collaborative Projects

10. You may want to team up with classmates to investigate how women's sports are prospering in local schools and area colleges. What can you find out about funding, morale, media coverage, unresolved issues?

Find It on the Web

Fitness magazines for women—with titles like *Shape, Fit,* and *Self*—tend to focus more on weight loss, aerobics, or trends in workouts than on team play and athletic competition. *Sports Illustrated* started to develop a spinoff focused on women and sports, and Condé Nast created a publication called *Women's Sports and Fitness* aimed at the same market. At the time this article was written, *Girljock* magazine focused on "hard-core" sports—like hockey, rugby, kickboxing, rock climbing. Websites recommended to sports and fitness enthusiasts included *Go, Girl* (www.gogirlmag.com) and *W.I.G.* (www.wigmag.com).

FACING DOWN ABUSERS

Im Jung Kwuon

> *Im Jung Kwuon is a Korean American woman who works in Los Angeles as a counselor in a domestic-violence-prevention program. The women's movement has everywhere raised public awareness of violence against women: Communities today have domestic-violence hotlines, shelters for battered women, and more effective police intervention. Kwuon is one of the countless anonymous dedicated professionals who make it their life's work to help others. At the same time, Kwuon's article makes it clear that there are no quick fixes or cheap solutions for the social pathologies that impact people's lives.*

Thought Starters: If you were to observe or witness a case of domestic violence, what would be your reaction? Would you be likely to intervene? Would you stay out of it? Would you tell others not to "get involved"?

I always wanted a safe life after recovering from alcoholism, two sui-   *1* cide attempts and abusive relationships. But could I truly be safe if others were in danger? Helping families became part of my recovery. Now I work with men who beat and sometimes kill the women they love. I counsel those who are court-ordered attendees to a yearlong domestic-violence prevention program. Some people hearing this step back startled, cringing at a familiar memory of abuse. Others glare, accusing me of coddling bad guys by teaching them anger-management skills.

Even cops twice my size say they would be scared to go into my classes. They say that domestic calls are the worst, too dangerous. I tell them, "Hey, my groups are as safe as you'll get. Come see what it's like. I'll protect you." They look skeptical since I'm a petite, 40-year-old, Korean-American woman. My bravado hides the fact that I've shopped for a bullet-proof Kevlar vest. I've fingered the high-tech, impenetrable material, wondering if it would be a good investment. I choose not to buy one, because fear is my worst enemy.

I wish I had been wearing a vest when enrolling some batterers into the classes. They scream curses and pace threateningly. They rarely admit to having beaten their partners or children. When they do, most cling to a jus-tification. "She made me punch her." I always suggest they take a timeout to cool off until the next class. When they choose to de-escalate, both class-mates and family are less likely to get hurt.

Recovery begins when men can express anger without intimidating others. It continues when they can recount how often they saw their moth-ers slapped, choked or hit with a two by four. I encourage them to share painful childhood experiences, but remind them there is no excuse for abuse.

I remain on guard even after healing days. When a group member shakes my hand or brings flowers in gratitude, I remember that emotional intimacy is dangerous for both victims and victimizers. Batterers usually injure only those they care about. Getting close to one is like building a home on the slopes of a dormant volcano. Occasionally, I hear encouraging reports from partners of former clients. One joyful wife called a year after her husband finished the class. She gushed, "We had a big fight and he didn't hit me. I should've called the police 10 years ago."

After working with batterers for four years, I no longer have unrealistic expectations of success. I remember a young man I'll call Joey. He attended 14 classes, entertaining us with clever jokes and reassuring us that he was getting along with his girlfriend. Then he dropped out. Two months later, I saw on TV that Joey had shot her in the chest and killed her. Six months earlier, she had given birth to their second son.

For weeks I cried and lost sleep, wondering if I could have saved her life. I pored over the newspaper, looking for names of former clients charged with homicide. Can the chain of domestic violence ever be broken? Recovery frequently includes relapse. So it wasn't surprising when a man called me after getting my number from his cellmate, a former client doing hard time for a second spousal-abuse charge. I reflected back to a decade ago when domestic-violence calls were less frequent and counseling haphazard. Today, an arrest often follows a 911 call. A criminal charge plus 52 classes encourages an abuser to give up violence and intimidation as control strategies. Families benefit because batterers can learn to become safer partners and fathers.

Without help abusers can also lose their lives. Last year after Father's Day weekend, one group talked about who among them got drunk, who picked a fight, who walked away for a timeout. Near the end of that session, a man I'll call John revealed how he had lost his father that past Sunday. "Just before midnight, my mom called me for help. Dad was drinking and beating her. Like times before, he pointed a shotgun at her, but this time they wrestled with it and she shot him." John choked up. "I got there too late," he explained.

John stayed behind to confess, "I know it was an accident. This has been going on since I was a kid, but even at Dad's funeral I couldn't forgive her. I couldn't look at my mom's face." He added, "I can't come back for a while." I hugged him goodbye, encouraging him to return soon.

I knew he needed our support as much as the group needed him. John's courage in telling other batterers about his loss could help prevent tragedy in their lives now. Confronting abusers with the consequences of their behavior increases the chance their families will survive and recover. Unfortunately, counseling cannot save or heal people who never try it. As a young adult, I took up with increasingly abusive boyfriends. I remember standing mute when a boyfriend punched a wall. He said my anger provoked him. I felt I was going to be hit next. Being a paralyzed victim or witness supports abusers. I learned this the hard way.

After salvaging my life through counseling, I've realized how powerful batterers are. They scare the world, because no one wants to face them. Often they are our family leaders. We still struggle to love and be loyal to them. I teach abusers how to be safe physically and emotionally. But no one is safe until every batterer is held accountable for his behavior.

For me, safety means that I'm prepared to call the police if anyone gets violent. This rule applies even to family and friends. But strengthening this basic security doesn't shield me from sadness and pain.

When I watched John walk away, I realized I had embraced someone experiencing my ultimate nightmare. No one in his family called 911 for the domestic violence, just the death. Breaking the chain of family abuse is a good job, even if it hurts.

The Responsive Reader

1. What would you include in a sketch of the counselor's own personal history? Do you think a person with her history would find it hard to be objective or professional, or do you think it is essential that a counselor or therapist should have lived through some of the experiences that she deals with in her professional capacity?

2. Kwuon talks about abusers on the basis of close personal observation and extended professional involvement. To judge from her article, what are major constants or predictable factors in the psychology of abusers? What are likely to be common elements in their background? What are recurrent patterns of behavior? What causes them to be the way they are, and what makes them act the way they do?

3. Kwuon says she no longer has "unrealistic expectations of success," and she offers no panacea. What is she trying to tell her readers about the successes and limits of counseling or therapy? What is the "bottom line" in the advice she gives to victims or to families?

4. What for you is the most revealing or thought-provoking case history in this article?

Talking, Listening, Writing

5. Kwuon works in a court-ordered program for offenders. Overall, how much good do you think her kind of work does? (Do you think she is "coddling bad guys"? Would you rather not hear about her kind of work in the first place?)

6. Do you think there is too much or not enough emphasis in our society today on women as victims?

Find It on the Web

Many publications have started to print the personal testimony of abused or battered women. An example was Vera Anderson's "Read My Face" (*Utne Reader* September/October 1997), which brought together interviews with seven women who were victims of domestic violence. You may want to check out websites of organizations devoted to combating spousal abuse or domestic violence.

THE COMMUNITY OF MEN
Robert Bly

Robert Bly is an award-winning poet, storyteller, showman, translator, and guru who lives on a lake in Minnesota. He grew up as his mother's favorite and as the son of a kindly but distant alcoholic father. He has traveled around the country doing sold-out poetry readings that bring back the days when poetry, interwoven with song and story, was a communal experience that helped shape people's views of themselves and of the world. He became a leader of the men's movement with his book Iron John: A Book about Men *(1990), which looked in myth and popular tradition for heroic archetypal figures who could serve as inspiration and role models for the disoriented modern male. He explored rites of initiation that would bring young males closer to their natural and instinctual roots and turn the overmothered boy into a man. One reviewer of* Iron John *said, "No poet in the United States in recent years has commanded so much attention. As a popularizer of archetypal psychology Bly has found a growing audience through public readings and lectures and more recently through a Bill Moyers television program which highlighted the wilderness 'gatherings' of men who have engaged with Bly on a ritualized variant of the 'talking cure'" (Stephen Kuusiso).*

Thought Starters: If you were to nominate a living contemporary as a role model for young boys, who would it be? How would you justify your choice?

We are living at an important and fruitful moment now, for it is clear   *1*
to men that the images of adult manhood given by the popular culture are worn out; a man can no longer depend on them. By the time a man is thirty-five he knows that the images of the right man, the tough man, the true man which he received in high school do not work in life. Such a man is open to new visions of what a man is or could be.

The hearth and fairy stories have passed, as water through fifty feet of soil, through generations of men and women, and we can trust their images more than, say, those invented by Hans Christian Andersen. The images the old stories give—stealing the key from under the mother's pillow, picking up a golden feather fallen from the burning breast of the Firebird, finding the Wild Man under the lake water, following the tracks of one's own wound through the forest and finding that it resembles the tracks of a god—these are meant to be taken slowly into the body. They continue to unfold, once taken in.

It is in the old myths that we hear, for example, of Zeus energy, that positive leadership energy in men, which popular culture constantly declares does not exist; from King Arthur we learn the value of the male mentor in the lives of young men; we hear from the Iron John story the importance of moving from the mother's realm to the father's realm; and from all initiation stories we learn how essential it is to leave our parental expectations entirely and find a second father or "second King."

The dark side of men is clear. Their mad exploitation of earth resources, devaluation and humiliation of women, and obsession with tribal warfare are undeniable. Genetic inheritance contributes to their obsessions, but also culture and environment. We have defective mythologies that ignore masculine depth of feeling, assign men a place in the sky instead of earth, teach obedience to the wrong powers, work to keep men boys, and entangle both men and women in systems of industrial domination that exclude both matriarchy and patriarchy.

Most of the language in my book speaks to heterosexual men but does not exclude homosexual men. It wasn't until the eighteenth century that people ever used the term homosexual; before that time gay men were understood simply as a part of the large community of men. The mythology as I see it does not make a big distinction between homosexual and heterosexual men.

We talk a great deal about "the American man," as if there were some constant quality that remained stable over decades, or even within a single decade.

The men who live today have veered far away from the Saturnian, old-man-minded farmer, proud of his introversion, who arrived in New England in 1630, willing to sit through three services in an unheated church. In the South, an expansive, motherbound cavalier developed, and neither of these two "American men" resembled the greedy railroad entrepreneur that later developed in the Northeast, nor the reckless I-will-do-without culture settlers of the West.

Even in our own era the agreed-on model has changed dramatically. During the fifties, for example, an American character appeared with some consistency that became a model of manhood adopted by many men: the Fifties male.

He got to work early, labored responsibly, supported his wife and children, and admired discipline. Reagan is a sort of mummified version of this dogged type. This sort of man didn't see women's souls well, but he appreciated their bodies; and his view of culture and America's part in it was boyish and optimistic. Many of his qualities were strong and positive, but underneath the charm and bluff there was, and there remains, much isolation, deprivation, and passivity. Unless he has an enemy, he isn't sure that he is alive.

The Fifties man was supposed to like football, be aggressive, stick up   *10*
for the United States, never cry, and always provide. But receptive space or
intimate space was missing in this image of a man. The personality lacked
some sense of flow. The psyche lacked compassion in a way that encouraged the unbalanced pursuit of the Vietnam war, just as, later, the lack of
what we might call "garden" space inside Reagan's head led to his callous-
ness and brutality toward the powerless in El Salvador, toward old people
here, the unemployed, schoolchildren, and poor people in general.

The Fifties male had a clear vision of what a man was, and what male
responsibilities were, but the isolation and one-sidedness of his vision were
dangerous.

During the sixties, another sort of man appeared. The waste and violence of the Vietnam war made men question whether they knew what
an adult male really was. If manhood meant Vietnam, did they want any
part of it? Meanwhile, the feminist movement encouraged men to actually
look at women, forcing them to become conscious of concerns and suf-
ferings that the Fifties male labored to avoid. As men began to examine
women's history and women's sensibility, some men began to notice what
was called their *feminine* side and pay attention to it. This process continues
to this day, and I would say that most contemporary men are involved in it
in some way.

There's something wonderful about this development—I mean the
practice of men welcoming their own "feminine" consciousness and nurturing it—this is important—and yet I have the sense that there is something
wrong. The male in the past twenty years has become more thoughtful,
more gentle. But by this process he has not become more free. He's a nice
boy who pleases not only his mother but also the young woman he is living with.

In the seventies I began to see all over the country a phenomenon that
we might call the "soft male." Sometimes even today when I look out at an
audience, perhaps half the young males are what I'd call soft. They're lovely,
valuable people—I like them—they're not interested in harming the earth
or starting wars. There's a gentle attitude toward life in their whole being
and style of living.

But many of these men are not happy. You quickly notice the lack of   *15*
energy in them. They are life-preserving but not exactly life-giving. Ironically, you often see these men with strong women who positively radiate
energy.

Here we have a finely tuned young man, ecologically superior to his
father, sympathetic to the whole harmony of the universe, yet he himself
has little vitality to offer.

The strong or life-giving women who graduated from the sixties, so
to speak, or who have inherited an older spirit, played an important part in
producing this life-preserving, but not life-giving, man.

I remember a bumper sticker during the sixties that read "WOMEN SAY YES TO MEN WHO SAY NO." We recognize that it took a lot of courage to resist the draft, go to jail, or move to Canada, just as it took courage to accept the draft and go to Vietnam. But the women of twenty years ago were definitely saying that they preferred the softer receptive male.

So the development of men was affected a little in this preference. Nonreceptive maleness was equated with violence, and receptive maleness was rewarded.

Some energetic women, at that time and now in the nineties, chose   20
and still choose soft men to be their lovers and, in a way, perhaps, to be their sons. The new distribution of "yang" energy among couples didn't happen by accident. Young men for various reasons wanted their harder women, and women began to desire softer men. It seemed like a nice arrangement for a while, but we've lived with it long enough now to see that it isn't working out.

I first learned about the anguish of "soft" men when they told their stories in early men's gatherings. In 1980, the Lama Community in New Mexico asked me to teach a conference for men only, their first, in which about forty men participated. Each day we concentrated on one Greek god and one old story, and then late in the afternoons we gathered to talk. When the younger men spoke it was not uncommon for them to be weeping within five minutes. The amount of grief and anguish in these younger men was astounding to me.

Part of their grief rose out of remoteness from their fathers, which they felt keenly, but partly, too, grief flowed from trouble in their marriages or relationships. They had learned to be receptive, but receptivity wasn't enough to carry their marriages through troubled times. In every relationship something *fierce* is needed once in a while: both the man and the woman need to have it. But at the point when it was needed, often the young man came up short. He was nurturing, but something else was required—for his relationship, and for his life.

The "soft" male was able to say, "I can feel your pain, and I consider your life as important as mine, and I will take care of you and comfort you." But he could not say what he wanted, and stick by it. *Resolve* of that kind was a different matter.

In *The Odyssey,* Hermes instructs Odysseus that when he approaches Circe, who stands for a certain kind of matriarchal energy, he is to lift or show his sword. In these early sessions it was difficult for many of the younger men to distinguish between showing the sword and hurting someone. One man, a kind of incarnation of certain spiritual attitudes of the sixties, a man who had actually lived in a tree for a year outside Santa Cruz, found himself unable to extend his arm when it held a sword. He had learned so well not to hurt anyone that he couldn't lift the steel, even to catch the light of the sun on it. But showing a sword doesn't necessarily mean fighting. It can also suggest a joyful decisiveness.

The journey many American men have taken into softness, or recep-   25
tivity, or "development of the feminine side," has been an immensely valuable journey, but more travel lies ahead.

The Responsive Reader

1. In recent years, males have come in for much negative criticism. How does Bly in his opening paragraphs acknowledge "the dark side of men"?
2. What are some models for the true American that Bly finds in the nation's early history? Do you recognize these early models of the typical American? (What is the meaning of *Saturnian* and *cavalier*?)
3. Do you recognize the fifties male as described by Bly? What are his key features? What are his strengths? What are his weaknesses?
4. Do you recognize the sixties male? What are his key qualities? What about the sixties male appeals to Bly? What does Bly think is lacking?
5. What is Bly's own vision of the ideal male? Do you recognize the mythical or literary precedents on which he draws?

Talking, Listening, Writing

6. Is the fifties man extinct? Do you identify with or feel attracted to the sixties man?
7. Are critics right who charge that Bly is merely in his own way rehabilitating the traditional patriarchal male?
8. Do you agree that our popular culture denies the existence of "positive leadership energy"? Is it true that we tend to debunk our leaders, cutting them down to size?
9. What would you include in your own portrait of the ideal male?

Collaborative Projects

10. Have images of American womanhood undergone a transformation similar to that of the images of manhood identified by Bly? Working with a group, you may want to prepare composite portraits of the fifties woman, the sixties woman, and the nineties woman.

HILLS LIKE WHITE ELEPHANTS
Ernest Hemingway

> *Next to Mark Twain, Ernest Hemingway is probably the most widely read American author and known as the most American of American authors. His great novels*—The Sun Also Rises *(1926),* A Farewell to Arms *(1929), and* For Whom the Bell Tolls *(1940)—were read by millions. Some think that as a writer of the modern short story he remains unsurpassed. Hemingway lives on in critical and media folklore as the poster child of an obsolete macho mentality—an image he himself promoted as a bullfight aficionado, deep-sea fisherman, and Great White Hunter. (He killed himself with a shotgun blast to the head in Idaho.) However, there are no Rambo types posturing as heroes in his fiction. Hemingway came away from volunteer service as an ambulance driver in Italy in World War I with a profound disillusionment with the oratory of politicians and with glib talk about heroism and sacrifice. The men in his best-known novels and stories are often shell-shocked, physically maimed or emotionally crippled, wary of any kind of shallow talk, looking for some worthwhile definition of manhood in a violent, corrupt, hypocritical world. They often, like the two people in the following story, are expatriates— exiles who have left behind whatever roots or sense of belonging they once had.*

Thought Starters: What does the word *macho* bring to mind? Do you expect men to be less sensitive than women?

The hills across the valley of the Ebro were long and white. On this side there was no shade and no trees and the station was between two lines of rails in the sun. Close against the side of the station there was the warm shadow of the building and a curtain, made of strings of bamboo beads, hung across the open door into the bar, to keep out flies. The American and the girl with him sat at a table in the shade, outside the building. It was very hot and the express from Barcelona would come in forty minutes. It stopped at this junction for two minutes and went on to Madrid.

"What should we drink?" the girl asked. She had taken off her hat and put it on the table.

"It's pretty hot," the man said.

"Let's drink beer."

"Dos cervezas," the man said into the curtain.

"Big ones?" a woman asked from the doorway.

"Yes. Two big ones."

The woman brought two glasses of beer and two felt pads. She put the felt pads and the beer glasses on the table and looked at the man and the girl. The girl was looking off at the line of hills. They were white in the sun and the country was brown and dry.

"They look like white elephants," she said.

"I've never seen one," the man drank his beer.   *10*

"No, you wouldn't have."

"I might have," the man said. "Just because you say I wouldn't have doesn't prove anything."

The girl looked at the bead curtain. "They've painted something on it," she said. "What does it say?"

"Anis del Toro. It's a drink."

"Could we try it?"   *15*

The man called "Listen" through the curtain. The woman came out from the bar.

"Four reales."

"We want two Anis del Toro."

"With water?"

"Do you want it with water?"   *20*

"I don't know," the girl said. "Is it good with water?"

"It's all right."

"You want them with water?" asked the woman.

"Yes, with water."

"It tastes like licorice," the girl said and put the glass down.   *25*

"That's the way with everything."

"Yes," said the girl. "Everything tastes of licorice. Especially all the things you've waited so long for, like absinthe."

"Oh, cut it out."

"You started it," the girl said. "I was being amused. I was having a fine time."

"Well, let's try and have a fine time."   *30*

"All right. I was trying. I said the mountains looked like white elephants. Wasn't that bright?"

"That was bright."

"I wanted to try this new drink. That's all we do, isn't it—look at things and try new drinks?"

"I guess so."

The girl looked across at the hills.   *35*

"They're lovely hills," she said. "They don't really look like white elephants. I just meant the coloring of their skin through the trees."

"Should we have another drink?"

"All right."

The warm wind blew the bead curtain against the table.

"The beer's nice and cool," the man said.   40

"It's lovely," the girl said.

"It's really an awfully simple operation, Jig," the man said. "It's not really an operation at all."

The girl looked at the ground the table legs rested on.

"I know you wouldn't mind it, Jig. It's really not anything. It's just to let the air in."

The girl did not say anything.   45

"I'll go with you and I'll stay with you all the time. They just let the air in and then it's all perfectly natural."

"Then what will we do afterward?"

"We'll be fine afterward. Just like we were before."

"What makes you think so?"

"That's the only thing that bothers us. It's the only thing that's made   50
us unhappy."

The girl looked at the bead curtain, put her hand out and took hold of two of the strings of beads.

"And you think then we'll be all right and be happy."

"I know we will. You don't have to be afraid. I've known lots of people that have done it."

"So have I," said the girl. "And afterward they were all so happy."

"Well," the man said, "if you don't want to you don't have to. I   55
wouldn't have you do it if you didn't want to. But I know it's perfectly simple."

"And you really want to?"

"I think it's the best thing to do. But I don't want you to do it if you don't really want to."

"And if I do it you'll be happy and things will be like they were and you'll love me?"

"I love you now. You know I love you."

"I know. But if I do it, then it will be nice again if I say things are like   60
white elephants, and you'll like it?"

"I'll love it. I love it now but I just can't think about it. You know how I get when I worry."

"If I do it you won't ever worry?"

"I won't worry about that because it's perfectly simple."

"Then I'll do it. Because I don't care about me."

"What do you mean?"   65

"I don't care about me."

"Well, I care about you."

"Oh, yes. But I don't care about me. And I'll do it and then everything will be fine."

"I don't want you to do it if you feel that way."

The girl stood up and walked to the end of the station. Across on the   70
other side, were fields of grain and trees along the banks of the Ebro. Far

away, beyond the river, were mountains. The shadow of a cloud moved across the field of grain and she saw the river through the trees.

"And we could have all this," she said. "And we could have everything and every day we make it more impossible."

"What did you say?"

"I said we could have everything."

"We can have everything."

"No, we can't."   75

"We can have the whole world."

"No, we can't."

"We can go everywhere."

"No, we can't. It isn't ours any more."

"It's ours."   80

"No, it isn't. And once they take it away, you never get it back."

"But they haven't taken it away."

"We'll wait and see."

"Come on back in the shade," he said. "You mustn't feel that way."

"I don't feel any way," the girl said. "I just know things."   85

"I don't want you to do anything that you don't want to do—"

"Nor that isn't good for me," she said. "I know. Could we have another beer?"

"All right. But you've got to realize—"

"I realize," the girl said. "Can't we maybe stop talking?"

They sat down at the table and the girl looked across at the hills on the   90
dry side of the valley and the man looked at her and at the table.

"You've got to realize," he said, "that I don't want you to do it if you don't want to. I'm perfectly willing to go through with it if it means anything to you."

"Doesn't it mean anything to you? We could get along."

"Of course it does. But I don't want anybody but you. I don't want any one else. And I know it's perfectly simple."

"Yes, you know it's perfectly simple."

"It's all right for you to say that, but I do know it."   95

"Would you do something for me now?"

"I'd do anything for you."

"Would you please please please please please please please stop talking?"

He did not say anything but looked at the bags against the wall of the station. There were labels on them from all the hotels where they had spent nights.

"But I don't want you to," he said, "I don't care anything about it."   100

"I'll scream," the girl said.

The woman came out through the curtains with two glasses of beer and put them down on the damp felt pads. "The train comes in five minutes," she said.

"What did she say?" asked the girl.

"That the train is coming in five minutes."

The girl smiled brightly at the woman, to thank her.   *105*

"I'd better take the bags over to the other side of the station," the man said. She smiled at him.

"All right. Then come back and we'll finish the beer."

He picked up the two heavy bags and carried them around the station to the other tracks. He looked up the tracks but could not see the train. Coming back, he walked through the barroom, where people waiting for the train were drinking. He drank an Anis at the bar and looked at the people. They were all waiting reasonably for the train. He went out through the bead curtain. She was sitting at the table and smiled at him.

"Do you feel better?" he asked.

"I feel fine," she said. "There's nothing wrong with me. I feel fine."   *110*

The Responsive Reader

1. Hemingway had a horror of big words and big speeches. How much of the talk in this story sounds like aimless chitchat? When do you first decide that something serious is going on? What is the issue? How do you know?

2. What kind of person is the man? What is his line of talk? What is his agenda? What do you think of him?

3. What kind of person is the woman? What is she looking for? How does she respond to the man's talk? Do you sympathize with her?

Talking, Listening, Writing

4. Do you think that in a different setting the same conversation could go on today, or has the relationship between the sexes changed in basic ways?

5. If the two people in the story were able to express their true feelings, would they be able to deal better with the situation or improve their relationship? (Do you think people tend to be too tongue-tied and uncommunicative? Or do you think people tend to be too gushy and sentimental?)

6. The "war of the sexes" has been a major theme in the literature of the West. Do you think that the relationship between the sexes in our society is becoming too adversarial? Is there too much hostility between the sexes?

A GLIMPSE

Walt Whitman

Through most of the history of our culture, gay men and lesbian women had to keep their sexual orientation secret. When it became a matter of public record, as in the case of the nineteenth-century poet and playwright Oscar Wilde, it wrecked careers and lives. (When Wilde came back from prison, one of his first acts was to write to the press pleading the cause of three children kept in the same brutal, dehumanizing jail where he had been confined.) In recent decades, gay and lesbian artists and writers have slowly emerged from the twilight in which they were kept by societal repression. Many of them admire the American poet Walt Whitman (1819–1892), author of Leaves of Grass *and the "poet of democracy," as a precursor and pioneer. Although he did not openly acknowledge his homosexuality, his celebration of the male human form and the love of comrades made him a prophet of gay liberation.*

Thought Starters: When did you first become aware of the gay lifestyle? How were your early impressions shaped?

A glimpse through an interstice caught,   *1*
Of a crowd of workmen and drivers in a bar-room around the stove
   late of a winter night, and I unremark'd seated in a corner,
Of a youth who loves me and whom I love, silently approaching and
   seating himself near, that he may hold me by the hand,   *5*
A long while amid the noises of coming and going, of drinking and
   oath and smutty jest,
There we two, content, happy in being together, speaking little,
   perhaps not a word.

The Responsive Reader

1. How does this poem go counter to stereotypes about gays?
2. Whitman uses the word *love* twice in this poem. Can you define love in such a way that it includes both heterosexual and homosexual love?
3. How do you think this poem should be read? How should it sound? (What should be the volume, speed, tone of voice?)

Talking, Listening, Writing

4. What prominent gays or lesbians are you aware of in contemporary American life? What do you know about them? How are they treated by the media?
5. What have you read or heard about gay-bashing or homophobia? What have you observed of it at first hand? What psychological or cultural mechanisms are at work?

FORUM: *Gay in America*

Are gays and lesbians becoming more widely accepted in American life, or is a conservative backlash reversing the movement toward gay rights? Openly gay or lesbian Americans have become a familiar feature of American politics and entertainment. In sitcoms, the squirming of family and friends when they are introduced to the gay lover of one of theirs became a familiar joke. Tom Hanks played a gay AIDS victim treated shabbily by a homophobic establishment. Gay rights initiatives asked voters to ban discrimination against gays in housing and employment; communities and corporations extended health benefits and pension rights to the domestic partners of gay employees.

At the same time, television evangelists and conservative politicians mounted a counterattack. State legislatures rushed to pass laws declaring same-sex marriages invalid; a "Defense of Marriage Act" was moving through Congress. In the United States Senate, Trent Lott of Mississippi classed homosexuals with alcoholics and kleptomaniacs (people driven by a pathological urge to steal). Pat Robertson, a multimillionaire televangelist, claimed that God was inflicting murderous tornadoes and hurricanes as punishment for communities' condoning of sexual deviation. Brutal and often fatal violence against gays made the headlines.

Richard Rodriguez is a Mexican American writer who first became known for his autobiographical *Hunger of Memory* (1982), which talked of immigrants and their children leaving their Old Country language behind as a necessary rite of passage in the process of joining fully in the American experience. Writing about legal challenges to laws banning discrimination against gays, he said:

> What I see is an astonishing change. I meet homosexual men and women now in every corner of American life. Everywhere people are "out" and, more remarkably, they are being accepted by their families and their friends and their coworkers. I know, like you, stories of parents who no longer speak to their children. But I am more impressed by the accommodation taking place throughout America. I think of two Catholic families in California. They have been united in recent years by the love of two dying men—lovers dying of AIDS. There they all were—50 smiling faces in a Christmas photograph. Three or four generations, standing alongside the two thinning men. That is the way the sexual revolution is taking place—by the Christmas tree, within the very family that Pat Buchanan and Pat Robertson invoke for their own purposes as unchanging and rigid. . . .

I am not being overly optimistic. I suspect that the great, perhaps even calamitous struggle in the next century will be a cultural war, pitting the secular against the fundamentalist. Do I think there will be more anti-gay legislation passed? Yes. Are we in for dangerous times? Yes. Do I think that there are many judges in America who will remain preoccupied by what I do in the dark? But the other day I received a letter from my first-grade teacher, a Catholic nun now in her 80's. "About your being gay," she writes, "I don't have any problem with it. I only pray that you will be a good man."

A DAY TO LEAVE THE CLOSET

Elizabeth Birch

> *Elizabeth Birch is executive director of the Human Rights Campaign, described as the largest U.S. gay political organization and was the director of litigation at the Apple Computer corporation in Silicon Valley in California, where she pushed for domestic partner benefits. She focuses her article on a basic choice that she says has faced millions of gay Americans. One alternative has traditionally been to stay in the closet—to deny or hide one's sexual orientation, conforming to the heterosexual lifestyle of the majority, leading a furtive, guilt-ridden life. The other alternative, increasingly available in recent years, has been to come out—to live one's life with "integrity," even if at the risk of facing rejection, discrimination, and antigay violence.*

Thought Starters: Have you seen evidence of increased visibility of gays and lesbians as the result of efforts by gay activists? Have you seen or read about Gay Pride parades or similar activities?

WASHINGTON—Since the inaugural National Coming Out Day 1
a decade ago, millions of Americans have taken the bold step of emerging from the closet. As more and more people realize their friends and family members are gay, their attitudes are changing, and they are joining the demand for basic fairness. Polls show more than two-thirds of Americans believe no one should lose a job or job opportunity because of sexual orientation.

This broad-based support for fairness is directly linked to individuals coming out and challenging misconceptions about gay people.

But it wasn't always this way—even in Silicon Valley, now recognized as progressive on gay and lesbian issues.

In 1992, as chief litigator at Apple Computer, I and colleagues in a gay employee group (led by Bennett Marks) began a push for health benefits for our domestic partners. We did not know how we would be received. Some feared that, by coming out, they would be jeopardizing their careers.

When we met with Chairman John Scully, he was magnificent. He 5
immediately saw the wisdom of instituting a fair policy. In 1993, Apple announced it would offer equal benefits to partners of gay and lesbian employees.

Following Apple's lead, many other employers came to recognize that treating all employees equally is good for business: It deepens commitment, boosts morale and inculcates the culture with a sense of fairness. Today, more than half of Fortune 500 companies offer domestic-partner benefits.

This success story underscores the impact of a simple tool for educating society and irreversibly improving the lives of gay Americans. Through the bold act of coming out at Apple, we helped blaze a trail.

Unfortunately, not everyone who comes out is embraced as we were.

Each year, thousands are fired, kicked out of their homes or even brutalized for being gay. It is still legal in 40 states to fire people for being gay, and gay Americans are the victims of 11.6 percent of all hate crimes reported. Attempts to pass federal legislation to remedy these problems are met with open hostility on Capitol Hill.

A MARATHON EFFORT

Under these circumstances, coming out is like running a marathon. It can be excruciating, exhausting and painful—and just when you think the race is over, you realize you aren't even at the halfway mark. Yet it is also liberating and empowering, and can provide some of life's most rewarding experiences.

The most difficult part of coming out is the constant anticipation of rejection. Sometimes those we thought would be accepting have deserted us. Other times, friends and relatives who we expected to snub us have opened their hearts and minds, resulting in new closeness. This constant foray into the murky, and scary, world of the unknown is what makes coming out a monumental act of courage.

National Coming Out Day, which falls on Oct. 11 this year, is a celebration for those who have successfully made this difficult journey. And it is a time of hope for those still struggling to love themselves in an often-hostile society.

But the decision to be honest does not end after a single declaration on a specific day. Coming out is a lifelong process that requires even the most open gay people to find new reservoirs of courage and fortitude daily.

Every time a gay person meets someone new, questions of sexuality come up directly or indirectly. Simple questions that the average heterosexual takes for granted, such as "Are you married?" or "What are you doing this weekend?" can cause great anxiety. We must decide whether to conjure up a tortured fiction or evasion, or simply tell the truth and potentially face the consequences.

Despite the constant juggling act—"Should I be brave today?" vs. "Should I be safe today?"—I and millions of others have found that the closet is not a safe place. It is a prison that produces self-hatred and validates those who would deny us our basic human dignity

Coming out is the ultimate weapon against politically motivated assaults on gay people in the guise of love or religion. And whatever the obstacles, gay people continue to come out in record numbers. Fear of societal reprisals cannot suppress the human need to live freely and with integrity.

A DIVERSE COMMUNITY

We are military heroes, like Vietnam Bronze Star recipient Col. Grethe Cammermeyer. We are successful entrepreneurs, like Quark founder and chairman Tim Gill.

We are conservative and liberal, often people of faith, of all races and socioeconomic classes. We are, and always have been, an integral part of America.

When I look back at what we accomplished at Apple, I marvel. I think, "How did we do it?" The answer is simple. We had the courage to come out, to take an immense risk to improve our lives and offer hope to the next generation of gay people.

Each day, and especially on National Coming Out Day, more people   20
are choosing to "risk it all"—because in the emptiness of the closet, surrendering self-respect and freedom, "all" can seem like nothing.

The Responsive Reader

1. What made her experience at Apple a test case for Birch? What features of the story stood out for her, and what did she learn from it?
2. Like Richard Rodriguez, Birch views society's progress toward acceptance and equal rights of gays and lesbians with mixed emotions. What developments for her stand out in the "success story" of improving conditions for gay Americans? What evidence does she cite of positive changes in public opinion? On the downside, how does she sum up the negatives in current developments?
3. According to Birch, what was it like for homosexual Americans to stay "in the closet"? What did it mean in everyday life? What was the psychological price? For her and many of her contemporaries, what were the pros and cons of "coming out"?
4. Have you seen evidence that social encounters and family relations between gays and straights can cause "great anxiety"? Have you seen evidence of the meeting of gay and straight causing strain or embarrassment in school? In the workplace?

Talking, Listening, Writing

5. You may want to team up with classmates to draft a "Miss Manners" set of guidelines for straight Americans interacting with gays and lesbians in social situations, in family relations, and in the workplace. You may want to draft a similar set of guidelines advising gay and lesbian Americans on how to act in the same situations.

Collaborative Projects

6. You may want to team up with classmates to investigate the role of openly gay and lesbian Americans in public life—in Congress, in local politics, in the news media. What is the role or influence of public figures like Frank Rich or Richard Rodriguez?

LOVE, MARRIAGE, AND THE LAW
William J. Bennett

> *William Bennett is one of the country's most prominent conservatives, marching under the banner of traditional values. With pundits like George Will and Roger Rosenblatt, he has been a leader of a gay-bashing, feminist-bashing, counterattack on multiculturalism and other mainstays of a liberal agenda. A chief instigator of the current culture wars, Bennett signed on as President Reagan's secretary of education at a time when the Reagan administration was trying to abolish the U.S. Department of Education. He has published tracts like* The Book of Virtues *to admonish America's poor to adopt higher moral standards. According to* Harper's *magazine, the author of* The Book of Virtues *earned $1,800,000 in speaking fees in a single year.*

Thought Starters: What does the term *family values* bring to mind? Where do you hear or see it used, and by whom?

We are engaged in a debate which, in a less confused time, would   *1*
be considered pointless and even oxymoronic: the question of same-sex marriage.

But we are where we are. The Hawaii Supreme Court has discovered a new state constitutional "right"—the legal union of same-sex couples. Unless a "compelling state interest" can be shown against them, Hawaii will become the first state to sanction such unions. And if Hawaii legalizes same-sex marriages, other states might well have to recognize them because of the Constitution's Full Faith and Credit Clause. Some in Congress recently introduced legislation to prevent this from happening.

Now, anyone who has known someone who has struggled with his homosexuality can appreciate the poignancy, human pain and sense of exclusion that are often involved. One can therefore understand the effort to achieve for homosexual unions both legal recognition and social acceptance. Advocates of homosexual marriages even make what appears to be a sound conservative argument: Allow marriage in order to promote faithfulness and monogamy. This is an intelligent and politically shrewd argument. One can even concede that it might benefit some people. But I believe that overall, allowing same-sex marriages would do significant, long-term social damage.

Recognizing the legal union of gay and lesbian couples would represent a profound change in the meaning and definition of marriage. Indeed, it would be the most radical step ever taken in the deconstruction of society's most important institution. It is not a step we ought to take.

The function of marriage is not elastic; the institution is already frag   5
ile enough. Broadening its definition to include same-sex marriages would stretch it almost beyond recognition—and new attempts to broaden the definition still further would surely follow. On what principled grounds could the advocates of same-sex marriage oppose the marriage of two consenting brothers? How could they explain why we ought to deny a marriage license to a bisexual who wants to marry two people? After all, doing so would be a denial of that person's sexuality. In our time, there are more (not fewer) reasons than ever to preserve the essence of marriage.

Marriage is not an arbitrary construct; it is an "honorable estate" based on the different, complementary nature of men and women—and how they refine, support, encourage and complete one another. To insist that we maintain this traditional understanding of marriage is not an attempt to put others down. It is simply an acknowledgment and celebration of our most precious and important social act.

Nor is this view arbitrary or idiosyncratic. It mirrors the accumulated wisdom of millennia and the teaching of every major religion. Among worldwide cultures, where there are so few common threads, it is not a coincidence that marriage is almost universally recognized as an act meant to unite a man and a woman.

To say that same-sex unions are not comparable to heterosexual marriages is not an argument for intolerance, bigotry or lack of compassion (although I am fully aware that it will be considered so by some). But it is an argument for making distinctions in law about relationships that are themselves distinct. Even Andrew Sullivan, among the most intelligent advocates of same-sex marriage, has admitted that a homosexual marriage contract will entail a greater understanding of the need for "extramarital outlets." He argues that gay male relationships are served by the "openness of the contract," and he has written that homosexuals should resist allowing their "varied and complicated lives" to be flattened into a "single, moralistic model."

But this "single, moralistic model" is precisely the point. The marriage commitment between a man and a woman does not—it cannot—countenance extramarital outlets. By definition it is not an open contract; its essential idea is fidelity. Obviously that is not always honored in practice.

But it is normative, the ideal to which we aspire precisely because we believe some things are right (faithfulness in marriage) and others are wrong (adultery). In insisting that marriage accommodate the less restrained sexual practices of homosexuals, Sullivan and his allies destroy the very thing that supposedly has drawn them to marriage in the first place.

There are other arguments to consider against same-sex marriage— for example, the signals it would send, and the impact of such signals on the shaping of human sexuality, particularly among the young. Former Harvard professor E. L. Pattullo has written that "a very substantial number of people are born with the potential to live either straight or gay lives." Societal indifference about heterosexuality would cause a lot of confusion. A remarkable 1993 article in the Washington Post supports this point. Fifty teen-agers and dozens of school counselors and parents from the local area were interviewed. According to the article, teen-agers said it has become "cool" for students to proclaim they are gay or bisexual—even for some who are not. Not surprisingly, the caseload of teen-agers in "sexual identity crisis" doubled in one year. "Everything is front page, gay and homosexual," according to one psychologist who works with the schools. "Kids are jumping on it . . . (counselors) are saying, 'What are we going to do with all these kids proclaiming they are bisexual or homosexual when we know they are not?'"

If the law recognizes homosexual marriages as the legal equivalent of heterosexual marriages, it will have enormous repercussions in many areas. Consider just two: sex education in the schools and adoption. The sex education curriculum of public schools would have to teach that heterosexual and homosexual marriage are equivalent. "Heather Has Two Mommies" would no longer be regarded as an anomaly; it would more likely become a staple of a sex education curriculum. Parents who want their children to be taught (for both moral and utilitarian reasons) the privileged status of heterosexual marriage will be portrayed as intolerant bigots; they will necessarily be at odds with the new law of matrimony and its derivative curriculum.

Homosexual couples will also have equal claim with heterosexual couples in adopting children, forcing us (in law at least) to deny what we know to be true: that it is far better for a child to be raised by a mother and a father than by, say, two male homosexuals.

The institution of marriage is already reeling because of the effects of the sexual revolution, no-fault divorce and out-of-wedlock births. We have reaped the consequences of its devaluation. It is exceedingly imprudent to conduct a radical, untested and inherently flawed social experiment on an institution that is the keystone in the arch of civilization. That we have to debate this issue at all tells us that the arch has slipped. Getting it firmly back in place is, as the lawyers say, a "compelling state interest."

The Responsive Reader

1. For Bennett, what is the essence of marriage as a traditional institution? What are the key values it represents? What in his praise of marriage seems idealized, and what seems valid to you?
2. Bennett's "I'm-not-a-bigot" stance keeps him from repeating any vulgar abuse directed at gays by homophobes. How does he talk about gay people at the beginning of his article? Later in the article, what use does he make of familiar antigay charges such as their proselytizing for homosexuality among the impressionable young or their encouraging of promiscuity (or "less restrained sexual practices," in Bennett's words)?
3. Conservatives demonize the trends they oppose as part of a threatened general breakdown of Western civilization. Besides gay marriage, what other items in Bennett's catalogue of societal evils signal the decay (or "deconstruction") of traditional values? A slippery slope argument attacks people not for what they advocate but for what else their success might bring in its wake. What other evils does Bennett envision once same-sex marriages open the door?

Talking, Listening, Writing

4. Do you think same-sex marriages are a threat from which the institution of marriage has to be protected?
5. The controversy about gay rights triggers highly emotionally charged rhetoric or loaded language. What is a fundamentalist? Do you think Bennett is a bigot? What kind of people use the words *faggot* and *queer?*
6. Have you seen evidence of an antigay backlash in your community or in society at large, or have you seen evidence of growing tolerance or acceptance?

THE MARRYING KIND

Tammerlin Drummond

> *In many cultures, marriage is a milestone event in a person's life history, with often elaborate marriage customs and wedding ceremonies. Marriage customs and marriage laws have varied and evolved over time: Many traditional cultures have featured multiple marriages or polygamy for the powerful and the privileged. Many cultures have relied on arranged marriages serving the economic interests of the involved families. A major challenge to the idea of a church-sanctioned union "till death do us part" was the slow, gradual acceptance of divorce and remarriage by most modern societies. Today same-sex unions as an equivalent of marriage are slowly becoming accepted in some states and abroad. Granting gay and lesbian couples married status not only helps them counteract traditional prejudices but has other important repercussions in*

their lives, such as enabling them to secure health benefits and pension rights for gay life partners or the right to visit sick or dying partners as family or next of kin. Sympathetic coverage of same-sex unions in the mainstream media, as in the following Time *article, is a sign of the times. At the same time, the movement toward same-sex marriage has been violently contested, and partnership rights and status have had to be negotiated state by state, city by city, or employer by employer.*

Thought Starters: Do you care whether couples are married or not? Do you care whether a marriage was a church marriage or a civil union? Are you comfortable around interracial couples? Are you comfortable around gay and lesbian couples?

Karen Kunz and Angela French had both been married once before, to men. Last month, after running the Boston Marathon, Kunz, 45, a nurse from Chandler, Ariz., and French, 42, a graduate student, made a symbolic pilgrimage to Vermont to wed each other. Tears streaming down their faces, the women, who have known each other for 18 years, exchanged rings; the Rev. Peter Denny proclaimed their union "the equivalent of marriage." That may be true in Vermont, but Arizona, where Kunz and French live with their nine-year-old daughter, doesn't recognize same-sex unions. They made the trip, says French, "because we wanted people to know how much it means for gay couples to get this kind of support."

One year ago, Vermont became the first state in the nation to recognize civil unions between two people of the same sex: marriages in virtually every legal respect but name. Kunz and French are among the 3,000 gays and lesbians who have come to Vermont since then to tie the knot. When the law was adopted, Vermont became the focus of a national debate over gay marriage. Opponents warned that it would become "a gay state" and that same-sex marriage would sweep the country as homosexuals in other states demanded the same rights.

None of that has happened. Instead, Vermont is enjoying a modest boomlet in gay tourism: 80% of the 2,000 gay civil-union licenses granted so far have been issued to out-of-state residents. (In that time, about 5,000 traditional marriage licenses have been granted.) Inns and B and Bs advertise civil-union packages on gay and lesbian websites. At the Moose Meadow Lodge in Waterbury, couples willing to pay $1,850 get two nights' accommodation for eight people, breakfast and the use of the pond meadow for their civil union or reception. K. C. David, CEO of an online concierge called gayweddings.com, has booked travel arrangements for couples from Russia, Indonesia and Australia who are planning civil unions in Vermont in the coming months. "It's snowballing," he says.

1

In economic terms, it's barely a snowflake. The gay and lesbian couples coming to Vermont to wed are but a tiny fraction of the 4 million visitors the state attracts each year. What's significant is that in some Vermont towns, civil unions have become a part of the fabric of everyday life. In Brattleboro, a bucolic community of 12,000 residents in liberal southern Vermont, there were 292 civil unions from July to December 2000 — the same number as there were straight marriages for the whole year. Even the Chamber of Commerce is a one-stop referral service. Along with the standard literature extolling the town's virtues, visitors get a list of gay-friendly B and Bs, florists, restaurants and justices of the peace.

Brattleboro is one of Vermont's more liberal enclaves. Conservative   5
farming communities, by contrast, saw a ferocious backlash shortly after the law's passage. Thousands of TAKE BACK VERMONT signs sprouted on lawns. Half a dozen town clerks quit rather than grant licenses to gay couples. Five state legislators who supported civil unions were defeated at the polls. But other civil-union proponents, such as Governor Howard Dean, survived, and the Take Back Vermont campaign eventually fizzled. Efforts by opponents to overturn the law have failed.

Nationally, the battle over gay marriage continues. [. . . S]even gay and lesbian couples in Massachusetts filed a lawsuit for the right to marry. So far, more than 30 states have passed "defense-of-marriage laws," which state that same-sex unions sanctioned elsewhere are null and void. Yet even though the licenses are worthless in their home states, for many gay couples making it legal in Vermont is better than nothing at all. "You wait all your life for something like that," says Vivienne Armstrong, a nurse from Dallas who has been with her partner Louise Young for 30 years. "We would have crawled to Vermont."

For some, marital bliss may be short-lived. No one in Vermont has yet filed for dissolution, but town clerks and local attorneys are already getting calls asking how to terminate a civil union. As it turns out, that's harder than getting hitched. Though residency isn't required for a civil union, it is to get out of one. That's six months' stay in Vermont for at least one partner. But couples in the throes of marital bliss rarely bother to read the fine print.

The Responsive Reader

1. Following a practice common in the glossy newsmagazines, this *Time* article starts with a human-interest case history or outstanding example. What are some of the human-interest details in this introduction? What here is different from what you might expect?
2. The *Time* writer furnishes some basic information and statistics to size up the developments in Vermont and put them in perspective. What would you include in a summary of facts and figures?
3. It is a cliché to say that major changes in society cannot just be legislated but must also happen in the hearts and minds of its citizens. What telltale

signs are there in this article of changes in the attitudes of straight fellow citizens?

4. What do you see in this article of the backlash that the same-sex marriage movement has generated? What form does it take? On balance, how does the writer size up its strength or its effect?

5. Some readers have felt that the final paragraph about the dissolution of civil unions may undermine the overall positive or encouraging effect of the article. As an editor, would you have advised the writer to leave it out? Why or why not?

Talking, Listening, Writing

6. "Let me not to the marriage of true minds / Admit impediments" begins one of Shakespeare's most widely known sonnets. In your view, should marriage be a "marriage of true minds"? Should it be a true meeting of soul mates? How important are economic factors? How important is acceptance by family and friends? How important is sex? You may want to help organize a symposium on what young people should expect of marriage in our changing modern world.

7. If same-sex unions became an issue in your state or community or in your place of employment, would you get involved? Why or why not? Would you take sides? Do you think this is an issue where persuasive arguments can change the minds of people strongly committed to their views?

Find It on the Web

Are same-sex unions or gay and lesbian marriages still in the news? What has been the fate of recent initiatives? In what states or communities has it become a major issue? What has been the fate of the movement in other countries, such as Holland?

TEACHING TOLERANCE BEFORE HATE TAKES ROOT

Elizabeth Bell

Confrontations over sex education in the schools raise a basic issue: Should parents reserve the right to teach values? Or do the schools have a role and hence an obligation to teach students about human sexuality? This issue becomes particularly inflamed when sex education includes information about alternative lifestyles or sexual orientation. As the following newspaper article shows, gay educators are concerned about homophobic, gay-bashing behavior and hateful language that takes root early. The article reports on various initiatives to "build tolerance of gays in middle and elementary schools."

Thought Starters: During your earlier school years, were you ever called names or the target of putdowns? What was the situation? Were you personally or a whole group the target? What was the effect on you? How did you react?

Charlotte Wood Middle School teacher Gary Leveque was stunned   *1*
when he read the hateful, homophobic remarks one of his students had posted about him on a Web site.

Within a week, 400 people had logged onto the student-run site, which targeted Leveque and a handful of students for a variety of reasons. There was little the [. . .] school could do to punish the students who contributed to the Web site, since it was not affiliated with the school in any way.

But the [. . .] gay community rushed to support Leveque, believing the Web site was more evidence that not enough had been done to build tolerance of gays in middle and elementary schools.

Gay activists and others are making uneven but gradual gains against homophobia in high schools, but they're already looking toward the next frontier: middle and elementary school. Hateful behavior starts early, they say, and festers until high school, when it may be too late to change attitudes.

"This starts out in kindergarten, you start hearing the words 'fag' and   *5*
'That's so gay,'" said Ann Acrey, co-chairwoman of the San Francisco East Bay chapter of the Gay, Lesbian and Straight Education Network (GLSEN).

"You have a huge population in your schools hearing that—gay teachers, people who have family members who are gay, kids being raised by two moms or two dads, the kids who may at some point grow up and decide they're gay."

Yet it's even tougher to get middle and elementary schools to address the dicey topic of homophobia than high schools. Schools worry about negative reactions from parents who don't want the topic introduced to impressionable youngsters.

In January, a new state law took effect designed to combat anti-gay sentiment on campuses. The law makes it clear that in addition to such traditionally protected characteristics as race, religion or disability, schools must not discriminate based on sexual orientation.

But gay activists believe schools must embrace the law to make true progress. Enthusiasm for promoting tolerance of gays has ranged from [. . .]

schools' establishing an office to serve "sexual minority youth," to school districts' refusing to do any training with staff on gay issues whatsoever.

San Ramon Valley schools fall toward the middle. The district has   10 hosted several staff workshops over the years to raise awareness of the harassment gay students often face at school, including an all-day training for high school faculty about five years ago.

In the last two years, the district has been promoting tolerance in general, but Leveque and several fellow teachers believe the district has been too timid in addressing homophobia. They want the district to do more staff training, and perhaps bring in gay youths to describe to peers the experience of being harassed.

The San Ramon teachers' union is responding by hosting a voluntary, after-school staff workshop this spring to deal with homophobia. Teachers' union President Janet Terranova said the district struggled to fit competing interests—including raising academic performance—into just three paid staff development days a year.

Parents, too, are nervous. Local parent clubs have embraced the concept of promoting tolerance of diversity with community workshops and multicultural presentations in schools. But they haven't addressed gay issues specifically, said Maureen Chang, Charlotte Wood's parent club president.

"You've got a lot of parents who don't want schools getting involved in teaching values," she said.

Gay activists argue they aren't teaching values, but simply trying to   15 create an atmosphere where it's as unacceptable to make fun of gays as it is to make racist or sexist remarks.

Discussing gay issues should be presented in a manner appropriate for each age level, said Acrey. With younger children it may simply be discouraging insults, or reading a story about different kinds of families, from group homes to those with two moms, two dads or single parents.

Student diversity clubs, often called Gay-Straight, Alliances, have taken hold at about 115 Bay Area high schools, up from 40 in 1998, according to Carolyn Laub with the Gay-Straight Alliance Network. Many deal with diversity in general, although some focus on gay issues specifically. Two middle schools have started Gay-Straight Alliances.

"Some folks believe parents are going to say we shouldn't be talking about sex with students this age," said Carolyn Lobb, executive director of the Gay-Straight Alliance Network. "But the reality is gay-straight alliances are not about sex. They're about student safety, respect, tolerance."

Many of the clubs flourish from the energy of a few students or a teacher, then disintegrate when the students graduate. A charismatic gay junior began such a club at San Ramon Valley High about a decade ago. He graduated—and then, a few years ago, the club's gay pride bulletin board was vandalized repeatedly.

"People were intimidated, and it brought up emotions and religion in   20 the community and all that stuff, and the kids didn't really want to go for it," said Mike Slater, the club's faculty adviser.

The controversy sapped the group's enthusiasm. Younger leaders have since steered the club toward general tolerance issues. There are no openly gay members of the club now, said Slater, and it rarely touches on gay issues.

Openly gay teacher Deborah Godner at King Middle School in Berkeley said she hadn't heard a bad word from her conservative parents about the gay-straight alliance she started 1½ years ago.

About 30 students attend the lunchtime meetings, with perhaps a third of them gay or unsure of their own sexual orientation. In one activity, they developed an anti-homophobia bingo game presented to all seventh graders. Some of the facts they imparted: not all gay men are effeminate; being gay doesn't rub off on others; most kids of gays are straight; and gay youths are three times more likely than straight youths to attempt suicide.

"Middle school is a really ripe age to get kids to unlearn their homophobia," said Godner. "It really cuts down on violence later on."

The Responsive Reader

1. Early in your career as a student, when and how did you become aware of the acceptance or rejection of gays and lesbians as an issue? Do you remember comments, incidents, or behavior by fellow students? Did you receive formal instruction on the subject of homosexuality or homophobia? How did you react to it?
2. What do you learn in Bell's article about various initiatives to raise awareness or raise consciousness of issues of antigay verbal harassment? What are their aims, or what is their strategy? What do you learn about methods employed and materials used? What is the involvement of straight students and educators?
3. This article provides a forum for articulate spokespersons in the movement to counteract anti gay prejudice in the schools. Who are they, or what kind of people are they? What are some revealing statements or quotable quotes?
4. What signs of obstacles, "nervousness," or opposition are part of this article?

Talking, Listening, Writing

5. Where do you stand on the basic issue of whether students should early learn about alternative lifestyles or sexual orientation in school? What to you are the basic arguments for and against? How would you answer some of the arguments of the side opposed to yours?
6. Popular television shows and movies increasingly feature gay and lesbian characters and gay and lesbian couples. Do you think this greater media exposure is helping to teach tolerance? Will wider visibility in the entertainment field lead to greater acceptance of gays and lesbians in everyday life? Why or why not?

WYOMING STUDENT DIES OF HIS WOUNDS

Tom Kenworthy

According to widely published statistics, crime in general has declined in recent years, but violence against gays has increased. Among reports of beatings and killings deplored in editorials and then forgotten, the story of a Wyoming student beaten and left to die crucified on a fence stood out. Matthew Shepard, a student of German and Arabic, died after being in a coma for nearly a week. He had been robbed, beaten, and pistol-whipped about the head so severely his skull was too crushed for surgery. He had been tied to a fence like a scarecrow and left there for eighteen hours in freezing cold weather. The father of one of the attackers said his son told him he committed the crime because he was embarrassed when Shepard flirted with him in front of his friends. Tony Kushner, a gay playwright writing on the editorial page of the Nation, *blamed Shepard's death on "theocrats, bullies, panderers, and hatemongers and their crazed murderous children." He called leading figures in church, synagogue, and state who claim to "hate the sin, not the sinner" homicidal liars. Addressing readers disapproving of such strong language, he said: "I worry less about the death of civil discourse than I worry about being killed if, visiting the wrong town with my boyfriend, we forget ourselves so much as to betray, at the wrong moment in front of the wrong people, that we love one another." A friend of Shepard called him "the most gentle soul I've ever met" and said, "sex wasn't his primary interest."*

Thought Starters: Have you observed antigay violence during your high school years or on your college campus? Who are the perpetrators? Are they just ordinary students like everyone else, or are they a special breed? What makes them act the way they do?

Golden, Colo.—Matthew Shepard, the University of Wyoming student who was savagely beaten last week in an apparent anti-gay attack, died early yesterday at a Fort Collins, Colo., hospital.   *1*

Authorities in Laramie immediately moved to upgrade criminal charges against the four suspects.

Russell Arthur Henderson, 21, and Aaron James McKinney, 22, will be charged with first-degree murder rather than attempted murder, and their girlfriends, Chastity Vera Pasley, 20, and Kristen Leann Price, 18, will be charged with being accessories after the fact to first-degree murder rather than being accessories to attempted murder. The two men also face charges of kidnapping and robbery.

Shepard, 21, was lured from a bar popular with University of Wyoming students last Tuesday night, beaten with a pistol butt and left tied to a fence just outside Laramie. He never regained consciousness during four days of hospitalization and died at Poudre Valley Hospital, with his parents at his bedside.

Responding to news of Shepard's death, Wyoming Governor Jim   5
Geringer said all Wyoming residents "feel a sense of tragedy and disbelief that a human life could be taken in such a brutal way."

"We must now find closure," said Geringer, "to first assure that justice will be effectively carried out and, second, to work with the determination that there will not be a repeat of this incident in any fashion in Wyoming."

Vigils were held nationwide for the slain student, including a memorial service yesterday attended by about 800 people on Prexy's Pasture, the sprawling green on the University of Wyoming campus that Shepard crossed countless [times] as a student.

That tribute was marred, however, by news that a scarecrow mocking homosexuals showed up on a homecoming parade float in Fort Collins sponsored by Pi Kappa Alpha fraternity and Alpha Chi Omega sorority. Colorado State University officials are investigating; spokesmen for the fraternity denied involvement, saying that their float had been vandalized.

Shepard's beating has been widely portrayed by gay rights advocates and others as a hate crime. But Price, McKinney's girlfriend, told the Denver Post that her boyfriend intended only to rob Shepard after the university student embarrassed him by flirting with him at a bar. Price is the only one of the four suspects who has been released on bond.

The beating of Shepard has shed a national spotlight on Wyoming and   10
the failure of the state Legislature to enact anti–hate crimes legislation. At a Sunday night vigil in Laramie, petitions urging the Legislature to act were circulated among several hundred people who paid tribute to Shepard.

Geringer, at a press conference in Cheyenne yesterday, continued to insist that one crime, no matter how brutal, should not be the basis for hastily considered legislation.

The Responsive Reader

1. Ordinary newspaper readers often respond to news stories like the one about the Shepard murder with a sense of disbelief—"Tell me it is not true." For you, what about this incident makes it hard to swallow or believe? Or, on the other hand, do you feel much of it sounds like something to be expected, predictable, given the current climate of opinion?

Talking, Listening, Writing

2. Do you think it is possible to "hate the sin, not the sinner"?
3. Do you think political and religious leaders who stir up antigay sentiment should be held responsible for antigay violence?
4. What do you think of the homecoming parade float featuring a scarecrow mocking the dead student? Do you believe members of fraternities and sororities are more likely to harbor racist and antigay prejudice than other students?

Student Voices

According to the *Washington Post,* Wyoming was one of the few states without hate-crime laws, which usually include harsher-than-usual penalties. While Shepard was still alive and unconscious in the hospital, Wyoming Republican governor Jim Geringer said he questioned whether any law would deter "perverted individuals" more than the state's already tough law-enforcement statutes. "We deal very toughly with criminals of any kind," he said. "In this case I don't know how you would make it tougher." Do you think the law and the courts should recognize a special category of hate crimes? Or should all crimes be covered by the same set of statutes? The following is a sampling of student reactions to these questions. Do you agree or disagree strongly with one or more of them? Write a response to one or more of these. Join in the conversation.

1   Yes, we need a special category of hate crimes, or violent crimes motivated by prejudice. However, we need to distinguish between two different kinds of hate. The first kind of hate exists between people who know each other. Hate may be caused by feelings of revenge against someone who has done serious harm or caused serious injury to another person. However, the kind of hate involved in a true hate crime is aimed at complete strangers. It is aimed at people who look different or belong to a specific race or are of a certain religion. True hate crimes do not just harm an individual and the person's family. They strike at a whole group, and they really attack society as a whole.

2   A crime is a crime. I personally don't believe criminals choose their crimes on the basis of the penalty they might receive. I am also against a protected status for every group around. If you say that a random beating of a gay man is more offensive than a random beating of a straight man, you value one life over another. Also, a law that involves the attitude of the alleged perpetrator is bound to be abused. Any prosecutor wanting to pile up years of jail on a defendant could accuse the defendant of a hate crime as long as the prosecutor could find a racial or other difference between the victim and the defendant. Even being acquitted in court would not be the end of the de-

fendant's troubles. Anyone involved in a high-profile hate-crime trial would be marked for life regardless of actual attitude or wrongdoing.

3   In my opinion, most criminals in situations like the Shepard case and in most others are uneducated individuals and are therefore more likely to commit hate crimes because of their lack of education. Whether or not imposing tougher laws would help prevent hate crimes I don't know. Maybe instead of dealing with the final result we should try to do something about the cause of these crimes. People need to learn tolerance and acceptance. The focus needs to be on education and not on special punishment.

4   I think the laws and the courts should recognize a special category for hate crimes to prove a point—if nothing else. States with special stricter laws for crimes inspired by racism or hatred for a specific group project to the public that they do not condone or tolerate violence directed at innocent people merely because of their lifestyle. Hate crimes are more likely to occur if someone like the governor of Wyoming seems to condone or dismiss something so despicable and flat out wrong. Hate crime laws send a message in hopes of deterring hate-filled people from acting on their prejudices. It is an insult to the gay community and other minorities persecuted in our society (for something so basic as the right to be an individual) for officials in high places to brush off and seem to condone vicious acts of violence. We need to assure our children that they can live in this country without fear of being persecuted because of differences of race, religion, or sexual orientation.

Comparing and Contrasting

Writers use comparison and contrast to make us see similarities and differences. They help readers understand something new by showing how it differs from something familiar. (Gentrification is different from earlier patterns of urban renewal—it does not raze existing structures. It renovates and upgrades them instead; it uses them to lure affluent buyers back to the city.) Comparison and contrast can help us put historical changes in perspective. They can help us choose among careers, mates, or places to live.

TRIGGERING   Writers make comparisons for a purpose. They typically have an agenda—to make us vote for the better candidate, prefer one plan to another, or move toward needed change.

- A writer may contrast the organic pattern of small neighborhood stores with new mega-outlets for large impersonal chains. He or she may be appealing to a zoning commission or to the voters to preserve the character of a neighborhood.

- It might be an eye opener to compare the cost and trauma of an elderly relative's terminal illness under two different systems of health insurance. In this country—with a largely privately operated system of health insurance—the death of an elderly relative might leave a family bankrupt and in disarray. In a country like Canada or Germany, where health care is considered a citizen's right, all costs might be assumed by the publicly financed system of universal insurance.

GATHERING   When you write to compare and contrast, the preliminary stock-taking is especially important. A key part of your prewriting may be **brainstorming** notes: You jot down features that might prove important as you chart similarities and differences. Suppose you are working on a paper that will show how changing gender roles have transformed traditional assumptions about marriage. The following might be your first jotting down of possibly relevant points:

TRADITIONAL	MODERN
church wedding	live together first
till death do us part	high divorce rate
virgin bride	family planning
subservient wife	both work
husband works	backyard weddings
take the good with the bad	equal relationships
husband handles finances	supportive, caring male
housewife cleans and cooks	share chores
wait on the husband	mixed marriages
sex on demand	marriage contract
talk about sex is taboo	mutual sex
marry your own kind	discuss problems
feminine wife	

Even while you jot down these items, you will be mentally making connections. Revealing contrasts emerge as you connect contrasting items: (traditional) the wife cooks and cleans/(modern) both share chores; (traditional) the husband works/(modern) both work; (traditional) subservient wife/(modern) equal partners. What other items should be linked to show a striking contrast between the old and the new?

SHAPING How would you organize the brainstorming notes about changing gender roles in the modern marriage? These notes might lead naturally to a **point-by-point** comparison. As each question is raised, the writer first shows the traditional answer and then the contrasting modern one. The following sequence might prove workable as an organizing strategy for the paper:

POINT ONE: Who supports the family financially? Who "provides"?

POINT TWO: Who is the dominant partner? Who is in charge?

POINT THREE: Who does the housekeeping?

POINT FOUR: What is the role of sex? (And what are the sex roles of the spouses?)

POINT FIVE: Who is considered an "eligible" marriage partner in the first place?

However, sometimes a **parallel-order** comparison might prove more workable or instructive. To give your readers a clear picture of two things you are comparing, you might decide to give them a complete, rounded picture of first the one and then the other. However, you help your readers see the connections. You take up key points in the same or nearly the same order—in parallel order. Here is the skeleton for a parallel-order comparison of two day-care centers:

It's Your Choice

preview	. . . In the light of these findings, working parents can perhaps suspend some of their feelings of guilt and instead concentrate on the hardest task: finding the right place for their children. *Three important qualities to look for in a daycare center are a stable staff, the right activities, and an active role for the parents.*
EXAMPLE A point 1	I have worked at two different centers. The first one I consider a bad example. The staff changed every few months, mainly because we were paid minimum wage. The teachers who stayed did so because they did not feel qualified to work for a higher salary elsewhere. . . .
point 2	The children's day was as follows: TV—inside play—outside play—lunch—nap—outside play—TV—parents pick up. The main goal was to make the children follow the rules and keep quiet. I remember one small girl particularly who was a very active child. . . .
point 3	Parents were not encouraged to participate; their role was to drop off the children and pick them up. . . .
EXAMPLE B point 1	The second school I worked at was quite different. There was a very low turnover of staff. . . .
point 2	The children's schedule was as follows: Play—story time—work time—music—outside play—lunch—nap—independent work or play—story time—outside play—art—parents pick up. . . .
point 3	Parents joined in all the outside activities and often stopped for lunch with the children. Parents should be wary of any school that does not allow drop-in visits. . . .
	In a world of two-career or single-parent families, day care is going to be part of growing up for thousands of children. Instead of dropping a child off at the nearest center, parents must shop around to find a place designed to help children grow.

Make sure that your organizing strategy works for the job at hand. Instead of the classic point-by-point or parallel-order pattern, a strategy like the following may prove right for your topic:

- *You may want to start with strong but misleading similarities.* You then alert your reader to important differences that may not meet the eye.

- *You may want to start with deceptive surface differences.* (For instance, race relations today are different than they were in the days of overt, legalized segregation and officially condoned violence.) However, you might then go on to show that basic similarities remain, though their current version takes a more subtle form. (For instance, there is de facto segregation in the schools; minorities hit a "glass ceiling" on their way up the promotion ladder; etc.)

REVISING A comparison-and-contrast paper necessarily follows a more complicated plan than a paper that states a main point and then lines up supporting examples. As you reread and revise a first draft, see whether you have taken your readers with you—or whether you have lost them along the way. You may need stronger **transitions**—stronger signposts to keep pointing your readers in the right direction.

- *Spell out clearly the main point of your comparison.* Have you summed up in a unifying thesis what your paper as a whole is trying to show? You may also need a stronger conclusion to pull together various points you made along the way.

- *Give your readers a preview of the itinerary.* Try to word your thesis in such a way that it gives away your overall plan. Give your readers a hint: point-by-point? parallel-order? similarities first? (But avoid a stodgy "In-this-paper-I-plan-to-do-the-following" style.)

- *Strengthen your network of transitions.* Signal turning points. Signal similarities by phrases like *similarly, in parallel fashion, as an exact counterpart, pointing in the same direction,* or *along the same lines.* Signal contrasts by phrases like *however, by contrast, on the other hand, as the direct opposite,* or *providing a counterweight* (or *a counterpoint*).

What is the overall plan in the following sample paper? How does the plan become clear to the reader? How effectively has the student writer followed through?

Wolves Mate for Life—Do You?

It is believed that the wolf mates for life. Spring is the breeding season. Six to seven in a litter is usual, but there may be as many as fourteen. The pups are born with big blue eyes, which soon fade in color. The family remains together while the pups are young, even when the mother breeds in successive years, and all members help take care of the family.

This could be compared to the traditional marriages of earlier times—married for life with six to fourteen children, and the family was a unit—unlike some of today's modern marriages where divorce dismantles half of them. What are the differences between the old traditional marriage and the new modern one that is so prominent in today's society? Where do these differences lie? I believe the substantial differences lie in the three general areas of work, family, and education, each stemming from changes in economics, values, or morality (or the lack of it, depending upon your viewpoint).

My grandpa and grandma lived in the little town of Yuba City and carried on a very traditional marriage. My grandfather did all of the out-of-house work while Grandma occupied herself with the domestic duties such as cleaning, cooking, and taking care of the children. My grandfather was a farmer and grew fruit and nut trees. He "brought home the bacon," while Grandma did the frying. This was very common in the traditional marriage, for the husband to work and the wife to stay at home, but this isn't too often seen in today's society.

Now we see the modern marriage as the only way to go. Because of the high cost of living both partners must work to support themselves. No longer can the husband deal with the outside job while his wife deals with the household. When I was younger my parents operated on a traditional-style marriage, but when I became a freshman in college, my mother went to work as an accountant. Our family could no longer live on what my father brought home, so my mother's joining the labor force was the only answer.

Family life in the traditional marriage is quite different from that in the modern marriage. My grandparents had three children—two boys and one girl. Having three or more children was not uncommon, but now in a modern marriage the third is usually "a mistake." My grandparents considered the family to be a very important institution and thus had many family activities together that brought closeness and harmony to the family. They often went camping at a cabin in Mt. Lassen, fed the ducks Wonder Bread at Ellis Lake, and played at the Sutter County park, which had four swings, a set of monkey bars, a slide, and a merry-go-round. Vacations were also family-oriented. They would pack the car and drive to Oklahoma to visit family out there, singing "She'll be comin' 'round the mountain" as they traveled.

In the modern marriage, people often forget the importance of the family. Often there isn't even a whole family present. Half of today's marriages end in divorce, thus leaving a single parent somewhere with children to take care of, and that parent working to support the children usually has little or no time for family activities. Even when both parents are present, often work schedules conflict, and differing individual wants and needs come into play. Dad's been working all week and wants to watch baseball and relax on Saturday, Mom has to work 10 to 6:30, the older child has a book report due on Monday, but the little six-year-old wants to feed the ducks the stale bread with the family. It just doesn't work as well as it used to. Families are lucky if they get a one-week vacation together at Big Basin to camp in an overcrowded tent and fight off savage ants and blood-sucking mosquitoes, eat overripe fruit, and use outhouses that reek and have doors that never quite latch.

Education is something that the whole family participates in in a traditional marriage. Not only do the children learn at school, but they are also taught important things at home. My grandma taught her daughter to cook, embroider, can fruits and vegetables, iron, and churn butter. She taught all her kids manners and how to behave. My grandpa taught all his children how to grade fruit—know what is acceptable for market—drive the vehicles, milk the cows, even ride a bike, swim and dive, hunt, and fish. He also taught his sons how to work on mechanical vehicles, prune trees, irrigate, and breed the livestock. He also took time to help his children learn the value of money, by helping them open up a savings account. Other relatives taught the children also. An aunt taught the girl to crochet and her great-grandmother taught her to sew and quilt. The boys' great-grandfather taught them to carve things out of wood.

Things are quite different in the modern marriages we see today. The parents have little time for teaching in the home because of their work responsibilities. Education occurs at school and through peers and other sources, and children learn more on their own without the family than ever before. They attend driving school to learn how to drive, and the local Parks and Recreation Department takes care of the swim lessons. Relatives aren't usually involved as much as in a traditional marriage either. As *Ms.* magazine says, "Grandma is 61. She looks 45, is divorced, has a job selling real estate, and spends her weekends with a retired banker whose wife died three years ago."

Why have marriages changed? Why aren't families the self-sufficient, close, "all for one and one for all" units they used to be? I believe the change stems from economics. Society hardly allows that type of lifestyle anymore. Values have changed also, along with changes in morality. I don't believe people put as high a priority on marriage and family as they used to. Maybe divorce, suicide, emotional breakdowns, and child abuse would decrease if people valued marriage and family more, and looked back to some of the traditional marriage ways, and even took after the wolf and mated for life, as it used to be.

Topics for Comparison and Contrast Papers (A Sampling)

1. In movie or television fare, have you observed a change from stereotypically feminine female characters to "strong woman" characters?
2. Have you ever lived in a homogeneous neighborhood (with people of very similar backgrounds or social status)—but also in a more diverse, mixed neighborhood? Or have you ever attended a school with a homogeneous student body—but also a school with a more diverse population? Write a paper working out the contrast between the two settings.
3. Have you ever converted from one religious or political group to another? Or have you had a chance to observe closely two such groups? How did they compare?
4. Have you experienced a major change in your lifestyle? Write a before-and-after paper on the subject.
5. Weigh the options on a topic like the following: What is preferable—a problem marriage or a divorce? What is preferable—single motherhood or an alternative?
6. In the men you have a chance to observe, do you find both the macho and the sensitive male? What sets them apart?
7. Have you observed a difference in outlook and values between recent immigrants (or Americans from immigrant families) and other Americans?

8. In your family or in other areas of your experience, is there a generation gap? Have you observed a marked contrast in values or outlook between the older and the younger generation?
9. Do men and women feel differently about love?
10. Have you experienced the difference between blue-collar and white-collar jobs?

7
MEDIA WATCH
Virtual Reality

> *On the front page*
> *of the daily fivestarfinal*
> ****** Edition a child*
> *is dying in the rubble*
> *of newsprint.*
> — *Olga Cabral*

The media have a vast potential for educating us and broadening our views. However, they also have the power to manipulate our minds. As some people are alcohol dependent, so many of us are media dependent. We choose political leaders in campaigns conducted in large part in the newspapers and on television with a constant barrage of polls, sound bites, and attack ads. Often these campaigns are orchestrated by consultants and spin doctors who have no qualms about working both sides of the political street.

Our views on race relations may have been shaped by TV images of violence and riots in places that few viewers have actually visited. Our fears and doubts about child molestation, rape, and incest are aroused and fueled by the media. People who have never been in a courtroom get their ideas about how the justice system works from watching televised trials on TV.

What we see and read on such subjects depends on editors' and network executives' judgment on what is newsworthy. Editorial and often marketing judgment decide what goes on page one and what is lost in the back pages. When the media focus on candidates for the Supreme Court or the presidency, the voter may learn more about their experiments with marijuana or the way they talk behind closed doors than about their stands on health insurance or abortion. For many viewers, the faces that people the small or the large screen—Madonna, Arnold Schwarzenegger, Michael Jackson, a favorite quarterback—are more real than their coworkers or neighbors.

We know some of our world at first hand and much of it through the media. Viewers may know almost no African Americans personally but only media stereotypes: the wise-cracking tough street kid, male or female; the kindly, ever-smiling, and self-deprecating entertainer; the violent and self-destructing black male athlete in trouble with the law. The news may play out in loving detail the personal disasters, heroic rescues, and petty scandals that viewers love. However, it may provide little insight into the politics of race, immigration, education, health care, or mental health.

How do the media shape or distort our reality? Do they always skim the surface, in sound bites that allow for no real thinking? Are we always helpless "target audiences," or can we influence the steady stream of images and ideas that the media aim at us?

GAME OVER

Amanda Fazzone

> *In her spectacularly successful book* The Beauty Myth: How Images of
> Beauty Are Used against Women *(1990), Naomi Wolf attacked "the icon
> of the anorexic fashion model" that drives out "most other images and stories
> of female heroines, role models, villains, eccentrics, buffoons, visionaries, sex
> goddesses and pranksters." She marshaled formidable statistics, insiders' testi-
> mony, and official reports in support of her charges against fashion magazines,
> the cosmetic surgery industry, the dieting industry, and other forces promoting
> an ideal of female beauty that robs women of their sense of self-worth. In the
> decade that followed, the "impossibly beautiful" stereotypical fashion model
> encountered formidable competition from a new kind of computer-generated
> video-game heroine that co-opted the new fashion of strong independent female
> characters while carrying the media cult of the "unnaturally perfect body" to a
> new extreme. Amanda Fazzone wrote the following article for the "Washing-
> ton Diarist" column of the* New Republic.

Thought Starters: The simulated reality of video games became a huge
marketing success. Are you or people you know well part of the target audience? For a journal entry, can you give a synopsis or vivid plot outline of
a current favorite?

I have more than a few things in common with Lara Croft, the   1
gun-toting, Bigfoot-slaying, back-flipping, treasure-hunting, aristocratic
English heroine who stars in the video game Tomb Raider, [. . .] spun off
into [. . . a] movie in the United States, *Lara Croft: Tomb Raider.* We both
have dark hair and dark eyes. We both enjoy music and the arts. We both
like corgis. We both write for a living. And we both have breasts. But while
Lara's 34Ds unwaveringly float mid-bicep, I, like most women, rely on an
armada of brassieres to ballast what nature never intended skin to buoy. The
5-foot-9-inch, 130-pound Lara—even with the enviable measurements of
34D-24-35—seems not to have any breast-control issues at all. Whether
she's fighting giant lizards or rappelling in the Himalayas, they invariably
stay put.

Her secret? Lara Croft isn't real. She doesn't actually weigh in at 130
pounds (and her breasts don't weigh anything at all), the "stats" in her
lengthy promotional "bio" notwithstanding. She's a synthespian: a computer-generated virtual woman with the pixels and the moxie to engender
crushes in the hearts of the millions of gamers who made Tomb Raider one
of the most successful video game series of all time. The game's tag line:
"Sometimes a killer body just isn't enough."

But not being human hasn't kept Lara from taking heat for her un-naturally perfect body. Feminists say that, with the advent of computer-generated cybermodels and synthespians, the bar for real women has been raised even higher. Asks Germaine Greer: "How many women do you know with broad chests and narrow waists like [Lara Croft]? Men should wake up to the fact that women have big bums. Whatever these characters are, they're not real women." Princeton University Professor Elaine Showalter claims that "Croft and the cybermodels epitomise the era of power grooming. No longer can women depend on a dab of powder and lipstick before they face the public." Today's woman, Showalter writes, employs "[l]iposuction, exfoliation, laser-blasting, Botox and collagen [to] take the skin to pix[e]lated smoothness and tautness." Life imitating art.

The outrage isn't surprising. Feminists have long decried the alchemy employed to create women of Barbie doll proportions, charging that such images cause men to objectify women, and contribute to the lack of female self-esteem that leads to depression, eating disorders, and the operating table. And with Lara and her virtual compatriots, that alchemy—and presumably the suffering it spawns—has taken a giant technological leap forward. Still, there may be an upside to all this pixelation. After all, feminists aren't the only ones infuriated by the emergence of cybermodels—the "real" modeling industry has good reason to be upset as well. Cybermodels may do more than put human models out of work; their explicit fakeness might just force people to admit that the whole modeling enterprise has been fake from the start.

From *Toy Story* to *Titanic* to *Shrek,* we're growing increasingly accustomed to recognizing synthespians for the man-made products they are. On the Internet, cybernewscasters Vandrea (modeled on British newscaster Andrea Catherwood) and Ananova have become celebs. And Webbie Tookay (that's "2-K"), the first virtual model, was dubbed "the most valuable model in the world" with an estimated market value last year of $15 million, thanks, in part, to contracts with Nokia and Sony. (By contrast, Gisele Bundchen, the world's highest-paid human model, earns a mere $5 million per year.) But cybermodel celebrity is a consciously cynical phenomenon. Their creators aren't trying to *trick* us into believing these images are real. They're just simulating reality.

What's more, even as girls' magazine *mary-kateandashley* dubs Lara "an Indiana Jones–esque girl" and as Angelina Jolie, the 26-year-old Academy Award–winning actress, doubles for Lara on film, it's almost impossible not to notice that Croft and her cyberpeers aren't real. It's true, as Naomi Wolf wrote in her 1991 book *The Beauty Myth,* that "'Computer imaging'—the controversial new technology that tampers with photographic reality—has been used for years in women's magazines' beauty advertising." But the whole point of computer imaging was that magazine readers didn't know—or at least didn't think much about the fact—that the woman on the cover didn't look that way in real life. And so young girls could aspire to look the

5

way Gisele looks on this month's cover of *Vogue*. But they can't ignore Lara's inauthenticity, because her inauthenticity is central to her fame. "When I first played the game, I thought [Lara's breast size] was ridiculous," said one 15-year-old girl I interviewed after the film. "How could she run and jump dressed like that?" And you can see it on the video screen. Lara barely speaks, is controlled by the player, and is primarily seen from behind. A clear case of art trying—and failing—to imitate life.

Of course it's possible that, as technology improves, it will become increasingly difficult to distinguish real women from their computer-generated counterparts. And if that's the case, beauty-industry handlers will have even more reason to prefer synthetic women. "She is the perfect model," cheers Webbie Tookay's agent, John Casablancas—the founder of Elite Model Management who left his post [. . .] to found the first-ever cyber-model agency, Illusion 2K. "Webbie can eat nothing and keep her curves. . . . [S]he will never get a pimple or ask for a raise." With a Screen Actors Guild strike looming, speculates a recent *Entertainment Weekly* article, the demand for synthespians may grow even higher. And, unlike most reed-thin models and actresses, cybermodels have no need for breast augmentation, airbrushing, padded bras, or industrial-strength double-stick tape.

Still, would it be so bad if technology grew sophisticated enough to trump reality, if synthespians replaced women in all those forms of entertainment feminists have historically derided—modeling, beauty pageants, pornography? Who would protest if we no longer expected women to look like models, just as we never expected anyone to climb walls like Spider-Man or have supersonic hearing like the Bionic Woman?

Perhaps cybermodels and synthespians will help us admit that what men have been getting off on all these years—and what women have been emulating at unrecoupable cost—are, like Lara Croft, little more than cartoon characters. And with that admission might come a more natural definition of what's sexy, by which the genuine confluence of health and DNA is deemed preferable to the handiwork of a Photoshop virtuoso. Were that truly to come to pass, of course, it wouldn't only be the human supermodels whose careers would suffer: Presumably, Lara's would as well. But she'd manage. After all, she'll always have her writing.

The Responsive Reader

1. In the course of her essay, Fazzone touches on many of the methods women employ to emulate the ideal created by the Beauty Myth. These range from the traditional "dab of powder and lipstick" to much more strenuous and costly methods and procedures. On which of these could you serve as somewhat of an expert to fill in your fellow students on the mysteries of the beauty trade?
2. What were the traditional objections of feminists to the Barbie doll image and to modeling shows and beauty pageants? What for them makes

the new computerized synthetic "thespians," or virtual actors, an even more formidable challenge? How do they raise the bar for women "even higher"?

3. Fazzone several times touches on the question of whether video game users really at some point confuse fantasy and reality. Overall, what seems to be her answer to the question? Do you think attitudes from the virtual reality of video games do in some way or to some extent carry over from the fantasy world into the real world of human behavior and human relationships?

Talking, Listening, Writing

4. Have you ever made a conscious effort to make yourself over or improve your appearance? What made you do it? What did you do? What was the result?

5. Do you or people you know object to makeup, perfume, or other beauty helps? Can you help with a presentation lining up arguments pro and con?

6. As Fazzone indicates, feminists have long agitated against fashion shows, beauty pageants, and Barbie dolls. Do you think their objections have had an impact?

Collaborative Projects

7. Working with a group, collect images from advertisements or commercials aimed at you and your peers or others of your age group. What kinds of faces, bodies, and clothes do you see? Do you think the grunge look, for instance, could be a rebellion of the young against the stereotypes of the Beauty Myth?

Find It on the Web

Much controversy has swirled about the Barbie doll as an icon of American popular culture. Studies have focused on the impact of the stereotypical Barbie doll image on young girls and on the manufacturer's initiatives designed to overcome charges of racism. Can you track some of the controversy in current or archived Internet sources?

UNGOOD FELLAS AND THE GODFATHER CULTURE

George de Stefano

The Godfather, *Mario Puzo's original Mafia epic with Marlon Brando as Don Corleone, spawned countless sequels and spinoffs. In some of the most popular American film and television entertainment, evil comes not from outer space or from the designs of a mad scientist but from your Italian neighbors around the block in the Bronx or other American city with a large ethnic population. The Sopranos, a trendy updating of the Godfather mystique, has become one of the most widely watched and critically acclaimed show on American television. Criminals still bully, conspire, and kill, but they share their concerns with a psychiatrist and operate in a society where brutal violence is no longer news. George de Stefano is a media watcher and culture critic for* Nation *magazine and other publications. As an Italian American author, de Stefano objects to the turning of ruthless criminals into audience favorites and to the continuing stereotyping of the Italian American community as a hotbed for organized crime.*

Thought Starters: Do you watch Mafia epics on television or on the big screen? Which of the *Godfather, Good Fellas,* or similar mafia epics are you familiar with? What identifies the gangsters and criminals as Italians or as Americans of Italian descent?

The last decade of the twentieth century was not a happy one for the Mafia. During the nineties both the United States and Italy made remarkable strides in curbing organized crime, imprisoning gangsters and dismantling their business interests. Though it would be premature to declare either the Italian or the American Mafia dead, both have been wounded, the latter perhaps mortally. But if the Mafia is a shadow of its former self, you'd hardly know it from pop culture. In fact, media images of La Cosa Nostra seem to be proliferating in direct proportion to the decline of organized crime. Not since Francis Ford Coppola's *The Godfather* reinvented the gangster genre in the early seventies have there been so many wiseguys on screen. The past year brought the films *Analyze This* and *Mickey Blue Eyes,* and with *i fratelli* Weinstein, Harvey and Bob, having acquired the rights to the late Mario Puzo's final novel, *Omertà,* for their Miramax Films, there's at least one other high-profile Mafia movie on the way. Another may well be the fourth installment of Coppola's *Godfather* saga. According to the *Hollywood Reporter,* Leonardo Di Caprio and Andy Garcia (Al Pacino's nephew in *Godfather III*) are keen to sign on to the project, pending a suitable script.

On television, gangsters with Italian surnames have been a surefire audience draw, from the days of *The Untouchables* to contemporary cop shows like *NYPD Blue*. A very partial list of recent programs includes the network miniseries *The Last Don* and *Bella Mafia*, as well as biopics about John Gotti and his turncoat lieutenant Sammy "The Bull" Gravano, and, on Showtime cable, an absurdly hagiographic one about Joseph Bonanno produced by his son, Bill. But no mob-themed show has generated the critical accolades and viewer enthusiasm accorded *The Sopranos*, the Emmy Award–winning HBO comedy-drama that has become the cable network's most-watched series, its recent second-season premiere attended by an avalanche of hype.

Moving from *The Sopranos'* suburban New Jersey turf to Palermo, HBO last fall premiered *Excellent Cadavers*, a feature-film adaptation of Alexander Stille's 1995 book about the anti-Mafia campaign launched by two courageous Sicilian magistrates. Why is Italian-American (and Italian) organized crime such a mainstay of American pop culture, and do these images reflect the reality of the Mafia? And does the persistence of the Mafioso as a pop-culture archetype constitute ethnic defamation of Italian-Americans?

That many of today's depictions of the American Mafia are in the comic mode — *The Sopranos, Analyze This, Mickey Blue Eyes,* the parody *Mafia!* — is possible only because organized crime is much less fearsome than in its heyday. Both *The Sopranos* and *Analyze This* feature Mafiosi on the verge of a nervous breakdown, their psychological crackups reflecting the disarray of their criminal enterprises under the pressure of law enforcement and the breaking of *omertà*, the code of silence, by gangsters who'd rather sing than serve time. V. Zucconi, a commentator for the Italian newspaper *La Repubblica,* analyzed this development in an article titled "America: The Decline of the Godfather." Zucconi claims that in the United States the Mafia survives mainly in its pop-culture representations, and that while it used to generate fear, today it is a source of humor. He says that in America one can observe "the funeral of the dying Mafia," an outcome he hopes one day will occur also in Italy. Is Zucconi overoptimistic?

Criminologist James Jacobs reaches a similar conclusion in his study   5
Gotham Unbound: How New York City was Liberated from the Clutches of Cosa Nostra (NYU Press). Organized-crime-control strategies "have achieved significant success in purging Cosa Nostra from the city's social, economic, and political life," he writes. Gangsters in New York, and also in other large and small cities, are losing their foothold in the labor and industrial rackets that have been the source of their power and influence; and there is a dearth of younger, rising stars to replace aging or incarcerated leaders. The decline, says Jacobs, has been so marked that "Cosa Nostra's survival into the next millennium . . . can be seriously doubted." It's a different story in Italy. The Sicilian Mafia's economic might, its alliances with politicians and indifferent law enforcement enabled it to grow so powerful that it threatened Italy's

status as a modern nation. As Alexander Stille observed in *Excellent Cadavers,* the war against the Mafia in Sicily is not a local problem of law and order but the struggle for national unity and democracy in Italy. HBO's film based on Stille's book promised to tell that story, but, at barely ninety minutes, it ended up too compressed to offer more than a skim on the events he reported and analyzed so compellingly. Talk about missed opportunities: Instead of the Z-like political thriller it could have been, *Cadavers* is a rather routine *policier.*

In the eighties, Mafia killings accelerated as ambitious upstarts from Corleone (a real place, *Godfather* fans) challenged the Palermo old guard for the control of organized crime. The body count included not only Mafiosi but also police officials, magistrates and politicians, who came to be called, with fine Sicilian mordancy, excellent cadavers. Two magistrates, Giovanni Falcone and Paolo Borsellino, began to pursue the Mafia with unprecedented persistence. Their efforts culminated in the historic "maxi-trials," which resulted in the imprisonment of hundreds of Sicily's most powerful gangsters.

The Mafia, of course, retaliated, assassinating Falcone in May 1992 and, two months later, Borsellino. The murders, however, ignited the simmering rage of Sicilians against the Mafia and the officials who protected it. The government was forced to respond, and the subsequent crackdown resulted in the arrest of numerous Mafiosi and connected businessmen and politicians.

Italians overwhelmingly regard Mafiosi as the other; they do not identify or empathize with criminals, nor do they feel that portrayals of organized crime in movies, television and other media tar them with the brush of criminality. Many Italian-Americans, however, regard the seemingly endless stream of Mafia movies and TV shows as a defamatory assault. In mid-January a coalition of seven Italian-American organizations issued a joint statement condemning *The Sopranos* for "defaming and assassinating the cultural character" of Americans of Italian descent.

It's undeniable that the dominant pop-culture images of Italian-Americans have been the mobster and the related, anti–working class stereotype of the boorish *gavone.* But there are important differences between these skewed portrayals and other forms of ethnic stereotyping. If the Mafia has been conflated with Sicilian/Italian culture, it's in large part because Italian-American filmmakers and writers have so expertly blended the two. Coppola's memorable and authentic depiction of an Italian-American wedding in *The Godfather* comes to mind. *The Sopranos,* created by veteran TV writer David Chase (né De Cesare), similarly gets many details right about *nouveau riche* suburban Italian-Americans, the eponymous mob family's noncriminal neighbors.

The Sopranos cleverly acknowledges Italian-American indignation 10 over Mafia stereotyping only to try to co-opt it. In an episode from the show's first season, Dr. Jennifer Melfi, Tony Soprano's psychiatrist, and her family have a lively dinnertime debate about the persistence of the mob image. The scene ends with the Melfis toasting the "20 million Italian Americans" who have nothing to do with organized crime. But Jennifer also mocks her ex-husband, an ethnic activist, for being more concerned about "rehabilitating Connie Francis's reputation" than with ethnic cleansing. The line neatly skewers the tunnel vision of conservative Italian-Americans who ignore forms of bias and social injustice that don't affect them. But it also poses a false dichotomy: caring passionately about the image of one's group need not preclude a broader perspective. At other times, the show suggests that Tony, a murderous criminal, is an Italian-American everyman. He's aware of his people's history—he informs his daughter that the telephone was invented not by Alexander Graham Bell but by Antonio Meucci—and he's depicted as more honest and vital than his snooty neighbors, or, as he calls them, the "Wonder-Bread wops."

The Mafia has become the paradigmatic pop-culture expression of Italian-American ethnicity for several reasons: the aura of glamour, sometimes tragic, surrounding the movie mobster, exemplified by Coppola's Corleones; the gangster genre's embodiment of the violent half of "kiss kiss, bang bang," Pauline Kael's famous distillation of the essential preoccupations of American movies; and, perhaps most important, the enduring appeal of the outlaw—the guy who, in a technocratic, impersonal society, has the personal power to reward friends, and, more important, whack enemies. Although real Mafiosi are venal and violent, films and TV too often have presented them far more sympathetically than they deserve—*The Sopranos* is just the latest case in point.

Italian-Americans, whose forebears fled *la miseria,* the crushing poverty of Southern Italy and Sicily, in numbers so vast that their departure has been likened to a hemorrhage, constitute one of the United States' largest ethnic groups. An Italian-American film critic and author told me some years ago that it was "selfish" of our *paesani* to complain about Mafia stereotyping given their largely successful pursuit of the American Dream and the more onerous discrimination faced by other minorities. He also insisted that most Americans are smart enough to realize that gangsters constitute only a tiny minority of the Italian-American population.

But it is dismaying—no, infuriating—to see one's group depicted so consistently in such distorted fashion. Unlike racist stereotyping of blacks, portrayals of Italian-American criminality don't reflect or reinforce Italian-American exclusion from American society and its opportunities. (Faced with a threatened NAACP boycott, both the NBC and ABC networks recently agreed to increase the hiring of blacks, Latinos and Asians, in front of and behind the TV cameras.) The pervasiveness of these images, however, does affect the perception of Italian-Americans by others. Surveys indicate that many Americans believe that most Italian-Americans are in some way "connected" and that Italian immigrants created organized crime in the United States, even though the Irish, Germans and others got there first.

Besides fostering such attitudes, the Mafia mystique also serves to obscure other, more interesting and no less dramatic aspects of the Italian-American experience. In 1997 the City University of New York hosted a conference on "The Lost World of Italian American Radicalism." Scholars discussed the immigrant anarchists Sacco and Vanzetti (executed by the US government), other major figures like the labor organizer Carlo Tresca, the New York City Congressman Vito Marcantonio and such icons of sixties activism as civil rights advocate Father James Groppi and Mario Savio of the Berkeley Free Speech movement. The conference also highlighted unsung men and women who were labor militants, anti-Fascist organizers and politically engaged writers and artists.

Besides such efforts to recover and understand the radical past, there has been a surge of cultural production and activism among Italian-Americans. In recent years the American-Italian Historical Association, a national organization of academics and grassroots scholars, has held conferences on such hot-button topics as multiculturalism and race relations. Fieri, an association of young Italian-American professionals, last year commemorated the life and work of Vito Marcantonio—an amazing choice given the far less controversial figures they could have honored. The New York–based Italian-American Writers Association and journals such as *Voices in Italian Americana* (VIA) and *The Italian American Review* promote and publish fiction, poetry and critical essays by writers whose vision of *italianità* flouts the pop-culture clichés. Italo-American gays and lesbians have come out with *Hey, Paisan!*, a new anthology, and *Fuori!*, a folio of essays published by VIA. Actor/playwright Frank Ingrasciotta's *Blood Type: Ragu,* currently enjoying a successful run at the Belmont Italian American Theater in the Bronx (several of whose productions have moved to Off Broadway), offers an exploration of Sicilian-American identity and culture free of *goombahs* with guns.

15

Ethnicity remains a powerful and contentious force in American life, and popular culture should illumine its workings. Italian-Americans who want to promote more diverse depictions might not only protest Hollywood film studios and TV production companies. They might put some of the onus on Italian-American creative talents who have built careers on the Mafia. And they could also support the alternative, community-level work being done. Other stories from Italo-America can and should be told.

The Responsive Reader

1. De Stefano mentions milestones and key features of the traditional gangster genre. What would you include in a description of the literature and media fare that feeds the public's appetite for entertainment with a Mafia or Cosa Nostra theme? (What is the Cosa Nostra? What is *omertà?*)

2. According to de Stefano, how has the gangster genre evolved in recent years? Does it show us the same types but seen from a more sophisticated, updated point of view? Does it reflect changes in the world of organized crime?

3. Media critics often accuse the mainstream media of co-opting voices of protest or criticism. They silence or undercut protest by adopting some of the protesters' language—"talking the talk without walking the walk." De Stefano claims that a recent media success co-opted the indignation of Italian Americans at the continued use of the gangster stereotype. How did it do so?

4. De Stefano mentions the "memorable and authentic depiction of an Italian-American wedding" in the original *Godfather* movie. If you remember the movie or similar scenes in other gangster movies, what makes such scenes so memorable or authentic for viewers like de Stefano? Other media critics are especially troubled by the role of family, and of the gangsters' wives and children, in the pop-culture Mafia movies. What do you think disturbs them?

Talking, Listening, Writing

5. De Stefano says that many Italian Americans "regard the seemingly endless stream of Mafia movies and TV shows as a defamatory assault." Do you think these media products defame or slander a whole group of Americans? Do you think Americans that are not of Italian descent should be concerned? Why or why not?

6. Producers and media executives often justify violent gangster epics as "just entertainment." Do you think they are just entertainment? Do you think that in the gangster genre criminals are glorified?

7. Do you think the trend in American popular entertainment is toward more brutal and more cynical violence?

8. Have you or people you know well felt you or they were the target of ethnic stereotyping in the media? What form did it take? How serious was it? What recourse do targeted groups have?

Find It on the Web

Have Americans come to think of organized crime as entertainment? De Stefano reminds them of the brutal realities of the struggle in his tribute to the murdered Italian crime fighters Falcone and Borsellino. What can you find out about Falcone, Borsellino, or other real-life crime fighters— their struggle against organized crime, their murders, and the attacks on their families? What would you include in an update on Italy's fight against organized crime?

TALK TV: TUNING IN TO TROUBLE

Jeanne Albronda Heaton and Nona Leigh Wilson

> *In the view of many media watchers, the media landscape has been radically transformed by the emergence of talk shows as a medium rivaling rock stations, news channels, or movie channels in popularity. Talk show hosts, whether on radio or TV, go out of their way to broach provocative topics that will get people to talk—and talk they do, often spilling out unedited raw popular opinion very different from the scripted prose of commentators with expensive hairdos. What view of reality and of other people do we derive from tuning in to the talk show world? The authors of the following article on talk television focus on the way the shows shape women's images of themselves, of other women, and of men. For better or for worse, how do the shows shape women's views of relationships between men and women? Heaton is a practicing psychologist who also teaches psychology at Ohio University. Wilson teaches counseling and human resource development at South Dakota State University. Their essay is adapted from their book* Tuning In to Trouble: Talk TV's Destructive Impact on Mental Health *(1995).*

Thought Starters: Do you listen to talk radio or watch talk TV? When you do, do you think of callers or guests as weird or as representative, ordinary people?

In 1967, *The Phil Donahue Show* aired in Dayton, Ohio, as a new daytime talk alternative. Donahue did not offer the customary "women's fare." On Monday of his first week he interviewed atheist Madalyn Murray O'Hair. Tuesday he featured single men talking about what they looked for in women. Wednesday he showed a film of a baby being born from the obstetrician's point of view. Thursday he sat in a coffin and interviewed a funeral director. And on Friday he held up "Little Brother," an anatomically correct doll without his diaper. When Donahue asked viewers to call in response, phone lines jammed.

For 18 years daytime talk *was* Donahue. His early guests reflected the issues of the time and included Ralph Nader on consumer rights, Bella Abzug on feminism, and Jerry Rubin on free speech. Never before had such socially and personally relevant issues been discussed in such a democratic way with daytime women viewers. But his most revolutionary contribution was in making the audience an integral part of the show's format. The women watching Donahue finally had a place in the conversation, and they were determined to be heard. The show provided useful information and dialogue that had largely been unavailable to housebound women, affording them the opportunity to voice their opinions about everything from politics to sex—and even the politics of sex.

No real competition emerged until 1985, when *The Oprah Winfrey Show* went national. Her appeal for more intimacy was a ratings winner. She did the same topics Donahue had done but with a more therapeutic tone. Donahue seemed driven to uncover and explore. Winfrey came to share and understand. In 1987, Winfrey's show surpassed Donahue's by being ranked among the top 20 syndicated shows. Phil and Oprah made it easier for those who followed; their successors were able to move much more quickly to the top.

At their best, the shows "treated the opinions of women of all classes, races, and educational levels as if they mattered," says Naomi Wolf in her book *Fire with Fire:* "That daily act of listening, whatever its shortcomings, made for a revolution in what women were willing to ask for; the shows daily conditioned otherwise unheard women into the belief that they were entitled to a voice." Both Donahue and Winfrey deserve enormous credit for providing a platform for the voices of so many who needed to be heard, and for raising the nation's consciousness on many important topics, including domestic violence, child abuse, and other crucial problems. But those pioneering days are over. As the number of shows increased and the ratings wars intensified, the manner in which issues are presented has changed. Shows now encourage conflict, name-calling, and fights. Producers set up underhanded tricks and secret revelations. Hosts instruct guests to reveal all. The more dramatic and bizarre the problems the better.

While more air time is given to the problems that women face, the 5 topics are presented in ways that are not likely to yield change. The very same stereotypes that have plagued both women and men for centuries are in full force. Instead of encouraging changes in sex roles, the shows actually solidify them. Women viewers are given a constant supply of the worst images of men, all the way from garden-variety liars, cheats, and con artists to rapists and murderers.

If there is a man for every offense, there is certainly a woman for every trauma. Most women on talk TV are perpetual victims presented as having so little power that not only do they have to contend with real dangers such as sexual or physical abuse, but they are also overcome by bad hair, big thighs, and beautiful but predatory "other" women. The women of talk are almost always upset and in need. The bonding that occurs invariably centers around complaints about men or the worst stereotypes about women. In order to be a part of the "sisterhood," women are required to be angry with men and dissatisfied with themselves. We need look no further than at some of the program titles to recognize the message. Shows about men bring us a steady stream of stalkers, adulterers, chauvinistic sons, abusive fathers, and men who won't commit to women.

The shows provide a forum for women to complain, confront, and cajole, but because there is never any change as a result of the letting loose, this supports the mistaken notion that women's complaints have "no weight," that the only power women have is to complain, and that they cannot effect real changes. By bringing on offensive male guests who do nothing but verify the grounds for complaint, the shows are reinforcing some self-defeating propositions. The idea that women should direct their energies toward men rather than look for solutions in themselves is portrayed daily. And even when the audience chastises such behavior, nothing changes, because only arguments and justifications follow.

On *The Jenny Jones Show* a woman was introduced as someone who no longer had sex with her husband because she saw him with a stripper. Viewers got to hear how the stripper "put her boobs in his face" and then kissed him. The husband predictably defended his actions: "At least I didn't tongue her." The next few minutes proceeded with insult upon insult, to which the audience "oohed" and "aahed" and applauded. To top it all off, viewers were informed that the offense in question occurred at the husband's birthday party, which his wife arranged, *stripper and all*. Then in the last few minutes a psychologist pointed out the couple weren't wearing rings and didn't seem committed. She suggested that their fighting might be related to some other problem. Her comments seemed reasonable enough until she suggested that the wife might really be trying to get her husband to rape her. That comment called up some of the most absurd and destructive ideas imaginable about male and female relationships—yet there was no explanation or discussion.

It is not that women and men don't find lots of ways to disappoint each other, or that some women and some men don't act and think like the women and men on the shows. The problem is talk TV's fixation on gender war, with endless portrayals of vicious acts, overboard retaliations, and outrageous justifications. As a result, viewers are pumped full of the ugliest, nastiest news from the front.

When issues affecting people of color are dealt with, the stereotypes   10
about gender are layered on top of the stereotypes about race. Since most of the shows revolve around issues related to sex, violence, and relationships, they tend to feature people of color who reflect stereotypical images—in a steady stream of guests who have children out of wedlock, live on welfare, fight viciously, and have complicated unsolvable problems. While there are less than flattering depictions of white people on these shows, white viewers have the luxury of belonging to the dominant group, and therefore are more often presented in the media in positive ways.

On a *Ricki Lake* show about women who sleep with their friends' boyfriends, the majority of the guests were African American and Hispanic women who put on a flamboyant display of screaming and fighting. The profanity was so bad that many of the words had to be deleted. The segment had to be stopped because one guest yanked another's wig off. For many white viewers these are the images that form their beliefs about "minority" populations.

The shows set themselves up as reliable sources of information about what's really going on in the nation. And they often cover what sounds like common problems with work, love, and sex, but the information presented is skewed and confusing. Work problems become "fatal office feuds" and "back-stabbing coworkers." Problems concerning love, sex, or romance become "marriage with a 14-year-old," "women in love with the men who shoot them," or "man-stealing sisters." TV talk shows suggest that "marrying a rapist" or having a "defiant teen" are catastrophes about to happen to everyone.

Day in and day out, the shows parade all the myriad traumas, betrayals, and afflictions that could possibly befall us. They suggest that certain issues are more common than they actually are, and embellish the symptoms and outcomes. In actuality, relatively few people are likely to be abducted as children, join a Satanic cult in adolescence, fall in love with serial rapists, marry their cousins, hate their own race, or get sex changes in midlife, but when presented over and over again the suggestion is that they are quite likely to occur.

With their incessant focus on individual problems, television talk shows are a major contributor to the recent trend of elevating personal concerns to the level of personal rights and then affording those "rights" more attention than their accompanying responsibilities. Guests are brought on who have committed villainous acts (most often against other guests). The host and audience gratuitously "confront" the offenders about their wrong-doing and responsibilities. The alleged offenders almost always refute their accountability with revelations that they too were "victimized." On *Sally Jessy Raphael,* a man appeared with roses for the daughter he had sexually molested. He then revealed that he had been molested when he was five, and summed it up with "I'm on this show too! I need help, I'll go through therapy."

His sudden turnabout was not unusual. Viewers rarely see guests admit error early in the show, but a reversal often occurs with just a few minutes remaining. This works well for the shows because they need the conflict to move steadily to a crescendo before the final "go to therapy" resolution. But before that viewers are treated to lots of conflict and a heavy dose of pseudo-psychological explanations that are really nothing more than excuses, and often lame ones at that. The guests present their problems, the hosts encourage them to do so with concerned questions and occasional self-disclosures, and the audience frequently get in on the act with their own testimonies. Anything and everything goes. 15

The reigning motto is "Secrets keep you sick." On a *Jerry Springer* show about confronting secrets, a husband revealed to his wife that he had been having an affair. Not only was the unsuspecting wife humiliated and speechless, but Springer upped the ante by bringing out the mistress, who kissed the husband and informed the wife that she loved them both. Conflict predictably ensued, and viewers were told this was a good idea because now the problem was out in the open. When Ricki Lake did a similar show, a man explained to his very surprised roommate that he had "finally" informed the roommate's mother that her son was gay, a secret the roommate had been hiding from his family.

Referring to these premeditated catastrophes as simply "disclosures" softens their edges and affords them a kind of legitimacy they do not deserve. On a program about bigamy, Sally Jessy Raphael invited two women who had been married to the same man at the same time to appear on the show. The man was also on, via satellite and in disguise. His 19-year-old daughter by one of the wives sat on the stage while these women and her father tore each other apart. Sally and the audience encouraged the fight with "oohs" and "aahs" and rounds of applause at the ever-increasing accusations. A "relationship therapist" was brought on to do the postmortem. Her most notable warning was that all this turmoil could turn the daughter "to women," presumably meaning that she could become a lesbian. The scenario was almost too absurd for words, but it was just one more show like so many others: founded on stereotypes and capped off with clichés. From the "catfight" to the "no-good father" to archaic explanations of homosexuality—cheap thrills and bad advice are dressed up like information and expertise.

These scenarios are often legitimized by the use of pseudopsychological explanations, otherwise known as psychobabble. This is regularly used as a "disclaimer," or as a prelude to nasty revelations, or as a new and more sophisticated way of reinforcing old stereotypes: "men are cognitive, not emotional," or "abused women draw abusive men to them." This not only leaves viewers with nothing more than platitudes to explain problems and clichés to resolve them, but it fails to offer guests with enormous conflicts and long histories of resentment and betrayals practical methods for changing their circumstances. The "four steps to get rid of your anger" may sound easy enough to implement, but what this kind of ready-made solution fails to acknowledge is that not all anger is the same, and certainly not everyone's anger needs the same treatment. Sometimes anger is a signal to people that they are being hurt, exploited, or taken advantage of, and it can motivate change.

Rather than encouraging discussion, exploration, or further understanding, psychobabble shuts it off. With only a phrase or two, we can believe that we understand all the related "issues." Guests confess that they are "codependents" or "enablers." Hosts encourage "healing," "empowerment," and "reclaiming of the inner spirit." In turn, viewers can nod knowingly without really knowing at all.

Talk TV initially had great potential as a vehicle for disseminating accurate information and as a forum for public debate, although it would be hard to know it from what currently remains. Because most of these talk shows have come to rely on sensational entertainment as the means of increasing ratings, their potential has been lost. We are left with cheap shots, 20 cheap thrills, and sound-bite stereotypes. Taken on its own, this combination is troubling enough, but when considered against the original opportunity for positive outcomes, what talk TV delivers is truly disturbing.

The Responsive Reader

1. Why do the authors see the early Phil Donahue show as a revolutionary departure? Was there a common pattern in choice of topics or of guests? What contribution did the early Oprah Winfrey show make? How did the two shows differ, and what did they have in common?
2. What is the difference between the pioneering early shows and today's fare? How did the shows change for the worse?
3. According to the authors, what is wrong with the way men are represented in today's shows? What is wrong with the way women are represented? What is wrong with the way people of color are represented? (Do you think the authors are too critical or negative?)
4. What function do the psychologists and counselors on these shows serve? On what grounds do the authors criticize the "experts" or "authorities"? (What is "psychobabble"?)

Talking, Listening, Writing

5. After watching several episodes of current shows, would you tend to agree with the authors or take issue with them? How or why?
6. Do you think media images or media talk has played a major role in shaping your own views on gender or race?

Collaborative Projects

7. Working with a group, you may want to tape several exchanges on a local talk radio show and analyze them for topics covered, people calling in, and the kind of interchange taking place.

MY BREAKFAST WITH FERGIE

Liz Smith

The gossip column has long been a staple of popular journalism. A major branch of the American cult of celebrity, it feeds the popular appetite for news of the comings and goings, romances and jealousies, and brushes with the law of rock stars, tennis champions, football players, and scandal-dogged politicians. Much news and entertainment revolve around the activities of those in the spotlight. Celebrities appear at multiple awards ceremonies where they give awards to one another. They make fun of one another at celebrity roasts. At the low end of the gossip industry, tabloids pry into private lives to expose secrets "never before revealed": furtive trips to alcoholism clinics, quarrels over marital infidelity, hushed-up, deadly medical problems. Liz Smith is the queen of gossip columnists, and in the following letter from the front lines of celebrity watching she speaks in the voice of a real or assumed Girl Friday, reporting on a favorite subject of gossip columnists: members of the British royal family.

Thought Starters: Do you follow or pay attention to news and other media coverage of celebrities? When, where, and how often? What kind of celebrities do you follow?

Dear Boss:

First, let me wish you a happy birthday. Remember how you warned   1
me about having breakfast with the Duchess of York? You said I should dress nicely, be courteous and remember that she is a member of the royal family and not to tell dirty jokes? Well, Boss, guess what? The first thing **Fergie,** I mean, the duchess, said to me wasn't exactly dirty, but it was certainly earthy. She said she is so busy traveling about the United States that she's like manure to roses. I said yes, and my boss, **Liz Smith,** is from Texas, and her dad said someone who is that ubiquitous is like horse manure at a rodeo. She yelped with joy and wrote that down. We hadn't had coffee yet.

She's really beautiful and fun and so energetic. I should think she could eat anything and have it waste away by 6 p.m. Naturally, she stays in the tower of the Palace Hotel. Perfect for a duchess to be up there in the belfry, so to speak, looking down on Manhattan.

She said she considers the United States her second home because Americans are so open and basically speak their minds. She said that as a girl she was always told not to cry, not to say what she felt or show any emotions. So she ate—to excess. Americans have taught her how to reinvent herself. So natch, she wrote a book called "Reinventing Yourself With the Duchess of York." It has a quote on the cover: "Start with your mind and your bottom will follow." (And you told me to be careful of what *I* might say.)

She was excited that new research was proving that diabetes has a direct tie-in to obesity. I said I knew because I have a cat. He was grossly overweight and became diabetic and is now surviving because of medication and diet. She thought that interesting. I could see the wheels in her incredibly hyperactive brain figuring out how to use this information in her next campaign against obesity. By now, the world knows that the duchess and Weight Watchers International are a match made in heaven. She hopes that soon Weight Watchers and its new Winners Program will be to excessive eating what Alcoholics Anonymous is to excessive drinking. Some 2,500 years ago, Hippocrates, the father of medicine, said, "Let thy food be thy medicine, and thy medicine, thy food." Now Sarah, as the spokeswoman for Weight Watchers, is saying, "Let food and exercise be your medicine."

The interesting thing about the duchess and her energy is that the   5
program has evolved into a philosophy and is now really about women: their needs, their deprivations and how they can turn their losses into gains. Not in pounds, but in hours, days, months and years—a lifetime of happiness. With her incredible energy, Fergie could take WW with her to the top. What's great is that all women will ultimately be better off for her efforts. Reading all this informative stuff and listening to Sarah has persuaded me to join.

I commented on how great I thought it was that **Prince Andrew** and their daughters are all so close—living in the same house and all. She smiled in a way that told me she was happy with the situation. But she wouldn't comment.

Gosh, boss, isn't it swell that all that nasty gossip and angst of a decade ago has disappeared? Now everything you read about Fergie is so positive. She is always "coming up roses," with or without—uh—fertilizer.

She said two men recently had become very important to her. Former President **Nelson Mandela** of South Africa and the **Dalai Lama,** who fled Tibet for India. Mandela, because he said that his 28 years in prison taught him that it was important to love, not hate (to hate your enemies reduced you to their level), and the Dalai Lama, because his philosophy is basic to freeing oneself from guilt (guilt is the essence of so many problems).

We were deep in a conversation about this philosophy when the duchess got up and excused herself and quickly returned with a box of tissues, which she placed beside me. (My single tissue had become a knot in my nervous hand.) Then, a few minutes later, she got up again and, this time, took my glasses off my face and disappeared into the bathroom, only to return two seconds later with them, sparkling.

This handsome woman has written four books for WW on saving   10
oneself, an autobiography, "My Story," two books about **Queen Victo-**

ria, and four children's books. She is the mother of two daughters who are fifth and sixth in line to the British throne. She is the spokeswoman for the National Heart Association, Weight Watchers International and Wedgwood. This woman, who at 41 has reinvented herself and found international success as a career woman, is mothering *me*. Me! Thank you, boss.

Your Girl Friday,
Diane Judge

The Responsive Reader

1. An undercurrent in much of celebrity reporting caters to the public's interest in the "troubled history" of the rich and famous. What hints are there in this generally flattering account of past "nasty gossip" about Sarah Ferguson, the duchess of York?

2. Although the lifestyles of celebrities and of the ordinary reader are often worlds apart, readers like to feel that in some way outstanding famous people are also ordinary and like them. How do the opening paragraphs satisfy both expectations? In what way does the subject of the article turn out to be "one of the people"? How do the opening paragraphs at the same time also have the snob appeal that allows readers to participate vicariously in the life of the rich and famous?

3. European news coverage of the United States can be snide and condescending, making fun of naive and uncouth Americans. How does the duchess go out of her way to overcome any possible negative expectations or apprehensions of her American audience?

4. Celebrity reporting often provides a mix of prying gossip and also, as if to compensate, flattering reporting on the philanthropies and good deeds of its subjects. How does the reporting of the duchess's current work and interest relate to a major preoccupation among women? What does the writer do to establish the duchess's credibility as a spokesperson or advocate? How does the writer satisfy the reader's interest in the personal angle or personal connection?

5. Name-dropping is a stock-in-trade of celebrity gossip. What names are being dropped as you proceed through the letter? Do you think the inspirational messages that some famous names bring into this essay serve mainly for favorable publicity, or do you think these messages are valuable and important?

6. The writer saves important personal data and background information about the duchess for the last paragraph. Why? Why do you think she did not give this background information by way of introduction? What does the conclusion reveal about the purpose of the article as a whole?

Talking, Listening, Writing

7. According to this letter, Weight Watchers "has evolved into a philosophy and is now really about women: their needs, their deprivations and

how they can turn their losses into gains." Does this sound to you like public relations prose, or do you think readers should take this assessment seriously? Why or why not?

8. In Britain, coverage of the royal family ranges from dutiful public relations material by palace staff to often snide coverage in the popular press. The American colonists drove out the British monarchy over two centuries ago and prided themselves on abolishing the pomp and prerogatives of the Crown. How do you explain the fascination of a large American audience with the lives of the British royal family and its hangers-on? Can you give some outstanding examples of this interest? Do you share it? Why or why not?

9. Students of American culture have seen in the celebrity worship focused on icons like Elvis Presley or the ex-Beatle John Lennon something more deeply anchored in the popular psyche than a superficial fan club phenomenon. Why or how did Elvis Presley become a mythical figure in American popular culture? What are people who travel to Graceland looking for? Is the role of the Beatles in the popular imagination a thing of the past?

Collaborative Projects

10. Working with a group, investigate the controversy about the American obsession with weight watching and dieting and prepare a presentation on this topic. The duchess of York became a Weight Watchers spokesperson after suffering ridicule for having gained weight. She lost the weight and is now working to promote Weight Watchers. Some activists have claimed that overweight people are the last group who can be ridiculed freely in the United States. Are they right? They say that obsession with weight and constant dieting is more unhealthy than obesity. Are they wrong?

Find It on the Web

Diana Spencer was a kindergarten teacher before she married the heir to the British throne and became the princess of Wales in a storybook marriage. She became one of the most photographed women of our time. Gossip magazines endlessly printed stories with the perfect mix of beauty, wealth, glamour, betrayal, sex, and tragedy for our celebrity-obsessed popular culture. At Lady Diana's death, there was an unprecedented outpouring of grief, with Elton John singing "Candle in the Wind" and mourners piling up mountains of flowers. Is her story already forgotten, or has she become part of a continuing popular mythology?

SISTER FROM ANOTHER PLANET PROBES THE SOAPS

Andrea Freud Loewenstein

> The ancient art of satire holds our human weaknesses and vices up to ridicule. The satirist's art is like a funhouse mirror that exaggerates our shortcomings for all to see. It employs humor as a weapon to shame us into acting more responsible or humane. Satire may be gentle and affectionate, but it may also turn cutting and bitter when ignorance, deviousness, or callousness offend the satirist's standards of acceptable behavior. The women's movement, sometimes stereotyped as humorless, is increasingly providing a stage for women's satirical humor. (Women's Glibber: State-of-the-Art Women's Humor *appeared in 1993.)* In the following example of feminist satire, a contributor to Ms. magazine directs her satirical barbs at a time-honored American institution. She has a visitor from outer space marvel at the strange rituals of courtship and "copulation" in the universe of the soaps. Andrea Freud Loewenstein is the author of The Worry Girl, *published by a women's press in the United Kingdom. This collection of interconnected stories, with its echoes of an Austrian Jewish past and the Holocaust, has been described as re-creating "the sorrows and terrors that inform a Jewish child's dreams." Loewenstein's study* Loathsome Jews and Engulfing Women *was published by New York University Press.*

Thought Starters: Why do people watch soap operas? Is it true that soap opera plots and a soap opera mentality are increasingly infiltrating prime-time television?

Dear Professor:

Enclosed is my research paper. As you may remember, I attended every one of your lectures (I float at a right angle in the front row; last Thursday I was an iridescent green with ocher spots) on that most fascinating subject, the human species North Americanus Soapus. For my research project, I viewed several weeks' worth of documentary videotapes from four different "Soaps," chosen because they were among the most widely watched programs in the Earthling year 1993, with some 50 million viewers combined. I will hereafter refer to the humanoids whose acquaintance I made in "The Young and the Restless," "The Bold and the Beautiful," "All My Children," and "General Hospital," as "Soapoids."

The name "Soaps," by the way, appears to derive from the obsessional recurrence of the cleanliness theme in the "commercials," which occur at rhythmic intervals throughout the tapes. These are short, ritualized hymns of thanksgiving and praise to selected objects of worship, such as toilet bowl cleaners and vaginal deodorants.

1

I must admit that during the first week of viewing, in which I used all 17 of my sensors, I was unable to distinguish one Soapoid from another. The only distinction I was immediately able to make was between male and female—the Soapoids' preoccupation with ritual ownership of the opposite sex causes them to go to amazing lengths to signal gender distinction. These signals include the compulsory arrangement and selective removal of facial and head hair, distinctive body coverings, and (for the adult female) symbolic facial markings and mutilations.

This species, in contrast to our own, is subdivided into a mere two fixed gender groupings: male and female. Contrary to the lecture in which you informed us that occasionally both male and female choose to couple with their own kind and that those humanoids tend to be ostracized by the majority, I observed no variation in gender identity or object choice. On the contrary, all of my sample were hostile toward their own gender, whom they perceived as rivals in their never-ending fight to possess the opposite sex. Although this goal appears to be the Soapoids' overwhelming motivational force, the humans in my sample spent almost no time actually copulating. Instead, their main behavior consisted of endless discussions of, preparations for, and references to the act.

Nevertheless, copulation, when it does occur, often leads to trouble and confusion, even for the viewer. I spent a great deal of time attempting to determine the name of the young woman from *All My Children* who works in a police station, is the daughter of one of the two possible fathers of Mimi's unborn child, and nosily looked up information to determine the date of conception. Since the records revealed that she had copulated with both men during the same week, Mimi was forced to confess and call off her wedding the day it was scheduled. I never did get the young woman's name.

Copulation does allow the females to exert ownership over the males. You had informed us that males are the dominant gender, and that their inability to express their feelings verbally leads to frequent acts of violence. I regret to inform you that this conclusion is no longer valid. Soapoid males are quite gentle and verbally expressive. Their preferred behavior consists of lengthy expositions on their feelings toward the females. The male is especially prone to elaborate courtship rituals in preparation for copulation. These include the repetition of such submissive phrases as: "I love you so much," "You're my whole life," and "You were amazing last night, darling!" In one typical behavior, a male in *The Bold and the Beautiful* prepared for intercourse by placing at least 20 floating water lilies containing small lit candles in a pool of water upon which floated an inflatable rubber raft, the intended scene of sexual activity.

The far more complex females are the actual aggressors. In a lecture, you had mentioned that some women, referred to as "feminists," join with one another toward a common goal. No such movement was evident in this sample. In fact, the females' most favored posture was the standoff, a highly aggressive position in which two women position themselves from one to

5

two feet apart and emit such statements as "I hated you the first time I saw you." This is accompanied by a full range of physical expressions, including crossing of the arms, curling of the lip, and advancing in a menacing manner.

Unlike the male, the female can be classified into several subtypes, all arranged around the notions of "good" and "evil." These inborn tendencies emerge at puberty, apparently along with the mammary glands. The Good Female mitigates her natural dominance by an exaggerated concern for the welfare and nourishment of "her" male. She is especially solicitous of his title—Writer, Actor, Businessman, Doctor, Lawyer, or Policeman—and is always ready to abandon her own title to have more time to support his efforts. In *The Young and the Restless,* for example, Nikki, a Businesswoman, repeatedly interrupts her own work to service Cole, a Writer who is also a Groomer of Horses. Attired in a series of low-cut red evening gowns, she waits on him at his workplace in the horse stable, serving him champagne and caviar, assuring him that publishers from the mythical city of New York will turn his novel into a "best-seller."

It is important to note, however, that these work titles are symbolic. Soapoids, who possess a limited will to action and often require several hours of "processing" conversation to accomplish a simple task, must limit themselves to the all-important Preparation for Copulation. They have neither the time nor the energy to engage in actual "work." (The now meaningless title *General Hospital* indicates that Soapoids did work at one time.)

Good Females can be recognized by their wide-open, forward-gazing eyes, modest demeanor, and light pink lip-paint. In old age they become wrinkled. Evil Females, on the other hand, remain slim, highly polished, and brightly painted throughout life, a certain tautness of the facial skin being the only visible sign of aging. The Evil Females' characteristics include unfaithfulness, sexual rapacity, and the need to manipulate others. Most Evil Females confine their ambition to collecting a large number of men, but a few exhibit a further will to power through the ownership of Titles, Land, Factories, Businesses, or Patents. These women, whom I call Controllers, have destroyed the lives of generations of Soapoids.

In your lecture on racial and ethnic diversity, you brought us almost to jellification with your tale of the oppression of darker-hued or "African American" humanoids at the hands of the lighter ones whom you labeled the subspecies "European American." I am happy to inform you that no such oppression exists among modern-day Soapoids. In fact, there seems to be no difference between the darker and lighter types. All hues mix and converse on terms of perfect equality and good-will and hold titles of equal symbolic significance. Dark-skinned females (who exhibit a wide range of coloration, unlike the more muted light-skinned humanoids) wear their head hair in the same fashion as all other females—raised two or three inches from the head, then flowing to the shoulders. Darker and lighter humanoids do not mate, and appear to have no desire to do so. Whether this is because of the force of taboo or physical incompatibility cannot be

10

determined at this juncture. It should be noted, however, that none of the African American females had attained the status of Controller, perhaps because they lack the necessary icy blue eyes.

Saul, an elderly male from *The Bold and the Beautiful,* speaks with an accent, wears a pink shirt, highly ornamented necktie, and thick spectacles; he appears to be a eunuch. My ethnosensor identified him as a member of the subspecies "Jew." Whether these characteristics are an honest reflection of this identity is hard for me to determine—he was the only member of the group in this sample. Maria from *All My Children* was identified as a member of the subspecies "Latina"; as far as I can tell from my viewing, this group is notable for wavy head hair and the ability to ride a Horse without a saddle. Unlike African Americans, these Latinas appear able to mate with the "European Americans."

The photographs you showed us of the unsavory dwelling places (known as "Ghettos") of some humanoids also appear to be out of date. As of now, all Soapoids inhabit spacious, carefully color-coordinated cubes, filled with plastic flowers and bright modular furniture, in which they engage in their activities of arguing, preparing for copulation, and discussing their feelings for one another. Since eating, cleaning, and evacuation are not part of these sequences (being reserved for the "commercials"), no rooms are provided for these activities. It is unclear whether this is by choice or necessity (perhaps the atmosphere outside these cubes is not pure enough to breathe).

No analysis of Soapoid society would be complete without a mention of the interlacing "commercials." These mini-documentaries demonstrate the Soapoids' unique ability to encapsulate and split off areas of behavior and their need to control their errant bodies. The mini-docs also provide a neat solution for any scholars who may, thus far in my narrative, have been puzzled by the absence of ingestion and excretion in the lives of these living organisms. All such functions are reserved for the mini-docs, during which Soapoids frantically ingest prepackaged slimness-controlling nourishments and rid their cubes, their eating utensils, their garments, and their bodies of all superfluous liquids and imperfections. "Dirty on the outside!" exclaims a voice-over as a female handles her mate's garment in horror. "Uh oh, what about the inside!" A typical hour in the lives of Soapoids contains countless mini-docs that utilize not only a cleaning fluid that will purify garments on the inside, but also: a garment that can absorb the excretions of even the most wiggly of infant young; a tablet that cleans the excreting instrument by providing 2,000 flushes; another tablet to be ingested by the enemy species Cockroach; and yet another to be taken by the female Soapoid in order to soften her stools and ease excretion.

The lower body of the female seems to be especially in need of such devices. A sequence that begins with the frightening words "Out of control!" introduces tablets that will "take control" of diarrhea in one day. The vaginal area is serviced by a pellet that cures yeast infections, a deodorant designed to "intercede" between the female's odor and her undergarments,

15

and—for those who would seem to have the opposite problem—an ointment for vaginal dryness. Is it because the female Soapoid's vagina is the seat of her dominance over the male, and thus the location of her power, that it requires such constant servicing? Or is the female's verbal aggression yet another mark of her need to "stay in control" of her wayward body?

I end this paper with a confession: I entered my research project with a certain amount of bias against humanoids, whom I had been taught to regard as primitive, quarrelsome creatures, frozen in their limited natures and bodily forms, unable to regulate their own lives and affairs. But slowly, I grew increasingly susceptible to the charm of these beings. Before long, I found myself growing impatient with the time spent in my ordinary occupations. As I went about my daily tasks, I couldn't wait to join those beings who, never challenging, always predictable, asked nothing more from me than to watch them. Now that the viewing is over, I feel empty.

As I beam this paper to your neurotransmitters and project it into the ozone, it is with both fondness and regret that, amid the busy whirl of my life, I pause to remember the Soapoids, a matriarchal people whose lives drag out in long luxurious segments lived within color-coordinated cubes, and who relegate the more messy business of life to quick one-minute segments, thus freeing themselves for a stress-free, germ-free, moisture-controlled existence.

The Responsive Reader

1. What trappings of research and science fiction help make this space visitor's field trip to the land of the humanoids humorous?
2. What is exaggerated and what is true to life in the visitor's naive observations of gender distinctions and gender roles? As here observed, what is revealing and funny about the treatment of sex in the soaps? about the treatment of "courtship"? What are some telling satirical touches on these subjects in this space traveler's log?
3. Does the episode about Mimi's intended marriage and unborn child from *All My Children* ring true? What does it show about the moral universe of the soaps?
4. What are Loewenstein's targets when she satirizes the treatment of race, ethnicity, or class differences in soapland?
5. How does life in the soaps go counter to what the visitor had been taught about the impact of feminism in the real human world? How else does the humanoid world of the soaps contradict what the visitor had been led to expect?

Talking, Listening, Writing

6. How much in the soaps as described here mirrors life? How much is fantasy? What kind of fantasy is it? Why is it so popular? What, if anything, is its central appeal?

7. Many college students reportedly are avid followers of the soap operas. What would you say or write in defense of the soaps? Or what would you say or write to wean people from this kind of entertainment?
8. Do male humor and female humor reflect different ways of looking at the world? Is what is funny to men often not funny to women, and vice versa?

Collaborative Projects

9. Working with a group, study typical plots of current soaps and examine what they show about the emotional and moral world of soap opera.

THE DEATH OF MARILYN MONROE
Sharon Olds

Sharon Olds is a widely published American poet who with uninhibited candor takes on the topics of a new generation: bad parenting, sex without love, sex with love, and the wars between mothers and daughters. In the following poem, Olds offers her own perspective on the myth of Marilyn Monroe, "goddess of the silver screen / the only original American queen" (Judy Grahn). In the popular imagination, Norma Jean, or Marilyn Monroe, stereotypical sex bomb and dumb blonde, became the ultimate Hollywood creation. A male admirer called her "every man's love affair," whose voice "carried such ripe overtones of erotic excitement and yet was the voice of a little child" (Norman Mailer). Feminist writers have tried to rediscover the human being behind the stereotype, who "tried, I believe, to help us see that beauty has its own mind" (Judy Grahn).

Thought Starters: What memories and associations does mention of Marilyn Monroe bring to mind? What do you remember about her career, her movies, her private life, her suicide?

The ambulance men touched her cold   *1*
body, lifted it, heavy as iron,
onto the stretcher, tried to close the
mouth, closed the eyes, tied the
arms to the sides, moved a caught   *5*
strand of hair, as if it mattered,
saw the shape of her breasts, flattened by
gravity, under the sheet,
carried her, as if it were she,
down the steps.   *10*

These men were never the same. They went out
afterwards, as they always did,
for a drink or two, but they could not meet
each other's eyes.

        Their lives took   *15*
a turn—one had nightmares, strange
pains, impotence, depression. One did not
like his work, his wife looked
different, his kids. Even death
seemed different to him—a place where she   *20*
would be waiting,

And one found himself standing at night
in the doorway to a room of sleep, listening to
a woman breathing, just an ordinary
woman   25
breathing.

The Responsive Reader

1. Poets often make us notice realities that to others might seem merely
   routine. In the account of the ambulance crew collecting the body, what
   details are striking, different, gripping, or unexpected?
2. Why did the death have such an impact on the ambulance men? How
   did it affect them and why?

Talking, Listening, Writing

3. A persona is an assumed identity that may serve as a mask hiding the real
   person. Have you ever discovered the private person or human being behind a public persona or media creation?
4. Has popular entertainment left the stereotype of the Hollywood blonde
   behind? Are other stereotypical females evident in the media today?

Collaborative Projects

5. Macho Norman Mailer and Gloria Steinem, a leading feminist, have
   both published books about Marilyn Monroe. What accounts for the
   wide range of perspectives on her life, work, and person? Your class may
   want to farm out different treatments of the Marilyn Monroe legend to
   members of a group and then have them compare notes and pool their
   resources.

FORUM: *The Fencing In of Cyberspace*

Freedom remains the essence of the innovation at the heart of Silicon Valley.

Sòlveig Singleton

Cyberspace—the world of electronic communication—opened up vast new uncharted areas. As in the Old West, the vast new spaces attract enterprising people staking out sites in the new territories—some of which prosper and some of which turn into ghost towns. The new opportunities attract empire-building entrepreneurs who make millions (or billions) as well as a fair share of adventurers, pirates, and scam artists. They also attract organizations and vigilantes trying to establish law and order—to regulate and fence in the free-for-all, anything-goes brave new world of the Internet.

Sòlveig Singleton, director of information studies at the Cato Institute, warns of continued pressure to impose regulations and require monitoring devices, sifting and blocking mechanisms, and rating systems:

> High-tech products will continue to be the focus of regulatory efforts because decentralized networks like the Internet give individuals unprecedented power of choice, a sure-fire way to irritate regulators. Consumers everywhere perversely seek out Web sites devoted to sex, gambling, bizarre political commentaries, off-label uses of medications . . . Silicon Valley can expect continued pressure to build certain choices out of its networks.

Some attempts to regulate, restrict, channel, or censor the flow of information and ideas on the Net take the form of highly visible legislation debated in the media and contested in the courts. Other initiatives take the form of stealth legislation—riders attached quietly to unrelated high-priority legislation that other lawmakers want. First Amendment watchdogs like the American Civil Liberties Union (ACLU) fight restrictive legislation as an infringement of constitutionally guaranteed free speech.

Since electronic communication ignores national borders, the attempts to regulate have become a world-wide phenomenon. According to news reports, the successor organization to the Soviet secret police (KGB) asked for legislation that would require Internet providers to install black-box surveillance devices. These Big Brother devices would allow Russian law enforcement to track tax evasion and illegal economic activities. Law enforcement agencies of several countries have collaborated to track down Internet users accused of downloading child pornography.

Do you side with those trying to control harmful or abusive uses of the Net or with those defending free access?

ON THE INTERNET,
WE ALL OWN A PRESS

Adair Lara

While the "talking heads" of television news programs debate national trends, Adair Lara is the kind of columnist who talks to her readers about the issues and annoyances of every day. In the following column, she talks about how e-mail and the Internet have become part of the daily lives of people and how they have changed the ways they communicate, do business, and cope.

Thought Starters: Have you used Internet messages to vent bad feelings or a sense of injustice?

The other day my friend Bob noticed a new Nissan Sentra advertised in the paper for $10,000. He called the dealer. "Is that the real price?" he asked. It was.

When he got to the lot, though, the salesman told him that price had been a typo.

Furious, Bob said fine. But he wanted the dealer to know that he taught English at Santa Rosa Junior College and that on Monday morning 1,200 of his colleagues on various campuses were going to know this whole story.

He got the Nissan for the advertised price.

Another story: A 12-year-old is missing in Tennessee. She has brown hair and eyes, stands 5 foot 3 and left home in the company of two teenage boys. They were in a green Ford F-150 extended-cab pickup. Her name is Emily Marie Tiger. She was last seen in Nashville on January 4. If anyone has seen her, please call. Her mother is worried.

I read this story on my e-mail, and there were a hundred addresses listed above mine. It was going out to a lot of people.

In recent months, I've read other messages like this. One came from a frantic woman whose husband had kidnapped their teenage son; she was imploring people to visit her Web site and look at the pictures posted there.

A woman named Jessica is using e-mail to search for donors for her friend Sachi, who has leukemia and desperately needs a bone-marrow transplant. She's half Caucasian and half Japanese, and people who think they might provide a match can call (800) 59-DONOR.

I got another one from a man who says he was plucked from a crowd of drivers on eastbound Highway 80, few of them wearing seat belts, and cited for violation of the seat belt law. He felt he received the citation because he was black, yet he could do nothing—except describe the incident over the Internet to hundreds of, he hoped, sympathetic fellow drivers.

Yet another was from a man in Forestville fuming because AOL was   *10*
charging him a $5 monthly service charge because he had no Visa card.

Before e-mail, when somebody did something mean to us, we just
raged impotently and stormed up and down in our own kitchens and kicked
the dog. We could threaten to sue, and sometimes did, but that was like
punishing ourselves, exposing ourselves to years of the expenses and continued bad feelings of a lawsuit—with no certainty that the other side's lawyers
would not in the end squash us and our little plea for justice like a bug.

But now. Now we can do what we wanted to do when we were little.
We can tell on them.

Even Kate Millett, author of the groundbreaking book "Sexual Politics," writes from her farm in Poughkeepsie—or allows her piece to be circulated, I can't tell which—that she can hardly support herself. "I cannot
earn money. Except by selling Christmas trees, one by one, in the cold
in Poughkeepsie. I cannot teach and have nothing but farming now. And
when physically I can no longer farm, what then? Nothing I write now has
any prospect of seeing print. I have no salable skill, for all my supposed accomplishments. I am unemployable."

Millett is probably telling the truth, but some of these stories may   *15*
be false. The classic story—you must have seen it by now—is the Internet
version of the urban legend about the woman who ordered cookies at
Neiman Marcus, asked for the recipe, was charged hundreds of dollars for
it and in retaliation printed the recipe on the Web. That is bunk, but people
keep forwarding it because they like the idea of it, getting back at the big
companies.

And because they like this feeling: The little guy has a voice now.
And, in at least one case, a new Nissan Sentra.

The Responsive Reader

1. What Internet stories does Lara tell to support her thesis that "the little
   guy has a voice now"? Which of her accounts seem most significant or
   convincing to you? Why?
2. What is an "urban legend"? How typical do you think is the one Lara
   mentions?

Talking, Listening, Writing

3. Do you sometimes respond to negative experiences with impotent
   rage? Have you observed people who punished themselves by exposing
   themselves to "years of the expenses and continued bad feelings of
   a lawsuit"? Do you think the Internet can provide people with valid
   alternatives?

4. Has the Internet broadened your range of contact with other people? Are you or people you know well interacting with others in new and different ways? Or do you agree with people who claim that the virtual reality of the net tends to isolate people from real human contact?

YES, VIRGINIA, THERE IS A FIRST AMENDMENT

Rob Morse

> *Both in Britain and in the American colonies, the printing press was a key weapon in the struggle to assert the rights of the people against an oppressive government. For civil libertarians, resistance to censorship of the press, of the media, and of teaching has always been a cornerstone of the defense of liberty. Adopted as part of the Bill of Rights in 1791, the First Amendment to the U.S. Constitution stipulates that "Congress shall make no law . . . abridging the fredom of speech, or of the press." Justice Hugo L. Black stated long-observed judicial doctrine when he said, "The Federal Government is without any power whatsover under the Constitution to put any type of burden on free speech and the expression of ideas of any kind (as distinguished from conduct)." The leapfrogging growth of access to printed and visual material on the Internet opened up a new front in the struggle between First Amendment "abolutists" and censorship forces. New legislative initiatives focused on restricting Internet access to adult material in libraries, schools, and private homes. A Communications Decency Act was passed by Congress but found by the Supreme Court to violate First Amendment rights. Various new initiatives aimed at imposing severe penalties on providers allowing access to material harmful to minors. Libraries and colleges began to rely on various kinds of filtering software or censoring services to block offensive or objectionable material. Rob Morse is an outspoken West Coast columnist who found that his columns were caught in the censorship web.*

Thought Starters: During your high school or college years, were you aware of any censorship controversy involving student publications, teaching content, library resources, or Internet access? What were the issues? Who were the key players? What was the outcome?

A guy from National Public Radio called me at home wanting to talk   *1*
about my lawsuit against the Loudoun County, Va., public libraries.
   "You won," he said.

Alas, I hadn't won any money. This was not a lawsuit over hot coffee in the lap.

It was more important than that. It was about the First Amendment, and what you as an adult may or may not read on the Internet in a public library.

It wasn't just my lawsuit. I was one of eight plaintiffs whose Web sites   5
had been blocked by a filtering device called X-Stop meant to block pornography from computers used by both adults and children in the Loudoun County public libraries.

I don't know what pornography the filter stopped, but it kept Loudoun County safe from a safe-sex Web page, as well as Web sites belonging to the Quakers, Beanie Baby collectors, the American Association of University Women and The San Francisco Examiner and the Chronicle.

That means me. I joined the suit to defend the First Amendment.

And we won. Now adults and children in Loudoun County libraries will be able to read about all the latest San Francisco perversions, such as pies being thrown in the faces of the mayor and other public figures.

Judge Leonie M. Brinkema of the United States District Court for Eastern Virginia decided last Monday that Loudoun County's Internet censorship policy violated the First Amendment because it blocked adults from accessing a wide variety of constitutionally protected material.

The guy from NPR asked a strange question: "When you found out   10
the newspapers were blocked, why didn't you just call the filtering company and ask to be unblocked?"

Maybe he was trying to goad me into a flip answer, so I gave one: "Yeah, and I could ask the guy who's burning my books to put out the match."

At least there's smoke when someone burns your book. When someone blocks your Web site in a faraway county's libraries, you don't even know it—unless you hear about it from a friend of a friend, as I did.

When I heard that the San Francisco newspapers were being electronically blocked from Loudoun County libraries, I thought it was a great joke.

Then I talked to lawyers at the American Civil Liberties Union, which had joined a group of Loudoun County citizens in bringing the suit against their libraries. I learned how Internet filtering devices work—or don't work.

Internet filters are stupid. The First Amendment protects against prior   15
restraint of speech on the basis of content. There's no restraint as capricious as a machine looking for key words.

The people who make X-Stop, Log-on Data Corp. of Anaheim, won't say how their filter works, but most filters involve punching in key words like "bondage." Then low-paid drones go through blocked sites and decide whether to unblock them. Thus Somerset Maugham's "Of Human Bondage" may or may not get through.

Lots of nonpornographic sites get blocked, while many pornographic sites go unblocked.

Harper's magazine has an excerpt from "Confessions of a Smut Blocker," which ran originally in Yahoo! Internet Life. This anonymous former employee for an Internet-filtering company (not Log-on Data) wrote:

"The main computer created a list of sites for us to check. . . . It was really an entry-level job. You didn't have to be computer-literate. They just showed you which buttons to push. We could choose to block a site, not block it, or even unblock it."

Just before I joined the suit against Loudoun County 10 months ago, I wrote, "If the Supreme Court can't define obscenity, how can some computer programmers in Anaheim do it?"   *20*

Or entry-level button pushers.

Some officials in Loudoun County complained that Judge Brinkema's decision overrode local standards of decency.

Local, where? In Loudoun or in Anaheim? The makers of X-Stop won't even tell Loudoun officials the criteria they use for blocking Web sites. It's proprietary information.

So how do public libraries deal with the Internet? They could just shut it off. However, the Internet is increasingly where information is to be found.

Judge Brinkema, a former librarian, cited some suggestions for keep-   *25* ing kids from Internet porn in public libraries while not violating adults' First Amendment rights—for example, filters that can be turned on or off for adult use.

Perhaps the most important thing is not to pass unnecessary and unconstitutional Net censorship laws, or otherwise get caught up in what Mike Godwin, author the book "Cyber Rights," calls "Net backlash," or "fear and loathing of the Net."

Loudoun County could point to only a single complaint arising from Internet use in a library in another Virginia county, and reports of three incidents in other libraries across the country.

It's not worth blocking the First Amendment for that.

The Responsive Reader

1. Who were the other plaintiffs joining Morse in his suit? What was the purpose of the X-Stop filter that the plaintiffs challenged? What are Morse's examples of communications or messages the filter blocked? Can you explain or speculate on why or how some of the examples were among those blocked?

2. Why would a journalist in California join in a lawsuit against a library system across the country in Virginia? How does Morse explain why he did not just ask to have his material unblocked?

3. Like much self-censorship or media censorship, the people running the filtering operation worked anonymously behind the scenes (and apparently not in Virginia but in Anaheim in southern California). What did Morse find out about the personnel and the MO, or operating mode, of the enterprise? According to Morse, what was wrong with the operation? What were the criteria they applied? (Why does he use Somerset Maugham's classic *Of Human Bondage* as a key example? Why does he object to censors appealing to local standards? What support did Loudoun County officials offer for their adoption of the filtering method?)

4. Morse writes for an audience that likes his amusing sidelights on the follies and weird happenings he observes in day-to-day politics of the city (like the incident when activists expressed their displeasure with the city's power structure by throwing a pie in the mayor's face). However, many of the topics he touches on in his informal, half-amused manner have serious undertones and implications, such as his "flip" reference to book burnings. What do you know about book burnings? Do they take place abroad or also in the United States? How are they similar to or different from current censorship initiatives?

5. Whistleblowers and other critics of prevailing practices are often dismissed as malcontents or "disgruntled" individuals. Does Morse offer any constructive suggestions for dealing with the issues causing the controversy? What for him is the most important lesson or warning we should heed?

Talking, Listening, Writing

6. If you were a member of a school board, library commission, or similar body, what stand would you take on the issues Morse raises? What arguments would you present to the opposing side? What counterarguments would you anticipate? What constructive suggestions would you offer?

7. In the early years of euphoria, the Internet was hailed as ushering in the era of the knowledge explosion and the information highway. Today many observers claim that we have entered an era of lowered expectations and second thoughts. What does Morse mean when he contends that the public libraries were succumbing to "Net backlash"? Have you observed second thoughts or a backlash concerning the promise of the Internet?

Collaborative Projects

8. Many controversies over censorship have hinged on definitions of key terms like *obscenity, community standards,* or *indecency.* Morse claims that even the "Supreme Court can't define obscenity." Working with a

group, you may want to study media coverage of court cases, legislation, or local controversies to see whether and how in your judgment one or more of these terms can be successfully defined.

THE INTERNET IS LEARNING TO CENSOR ITSELF

John Browning

While anticensorship organizations were fighting attempts at government regulation of the Internet, enterprising organizations were developing filtering systems, blocking systems, and rating systems that could be used by individuals and institutions. One employee described an operation employing fifty to sixty staffers working full shifts to call up suspect images and screen sites whose labels included clues to possibly offensive content. John Browning, writing in the Scientific American, *sees this privatizing of censorship as a welcome compromise between die-hard defenders of freedom of speech and die-hard defenders of traditional moral standards.*

Thought Starters: Do you pay attention to the self-ratings used by the television and movie industry to identify possibly offensive programs and movies? How do they work? What purpose do they serve? How effective are they?

Of all the arguments over the future of the Internet, censorship has   *1* sparked the most heated debates. Libertarians see any attempt to censor the net as the death of freedom of speech. Traditionalists see its continued liberties as the death of moral standards. Mercifully, some of the very technologies that have created this argument now are paving the way for a compromise. The Platform for Internet Content Selection (PICS) promises to create a sort of do-it-yourself censorship that will allow everybody both freedom to speak and freedom not to listen. It could also make the net a richer and more interesting place.

PICS is being developed by the World Wide Web Consortium, a group based at the Massachusetts Institute of Technology. Led by Web inventor Tim Berners-Lee, PICS resolves the moral contradiction that lies at the heart of existing schemes to regulate the net. Because they inherit the assumptions of broadcasting regulation, content-regulation schemes try to impose uniform moral standards on a world in which tolerance for diversity is highly valued. One of the most offensive aspects of the Communications Decency Act—declared unconstitutional by a court in Philadelphia—is that it would have forced federal courts to decide for all Americans what is and is not "offensive." PICS allows each individual American to decide.

Instead of creating a single rating system that applies the same set of values to all Web content, PICS encourages the creation of a variety of rating systems. Web sites can either rate themselves, or they can ask to be rated by a (supposedly objective) agency. Rating systems can apply any desired criteria—from the amount of sex and violence a site contains to individual reviewers' judgments on how entertaining it is. PICS is in effect a system for disseminating reputations throughout the global village.

PICS works because everything on the Internet is connected to everything else. Each PICS rating has two parts: the rating itself and the URL, or address, of the rating agency. The actual text of the ratings is abbreviated and hard to decipher. But when a surfer (or, to be specific, the browser) wants to know how a site measures up under some particular rating system, he or she simply contacts the rating agency, sends in the abbreviated rating and receives in return as much explanation as desired.

Ratings can either be distributed with the document being requested 5 or separately, by contacting the rating service directly to see if it has a rating at the URL of the document in question. This second option means that third parties can rate those sites that might not necessarily welcome their judgments; the Simon Wiesenthal Center, for example, could rate Nazi sites on the viciousness of their anti-Semitism, even though the sites themselves are highly unlikely to include the center's rating in their Web home pages.

Whatever the source of the ratings, they enable surfers to anticipate what they are likely to see. By building the ability to read ratings directly into the browser, parents can automatically restrict their children's access only to sites rated safe. Similarly, software "firewalls" can block a whole network's access to some sites; for example, a business could limit employees' access to recreational sites during working hours.

Both Netscape and Microsoft have promised to build PICS capabilities into forthcoming browsers. CompuServe has said it will put PICS ratings on all its content as it moves onto the Web. Britain's Internet service providers agree to adopt PICS ratings voluntarily, although their willingness was in part motivated by threatened regulation. France's new regulations require Internet service providers to make the ratings available to surfers. Although the regulations do not specify a particular rating scheme, most French service providers are expected to adopt a method that is compliant with PICS.

PICS already offers a choice of rating schemes. The recreational Software Advisory Council, the rating system adopted by CompuServe, has a self-rating scheme based on four simple categories: violence, nudity, sex and language. Each Web site is asked to rate itself in each category on a scale from one (damage to objects, revealing attire and kissing) to four (torture, explicit sex and filthy speech). SafeSurf offers a rating system involving more categories of information—from homosexuality to drug use and gambling. Because the categories and criteria are more complicated, the scheme does not allow sites to rate themselves directly; instead SafeSurf asks managers of each site to fill out a form from which a rating is automatically created.

Accept the underlying principle of PICS—that there is no need for government to choose what citizens can experience when they can choose for themselves—and the role of government in content regulation changes completely. Instead of trying to thrash out a single value system for multicultural societies, government's first job is simply to ensure that sites do not misrepresent themselves under whatever rating systems they choose to advertise.

But the potential of PICS is far greater than simply managing smut. *10* It can fortify the Web with a vast, interlinked system of reference, recommendation and reputation. It creates automatic, electronic analogs to the bonds of judgment and trust that make sense of the information people use day to day. It allows one person to vouch for the trustworthiness of another's information, to recommend a funny piece of entertainment or to warn surfers away from a boring or offensive site. It adds to the fullness of discussion on the net. Everybody can speak, and everybody can also pass judgment.

The Responsive Reader

1. Browning discusses different options for those interested in "do-it-yourself censorship." What would be the differences separating self-rating, rating by interested third parties (like the Simon Wiesenthal Center), and ratings by "supposedly objective" rating agencies? (Why "supposedly objective"?) How would each work? What are the justifications and intended uses for each? Who are the intended users?
2. Under Browning's system of do-it-yourself censorship, who would be the censors? Who would be the citizens who "can choose for themselves"? Who would have the choices made for them by others?
3. What is the role of government in Browning's system? Would the government keep hands off? What does Browning mean when he says "the role of government in content regulation changes completely"?

Talking, Listening, Writing

4. According to Browning, how would the system of "do-it-yourself" censorship create "bonds of judgment and trust" to make sense of information? How would it "vouch," "recommend," and "warn"?
5. Do you believe that the options Browning describes will add to "the fullness of discussion on the net" instead of restricting it or hemming it in? Do you believe they will head off people trying to impose "a single value system" on a multicultural society?

CENSORSHIP DEVICES
ON THE INTERNET

J. D. Lasica

In a case described as the first of its kind, a federal judge who was a former librarian ruled against a library board in Virginia that had decided (in a 5-to-4 vote) to use computer filters in a local library. The board had voted a year earlier to equip public terminals with software blocking thousands of Internet sites that could be considered harmful to minors. The attorney representing a group of residents that had challenged the board said, "This is a landmark decision for public libraries and mainstream citizens who want to decide for themselves what they want to read." J. D. Lasica is the editor of an online publication who sees the trend toward "censorware" and the privatizing of censorship as a threat to the Internet "as an open forum of ideas."

Thought Starters: Do you think "cybersmut" is a serious threat to young people?

When the U.S. Supreme Court struck down the pernicious Communications Decency Act . . . the online community roundly celebrated the victory as a milestone for free speech in cyberspace. [1]

But this is no time to relax. A new threat—nearly as insidious as the CDA—now looms over freedom of speech on the net: censorware.

"We're seeing a move toward the privatizing of censorship," warns David Sobel, legal counsel for the Electronic Privacy Information Center in Washington, D.C. "It's likely to destroy the Internet as it's existed until now."

Overstated? Not at all.

Filtering programs like SurfWatch, Cyber Patrol, CYBERsitter and [5] Net Nanny Pro—touted as industry's solution to protecting children from pornography on the net—have already sold millions of copies. While they do block most smut sites, they also screen out much more:

- The Web browser included with Sega's Saturn game console allows users to block out "alternative lifestyles"—not merely Satanic cults and the like, but all information regarding gays and lesbians.

- For certain age groups, Cyber Patrol blocks such sites as Planned Parenthood and the Usenet news groups alt.journalism.gay-press, clari.news.gays (home to AP and Reuters articles), alt.atheism and soc.feminism.

- CYBERsitter, which has drawn the greatest wrath of Netizens, has in the past blocked the sites of the National Organization for Women, gay rights groups, animal rights groups and progressive political causes. It also filters words and phrases like "safe sex," "violence," "Sinn Fein," "lesbian," "fascism" and "drugs" from e-mail messages and Web pages—including newspaper sites.

Marketed largely by the Christian watchdog group Focus on the Family, the program's manufacturer, Solid Oak Software Inc., has responded to its critics by saying that parents have the right to prevent "objectionable material" from coming into their homes.

Some of the sites listed above are no longer blocked; the black list *10* changes weekly. Often, neither users nor operators of the censored sites know about the blockage.

I have no quarrel with parents who want to protect their children from some of the net's excesses. But parents also have a right to know the kinds of sites that are being censored.

"I think parents would be surprised to learn what's being blocked," Sobel says. "Frankly, I don't know why any parent would want to buy these kinds of shrink-wrapped values, which amount to someone else's idea of what's good for your kid."

Children may be only the first casualties in the rush to muzzle the net. Corporate America may be next. Net Nanny Pro is being pitched to major businesses as a way "to ensure that employee productivity and corporate policies are maintained within the workplace."

It's unknown if any newspapers have installed such censorware in their newsrooms, but it may be only a matter of time. Meanwhile, censorware has made its way into public libraries and public schools.

The American Library Association in July adopted a resolution against *15* the use of any filtering software in libraries because they also block constitutionally protected medical, artistic and political information. But public libraries in Austin, Texas, and elsewhere have already installed Cyber Patrol on their computer systems.

So what is journalism's stake in this? Plenty.

As content providers, newspapers have an interest in not having a third party censor their content before it reaches the eyes of young readers. Pity the poor censorware-shackled student who accesses his local newspaper's archives to write a report on the Middle East or the Oklahoma City bombing.

Journalists and publications not in the safe center of the political spectrum will be marginalized if a large portion of net readers cannot access their views.

All journalists have an interest in preserving the free flow of constitutionally protected information on the Internet. As guardians of the First Amendment, we have an obligation to ensure that a broad range of voices continues to flourish in this new medium.

Up until now, some news organizations have shirked their responsi- *20* bility to the public by touting these censorial tools—but telling only half the story. It's time for a healthy dose of public education, discussion and careful reporting to make it clear what each of these products actually does.

Warns Sobel: "If this trend continues, the Internet is not going to be the open forum of ideas that it has been. This kind of technology will sanitize content to the point that it's even safer and less controversial than the mainstream media."

And that would be the biggest tragedy of all.

The Responsive Reader

1. Lasica claims that the new censorware, sold in the millions of copies, screens out "much more" than pornography. According to Lasica, what topics, organizations, views, or lifestyle choices are being blocked by various kinds of censorship software? Which exclusions or blockages seem to be most disturbing to him? Are any of them unexpected or especially disturbing to you?
2. According to Lasica, newspapers and print journalism have a major stake in the controversy over censoring the Internet. Why or how?

Talking, Listening, Writing

3. As a parent, would you "buy these kinds of shrink-wrapped values, which amount to someone else's idea of what's good for your kid"?
4. Do you think that the newspapers or newsmagazines you see "sanitize content"? Do you think the mainstream media are striving to make the media "safer and less controversial"? Are there topics on which you expect less timid, less bland, and more aggressive treatment?

PUSH TO SQUASH SPAM

Jon Swartz

Junk mail has long been as American as pizza. Mailboxes are stuffed with outdoor-clothing catalogs, glossy gift-suggestion mailers, coupon books, "You-may-already-have-won . . ." come-ons, and unsolicited ties or mailing labels promoting good causes. The shift from snail mail to e-mail has multiplied the potential for unwanted solicitations. It has hugely extended the reach of junk mailers, who are jamming e-mail boxes with unsolicited promotional mail, or spam. What to do? Jon Swartz, a staff writer for a metropolitan newspaper, tracks cutting-edge developments in cyberspace.

Thought Starters: How do you feel about junk mail? What kind of junk mail have you seen? Do you have any use for it?

Congress has declared war on junk e-mail with a blitzkrieg of bills *1*
banning the annoying messages.

But in their haste to can spam, overzealous lawmakers may be trampling
individuals' First Amendment rights, civil libertarians claim and politicians
concede.

"Everyone hates spam, but you don't stop the problem by compromis-
ing free speech," said Stanton McCandlish, program director at the Electronic Frontier Foundation, a nonprofit organization in San Francisco.

Pending legislation would force Internet service providers to scan any
suspicious e-mail for sales pitches and impose the use of strict language by
commercial ventures in their e-mail.

Privacy advocates fear that personal correspondence may land in the *5*
lap of ISPs during e-mail screenings. Junk mailers, meanwhile, claim that
government-ordered mandatory language in their messages undercuts their
right to communicate freely under the First Amendment.

Internet proponents are particularly galled by the Consumer Anti-
slamming and Spamming Prevention Act, currently floating in the House.
It would require spammers to use the phrase "unsolicited commercial mail"
within the text of messages. Then Internet service companies would be obligated to check e-mail for that phrase and block it from subscribers who
don't want spam. Opponents say the bill would illegally infringe spammers'
rights to free speech and, more ominously, strong-arm ISPs into a law enforcement role.

Another bill—co-sponsored by Senator Robert Torricelli, D-N.J.,
and unanimously approved in the Senate—would fine junk e-mailers up to
$15,000 if they mask their identities with forged addresses. It, too, includes
a provision requiring cyber businesses to tag e-mail subject headers with
disclaimers such as "solicitation" and "$$."

"I find it objectionable from a privacy and content standpoint," said
Deirdre Mulligan, staff counsel for the liberal Center for Democracy and
Technology in Washington, D.C. "Anytime you regulate speech on the
Internet, you have to ask, 'Are there non–First Amendment (infringing)
ways to deal with it?' There aren't many."

Even lawmakers—like Representative Billy Tauzin. R-La., who au-
thored The Consumer Anti-slamming and Spamming Prevention Act—
admit they are hamstrung in attempting to protect consumers from a deluge
of spam while being "sensitive" to free speech.

Phil Singer, a spokesman for Senator Torricelli, noted the difficulty of *10*
preparing a bill that "tries to nurture e-commerce and protect free-speech
rights while reducing spam—all at the same time."

"It's a delicate balancing act," acknowledged Tauzin, chairman of the
influential House Telecommunications Subcommittee. "I've heard the con-
cerns about its constitutionality and agree. We're working on them."

"But people also have the right to listen as well as speak," Tauzin said.
"No one should be paying for an e-mail account crammed with spam."

An estimated 10 billion pieces of spam—messages shilling sex sites, miracle cures and fly-by-night business scams—course through the Internet each year, jamming pipelines and individuals' e-mail accounts, according to industry experts.

Consumer outrage has prompted—some say forced—politicians to hurriedly draft legislation that may have cut constitutional corners, online legal experts said.

Politicians' task may have been made even more ticklish, they say, by   15
the lack of laws that apply to the fledgling Internet industry.

"There is no good way, legislatively, to solve the problem," said David Sobel, legal counsel at the nonpartisan Electronic Privacy Information Center in Washington, D.C. "Any law that mandates certain language in e-mail poses constitutional problems."

The Responsive Reader

1. What is the issue here? What is the nature or extent of the problem? How would you sum up the key arguments of people trying to stop "junk e-mail"? How would you sum up the arguments of those on the opposing side?

2. What are the solutions being discussed here? Do you see prospects for a reasonable compromise?

3. Could you help initiate outsiders into the lingo of this cyberspace controversy? What are civil libertarians? Are they different from other libertarians? What are ISPs, or Internet service providers? (What's a blitzkrieg, and why do football commentators talk about teams "blitzing" their opponents?)

Talking, Listening, Writing

4. Are you the kind of person who would post a "No Soliciting" sign on your property to keep out Avon sales representatives and other door-to-door promoters? Or would you rather post a "Welcome" sign and talk to people who peddle magazine subscriptions or hand out religious tracts?

5. Some Americans are First Amendment fanatics. (One prominent East Coast journalist called herself a "First Amendment junkie.") Other Americans are equally passionate Second Amendment supporters. What is the actual text of the two amendments? Why or how have they provided rallying cries for their respective constituencies? What is the basic contrast between the two constituencies or mentalities?

Weighing Alternatives

Writing about a current issue, you will often be looking at a problem with more than one possible solution. Often there is more than one side to an issue. Thinking the matter through often means sorting out the pros and cons. You weigh the arguments for and against. You lean to one side, but then you listen to those who disagree, and you find that there is something to be said for the other side. Ideally, after giving due weight to opposing views, you reach a balanced conclusion.

Of course, you will never approach an issue with a totally open mind. You are likely to incline one way or the other on tax money for public transportation, on affirmative action in college admissions, on health services for illegal immigrants, on smoking bans for restaurants, or on mandatory helmets for bicycle riders. However, the test of a thinking person is the willingness to consider alternative views and to judge them on their merits.

Weighing the pros and cons is not just a matter of helping you make up your own mind. To convince a fair-minded audience, you need to show that you have looked at relevant evidence. You have considered alternatives. You have considered valid objections—instead of sweeping unwanted facts under the carpet. If you honestly look at conflicting evidence and weigh conflicting opinions, your readers can feel that they are not being manipulated and that you respect their intelligence.

TRIGGERING Many people's minds are set on controversial subjects. (Sometimes they seem set in cement.) Such people often voice their opinions confidently, sometimes at the top of their voice. But many other people are genuinely challenged by issues where there is something to be said on both sides. Here are some issues that you may want to think and write about:

- Traditionally, Americans have prided themselves on their opposition to censorship. However, we encounter situations that test our commitment to freedom of speech. Do we have to protect hate literature circulated by neo-Nazis, rap songs endorsing the killing of cops, or art that seems blasphemous to religious groups? Where do we draw the line? Is there a line? What do we learn from listening to those who radically oppose and those who seem to endorse censorship?

- Most Americans endorse equal educational opportunity. However, what happens when those students reach college age whose previous schooling has been hampered by poverty, a violent environment, substandard schools with burnt-out teachers and no money for up-to-date textbooks? Do we apply the same admission standards to them as to preppies? Or do we make allowances—and how? Do we "water down" our standards and our curriculum?

- Traditionally, Americans have prided themselves on freedom of choice. If someone continues to smoke in spite of health warnings, it is that person's choice. However, nonsmokers who inhale secondary smoke in offices, restaurants, or airplanes do not make that choice. Do smokers have rights, and how do we balance them against those of nonsmokers?

GATHERING As with any other substantial paper, with your pro-and-con paper, input has to come before output. You need to explore the issue—listening, reading, taking notes. Try to develop the mental habits that will help you profit from the play of pro and con:

- *Learn to listen to people you think are wrong.* (The natural impulse is to ridicule them or shout them down.) What are they actually saying? *Why* do they disagree with you? What do they know that you don't know? What do they value that you disregard—and why?

- *Try playing the devil's advocate.* To come to know an opposing view from the inside, try to present your opponents' position as if you were on their side.

- *Look for the informed impartial observer.* Listen to some voices that do *not* represent the opposing factions. Is there someone who is knowledgeable but above the fray? Can you find someone who might care but not have an axe to grind? Much of what you encounter will be "facts" and arguments presented by interested parties or by PR people promoting an agenda. Who might be unbiased and yet be in a position to know?

To help you explore the pros and cons of an issue, you might want to participate in a group writing activity. Different members of the class would suggest arguments to be lined up in pro and con columns on the board. Or your class might want to stage a mock debate, with opposing speakers presenting arguments that members of the class would have to ponder in their pro-and-con papers.

SHAPING As with other kinds of papers, there is no "one-size-fits-all" formula for writing a paper weighing alternatives. To start getting your material under control, try lining up arguments in separate columns. Preparing contrasting lists will help clarify the issue for you. It will at the same time be a big step toward structuring your paper.

Here is a tentative lining up of the pros and cons of the issue of drug testing on the job: As a condition of employment, should people in sensitive occupations agree to submit to unannounced testing for illegal drugs? (Which side do you find yourself on when looking over these notes? Or are you torn between the opposing positions?)

PRO	CON
1. Pilots, engineers, and operators of heavy equipment literally take others' lives into their hands.	1. The "war on drugs" makes no distinction between recreational drug users and addicts.
2. Drug users are responsible for absenteeism, low productivity, and high injury rates on the job.	2. The tests are notoriously inaccurate (sesame seeds cause false positives) and ruin the careers of people falsely accused.
3. "Recreational" drug users support a murderous drug trade responsible for unprecedented levels of crime.	3. Employers become agents of a police state, poisoning employer-employee relations.
4. Drug users in prestigious occupations are the worst possible role models for endangered American youth.	4. Drug testing undermines basic American traditions of due process and protection against self-incrimination.
5. Testing is above-board and better than snooping and spying.	5. We already have too much government meddling in people's private lives.

By looking at what you have on each side of the issue, you can decide what organizational strategy might be more effective: presenting the position of each side in its entirety—or presenting the pros and cons point by point.

Should you present and explain major arguments on one side first and then look at those on the opposing side? This way the inner logic of each position might become clear. Your readers would see how major planks in the opposing positions are related, how they fit together.

Or should you present one argument on one side at one time—and then immediately show what the other side would say in return? This way your readers could share in the excitement of the debate. They could become involved in the give-and-take of assertion and rebuttal.

REVISING   In spite of your good intentions, a first draft is still likely to be too one-sided. It is likely to be too polemical—pushing your own side of the argument while giving a nod to the other (with too many barbs at those who disagree with you). Try the following to make your paper read more like a true weighing of the options:

■ *Try to apply the equal time rule.* The treatment of the other side is likely to be too brief—or too biased. A rule of thumb: Are the arguments for given roughly as much space as the arguments against?

- *Lower the emotional thermostat.* Use your revision to tone down heated statements—to make your treatment more objective, more balanced. A sentence like "Again our First Amendment rights are encroached upon, ignored, and violated by the pro–censorship forces" is not likely to make the other side listen to your arguments (it is going to make them mad).

- *Edit out outright invective or abuse.* Check for terms like *extremists, lunatic fringe, safety nazis, gun nuts, femlibbers*—all such expressions generate more heat than light. (If any such appear in your paper, make sure to show that you are merely *quoting* them and that they are not yours.)

Study the following sample student paper. How successful is it? How good a model does it make?

Warning: Material May Not Be Suitable for Members of Congress

We drink the vomit of priests, make love with the dying whore.
We suck the blood of the beast and hold the key to death's door.

This song by a heavy metal band shows the kind of lyrics that have brought organizations like the Parents' Music Resource Center (PMRC) into the censorship arena. With the aim of fighting explicit lyrics promoting violence, racism, suicide, sexual abuse, drugs, and alcohol, the PMRC has supported numerous bills mandating the labeling and censorship of offending recording artists and their albums. An in-house legal research service advised the U.S. Congress in 1987 that it has the "constitutional authority to regulate explicit sound recording lyrics and restrict minors' access to them." Albert Gore, then Democratic senator from Tennessee, went on record as saying that he would be "looking to find if there is some constitutional means to regulate lyrics." Phyllis Pollack, the executive director of Music in Action, an anti-censorship group, replied that "this is very dangerous, strange stuff. We've always said that the issue is not rock music; it's trying to take away freedom of speech. Once they convince people that censorship is O.K. in rock, they'll move on to other media."

The basic argument of the groups asking for warning labels on offensive recordings is that parents have the responsibility to bring up their children in a way that is acceptable to the parents' moral and ethical beliefs. Parents cannot exercise this responsibility when material diametrically opposite to their religious and moral views is everywhere easily accessible to their children. As one supporter of the labeling laws explained, our thoughts are influenced by the words and images we put in our minds. We should try to supply our minds with input that will promote healthy thoughts, "which in turn will produce healthy lives." Many supporters of warning labels for offensive material are members of the Christian right who attribute the rise of teenage suicides, teenage sex, and violence in our society to the constant presence of sex and violence in the media.

In rebuttal, defenders of rock musicians have challenged the alleged links between teen murderers or suicide victims and the rock lyrics that are being made the "scapegoat." As Jean Dixon, member of Congress from Missouri, said, there must have been something terribly wrong with these children before they listened to any particular song. The proposed laws would require large warning stickers or parental advisory labels on certain albums. Who would make the decisions? Retailers are not experts on the political and religious ideologies involved. More than one skeptic has warned, "a sticker may just entice kids to buy a record." Warning labels might actually encourage people to purchase records they otherwise would pass by.

As with similar issues, charges and countercharges are heated. Pro-censorship groups freely use terms like "filth" and "garbage of the mind." Anti-censorship forces call their opponents "book burners." What is the answer?

We are not going to control our children's minds. We cannot dictate what they can see and hear and think. The best we can hope for is open and honest communication between parents and their children. I agree we must help create positive images for our children. I also agree that there is much offensive or borderline material in today's popular music. However, if there is to be any labeling of recordings, it should be worked out on a voluntary basis by representatives of the industry and the artists concerned. The federal, state, and local governments should keep their hands off. The basic challenge is to provide some voluntary system of rating, similar to the one used for movies. The music industry professionals should create their own system of labeling while protecting the free speech rights of their artists.

QUESTIONS How and how well does the student writer set up the issue? Do you think both sides are fairly represented in this paper? Are you willing to accept the writer's solution as a balanced, rational conclusion? Do you think the paper as a whole leads up to it effectively? Why or why not?

Topics for Papers Weighing Alternatives (A Sampling)

1. Are efforts to protect or bring back predators—coyotes, wolves, grizzlies—well intentioned but ill advised?
2. Should college bookstores take from the shelves materials (magazines, calendars) accused of being sexist or exploitative of women?
3. Are the courts justified in banning school prayer? (Do they have the right to ban invocations at ceremonies at public colleges or universities?)
4. Should colleges have special admission standards for members of minorities? (Should they lower or adjust their requirements for special groups?)
5. Should public funds be used to support art that is offensive to the majority? (Study test cases like exhibits supported in part by funds from the National Endowment for the Arts and criticized by conservative groups.)
6. Should anything be done to stem the flood of violence in movies and television programs?

7. Are the private lives and past histories of political candidates fair game for the news media, or do public figures have a right to privacy?
8. Do people teaching minority literature have to be members of minorities themselves? (Is a white teacher qualified to teach a course in African American literature, for instance?)
9. Are you in favor of sting operations, or do they constitute entrapment? (For instance, is the government or the post office justified in conducting sting operations to combat child pornography?)
10. Do smokers have rights?

8
ROLE MODELS
The Search for Heroes

When I hear the people praising greatness, then I know that I too
shall be recognized; I too when my time comes shall achieve.
                                                    —from the Chippewa

What does it take to be a hero in today's America? In the fall of 1998, John Glenn, who had been one of America's first astronauts, joined the crew of the space shuttle *Discovery* for his second flight in space. An estimated one million spectators and the president of the United States came to watch the launch. Media celebrities, Hollywood megastars, and a heavyweight champion were in attendance. What heroes does our country set up for its youth other than astronauts, star athletes, and movie stars?

Our society finds it hard to worship heroes—or to find heroes to worship. Americans have a tradition of debunking, or iconoclasm (or idol-smashing). Historians scour the history books "in search of heroes to lay low" (Mark Leyner). Biographers and offspring of famous people lay bare the private traumas and meannesses behind the glamorous or warmhearted façade. The media thrive on scandal. Political leaders spend millions investigating one another, trying to prove the other side guilty of influence peddling and illegal activities.

The idols the media glorify often have feet of clay: Celebrities endorse products they don't use. The heroes of financial newsletters and the *Wall Street Journal* are cost-cutting executives who engineer mass layoffs and downgrade the jobs of the remaining employees. Nevertheless, people who are struggling or faced with barriers have a need for someone to admire, to look up to, to emulate. They look for role models that can symbolize for them their hopes and aspirations. Eve Merriam said in her poem dedicated to Elizabeth Blackwell, who braved centuries of precedent to become a female M.D., "don't let it darken, / the spark of fire; / keep it aglow." Amelia Earhart, before she left on the flight around the world from which she did not return, wrote a letter that said:

> Please know that I am quite aware of the hazards. I want to do it because I want to do it. Women must try to do things as men have tried. When they fail, their failure must be but a challenge to others.

Thousands of Americans each year visit the Martin Luther King Memorial in Atlanta to remind themselves of the eloquence and vision of the preacher who spoke of his dream that "the rough places will be made plain, and the crooked places will be made straight, and the glory of the Lord shall be revealed, and all flesh shall see it together."

In the aftermath of the September 11 attack on the World Trade Center in New York, Americans rediscovered everyday heroes who risk their lives in the service of the public: firefighters, police officers, rescue workers. In our diverse culture, what role models do we have who are not athletes, generals, or astronauts? What do we hear when we do not merely put people we admire on a pedestal but listen to what they have to say?

A BLACK ATHLETE LOOKS AT EDUCATION

Arthur Ashe

> *Arthur Ashe was one of the first African Americans to achieve an international reputation in tennis, until then often thought of as a sport for white players with money and social aspirations. Althea Gibson had been the first black woman to win the English Wimbledon tournament, in 1957 and 1958. Ashe defeated the seemingly invincible Jimmy Connors for the Wimbledon title in men's tennis in 1975. Ashe was ranked first in the world at the time, but injuries and finally a heart attack cut short his career. He used his influence as a sports celebrity to promote civil rights causes; he helped get South Africa banned from the Davis Cup when its government was still identified with apartheid policies. The following is one of the articles he wrote for the* New York Times *and the* Washington Post, *trying to convince "not only black athletes but young blacks in general to put athletics in its proper place." Ashe said about this article, "Some teacher probably read it and put it on the bulletin board. . . . The people who have the problems may not read it, but the ones who are in a position to influence them will." Do you think the kind of advice Ashe gives in this article influences people? Do you think attitudes and policies have changed since he wrote the article?*

Thought Starters: Have you ever read or heard enough about an outstanding athlete to make you feel you knew the person behind the media image?

Since my sophomore year at UCLA, I have become convinced that we blacks spend too much time on the playing fields and too little time in the libraries. Consider these facts: for the major professional sports of hockey, football, basketball, baseball, golf, tennis and boxing, there are roughly only 3170 major league positions available (attributing 200 positions to golf, 200 to tennis and 100 to boxing). And the annual turnover is small.

There must be some way to assure that those who try but don't make it to pro sports don't wind up on street corners or in unemployment lines. Unfortunately, our most widely recognized role models are athletes and entertainers—"runnin'" and "jumpin'" and "singin'" and "dancin'."

Our greatest heroes of the century have been athletes—Jack Johnson, Joe Louis, and Muhammad Ali. Racial and economic discrimination forced us to channel our energies into athletics and entertainment. These were the ways out of the ghetto, the ways to get that Cadillac, those regular shoes, that cashmere sport coat.

Somehow, parents must instill a desire for learning alongside the desire to be Walt Frazier. Why not start by sending black professional athletes into high schools to explain the facts of life?

I have often addressed high school audiences and my message is always the same: "For every hour you spend on the athletic field, spend two in the library. Even if you make it as a pro athlete, your career will be over by the time you are 35. You will need that diploma."

Have these pro athletes explain what happens if you break a leg, get a sore arm, have one bad year or don't make the cut for five or six tournaments. Explain to them the star system, wherein for every star earning millions there are six or seven others making $15,000 or $20,000 or $30,000. Invite a bench-warmer or a guy who didn't make it. Ask him if he sleeps every night. Ask him whether he was graduated. Ask him what he would do if he became disabled tomorrow. Ask him where his old high school athletic buddies are.

We have been on the same roads—sports and entertainment—too long. We need to pull over, fill up at the library and speed away to Congress and the Supreme Court, the unions and the business world.

I'll never forget how proud my grandmother was when I graduated from UCLA. Never mind the Davis Cup. Never mind the Wimbledon title. To this day, she still doesn't know what those names mean. What mattered to her was that of her more than thirty children and grandchildren, I was the first to be graduated from college, and a famous college at that. Somehow, that made up for all those floors she scrubbed all those years.

The Responsive Reader

1. Where does Ashe state his central thesis? How does he echo or reinforce it? How does he support it with examples, explanations, statistics?
2. Does Ashe look at the larger political or cultural context of the issue? Does he try to get at underlying causes?

Talking, Listening, Writing

3. Do you think this article persuaded its intended audience? Why or why not?
4. Some observers say that the lionizing of black athletes and entertainers perpetuates damaging stereotypes: African Americans can succeed only as ballplayers, singers, or comedians. Others answer that successful athletes from nonwhite backgrounds give both nonwhite and white youngsters people from other backgrounds to admire. Widely admired athletes thus help break down the barriers of prejudice. What do you think? How would you defend your stand on this issue?
5. In 1992 Ashe announced at a news conference that he had been infected with the AIDS virus, apparently as the result of a blood transfusion dur-

ing open-heart surgery. He made the announcement reluctantly, after *USA Today* confronted him with a rumor of his condition and asked him to confirm or deny. Anna Quindlen examined the question of journalistic ethics involved when she wrote in her column in the *New York Times:*

> Anyone who tries to make readers believe the questions are simple ones, who automatically invokes freedom of the press and the public's right to know, is doing a disservice to America's newspapers. . . . Naming rape victims. Outing gay people. The candidate's sex life. The candidate's drug use. Editors are making decisions they have never made before, on deadline, with competitors breathing down their necks. . . . Like victims of rape, perhaps the victims of this illness deserve some special privacy. . . . The white light of the press and the closed doors of our homes are two of the most deeply prized assets of our lives as Americans. It just so happens that they are often in direct opposition.

Toward the end of her column, Quindlen asked: "Need we know the medical condition of every public figure? . . . What are the parameters?" How would you answer the questions raised by her column?

Collaborative Projects

6. Critics attack the passive role of the audience in the popular spectator sports, which the fans follow from their seats in the stadium or from the couch in front of the small screen. On your campus or in your community, is there a trend away from spectator sports and toward more active participation in sports? Working with other students, you may want to organize an investigation or survey to find answers to this question.

Find It on the Web

Studies of how student athletes fare in commercialized college athletics programs have included Thad Williamson's "Bad As They Wanna Be" (*Nation* 10/17 August 1998). Williamson claimed that "graduation rates for Division I football and basketball players in the NCAA [National Collegiate Athletic Association] hover at roughly 50 percent" and that NCAA rule changes enabled coaches to terminate athletic scholarships when students became dispensable. Williamson wrote a column for *Inside Carolina* (north-carolina.com), an independent magazine and website devoted to University of North Carolina sports. You may want to do a first search on the Internet for more recent discussions on subjects like career prospects and minimum academic standards for college athletes.

E-MAIL FROM BILL

John Seabrook

> *The story of Bill Gates was one of the great American success stories of the twentieth century. He was the brilliant example of a new kind of billionaire entrepreneur who outdistanced the old business elite by riding the wave of a revolutionary new technology. Gates and other cyberspace pioneers wore jeans and running shoes rather than three-piece suits and designer footwear; they tinkered in garages and makeshift workshops rather than making deals on the golf course. Taking over and improving on someone else's software, Gates developed what is now the operating system of most of the world's personal computers. His marketing and "preselling" of the updated Microsoft Windows 95 with a $200 million promotional campaign was an extravaganza of glitz and hype, with media stars and corporate sponsors lining up to help usher in a new era whose motto, in the words of a Microsoft vice president, was: "Software is now the center of the world." Gates's story turned into a modern morality play because of the speed with which he went from hero to goat. Gates-bashing became a familiar phenomenon among computer aficionados around the globe. He is accused of pushing inferior product through sheer muscle and intimidation and destroying competitors by boa constrictor deals and mergers. The U.S. Justice Department for several years was engaged in antitrust proceedings against the Microsoft empire. A few years earlier, John Seabrook researched a piece on Bill Gates for the* New Yorker, *exchanging extensive e-mail messages with him and finding him astonishingly accessible and ready to talk about his ideas and his work. Seabrook is a science writer who had previously done a long* New Yorker *piece on another cutting-edge field—biotechnology.*

Thought Starters: Do the names of the legendary entrepreneurs of the American past mean anything to the current generation? For instance, does anyone remember the automotive pioneer Henry Ford? the inventor Thomas Edison? the newspaper tycoon Randolph Hearst? Are they still admired? Why or why not?

Bill Gates, aged thirty-eight, [was] one of the richest men in the   *1*
country—the richest in 1992, and the second richest, after the investor Warren Buffett, in 1993, with a fortune of six billion one hundred and sixty million dollars, according to *Forbes*. . . . [W]hen he announced his engagement to Melinda French, a twenty-nine-year-old manager at Microsoft, the news made the front page of the *Wall Street Journal*. Gates controls the computer industry to an extent matched by no other person in any other

major industry. The Justice Department is currently trying to determine whether his control constitutes a monopoly. Microsoft now supplies eighty per cent of all the personal-computer operating-system software in the world—that is, the layer of software that translates your commands so that the computer can act on them—and fifty per cent of all the application software, which is the tools, like Microsoft Word (writing) and Excel (accounting), that run on top of the operating system. Microsoft uses its leverage in the operating-system market as a competitive advantage in the applications market—a practice that is not nice but is not necessarily illegal. "You could say, as I have said to Bill, that having achieved this much power you should turn your attention to being magnanimous," a rival software executive told me, "But Bill believes that now is not the time for statesmanship. Now is the time to conquer new foes, plunder new lands. He doesn't like being compared to John D. Rockefeller—he goes, 'Hey, I'm not a grasping monopolist, am I?'—but he doesn't know how to behave any other way. To hold war councils and to design strategies with the explicit aim of crushing an opponent—this is very American. You know, Mother Teresa is not going to build the broadband network of the future."

Recently, the wife of a software developer was listening to her husband describe for me what it was like to be in the same industry as Bill Gates: he was saying, in a pained but stoical way, that maybe Gates didn't have to be quite so competitive now that he had achieved great power, and that it might be better for the computer industry as a whole if he behaved in a more benevolent way, when his wife interrupted and said to me, "No. You don't understand. We talk about Bill Gates every night at home. We think about Bill Gates all the time. It's like Bill Gates lives with us." This enveloping sense of Bill Gates is hard for someone outside the computer industry to fathom. To people who are unfamiliar with computers, Gates is just a nerd, and if you try to get them to square the negative connotation of the word "nerd" with Gates' incredible success, and with the fact that, far from being on the margin of society, Gates is now in a position to determine what society is like, they're likely to say, "Well, I guess it really is the revenge of the nerds." Actually, Gates probably represents the end of the word "nerd" as we know it.

But all Gates' influence and success are small potatoes compared with the influence he could have and with the opportunity that now lies before him. The computer, which in twenty-five years has evolved from a room-size mainframe into a laptop device, appears to be turning into a new kind of machine. The new machine will be a communications device that connects people to the information highway. It will penetrate far beyond the fifteen per cent of American households that now own a computer, and it will control, or absorb, other communications machines now in people's homes—the phone, the fax, the television. It will sit in the living room, not in the study. The problem of getting people to feel comfortable with such a powerful machine will be partly solved by putting it inside one of the most

unobtrusive objects in the house—the set-top converter, which is the fea-
tureless black box on top of a cable-connected TV set (the one the cat likes
to sit on if the VCR is occupied).

Gates would like to have his software inside that box. Microsoft's
ambition is to supply the standard operating-system software for the
information-highway machine, just as it now supplies the standard
operating-system software, called Windows, for the personal computer.
Microsoft has two billion dollars in cash, and no debt, and is spending a
hundred million dollars a year developing software for the new machine,
which is a lot more than anyone else is spending. The plan is first to supply
the software that allows people to rent videos over the TV and makes home
shopping more attractive, and then to use money from the video-rental and
home-shopping businesses to pay for the development of the rest of the
software. Therefore, Gates is now meeting with people like Mike Ovitz and
Barry Diller to discuss better ways of delivering their products into people's
homes. "I actually requested a meeting with him," Ovitz told me last October. "I flew up to Seattle and we had dinner together and spent three or
four hours just talking about the future."

"Could you say specifically what you talked about?"   5

"It was just very deep stuff about the future."

"Well, for example, did you talk about information-highway
software?"

"It goes much deeper than that."

At Microsoft's main office, in Redmond, a suburb of Seattle, I saw
a demo of an early version of the company's operating software for the
information-highway machine, in which the user points at the TV screen
with a remote control, clicks onto icons, and selects from menus. I heard a
lot about "intelligent agents," which will at first be animated characters that
occasionally appear in the corner of your TV screen and inform you, for example, that President Aristide is on "Meet the Press," because they know
you're interested in Haitian politics, but will eventually be out there on the
information highway, filtering the torrent of information roaring along it,
picking out books or articles or movies for you, or receiving messages from
individuals. As the agents become steadily more intelligent, they will begin
to replace more and more of the functions of human intelligent agents—
stockbrokers, postal workers, travel agents, librarians, editors, reporters.
While I was at Microsoft, I sometimes felt like prey.

Gates' greatest disadvantage in this new market is that Microsoft   10
doesn't own any wires into people's homes, nor does it have the computers
installed to handle all the switching and billing that two-way communication requires. To solve this problem, Microsoft needs to make an alliance
with a cable company or a telephone company, or both. Microsoft has an
alliance with Intel Corporation, the world's leading manufacturer of microprocessors, and General Instrument, a maker of set-top converters, but it
is not a very powerful alliance compared with Bell Atlantic's alliance with

Tele-Communications, Inc., the largest cable company in the United States, or with U S West's alliance with Time Warner, the second-largest cable company. Gates is currently negotiating an alliance involving Time Warner and Tele-Communications, Inc.—a kind of granddaddy of all alliances, which would have the power to set the standard for the information-highway machine. A major issue in the negotiations will be the extent to which Microsoft would own the software in the machine. Gates would like to retain the rights to the software; Gerald Levin, the C.E.O. of Time Warner, and John Malone, the C.E.O. of T.C.I., will not want to give Gates those rights.

If Gates does succeed in providing the operating system for the new machine, he will have tremendous influence over the way people communicate with one another: he, more than anyone else, will determine what it is like to use the information highway. His great advantage is that Microsoft knows how to make software. Another advantage Bill Gates has is that he already lives on the information highway.

New employees at Microsoft are likely to encounter Bill Gates electronically long before they meet him in person. Some get to thinking of him by his e-mail handle, which is "billg," rather than by his real name. You'll be chatting with a Microsoft employee in the employee's office, the computer will make a little belch or squeak, indicating an incoming piece of electronic mail, and it'll be e-mail from Bill. It is not unusual to hear a young employee say, "Hey, that's a good idea, I'm going to e-mail Bill about that." While I was attending a lunchtime cookout at Microsoft headquarters one day, I heard several people start conversations by asking about e-mail from Bill: "Did you get mail from Bill today?" "Did you see Bill's mail?" Bill and Melinda were in Africa at the time, touring the valley where the oldest human skeleton, Lucy, was discovered, but I had the sense that he was present, in the network, flying around the Microsoft campus and popping into people's computers.

The Microsoft campus looks like a college campus: there are playing fields, and employees in T-shirts and jeans who aren't much older than college students. Nowhere on earth do more millionaires and billionaires go to work every day than do so here—about twenty-two hundred of the fifteen thousand employees own at least a million dollars' worth of Microsoft stock—but the campus is in no respect worldly. Workers spend much of their day staring into large computer monitors and occasionally exploding into a rapid fingering of keys. Empty soda cans and cardboard latte cups collect on their desks. Designing software—or "writing code," as people in the trade say—is a sort of intellectual handiwork. Operating systems, the most monumental of all software constructions, are like medieval cathedrals: thousands of laborers toil for years on small parts of them, each one working by hand, fashioning zeroes and ones into patterns that control switches inside microprocessors, which constitute the brains of a computer. The platonic nature of software—it is invisible, weightless, and odorless; it doesn't exist in the physical world—determines much of the culture that surrounds it. At Microsoft, workers often describe each other as "smart" or "supersmart" or "one of the smartest people you'll meet around here," and it is almost an article of faith that Bill Gates, who co-founded the company with Paul Allen, a friend from his high-school days, in 1975, when he was nineteen years old, is the smartest person of all. "Bill is just smarter than everyone else," Mike Maples, an executive vice-president of Microsoft, says. "There are probably more smart people per square foot right here than anywhere else in the world, but Bill is just smarter."

Gates' office is exactly twice as large as the offices of junior employees, and his carpeting is a little richer than the carpeting in other offices; otherwise, there is nothing fancy about the place. A large monitor sits on his desk, and on the wall behind the desk are pictures from important moments in Gates' career, many of which coincide with important moments in the history of the personal computer. There are also pictures of Gates' two sisters, and of his mother and father. (No picture of Melinda French is visible, partly because Gates wants to keep her job as normal as he can.) As in all the Microsoft offices, one rarely hears the sound of a ringing phone. The employees send a total of two hundred million e-mail messages to each other every month. (Over at McCaw Cellular Communications, another prominent high-tech company, whose headquarters is a few miles from Microsoft's, phones ring all the time, and everyone wears a beeper.) Gates spends at least two hours a day at his desk staring into his monitor, reading and writing e-mail. E-mail allows Gates to run the company in his head, in a sense. While he is working, he rocks. Whether he is in business meetings, on airplanes, or listening to a speech, his upper body rocks down to an almost forty-five-degree angle, rocks back up, rocks down again. His elbows are often folded together, resting in his crotch. He rocks at different levels of intensity according to his mood. Sometimes people who are in the meetings begin to rock with him. "I think it's just excess energy," Gates said to me about his rocking. "I should stop, but I haven't yet. They claim I started at an extremely young age. I had a rocking horse and they used to put me to sleep on my rocking horse, and I think that addicted me."

Gates does not have the physical charisma of, say, Steve Jobs, the co-founder of Apple Computer. Like Lenin, Gates leads by sheer force of intellect. He looks like a teen-ager, but not because he actually looks younger than thirty-eight. In some ways, he looks older—a very old little boy. It is the oddly undeveloped quality in his pale, freckled face that makes him seem boyish. His hair is brown and is almost always uncombed. He has heavy lips, which contort into odd shapes when he talks. His characteristic pose when he is standing is pelvis pushed forward slightly, one arm wrapped around his body, the other arm occasionally going up into the air as he talks—kind of flying up, almost spastically, with the palm outstretched, then settling again somewhere on his chest. His voice is toneless, with a some-

15

what weary note of enthusiasm permanently etched into it, and his vocabulary is bland: "stuff" is "cool," "neat," "crummy," "super," "supercool."

When Gates was in his twenties, his mother color-coordinated his clothes—he had green days, beige days, blue days—and then the job was taken over by girlfriends, and now it will presumably fall to his wife, but so far no one has really handled the task successfully. "A lot of his friends have said, 'Bill, come on, let's go on a shopping spree, we'll buy you some clothes,' but it never works," Ann Winblad, who is now a highly respected venture capitalist in Silicon Valley, and was the woman in Bill's life for five years, told me. "Bill just doesn't think about clothes. And his hygiene is not good. And his glasses—how can he see out of them? But Bill's attitude is: I'm in this pure mind state, and clothes and hygiene are last on the list." Esther Dyson, who edits a computer-industry newsletter called *Release 1.0,* says, "I'm told that within Microsoft certain people are allowed to take Bill's glasses off and wipe them, but I've never done it. You know, it's like— 'Don't try this at home.'"

Gates is famously confrontational. If he strongly disagrees with what you're saying, he is in the habit of blurting out, "That's the stupidest fucking thing I've ever heard!" People tell stories of Gates spraying saliva into the face of some hapless employee as he yells, "This stuff isn't hard! I could do this stuff in a weekend!" What you're supposed to do in a situation like this, as in encounters with grizzly bears, is stand your ground: if you flee, the bear will think you're game and will pursue you, and you can't outrun a bear.

All the executives directly under Gates are male, and almost all are in their mid-thirties. Nathan Mhyrvold, thirty-four, who as a graduate student at Cambridge University interpreted for Stephen Hawking, is in charge of new technology. Steve Ballmer, thirty-seven, who is Gates' best friend, runs the numbers side of the business. He and Gates met during freshman year at Harvard, when they lived down the hall from each other. Cramming together for an advanced-economics exam was a determining event in their relationship. Ballmer acted this scene out for me, pacing around the room, waving his arms, the shirttail of his oxford shirt poking out of his khakis, as he cried, "'Yes! We're golden! We're going to pass! No! Shit! We're screwed! We're going to fail! No! Yes! We're golden! We're screwed!' We'd get real up or real down, and it's still that way. We love to get up and down."

Ballmer is the reason Gates always flies coach when he is travelling on business. "If you're going to work for this company," Ballmer told me, "you're going to rent a certain kind of car and stay in a certain kind of hotel and fly coach, because that's business, and anything else is just aggrandizement." Gates once chartered a plane because he had to get somewhere in a hurry, but Ballmer gave him so much grief that Gates is still explaining why he did it. Experienced fliers into and out of Seattle know to scan the cabin for a man with a blanket over his head—that's Bill Gates, taking a nap.

The Responsive Reader

1. Psychologists identify personality types. If you were to sketch a personality type that Gates represents, what key features would you include? Or would you argue that people like Gates do not represent a type at all but are unique individuals? What makes him different?
2. Defending the aggressive behavior of Microsoft, Gates told Seabrook that according to Moore's law microprocessors get twice as powerful, or twice as cheap, every eighteen months. As a result, only companies that are constantly moving aggressively into the future have a chance to survive, with many earlier competitors having already fallen by the wayside. Have you seen striking evidence of the speed of change in the computer field?
3. The fight against the power of monopolies has played a major role in American history. In what sense did Microsoft become a monopoly?

Talking, Listening, Writing

4. From what you know or have read about Bill Gates, do you consider him admirable? Would you consider him as a possible role model for yourself or for others? Why or why not?
5. Do you think you could be happy working for the Microsoft organization? Do you think there is a contradiction between the laid-back dress code and the low-budget perks on the one hand and the power and competitive ethic on the other? Would you be one of the critics of the organization?
6. According to *Harper's* magazine, Microsoft offered $200 to any computer science professor who mentioned its programs in an academic presentation. Would you call this offer a justified incentive? Would you call accepting such an offer unprofessional behavior or legitimate cooperation with American business?
7. Recently there has been much talk about differences in "corporate culture"—with a certain look and outlook and way of doing business expected of people in a company's orbit. Have you had experience with employers or organizations that expect people to "fit in"? Have you ever had a problem with the right or expected way to look, to dress, to talk, or to socialize?

Collaborative Projects

8. Books on Gates have included *Gates* by Stephen Manes and Paul Andrews and *Barbarians Led by Bill Gates* by Jennifer Edstrom and Marlin Eller, as well as Wendy Goldman Rohm's *The Microsoft File: The Secret Case against Bill Gates,* drawing on hundreds of interviews with Microsoft insiders and CEOs of companies doing business with the company. Working with a group, you may want to take part in preparing a set of reviews of more recent articles or books updating the "Microsoft File."

DREAM CATCHER

Mark Leiren-Young

Much traditional history focused on political struggles and political leaders, unrest and revolutions, and famous battles and generals. Today cultural historians stress the forces that shape the day-to-day quality of life for ordinary people. They study the work of the architects and other creative artists who create the environment in which people live and find meaning and direction for their lives. In cities from Chicago to New York City and Los Angeles, magnificent public and private museums and concert halls have always been a center of community life and a source of civic pride. Today spectacular new museums and cultural centers are springing up here and abroad that attract huge numbers of visitors hungering for experiences that will uplift the spirit and reinforce their sense of human solidarity. The following article from the Utne Reader *pays tribute to a pioneering modern architect rediscovering his ethnic roots and engaging in "consensus-building" to develop projects that will "bring other people's visions into reality."*

Thought Starters: Are you aware of a burgeoning movement to enhance the cultural and spiritual life of our communities? Do you know of new art centers and museums, community concerts and festivals, theater-in-the-park and other similar initiatives and activities? What, if any, has been your own exposure or involvement?

The folks in Washington, D.C., are famous for designing by committee, but this was ridiculous. Shortly after the Smithsonian Institution hired Calgary-based architect Douglas Cardinal to design the new National Museum of the American Indian, he flew in two dozen native elders from across the country to discuss the project. "We all gathered in a circle and everybody was respected and heard," Cardinal recalls. "Even opposing views were respected and heard, because the elders always said, 'When you have a circle, if you have everybody agree with you there's only half the circle there.'" Then after convening with tribal leaders in Seattle and Arizona. Cardinal sat down with "the elders here in Washington—all the approval agencies."

In anyone else's hands, this style of consensus-building would be a recipe for mediocrity, but somehow Cardinal, arguably North America's leading Native American architect, elevates it to high art. In 1992, he designed a new village for the small Cree community of Ouje-Bougoumou in Quebec with the ongoing input of 500 or so future residents. The results not only delighted the residents but also won him a United Nations award for community design. "My job is to listen," he says. "My job is to bring other people's visions into reality."

Cardinal, 63, has been applying those principles to high-profile projects in both Canada and the United States ever since he startled the architectural establishment by winning the competition to design the $257 million Canadian Museum of Civilization in Ottawa. As one critic wrote, "Nobody knew how to deal with an architect who achieved the bulk of his inspiration for the design of a major museum during a sweat lodge ceremony."

When the building was unveiled in 1989, a few critics derided its "primitivist" style. (An ironic label, considering the fact that the museum was one of the first large buildings to be rendered by computer.) But many were enchanted by the deeply ecological nature of his work. *The Ottawa Citizen* praised his "distinctive style with curves that bring to mind the natural forms of drifting snow and hills." Such analogies make sense to Cardinal, whose architectural vision was shaped by the environment where he grew up—"the wonderful sculptural forms of nature," as he puts it—in the Canadian prairies and the nearby Rocky Mountains.

He has also been strongly influenced by native metis roots. But it wasn't always so. Cardinal's father, Joseph, was half Blackfoot and was so determined to shield his son from "the stigma of being native" that he never discussed their heritage and once took Douglas to visit his great-grandmother on a reserve and pretended that she wasn't a family member. The "stigma" wasn't easy to erase though. After falling in love with architecture as a child, Cardinal went to the University of British Columbia but was told by the department head after a year that he had "the wrong family background" to be an architect. So he transferred to the University of Texas where, he says, "I received my education—not only in architecture but also in human rights."

Cardinal returned to Alberta in 1964 to set up his practice and did quite well—until he started getting involved in native politics. "One day I was a successful architect; the next day I was an Indian who couldn't be trusted with money," he says. "My father just thought he had passed on to me a terrible legacy."

But in 1970, when his father lay dying, he told Cardinal to stick to his path. "He said, 'I was wrong. You're right to make the stand that you're making for the people.'" recalls Cardinal. "Those were his last words to me." Shaken by his father's death, Cardinal went with some elders he knew to a traditional native camp, where, he says, he fully embraced his roots.

The elders taught him to approach each new project with a shared vision, to always look beyond himself. Such philosophizing might be anathema to most architects, but Cardinal can't understand why anyone would dream of building any other way. "I learned a long time ago that if I was just to bring my own visions into reality it was like looking at a mirror all the time," he adds. "But if you are bringing other people's visions into reality it's very broadening."

The Responsive Reader

1. In Douglas Cardinal's history and mission as a creative artist, his relationship to his roots plays a central role. How does the article trace the far-reaching change or evolution of the architect's relation to his family history? What was the crucial or central role of his father? Do you think Cardinal's experience has parallels in the experience of other Americans from minority backgrounds? (Is it in some ways an archetypal journey in search of roots that many Americans have reenacted?)

2. In the eighties and nineties, a new search for community became a watchword in the media. What do you learn in this article about the community involvement that Cardinal fostered? What were some of the obstacles or doubts he encountered? What were some of his successes and rewards? (How do you like the title of this article?)

Talking, Listening, Writing

3. Have you had any experience with consensus-building? Are you good at respecting opposing views? Are you likely to listen to elders, or are you inclined to discount their views as having been left behind by modern times?

4. In your area or community, are the public buildings you know best mostly practical and functional, serving the everyday purposes of their users? Or do any to you project a sense of mission, a vision, or a philosophy? You may want to write a journal entry or a letter to the editor about the "sense of mission"—or the lack of it—in a current civic building project in your area or community or on your college campus.

Collaborative Projects

5. People involved in political campaigns, advertising campaigns, or filmmaking stress the varied contributions, big and small, and the interplay of conflicting interests that go into such cooperative endeavors. Major articles in newsmagazines and media documentaries often credit numerous contributors and collaborators. Working with a group, you may want to study the workings, challenges, and pitfalls of collaboration in one major line of creative endeavor in which you and your group have a special interest or about which you have a chance to get the inside story.

ARCHITECTURE: The Spirit of the Age

The Guggenheim Museum in New York was one of the first of the bold new museums expressing the spirit of a new age. Have you had a chance to visit or to read about and study one of these museums that have been receiving much press coverage? How does the building, or how do the buildings, express the spirit of the age?

THE DECLINE OF FATHERHOOD

David Popenoe

> *Much current writing about the changing American family assumes that the traditional two-parent family is rapidly becoming a thing of the past. Millions of American children are not living with their fathers, and more than half of them have never been in the father's home. Politicians and pundits who promote family values (even if they themselves are divorced) call this trend toward fatherlessness the single most harmful demographic trend of this generation—blaming it for adolescent pregnancy, child sexual abuse, and juvenile crime. How important is the father to the intellectual, emotional, and moral growth of a child? In particular, how important is it for young males to have a male role model in the immediate family? David Popenoe is a professor of sociology at Rutgers University who believes that government policies should be designed to favor married, child-rearing couples. He sees the phenomenon of the absent father as part of a larger ominous picture including "rising crime rates, growing personal and corporate greed, deteriorating communities, and increasing confusion over moral issues." The following is the first part of an article he published in the* Wilson Quarterly.

Thought Starters: Is it true that fathers have been getting a bad press in recent years? How much do the media dwell on deadbeat dads or emotionally absent fathers?

The decline of fatherhood is one of the most basic, unexpected, and extraordinary social trends of our time. Its dimensions can be captured in a single statistic: In just three decades, between 1960 and 1990, the percentage of U.S. children living apart from their biological fathers more than doubled, from 17 percent to 36 percent. By the turn of the century, nearly 50 percent of American children may be going to sleep each evening without being able to say good night to their dads.

No one predicted this trend, few researchers or government agencies have monitored it, and it is not widely discussed, even today. But the decline of fatherhood is a major force behind many of the most disturbing problems that plague American society: crime and delinquency; teenage pregnancy; deteriorating educational achievement; depression, substance abuse, and alienation among adolescents; and the growing number of women and children living in poverty. The current generation of children may be the first in our nation's history to be less well off—psychologically, socially, economically, and morally—than their parents were at the same age. The United States, observes Senator Daniel Patrick Moynihan, "may be the first society in history in which children are distinctly worse off than adults."

Even as this calamity unfolds, our cultural view of fatherhood itself is changing. Few people doubt the fundamental importance of mothers. But fathers? More and more, the question of whether fathers are really necessary is being raised. Fatherhood is said by many to be merely a social role that others—mothers, partners, stepfathers, uncles and aunts, grandparents— can play.

There was a time in the past when fatherlessness was far more common than it is today, but death was to blame, not divorce, desertion, and out-of-wedlock births. In early-17th-century Virginia, only an estimated 31 percent of white children reached age 18 with both parents still alive. That figure climbed to 50 percent by the early 18th century, to 72 percent by the start of the 20th century, and close to its current level by 1940. Today, well over 90 percent of America's youngsters turn 18 with two living parents. Almost all of today's "fatherless" children have fathers who are alive, well, and perfectly capable of shouldering the responsibilities of fatherhood. Who would have thought that so many men would relinquish them?

Not so long ago, social scientists and others dismissed the change in the cause of fatherlessness as irrelevant. Children, it was said, are merely losing their parents in a different way than they used to. You don't hear that very much anymore. A surprising finding of recent research is that it is decidedly worse for a child to lose a father in the modern, voluntary way than through death. The children of divorced and never-married mothers are less successful in life by almost every measure than the children of widowed mothers. The replacement of death by divorce as the prime cause of fatherlessness is a monumental setback in the history of childhood. 5

Until the 1960s, the falling death rate and the rising divorce rate neutralized each other. In 1900 the percentage of American children living in single-parent families was 8.5 percent. By 1960 it had increased to just 9.1 percent. Virtually no one during those years was writing or thinking about family breakdown, disintegration, or decline.

Indeed, what is most significant about the changing family demography of the first six decades of the 20th century is this: Because the death rate was dropping faster than the divorce rate was rising, more children were living with both of their natural parents by 1960 than at any other time in world history. The figure was close to 80 percent for the generation born in the late 1940s and early 1950s. But then the decline in the death rate slowed, and the divorce rate skyrocketed. "The scale of marital breakdowns in the West since 1960 has no historical precedent that I know of," says Lawrence Stone, a noted Princeton University family historian. "There has been nothing like it for the last 2,000 years, and probably longer."

Consider what has happened to children. Most estimates are that only about 50 percent of the children born during the 1970–84 "baby bust" period will still live with their natural parents by age 17—a staggering drop from nearly 80 percent.

In theory, divorce need not mean disconnection. In reality, it often does. A large survey conducted in the late 1980s found that about one in five divorced fathers had not seen his children in the past year and that fewer than half of divorced fathers saw their children more than several times a year. A 1981 survey of adolescents who were living apart from their fathers found that 52 percent hadn't seen them at all in more than a year; only 16 percent saw their fathers as often as once a week—and the fathers' contact with their children dropped off sharply over time.

The picture grows worse. Just as divorce has overtaken death as the leading cause of fatherlessness, out-of-wedlock births are expected to surpass divorce in the 1990s. They accounted for 30 percent of all births by 1991; by the turn of the century they may account for 40 percent (and 80 percent of minority births). And there is substantial evidence that having an unmarried father is even worse for a child than having a divorced father.   10

Across time and cultures, fathers have always been considered essential—and not just for their sperm. Indeed, no known society ever thought of fathers as potentially unnecessary. Marriage and the nuclear family—mother, father, and children—are the most universal social institutions in existence. In no society has the birth of children out of wedlock been the cultural norm. To the contrary, concern for the legitimacy of children is nearly universal.

In my many years as a sociologist, I have found few other bodies of evidence that lean so much in one direction as this one: On the whole, two parents—a father and a mother—are better for a child than one parent. There are, to be sure, many factors that complicate this simple proposition. We all know of a two-parent family that is truly dysfunctional—the proverbial family from hell. A child can certainly be raised to a fulfilling adulthood by one loving parent who is wholly devoted to the child's well-being. But such exceptions do not invalidate the rule any more than the fact that some three-pack-a-day smokers live to a ripe old age casts doubt on the dangers of cigarettes.

The collapse of children's well-being in the United States has reached breathtaking proportions. Juvenile violent crime has increased from 18,000 arrests in 1960 to 118,000 in 1992, a period in which the total number of young people in the population remained relatively stable. Reports of child neglect and abuse have quadrupled since 1976, when data were first collected. Since 1960, eating disorders and depression have soared among adolescent girls. Teen suicide has tripled. Alcohol and drug abuse among teenagers, although it has leveled off in recent years, continues at a very high rate. Scholastic Aptitude Test scores have declined more than 70 points, and most of the decline cannot be accounted for by the increased academic diversity of students taking the test. Poverty has shifted from the elderly to the young. Of all the nation's poor today, 38 percent are children.

One can think of many explanations for these unhappy developments: the growth of commercialism and consumerism, the influence of television and the mass media, the decline of religion, the widespread availability of guns and addictive drugs, and the decay of social order and neighborhood relationships. None of these causes should be dismissed. But the evidence is now strong that the absence of fathers from the lives of children is one of the most important causes.

What do fathers do? Partly, of course, it is simply being a second adult in the home. Bringing up children is demanding, stressful, and often exhausting. Two adults can support and spell each other; they can also offset each other's deficiencies and build on each other's strengths. 15

Beyond that, fathers—men—bring an array of unique and irreplaceable qualities that women do not ordinarily bring. Some of these are familiar, if sometimes overlooked or taken for granted. The father as protector, for example, has by no means outlived his usefulness. And he is important as a role model. Teenage boys without fathers are notoriously prone to trouble. The pathway to adulthood for daughters is somewhat easier, but they still must learn from their fathers, as they cannot from their mothers, how to relate to men. They learn from their fathers about heterosexual trust, intimacy, and difference. They learn to appreciate their own femininity from the one male who is most special in their lives (assuming that they love and respect their fathers). Most important, through loving and being loved by their fathers, they learn that they are worthy of love.

Recent research has given us much deeper—and more surprising—insights into the father's role in child rearing. It shows that in almost all of their interactions with children, fathers do things a little differently from mothers. What fathers do—their special parenting style—is not only highly complementary to what mothers do but is by all indications important in its own right.

For example, an often-overlooked dimension of fathering is play. From their children's birth through adolescence, fathers tend to emphasize play more than caretaking. This may be troubling to egalitarian feminists, and it would indeed be wise for most fathers to spend more time in caretaking. Yet the fathers' style of play seems to have unusual significance. It is likely to be both physically stimulating and exciting. With older children it involves more physical games and teamwork that require the competitive testing of physical and mental skills. It frequently resembles an apprenticeship or teaching relationship: Come on, let me show you how.

Mothers generally spend more time playing with their children, but mothers' play tends to take place more at the child's level. Mothers provide the child with the opportunity to direct the play, to be in charge, to proceed at the child's own pace. Kids, at least in the early years, seem to prefer to play with daddy. In one study of 2½-year-olds who were given a choice, more than two-thirds chose to play with their fathers.

The way fathers play affects everything from the management of emo-   *20*
tions to intelligence and academic achievement. It is particularly important
in promoting the essential virtue of self-control. According to one expert,
"Children who roughhouse with their fathers . . . usually quickly learn that
biting, kicking, and other forms of physical violence are not acceptable."
They learn when enough is enough.

Children, a committee assembled by the Board on Children and Families of the National Research Council concluded, "learn critical lessons
about how to recognize and deal with highly charged emotions in the context of playing with their fathers. Fathers, in effect, give children practice
in regulating their own emotions and recognizing others' emotional clues."
A study of convicted murderers in Texas found that 90 percent of them either didn't play as children or played abnormally.

At play and in other realms, fathers tend to stress competition, challenge, initiative, risk taking, and independence. Mothers, as caretakers, stress
emotional security and personal safety. On the playground, fathers will try
to get the child to swing higher than the person on the next swing, while
mothers will worry about an accident. It's sometimes said that fathers express more concern for the child's long-term development, while mothers
focus on the child's immediate well-being. It is clear that children have dual
needs that must be met. Becoming a mature and competent adult involves
the integration of two often-contradictory human desires: for *communion,*
or the feeling of being included, connected, and related, and for *agency,*
which entails independence, individuality, and self-fulfillment. One without the other is a denuded and impaired humanity, an incomplete realization of human potential.

For many couples, to be sure, these functions are not rigidly divided
along standard female-male lines, and there may even be a role reversal. But
the exceptions prove the rule. Gender-differentiated parenting is so important that in child rearing by gay and lesbian couples, one partner commonly
fills the male role while the other fills the female role.

It is ironic that in our public discussion of fathering, it's seldom acknowledged that fathers have a distinctive role to play. Indeed, it's far more
often said that fathers should be more like mothers (and that men generally
should be more like women—less aggressive, less competitive). While such
things may be said with the best of intentions, the effects are perverse. After all, if fathering is no different from mothering, males can easily be replaced in the home by women. It might even seem better. Already viewed
as a burden and obstacle to self-fulfillment, fatherhood thus comes to seem
superfluous and unnecessary as well.

We know that fathers have a surprising impact on children. Fathers' in-   *25*
volvement seems to be linked to improved quantitative and verbal skills, improved problem-solving ability, and higher academic achievement. Several

studies have found that the presence of the father is one of the determinants of girls' proficiency in mathematics. And one pioneering study found that the amount of time fathers spent reading was a strong predictor of their daughters' verbal ability.

For sons, who can more directly follow their fathers' example, the results have been even more striking. A number of studies have uncovered a strong relationship between father involvement and the quantitative and mathematical abilities of their sons. Other studies have found a relationship between paternal nurturing and boys' verbal intelligence.

How fathers produce these intellectual benefits is not yet clear. No doubt it is partly a matter of the time and money a man brings to his family. But it is probably also related to the unique mental and behavioral qualities of men; the male sense of play, reasoning, challenge, and problem solving, and the traditional male association with achievement and occupational advancement.

Men also have a vital role to play in promoting cooperation and other "soft" virtues. We don't often think of fathers as teachers of empathy, but involved fathers, it turns out, may be of special importance for the development of this character trait, essential to an ordered society of law-abiding, cooperative, and compassionate adults. Examining the results of a 26-year longitudinal study, a trio of researchers at McGill University reached a "quite astonishing" conclusion: The single most important child-hood factor in developing empathy is paternal involvement in child care. Fathers who spent time alone with their children more than twice a week—giving meals, baths, and other basic care—reared the most compassionate adults.

It is not yet clear why fathers are so important in instilling this quality. Perhaps merely by being with their children they provide a model for compassion. Perhaps it has to do with their style of play or mode of reasoning. Perhaps it is somehow related to the fact that fathers typically are the family's main arbiter with the outside world. Or perhaps it is because mothers who receive help from their mates have more time and energy to cultivate the soft virtues. Whatever the reason, it is hard to think of a more important contribution that fathers can make to their children.

Men, too, suffer grievously from the growth of fatherlessness. The *30* world over, young and unattached males have always been a cause for social concern. They can be a danger to themselves and to society. Young unattached men tend to be more aggressive, violent, promiscuous, and prone to substance abuse; they are also more likely to die prematurely through disease, accidents, or self-neglect. They make up the majority of deviants, delinquents, criminals, killers, drug users, vice lords, and miscreants of every kind. Senator Moynihan put it succinctly when he warned that a society full of unattached males "asks for and gets chaos."

The Responsive Reader

1. What would you include in a statistical digest of figures on the changing demography of the American family that Popenoe presents in the first few pages? What figures are most predictable or familiar? Which statistics for you are startling or thought-provoking? What has happened to the nuclear family?

2. What support does Popenoe offer for his claim that "the collapse of children's well-being in the United States has reached breathtaking proportions"?

3. What are key ideas in Popenoe's discussion of the father's role in a child's play? Does he convince you that some or all of that role is "gender-specific"?

4. In what other areas does Popenoe see a need for the "array of unique and irreplaceable qualities" that fathers bring to a child's development?

Talking, Listening, Writing

5. Are fathers necessary? Do you think father and mother should be equal partners in parenting? Or do you agree with Popenoe that fathers have a special, important "masculine" role to play?

6. Whether the fatherless family is bound to be bad for a child is a subject of vigorous debate. In a reply to Popenoe's article, Judith Stacey, a professor of sociology and women's studies at the University of California at Davis, said: "The evidence resoundingly supports the idea that a high-conflict marriage injures children more than divorce does. Instead of protecting children, the current assault on no-fault divorce endangers them by inviting more parental conflict, desertion, and fraud." To judge from your own experience and that of friends and relatives, is a high-conflict marriage with a father present better or worse than a family situation without one?

7. Alix Kates Shulman, who says that all her novels were centered on the mother–child relationship, has written, "Mothering is so unsupported in our society that every attempt to raise a child is a complex juggling act. . . . In the end, I think all you can do, feminist or not, is try to raise your children lovingly as best you can, pass on what you know, and keep your fingers crossed." Do you agree that mothering is unsupported in our society?

Collaborative Projects

8. Working with a group, you may want to ask: Is there a movement to reconsider no-fault divorce? Who is behind it? What are the arguments?

MISTER TOUSSAN

Ralph Ellison

Ralph Ellison, born in Oklahoma City, became famous for his novel Invisible Man *(1952). One reviewer said about this book that it "has been viewed as one of the most important works of fiction in the twentieth century, has been read by millions, influenced dozens of younger writers, and established Ellison as one of the major American writers" of his time. Ellison's semi-autobiographical hero embarked on an archetypal journey of a Southern black in search of his true identity. He experienced segregated schools in the South. He rebelled against white coworkers considering him inferior ("Were they all Ph.D.s?"). In the big Northern city, he first tried to deny and then came to accept his Southern roots—grits and hot yams and all ("I yam what I yam!"). He watched political groups—Communists, black nationalists— trying to use him for their own purposes. Everywhere he felt no one saw him as a human being in his own right. He was typed as a member of a racial group—he was invisible as his own person. In the following short story, two young boys are learning pride in who they are. The "Mister Toussan" of the title is Toussaint L'Ouverture (1743–1803), who led the people of Haiti in their fight against French colonial rule. Napoleon was rising to power as emperor of France at the time.*

Thought Starters: What do you know about the colonial history of the Caribbean?

Once upon a time
The goose drink wine
Monkey chew tobacco
And he spit white lime.
—*Rhyme used as a prologue*
to Negro slave stories

"I hope they all gits rotten and the worms git in 'em," the first boy   1
said.

"I hopes a big windstorm comes and blows down all the trees," said the second boy.

"Me too," the first boy said. "And when old Rogan comes out to see what happened I hope a tree falls on his head and kills him."

"Now jus' look a-yonder at them birds," the second boy said, "they eating all they want and when we asked him to let us git some off the ground he had to come calling us names and chasing us home!"

"Doggonit," said the second boy, "I hope them birds got poison in   5
they feet!"

The two small boys, Riley and Buster, sat on the floor of the porch, their
bare feet resting upon the cool earth as they stared past the line on the paving where the sun consumed the shade, to a yard directly across the street.
The grass in the yard was very green and a house stood against it, neat and
white in the morning sun. A double row of trees stood alongside the house,
heavy with cherries that showed deep red against the dark green of the
leaves and dull dark brown of the branches. They were watching an old man
who rocked himself in a chair as he stared back at them across the street.

"Just look at him," said Buster. "Ole Rogan's so scared we gonna
git some of his ole cherries he ain't even got sense enough to go in outa
the sun!"

"Well, them birds is gitting theirs," said Riley.

"They mockingbirds."

"I don't care what kinda birds they is, they sho in them trees."   10

"Yeah, old Rogan don't see *them*. Man, white folks ain't got no sense."

They were silent now, watching the darting flight of the birds into the
trees. Behind them they could hear the clatter of a sewing machine: Riley's
mother was sewing for the white folks. It was quiet and, as the woman
worked, her voice rose above the whirring machine in song.

"Your mamma sho can sing, man," said Buster.

"She sings in the choir," said Riley, "and she sings all the leads in
church."

"Shucks, I know it," said Buster. "You tryin' to brag?"   15

As they listened they heard the voice rise clear and liquid to float upon
the morning air:

> I got wings, you got wings,
> All God's chillun got a-wings
> When I git to heaven gonna put on my wings
> Gonna shout all ovah God's heaven.
> Heab'n, heab'n
> Everybody talkin' bout heab'n ain't going there
> Heab'n, heab'n, Ah'm gonna fly all ovah God's heab'n. . . .

She sang as though the words possessed a deep and throbbing meaning for her, and the boys stared blankly at the earth, feeling the somber,
mysterious calm of church. The street was quiet and even old Rogan had
stopped rocking to listen. Finally the voice trailed off to a hum and became
lost in the clatter of the busy machine.

"Sure wish I could sing like that," said Buster.

Riley was silent, looking down to the end of the porch where the sun
had eaten a bright square into the shade, fixing a flitting butterfly in its
brilliance.

"What would you do if you had wings?" he said.   *20*

"Shucks, I'd outfly an eagle, I wouldn't stop flying till I was a million, billion, trillion, zillion miles away from this ole town."

"Where'd you go, man?"

"Up north, maybe to Chicago."

"Man, if I had wings I wouldn't never settle down."

"Me, neither. With wings you could go anywhere, even up to the sun   *25* if it wasn't too hot. . . ."

". . . I'd go to New York. . . ."

"Even around the stars . . ."

"Or Dee-troit, Michigan . . ."

"You could git some cheese off the moon and some milk from the Milky Way. . . ."

"Or anywhere else colored is free. . . ."   *30*

"I bet I'd loop-the-loop. . . ."

"And parachute. . . ."

"I'd land in Africa and git me some diamonds. . . ."

"Yeah, and them cannibals would eat you too," said Riley.

"The heck they would, not fast as I'd fly away. . . ."   *35*

"Man, they'd catch you and stick soma them long spears in you!" said Riley.

Buster laughed as Riley shook his head gravely: "Boy, you'd look like a black pin cushion when they got through with you," said Riley.

"Shucks, man, they couldn't catch me, them suckers is too lazy. The geography book says they 'bout the most lazy folks in the whole world," said Buster with disgust, "just black and lazy!"

"Aw naw, they ain't neither," exploded Riley.

"They is too! The geography book says they is!"   *40*

"Well, my ole man says they ain't!"

"How come they ain't then?"

"'Cause my ole man says that over there they got kings and diamonds and gold and ivory, and if they got all them things, all of 'em cain't be lazy," said Riley. "Ain't many colored folks over here got them things."

"Sho ain't, man. The white folks won't let 'em," said Buster.

It was good to think that all the Africans were not lazy. He tried to   *45* remember all he had heard of Africa as he watched a purple pigeon sail down into the street and scratch where a horse had passed. Then, as he remembered a story his teacher had told him, he saw a car rolling swiftly up the street and the pigeon stretching its wings and lifting easily into the air, skimming the top of the car in its slow, rocking flight. He watched it rise and disappear where the taut telephone wires cut the sky above the curb. Buster felt good. Riley scratched his initials in the soft earth with his big toe.

"Riley, you know all them African guys ain't really that lazy," he said.

"I know they ain't," said Riley, "I just tole you so."

"Yeah, but my teacher tole me, too. She tole us 'bout one of them African guys named Toussan what she said whipped Napoleon!"

Riley stopped scratching the earth and looked up, his eyes rolling in disgust:

"Now how come you have to start lying?"   50

"Thass what she said."

"Boy, you oughta quit telling them things."

"I hope God may kill me."

"She said he was a *African?*"

"Cross my heart, man. . . ."   55

"Really?"

"Really, man. She said he come from a place named Hayti."

Riley looked hard at Buster and seeing the seriousness of the face felt the excitement of a story rise up within him.

"Buster, I'll bet a fat man you lyin'. What'd that teacher say?"

"Really, man, she said that Toussan and his men got up on one of them 60 African mountains and shot down them peckerwood soldiers fass as they'd try to come up. . . ."

"Why good-a-mighty!" yelled Riley.

"Oh boy, they shot 'em down!" chanted Buster.

"Tell me about it, man!"

"And they throwed 'em all off the mountain. . . ."

". . . Goool-leee! . . ."   65

". . . And Toussan drove 'em cross the sand. . . ."

". . . Yeah! And what was they wearing, Buster? . . ."

"Man, they had on red uniforms and blue hats all trimmed with gold, and they had some swords, all shining what they called sweet blades of Damascus. . . ."

"Sweet blades of Damascus! . . ."

". . . They really had 'em," chanted Buster.   70

"And what kinda guns?"

"Big, black cannon!"

"And where did ole what-you-call-'im run them guys? . . ."

"His name was Toussan."

"Toussan! Just like Tarzan . . ."   75

"Not *Taar*-zan, dummy, *Toou*-zan!"

"Toussan! And where'd ole Toussan run 'em?"

"Down to the water, man . . ."

". . . To the river water . . ."

". . . Where some great big ole boats was waiting for 'em. . . ." 80

". . . Go on, Buster!"

"An' Toussan shot into them boats. . . ."

". . . He shot into 'em. . . ."

"With his great big cannons . . ."

"... Yeah! ..."   85

"... Made a-brass ..."

"... Brass ..."

". . . An' his big black cannonballs started killin' them peckerwoods. . . ."

"... Lawd, Lawd ..."

". . . Boy, till them peckerwoods hollowed '*Please, please, Mister Tous-*   90
san, we'll be good!'"

"An' what'd Toussan tell em, Buster?"

"'Boy,' he said in his big deep voice, '*I oughta drown all a-you.*'"

"An' what'd the peckerwoods say?"

"They said, 'Please, Please, *Please, Mister Toussan* . . .'"

"... 'We'll be good,'" broke in Riley.   95

"Thass right, man," said Buster excitedly. He clapped his hands and
kicked his heels against the earth, his black face glowing in a burst of rhythmic joy.

"Boy!"

"And what'd ole Toussan say then?"

"He said in his deep voice: 'You all peckerwoods better be good, *'cause
this is sweet Papa Toussan talking and my men is crazy 'bout white meat!*'"

"Ho, ho, ho!" Riley bent double with laughter. The rhythm still   100
throbbed within him and he wanted the story to go on and on. . . .

"Buster, you know didn't no teacher tell you that lie," he said.

"Yes she did, man."

"That teacher said there was really a guy like that what called hisself
Sweet Papa Toussan?"

Riley's voice was unbelieving and there was a wistful expression in his
eyes which Buster could not understand. Finally he dropped his head and
grinned.

"Well," he said, "I bet thass what ole Toussan said. You know how   105
grown folks is, they cain't tell a story right, 'cepting real old folks like
grandma."

"They sho cain't," said Riley. "They don't know how to put the right
stuff to it."

Riley stood, his legs spread wide, and stuck his thumbs in the top of
his trousers, swaggering sinisterly.

"Come on, watch me do it now, Buster. Now I bet ole Toussan looked
down at them white folks standing just about like this and said in a soft easy
voice: 'Ain't I done begged you white folks to quit messin' with me? . . .'"

"Thass right, quit messing with 'im," chanted Buster.

"'But naw, you-all had to come on anyway. . . .'"   110

". . . Jus' 'cause they was black . . ."

"Thass right," said Riley. "Then ole Toussan felt so bad and mad the
tears come a-trickling down. . . ."

"... He was really mad."

"And then, man, he said in his big bass voice: 'white folks, how come you-all cain't let us colored alone?'"

"... An' he was crying. ..."   *115*

"... An' Toussan tole them peckerwoods: 'I been beggin' you-all to quit bothering us. ...'"

"... Beggin' on his bended knees! ..."

"Then, man, Toussan got real mad and snatched off his hat and started stompin' up and down on it and the tears was tricklin' down and he said: 'You-all come tellin' me about Napoleon. ...'"

"They was tryin' to make him scared, man. ..."

"Toussan said: 'I don't care about no Napoleon. ...'"   *120*

"... Wasn't studyin' 'bout him. ..."

"... Toussan said: 'Napoleon ain't nothing but a man!' Then Toussan pulled back his shining sword like this, and twirled it at them peckerwoods' throats so hard it z-z-z-zinged in the air!"

"Now keep on, finish it, man," said Buster. "What'd Toussan do then?"

"Then you know what he did, he said: 'I oughta beat you peckerwoods!'"

"Thass right, and he did it too," said Buster. He jumped to his feet   *125* and fenced violently with five desperate imaginary soldiers, running each through with his imaginary sword. Buster watched from the porch, grinning.

"Toussan musta scared them white folks almost to death!"

"Yeah, thass 'bout the way it was," said Buster. The rhythm was dying now and he sat back upon the porch, breathing tiredly.

"It sho is a good story," said Riley.

"Heck, man, all the stories my teacher tells us is good. She's a good ole teacher—but you know one thing?"

"Naw; what?"   *130*

"Ain't none of them stories in the books! Wonder why?"

"You know why, ole Toussan was too hard on them white folks, thass why."

"Oh, he was a hard man!"

"He was mean. ..."

"But a good mean!"   *135*

"Toussan was clean. ..."

"... He was a good, clean mean," said Riley.

"Aw, man, he was sooo-preme," said Buster.

"Riiiley!!"

The boys stopped short in their word play, their mouths wide.   *140*

"Riley I say!" It was Riley's mother's voice.

"Ma'am?"

"She musta heard us cussin'," whispered Buster.

"Shut up, man. ... What you want, Ma?"

"I says I wants you-all to go around in the backyard and play, you *145* keeping up too much fuss out there. White folks says we tear up a neighborhood when we move in it and you-all out there jus' provin' them out true. Now git on round in the back."

"Aw, ma, we was jus' playing, ma. . . ."

"Boy, I said for you-all to go on."

"But, ma . . ."

"You hear me, boy!"

"Yessum, we going," said Riley. "Come on, Buster." *150*

Buster followed slowly behind, feeling the dew upon his feet as he walked upon the shaded grass.

"What else did he do, man?" Buster said.

"Huh? Rogan?"

"Heck, naw! I mean Toussan."

"Doggone if I know, man—but I'm gonna ask that teacher." *155*

"He was a fightin' son-of-a-gun, wasn't he, man?"

"He didn't stand for no foolishness," said Riley reservedly. He thought of other things now, and as he moved along he slid his feet easily over the short-cut grass, dancing as he chanted

Iron is iron,
And tin is tin,
And that's the way
The story . . .

"Aw come on man," interrupted Buster. "Let's go play in the alley. . . ."

And that's the way . . .

"Maybe we can slip around and git some cherries," Buster went on.

". . . the story ends," chanted Riley. *160*

The Responsive Reader

1. In much of his fiction, Ellison has fought racial stereotypes. How does he do so in this story?
2. The boys in this story delight in word play, in playing games with words. Can you describe their way of talking, their use of language?
3. What is the role of the mother in the story?

Talking, Listening, Writing

4. The boys claim that stories like the ones about Toussaint are not in their schoolbooks. Should they be?
5. Are treatments of black history in the media too downbeat? Are blacks or other minorities too often associated in the viewers' or readers' minds with problems or trouble?

6. Have you observed or participated in recent efforts to help African Americans or members of other groups to feel pride? What are these efforts? How successful are they?

Collaborative Projects

7. You may want to do some background reading for a capsule portrait of, or short tribute to, one of the following famous people: Paul Laurence Dunbar, Harriet Tubman, Frederick Douglass, Sojourner Truth, William E. B. Du Bois, Marian Anderson, Paul Robeson, Leontyne Price, Mahalia Jackson, Alexander Haley, Thurgood Marshall, Lorraine Hansberry, Cicely Tyson. You may want to start with but also go beyond entries in encyclopedias or biographical dictionaries.

NADINE, RESTING ON HER NEIGHBOR'S STOOP

Judy Grahn

> *Judy Grahn is a feminist and lesbian poet who has published eight volumes of poetry, including* The Work of a Common Woman *(1978) and* Queen of Swords. *She has also written books about poetry and language as well as a novel,* Mundane's World. *She founded the Women's Press Collective and has taught writing and mythology. In her cycle of poems devoted to the Helen myth, she takes it beyond the story of Helen of Troy, former queen of Sparta, who as the "stolen queen" was "hated and blamed for the most famous war of western history and literature, the model war of Troy." Grahn makes Helen the archetypal creation goddess who appears in various forms in many early religions. Helen is the goddess of beauty and love, of the womb and the source of life, of life and fire. Grahn associates her with the tradition of the weaver, or webster, symbolized by the spider, from whose very body comes the cloth of life. The following is one of the poems in which Grahn pays tribute to "common women." How common is the "common woman" in the following poem? How does she challenge traditional definitions of femininity or womanhood?*

Thought Starters: Do the media today project images of ordinary women—women who are not fashion models, sex workers, or overachievers in the world of business and law?

She holds things together, collects bail, | *1*
makes the landlord patch the largest holes.
At the Sunday social she would spike
every drink, and offer you half of what she knows,
which is plenty. She pokes at the ruins of the city | *5*
like an armored tank; but she thinks
of herself as a ripsaw cutting through
knots in wood. Her sentences come out
like thick pine shanks
and her big hands fill the air like smoke. | *10*
She's a mud-chinked cabin in the slums,
sitting on the doorstep counting
rats and raising 15 children,
half of them her own. The neighborhood
would burn itself out without her; | *15*
one of these days she'll strike the spark herself.

She's made of grease
and metal, with a hard head
that makes the men around her seem frail.
The common woman is as common as a nail.   20

The Responsive Reader

1. What are striking images or details in this poem that the reader is likely
   to remember?
2. Do you recognize this person? Does she seem like a real person to you?
3. Compare and contrast what you take to be a more traditional "feminine
   image" with Grahn's portrait of a "common woman."

Talking, Listening, Writing

4. What images of femininity or womanhood are dominant in our culture?
   How obsolete or how alive are such stereotypes as the homemaker, the
   cover girl, the beauty queen, the cheerleader, the dumb blonde, the sex
   bomb? What, if anything, has taken their place?
5. Have you encountered "strong women" in your own family or among
   friends, neighbors, coworkers, business associates?

FORUM: *The American Dream*

The most popular stories in American lore are not about someone who inherited a fortune or was chauffeured to a private school in a limousine. Instead, they are the biographies of people who started in life without money or privilege and became a legend in their own time. They may be the stories of people whose families arrived penniless from a war-torn country and who became movie moguls or advisers to presidents. Among American presidents in the twentieth century, one came from a family that ran a corner grocery store, one had taught Mexican American children in a country school in Texas, and one was born after his father died, leaving the son to grow up with an abusive alcoholic stepfather. One of the great American myths is the log cabin myth—the story of those making it on their own.

What does it take? What mixture of admiration, envy, or resentment do people who stand out inspire?

THE AUTOBIOGRAPHY
OF BILLY GRAHAM

Andrew Delbanco

> *If name recognition is a test of success, the evangelist Billy Graham is one of the great success stories of American history. Adviser to presidents, he has been organizer of megacrusades around the globe, earning his reputation "as having preached Christianity to more people than anyone in history." He transplanted to the world of today's media the American tradition of the revival tent, the itinerant or traveling preacher, and the converts swearing off a life of sin. Graham has been admired for not allowing religion to become a divisive force. He has said that although homosexuality is a sin, God's love extends to homosexuals.*

Thought Starters: Do you watch religious broadcasts? Have you ever attended a revival meeting? What do you think of evangelists?

There is a striking moment in Benjamin Franklin's *Autobiography* in   *1*
which two main currents of American life converge. Skeptical Ben, a man
who "seldom attended any public worship," and for whom "Revelation had
indeed no weight," goes out one day in 1739 to hear a famous evangelical
preacher whom he regards as a holdover from the age of credulity. The
place is Philadelphia, the preacher is the visiting English Methodist George
Whitefield, and the charity on Whitefield's mind that day is an orphanage
in Georgia. Before the appeal, Franklin "did not disapprove of the design"
for an orphans' home. Ever the booster of local interests, he "thought it
would have been better to have built the House here & [to have] Brought
the Children to it." By the time Whitefield finished his soaring plea, however, Franklin had "emptied my pocket wholly into the collector's dish,
gold and all." A wealthy friend, whose wariness of the preacher's blandish-
ments had led him to attend the service without a cent on his person, found
himself begging in the crowd for a loan with which he could make a gift of
his own.

If Whitefield was the first great practitioner of itinerant revival
preaching in America, Billy Graham is its modern master. His story begins
fifty years ago, when Americans outside the South first came to know this
dentally impeccable farmboy from North Carolina with a taste for Dr. Pepper and goofy suits, who traveled with a supporting cast of musicians,
notably George Beverly Shea, the baritone who sings what Graham's biographer Marshall Frady aptly calls the "lanolin-lubricated solos" that are a
standard part of a Graham service. In 1949, Billy and his Crusade Team (the

initial letters are always capitalized) made their first incursion into the urban Northeast. Preaching on the Boston Common in a city full of theological liberals, Catholics and egghead unbelievers, he borrowed his topic from a sermon that Whitefield had preached there some two centuries before: "Shall God Reign in New England?" The result was a "harvest" of contributions and converts, and a sense among some in the infidel city that God's messenger had come to town. Even some latter-day skeptics, in the tradition of Franklin, were impressed.

Journey, Arrival, Doubt, Triumph: this is the four-part movement of Billy Graham's autobiography, which bears the belligerently modest title *Just As I Am*. It is a monotonous tale—how the ministry went national and then international, how it reached out through radio, film and (most of all) television—that makes for a book with a repetitive structure rather like the structure of pornography. Virtually every chapter tells the same story in the same vocabulary. Billy flies into town in a rickety chartered plane that is running low on fuel or in the hands of an unlicensed pilot or buffeted by a thunderstorm. At first, the press as well as local civic and religious leaders are dubious or hostile (Billy's handlers are always fretting that the plane is late or the weather bad), but the great man remains undaunted, the rally goes on, and it ends with a throng of converts approaching the sundrenched or moonlit platform to declare their "decisions for Christ."

Billy Graham probably deserves his reputation as having preached Christianity to more people than anyone in history. Pastor to presidents, inventor of (in Garry Wills's phrase) "golf course spirituality," author now of a bestselling memoir, he has been on the lists of most admired Americans for most of the last forty years. But who is this Elvis of the evangelicals? What does he believe? And what kind of religious experience does he offer his followers?

Just As I Am does not help much with these questions. Despite its   5
length, it is not really a book. It is what Robert Giroux used to call an "ook": a gesture toward an idea or a sentiment or a story that is packaged as a book, but never quite becomes one. Considering how important strenuous self-reflection is in the religious tradition to which Graham belongs, one of its oddest features is how little it reveals of its author's inner life. We do catch glimpses of Billy in times of edginess and exhaustion; we learn that on tour he misses his wife and children; we witness a fleeting moment of doubt about the inerrancy of scripture. He expresses regret over a few public gaffes—such as when he and the Team, after a chilly visit with President Truman, knelt in posed prayer for photographers on the White House lawn. Put together with help from various writers, secretaries and "editorial coordinators," this memoir has the feeling of having been dictated on the run. There are flashes of self-deprecating humor, as when Billy looks back and discovers his youthful resemblance to Li'l Abner; but most of the humor is unwitting, as when we encounter "Bev" Shea at the Helsinki Crusade crooning "I'd Rather Have Jesus" in Finnish.

"To be honest," Graham says, "I never thought I would write this book . . . [and] one of the hardest parts has been deciding what to leave out." It is not always easy to grasp just what has guided him in choosing what to put in. Skipping quickly over the war years (he was 23 when Pearl Harbor was bombed), he says little more than that his hopes for an army chaplaincy were thwarted when he turned out to be underweight. Yet certain small childhood incidents are carefully preserved for their allegorical value, as when the future preacher of love and reconciliation shuts up the family collie in the doghouse overnight with a cat—an experiment by which he learns, presumably, that creatures who go into a situation as enemies can come out friends.

Graham's first stirrings of conviction came when he was turning 16, in response to the voice and the gaze of a traveling preacher with the splendid name of Mordecai Ham, who had come to Charlotte to denounce sin. Dr. Ham seemed especially attuned to the dark secrets of the young, and Billy, whose participation in the local Presbyterian church had until then been merely dutiful, found himself feeling accused by the man's stare. "Billy was always a ladies man," as one friend (quoted not in *Just As I Am,* but in an admiring biography by William Martin) has put it. "He was quite a thinker, too. That's all he thought about." Surprising himself in feeling drawn to the revival meeting for a second night, he and his lifelong friend Grady Wilson decided to join the choir so they could mouth the words (neither could sing) while using their hymn books to hide from Ham's dread gaze.

Evidently, Graham came to his faith out of standard adolescent anxiety. "As a teenager, what I needed to know for certain was that I was right with God." *Just As I Am* does not elaborate on this quest for certainty, which concluded successfully when he was 16 and seems never to have faltered in the ensuing sixty-four years. It was a conversion of what William James called the "volitional type," a spiritual event without much sense of upheaval. "No bells went off inside me," Billy says. "No signs flashed across the tabernacle ceiling. No physical palpitations made me tremble." Now, nearly 80, he indulges in scant retrospective analysis of his adolescent self, but he does recall that after being smitten by Dr. Ham, he worried about ridicule from his peers. "How could I face school tomorrow? . . . There seemed to be a song in my heart, but it was mixed with a kind of pounding fear as to what might happen when I got to class." There are hints that even before his conversion he may already have been regarded as overscrupulous:

> Once in my senior year, when we were in a night rehearsal of a school play at Sharon High, one of the girls in the cast coaxed me aside into a dark classroom. She had a reputation for "making out" with the boys. Before I realized what was happening, she was begging me to make love to her. My hormones were as active as any other healthy

young male's, and I had fantasized often enough about such a moment. But when it came, I silently cried to God for strength and darted from that classroom the way Joseph fled the bedroom of Potiphar's philandering wife in ancient Egypt.

What Mordecai Ham gave to this boy was a new sense of the dignity of his scruples. To this was added the gift of a vocation: Billy would be a preacher. At Bible school and college, Graham discovered his own oratorical gifts and developed chaste friendships with several pious girls, eventually courting Ruth Bell, the daughter of missionaries, to whom he has now been married for more than fifty years. While studying to be a purveyor of the gospel, he spent some time hawking Fuller brushes door to door, an experience by which he tested and refined his salesman's knack. In 1940, at the New York World's Fair, Graham saw his first television. "They had a camera there, and as you walked by, you could see yourself on a screen. We never thought it would amount to anything, though. It seemed too incredible!" The rest is evangelical history.

The Responsive Reader

1. In the beginning of this review, you hear echoes of the vocabulary of old–time religious crusades, which pitted "infidels," "skeptics," and "unbelievers" against "Revelation" or else "credulity." Is this language obsolete or old-fashioned today, or are people still using it? Where and how? (What is the "inerrancy of scripture"? Is it an issue for you or people you know?)
2. According to this review, how does Graham describe the basic scenario, or MO, of his traveling ministry? Do you find it inspirational or self-admiring?
3. What key traits of Graham's personality emerge for you from this portion of a longer review? What were key factors in his conversion or major stages in his spiritual history? What temperament suited him for his life work? For you, what about his personality was predictable, and what was surprising?

Talking, Listening, Writing

4. Do you think that the ministry of the individual crusading evangelist is more American than the organization and ritual of a traditionally structured church? Why or why not?
5. Many television evangelists have built business empires and become millionaires. Do you think large personal wealth is compatible or incompatible with the teachings of the gospels?
6. What major experiences or what influences played a role in your own spiritual or intellectual history?

THE DIGITAL AMAZON

Leslie Gornstein

A standard feature of feminist publications like Ms. *or minority-oriented publications like* Ebony *has been tributes to Americans from unconventional backgrounds who succeeded against odds. Often the journalist writing about an outstanding woman will ask: What set her on the path to success? What did she consider her mission? What obstacles did she have to overcome? How can she serve as an inspiration to others? The following article focuses on an outstanding woman making her way in the "brutally male" medium of cyberspace. At the time she wrote this article, Gornstein encouraged readers to check out Amazon City at www.amazoncity.com*

Thought Starters: What do you know about the original Amazons? Have you encountered current revivals of the word or the concept? Where or in what context?

Five-feet-eight and skinny as a model, ramrod-poised in DKNY sunglasses and high-heeled mules, the 28-year-old blond in stretch pants is blowing away the bums along the Venice Beach boardwalk. They tell her she looks "just fi-i-ne," but her head never turns. The mules maintain their clip as she heads back to the candlelit apartment that doubles as the worldwide headquarters for her unlikely online empire.

Stephanie Brail is a digital Amazon.

More specifically, she's the founder of Digital Amazon, a Web consulting firm with clients ranging from healthcare giant Kaiser Permanente to the nonprofit Los Angeles Commission on Assaults Against Women. She's also the brains behind Amazon City, an online women's community, and one of the driving forces behind the growing women's presence in cyberspace.

The whole idea behind Digital Amazon, she says, is to support and promote women as they strive for success. That's a daunting mission, given the testosterone coursing through the net, and Brail knows firsthand how brutally male the medium can be. In 1993 she found herself in the middle of a flame war that morphed into a case of e-mail stalking so terrifying that she began practicing martial arts for self-defense. "That's when I decided that I wanted to get more women on the Internet, to even things out," she says.

Five years later, things *are* beginning to even out—more women are getting online—partly because of Brail's work. Like any young entrepreneur with no venture capital, she logs 60- to 80-hour workweeks. She also

1

5

fights a constant battle with chronic fatigue immunodeficiency syndrome, which requires daily naps and causes occasional bouts of "brain fog." Still, Brail has managed, on a shoestring, to develop some of the most successful women-oriented sites on the net. Her Amazon City Radio, launched last year, is the only radio station on the Web offering women-oriented music, talk, news, and public affairs programming. The Amazon City online community attracts as many as half a million page views a month.

Meanwhile, women-oriented sites are attracting corporate sponsors. "This is not a bad thing," Brail says, "but I think a lot of women are downright suspicious of glitzy, advertisement-driven Web sites."

And many of these sites avoid political content at all costs. "Say the word *bitch* on your Web site and that's enough for an ad campaign to be pulled," Brail says. "Sometimes you'll actually find more controversial stuff in the traditional women's magazines."

Brail, who grew up in Jackson, Michigan, got turned on to computers at 10, when her father brought one home and told her she'd be needing it if she wanted a career. Her feminist leanings also began at an early age. "I grew up in an environment where I was always told I could be whatever I wanted to be," she says.

By 1993—when most of the world still didn't know what the Internet was—Brail was typing away on cyberspace bulletin boards. At 24, she was teaching Internet classes. But with chronic fatigue occasionally draining her energy, she knew she couldn't fit into a 9-to-5 grind. So she started building Web pages for pay, mooching a free Internet connection from a friend and sharing a server with a few colleagues.

Today, her Digital Amazon empire is profitable and supports seven part-time off-site employees. She's hoping to move the entire operation into an office next year.   10

But is all this enough to revitalize the women's movement? "I don't think technology is the key to advancing feminist goals," she explains. "It is certainly, helpful, but not essential. It is more important that women, individual women, have a shift in their perceptions of themselves, that they start to believe in their dreams and follow them."

The Responsive Reader

1. What key details would you include in a portrait of the cyberspace entrepreneur featured in this article? Do any of the biographical data seem especially significant? Do any seem surprising or nonstereotypical?
2. What concrete evidence do you see in this article of the success or promise of Brail's business venture? If you were a budding cyberspace entrepreneur, what key points—or what sidelights—would you note especially?
3. How much does this article focus on obstacles in Brail's path?

4. Where in the article do Brail's feminist convictions or commitments come through most strongly? What kind of feminist is she? What is her advice to other feminists?

Talking, Listening, Writing

5. The magazine where this article was printed included a picture of Brail with the caption "Maverick." What makes her a maverick, or what kind of maverick is she?
6. Would you turn to articles like this one for inspiration and guidance? Or are you a reader suspicious of too much hype that might create unrealistic expectations?

HILLARY IN THE CROSSFIRE

Gloria Steinem

> Gloria Steinem became America's most widely known and admired as well as attacked feminist. She is the granddaughter of a prominent American suffragist—an activist fighting for women's right to vote. Steinem grew up in poverty in Toledo, Ohio, in a family traumatized by mental illness. She came to New York to work as a journalist and became a cofounder and editor of Ms., the country's leading feminist magazine. Her widely read and influential publications range from her early Outrageous Acts and Everyday Rebellions and a book about Marilyn Monroe to her best-selling Revolution from Within: A Book of Self-Esteem (1992). In the following article, she draws a feminist's conclusion from the successful run for U.S. senator from New York of the former first lady of the Clinton White House.

Thought Starters: Next to Lady Diana and Mother Theresa, Hillary Rodham Clinton was one of the most prominent women in the news during the years of the Clinton presidency. What do you recall, good or bad, of news coverage and controversy concerning her before she became a U.S. senator?

Why did Hillary Rodham Clinton want to run for the Senate—from *1* New York, Illinois, or anywhere? Imagine the scenario if she lost: all the right-wingers who sported "Impeach Hillary's husband" bumper stickers would claim victory, as would those behind the TV ads that burlesque Hillary as the Statue of Liberty. If she wins, what happens? She gets to live in the free-floating hostility of Washington again, this time without the protection of the White House, working every day under such senior senators as Jesse Helms and Strom Thurmond.

Is this a lose-lose situation or what?

As one of the most famous and admired women on the world stage, she had plenty of alternatives. For example, she could have raised a huge pot of foundation money and become an international force on the women's and children's issues that have always been close to her heart. Instead, she was doing daily combat with New York's Mayor Rudolph Giuliani, one of the most vindictive and racially divisive politicians of our time, and also discovering a fact of life for any female candidate: there is no "right" way for a woman to seek power.

So why did she choose this path of maximum resistance?

After months of listening to her around New York State, I think the answer is simple: she wanted to use the lessons she learned as the partner of a politician, and to do so in Washington, where she also witnessed the power that even one U.S. senator can have over the issues she cares about. Though her goals have been created by experience and interests that are different from her husband's—her work as a lawyer for the Watergate Committee, a top corporate lawyer, a children's rights advocate, a policy wonk on health care, and an international activist on women's issues—she wants to advance them by using her derived experience in campaigning, building coalitions, dealing with the press, cultivating a thick skin, making Washington work, and other time-honored secrets of getting and using elected power.

This bridging of worlds is a new possibility. Eleanor Roosevelt was an intimate lobbyist with her husband, but not a practitioner of elected power. As for such beneficiaries of derived power as Senator Margaret Chase Smith and Representative Lindy Boggs, they waited for husbands to die before taking over their Congressional seats, thus obeying the rule that in a patriarchy, it's only widows who are honored in authority.

Perhaps these differences are part of the reason that Hillary Clinton is accused of exploiting her wifely position—even by some feminists. They ask, "Why doesn't she stick to her own professional experience? Isn't she setting feminism back by exploiting the power she gained as a wife?"

But those questions betray a double standard. They also ignore the wisdom gained in traditionally female roles. The fact is, the Bush boys would be nowhere without the derived power of their father's presidency; John Glenn used the male-only privilege of being an astronaut to become a U.S. senator; and John McCain went from prisoner of war to the Senate and almost to the White House. Those experiences were far less relevant to the political job at hand than Hillary's eight years in Washington, yet they were highly valued. Meanwhile, such largely female experiences as parenting, teaching, community organizing, and living on welfare have been undervalued as political training grounds.

This double standard wouldn't last if it hadn't been internalized by women ourselves. That's one of the reasons for a disheartening fact: female registered voters in New York State were almost equally divided between Hillary Clinton and Rudolph Giuliani. Of course, women are not immune to the law-and-order, wealth-protecting Republican platform, especially because Republican leadership in New York is slightly less bad on gender-gap issues. (For example, the governor and New York City's mayor both opposed the criminalization of abortion.)

Still another reason for some women voter's hesitancy was the anger   *10*
they felt toward Hillary for remaining married to an unfaithful husband, especially women who themselves had been hurt by faithless men. And then there were the women who have been exposed only to the right-wing image of Hillary.

For all those who didn't support her the bottom-line question is: would you support a male candidate with the same issue positions? If the answer is yes, it's worth rooting out the double standard.

Because Hillary Clinton's success as the first crossover candidate was a landmark for a larger issue: making partnered and other female experience a source of talent, honor, and credit.

The Responsive Reader

1. Steinem briefly summarizes the candidate's credentials in two major areas. The first is her work as a lawyer and on issues that were her special interest. Is there a connecting thread in her interests? The second is her insider's participation in the power politics of Washington. According to Steinem, what assets did she acquire in that role?

2. What precedents for a woman's prominent role in American politics does Steinem mention? How familiar are you with them? For Steinem, why was Hillary's candidacy an important departure or step forward? What is the double standard concerning family connections or experience outside politics that Steinem objects to?

3. Steinem says that "such largely female experiences as parenting, teaching, community organizing, and living on welfare have been undervalued as political training grounds." Do you think that in the years ahead such experiences should be valued more highly as qualifications for office? Why or why not?

4. Political pundits observed that the candidate succeeded in winning over women wary of or hostile to her. How does Steinem explain the lack of unanimous support by women?

Talking, Listening, Writing

5. Steinem calls Hillary "one of the most famous and admired women on the world stage." What do you think explains the special animosity and

ridicule that the first lady attracted? How much was political? How much was personal? How much represented the misogyny and distrust of women of a cultural rearguard?

6. Do you think women still labor under special disadvantages when running for public office? What evidence can you offer in support of your answer?

7. Do you think that a candidate's private life or marital history should be an issue in a political campaign? Why or why not?

8. *Time* magazine declared New York mayor Rudolph Giuliani, Hillary's original opponent in the Senate race, its Person of the Year for 2001 after he was featured prominently in the aftermath of the attack on the twin towers of the World Trade Center in September 2001. Why does Steinem call him "one of the most vindictive and racially divisive politicians of our time"? You may want to research Giuliani's role in controversies focused on funding and admission policies for the City University of New York and on his attempted censorship of art exhibits at the Brooklyn Museum of Art.

Collaborative Projects

9. In other countries, women have become powerful political figures and national leaders, including Golda Meir in Israel, Margaret Thatcher in England, Indira Gandhi in India, and Benazir Bhutto in Pakistan. Working with a group, you may want to research the personal qualities, political circumstances, cultural factors, or family connections that contributed to their rise to power and to the opposition they encountered.

Arguing from Principle

As rational, objective people, we pride ourselves on our ability to approach a subject with an open mind. We feel capable of looking at the evidence and drawing logical conclusions. Three major reasoning patterns help writers structure papers that present a strong argument:

- The **inductive,** generalizing, kind of reasoning is the most easily demonstrated of the procedures that our minds use to process information. The inductive think scheme, moving from fact to inference, has for centuries been the model for Western science. Early scientists took in such facts as that the moon is kept in orbit around Earth, that pens fall to the floor and not to the ceiling, that apples drop to the ground instead of flying off toward the sky. They concluded that there is an all-pervading physical force—gravity—that pulls material objects toward one another.

- The playing off of **pro and con** mirrors the way a public consensus takes shape on many debatable issues. By listening to both sides, we can hope to weed out what is clearly self-serving, partisan, or extreme in order to find common ground. We move from statement to counterstatement and, ideally, to a balanced conclusion.

- Much formal, structured argument follows a third reasoning pattern. Much of our reasoning follows the opposite of the inductive procedure. **Deduction,** or deductive reasoning, starts with something that we believe—something that we already accept as true. It then shows how the general principle applies to a specific situation. The inductive and deductive kinds of reasoning work together if we first develop general physical laws or patterns of behavior and then use them to predict behavior in a specific situation. For instance, if the law of gravity holds true, a space module passing Venus or Mars should be pulled toward the planet or deflected into an orbit around the planet.

Deductive reasoning moves from the general to the specific. It invokes principles that we expect the reader to share. It then applies these to the situation in question. Many arguments concerning values or behavior follow a deductive pattern:

- If all human beings, regardless of race, are created equal, then slavery is evil.

- If the foundation of democracy is an educated citizenry, then providing universal public education is a civic duty.

- If all Americans are equal before the law, then the offspring of a senator or a corporation president should not get a special exemption from military service.

Many such arguments hinge on the initial *if*—the initial assumption, or initial **premise.** If the premise does not hold true, the argument does not convince.

The same basic pattern structures many arguments on public issues:

IF: The U.S. Constitution separates church and state, religion and government.
AND IF: The nativity scene is a religious symbol.
THEN: The nativity scene should not be displayed at city hall.

A three-step argument, moving from two accepted premises to a justified conclusion, is called a syllogism:

FIRST PREMISE: All full-time students are eligible for the loan program.
SECOND PREMISE: You are a full-time student.
CONCLUSION: Therefore, you are eligible.

FIRST PREMISE: No undocumented aliens will be hired.
SECOND PREMISE: I am an undocumented alien.
CONCLUSION: Therefore, I need not apply.

FIRST PREMISE: No one with an arrest record will be hired.
SECOND PREMISE: I do not have an arrest record.
CONCLUSION: Therefore, I am eligible.

In each of these arguments, the first premise specifies what it includes or rules out. The conclusion necessarily follows because the premise includes or rules out *all* members of a group. In practice, many arguments are not true syllogisms. Arguments that use *some* or *many* instead of *all* or *no* in the first premise are less airtight. They lead to a *probable* conclusion:

IF: Most members of the Achievement Club are business majors.
AND IF: Maria is a member of the Achievement Club.
THEN: Maria is *likely to be* a business major.

A Checklist of Logical Fallacies

Advocates of straight thinking take inventory of familiar **logical fallacies**—familiar kinds of shortcut thinking or predictable ways of reaching the wrong conclusion. Problems like the following will hurt your credibility as a writer:

1 **scapegoating** Politicians looking for "wedge issues" to exploit may blame the trend toward low-wage jobs without job security or health benefits on immigrants or illegal aliens rather than on the transfer of manufacturing to third-world nations. They may blame high taxes on welfare mothers.

2 **ad hominem** Ad hominem arguments aim "at the person" instead of addressing the issue. Instead of discussing your ideas about health care, your opponent might call attention to a bitter divorce, an alcoholic relative, your visits to a psychiatrist, or your sexual orientation.

3 **hasty generalization** Knowing a few Vietnamese students hardly gives us the right to generalize about "how Asians think." (Filipino, Japanese, Chinese, and Vietnamese students might think alike in some ways, but it would be a formidable task to pinpoint the similarities and test our conclusions.) Similarly, we should not make sweeping generalizations about "what the American people want" or "the world view of the younger generation."

4 **unrepresentative sample** What makes a good cross section of a group or a population that you are discussing? We cannot determine student sentiment on current issues by talking only to friends who are members of fraternities and sororities. We need to listen as well to co-op dwellers, people living on their own close to the campus, and commuters. We should probably talk to re-entry students, minority students, and part-time students.

5 **post-hoc fallacy** Post hoc is short for the Latin for "after this, therefore because of this." "First this and then that" does not always mean cause and effect. If it rained after the rainmaker performed a ceremony, it might have rained anyway without his help. If a hurricane strikes after a nuclear test, there might or might not be a causal connection.

6 **false analogy** Is our nation like a lifeboat—with only so many spaces? Would it be swamped if we allowed an unlimited number of the people floundering in the water to climb aboard? It is true that no nation has unlimited resources and absorbing too many immigrants might "swamp" cities and institutions. However, sooner or later the analogy breaks down. Immigrants have often developed new resources and taken new initiatives (which newcomers to a lifeboat could not do). And as a nation,

A Checklist of Logical Fallacies

we depend on people *outside* the lifeboat for resources and for trade that brings employment.

7 **rationalization** When we rationalize, we go for explanations that make us look good. When something goes wrong, we look for explanations that sound reasonable and at the same time clear us of blame. When you do poorly in a class with a teacher of a different gender or ethnicity, the reason may well be that the teacher is prejudiced against your group. But the reason may also be that the subject is difficult or that you did not have enough time to study.

8 **slanting** Court procedures require prosecutors and defense attorneys to share evidence favoring the other side. The wary reader knows that interested parties tend to slant the data or suppress damaging evidence. They exaggerate what favors their cause and leave out complicating or contrary testimony.

9 **bandwagon** Advertisers and public relations experts try to sway us by letting us know that "everybody does it" or "everyone thinks so." What is fashionable or trendy carries people along when it comes to selling ideas as well as shoes.

10 **smokescreen** Propagandists know how to hide damaging information behind a verbal smokescreen. How are our reactions being steered when the cutting down of trees is described as "harvesting"? The word *harvest* might lead us to believe that in a few years the trees will grow again. They would provide another crop—although, in the case of redwood trees, the last "crop" took between two hundred and eight hundred years to grow.

TRIGGERING As with other kinds of reasoning, we may think about the principles at stake in a current issue at least in part to make up our own minds. But more often we use an appeal to principle to bring others around to our point of view. We invoke basic principles when defending our position on public education, drunken driving laws, Christmas displays on public property, welfare reform, military service, or capital punishment.

In his famous "I Have a Dream" speech, Martin Luther King, Jr., invoked basic principles of the American political tradition:

■ In the country of the free, one large segment of the population should not be denied the freedom to live, eat, and go to school where they choose.

■ In a country founded on the principle of human dignity, a large number of fellow citizens should not be subjected to demeaning restrictions and exclusions.

GATHERING   To appeal effectively to shared values, you might need to invoke precedents and established legal principles. For instance, what is the history of our protections for freedom of speech? (Why were printers and journalists in the colonies concerned about their freedom to print? What are the roots of First Amendment rights in earlier British history? Where in modern times have censorship forces been especially repressive?) On our obligation to the poor, you might want to quote an eloquent statement by a widely respected leader, or you might present a modern rereading of a parable from the New Testament. On an unpopular law, you might present impressive evidence of public opinion.

Perhaps you want to appeal to the principle of compassion in arguing against "heroic" medical procedures that needlessly prolong the suffering of the terminally ill. Your reading notes for the paper might include entries like the following:

> Public opinion polls show that most Americans oppose the use of "heroic measures" to keep patients alive when there is no hope of recovery. A Louis Harris poll found that 82% supported the idea of withdrawing feeding tubes if it was the patient's wish. . . .
>
> In many cases, the family and the staff agree that the patient in question "derives no comfort, no improvement, and no hope of improvement" from further medical treatment. . . .
>
> Many Americans linger in a hopeless twilight zone between life and imminent death. Recent studies show the tremendous financial burden and the anguish suffered by their families. . . .

SHAPING   A classic pattern for an argument from principle first dramatizes the current situation that raised the issue. It then spells out the principle (or principles) involved, presented in such a way that the argument will speak strongly to the shared values of the intended audience. Then the writer applies the principle (or principles) to specific authentic examples.

What are the principles invoked in the following paper? Do you think they will command the assent or at least the respect of the intended readers? How authentic or convincing do the test cases or key examples seem to you? How do *you* react to this paper as a reader?

Thou Shalt Not

As we hear about prayer vigils and last-minute pleas protesting the current spate of executions, we realize that an issue that has lain dormant for many years is again dividing the citizens into hostile camps. The weakness of the passionate last-minute appeals for clemency played up by the media is that they tend to focus on the special circumstances of the individual case. A murderer was the victim of child abuse. A rapist suffered brain damage. By focusing on the individual history of those waiting on death row, we run the danger of losing sight of the basic principles at stake when a civilized society reinstitutes capital punishment.

In spite of strong current arguments in favor of the death penalty, capital punishment violates basic principles underlying the American system of justice. Most basic to our legal system is the commitment to even-handed justice. We believe that equal crimes should receive equal punishment. However, the death penalty has always been notorious for its "freakish unfairness." Some murderers walk the streets again after three or five or seven years, whereas others—because of ineffectual legal counsel, a vindictive prosecutor, or a harsh judge—join the inmates waiting out their appeals on death row. In one celebrated case, two partners in crime were convicted of the same capital crime on identical charges. One was executed; the other is in prison and will soon be eligible for parole. In the words of one study, "Judicial safeguards for preventing the arbitrary administration of capital punishment are not working." Judges and juries apply widely different standards.

We believe that all citizens are equal before the law. Justice should be blind to wealth, race, or ethnic origin. However, poor defendants are many times more likely to receive the death penalty than wealthy ones, protected by highly paid teams of lawyers whose maneuvers stymie the prosecution and baffle the jury. Minority defendants convicted of capital crimes have a much higher statistical chance of being executed than white defendants. A black person killing a white person is more likely to receive the death penalty than a white person killing a black person.

Fairness demands that the judicial system make provision for correcting its own mistakes. If someone has been unjustly convicted, there should be a mechanism for reversing the verdict and setting the person free. No one doubts that there are miscarriages of justice. Citizens of Northern Ireland convicted as terrorists are set free after many years because of evidence that they were framed and their confessions coerced by the police. Victims withdraw rape charges; witnesses admit to mistaken identification of suspects. A convict confesses on his deathbed to a crime for which someone else was convicted.

However, in the case of the death penalty, any such correction of error is aborted. We are left with futile regrets, like the prosecutor who said, "Horrible as it is to contemplate, we may have executed the wrong man."

REVISING When we write with special conviction, we are likely to come on strong. We may use emotional language. We are often impatient with the opposition. We may sound very sure—probably too sure—of ourselves. Give yourself time to reread a paper that you wrote in the heat of passion. Rereading the paper in the sober light of next morning, you have a chance to take some of the heat and steam out of the argument. You have a chance to make sure the argument stands on its merits. In revising your paper, consider advice like the following:

- *Do not invoke large abstractions like Science or History or Common Sense.* "Science says . . ." is a weak argument, because specific scientists make limited assertions—and often scientists disagree among themselves. (Quote specific scientists, and try to show that they are recognized authorities or people in the mainstream of current scientific opinion.) Remember that common sense told people that Earth was flat.

- *Try not to dismiss (or brush off) opposing points of view.* People who feel insulted or ignored are not likely to listen attentively—and perhaps change their minds. (Not everyone who more or less reluctantly endorses the reinstatement of the death penalty is a fascist, a sadist, a vigilante, or a believer in primitive eye-for-an-eye justice.)

- *Tone down passages that make you sound bigoted or prejudiced.* ("The average criminal is a brutal individual who deserves exactly what he got." "To rid our streets of violent crime, we should lock up violent criminals and throw away the key.")

- *Strengthen logical links.* Signal turns in the argument. Use the transitions that are needed to hold an argument together. Insert a strategic *therefore* or *consequently* to signal that you are drawing a logical conclusion. Use *however* or *nevertheless* to signal that you are raising a major objection. Use links like *on the one hand* and *on the other hand* to show that you are playing off the pro and con.

Topics for Papers Arguing from Principle (A Sampling)

1. Should a college assure parity in funding for men's and women's sports? Why or why not? If you answer in the affirmative, how would parity be achieved?
2. Should women receive equal pay not only for the same jobs but also for jobs of "comparable worth"? What principles are involved?
3. Does society have the right to deny welfare payments to unwed teenage mothers? What principles are at stake?
4. Should employers have the right to hire permanent replacements for striking workers? (Are there limits to the right to strike?)
5. Should employers have the right to ban romantic relationships among employees? On what grounds?
6. Do traditional tests or qualifying exams work against equal opportunity for candidates from other than conventional white, middle-class backgrounds? What principles are at stake?
7. In awarding custody of children in divorce cases, should the courts give preference to the mother? Why or why not?

8. Should cities or other local jurisdictions have the right to enact their own gun control measures? What are the principles at stake?

9. Should the military have the right to exclude Americans who are openly gay or lesbian?

10. Does the United States have a humanitarian obligation to accept refugees escaping from war, poverty, or repression?

9
LANGUAGE
Bond and Barrier

*An education for freedom (and for the love and intelligence which are
at once the conditions and the results of freedom) must be, among other
things, an education in the proper uses of language.*

—*Aldous Huxley*

*Languages are far-reaching realities. They go far beyond those political
and historical structures we call nations.*

— *Octavio Paz*

Language is the greatest human invention. It gives us more than neutral information of the kind that could be stored in a computer—or recited
by a computerized voice. Words do not just give directions ("This way to
the center of the city"). They tell us something about the speaker—as if
a telephone while carrying a message were to tell us whether it liked its job.
Bureaucrat, politician, schoolmarm, welfare cheat, redneck, and *woman driver* are
not neutral labels like *detergent* or *soap.* They give vent to the speaker's feelings. They carry messages of dislike, of antagonism. They say, "I am not as
dense or obstructing or incompetent or bigoted as you are."

Many of the following selections raise a crucial question about language: Is it boon or bane in relationships between individuals or groups?
Does it further human understanding, or does it serve to muddy the waters
or poison the wells? We like to think of language as a bond. It helps people
to break out of their isolation, to break down the wall of separateness. In
the prehistoric past, it enabled human beings to band together, to make
plans, to coordinate their efforts. Language enables us to offer other human
beings help and comfort. ("Be of good cheer; we will not abandon you" is
chalked on a message board held up on a rescue vessel to comfort the people
on a shipwrecked ship in one of Walt Whitman's poems.) However, language also carries messages of rejection, condescension, and contempt, as
with words like *stud, slut, young punk, dirty foreigner, greaser, dago,* and other
racial or ethnic slurs too ugly to mention. Language often reinforces divisions; it serves to outgroup people who are "not one of us." Language is the
medium of love, but it is also the medium of quarrels, of hate propaganda,
of incitement to violence.

Many people in our modern world have been suspicious of language—
wary of its potential for abuse. Others have maintained their faith in the capacity of language to help human beings communicate. The critic Margaret
Laurence said about the Nigerian novelist Chinua Achebe, author of *Things
Fall Apart,*

In Ibo villages, the men working on their farm plots in the midst of the
rain forest often shout to one another—a reassurance, to make certain
the other is still there, on the next cultivated patch, on the other side
of the thick undergrowth. The writing of Chinua Achebe is like this.
It seeks to send human voices through thickets of our separateness.

TALK IN THE INTIMATE RELATIONSHIP: HIS AND HERS

Deborah Tannen

Deborah Tannen is a language scholar who says her marriage broke up because of a classic breakdown in communication: She employed a literal style, trying to say exactly what she meant, whereas her husband used the indirect style of people who hint at what they want and expect other people to pick up the hints. Tannen, who studied at Berkeley under linguists focusing on language as an interactive social medium, reached a large public with two books on the undercurrents and hidden messages in how people talk: You Just Don't Understand: Women and Men in Conversation *and* That's Not What I Meant: How Conversational Style Makes or Breaks Relationships. *Her focus is on the metamessages we send—the messages that go beyond what we say outright. Literal-minded people miss much of the subtext of communication—what lies below surface meanings. The mere fact that people bother to talk to us already sends a message (they care enough to give us some of their time), just as their refusal to talk to us also sends a message. Tannen's most recent book is* Talking from 9 to 5 *(1994), on the role of language in the workplace. A reviewer of the book said that much of the secret of her success is "that she is writing about the single most common social activity in the world; everyone talks, although not everyone reads, writes, or reasons." Dr. Tannen's scholarly essays have been collected in* Gender and Discourse, *published by Oxford University Press.*

Thought Starters: Is it true that as far as language goes, boys and girls "grow up in different worlds"? Is a conversation between a man and a woman truly "cross-cultural" communication?

Male-female conversation is cross-cultural communication. Culture is simply a network of habits and patterns gleaned from past experience, and women and men have different past experiences. From the time they're born, they're treated differently, talked to differently, and talk differently as a result. Boys and girls grow up in different worlds, even if they grow up in the same house. And as adults they travel in different worlds, reinforcing patterns established in childhood. These cultural differences include different expectations about the role of talk in relationships and how it fulfills that role.

Everyone knows that as a relationship becomes long-term, its terms change. But women and men often differ in how they expect them to change. Many women feel, "After all this time, you should know what I want without my telling you." Many men feel, "After all this time, we should be able to tell each other what we want."

These incongruent expectations capture one of the key differences between men and women. Communication is always a matter of balancing conflicting needs for involvement and independence. Though everyone has both these needs, women often have a relatively greater need for involvement, and men a relatively greater need for independence. Being understood without saying what you mean gives a payoff in involvement, and that is why women value it so highly.

If you want to be understood without saying what you mean explicitly in words, you must convey meaning somewhere else—in how words are spoken, or by metamessages. Thus it stands to reason that women are often more attuned than men to the metamessages of talk. When women surmise meaning in this way, it seems mysterious to men, who call it "women's intuition" (if they think it's right) or "reading things in" (if they think it's wrong). Indeed, it could be wrong, since metamessages are not on record. And even if it is right, there is still the question of scale: How significant are the metamessages that are there?

Metamessages are a form of indirectness. Women are more likely to   5
be indirect, and to try to reach agreement by negotiation. Another way to understand this preference is that negotiation allows a display of solidarity, which women prefer to the display of power (even though the aim may be the same—getting what you want). Unfortunately, power and solidarity are bought with the same currency: Ways of talking intended to create solidarity have the simultaneous effect of framing power differences. When they think they're being nice, women often end up appearing deferential and unsure of themselves or of what they want.

When styles differ, misunderstandings are always rife. As their differing styles create misunderstandings, women and men try to clear them up by talking things out. These pitfalls are compounded in talks between men and women because they have different ways of going about talking things out, and different assumptions about the significance of going about it.

Sylvia and Harry celebrated their fiftieth wedding anniversary at a mountain resort. Some of the guests were at the resort for the whole weekend, others just for the evening of the celebration: a cocktail party followed by a sit-down dinner. The manager of the dining room approached Sylvia during dinner. "Since there's so much food tonight," he said, "and the hotel prepared a fancy dessert and everyone already ate at the cocktail party anyway, how about cutting and serving the anniversary cake at lunch tomorrow?" Sylvia asked the advice of the others at her table. All the men agreed: "Sure, that makes sense. Save the cake for tomorrow." All the women disagreed: "No, the party is tonight. Serve the cake tonight." The men were focusing on the message: the cake as food. The women were thinking of the metamessage: Serving a special cake frames an occasion as a celebration.

Why are women more attuned to metamessages? Because they are more focused on involvement, that is, on relationships among people, and it is through metamessages that relationships among people are established and maintained. If you want to take the temperature and check the vital signs of a relationship, the barometers to check are its metamessages: what is said and how.

Everyone can see these signals, but whether or not we pay attention to them is another matter—a matter of being sensitized. Once you are sensitized, you can't roll your antennae back in; they're stuck in the extended position.

When interpreting meaning, it is possible to pick up signals that   10
weren't intentionally sent out, like an innocent flock of birds on a radar screen. The birds are there—and the signals women pick up are there—but they may not mean what the interpreter thinks they mean. For example, Maryellen looks at Larry and asks, "What's wrong?" because his brow is furrowed. Since he was only thinking about lunch, her expression of concern makes him feel under scrutiny.

The difference in focus on messages and metamessages can give men and women different points of view on almost any comment. Harriet complains to Morton, "Why don't you ask me how my day was?" He replies, "If you have something to tell me, tell me. Why do you have to be invited?" The reason is that she wants the metamessage of interest: evidence that he cares how her day was, regardless of whether or not she has something to tell.

A lot of trouble is caused between women and men by, of all things, pronouns. Women often feel hurt when their partners use "I" or "me" in a situation in which they would use "we" or "us." When Morton announces, "I think I'll go for a walk," Harriet feels specifically uninvited, though Morton later claims she would have been welcome to join him. She felt locked out by his use of "I" and his omission of an invitation: "Would you like to come?" Metamessages can be seen in what is not said as well as what is said.

It's difficult to straighten out such misunderstandings because each one feels convinced of the logic of his or her position and the illogic—or irresponsibility—of the other's. Harriet knows that she always asks Morton how his day was, and that she'd never announce, "I'm going for a walk," without inviting him to join her. If he talks differently to her, it must be that he feels differently. But Morton wouldn't feel unloved if Harriet didn't ask about his day, and he would feel free to ask, "Can I come along?," if she announced she was taking a walk. So he can't believe she is justified in feeling responses he knows he wouldn't have.

These processes are dramatized with chilling yet absurdly amusing authenticity in Jules Feiffer's play *Grown Ups*. To get a closer look at what happens when men and women focus on different levels of talk in talking things out, let's look at what happens in this play.

Jake criticizes Louise for not responding when their daughter, Edie,   *15* called her. His comment leads to a fight even though they're both aware that this one incident is not in itself important.

Jake: Look, I don't care if it's important or not, when a kid calls its mother the mother should answer.
Louise: Now I'm a bad mother.
Jake: I didn't say that.
Louise: It's in your stare.
Jake: Is that another thing you know? My stare?

Louise ignores Jake's message—the question of whether or not she responded when Edie called—and goes for the metamessage: his implication that she's a bad mother, which Jake insistently disclaims. When Louise explains the signals she's reacting to, Jake not only discounts them but is angered at being held accountable not for what he said but for how he looked—his stare.

As the play goes on, Jake and Louise replay and intensify these patterns:

Louise: If I'm such a terrible mother, do you want a divorce?
Jake: I do not think you're a terrible mother and no, thank you, I do not want a divorce. Why is it that whenever I bring up any difference between us you ask me if I want a divorce?

The more he denies any meaning beyond the message, the more she blows it up, the more adamantly he denies it, and so on:

Jake: I have brought up one thing that you do with Edie that I don't think you notice that I have noticed for some time but which I have deliberately not brought up before because I had hoped you would notice it for yourself and stop doing it and also—frankly, baby, I have to say this—I knew if I brought it up we'd get into exactly the kind of circular argument we're in right now. And I wanted to avoid it. But I haven't and we're in it, so now, with your permission, I'd like to talk about it.
Louise: You don't see how that puts me down?
Jake: What?
Louise: If you think I'm so stupid why do you go on living with me?
Jake: Dammit! Why can't anything ever be simple around here?!

It can't be simple because Louise and Jake are responding to different levels of communication. As in Bateson's example of the dual-control electric blanket with crossed wires, each one intensifies the energy going to a different aspect of the problem. Jake tries to clarify his point by overelaborating it, which gives Louise further evidence that he's condescending to her, making it even less likely that she will address his point rather than his condescension.

What pushes Jake and Louise beyond anger to rage is their different perspectives on metamessages. His refusal to admit that his statements have implications and overtones denies her authority over her own feelings. Her attempts to interpret what he didn't say and put the metamessage into the message makes him feel she's putting words into his mouth—denying his authority over his own meaning.

The same thing happens when Louise tells Jake that he is being manipulated by Edie:

Louise: Why don't you ever make her come to see you? Why do you always go to her?

Jake: You want me to play power games with a nine year old? I want her to know I'm interested in her. Someone around here has to show interest in her.

Louise: You love her more than I do.

Jake: I didn't say that.

Louise: Yes, you did.

Jake: You don't know how to listen. You have never learned how to listen. It's as if listening to you is a foreign language.

Again, Louise responds to his implication—this time, that he loves Edie more because he runs when she calls. And yet again, Jake cries literal meaning, denying he meant any more than he said.

Throughout their argument, the point to Louise is her feelings—that Jake makes her feel put down—but to him the point is her actions—that she doesn't always respond when Edie calls:

Louise: You talk about what I do to Edie, what do you think you do to me?

Jake: This is not the time to go into what we do to each other.

Since she will talk only about the metamessage, and he will talk only about the message, neither can get satisfaction from their talk, and they end up where they started—only angrier:

Jake: That's not the point!

Louise: It's *my* point.

Jake: It's hopeless!

Louise: Then get a divorce.

American conventional wisdom (and many of our parents and English teachers) tell us that meaning is conveyed by words, so men who tend to be literal about words are supported by conventional wisdom. They may not simply deny but actually miss the cues that are sent by how words are spoken. If they sense something about it, they may nonetheless discount what they sense. After all, it wasn't said. Sometimes that's a dodge—a plausible defense rather than a gut feeling. But sometimes it is a sincere conviction.

Women are also likely to doubt the reality of what they sense. If they don't doubt it in their guts, they nonetheless may lack the arguments to support their position and thus are reduced to repeating, "You said it. You did so." Knowing that metamessages are a real and fundamental part of communication makes it easier to understand and justify what they feel.

An article in a popular newspaper reports that one of the five most [20] common complaints of wives about their husbands is "He doesn't listen to me anymore." Another is "He doesn't talk to me anymore." Political scientist Andrew Hacker noted that lack of communication, while high on women's lists of reasons for divorce, is much less often mentioned by men. Since couples are parties to the same conversations, why are women more dissatisfied with them than men? Because what they expect is different, as well as what they see as the significance of talk itself.

First, let's consider the complaint "He doesn't talk to me."

One of the most common stereotypes of American men is the strong silent type. Jack Kroll, writing about Henry Fonda on the occasion of his death, used the phrases "quiet power," "abashed silences," "combustible catatonia," and "sense of power held in check." He explained that Fonda's goal was not to let anyone see "the wheels go around," not to let the "machinery" show. According to Kroll, the resulting silence was effective on stage but devastating to Fonda's family.

The image of a silent father is common and is often the model for the lover or husband. But what attracts us can become flypaper to which we are unhappily stuck. Many women find the strong silent type to be a lure as a lover but a lug as a husband. Nancy Schoenberger begins a poem with the lines "It was your silence that hooked me, / so like my father's." Adrienne Rich refers in a poem to the "husband who is frustratingly mute." Despite the initial attraction of such quintessentially male silence, it may begin to feel, to a woman in a long-term relationship, like a brick wall against which she is banging her head.

In addition to these images of male and female behavior—both the result and the cause of them—are differences in how women and men view the role of talk in relationships as well as how talk accomplishes its purpose. These differences have their roots in the settings in which men and women learn to have conversations: among their peers, growing up.

Children whose parents have foreign accents don't speak with accents. [25] They learn to talk like their peers. Little girls and little boys learn how to have conversations as they learn how to pronounce words: from their playmates. Between the ages of five and fifteen, when children are learning to have conversations, they play mostly with friends of their own sex. So it's not surprising that they learn different ways of having and using conversations.

Anthropologists Daniel Maltz and Ruth Borker point out that boys and girls socialize differently. Little girls tend to play in small groups or, even more common, in pairs. Their social life usually centers around a best friend, and friendships are made, maintained, and broken by talk—especially "secrets." If a little girl tells her friend's secret to another little girl, she may find herself with a new best friend. The secrets themselves may or may not be important, but the fact of telling them is all-important. It's hard for newcomers to get into these tight groups, but anyone who is admitted is treated as an equal. Girls like to play cooperatively; if they can't cooperate, the group breaks up.

Little boys tend to play in larger groups, often outdoors, and they spend more time doing things than talking. It's easy for boys to get into the group, but not everyone is accepted as an equal. Once in the group, boys must jockey for their status in it. One of the most important ways they do this is through talk: verbal display such as telling stories and jokes, challenging and sidetracking the verbal displays of other boys, and withstanding other boys' challenges in order to maintain their own story—and status. Their talk is often competitive talk about who is best at what.

Feiffer's play is ironically named *Grown Ups* because adult men and women struggling to communicate often sound like children: "You said so!" "I did not!" The reason is that when they grow up, women and men keep the divergent attitudes and habits they learned as children—which they don't recognize as attitudes and habits but simply take for granted as ways of talking.

Women want their partners to be a new and improved version of a best friend. This gives them a soft spot for men who tell them secrets. As Jack Nicholson once advised a guy in a movie: "Tell her about your troubled childhood—that always gets 'em." Men expect to *do* things together and don't feel anything is missing if they don't have heart-to-heart talks all the time.

If they do have heart-to-heart talks, the meaning of those talks may be   *30* opposite for men and women. To many women, the relationship is working as long as they can talk things out. To many men, the relationship isn't working out if they have to keep working it over. If she keeps trying to get talks going to save the relationship, and he keeps trying to avoid them because he sees them as weakening it, then each one's efforts to preserve the relationship appear to the other as reckless endangerment.

If talks (of any kind) do get going, men's and women's ideas about how to conduct them may be very different. For example, Dora is feeling comfortable and close to Tom. She settles into a chair after dinner and begins to tell him about a problem at work. She expects him to ask questions to show he's interested; reassure her that he understands and that what she feels is normal; and return the intimacy by telling her a problem of his. Instead, Tom sidetracks her story, cracks jokes about it, questions her interpretation of the problem, and gives her advice about how to solve it and avoid such problems in the future.

All of these responses, natural to men, are unexpected to women, who interpret them in terms of their own habits—negatively. When Tom comments on side issues or cracks jokes, Dora thinks he doesn't care about what she's saying and isn't really listening. If he challenges her reading of what went on, she feels he is criticizing her and telling her she's crazy, when what she wants is to be reassured that she's not. If he tells her how to solve the problem, it makes her feel as if she's the patient to his doctor—a metamessage of condescension, echoing male one-upmanship compared to the female etiquette of equality. Because he doesn't volunteer information about his problems, she feels he's implying he doesn't have any.

His way of responding to her bid for intimacy makes her feel distant from him. She tries harder to regain intimacy the only way she knows how—by revealing more and more about herself. He tries harder by giving more insistent advice. The more problems she exposes, the more incompetent she feels, until they both see her as emotionally draining and problem-ridden. When his efforts to help aren't appreciated, he wonders why she asks for his advice if she doesn't want to take it. . . .

When women talk about what seems obviously interesting to them, their conversations often include reports of conversations. Tone of voice, timing, intonation, and wording are all re-created in the telling in order to explain—dramatize, really—the experience that is being reported. If men tell about an incident and give a brief summary instead of re-creating what was said and how, the women often feel that the essence of the experience is being omitted. If the woman asks, "What exactly did he say?," and "How did he say it?," the man probably can't remember. If she continues to press him, he may feel as if he's being grilled.

All these different habits have repercussions when the man and the woman are talking about their relationship. He feels out of his element, even one down. She claims to recall exactly what he said, and what she said, and in what sequence, and she wants him to account for what he said. He can hardly account for it since he has forgotten exactly what was said—if not the whole conversation. She secretly suspects he's only pretending not to remember, and he secretly suspects that she's making up the details. 35

One woman reported such a problem as being a matter of her boyfriend's poor memory. It is unlikely, however, that his problem was poor memory in general. The question is what types of material each person remembers or forgets.

Frances was sitting at her kitchen table talking to Edward, when the toaster did something funny. Edward began to explain why it did it. Frances tried to pay attention, but very early in his explanation, she realized she was completely lost. She felt very stupid. And indications were that he thought so too.

Later that day they were taking a walk. He was telling her about a difficult situation in his office that involved a complex network of interrelationships among a large number of people. Suddenly he stopped and said, "I'm sure you can't keep track of all these people." "Of course I can," she said, and she retraced his story with all the characters in place, all the details right. He was genuinely impressed. She felt very smart.

How could Frances be both smart and stupid? Did she have a good memory or a bad one? Frances's and Edward's abilities to follow, remember, and recount depended on the subject—and paralleled her parents' abilities to follow and remember. Whenever Frances told her parents about people in her life, her mother could follow with no problem, but her father got lost as soon as she introduced a second character. "Now who was that?" he'd ask. "Your boss?" "No, my boss is Susan. This was my friend." Often he'd still be in the previous story. But whenever she told them about her work, it was her mother who would get lost as soon as she mentioned a second step: "That was your tech report?" "No, I handed my tech report in last month. This was a special project."

Frances's mother and father, like many other men and women, had   40 honed their listening and remembering skills in different arenas. Their experience talking to other men and other women gave them practice in following different kinds of talk.

Knowing whether and how we are likely to report events later influences whether and how we pay attention when they happen. As women listen to and take part in conversations, knowing they may talk about them later makes them more likely to pay attention to exactly what is said and how. Since most men aren't in the habit of making such reports, they are less likely to pay much attention at the time. On the other hand, many women aren't in the habit of paying attention to scientific explanations and facts because they don't expect to have to perform in public by reciting them—just as those who aren't in the habit of entertaining others by telling jokes "can't" remember jokes they've heard, even though they listened carefully enough to enjoy them.

So women's conversations with their women friends keep them in training for talking about their relationships with men, but many men come to such conversations with no training at all—and an uncomfortable sense that this really isn't their event.

Most of us place enormous emphasis on the importance of a primary relationship. We regard the ability to maintain such relationships as a sign of mental health—our contemporary metaphor for being a good person.

Yet our expectations of such relationships are nearly—maybe in fact—impossible. When primary relationships are between women and men, male-female differences contribute to the impossibility. We expect partners to be both romantic interests and best friends. Though women and men may have fairly similar expectations for romantic interests, obscuring their differences when relationships begin, they have very different ideas about how to be friends, and these are the differences that mount over time.

In conversations between friends who are not lovers, small misunder-   45 standings can be passed over or diffused by breaks in contact. But in the context of a primary relationship, differences can't be ignored, and the pressure cooker of continued contact keeps both people stewing in the juice of accumulated minor misunderstandings. And stylistic differences are sure to cause misunderstandings—not, ironically, in matters such as sharing values and interests or understanding each other's philosophies of life. These large and significant yet palpable issues can be talked about and agreed on. It is far harder to achieve congruence—and much more surprising and troubling that it is hard—in the simple day-to-day matters of the automatic rhythms and nuances of talk. Nothing in our backgrounds or in the media (the present-day counterpart to religion or grandparents' teachings) prepares us for this failure. If two people share so much in terms of point of view and basic values, how can they continually get into fights about insignificant matters?

If you find yourself in such a situation and you don't know about differences in conversational style, you assume something's wrong with your partner, or you for having chosen your partner. At best, if you are forward thinking and generous minded, you may absolve individuals and blame the relationship. But if you know about differences in conversational style, you can accept that there are differences in habits and assumptions about how to have conversation, show interest, be considerate, and so on. You may not always correctly interpret your partner's intentions, but you will know that if you get a negative impression, it may not be what was intended—and neither are your responses unfounded. If he says he really is interested even though he doesn't seem to be, maybe you should believe what he says and not what you sense.

Sometimes explaining assumptions can help. If a man starts to tell a woman what to do to solve her problem, she may say, "Thanks for the advice but I really don't want to be told what to do. I just want you to listen and say you understand." A man might want to explain, "If I challenge you, it's not to prove you wrong; it's just my way of paying attention to what you're telling me." Both may try either or both to modify their ways of talking and to try to accept what the other does. The important thing is to know that what seem like bad intentions may really be good intentions expressed in a different conversational style. We have to give up our conviction that, as Robin Lakoff put it, "Love means never having to say 'What do you mean?'"

The Responsive Reader

1. Tannen once said that readers of her work reported an "Aha!" response. They found that what they thought was their personal problem was actually part of a larger pattern. Did you have an "Aha!" response to any part of this selection? Can you give examples from your own experience for the clashing assumptions or expectations that Tannen ascribes to men and women?

2. What are key examples that Tannen gives for the difficulties of communication between men and women? How real or convincing do they seem to you? (How convincing are the examples from the Feiffer play?) Do you interpret the examples the same way she does?
3. How does Tannen explain how misunderstandings "intensify" or escalate?
4. How familiar are the stereotypes about males that Tannen claims are widespread in our culture and shape male behavior? How strong are they?
5. Is there hope for miscommunicating couples? What is the gist of the positive advice, explicit or implied, that Tannen would give to couples who have trouble communicating?

Talking, Listening, Writing

6. There is much debate over what is truly gender-specific in our culture. Do you think Tannen exaggerates the differences between the talking styles of the sexes? Where and how?
7. Tannen has challenged the feminist claim that men dominate women in conversation. Is it true that men tend to interrupt women, cutting them off or brushing off their opinions? Or are women right who claim that "men never talk"?
8. Have you ever rebelled against a style of talking expected of you? Have you ever found yourself using language that was not "you"? What was the occasion or situation? What was the problem? What was the outcome?

Collaborative Projects

9. Working alone or in a group, you may want to investigate the "women's language" of fashion sections or society pages or the "men's language" of the sports pages. Or you may want to work out significant contrasts between the two.

CULTURAL ETIQUETTE: A GUIDE

Amoja Three Rivers

> Ms. *magazine published the following article as part of a series on race and women. The editors called it a "creative attempt to shed some light—and levity—on the serious task of dispelling racial myths and stereotypes." The author is a cofounder of the Accessible African Herstory Project and was described by the editors of* Ms. *as a "lecturer, herstorian, and craftswoman." Much of the article focuses on how language—ready-made phrases, loaded words—channel or distort our thinking. The article provides a guide to words that can raise hackles or short-circuit communication—in short, make people see red. This article should make you think about the power of words to shape our thinking and our views of other people.*

Thought Starters: Whatever the color of their skin, people tend to be thin-skinned when they encounter words that they perceive to be slurs on their group, religion, or background. Do you encounter ways of talking about a group with which you identify that you find embarrassing or offensive?

Cultural Etiquette is intended for people of all "races," nationalities, and creeds, not necessarily just "white" people, because no one living in Western society is exempt from the influences of racism, racial stereotypes, race and cultural prejudices, and anti-Semitism. I include anti-Semitism in the discussion of racism because it is simply another manifestation of cultural and racial bigotry.

All people are people. It is ethnocentric to use a generic term such as "people" to refer only to white people and then racially label everyone else. This creates and reinforces the assumption that whites are the norm, the real people, and that all others are aberrations.

"Exotic," when applied to human beings, is ethnocentric and racist.

While it is true that most citizens of the U.S.A. are white, at least four fifths of the world's population consists of people of color. Therefore, it is statistically incorrect as well as ethnocentric to refer to us as minorities. The term "minority" is used to reinforce the idea of people of color as "other."

A cult is a particular system of religious worship. If the religious practices of the Yorubas constitute a cult, then so do those of the Methodists, Catholics, Episcopalians, and so forth.

A large radio/tape player is a boom-box, or a stereo or a box or a large metallic ham sandwich with speakers. It is not a "ghetto blaster."

Everybody can blush. Everybody can bruise. Everybody can tan and get sunburned. Everybody.

Judaism is no more patriarchal than any other patriarchal religion.

Koreans are not taking over. Neither are Jews. Neither are the Japanese. Neither are the West Indians. These are myths put out and maintained by the ones who really have.

All hair is "good" hair. Dreadlocks, locks, dreads, natty dreads, et   *10* cetera, is an ancient traditional way that African people sometimes wear their hair. It is not braided, it is "locked." Locking is the natural tendency of African hair to knit and bond to itself. It locks by itself, we don't have to do anything to it to make it lock. It is permanent; once locked, it cannot come undone. It gets washed just as regularly as anyone else's hair. No, you may not touch it, don't ask.

One of the most effective and insidious aspects of racism is cultural genocide. Not only have African Americans been cut off from our African tribal roots, but because of generations of whites pitting African against Indian, and Indian against African, we have been cut off from our Native American roots as well. Consequently, most African Native Americans no longer have tribal affiliations, or know for certain what people they are from.

Columbus didn't discover diddly-squat.

Slavery is not a condition unique to African people. In fact, the word "slave" comes from the Slav people of Eastern Europe. Because so many Slavs were enslaved by other people (including Africans), their very name came to be synonymous with the condition.

Native Americans were also enslaved by Europeans. Because it is almost impossible to successfully enslave large numbers of people in their own land, most enslaved Native Americans from the continental U.S. were shipped to Bermuda, and the West Indies, where many intermarried with the Africans.

People do not have a hard time because of their race or cultural   *15* background. No one is attacked, abused, oppressed, pogromed, or enslaved because of their race, creed, or cultural background. People are attacked, abused, oppressed, pogromed, or enslaved because of racism and anti-Semitism. There is a subtle but important difference in the focus here. The first implies some inherent fault or shortcoming within the oppressed person or group. The second redirects the responsibility back to the real source of the problem.

Asians are not "mysterious," "fatalistic," or "inscrutable."

Native Americans are not stoic, mystical, or vanishing.

Latin people are no more hot-tempered, hot-blooded, or emotional than anyone else. We do not have flashing eyes, teeth, or daggers. We are lovers pretty much like other people. Very few of us deal with any kind of drugs.

Middle Easterners are not fanatics, terrorists, or all oil-rich.

Jewish people are not particularly rich, clannish, or expert in money 20 matters.

Not all African Americans are poor, athletic, or ghetto-dwellers.

Most Asians in the U.S. are not scientists, mathematicians, geniuses, or wealthy.

Southerners are no less intelligent than anybody else.

It is not a compliment to tell someone: "I don't think of you as Jewish/ Black/Asian/Latina/Middle Eastern/Native American." Or "I think of you as white."

Do not use a Jewish person or person of color to hear your confession 25 of past racist transgressions. If you have offended a particular person, then apologize directly to that person.

Also don't assume that Jews and people of color necessarily want to hear about how prejudiced your Uncle Fred is, no matter how terrible you think he is.

If you are white and/or gentile, do not assume that the next Jewish person or person of color you see will feel like discussing this guide with you. Sometimes we get tired of teaching this subject.

If you are white, don't brag to a person of color about your overseas trip to our homeland. Especially when we cannot afford such a trip. Similarly, don't assume that we are overjoyed to see the expensive artifacts you bought.

Words like "gestapo," "concentration camp" and "Hitler" are only appropriate when used in reference to the Holocaust.

"Full-blood," "half-breed," "quarter-blood." Any inference that a 30 person's "race" depends on blood is racist. Natives are singled out for this form of bigotry and are denied rights on that basis.*

"Scalping": a custom also practiced by the French, the Dutch, and the English.*

Do you have friends or acquaintances who are terrific except they're really racist? If you quietly accept that part of them, you are giving their racism tacit approval.

As an exercise, pretend you are from another planet and you want an example of a typical human being for your photo album. Having never heard of racism, you'd probably pick someone who represents the majority of the people on the planet—an Asian person.

How many is too many? We have heard well-meaning liberals say things like "This event is too white. We need more people of color." Well, how many do you need? Fifty? A hundred? Just what is your standard for personal racial comfort?

* Reprinted with permission from *The Pathfinder Directory,* by Amylee, Native American Indian Resource Center. [Author's note]

People of color and Jewish people have been so all their lives. Further, *35* if we have been raised in a place where white gentiles predominate, then we have been subjected to racism/anti-Semitism all our lives. We are therefore experts on our own lives and conditions. If you do not understand or believe or agree with what someone is saying about their own oppression, do not automatically assume that they are wrong or paranoid or oversensitive.

It is not "racism in reverse" or "segregation" for Jews or people of color to come together in affinity groups for mutual support. Sometimes we need some time and space apart from the dominant group just to relax and be ourselves. If people coming together for group support makes you feel excluded, perhaps there's something missing in your own life or cultural connections.

The various cultures of people of color often seem very attractive to white people. (Yes, we are wonderful, we can't deny it.) But white people should not make a playground out of other people's cultures. We are not quaint. We are not exotic. We are not cool.

Don't forget that every white person alive today is also descended from tribal peoples. If you are white, don't neglect your own ancient traditions. They are as valid as anybody else's, and the ways of your own ancestors need to be honored and remembered.

"Race" is an arbitrary and meaningless concept. Races among humans don't exist. If there ever was any such thing as race, there has been so much constant crisscrossing of genes for the last 500,000 years that it would have lost all meaning anyway. There are no real divisions between us, only a continuum of variations that constantly change, as we come together and separate according to the movement of human populations.

Anyone who functions in what is referred to as the "civilized" world *40* is a carrier of the disease of racism.

Does reading this guide make you uncomfortable? Angry? Confused? Are you taking it personally? Well, not to fret. Racism has created a big horrible mess, and racial healing can sometimes be painful. Just remember that Jews and people of color do not want or need anybody's guilt. We just want people to accept responsibility when it is appropriate, and actively work for change.

The Responsive Reader

1. The writer attacks stereotypes about hot-blooded Latins, inscrutable Asians, athletic blacks, rich Jews, Middle Eastern terrorists, and others. Which of these stereotypes have you encountered—where and how? Have they shaped your own thinking?
2. What are the author's objections to the terms *minority, exotic, cult, half-breed, racism in reverse,* and *race* itself? What other uses of language does

she ask you to reconsider? How serious or valid do her objections seem to you?

3. When conversations turn on sensitive subjects, it is easy to say the wrong thing. What advice does this guide to etiquette give for conversations with people from different ethnic or cultural backgrounds? What pitfalls does Three Rivers warn against? How helpful or valid are her warnings?

4. The author uses weighty words like *ethnocentric, anti-Semitism, bigotry, genocide*. What do these words mean to you? How does the author use them?

5. The writer defends herself against the charge of being oversensitive — do you think she is?

Talking, Listening, Writing

6. The author says that "no one living in Western society is exempt from the influences of racism." Do you agree?

7. At the end, Three Rivers asks, "Does reading this guide make you uncomfortable? Angry? Confused? Are you taking it personally?" What are your answers to these questions?

8. What has been your own experience with the power of language to hurt people, to divide them, or to hold them back?

Collaborative Projects

9. Many colleges have considered speech codes aimed at hate speech or offensive language. Working with a group, investigate the history and the pros and cons of such initiatives.

A BATTLE OVER A NAME IN THE LAND OF THE SIOUX

Andrew Brownstein

> *What's in a name? In the seventies, the Stanford University football team ceased to be the Stanford Indians and became the Stanford Cardinals. A student vote had agreed that the Indian label brought negative stereotypes into play. Professional football teams still call themselves the Redskins or the Braves, although there is no team calling itself the Palefaces. One team still calls itself the Buffalo Bills, after a notorious killer of Native Americans. The following article is a shortened version of an article in* The Chronicle of Higher Education, *a professional journal for educators that examines issues affecting colleges and faculties in carefully researched and documented articles. As the author says, "mascot controversies come and go" in the academic world, but some are more costly, long-drawn-out, and divisive than others.*

Thought Starters: How important are sports teams to the image of a college or university? What would Notre Dame be without its football team? Do any traditional names, logos, or mascots of college teams have a special meaning for you? Do you know of any that have been changed in reponse to pressure or criticism?

GRAND FORKS, N.D.

The message came in March, when winter lingers and the frost still   *1*
covers the silent prairie that surrounds the University of North Dakota.

The sender was anonymous. The recipient was Ira Taken Alive, a former student at the university who is a Lakota Sioux and the son of a tribal elder at the Standing Rock Indian Reservation.

"I assume this is the guy who wants to change the Fighting Sioux name," the e-mail message began. Mr. Taken Alive, a junior in 1999, when he received the message, had challenged the name of the university's sports teams, which he felt demeaned his people and stood as a barrier to the progress of American Indians in general.

As he sat in front of his computer, he read on: "There are many people who want your head, no joking. I am not one of those people, but I have heard some nasty talk by people about doing stuff to you. So take this from me, a concerned human being, watch out for your life."

University officials were never able to trace the source. But Mr. Taken   *5*
Alive says he had had enough—of the endless debates, the taunts, the

vandalism to his car—that came from fighting the Fighting Sioux. In the fall, he transferred to another university; he returned quietly last summer to finish his degree.

Withdrawing a Huge Gift

Mascot controversies come and go in academe. But words can be costly in the ancestral home of Crazy Horse and Sitting Bull, on a campus where American Indians are the largest minority group.

This past December, it looked like the name debate might exact a very specific price: $100-million. That was the amount that Ralph Engelstad, a Las Vegas casino owner, had promised to his alma mater, largely to build a luxurious new hockey arena that would bear his name. In a sharply worded letter addressed to the university's president, he threatened to abandon the half-completed project, which he was personally overseeing, if the university dropped the Fighting Sioux name.

President Charles E. Kupchella, following protests by students and tribal leaders, had formed a commission that had been investigating the naming controversy for five months. He planned to announce his decision after New Year's. But a day after he and members of the State Board of Higher Education received the letter, the board launched a pre-emptive strike, voting 8-0 to keep the name.

It has not helped public relations at the university that its benefactor has a troubled past in the area of racial sensitivity. In 1988, Nevada authorities discovered that Mr. Engelstad had held two parties on Hitler's birthday, and kept a trove of Nazi paraphernalia at his Imperial Palace hotel and casino. He was fined $1.5-million for damaging the reputation of the State of Nevada.

That the episode has turned surreal is a fact that not even the univer- *10*
sity's seasoned flacks try to conceal. "Oh, it's strange," says Peter B. Johnson, the college's spokesman. "It could be a movie script."

Where Two Worlds Converge

Grand Forks, population 49,000, sits where the Red Lake River meets the Red River of the North. But the university here may as well be the convergence of two worlds.

For most of the athletes and fans on this campus of 11,000, the Fighting Sioux name is a source of pride and honor. The powerhouse men's hockey team won Division I's "Frozen Four" championship last year; over the decades, the team has sent 54 players to the National Hockey League.

The university can also lay claim to being one of the top institutions for American Indians in the country. It houses 25 American Indian programs—mostly financed with federal grants—including *Native Directions,* a quarterly student magazine of American Indian life and culture; an Indian studies major; and the Indians Into Medicine program, which credits itself with training a fifth of the Native American doctors in the country.

Yet, there is a disconnect. Many of the 350 American Indian students at North Dakota say that beneath the campus's Main Street friendliness lies a dark current of racism, a facet of university life that the name controversy has brought uncomfortably to the surface.

"They say they keep the name to honor and respect us, but those   *15* words have lost all meaning," says Alva Irwin, a Hidatsa Indian and senior majoring in social work and Indian studies. "How can they honor us by keeping something we clearly don't want?"

Once known as the Flickertails, the university's intercollegiate sports teams have been called the Sioux since 1930, when the name was changed to strike fear into the hearts of the Bison at rival North Dakota State University, in Fargo. There were no protests at the time, because there were virtually no American Indian students here. Native Americans didn't start attending the university in large numbers until the 1960's.

Ugly Incidents

Once on campus, they saw that the use of the name extended far beyond athletics. In 1972, fraternity members at the now-defunct King Kold Karnival created a lurid sculpture of a naked Indian woman, with a sign reading "Lick 'em Sioux"; an American Indian student was briefly jailed after he got into a fight over the sculpture with fraternity members, sending three of them to the hospital.

Tensions ran high again in 1992, when onlookers at a homecoming parade performed the Atlanta Braves' "tomahawk chop" as dancing American Indian children passed on a float, and then yelled at them to "go back to the reservation."

As recently as this past fall, says one student, Michael Grant, fraternity members dressed as cowboys and Indians flashed a cap gun at his wife and infant daughter. "Do you realize what would have happened if I had been there?" says Mr. Grant, an Omaha Indian and a sophomore majoring in Indian studies. "I wouldn't be here, man. I'd be in jail."

The name always takes center stage whenever the Bison come to   *20* town. In the 1990's, North Dakota State fans started chanting "Sioux suck" during games, and, over the years, the slogan has taken on ever more inventive permutations.

For years, it was impossible to drive down Interstate 29 from Grand Forks to Fargo without seeing the abandoned barn with the giant slogan painted on it. And then there's the T-shirt worn by North Dakota State fans. It shows a stereotypical American Indian suggestively between the legs of a bison. A caption reads, "We saw. They sucked. We came."

"It's like we're not even human," says Anjanette Parisien, a Chippewa senior majoring in biology and Indian studies.

"This Is Sioux Territory"

Earl Strinden doesn't see it that way. The semi-retired chief executive officer of the university's alumni association and Mr. Engelstad's friend for 40 years, Mr. Strinden helped clinch the 1998 deal that culminated in the $100-million pledge.

Wearing a sports coat in the school's signature green, he marches over to a framed map of the Dakota territories that graces a wall in his campus office. He points to faded print marking what was once the Great Sioux Nation. "This is Sioux territory, for crying out loud!" he says.

The point is made again and again by alumni: The Sioux are indeli- 25 bly etched into the state's lore and culture. To rid the campus of the name would be to rob the state of one of its great traditions and to further isolate American Indians.

"When the hockey team plays in Boston, the people will think, 'Fighting Sioux, what's that?'" Mr. Strinden says. "They'll want to find out about the Sioux. There are those on this campus who want to make sure that Native Americans are always victims."

During the interview, two American Indian students in his office nod vigorously, as if the notion of hockey as export of Indian culture is self-evident.

"If we lose the name, it's going to help erase our culture," says Greg Holy Bull, a Lakota Sioux and a graduate student in fine arts.

A "Deplorable" Name

At the *Dakota Student,* the semi-weekly student newspaper, the subject of Mr. Engelstad and the name is something of a newsroom obsession. One Sunday, staff members vowed not to talk about the issue all day. The silence lasted until 3 p.m.

When Evan Nelson, the sports editor, first came to the university, he 30 thought "the whole issue was garbage." But after working the sports beat for a year and a half, he came to view the name as "deplorable."

"It was hearing all those ignorant bastards—the alumni, the athletes, the fans—talking about Indians that did it for me," says Mr. Nelson, a junior and a communications major from Sioux Falls, S.D.

He raised eyebrows among his sources with a recent column, in which he wrote that the state board's decision on the Fighting Sioux name was "an act of malice and contempt." The racism behind the name is subtle, Mr. Nelson says. "There are no hate crimes. It's not like the Deep South in the 60's, where police were brushing crowds with fire hoses." It's the "Injun" jokes and terms like "prairie nigger." It's in the oft-repeated comments that

Indians are all drunks or are going to college on the government dole. It's the person who will wear a jacket with the mascot of an Indian, but won't talk to one.

"My grandparents have been telling me since I was 2 years old that the Indians are stealing from us," he says. "This is a very white-bread part of the world."

To the majority of students—82 percent, according to a recent poll—the issue has nothing to do with racism. It's just the name of a sports team. Kim Srock, a sophomore discussing the debate in Jim McKenzie's advanced-composition class, expresses annoyance that so much is being made of a five-letter word.

"It's like, get a life," she says. "This is a game—it's not about Indians.   *35* They're like a bunch of crybabies. Get over it."

If the subject of race is the university's most divisive issue, hockey is its No. 1 passion. So it makes sense that the biggest controversy in recent years would be a combination of both.

The joke in this corner of the world is that children learn to skate before they can walk. The enthusiasm for the sport is hard to miss. On game day against the rival Golden Gophers of the University of Minnesota, ticket lines will start forming around noon, even in the sub-zero chill. Local merchants sell coffee and barbecued ribs as tailgaters, often in green and white face paint, warm themselves near bonfires.

They come to see players like Jeff Panzer, the center and a Grand Forks native, who is Division I's top scorer and a leading candidate for the Hobey Baker trophy, college hockey's equivalent of the Heisman.

The new arena, now estimated at over $85-million, promises to be an even bigger draw. Billed as one of the finest hockey stadiums in the nation, the complex will house 11,400 fans, 48 luxury skyboxes, and a second ice rink for Olympic-style play.

The Responsive Reader

1. How does Brownstein's introduction use the anonymous e-mail message to Ira Taken Alive to dramatize the issue? How would you have reacted to the message? How would you have reacted to the anonymous correspondent identifying himself as a "concerned human being"? How does the introduction sum up the basic issue?
2. How much do you learn here about the history or various stages of the controversy and the major players involved? Are you surprised by the action or actions of the university president? Are you surprised by the action of the State Board of Education? Are you surprised by the stance taken by the multimillion-dollar benefactor?
3. As you would expect in a professional journal, Brownstein tries to present both sides of the controversy. What evidence does he cite that for many athletes and fans "the Fighting Sioux name is a source of pride and

honor"? What evidence does he cite that the university is "one of the top institutions" for Native Americans in this country?

4. On the other hand, what evidence does Brownstein cite of the "dark current of racism" beneath the surface friendliness of the campus? What seems to have been the special role of fraternity members? (Do you think it is fair that fraternities are often mentioned in this kind of context?) Why was the benefactor's "troubled past" a special problem for the university? (The benefactor went on record saying that he despises everything Hitler stood for, that many other collectors collect Nazi memorabilia, and that the Hitler's birthday party was a joke.)

5. Some of the uglier details and incidents Brownstein describes relate to the taunting and juvenile rivalry between fans of competing teams. To you, do they seem more serious than that? Did they bring an ugly undercurrent of racism into play? Why or why not?

6. To judge from this article, do the protesters speak for themselves or for all or most Native American students on the campus? Do the students showing racist attitudes seem to represent a sizable portion or a majority of the student body? When you try to decide who is right and who is wrong, does it matter how strong or widespread support is on either side?

Talking, Listening, Writing

7. What images and associations do you and members of your generation associate with names like the Sioux, Chief Crazy Horse, and Sitting Bull? What do you think of the argument that keeping the team name will help honor the Native American past and keep the history of a proud people alive?

8. If you were of Irish American descent, would you object to a college team being named the "Fighting Irish"? Why or why not? Would this be a different matter from calling a college team the "Fighting Sioux"?

9. Have you seen instances of people protesting against prejudice or injustice being accused of perpetuating a "victim mentality"?

BILINGUALISM: ASSIMILATION IS MORE THAN ABCs

Jorge R. Mancillas

> Even the most acculturated Mexican–American writer faces the dilemma of straddling two languages and two cultures.
>
> Alejandro Portes

Like millions of immigrants and children of immigrants, Jorge R. Mancillas speaks English as a second language. He came to this country from Ensenada in Mexico and wrote the following article in 1993 while an assistant professor of anatomy and cell biology at the UCLA School of Medicine. He takes a stand on an issue of special concern in areas with large Spanish-speaking school populations, such as New York City, Miami, Texas, and California. What should the schools do for students whose proficiency in English is limited or nonexistent? The traditional policy had been immersion (or, more informally, sink or swim). Everyone was taught all subjects in English, and the use of any other language even during recess was discouraged or banned outright. This policy was once credited with turning the children of Jewish, Polish, German, Armenian, and Czech immigrants into Americans after a few years of schooling. In the seventies and eighties, with high dropout rates for ESL (English as a second language) students, a different policy was mandated by the federal government. Bilingual education provides instruction in subjects like reading, math, geography, and history in the students' original language, to keep them from falling behind while they are still learning English. Bilingual education has come in for much criticism: It has been charged with perpetuating the linguistic and cultural separation of immigrant children. It has had to grapple with inadequate funding, a shortage of bilingual teachers, and the proliferation of foreign languages among our school populations, ranging from Spanish to Vietnamese, Chinese, Tagalog, Lebanese, and Russian.

Thought Starters: Do you know people who are bilingual? How many of your classmates are bilingual? What is meant by "bilingual education"?

Imagine going from a working-class neighborhood in Ensenada to the   *1*
University of California at Berkeley. Having graduated from high school with the Mexican equivalent of a 4.0 GPA, having studied English and worked in my hometown's tourist industry, and having passed the TOEFL

(Test of English as a Foreign Language) without difficulties, I sat in my first lecture at Berkeley full of confidence and excitement.

I had just been exposed to the United States' dual immigration policy. For the first time in my life, I had been treated courteously by immigration officials: With a letter of acceptance from one of the world's most prestigious universities, my expected contribution to Mexico's brain drain was greeted with the prompt dispensation of a student visa. Now, sitting in the front row of a large lecture hall, I opened my notebook as the professor began to speak. A few minutes later, I was devastated.

Engaging in conversation with tourists at a hotel desk and passing the TOEFL were quite different from trying to grasp complex concepts in psychology delivered at the pace required by 10-week quarter terms. I was lost. Trying to absorb the material from the 600-page psychology textbook was no easier.

Still, that was the easiest part. I also had to fulfill the English 1A requirement, for which we had to read a text and write a report at the end of each week. Assigned reading for the first two weeks: Theodore Roszak's "The Making of the Counter-Culture" and Norman Mailer's "Miami and the Siege of Chicago." Quite a tall order for a boy who had grown up in Ensenada. It was more than the language that I was "deficient" in; it was the implied understanding of the culture and politics.

Sitting in the back of the classroom, I struggled for two quarters as   5 I had never struggled before in my life, and I barely managed to maintain a C average. My self-esteem was shattered. I forged ahead, however, understanding very well what the educational opportunity that I had before me meant to my future prospects. By the time I graduated, my grade average was up to an A, although my overall average was much lower due to the impact of the first quarters.

Years later, I find myself part of the faculty at the UCLA School of Medicine and the director of a research laboratory affiliated with UCLA's Brain Research Institute. Had I not been able to overcome the hurdles of my first few months at Berkeley, emotional as well as practical—and I almost didn't—my life and any contribution I may be able to make to society would have been very different.

This experience comes to mind when I hear arguments about bilingual education for the substantial proportion of children with limited English proficiency in the Los Angeles Unified School District. It is easy for me to understand the experience of children finding themselves in a new culture, wanting and struggling to master the English language but lagging behind in other subjects while they do. By the time they learn English— and almost invariably they do—they are behind academically; they are left with gaps in their academic development. Even worse, their self-esteem has suffered considerably, for at that tender age, their sense of self-worth is shaped to a large degree by their perception of how they measure up in comparison to, and in the eyes of, their peers.

Why would we want to academically disable and emotionally impair thousands of children instead of providing them with the mechanisms that allow for a healthy transition to their adopted culture?

The Mexican government's recent contribution of school texts and bilingual teachers to the LAUSD was born of compassion for Spanish-speaking children. It also was influenced by the government's intelligent understanding of Mexico's need to respond to ongoing changes in contemporary society; the Mexican educators who will be exposed to the U.S. educational system and culture will be a valuable resource upon returning to their country.

Children with limited English proficiency must be seen, like other 10 children, as a valuable resource, not as a hindrance or a burden. If we help them to integrate successfully into the mainstream while preserving their original language and cultural skills, they will be the bridge-builders this country needs to succeed in the global community.

This is a priceless resource: a new generation of Americans committed to preserving and strengthening a democratic and pluralistic U.S. society, but also having a birthright familiarity with Latin American, Asian or Middle Eastern societies. Think of what these children might contribute in an age of revolutions in communications and development that we, today, can hardly imagine.

Against this possibility, the alternative is ludicrous: to create a large population of school dropouts, hostile to the mythical "mainstream American culture" to which, they are made to feel, they have nothing to contribute because they are culturally and linguistically deficient.

Those who oppose bilingual education are propelled more by fear of others and insecurity about their own capabilities, identity, and culture. To follow them is to go against the current of history and embark on a futile attempt to become culturally insular and ethnically "clean." Our only other choice is to embrace change and learn the value of diverse expressions of the human experience as a strong basis for our place in the global society of the 21st Century. From that perspective, the monetary cost of bilingual education is trivial and a sound investment in the future.

The Responsive Reader

1. Advocates of bilingual education stress the adverse effect that English-only instruction has on students' overall academic performance and on their self-image or self-esteem. What light does Mancillas's experience throw on this issue?
2. What for Mancillas are the social costs of failure to integrate second-language students "successfully into the mainstream"?
3. A much-debated question is whether bilingual education should be a "transition" to full English proficiency or whether students should at the same time "maintain" their first language and culture. What is Mancillas's answer to this question? What are the reasons for the stand he takes?

Talking, Listening, Reading

4. What has been your own experience or what has shaped your own views on the issue of bilingualism? Is it an issue in schools you know?
5. Mancillas uses or alludes to buzzwords that have played a prominent role in public discourse in recent years: *ethnic cleansing, pluralism, diversity, a global perspective.* Why and where does he use them and with what effect?

Find It on the Web

During strong English-only agitation in the late nineties, the controversy over bilingual education escalated. Various legislative initiatives were aimed at ending bilingual education, and voters in California passed an anti-bilingual referendum. Rosalie Pedalino Porter's "The Case against Bilingual Education" (*Atlantic* May 1998) forcefully stated the arguments of those who declared bilingual education "a failure" and were forcing school districts to abandon their bilingual programs. You may want to do a quick-search on the Internet to find news on recent developments or initiatives.

RETURN OF THE CLICHÉ EXPERT
Roger Angell

> *Some people sound like a commercial that has been run too many times. They speak and write in clichés—tired and predictable phrases that sound as if they came to the speaker all ready-made and strung together ready for use:* a run for their money, throw in the towel, only the tip of the iceberg, the window of opportunity, the cutting edge, *and* the bottom line. *Some of these may at one time have been clever or imaginative, but they have lost their flavor, like stale bread. To say it in the language of clichés:* To be brutally frank, and not to put too fine a point on it, the bloom is off such expressions (to coin a phrase), and in this day and age they are far from being a sure winner in the hearts and minds of men and women from all walks of life, and in the final analysis, when all is said and done, they do more harm than good. *The* New Yorker *magazine for many years ran a feature with the cliché expert parodying contemporaries who fall back on trite, ready-made expressions rather than using fresh language to communicate some fresh thinking of their own. Recently, the cliché expert returned to take stock of the buzzwords of a new, proactive, computer-literate generation.*

Thought Starters: How aware are you of changing fashions in the way people use words? Do you or your friends use expressions like, "You don't want to go there," or, "It doesn't get any better than this"? Do you ever say, "No problema"? Does anyone still say, "You've made my day"?

Q: Good morning, Mr. Arbuthnot. It's a pleasure to see you again, and to hear further testimony from you on the subject of clichés.   1

A: Wrong man. You're thinking of my uncle, Dr. Magnus Arbuthnot, who is no longer with us. Bought the farm, checked out, fumed out, popped off, slipped his cable, went over the pass, hit the throughway. I mean, he's gone-zo. I'm Chip Arbuthnot, his heir. His *spiritual* heir.

Q: But you are here to give us your views on current and established clichés, are you not?

A: No way.

Q: You're not?   5

A: I'm here to share my views.

Q: I see. And you are an expert in the field, are you not?

A: Arguably.

Q: You wish to argue with the court?

A: No, I'm arguably an expert. The adverb allows me to say some-   10
thing and then partly take it back.

Q: I think I understand.

A: Don't worry about it. This stuff isn't written in stone.

Q: You're very kind.

A: There's a reason for that.

Q: I can almost guess what it is. It's on the tip of my tongue.   *15*

A: I'm a people person.

Q: I knew it! Now, Mr. Arbuthnot, may I ask a strange question? What's that on your head?

A: This is my other hat.

Q: Your *other* hat?

A: This is the hat I wear when I'm being the cliché expert. When I'm   *20*
doing something else, I wear a different other hat, not this one.

Q: Hmm. Are you telling us that being a cliché expert is not a full-time occupation?

A: As if. Get a grip.

Q: You must be a busy man, holding so many demanding jobs.

A: None of this is rocket science. But, yes, my plate is full.

Q: And you must have to maintain a constant schedule of travels to   *25*
different parts of the country, if not the world, to keep up with regional as
well as occupational clichés, is that not the case?

A: Been there, done that.

Q: Tell me, do most people know when they're speaking in clichés?
Or is that a dumb question?

A: I'm not comfortable with it. If I said it was a no-brainer, I'd be
sending the wrong message. Let's say that some folks who think they're
pushing the envelope conversationwise ain't.

Q: Mr. Arbuthnot, are there specific occupations that produce a
greater preponderance of clichés in daily human intercourse than others do?

A: "Daily human intercourse" is very fine. Congratulations.   *30*

Q: Shall I repeat the question?

A: No, because I'm going to pass. This is a slippery slope.

Q: What about the sexes? Are women more likely than men to—

A: Whoa. Back off, Mister. Don't go there. It's a no-win situation.

Q: Oh, I'm sorry.   *35*

A: You're putting me between a rock and a hard place.

Q: I didn't mean to upset you. I apologize.

A: You mean you empathize.

Q: That's what I meant to say.

A: You feel my pain.   *40*

Q: Yes, I do, I do!

A: Historically, you have concerns.

Q: That's right!

A: Unless I miss my guess, you're also pro-active.

Q: Yup.   *45*

A: At the same time, you're a very private person.

Q: Absolutely. How did you know?

A: Trust me, it's easy. All you have to do is listen to your inner child.

Q: So any of us can become a cliché expert—is that what you're saying?

A: How did we end up here? Hello?   *50*

Q: Oop, I'm going too fast again, aren't I? Just *using* clichés doesn't do the trick—is that right?

A: No. You have to talk the talk and walk the walk.

Q: But of course. I wish we could go on with this and perhaps find out how you got to ask all the questions, instead of the court. But our time is up. I hope you've enjoyed our little meeting.

A: You've made my day.

Q: You have enlightened us all.   *55*

A: It doesn't get any better than this.

Q: Thank you, Mr. Arbuthnot.

A: No problema.

The Responsive Reader

1. How up-to-date are you on buzzwords and current clichés? Have you heard people talk about wearing different hats? When do people talk about a no-win situation? What do people mean when they use the terms *no-brainer, counter-intuitive, pushing the envelope,* and *a full plate?*

2. People may pick up new buzzwords because they fit in well with the way they think or with their personal agendas. Who uses the expression *the bottom line*—when, where, and for what purpose? When do people use expressions like, "It's not written in stone," or, "This is not rocket science"? Why do they say, "I'm not comfortable with it"? What signal do they give when they say, "We have concerns"? What purposes does the expression *slippery slope* serve? What's the difference between giving your views and sharing your views? Why does Angell think there is something wrong with the term *arguably?*

Talking, Listening, Writing

3. Do you use one kind of language when you are trying to impress people and another kind of language when relaxing with your friends? Can you give examples of the two contrasting ways of saying things?

Collaborative Projects

4. The language of politics and political campaigns is shot through with buzzwords and clichés. For instance, when and why did politicians start to talk about a color-blind society? When and how did "preferences" get to be a dirty word? Working with a group, you may want to investigate current trends in political rhetoric.

HOW AVERY GOT TO BE A PREACHER

August Wilson

> *August Wilson is a spectacularly successful African American playwright whose endlessly talkative characters speak a version of Black English. His widely discussed and reviewed plays include* Joe Turner's Come and Gone *and* Seven Guitars. *The following excerpt is from Wilson's* The Piano Lesson, *a play first staged by the Yale Repertory Theatre in 1988. An interviewer asked Wilson, "Don't you grow weary of thinking black, writing black, being asked questions about being black?" Wilson answered, "Whites don't get tired of thinking white or being who they are. I'm just who I am. You never transcend who you are. Black is not limiting. There's no idea in the world that is not contained by black life. I could write forever about the black experience in America."*

Thought Starters: In your own everyday encounters, where are you most aware of language differences? What are some examples? How do you react?

BOY WILLIE How you get to be a preacher, Avery? I might want to be a   *1*
preacher one day. Have everybody call me Reverend Boy Willie.

AVERY It come to me in a dream. God called me and told me he wanted
me to be a shepherd for his flock. That's what I'm gonna call my
church . . . The Good Shepherd Church of God in Christ.

DOAKER Tell him what you told me. Tell him about the three hobos.

AVERY Boy Willie don't want to hear all that.

LYMON I do. Lots a people say your dreams can come true.   *5*

AVERY Naw. You don't want to hear all that.

DOAKER Go on. I told him you was a preacher. He didn't want to believe
me. Tell him about the three hobos.

AVERY Well, it come to me in a dream. See . . . I was sitting out in this
railroad yard watching the trains go by. The train stopped and these
three hobos got off. They told me they had come from Nazareth and
was on their way to Jerusalem. They had three candles. They gave me
one and told me to light it . . . but to be careful that it didn't go out.
Next thing I knew I was standing in front of this house. Something
told me to go knock on the door. This old woman opened the door
and said they had been waiting on me. Then she led me into this
room. It was a big room and it was full of all kinds of different people.
They looked like anybody else except they all had sheep heads and
was making noise like sheep make. I heard somebody call my name. I
looked around and there was these same three hobos. They told me

to take off my clothes and they give me a blue robe with gold thread. They washed my feet and combed my hair. Then they showed me these three doors and told me to pick one.

I went through one of them doors and that flame leapt off that candle and it seemed like my whole head caught fire. I looked around and there was four or five other men standing there with these same blue robes on. Then we heard a voice tell us to look out across this valley. We looked out and saw the valley was full of wolves. The voice told us that these sheep people that I had seen in the other room had to go over to the other side of this valley and somebody had to take them. Then I heard another voice say, "Who shall I send?" Next thing I knew I said, "Here I am. Send me." That's when I met Jesus. He say, "If you go, I'll go with you." Something told me to say, "Come on. Let's go." That's when I woke up. My head still felt like it was on fire . . . but I had a peace about myself that was hard to explain. I knew right then that I had been filled with the Holy Ghost and called to be a servant of the Lord. It took me a while before I could accept that. But then a lot of little ways God showed me that it was true. So I became a preacher.

LYMON I see why you gonna call it the Good Shepherd Church. You   *10*
dreaming about them sheep people. I can see that easy.

(Act One, Scene 1)

The Responsive Reader

1. Students of religious history have been fascinated with how different parts of the world have adapted religious traditions to new situations and brought them close to the thinking and lives of local congregations. What ideas and what of the language of traditional Christian teaching play a role in this passage? How have they been changed or adapted to a different audience or a different context?

2. The language of this passage shows some basic features of Black English, while at the same time it stays closer than other versions to the more formal language of the Bible and traditional preaching. Can you describe some of the features of Black English illustrated here? How do they contrast with school English or media English?

Talking, Listening, Writing

3. In the past, regional varieties or social dialects of English have often been the butt of dialect jokes and ethnic humor. Do you think audiences of your generation are ready to respond seriously to the use of language in this play? Why or why not?

4. If you had been involved in the original production of Wilson's play, would you have recommended that he change the language to something closer to standard English? Why or why not?

5. One African American playwright said that productions about black singers or musicians or other entertainers have "left the lives of millions of black people who don't sing and dance for a living unattended to" in the theater or in the media. Is the media treatment of African Americans still tilted toward entertainers? Where and how?

A GATHERING OF DEAFS

John Heaviside

> *Researchers like Oliver Sacks have written about the heightened sensitivity, or acuteness of other senses, that people who are color-blind or have other impairments may develop to compensate for what we normally see as deficiencies. Authors writing about the deaf community have written about the hearing-impaired not as medical cases or people with disabilities but as people who share a rich culture, historically conditioned and transmitted across generations. In that culture, signed languages (sign languages or gesture languages) play a central role. Authors writing about the structure and uses of American Sign Language (ASL) have stressed the "linguistic richness" of the languages of the deaf, describing them as "rich systems with complex structures that reflect their long histories." John Heaviside wrote the following poem about the deaf as a student and published it in the* Olivetree Review, *a publication devoted to student work at Hunter College of the City University of New York.*

Thought Starters: What do you know about or what experience have you had with alternative language or writing systems like braille or ASL?

By the turnstiles   *1*
in the station
where the L train greets
the downtown six there was
a congregation of deafs   *5*
passing forth
a jive wild
and purely physical
in a world dislocated
from the subway howling   *10*
hard sole shoe stampede
punk rock blasted radio
screaming, pounding, honking
they gather in community
lively and serene, engaging   *15*
in a dexterous conversation

An old woman
of her dead husband tells
caressing the air
with wrinkled fingers that demonstrate the story with   *20*
delicate, mellifluous motion
she places gentle configurations before the faces of the group

A young Puerto Rican
describes a fight with his mother emphasizing each word
with abrupt, staccato movements jerking his elbows   *25*
and twisting his wrists
teeth clenched and lips pressed
he concluded the story
by pounding his fist
into his palm   *30*

By the newsstand
two lovers express emotion
caressing the air
with syllables
graceful and slow   *35*
joining their thoughts
by the flow of fingertips

The Responsive Reader

1. How does the world of sound acquire negative connotations in this poem? How does it set the scene for the contrasting world of the deaf?
2. What do you learn from this poem about the signed language of the deaf as a language? What are key features it shares with spoken language? How is it different?
3. What are the usual meanings of *serene, dexterous, mellifluous, staccato, congregation?* How does the poet transpose these words to the culture of the deaf?
4. Why or how did the poet select the "speakers" that he asks us to focus on in this poem?

Talking, Listening, Writing

5. What has been your experience with people with impaired sight, hearing, or mobility? How much do you know from firsthand experience or observation? How much is hearsay or stereotype?
6. What is the reaction of people in our society to the hearing-impaired? How are attitudes in our society changing toward people with disabilities? How much progress has society made toward recognizing the needs and rights of the disabled?

Collaborative Projects

7. Many colleges now employ interpreters who translate oral instruction into signed language. If you can, arrange for such a person to come and speak to your class about the language of the deaf.

FORUM: *Language and Social Class*

The way we talk enables people to put us into mental bins. They stereotype us as "one of us" or "one of them." They mentally earmark us as middle class or lower class, educated or uneducated, Southerner or Yankee, American-born or immigrant. In many other countries, language differences are even more conspicuous as telltale signs of social class or regional identity than in ours. In London, bankers speak a kind of BBC English that sounds snooty to most Americans, while cab drivers speak a Cockney dialect that is nearly unintelligible to the visitor.

It is often said that in this country language differences are less obvious than in countries where people in isolated rural areas speak a local dialect hardly understood by their city cousins. The way Americans move and mingle has prevented the development of regional differences that could become true barriers. In addition, first the movies and radio and then television have had a leveling effect. Nevertheless, language differences continue to play a huge but often unexamined role as markers of social class and of ethnic or regional origin.

Millions of Americans have always been bilingual. They learned American English as a second language, allowing them to function and do business beyond the circle of their family and friends or tightly knit ethnic group. Their English showed traces of the Italian, Polish, Chinese, or Yiddish they brought from across the sea—or of the Spanish their ancestors spoke in what was once part of Mexico. Other millions of Americans have always been bidialectal. They grew up with a variety of English different from school English and media English. They spoke a rural dialect or downhome variety of English at home, in the neighborhood, and with their friends. They learned to speak and write standard English as the language of school and office, of the media and public life.

Since our accents or dialects serve others as a class marker or as a means of outgrouping and ingrouping, many have always worked at "crossing over" to a prestige dialect. They have tried hard to move from country talk to city talk, from a heavy Irish brogue to refined Harvard English, from a Yiddish-tinged New Yorkerese to something less ethnic. School systems have often held out the promise of linguistic assimilation. If minority students learned to "talk white," then maybe society—teachers, employers—would treat them as if they were white. Today this program of linguistic upgrading or language assimilation works for some, but it fails to work for many others. Why?

SMALL TAWK

Mark Francis Cohen

> *Outside your family or group of friends, do you "watch your language"? The novelist Tom Wolfe, noted for his flashy, flamboyant style, said that in the South it is "considered very good form, and very macho" for successful or upper-class males to speak with "downhome accents." He said that this would never happen in New York—successful people or wannabe sophisticates would never slip "into a Brooklyn street accent." Other observers have noticed people from Texas or the Midwest changing their way of talking: The world-renowned American poet T. S. Eliot, from St. Louis, moved to England and spoke with an acquired Oxford accent. The widely syndicated pundit George Will name-drops Harvard and Oxford and hardly ever mentions that he is a homeboy from a small burg in Illinois. The following article looks at both the funny side and the serious side of a basic fact of American life: The natural way of talking of many working-class Americans in our big cities is different from what English teachers and media pundits consider good English. Mark Francis Cohen is a New York–based freelance journalist who used to cover Brooklyn for the staid* New York Times.

Thought Starters: Do you adjust the way you talk for different groups, different contexts, different situations? Where and how?

Sitting in his cluttered Manhattan office, Sam Chwat, accent coach   *1*
to the stars, is holding court with one of his not-so-famous clients in what amounts to a public flogging. The subject of the flogging is an upwardly mobile woman with short, chestnut-colored hair and a knit sweater wrapped around her shoulders, who has come here to eliminate her cumbersome Brooklyn accent. Every session costs $185, but it's worth it, she says, for a chance to learn from the man who once tutored—and cured—Tony Danza.

Chwat (whose name, he tells me, is pronounced Sh-wah but is usually mispronounced by New Yorkers as Sh-whaat?) implores the woman to begin chatting about her children just so he can pounce on every offensive sound she emits. Soon, in the middle of her sixth attempt to say "six-yeehshuld" like a Midwesterner, Chwat erupts: "Wai, wai, wait! You're screwing it up. If you pucker, it's going to screw it up. A puckered 's' is going to give you a 'sh.' Like 'In the office she . . .' try *that*—without puckering."

"In-thuh-aw-fish-she," she gurgles.

"I need an 's,'" he chimes.

"In the aw-fis-she."   *5*

"That's it! And—"

"Six-yeers-old."

"You got it, and she had a list of what?"

"She hadda lish ah . . ."

"Don't pucker!"

"She hadda lish ah quesh-chuns."

"You blew it!"

Slowly, she says: "She had a list of quest-chuns."

"You're right!" Later, Chwat declares: "It's important to note she doesn't have a lisp. This is just a local thing."

Of course, Brooklynese is more than a local thing. It is perhaps the most recognizable regionalism in the world, thanks mainly to movies and television, which have transformed it into an emblem of class as much as of place. Yet, in the borough of Brooklyn, of all places, Brooklynese is suddenly on the brink of extinction or at least some serious evolution—thanks to the old ethnic Brooklynites, who no longer want to speak it, and to the new ethnic Brooklynites, who are changing it beyond recognition.

Of course, it was ethnic groups that created Brooklynese in the first place. First it was the early Dutch and French settlers, trying to learn English after the British captured Brooklyn in 1664. These groups, which already had trouble pronouncing the King's "th"s, assumed the Cockney sounds around them—and that meant eliminating the final "r" in many words, just like the colonists. And so the ancestors of Brooklyn's mudduhs were born.

In the 1840s, Irish immigrants added a muscularity to the dialect. The Irish tongue made "th"s into hard "t"s and "ir"s into "oi"s—thirty-third became "toity-tird." Turn-of-the-century Italian immigrants found the Brooklyn tone flat and flavorless, devoid of rhythm, and so they imbued the vowels with a sing-songy passion. Thus, "mayyn." But—whoops!—they robbed some words of their consonants. Ergo, "tawwk." Meanwhile, Jews speaking Yiddish were arriving in droves, striking new intonation riffs as well as word substitutions. Declarative sentences sounded like questions? Wordsrantogether, and "v"s replaced "w"s. Ultimately, on a steamy summer day, as kids played stickball and fire hydrants sprayed water on the streets below, it was not uncommon to hear an apartment dweller produce a hands-in-the-air wail of "Oh-pin-duh-vinda-awe-red-de!"

By 1950, Brooklynese had become nationally recognized—and derided. According to Margaret Mannix Flynn, a former professor of speech at Brooklyn College who is generally considered the doyenne of Brooklynese, the advent of radio, movies, and television would, oddly enough, diminish its real use. For one thing, whenever a movie character invoked the Brooklyn warble, Flynn observes, "he was always the poor schlump. And he spoke the language that the average guy and gal could identify with." Meanwhile, radio and television broadcasts were entering more homes. To the extent that news segments were suddenly being heard and seen all over, announcers had to be starkly accentless and regionally unspecific. With this need for crushing universality, a standard American English was born—the so-called newscaster's speech. Whereas Brooklynites once took pride in the fraternity of the accent, people now understood it to be a feature of the working class, an association that sticks to this day. As the borough's aspiring eggheads and social climbers became conscious of the accent's symbolism, they decided to rid themselves—and their children—of it. In the ensuing years, as the aspiring middle class fled to the suburbs of Long Island and New Jersey, a new wave of Southern blacks and Puerto Ricans took their place and made their own mark. Spanish, for example, has pushed the accent in a different direction—providing us with the quick, guttural sounds we have today.

Not that Brooklynese has lost all of its familiar features: it's still blind to things like final "r"s and, in some of the neighborhoods, still home to "youse," as in "youse guyz." Yet, given the dizzying variety of Brooklyn's new immigrants—remember, it's not just Hispanics, but Russians, Chinese, Dominicans, Jamaicans, and Haitians, too—most linguistic experts predict it's only a matter of time before traditional Brooklynese morphs into something wholly different. "It's dying," announces William Stewart, a linguist at the CUNY Graduate Center. "Any place you have immigration, differences are created; and, as children interact, these differences get leveled off, and a new variety is formed."

A week has passed since the session in Sam Chwat's office. Alan Rodin, 20
a speech pathologist who teaches accent elimination, is giving me a tour of Brighton Beach, which is now predominantly Russian. He's conducting an informal survey of how young people speak, and at one point near the boardwalk he approaches an eleven-year-old boy who has brown hair, deeply set blue eyes, and a down-to-his-knees black T-shirt. When the boy confirms his Russian origins, Rodin flashes a clipboard and asks, "Would you read these words for me?"

"Sure," the boy says in a formal-sounding English, as he glances up at the page and ticks off the answers. "Three. Dog. Soda. Water. Give me this."

"Have you ever heard someone say 'dis' instead of 'this'?" Rodin asks.

"Well, sure," he says. "You know—dis! Don't 'dis' me."

"Oh boy," Rodin says, shaking his head. "There's not going to be a Brooklynese for long."

The Responsive Reader

1. Which of the language features treated in this article do you recognize? Which can you demonstrate or explain to classmates who might have less of an ear for language differences than you do?
2. What do you think is the major purpose of this article, or what are its major effects on the reader? Do you tend to think of the language differences treated here as a source of amusement, or of embarrassment, or of important pointers for human interaction?

Talking, Listening, Writing

3. What is the difference between a language and a dialect? One language scholar said jokingly that a dialect is a language that has an army and a navy. You might want to check out the treatment of "dialect" in a major online encyclopedia or other authoritative source.

4. Have you known or observed people who consciously or deliberately speak a regional or "downhome" kind of speech? Have you known or observed others who have tried hard to change speech patterns that might reveal their ethnic, social, or regional origins? How successful were they?

5. Much ethnic humor is dialect humor or foreign-accent humor. Can you imitate the speech patterns of others? Can you give your classmates a sample? Is dialect humor always mean-spirited or condescending, or can it be nonoffensive?

Collaborative Projects

6. Both in this country and in Europe, there has been a revival of interest in dialects as a rich source of nostalgia and regional pride. You may want to team up with classmates to stage a festival of American dialects with stories, poetry, or humor from dialect sources—including perhaps Minnesota-Scandinavian, Cajun, Yiddish-tinged American, deep South, Irish American, Mexican American, Puerto Rican American, Hawaii pidgin, and others.

EBONICS: OPENING PANDORA'S BOX

Toni Cook

The school board in the predominantly African American city of Oakland in California caused a huge media flap when it called the Black English spoken by many of its students "Ebonics" and said that it should be recognized as a separate language showing the influence of African roots. Soon amended or "clarified," the school board's resolution called for "maintaining the richness and legitimacy" of the students' "primary language" while teaching them standard English. The Oakland initiative caused an outpouring of criticism and of vicious racist humor on the Internet, with the voices of scholars and teachers concerned about the failure of traditional methods at first largely drowned out. Linguists, or language scholars, say that calling the Spanish, rural dialect, or Black English that students bring to school inferior or illiterate is counterproductive. In the past, it has not produced large numbers of well-educated students with perfect accents but instead has created large numbers of hostile dropouts. Dialect features like the double negative, from Chaucer's "He never yet no villainy ne said" to the blues singer's "I ain't got nobody," have been part of English for centuries. Slaves brought to the New World from

*Africa developed various kinds of Creole or Creolized languages with vocabu-
lary items (like* gumbo*) and speech patterns indebted to African languages.
(Gullah, spoken in the isolated islands off the shore of Georgia and South
Carolina, has been described as the African American dialect closest to becoming a separate language.) In the following interview, Toni Cook, a member of
the Oakland school board, talks about the thinking that went into the board's
resolution. Cook has B.A. and M.A. degrees with honors from UCLA. She
has served as associate dean at Howard University and as national director of
advance for Jesse Jackson's presidential campaign in 1984.*

Thought Starters: Are people you know well bilingual? Are any bidialectal? When and how do they shift from one language or one dialect to
another?

Q: Other than making a lot of people mad, what have you done here?   1
A: I've sounded a bell that everyone is talking about. We got a call
from Amsterdam, and another one from South Africa. I'm finding that
more people are becoming anywhere from supportive to understanding
about this.
Q: Has anyone given you serious trouble?
A: Someone called from a radio talk show and played real raw, racist
stuff live and on air. My reaction to the first flood of phone calls (on my answering machine) was to deep-six every call.
Q: Why?   5
A: I was broadsided by the controversy. I didn't get home (from the
board meeting) until 2 A.M. and I didn't listen to any news the next day because I didn't think anything we did was newsworthy. I'm just thinking,
"I can't function." So I get up and make the call (to my job at the San Francisco Housing Authority): "I'm not coming." Then Edgar, our board's
assistant, calls and says, "Can you come over?" I said, "Edgar, I'm trying
to put a lie together about why I'm not going to work." He said, "All hell
has broken loose on the resolution." I said, "What resolution?" He said,
"The one put out by the African American task force. The mayor's on a
rampage."
Q: Why was (Mayor) Elihu Harris so mad?
A: I used to work for Elihu. He could be mad at anything! And when
I got there, he had already gone off to (Superintendent) Carolyn Getridge.
And he asked me, "Do you know what you have done? I'm getting calls
from everybody in the world! This is embarrassing to Oakland! You all have
adopted a policy that's going to teach black English!"
I said, "Elihu, I know you're cheap, but do you have television? Did
you watch the school board meeting last night? We meant you no ill will
in terms of your challenges with the city. But our kids are being ridiculed

if they speak standard English—'Ugh, you talk like a white girl!' So this is the problem we're faced with, and this is how we're going to deal with it." Elihu kind of calmed down a little and began to focus on why we did it like we did it.

Q: What did you do and why did you do it? *10*

A: I asked the superintendent to form a task force to look at the performance of African American kids. Since I've been on the board, drop-out rates, suspensions, expulsions, truancy—all have gone up for African American kids. But enrollment in the gifted and talented program and presence in college-bound, honors and advanced-placement classes were not proportionate to black enrollment, which is 53 percent.

Q: What about special education?

A: Of 5,000 kids in that, 71 percent are African American. And they were in there for "causing disruption."

Q: Aren't special education classes supposed to be for students who are disabled or have learning disabilities?

A: Yes. And you have to have a referral to be placed in the program. *15* The referrals disproportionately were because of a "language deficiency."

Q: What's that?

A: When you really dug down, it's that they weren't writing or speaking standard English. We found there were white and black teachers making referrals. And white and black principals—disproportionately black—saying yes. So when the task force began to talk with teachers, it was like, "Well, we don't have any strategies for these kids." The only one they had was the (state's) Standard English Proficiency Program for a few teachers who got that training.

Q: So what did you do?

A: You know, there's an old guy who comes to the board meetings named Oscar Wright. He came to every board meeting until his wife died about a year ago. And he would stand with those trembling hands and talk about the performance of African American kids—test scores, truancy— and he said, "I see having four black board members has made no difference in what these kids are doing."

And we hung our heads, because it was true! We had a crisis situation *20* and we kept coming up with old ways. Or ways that were so homogenized they didn't really wake anybody up.

Q: You're saying that test scores will go up as African American students begin speaking standard English?

A: Yes. Which ultimately means—more critically—that they can go from high school to college if that's their choice. You can no longer drop your kid off in kindergarten and expect to pick him up in the 12th grade with a diploma that means he's ready for college. We should quit making these promises that we're going to do that by adding health programs, and all those other kinds of things. That is not about education. I know they need all that, but there isn't any education strategy here. When it's directed to African American kids, it's basically the assumption that we have to control them before we can educate them.

Q: You don't feel that way?

A: No.

Q: How can you teach a kid who's out of control—whether threatening a teacher or just making noise?   25

A: Teachers need the teaching and learning tools to know how to communicate with these youngsters to capture their attention. We have some kids with a proven record of suspension in the third grade, and they're going like this (waves wildly) in the math class! I've seen that at some of our schools in the deepest parts of the flatlands.

Q: Are you saying their teachers caught their attention because they spoke ebonics?

A: What they knew was how to hear the child, listen to the child, correct the child, and make the child feel good about being corrected. These are teachers who have been through our Standard English Proficiency Program.

Q: Give me an example.

A: Well, I go to classes to read to the kids. Everybody knows Dr. Seuss,   30
so I made the presumption that I could read a page and the child would read a page. I found two things: Either the kids could not read, or they could read, but the words they pronounced were definitely not on that piece of paper.

Q: What were they saying?

A: -*ing*'s left off of words, consonants left off words, and you begin to think: "Does this kid have dyslexia? Half the word is falling off." And then I went to Prescott Elementary, and I noticed that in (teacher) Carrie Secret's class, where most of the kids are from the housing projects, they were excited about learning. They could read, and tell you what they had read, had great diction, good reasoning skills. And this was the third grade.

Q: You're saying that the kids in this class had better diction than kids in other classes with the same background?

A: Yes. And I began to ask Carrie Secret, "What are you doing differently?" She told me about the Standard English Proficiency Program. So when a kid did not make the -*ing* sound, or left off a consonant or made a word singular when it should be plural, or plural when it should be singular, Carrie would repeat back to the young people until they began to hear the correct word.

Q: How did she do it?   35

A: The child says, "I'm going wif my mother." Or, "I'm goin home." She says, "Where?" And the child says, "I'm going to go home."

Q: When you heard children speaking standard English, you were thrilled. You're sounding like the critics of your own ebonics resolution.

A: Standard English is (necessary) to go to a four-year college, to being accepted in an apprenticeship program, to understanding the world of technology, to communicating. We owe it to our kids to give them the best that we've got.

Q: There's great disagreement over black English as a language, language "pattern" or just street slang. What is black English?

A: All I know is that it's not slang. The linguists call that "lazy English." But our children come to school with this language pattern. Go back to what they call the Negro spiritual: "I'm going to lay my 'ligion down." That was the code song that got you your ticket on the Underground Railroad. It's the way the words were used. So they might have thought we were old dumb slaves, but it served a purpose. It was communication.

Q: Do some parents and children resist speaking standard English because they really see it as white English?

A: I don't think they consciously resist. My youngest daughter has had that criticism: "You talk like a white girl." It's another way of saying, "How come you don't sound like us?" It hurts to be accused of that. When I was a girl, it was a goal to speak standard English, not a ridicule. I have no idea how that changed.

Q: Why don't children automatically know standard English, since they hear it all the time on television and at school?

A: Two things. African Americans whose economic status and exposure is closer to that of the Huxtables have the exposure to work with the youngsters, and teach them about the "two-ness" of the world they're involved in. But some schools are located in very depressed areas, have a primary population of African Americans on a fixed income. They see very little, the young people are exposed to very little, and there isn't a whole lot of reason in the home—this is just my guess—to adopt the behavior of duality.

Q: Do you believe that the language pattern of black English is genetic?

A: It's ancestral. "Genetic" doesn't say "in your blood, in your biology." It says, "in the beginning!"

Q: Following that logic, why don't other ethnic groups use the grammar of their immigrant ancestors?

A: No other group in America, outside the Native American, ever had to grope (as we did) with the new language. If you didn't get off the Good Ship Lollypop speaking English, learning it was exacerbated by the fact that you had to sneak to teach yourself. Then if you stay together in an isolated, segregated environment, the language pattern persists over time.

Q: And yet there are millions of African Americans who speak with no trace of ebonics.

A: And there are an awful lot of second- and third-generation Chinese who speak perfect English, but when they go home to grandmother, they make the switch.

Q: And many African Americans don't. Is this an issue of class?

A: In some instances, it is class. You know, having come from a family of educators, it was a symbol of your ability to speak the King's English. I remember my mother telling me the tragedy is that as those kids became comfortable with the tools of the middle class, one of which was language, they began to turn their backs on their parents. They were embarrassed about their language style.

Q: This is the traditional immigrant experience. What's unusual is for children to cling to the language patterns of their elders.

A: Here is where it's confusing to some, but to others, I think they have ulterior motives.

Q: What's the ulterior motive? 55

A: The English Only campaign. We talked informally among the school board members. Be careful, don't get caught up in the English Only campaign.

Q: And the ulterior motive is the anti-affirmative action movement?

A: The funding is from the same platform. Right-wing America. It used to be that we'd just simply say it was racism. But now they are so sophisticated that it's about being anti-black, anti-Jewish, anti-immigrant, anti anything that's not Christian. Anti-urban, anti-female, I mean they just kind of took everybody and just threw us all over there together. We have no allies over there. None whatsoever.

Q: If nothing else, you've gotten them to add anti-ebonics to the list. But you've also gotten many people on your side, haven't you?

A: I'd love to be able to tell you how we plotted and planned to be- 60 come the topic of everybody's conversation in the world. That's dishonest. It took me by surprise.

Q: You had been very opposed to changing any of the controversial wording in your resolution—that ebonics is "genetically based," for instance, and that students will be taught "in ebonics." Yet you changed your mind. What happened?

A: Sometimes you have to look: Are you winning the battle but losing the war? The African American Task Force met (for about 10 hours) last week and got no closure on the word "genetics." Then Oscar Wright, the old man of the group, said, "If removal of this word will heal the pain of the African American community, then remove the word." When that old man gave the word, we moved on. I felt fine about that. I would have stayed on course, but the village said to do things differently.

Q: Did you grow up speaking ebonics?

A: No, but I heard it. You've got to think about coming up in a segregated time. In 1954, when the school desegregation decision came, I was 10. But the more I think about it, the more I think about how blessed I've been. Both of my parents had graduate degrees. My dad was a dentist. My mom was a linguist with the National Security Agency. We were never quite sure what she really did. We knew she spoke perfect Russian. We used to say Mom was a spy for the FBI. And we always thought that Mommy was the smartest thing we ever saw.

Q: So language and politics were always entwined in your family? 65

A: Everyone in my family, whether it was Mom or Dad, they were always crusaders. You never earned the right to snub your nose at anybody based on speech patterns. I remember a time we went down the street, and a drunk said something to my sister Twink, and she laughed. Mom gave her a backhand, and said, "That man meant nothing but to be kind. Go back and say: 'How do you do, sir?'" She was serious. My mother was 4-foot-9, and 89 pounds, boy. And she spoke perfect English.

Q: Did you send your own children to private schools?

A: Both (religious and public) schools. I have two girls. Arlene, 31, is teaching in San Francisco. Leslie will be 33 this year. They got exposed to some things in all environments. But only in California was the diversity. Here they've got everybody. I like that. This is real.

Q: California's diversity is unusual even in America, isn't it?

A: But that's the advantage. That's the gift. If we are really taking 70 pride in the diversity, is it not important that we know something about everything that makes us Americans? Because the tragedy is that really, multicultural curricula in our schools are predicated in the philosophy of, "Can't we all get along?"

I don't care whether we all get along. I care whether you respect me and know something about me.

Q: Why is that the job of teachers? Why isn't that the job of parents and neighbors and friends?

A: It's all of our jobs. But I think what this (ebonics issue) does is show we are a long way from being a multicultural society. Somehow, talking about anything African American makes people very tight-lipped and angry, and wondering, "Am I being politically correct?" Our prejudice comes out.

Q: Or our ignorance?

A: Yeah. If you ever want to see how segregated our schools are, go 75 to the teachers' lounge. Very segregated. We are all operating from a state of ignorance.

Q: How will the Oakland school board pay for expanding this program to teach standard English?

A: The program is now paid for by federal Title I money. So we'll move money from other Title I programs that are less effective, and into this one, which makes more sense. And we'll evaluate how well it's going.

Q: In Los Angeles, school board member Barbara Boudreaux said she will try to get federal funding if the board approves her ebonics resolution. Will Oakland do the same?

A: It's a useless fight. Those bilingual kids don't get enough money already. Besides, those are federally mandated funds. When you start using those funds for other than what the law mandates, you get into a very dangerous zone called "supplanting." That is not our goal.

Q: And that's illegal? 80

A: Hell, yes.

Q: Was your resolution a trial balloon for bilingual funds that Riley did not go for?

A: No. There was never any intent on the part of the board to ask for bilingual funds. No. The intent is to expand the Standard English Proficiency Program.

Q: Why did you and the board make it so difficult for the public to get copies of your resolution? The board seemed to be hiding it.

A: I know, I looked for it on the Web site and I didn't see it, either. 85
I don't understand why.

Q: Is it because the resolution didn't stand on its own until the board prepared to change its controversial wording on Wednesday?

A: For me it always stood on its own. But it was getting to be ugly—which black leader can we find to kick y'all in the butt now? They were not focusing on the problems of kids that brought us to this point.

While Rome is burning, we're trying to figure out whether the song we're singing is politically correct. But now that we've gotten past the wordsmithing, it's time to roll up our sleeves and do the work. We've got a class that is getting ready to graduate and may not even have a grade-point average of 1.8! Rome is burning, folks. It's burning! I don't know how much more pitiful we've got to get.

The Responsive Reader

1. How does Cook sketch out the concerns that led the school board to adopt the controversial resolution? What were typical student attitudes toward language in her district? What were typical attitudes of teachers and administrators? What is Cook's view of the connection between poor academic performance on the one hand and students' and teachers' attitudes toward language on the other?

2. Some of the critics of the Oakland resolution called Black English "slang." What is Cook's answer? What is your own definition of slang, and what to you are typical current examples?

3. What does Cook mean by the "two-ness" of the world of her students? What does she mean by the "behavior of duality"? Why do some African American students learn it while others don't?

4. How would you describe Cook's basic attitude toward standard English? What was her own experience with standard English? What did her parents teach her about language? How were language and politics entwined in her upbringing?

5. According to Cook, what makes the relationship of African Americans to the English language different from that of immigrant groups from

non-English-language backgrounds? Why does she think, for instance, that language issues are different for the many Asian students in her area of California?

6. Charges of racism started flying both ways in the Ebonics controversy. What "ulterior motives" does Cook identify or suspect on the part of people who attacked the initiative? How does she think the politics of racism have changed from earlier days of crude, overt antiblack prejudice? (What do you know about the English Only movement?)

Talking, Listening, Writing

7. Do you know people who are or were embarrassed by the language of their parents, family, or neighborhood? Are you?

EBONICS PLAN IS WORTH A LISTEN
Angelo Figueroa

Many of those vocal in the Ebonics controversy were people never seen visiting inner-city schools or drumming up funds for the improved recruitment and training of minority teachers. In the words of one African American commentator, for a while "it was hard to sort everything out, what with all the hollering and the blood and the hum of the chainsaws." Finally people talking about their own experiences with becoming bilingual or bidialectal or with teaching bilingual or bidialectal students were beginning to be heard. Angelo Figueroa is a Latino columnist who went to school in a predominantly black neighborhood in Detroit and who now works for a newspaper in San Jose, another city with a large minority population. The ethnic mix in the area includes Mexican Americans, Filipinos, Vietnamese, and Koreans, among others.

Thought Starters: In a widely publicized sensational court case, a prominent African American lawyer criticized a witness for saying he heard "a black voice." Do you think you can tell whether a person calling you on the telephone is black, or from a Spanish-speaking background, or from some other distinct linguistic group? Why or why not? How can you be sure?

If you're like me, you probably never heard of the word Ebonics. 1
Well, the word will probably become part of our collective lexicon.
Ebonics, as I understand it, is a word to describe black vernacular or more simply, the way some black people talk. The term derives from the words ebony and phonics.

Oakland public school officials made national headlines when they declared that Ebonics is so radically different from English that it merits special recognition. The district wants to train Oakland teachers to understand Ebonics so they can use it as a springboard to teach black students standard English.

Now, I suspect that many of you—or least the guy who called me Friday to rant about the issue—believe that this is insane.   5

Why should tax dollars be used to teach teachers how to use a fractured form of English?

I can understand the stick-to-the-basics sentiment, but don't agree with it.

How, for example, is our average school teacher supposed to translate something like this if they don't understand it:

> *Yo, what up, dog? What it be like? I's fixin' to scoop you in my hoopty so we can jet to Jerome's crib and kick it. I likes to listen to some mad tunes, if Jerome's moms don't be trippin, all-ight?*

While this may be a hack's example of Ebonics and common street slang, this fact remains: Black kids who grow up in the inner-city speak in a distinct dialect that makes learning standard English a major challenge.

I grew up in a predominantly black neighborhood in Detroit. I   10
learned the street slang and sentence structure that everyone else around me employed.

Spanish was my first language, adding to my language confusion.

Fortunately, I've always loved to read and learned standard English more from books than grammar classes. Otherwise, I wouldn't be writing this column.

For many kids, the language barrier created by a mixture of slang and Ebonics places them at a disadvantage when they have to work or study outside their communities. Many are so intimidated, in fact, that they simply drop out—out of school and the mainstream.

That's why I applaud the Oakland school system if the goal is to make teachers aware of Ebonics so that they can help students overcome its potentially crippling impact.

Some may counter that it would be better if the black community   15
simply abandoned black English. But that's like expecting Latinos to stop speaking Spanish because a law making English the official language is passed.

It's not realistic.

Black folks have been speaking a different dialect and using different phrasing to express themselves since the days of slavery. There's nothing wrong with that. If there were, Texans and New Yorkers would have been forced to take diction classes long ago.

Language isn't static. It's constantly evolving. Ebonics and street slang add spice to our language and give its speakers a sense of cultural identity they can be proud of.

But let's be clear about one thing: Ebonics and slang don't play in the boardroom. In other words, it doesn't work in a marketplace where standard English rules.

Both blacks and Latinos must recognize that mastering English is vi-   *20* tal to their success in the United States.

That's the way it be's whether we likes it or not.

The Responsive Reader

1. How does Figueroa's own experience give him a special insider's perspective on the controversy? A major issue was whether or not the challenges facing Spanish-speaking students and students with Black English are similar.
2. What do you think is Figueroa's answer? How would you sum up his position on the relation between "dialects," or "vernaculars," and standard English? What should be the teachers' goals? What methods might work?

Talking, Listening, Writing

3. Do both sides in the controversy accuse each other of "stigmatizing" the students? Why or how? Why would the students be stigmatized, and what could or should be done about it?
4. Some Americans retain a first language or downhome dialect. Others seem to leave it behind at least in part more quickly than others. And some rediscover a first language or dialect as they go back to their roots. To judge from your own experience or observation, what makes the difference? Do you think of a first language or downhome dialect as a liability or as an asset?
5. The playwright Imamu Amiri Baraka once said, "I heard an old Negro street singer, Reverend Pearly Brown, singing, 'God don't never change!' This is a precise thing he is singing. He does not mean 'God does not ever change!' He means 'God don't never change!'" What is the difference? What is Baraka talking about?

Writing to Define

Definition stakes out the territory a term covers. Sometimes it simply fills in a blank in the reader's mind. If you suspect that some of your readers do not know the term *recidivism,* you may briefly explain it as the pattern of released convicts becoming repeat offenders. More often, however, definition is needed to give exact meaning to terms that on closer inspection turn out to be vague, slippery, or misleading.

To define means to draw the line. Who is poor in our society? It depends on where we draw the "poverty line." Who is a "qualified applicant" for a job or a promotion? It depends on the criteria of the people who do the hiring. (They are sometimes second-guessed by an arbitration board or by the courts.) What is obscene in our society depends on how explicit the treatment of sex has to become before viewers or readers stop saying, "This is sexy!" and start saying, "This is sick!" Ultimately, what is obscene in our society depends on where the members of the United States Supreme Court draw the line.

TRIGGERING Definition becomes an issue whenever someone says: "Just a minute—what exactly do we mean by this word?" The French philosopher Voltaire said, "Before you start arguing with me, define your terms!" Here are some typical situations where a writer might say: "Time out to define a key term!"

- *You may have to pin down the meaning of a catch-all label.* What for you is the core meaning of *conservative, liberal, radical, feminist,* or *activist?* People you label liberals or feminists or conservatives may resist a label that commits them to more than they bargained for. A person who says, "I'm not a feminist, but . . ." often turns out to be a feminist—in the sense of someone promoting women's causes and standing up for women's rights. However, the person might not want to buy into other positions the label might imply—whether a generally negative view of men, or a commitment to aggressive legal or political tactics. Your definition of such a term can highlight the common core, telling the reader: "This is what the term basically means. Much else is optional!"

540

- *You may have to pin down the exact meaning of a catch phrase.* Definition makes sure that words do not remain "just words." The more sweeping and uplifting the terms are, the easier it is for everyone to pay lip service to them. Everyone today is an "equal opportunity employer." What does that mean? What equal opportunities can two students have if one struggled to stay in school in a violence-prone neighborhood and the other grew up with good schools, regular homework, and much help from well-educated parents? If you commit yourself to "equal opportunity," how are you going to ensure the legendary "level playing field"? Are you going to provide the kind of second chance (or third chance) without which "equal opportunity" remains just words?

- *You may have to reexamine slippery categories.* The boxes you are expected to check on a questionnaire may make you ask: "What do you mean?" Is a person with two French and two Hawaiian grandparents of "European descent"? Is a person with an Irish father and an African American mother white or black? Who is white or black in our society is a matter of definition.

GATHERING You may be tempted to start a definition paper by saying, "*Webster's Dictionary* defines *equity* as the practice of being fair and equal." Noah Webster, of course, is dead, and several publishers of dictionaries have appropriated his name to help peddle their wares. (So what reference book are you quoting?) Moreover, the dictionary definition is often a **circular definition:** It tells us that being equitable means being fair but does nothing to show what that means in practice.

To make your readers see what a key word means in practice, ask yourself questions like the following: Who uses the word? In what situations? For what purpose? Are there several main uses? How are they related? Is there a common denominator? What do you think is the prevailing or most useful meaning of the term? What are possible abuses or dishonest uses?

Here are some categories a student might set up to collect material for a definition of the term *feminism.* Such categories serve as a **discovery frame,** charting a program for a systematic stock-taking of relevant material:

> What popular associations and misunderstandings cluster around the term? What stereotypes do you hear invoked on talk shows, for instance?
>
> What is the history of the movement—what famous names and events come to mind?
>
> How do the media reflect changing definitions of gender roles? (Do commercials, action movies, or soap operas feature more independent, less vulnerable women than they used to?)
>
> Where have feminist issues played a role in my own experience?

What related terms (*women's liberation, emancipation, sexism, patriarchy*) cluster around the term?

What is the core meaning of the term? What is the common denominator?

SHAPING   Strategies for presenting an **extended definition**—a definition in depth of a much-used important term—will vary.

- You may want to set your paper in motion by focusing on a common misunderstanding of the term—and then correcting it. You lead from the misuse or misunderstanding of the term to what you consider its true meaning. You then give several examples of situations where your definition fits especially well.

- You may want to focus on providing a historical perspective. For instance, you might trace key meanings of the term *democracy* from its original Greek meaning—"rule by the people"—to modern times. You move from the *direct* democracy of ancient Greece (with the whole electorate voting on major decisions) to the *representative* democracy of modern times (voting on major issues by proxy). From there, you move to the participatory, "town meeting" kind of democracy advocated by those who feel that democratic institutions have become too isolated from the people.

- You may want to examine several key examples of affirmative action to find what they have in common, or you may want to focus on one extended **case history** that puts possible definitions of the term to the test.

What is the overall plan in the following student paper? What problems of definition does the writer recognize? What is the core definition that emerges from the paper?

Dem's Fightin' Words!

When does ordinary name-calling turn into offensive slurs? Where do we draw the line when people use racial epithets or demeaning language directed at other groups? What do we do about it?

"Faggot! Hope you die of AIDS! Can't wait till you die!" These words were shouted, not by an ignorant twelve-year-old, but by Keith R., a law student at Stanford University. Weeks later, when confronted, he said he had used offensive language on purpose in order to test the limits of freedom of speech at Stanford. Others doubt that his use of language was an experiment; they say it closely coincided with opinions he had expressed in *The Stanford Review*.

When dealing with abusive individuals like R., the natural impulse is to legislate, to pass ordinances, to enforce guidelines. If we could only ban offensive language, expel the offender, or shut down an offending magazine, we would get rid of the problem. Many colleges have tried this tack by instituting "Fighting Words" rules. Responding to the pain felt by the victims of racism, sexism, and homophobia, these schools have as necessary amended their constitutions to forbid certain offensive expressions. Violators may be reprimanded or even expelled. At Dartmouth, for instance, a student was called on the carpet for asking in class whether it was possible to "cure" homosexuals.

The objection to such rules is that they inevitably have what lawyers call "a chilling effect" on the free expression of ideas. These rules inevitably pose a problem of definition: Where do we draw the line? Who decides what is offensive, and to whom? Stanford's "Speech Code" made a brave attempt to minimize the problem by being very specific. It read in part: "Speech or other expression constitutes harassment or personal vilification if it: (1) intends to insult or stigmatize an individual or group of individuals on the basis of sex, race, color, handicap, religion, sexual orientation, or national or ethnic origin; (2) is addressed directly to the individual; (3) makes use of insulting or fighting words or gestures."

Nevertheless, drawing the line between offensive speech and legitimate expression is not easy. How would this rule apply to the speeches of Malcolm X, who for a time referred to whites as "white devils"? On the other hand, what set of rules could stop a person like Keith R. from being personally offensive? He could have expressed his hostility by gestures instead of words— a wink, a leer, a walk, humming a few bars of "Here Comes the Bride."

The British writer Christopher Isherwood (who often referred to himself as Christopher Swisherwood) insisted on using words like *faggot* and *queer*. He said that by using them and making them ordinary, he could help take away their power to insult and to hurt. Would Mr. Isherwood be censored today on Stanford's green and pleasant lawn? No, say supporters of the Speech Code, because his use of language was not intended to offend. But this puts the censors into the business of judging the intent of an expression—looking into people's heads to judge what made them say what they said. Who is going to say if an expression was used insultingly, kiddingly, or ignorantly?

At Stanford, the reaction to the incident was a petition condemning R.'s behavior, signed by almost five hundred students and faculty members. At the law school, a large poster read: "Exercise your right of free speech. Tell this law student what you think of his behavior. It may be legal, but it isn't right." This has to be the definition of offensive language in a free society: What bigots and racists say may be offensive, but they have the right to say it, and we have the right and duty to talk back to them. That is what free speech is all about.

If you take away the bigot's right to shout "Faggot!" you may also be taking away my right to say: "Shut up, you creep!" You may be taking away my right to call a religious fanatic a bigot or my gun-toting neighbor a redneck. Bad ideas and bad language cannot be legislated against; they must be driven out by better ideas.

Topics for Definition Papers (A Sampling)

1. What kind of group qualifies as a minority? Who decides? Is it an advantage today to have minority status?

2. What is meant by terms like the *culture of victimization* or *victimology?* Why have such terms become widely used? What controversies revolve around them?

3. What does *macho* mean? Who uses the term, and why? How do you react to it?
4. What is meant by *welfare dependency?* Who uses the term, and why?
5. Is the term *feminine* obsolete? Does anyone still want to be feminine?
6. Is there such a thing as an ideal marriage? (Or does it exist only in reruns of fifties television shows or movies?)
7. What kind of movie would you call a romantic movie? Is romance making a comeback in popular entertainment?
8. What is meant by "assertiveness training"? Why is it needed? How would it be taught?
9. Is there such a thing as reverse racism or reverse discrimination?
10. What is homophobia, and how widespread is it in our society?

10

VIOLENCE
Living at Risk

A 16-year-old high school girl blazed away with a .22-caliber rifle at an elementary school near her house, killing the principal and a janitor. She later said, "I don't like Mondays. This livens up the day." The Boomtown Rats, an Irish group, sold half a million copies of a record whose lyrics went, "I don't like Mondays / I want to shoot / the whole day down."

MTV's animated Celebrity Deathmatch pitted past and present celebrities against each other in bloody, gory battles. In one episode, Genghis Khan ripped into Mahatma Gandhi. In another, Hillary Clinton and Monica Lewinsky fought it out with metal fence railings and chairs.

The American culture of drive-by shootings, homicidal youth gangs, drug vendettas, serial killers, celebrity murders, and mass cult suicides has a global resonance: In countries that pride themselves on a tradition of law and order, young killers appear out of nowhere, without a psychiatric history or any intelligible motive. In a mansion in Switzerland, 48 bodies are found, sacrificed to the apocalyptic vision of a messianic leader. Media phenomena like *Natural Born Killers* and the latest Schwarzenegger movie travel around the globe, reinforcing what a French journalist called the "culture of brutality."

Violence is an integral part of our historical and cultural legacy. The twentieth century brought wars deploying an unprecedented technology of mass destruction. A generation of young men was killed in the trench warfare of World War I. In World War II, civilian casualties—from scorched-earth policies, bombings, and campaigns of extermination—rivaled the numbers of those killed in combat. Many Americans first came here as refugees—from Germany, Russia, Southeast Asia—carrying with them the scars, physical and psychological, of repression, starvation, and genocide. Young Americans (many from minority backgrounds) were sent to fight in North Africa, Italy, France, and the Pacific in World War II; in Korea; in Vietnam; and in Iraq. Thousands of veterans suffer from the disabilities and traumas left in the wake of their war experience overseas.

At home, American cities have rates of violent crime and murder unprecedented in the developed countries of the West. Serial murders and gang wars are features of our news and entertainment. Americans live in fear of violence. Often that fear pits members of different racial or ethnic groups against one another. Are we going to live in a society where a white police officer is assumed to be the enemy of a black citizen? Are we going to live in communities where a Korean grocer and a customer from the barrio regard one another with hatred and distrust?

Have Americans come to accept violence as an inevitable fact of life? Do we have any blueprints for making ours a safer world?

FRIENDS KNEW ALLEGED GUNMAN'S PLANS

Ben Fox

> *In the nineties, a spate of bloody school shootouts shook up parents and students long used to murderous gunplay as entertainment on the television and movie screen. Parents who said they bought guns to protect their families and homes discovered that they had not protected their children and their teachers when they attended school. While relatives of the dead and of maimed survivors often reacted with stunned disbelief, media commentators and an outpouring of online popular comment tried to fix blame. One psychologist blamed a lack of "impulse control" on the part of immature young people—in a society where most of the murderers killing family, ex-lovers, coworkers, or other targets of gun violence are adults. How much of the following Associated Press report is "just the facts, please"? How much is interpretation, editorializing, finger-pointing, or attributing blame?*

Thought Starters: How close have you been to gun violence? Do you know anyone who has been shot, or do you remember a report of a shooting that made a special impression on you? What was the person's story? Who did what? What led up to what? What was the aftermath of the shooting? Who was blamed? How could what happened been prevented or avoided?

SANTEE, Calif. (March 6)—A 15-year-old boy fired randomly at 1
fellow students and had eight bullets left in his gun when police cornered him in a bathroom after he killed two teen-agers at school, investigators said Tuesday.

Friends said the scrawny freshman accused in the nation's latest high school bloodbath talked about his plans over the weekend, and they took him seriously enough to pat him down before school started Monday.

One adult even warned Charles Andrew "Andy" Williams not to commit "a Columbine," and tried to call the boy's father but didn't follow through. But no one is known to have reported the threats that preceded Monday's attack that also wounded 13.

During a news conference, authorities said the carnage could have been much worse if not for the swift actions of a sheriff's deputy and an off-duty police officer who was on campus.

When the boy surrendered, his gun, a .22-caliber long rifle revolver, 5
was fully loaded with eight rounds of ammunition, its hammer cocked, investigators said.

"I do believe that if it had not been for the conduct of the people involved . . . it would have been even worse," Sheriff Bill Kolender said.

The gunman appeared to be firing indiscriminately, sheriff's Lt. Jerry Lewis said. Most of the students who were hit were struck as they fled down a hallway between the school's library and administration office.

"The information we have from the evidence and the witnesses (is) the suspect was firing randomly at anybody who was going by," Lewis said. "Any student who was going by he was shooting at."

Although Santana High closed Tuesday, students, parents and others gathered outside to place flowers at a makeshift memorial site and share their grief. Some expressed anger that acquaintances of Williams heard him make threats in recent days but failed to warn authorities.

"I think they're to blame, too," said Helen Howard, a 10-year resident 10 of the community who came to the high school with her husband. "I just can't understand why they didn't say anything."

During a morning counseling session at a church, an American Red Cross representative asked for a show of hands of people who had trouble sleeping the previous night. About a third of the 200 people who attended indicated they did.

"You may just feel like your heart is beating all the time and you can't calm down," Robert Bray, a Red Cross disaster mental health worker, told the audience. "I want to reassure you that people do get through this."

Teachers were told to report to school district headquarters.

As authorities dug into the case, the first question for many was: How could so many people see the warning signs and fail to act?

"That's going to be haunting me for a long time," said Chris Reynolds, 15 29, who heard the threats and didn't report them.

Williams, held in a juvenile facility Tuesday, will be charged as an adult with murder, assault with a deadly weapon and gun possession, District Attorney Paul Pfingst said. The adult prosecution is mandatory under a ballot measure approved last year, and the boy could face multiple life terms. Arraignment was set for Wednesday.

Pfingst said the gun belonged to Williams' father, Charles, a lab technician at the Naval Medical Center–San Diego, since July. It had been stored in a locked cabinet, investigators said. Sheriff's and FBI officials Monday night searched the Williams' apartment and said they removed seven rifles, a computer, a plastic crate filled with papers and files, and about a half dozen bags filled with evidence.

Bryan Zuckor, 14, and 17-year-old Randy Gordon were killed; 11 other students and two adults—a student teacher and a campus security worker—were wounded. The adults and four students remained hospitalized in good or fair condition.

The shooting happened Monday morning in this overwhelmingly white, middle-class suburb of San Diego, a town that prides itself on its country atmosphere and low crime rate.

Youngsters were out and about as one "block" of students who start   *20*
early in the day headed to their next classes and another group—Williams'
"block"—arrived for their first classes.

The boy shot two people in a restroom, then walked into a quad and
fired randomly, sheriff's Lt. Jerry Lewis said. He stopped to reload as many
as four times, getting off 30 or more shots, Lewis said.

"It was total chaos. People were trying to take cover," said student
John Schardt, 17, who was in a nearby classroom when the shooting started.
He said the shooter had a smile on his face.

"Pop, pop, pop and everyone started ducking," recalled student Nika
Ocen-Odoge.

Barry Gibson, 18, said he ran at the sound, then returned with two
others when they saw a friend fall to the ground. The friend rolled onto his
side, spitting up blood.

"We were asking him, 'Are you OK?'" Gibson told the *Los Angeles*   *25*
Times. Amid another burst of fire, Gibson ran. "I got hit in the leg," he said.
"It went numb."

Authorities have said little about a motive for the rampage, but the
suspect's life abounds in warning signs that have become as familiar as the
TV images of frightened students being herded to safety from the presumed
safe harbor of a suburban school.

Williams, whose parents are divorced, occasionally visited his mother,
Linda Wells, in North Augusta, S.C. He and his father moved to California
from Frederick County, Md., last year.

He's a skinny kid, a skateboarder "wannabe" friends said. There's talk
of recent scrapes with booze and a girl, a breakup, and a beating by another
teen-ager at the skateboard park where he hung out. His skateboard was
stolen twice, one friend recalled.

"He was picked on all the time," student Jessica Moore said. "He was
picked on because he was one of the scrawniest guys. People called him
freak, dork, nerd, stuff like that."

While staying overnight Saturday with his friend Joshua Stevens, 15,   *30*
Williams spoke specifically about shooting up the school, according to
Stevens and Reynolds, who is dating Stevens' mother.

Both moved tentatively to head off trouble, but failed.

"My friend A.J. patted him down this morning for guns, but he said
he was joking," Stevens told *The San Diego Union-Tribune*. "I guess he had
(the gun) by his crotch."

Alex Ripple, a 14-year-old who was present, said they searched
Williams' body but not his backpack.

Reynolds said he warned Williams: "I even mentioned Columbine to
him. I said I don't want a Columbine here at Santana. But he said, 'No,
nothing will happen, I'm just joking,'" Reynolds told the AP.

Reynolds tried to call Williams' father on Sunday, but gave up after   *35*
getting no answer and then a busy signal, the *Los Angeles Times* reported.

There have been signs since the 1999 Columbine High massacre that left 15 dead in Colorado that teens and those around them have become more willing to report threatening behavior. At least four times around the country in recent months students reported threats and possibly averted violent episodes at school.

The Responsive Reader

1. How many press reports or television news accounts like this Associated Press story have you read or watched? Can you construct a "generic" or archetypal news report of a school shooting that would include most of the common or recurrent elements? What "bottom-line" details would you include that most of the time seem to be part of the story? Compare your "Profile of a School Shooting" with those prepared by your fellow students. What did they include that you left out?

2. Most groups have a code of honor about not informing, or "snitching," on their friends. Do you think the friends in this instance did not care enough? What precautions did they take, and do you think these were insufficient? What would you have done that they did not do? Should the adults have done more?

3. An explanation surfacing often in this and similar accounts is the bullying and outgrouping that unpopular kids undergo in school. What form did it take in this case? Does what happened seem familiar or unusual to you? How common or widespread is this kind of thing? How serious is it? Does anyone have an answer to the problem? What can or should be done?

4. Although the familiar slogan says that guns do not kill people, two young people in this incident were killed by shots fired from a gun that was still "fully loaded," with plenty of ammunition to kill many additional people. In this long press report, how many lines are devoted to the gun? What kind was it? Where did it it come from? Why did the boy have it? Why do you think the father had seven guns?

Talking, Listening, Writing

5. This report says that after the "bloodbath" the first question many asked was: "How could so many people see the warning signs and fail to act?" What would have been your first question?

Collaborative Projects

6. After a tragedy such as this, are the victims often briefly mourned and then forgotten? How much attention is devoted to the victims? Working with a group, you may want to explore the aftermath of a school shooting or prepare a tribute to a victim or victims of gun violence you knew or read about and especially cared about.

THE VIOLENT POLITICS OF CRIME

Bruce Shapiro

> *Media critics complain that our treatment of crime tends to focus on the accused or on sensational criminal trials where the prosecution and defense lawyers decide the fate of the accused. Do we tend to forget about the victim? The author of the following article presents his personal testimony as a crime victim. He writes about a violent incident that seemed to come out of nowhere. It occurred in an everyday setting, and many of his readers should be able to imagine themselves in his place. The event inflicted physical and psychological trauma of the kind the media tend to bypass or ignore. What does the writer want his readers to learn from his experience? Shapiro is an editor for* Nation *magazine, where this story of his encounter with violent crime first appeared.*

Thought Starters: Crime-fighting organizations and law enforcement agencies draw up profiles of potential lawbreakers. What would you include in your own profile of a violent criminal?

Alone in my home I am staring at the television screen and shouting. On the local evening news I have unexpectedly encountered video footage, several months old, of myself writhing on an ambulance gurney—skin pale, shirt open and drenched with blood, trying desperately to find relief from pain.

On the evening of August 7, 1994, I was among seven people stabbed and seriously wounded in a café a few blocks from my house. Any televised recollection of this incident would be upsetting. But tonight's anger is quite specific, and political, in origin: My picture is being shown on the news to illustrate why my state's legislature plans to lock up more criminals for a longer time. A picture of my body, contorted and bleeding, has become a propaganda image in the crime war. I had not planned to write about this assault. But for months now the politics of the nation have in large part been the politics of crime, from last year's federal crime bill to the "Taking Back Our Streets" clause of the Contract with America. Among a welter of reactions to my own recent experience, one feeling is clear: I am unwilling to be a silent poster child in this debate.

Here is what happened: At about 9:45 P.M. I arrived at the coffeehouse on Audubon Street with two neighborhood friends, Martin and Anna. We sat at a small table near the front; about fifteen people were scattered around the room. Just before ten, as Martin went over to the counter for a final refill, chaos erupted. I heard him call Anna's name. I looked up and saw his arm raised and a flash of metal and people leaping away from

1

a thin, bearded man with a ponytail. Tables and chairs toppled. Without thinking I shouted to Anna, "Get down!" Clinging to each other, we pulled ourselves along the wall toward the door.

What actually happened I was only tentatively able to reconstruct later. Apparently, as Martin headed toward the counter the thin, bearded man, whose name we later learned was Daniel Silva, asked the time from another patron, who answered and then turned to leave. Without warning, Silva pulled out a hunting knife and began moving about the room with demonic speed, stabbing six people in a matter of seconds. Among these were Martin, stabbed in the thigh and the arm, the woman behind the counter, stabbed in the chest and abdomen while phoning the police, and Anna, stabbed in the side as we pulled each other toward the door.

I had gone no more than a few steps down the sidewalk when I felt a ⁵ hard punch in my back followed instantly by the unforgettable sensation of skin and muscle tissue parting. Silva had stabbed me about six inches above my waist, just beneath my rib cage. Without thinking, I clapped my hand over the wound before the knife was out, and the exiting blade sliced my palm and two fingers.

"Why are you doing this?" I cried out. I fell, and he leaned over my face, the knife's glittering blade immense. He put the point into my chest. I remember his brown beard, his clear blue-gray eyes looking directly into mine, and the round globe of a streetlamp like a halo above his head.

"You killed my mother," Silva answered. At my own desperate response—"Please don't"—he pulled the knifepoint out of my chest and disappeared. A moment later I saw him flying down the street on a battered bicycle.

I lay on the sidewalk, screaming in pain. Every muscle in my back felt locked and contorted; breathing was excruciating. A woman in a white-and-gray plaid dress was sitting on the curb in a stupor, covered with blood. Up the street I saw a police car's flashing lights, then another's, then an officer with a concerned face and a crackling radio was crouching beside me. I stayed conscious as the medics arrived and I was loaded into an ambulance.

Until August 7 Daniel Silva was a self-employed junk dealer and a homeowner. He lived with his mother and several dogs. He had no arrest record. A police detective who was hospitalized across the hall from me recalled Silva as a socially marginal neighborhood character. He was not, apparently, a drug user. He had told neighbors about much violence in his family—showing one a scar on his thigh he said was from a stab wound.

A week earlier, Silva's seventy-nine-year-old mother had been hospi- ¹⁰ talized for diabetes. After a few days the hospital moved her to a new room; when Silva saw his mother's empty bed he panicked, but nurses swiftly took him to her new location. Still, something seemed to have snapped. On the day of the stabbings, police say, Silva released his dogs, set fire to his house, and rode away on his bicycle as his home burned. He arrived on Audubon Street evidently convinced that his mother was dead.

While I lay in the hospital, the big story on CNN was the federal crime bill then being debated in Congress. Even fogged by morphine I was aware of the irony. I was flat on my back, with tubes in veins, chest, penis, and abdomen, the result of a particularly violent assault, while Congress was busy passing the anticrime package that I had criticized in print just a few weeks earlier. Night after night, unable to sleep, I watched Republicans and Democrats fall over one another to prove who could be the toughest on crime.

A few days after I returned home, the bill passed. What I found when I finally read its 412-page text was this: Not a single one of those pages would have protected me or Anna or Martin or any of the others from our assailant. Not the extended prison terms, not the forty-four new death-penalty offenses, not the three-strikes-and-you're-out requirements, not the summary deportations of criminal aliens. The even stiffer provisions of the Contract with America, including the proposed abolition of the Fourth Amendment's search-and-seizure protections, still would have offered me no practical protection.

On the other hand, the mental-health and social-welfare safety net shredded during the 1980s might have made a difference in the life of someone like my assailant—and thus in the life of someone like me. Silva's growing distress in the days before August 7 was obvious to his neighbors. He had muttered darkly about relatives planning to burn down his house. A better-funded, more comprehensive social-service infrastructure might have saved me and six others from untold pain and trouble.

In fact, it was in no small measure the institutions of an urban community that saved my life that night. The police officer who found me was joined in a moment by a phalanx of emergency medics, and his backups arrived quickly enough to chase down my assailant three blocks away. In minutes I was taken to nearby Yale–New Haven hospital—built in part with the kind of public funding so hated by the right—where several dozen doctors and nurses descended to handle all the wounded. If my stabbing had taken place in the suburbs, I would have bled to death.

One thing I could not properly appreciate in the hospital was how deeply other people were shaken by the stabbings. The reaction of most was a combination of decent horrified empathy and a clear sense that their own presumption of safety had been undermined. But some who didn't bother to acquaint themselves with the facts used the stabbings as a sort of Rorschach test on which they projected their own preconceptions. Some present and former Yale students, for instance, were desperate to see in my stabbing evidence of the great dangers of New Haven's inner city. One student newspaper wrote about "New Haven's image as a dangerous town fraught with violence." A student reporter from another Yale paper asked if I didn't think the attack proved that New Haven needs better police protection. Given the random nature of this assault, it's tempting to dismiss such sentiments. But city-hating is central to today's political culture. Newt

Gingrich excoriates cities as hopelessly pestilent, crime-ridden, and corrupt. Fear of urban crime is the right's basic fuel, and defunding cities is a central agenda item for the new congressional majority.

"Why didn't anyone try to stop him?" That question was even more common than the reflexive city-bashing. I can't begin to guess the number of times I had to answer it. Each time, I repeated that Silva moved too fast, that it was simply too confusing. And each time, I found the question not just foolish but offensive.

"Why didn't anyone stop him?" To understand that question is to understand, in some measure, why crime is such a potent political issue. To begin with, the question carries not empathy but an implicit burden of blame; it really asks, "Why didn't *you* stop him?" It is asked because no one likes to imagine oneself a victim. It's far easier to imagine assuming the aggressive power of the attacker, to embrace the delusion of oneself as Arnold Schwarzenegger: *If I am tough enough and strong enough, I can take out the bad guys.*

The country is at present suffering from a huge version of this same delusion, a myth nurtured by historical tales of frontier violence and vigilantism and by the action-hero fantasies of film and television. Bolstered by the social Darwinists of the right, who see society as an unfettered marketplace in which the strongest individuals flourish, this delusion frames the crime debate.

To ask, "Why didn't anybody stop him?" is to imply only two choices: Rambo-like heroism or abject victimhood, fight or flight. And people don't want to think of themselves choosing flight. In last year's debate over the crime bill, conservatives successfully portrayed themselves as those who would stand and fight; liberals were portrayed as ineffectual cowards.

But on the receiving end of a violent attack, the fight-or-flight dichotomy didn't apply. Nor did that radically individualized notion of survival. At the coffeehouse that night there were no Schwarzeneggers, no stand-alone heroes. But neither were there abject victims. The woman behind the counter helped one of the wounded out the back window; Anna, Martin, and I clung to one another as we escaped; and two patrons who had never met sought a hiding place together around the corner. In the confusion and panic of life-threatening attack, people reached out to one another. This sounds simple, yet it suggests that there is an instinct for mutual aid that poses a profound challenge to the atomized individualism of the right. 20

I do understand the rage and frustration behind the crime-victim movement, and see how the right has harnessed it. Anyone trying to deal with the reality of crime, as opposed to the fantasies peddled to win elections, needs to understand the complex suffering of those who are survivors of such traumas, and the suffering and turmoil of their families. I have impressive physical scars, but to me the disruption of my psyche is more significant. For weeks after the attack, I awoke nightly, agitated, drenched with sweat. Any moment of mental repose was instantly flooded with images from that night. Sometimes my mind simply would not tune in at all. My reactions are still out of balance and disproportionate. I shut a door on my finger, not too hard, and my body is suddenly flooded with adrenaline, nearly faint. Walking on the arm of my partner, Margaret, one evening I abruptly shove her to the side of the road because I have seen a tall, lean shadow a block away. An hour after an argument, I find myself quaking with rage, completely unable to restore my sense of calm.

What psychologists call post-traumatic stress disorder is, among other things, a profoundly political state, in which the world has gone wrong, in which you feel isolated from the broader community by the inarticulable extremity of experience. I have spent a lot of time in the past few months thinking about what the world must look like to those who have survived repeated violent attacks—to children battered in their homes and prisoners beaten or tortured behind bars—and to those, like rape victims, whose assaults are rarely granted the public ratification that mine was.

If the use of my picture on television unexpectedly brought me face-to-face with the memory of August 7, some part of the attack is relived for me daily as I watch the gruesome, voyeuristically reported details of the deaths of Nicole Brown Simpson and Ronald Goldman. And throughout the Colin Ferguson trial, as he spoke of falling asleep and having someone else fire his gun, I heard Daniel Silva's calm, secure voice telling me I had killed his mother. When I hear testimony by the survivors of that massacre—on a train as comfortable and familiar to them as my neighborhood coffee bar is to me—I feel a great and incommunicable fellowship.

But the public obsession with these trials, I am convinced, has no more to do with the real experience of crime victims than do the posturings of politicians. I do not know what made my assailant act as he did. Nor do I think crime and violence can be reduced to simple political categories. I do know that the answers will not be found in social Darwinism and individualism, in racism, in dismantling cities and increasing the destitution of the poor. To the contrary: every fragment of my experience suggests that the best protection from crime and the best aid to victims are the very social institutions most derided by the right. As a crime victim and a citizen, what I want is the reality of a safe community—not a politician's fantasyland of restitution and revenge. That is my testimony.

The Responsive Reader

1. To help us make sense of an instance of "senseless violence," Shapiro chronicles his traumatic experience in painstaking detail. How much do you learn about the circumstances? What would you include in a report on the basic facts?
2. How much do you learn about the assailant? What do you learn about his history, his condition, or his motives? What is Shapiro's attitude toward him?

3. What does Shapiro say about "the delusion of oneself as Arnold Schwarzenegger" and about "Rambo-like heroism"? To him, what makes it an illusion?

4. What does Shapiro say about the aftermath of violence for the victims? Encounters with irrational violence may leave people cynical about human nature. For Shapiro, were there any redeeming positive or encouraging aspects of his experience?

5. Charles Darwin described the state of nature as a struggle for survival and as a war of all against all. What is social Darwinism? Why is it an issue in this essay?

Talking, Listening, Writing

6. Shapiro wants to do more than tell his personal story. He wants us to take a new look at the politics of crime. What is his criticism of the treatment of crime by the media? What is his criticism of the treatment of crime on the part of politicians?

7. Was what happened to Shapiro an "isolated incident"? Or do you think what happened to him "could have happened to anybody"? Was he "in the wrong place at the wrong time"?

8. Do you think the media spend too much time exploiting sensational crimes or refereeing sensational court battles and too little on what the aftermath of crime means for victims or their families?

9. Have you or people you know well been the victims of violent crime? What is your story, or what is their story?

Collaborative Projects

10. You may want to team up with classmates to find out about the movement toward victims' rights. What is the agenda of victims' rights organizations? What are reasons, initiatives, accomplishments? What are possible roadblocks, pitfalls, objections? How much popular support is there for the movement?

A PEACEFUL WOMAN EXPLAINS WHY SHE CARRIES A GUN

Linda M. Hasselstrom

For a time it seemed that the argument over gun control had divided the American public into two camps. Debate seemed polarized: Liberals were asking citizens to hand in their guns as a first step toward a safer, saner world. Conservatives seemed to be defending the constitutional right of citizens to assemble arsenals of lethal weapons for armed resistance against an evil government. In recent years, however, women especially have been rethinking their attitude toward guns as the symbol of a violence-prone civilization. Increasingly, law enforcement seemed incompetent to protect women from battering abuse and homicidal violence. Linda M. Hasselstrom originally wrote the following widely read call for women's self-reliance and self-defense for the High Country News, *a regional* Rocky Mountain *publication. She is from the grasslands of western South Dakota near the Black Hills. Her family had homesteaded in the late 1800s in the "vast emptiness" of the South Dakota prairie along with other Swedes and Norwegians. She has worked as a cattle rancher, saying that "someone who pays attention to the messages the natural world sends can bring cattle home the day* before *a blizzard nine times out of ten." A poet and environmental activist, she for years operated her own small press, named Lame Johnny after a horse thief.*

Thought Starters: What advice does law enforcement give to women concerned about safety? Is it helpful? Is it useless? Does it reflect a male point of view?

I am a peace-loving woman. But several events in the past 10 years   *1* have convinced me I'm safer when I carry a pistol. This was a personal decision, but because handgun possession is a controversial subject, perhaps my reasoning will interest others.

I live in western South Dakota on a ranch 25 miles from the nearest town: for several years I spent winters alone here. As a free-lance writer, I travel alone a lot more than 100,000 miles by car in the last four years. With women freer than ever before to travel alone, the odds of our encountering trouble seem to have risen. Distances are great, roads are deserted, and the terrain is often too exposed to offer hiding places.

A woman who travels alone is advised, usually by men, to protect herself by avoiding bars and other "dangerous situations," by approaching her car like an Indian scout, by locking doors and windows. But these precautions aren't always enough. I spent years following them and still found myself in dangerous situations. I began to resent the idea that just because I am female, I have to be extra careful.

A few years ago, with another woman, I camped for several weeks in the West. We discussed self-defense, but neither of us had taken a course in it. She was against firearms, and local police told us Mace was illegal. So we armed ourselves with spray cans of deodorant tucked into our sleeping bags. We never used our improvised Mace because we were lucky enough to camp beside people who came to our aid when men harassed us. But on one occasion we visited a national park where our assigned space was less than 15 feet from other campers. When we returned from a walk, we found our closest neighbors were two young men. As we gathered our cooking gear, they drank beer and loudly discussed what they would do to us after dark. Nearby campers, even families, ignored them: rangers strolled past, unconcerned. When we asked the rangers point-blank if they would protect us, one of them patted my shoulder and said, "Don't worry, girls. They're just kidding." At dusk we drove out of the park and hid our camp in the woods a few miles away. The illegal spot was lovely, but our enjoyment of that park was ruined. I returned from the trip determined to reconsider the options available for protecting myself.

At that time, I lived alone on the ranch and taught night classes in town. Along a city street I often traveled, a woman had a flat tire, called for help on her CB radio, and got a rapist who left her beaten. She was afraid to call for help again and stayed in her car until morning. For that reason, as well as because CBs work best along line-of-sight, which wouldn't help much in the rolling hills where I live, I ruled out a CB.

As I drove home one night, a car followed me. It passed me on a narrow bridge while a passenger flashed a blinding spotlight in my face. I braked sharply. The car stopped, angled across the bridge, and four men jumped out. I realized the locked doors were useless if they broke the windows of my pickup. I started forward, hoping to knock their car aside so I could pass. Just then another car appeared, and the men hastily got back in their car. They continued to follow me, passing and repassing. I dared not go home because no one else was there. I passed no lighted houses. Finally they pulled over to the roadside, and I decided to use their tactic: fear. Speeding, the pickup horn blaring, I swerved as close to them as I dared as I roared past. It worked: they turned off the highway. But I was frightened and angry. Even in my vehicle I was too vulnerable.

Other incidents occurred over the years. One day I glanced out a field below my house and saw a man with a shotgun walking toward a pond full of ducks. I drove down and explained that the land was posted. I politely asked him to leave. He stared at me, and the muzzle of the shotgun began to rise. In a moment of utter clarity I realized that I was alone on the ranch, and that he could shoot me and simply drive away. The moment passed: the man left.

One night, I returned home from teaching a class to find deep tire ruts in the wet ground of my yard, garbage in the driveway, and a large gas tank

5

empty. A light shone in the house: I couldn't remember leaving it on. I was too embarrassed to drive to a neighboring ranch and wake someone up. An hour of cautious exploration convinced me the house was safe, but once inside, with the doors locked, I was still afraid. I kept thinking of how vulnerable I felt, prowling around my own house in the dark.

My first positive step was to take a kung fu class, which teaches evasive or protective action when someone enters your space without permission. I learned to move confidently, scanning for possible attackers. I learned how to assess danger and techniques for avoiding it without combat.

I also learned that one must practice several hours every day to be   10
good at kung fu. By that time I had married George: when I practiced with him, I learned how *close* you must be to your attacker to use martial arts, and decided a 120-pound woman dare not let a six-foot, 220-pound attacker get that close unless she is very, very good at self-defense. I have since read articles by several women who were extremely well trained in the martial arts, but were raped and beaten anyway.

I thought back over the times in my life when I had been attacked or threatened and tried to be realistic about my own behavior, searching for anything that had allowed me to become a victim. Overall, I was convinced that I had not been at fault. I don't believe myself to be either paranoid or a risk-taker, but I wanted more protection.

With some reluctance I decided to try carrying a pistol. George had always carried one, despite his size and his training in martial arts. I practiced shooting until I was sure I could hit an attacker who moved close enough to endanger me. Then I bought a license from the county sheriff, making it legal for me to carry the gun concealed.

But I was not yet ready to defend myself. George taught me that the most important preparation was mental: convincing myself I could actually *shoot a person.* Few of us wish to hurt or kill another human being. But there is no point in having a gun—in fact, gun possession might increase your danger—unless you know you can use it. I got in the habit of rehearsing, as I drove or walked, the precise conditions that would be required before I would shoot someone.

People who have not grown up with the idea that they are capable of protecting themselves—in other words, most women—might have to work hard to convince themselves of their ability, and of the necessity. Handgun ownership need not turn us into gunslingers, but it can be part of believing in, and relying on, *ourselves* for protection.

To be useful, a pistol has to be available. In my car, it's within instant   15
reach. When I enter a deserted rest stop at night, it's in my purse, with my hand on the grip. When I walk from a dark parking lot into a motel, it's in my hand, under a coat. At home, it's on the headboard. In short, I take it with me almost everywhere I go alone.

Just carrying a pistol is not protection; avoidance is still the best approach to trouble. Subconsciously watching for signs of danger, I believe

I've become more alert. Handgun use, not unlike driving, becomes instinctive. Each time I've drawn my gun—I have never fired it at another human being—I've simply found it in my hand.

I was driving the half-mile to the highway mailbox one day when I saw a vehicle parked about midway down the road. Several men were standing in the ditch, relieving themselves. I have no objection to emergency urination, but I noticed they'd dumped several dozen beer cans in the road. Besides being ugly, cans can slash a cow's feet or stomach.

The men noticed me before they finished and made quite a performance out of zipping their trousers while walking toward me. All four of them gathered around my small foreign car, and one of them demanded what the hell I wanted.

"This is private land. I'd appreciate it if you'd pick up the beer cans."

"What beer cans?" said the belligerent one, putting both hands on the   20
car door and leaning in my window. His face was inches from mine, and the beer fumes were strong. The others laughed. One tried the passenger door, locked; another put his foot on the hood and rocked the car. They circled, lightly thumping the roof, discussing my good fortune in meeting them and the benefits they were likely to bestow upon me. I felt very small and very trapped and they knew it.

"The ones you just threw out," I said politely.

"I don't see no beer cans. Why don't you get out here and show them to me, honey?" said the belligerent one, reaching for the handle inside the door.

"Right over there," I said, still being polite. "—there, and over there." I pointed with the pistol, which I'd slipped under my thigh. Within one minute the cans and the men were back in the car and headed down the road.

I believe this incident illustrates several important principles. The men were trespassing and knew it: their judgment may have been impaired by alcohol. Their response to the polite request of a woman alone was to use their size, numbers, and sex to inspire fear. The pistol was a response in the same language. Politeness didn't work: I couldn't match them in size or number. Out of the car, I'd have been more vulnerable. The pistol just changed the balance of power. It worked again recently when I was driving in a desolate part of Wyoming. A man played cat-and-mouse with me for 30 miles, ultimately trying to run me off the road. When his car passed mine with only two inches to spare, I showed him my pistol, and he disappeared.

When I got my pistol, I told my husband, revising the old Colt slo-   25
gan, "God made men *and women,* but Sam Colt made them equal." Recently I have seen a gunmaker's ad with a similar sentiment. Perhaps this is an idea whose time has come, though the pacifist inside me will be saddened if the only way women can achieve equality is by carrying weapons.

We must treat a firearm's power with caution. "Power tends to corrupt, and absolute power corrupts absolutely," as a man (Lord Acton) once said. A pistol is not the only way to avoid being raped or murdered in today's world, but, intelligently wielded, it can shift the balance of power and provide a measure of safety.

The Responsive Reader

1. Why was Hasselstrom dissatisfied with the advice she was given about how to avoid danger? What alternatives did she check out before she turned to guns? What were her conclusions?
2. What about where and how she lived put Hasselstrom especially at risk? What are the key points she is trying to make about the incidents she describes? Do you think these are "isolated incidents" or parts of a familiar pattern of male behavior?
3. How concerned is Hasselstrom about the "intelligent" use of guns? What does she think it takes for women to use guns successfully for protection? What warnings or advice does she have for other women?

Talking, Listening, Writing

4. The incidents that Hasselstrom reports took place in an isolated rural setting. Do you think her arguments could apply equally in a crowded urban environment? Why or why not?
5. Do you think that safeguards or precautions could be developed to limit the use of guns to self-defense or to make them safer for their owners and their families?
6. Are there still men who think that female victims of rape or male violence probably "asked for it"?

WHITE MAN
Tobias Wolff

Tobias Wolff became known for his autobiographical This Boy's Life, *which has been called "an unforgettable memoir of an American childhood." Like other young Americans of his generation, Wolff found himself in the army in Vietnam—in a nightmarish losing war, in a disorienting different culture, and in alien natural surroundings. After World War II, the French had lost a disastrous colonial war to reestablish their rule over their Indochinese territories. The independence movement in the former Indochina was led by the communist Vietminh in Vietnam and the Khmer Rouge in Cambodia, and the United States joined in the fight to defend Western-sponsored local governments in the name of the Cold War struggle against communist aggression. The Vietcong, the southern arm of the North Vietnamese liberation movement, led a classic guerilla war against conventionally trained American troops. In his* In Pharaoh's Army: Memories of the Lost War *(1994), Wolff wrote a searingly honest eyewitness account from the point of view not of the generals, the propagandists, or the political commentators but of the unknown ordinary soldiers sent out to fight, to die, or to return shell-shocked and traumatized to society.*

Thought Starters: Is the Vietnam War ancient history for you or others of your generation? Do you know anyone who, like Wolff, is still close to the traumas and controversies of the lost war? Has the war and its aftermath disappeared from the news?

A week or so after Sergeant Benet and I made our Thanksgiving raid on Dong Tam, the division was ordered into the field. The plan called for our howitzers and men to be carried by helicopter to a position in the countryside. I was sent ahead with the security force responsible for preparing the ground and making sure it was safe to land. My job was to call in American gunships and medevacs if any were needed. I could even get F-4 Phantom jets if we ran into serious trouble, or trouble that I might consider serious, which would be any kind of trouble at all.

The designated position turned out to be a mudfield. We were ordered to secure another site some four or five kilometers away. Our march took us through a couple of deserted villages along a canal. This was a free-fire zone. The people who'd lived around here had been moved to a detention camp, and their home ground declared open to random shelling and bombing. Harassment and interdiction, it was called, H and I. The earth was churned up by artillery and pocked with huge, water-filled craters from

B-52 strikes. Pieces of shrapnel, iridescent with heat scars, glittered under-foot. The dikes had been breached. The paddies were full of brackish wa-ter covered by green, undulant slime, broken here and there by clumps of saw grass. The silence was unnatural, expectant. It magnified the sound of our voices, the clank of mess kits and weapons, the rushing static of the ra-dio. Our progress was not stealthy.

The villes were empty, the hooches in shreds, but you could see that people had been in the area. We kept coming across their garbage and cooking fires. Cooking fires—just like a Western. In the second village we found a white puppy. Someone had left him a heap of vegetable slops with some meat and bones mixed in. It looked rotten, but he seemed to be do-ing okay, the little chub. One of the soldiers tied a rope around his neck and brought him along.

Because the paddies were flooded and most of the dikes broken or collapsed, we had only a few possible routes of march, unless we moved off the trail; but mucking through the paddies was a drag, and our boys wouldn't dream of it. Though I knew better I didn't blame them. Instead we kept to what little remained of dry land, which meant a good chance of booby traps and maybe a sniper. There were several troops ahead of me in the column and I figured they'd either discover or get blown up by any-thing left on the trail, but the idea of a sniper had me on edge. I was the tallest man out here by at least a head, and I had to stay right next to the ra-dio operator, who had this big squawking box on his back and a long an-tenna whipping back and forth over his helmet. And of course I was white. A perfect target. And that was how I saw myself, as a target, a long white face quartered by crosshairs.

I was dead sure somebody had me in his sights. I kept scanning the tree lines for his position, feeling him track me. I adopted an erratic walk, slowing down and speeding up, ducking my head, weaving from side to side. We were in pretty loose order anyway so nobody seemed to notice ex-cept the radio operator, who watched me curiously at first and then went back to his own thoughts. I prepared a face for the sniper to judge, not a brave or confident face but not a fearful one either. What I tried to do was look well-meaning and slightly apologetic, like a very nice person who has been swept up by forces beyond his control and set down in a place where he knows he doesn't belong and that he intends to vacate the first chance he gets.

But at the same time I knew the sniper wouldn't notice any of that, would notice nothing but my size and my whiteness. I didn't fit here. I was out of proportion not only to the men around me but to everything else— the huts, the villages, even the fields. All was shaped and scaled to the people whose place this was. Time had made it so. I was oafish here, just as the Vietnamese seemed oddly dainty on the wide Frenchified boulevards of Saigon.

And man, was I white! I could feel my whiteness shooting out like sparks. This wasn't just paranoia, it was what the Vietnamese saw when they looked at me, as I had cause to know. One instance: I was coming out of a bar in My Tho some months back, about to head home for the night, when I found myself surrounded by a crowd of Vietnamese soldiers from another battalion. They pressed up close, yelling and pushing me back and forth. Some of them had bamboo sticks. They were mad about something but I couldn't figure out what, they were shouting too fast and all at once. *Tai sao?* I kept asking—Why? Why? I saw that the question infuriated them, as if I were denying some outrage that everyone there had personally seen me commit. I understood that this was a ridiculous misunderstanding, that they had me confused with another man, another American.

"I'm the wrong man," I said. "The wrong man!"

They became apoplectic. I couldn't get anywhere with them, and I soon wearied of trying. As I pushed my way toward the jeep one of them slashed me across the face with his stick and then the rest of them started swinging too, shoving for position, everyone trying to get his licks in. I fought back but couldn't hold them off. Because of my height I took most of the punishment on my shoulders and neck, but they managed to hit me a few more times in the face, not heavy blows but sharp and burning, as from a whip. Blood started running into my eyes. They were swinging and screaming, totally berserk, and then they stopped. There was no sound but the feral rasp and pant of our breathing. Everyone was looking at the bar, where an American lieutenant named Polk stood in the doorway. He was the one they were after, that was clear from his expression and from theirs.

With an unhurried movement Polk unsnapped his holster and took out his .45 and cocked it. He slowly aimed the pistol just above their heads, and in the same dream time they stepped back into the street and walked silently away.

Polk lowered the pistol. He asked if I was all right.

"I guess," I said. "What was that all about, anyway?"

He didn't tell me.

I was halfway home before it occurred to me that I could have saved myself a lot of trouble by pulling my own pistol. I'd forgotten I had it on.

Sergeant Benet cleaned my wounds—a few shallow cuts on my forehead. He had a touch as gentle as a woman's, and feeling him take me so tenderly in hand, dabbing and clucking, wincing at my pain as if it were his own, I started to feel sorry for myself. "I don't get it," I said. "Polk doesn't look anything like me. He's almost as big as you are. He doesn't have a moustache. He's got these piggy little eyes and this big moon face. We don't look *anything* alike!"

We found the second position to be satisfactory and set up camp for the night. Though the troops weren't supposed to build fires, they did, as always. They dropped their weapons any old place and took off their boots

and readied their pans for the fish they'd collected earlier that day by tossing hand grenades into the local ponds. While they cooked they called back
and forth to each other and sang along with sad nasal ballads on their radios.
The perimeter guards wouldn't stay in position; they kept drifting in to visit
friends and check on the progress of the food.

   Nights in the field were always bad for me. I had a case of the runs.
My skin felt crawly. My right eye twitched, and I kept flinching uncon-
trollably. I plotted our coordinates and called them in to the firebase and
the air support people, along with the coordinates of the surrounding tree
lines and all possible avenues of attack. If we got hit I intended to call down
destruction on everything around me—the whole world, if necessary. The
puppy ran past, squealing like a pig, as two soldiers chased after him. He
tumbled over himself and one of the troops jumped for him and caught him
by a hind leg. He lifted him that way and gave him a nasty shake, the way
you'd snap a towel, then walked off swinging the puppy's nose just above
the ground. After I finished my calls I followed them over to one of the
fires. They had tied the puppy to a tree. He was all curled in on himself,
watching them with one wild eye. His sides were heaving.

   I greeted the two soldiers and hunkered down at their fire. They were
sitting face-to-face with their legs dovetailed, massaging each other's feet.
The arrangement looked timeless and profoundly corporeal, like two horses
standing back to front, whisking flies from one another's eyes. Seeing them
this way, whipped and sore, mired in their bodies, emptied me of anger. I
shared my cigarettes. We agreed that Marlboros were number one.

The Responsive Reader

1. What was Wolff's assignment or role in the military dimension of the
   conflict? What early in his story can be read as if it were part of a
   straightforward bulletin from the front? Where does his account first become colored by the surreal or nightmarish quality that many participants came to associate with the Vietnam war?
2. White Americans are used to being lectured about using or abusing their
   race as a badge of privilege. How does Wolff's account turn the tables
   on this assumption of white superiority and privilege? What details and
   what incidents dramatize the traumatizing changed perspective that
   makes the white man see himself as target, as enemy, and as resented
   alien intruder? How did Wolff cope with his role as the designated target and enemy?
3. What do you learn from Wolff's account about the ordinary unglam-
   orous, unheroic day-to-day reality of war for the foot soldiers between
   murderous combat encounters? How serious or how casual are they
   about their assigned duties? What occupies their time? What signs are
   there of the camaraderie of the doomed?

4. Volumes have been written and countless documentaries produced about the motives, war aims, political movements, strategies, and changing fortunes of the Vietnam war. What is Wolff's perspective, attitude, or involvement concerning the war?

5. Racism became a poisonous undercurrent during the Vietnam war. Does it play a role in this account?

Talking, Listening, Writing

6. What war movies about Vietnam have you watched? How does Wolff's account compare with the picture they present of the war? What is similar, and what is different?

Collaborative Projects

7. Among books honoring the grunt or the high-risk FNG (fucking new guy), Tobias Wolff's *In Pharaoh's Army,* Larry Heinemann's *Close Quarters,* and Tim O'Brien's *Going after Cacciato* stand out. Working with a group, you may want to organize a reading and discussion of selections from these and other survivors' testimonies. Denise Levertov's "What Were They Like?," Alberto Rios's "Vietnam Wall," and Jeffrey Harrison's "Reflection of the Vietnam Memorial" are among poems you may want to include in a reading paying tribute to the Vietnam war dead and victims of war.

THE BUCK PRIVATE (*SOLDADO RAZO*)

Luis Valdez

> If you can sing, dance, walk, march, hold a picket sign, play a gui-
> tar or harmonica or any other instrument, you can participate! No
> acting experience required.
>
> From a recruiting leaflet for the *Teatro Campesino*

Luis Valdez (born 1940) founded the Teatro Campesino, *which has
been honored in both the United States and Europe. (A* campesino *is someone who works in the fields.) Valdez himself was working in the fields by the
time he was six years old, with the much-interrupted schooling of the children
of America's migrant workers. He eventually accepted a scholarship at San Jose
State University and graduated with a B.A. in English in 1964. The theater
group that Valdez founded in 1965 began by performing* actos—*short, one-
act plays—in community centers, church halls, and fields in California. Under his leadership, the* Teatro Campesino *explored the lives of urban Chicano
youth, Mexican Indian legend and mythology, and materials from Third
World sources. At the beginning of his play* Los Vendidos (The Sellouts,
1967), *a secretary from the governor's office comes to Honest Sancho's Used
Mexican lot to look for a suave, not-too-dark Chicano to become a token Mexican American at social functions in the state capital. In 1987, Valdez wrote
and directed the movie* La Bamba, *a biography of the Chicano rock 'n' roll singer
Ritchie Valens. His PBS production of* Corridos: Tales of Passion and Revolution, *with Linda Ronstadt, won the Peabody Award.* Soldado Razo, *or*
The Buck Private, *was first performed by the* Teatro Campesino *in 1971.*

Thought Starters: What is the history of minorities in the American military? Have the least privileged in our society borne a disproportionate
share of the burden of defending it?

Characters

Johnny	The Mother
The Father	Cecilia
Death	The Brother

DEATH (*enters singing*). I'm taking off as a private, I'm going to join the   *1*
    ranks . . . along with the courageous young men who leave behind be-
    loved mothers, who leave their girlfriends crying, crying, crying their
    farewell. Yeah! How lucky for me that there's a war. How goes it, bro?

I am death. What else is new? Well, don't get paranoid because I didn't come to take anybody away. I came to tell you a story. Sure, the story of the Buck Private. Maybe you knew him, eh? He was killed not too long ago in Vietnam.

[JOHNNY *enters, adjusting his uniform.*]

DEATH. This is Johnny, The Buck Private. He's leaving for Vietnam in the morning, but tonight—well, tonight he's going to enjoy himself, right? Look at his face. Know what he's thinking? He's thinking (Johnny *moves his lips*) "Now, I'm a man!"

[THE MOTHER *enters.*]

DEATH. This is his mother. Poor thing. She's worried about her son, like all mothers. "Blessed be God," she's thinking; (The Mother *moves her mouth*) "I hope nothing happens to my son." (The Mother *touches* Johnny *on the shoulder.*)

JOHNNY. Is dinner ready, mom?

MOTHER. Yes, son, almost. Why did you dress like that? You're not leaving until tomorrow. 5

JOHNNY. Well, you know. Cecilia's coming and everything.

MOTHER. Oh, my son. You're always bringing girlfriends to the house but you never think about settling down.

JOHNNY. One of these days I'll give you a surprise, ma. (*He kisses her forehead. Embraces her.*)

DEATH. Oh, my! What a picture of tenderness, no? But, watch the old lady. Listen to what she's thinking. "Now, my son is a man. He looks so handsome in that uniform."

JOHNNY. Well, mom, it's getting late. I'll be back shortly with Cecilia, okay? 10

MOTHER. Yes, son, hurry back. (*He leaves.*) May God take care of you, mom's pride and joy.

[JOHNNY *re-enters and begins to talk.*]

DEATH. Out in the street, Johnny begins to think about his family, his girl, his neighborhood, his life.

JOHNNY. Poor mom. Tomorrow it will be very difficult for her. For me as well. It was pretty hard when I went to boot camp, but now? Vietnam! It's a killer, man. The old man, too. I'm not going to be here to help him out. I wasn't getting rich doing fieldwork, but it was something. A little help, at least. My little brother can't work yet because he's still in school. I just hope he stays there. And finishes. I never liked that school stuff, but I know my little brother digs it. He's smart too—maybe he'll even go to college. One of us has got to make it in this life. Me—I guess I'll just get married to Cecilia and have a bunch of kids. I remember when I first saw her at the Rainbow Ballroom. I couldn't even dance with her because I had had a few beers. The next week was pretty good, though. Since then. How long ago was that? June . . . no, July. Four months. Now I want to get hitched. Her parents don't like me, I know. They think I'm a good for nothing. Maybe they'll feel different when I come back from Nam. Sure, the War Veteran! Maybe I'll get wounded and come back with tons of medals. I wonder how the dudes around here are going to think about that? Damn neighborhood—I've lived here all my life. Now I'm going to Vietnam. (*Taps and drum*) It's going to be a drag, man. I might even get killed. If I do, they'll bring me back here in a box, covered with a flag . . . military funeral like they gave Pete Gomez . . . everybody crying . . . the old lady—(*Stops*) What the hell am I thinking, man? Damn fool! (*He freezes.*)

[DEATH *powders* JOHNNY's *face white during the next speech.*]

DEATH. Foolish, but not stupid, eh? He knew the kind of funeral he wanted and he got it. Military coffin, lots of flowers, American flag, women crying, and a trumpet playing taps with a rifle salute at the end. Or was it goodbye? It doesn't matter, you know what I mean. It was first class all the way. Oh, by the way, don't get upset about the makeup I'm putting on him, eh? I'm just getting him ready for what's coming. I don't always do things in a hurry, you know. Okay, then, next scene. (Johnny *exits.*)

[JOHNNY *goes on to* CECILIA's *and exits.*]

DEATH. Back at the house, his old man is just getting home.   15

[THE FATHER *enters.*]

FATHER. Hey, old lady, I'm home. Is dinner ready?

[THE MOTHER *enters.*]

MOTHER. Yes, dear. Just wait till Juan gets home. What did you buy?
FATHER. A sixpack of Coors.
MOTHER. Beer?
FATHER. Well, why not? Look—This is my son's last night.   20
MOTHER. What do you mean, his last night? Don't speak like that.
FATHER. I mean his last night at home, woman. You understand—hic.
MOTHER. You're drunk, aren't you?
FATHER. And if I am, what's it to you? I just had a few beers with my buddy and that's it. Well, what is this, anyway . . . ? It's all I need, man. My son's going to war and you don't want me to drink. I've got to celebrate, woman!
MOTHER. Celebrate what?   25
FATHER. That my son is now a man! And quite a man, the twerp. So don't pester me. Bring me some supper.

MOTHER. Wait for Juan to come home.

FATHER. Where is he? He's not here? Is that so-and-so loafing around
again? Juan? Juan?

MOTHER. I'm telling you he went to get Cecilia, who's going to have dinner with us. And please don't use any foul language. What will the girl
say if she hears you talking like that?

FATHER. To hell with it! Who owns this damn house, anyway? Aren't I the   30
one who pays the rent? The one who buys the food? Don't make me
get angry, huh? Or you'll get it. It doesn't matter if you already have a
son who's a soldier.

MOTHER. Please. I ask you in your son's name, eh? Calm down. (*She exits.*)

FATHER. Calm down! Just like that she wants me to calm down. And
who's going to shut my trap? My son the soldier? My son . . .

DEATH. The old man's thoughts are racing back a dozen years to a warm
afternoon in July. Johnny, eight years old, is running toward him between the vines, shouting: "Paaa, I already picked 20 trays, paaapá!"

FATHER. Huh. Twenty trays. Little bugger.

[THE BROTHER *enters.*]

BROTHER. Pa, is Johnny here?   35

DEATH. This is Johnny's little brother.

FATHER. And where are you coming from?

BROTHER. I was over at Polo's house. He has a new motor scooter.

FATHER. You just spend all your time playing, don't you?

BROTHER. I didn't do anything.   40

FATHER. Don't talk back to your father.

BROTHER (*shrugs*). Are we going to eat soon?

FATHER. I don't know. Go ask your mother.

[THE BROTHER *exits.*]

DEATH. Looking at his younger son, the old man starts thinking about
him. His thoughts spin around in the usual hopeless cycle of defeat,
undercut by more defeat.

FATHER. That boy should be working. He's already fourteen years old. I   45
don't know why the law forces them to go to school till they're sixteen. He won't amount to anything, anyway. It's better if he starts
working with me so that he can help the family.

DEATH. Sure, he gets out of school and in three or four years, I take him
the way I took Johnny. Crazy, huh?

[JOHNNY *returns with* CECILIA.]

JOHNNY. Good evening, pa.

FATHER. Son! Good evening. What's this? You're dressed as a soldier?

JOHNNY. I brought Cecilia over to have dinner with us.

FATHER. Well, have her come in, come in.   50

CECILIA. Thank you very much.

FATHER. My son looks good, doesn't he?

CECILIA. Yes, sir.

FATHER. Damn right. He's off to be a buck private. (*Pause*) Well, let's see . . . uh, son, would you like a beer?!

JOHNNY. Yes, sir, but couldn't we get a chair first? For Cecilia?   55

FATHER. But, of course. We have all the modern conveniences. Let me bring one. Sweetheart? The company's here! (*He exits.*)

JOHNNY. How you doing?

CECILIA. Okay. I love you.

DEATH. This, of course, is Johnny's girlfriend. Fine, ha? Too bad he'll never get to marry her. Oh, he proposed tonight and everything— and she accepted, but she doesn't know what's ahead. Listen to what she's thinking. (Cecilia *moves her mouth.*) "When we get married I hope Johnny still has his uniform. We'd look so good together. Me in a wedding gown and him like that. I wish we were getting married tomorrow!"

JOHNNY. What are you thinking?   60

CECILIA. Nothing.

JOHNNY. Come on.

CECILIA. Really.

JOHNNY. Come on, I saw your eyes. Now come on, tell me what you were thinking.

CECILIA. It was nothing.   65

JOHNNY. Are you scared?

CECILIA. About what?

JOHNNY. My going to Vietnam.

CECILIA. No! I mean . . . yes, in a way, but I wasn't thinking that.

JOHNNY. What was it?   70

CECILIA (*Pause*). I was thinking I wish the wedding was tomorrow.

JOHNNY. Really?

CECILIA. Yes.

JOHNNY. You know what? I wish it was too. (*He embraces her.*)

DEATH. And, of course, now he's thinking too. But it's not what she was   75
thinking. What a world!

[THE FATHER *and* THE BROTHER *enter with four chairs.*]

FATHER. Here are the chairs. What did I tell you? (*To* The Brother) Hey, you, help me move the table, come on.

JOHNNY. Do you need help, pa?

FATHER. No, son, your brother and I'll move it. (*He and* The Brother *move imaginary table into place.*) There it is. And your mom says you should start sitting down because dinner's ready. She made tamales, can you believe that?

JOHNNY. Tamales?

BROTHER. They're Colonel Sanders, eeehh.   80

FATHER. You shut your trap! Look . . . don't pay attention to him, Cecilia;
this little bugger, uh, this kid is always saying stupid things, uh, silly
things. Sit down.

MOTHER (*entering with imaginary bowl*). Here come the tamales! Watch out
because the pot's hot, okay? Oh, Cecilia, good evening.

CECILIA. Good evening, ma'am. Can I help you with anything?

MOTHER. No, no, everything's ready. Sit down, please.

JOHNNY. Ma, how come you made tamales? (Death *begins to put some more*   85
makeup on Johnny's *face*.)

MOTHER. Well, because I know you like them so much, son.

DEATH. A thought flashes across Johnny's mind: "Too much, man. I
should go to war every day." Over on this side of the table, the little
brother is thinking: "What's so hot about going to war—tamales?"

BROTHER. I like tamales.

FATHER. Who told you to open your mouth? Would you like a beer, son?

JOHNNY (*nods*). Thanks, dad.   90

FATHER. And you, Cecilia?

CECILIA (*surprised*). No, sir, uh, thanks.

MOTHER. Juan, don't be so thoughtless. Cecilia's not old enough to drink.
What are her parents going to say? I made some Kool-Aid, sweetheart;
I'll bring the pitcher right out. (*She exits.*)

DEATH. You know what's going through the little brother's mind? He is
thinking: "He offered her a beer! She was barely in the eighth grade
three years ago. When I'm 17 I'm going to join the service and get really drunk."

FATHER. How old are you, Cecilia?   95

CECILIA. Eighteen.

DEATH. She lied, of course.

FATHER. Oh, well, what the heck, you're already a woman! Come on son,
don't let her get away.

JOHNNY. I'm not.

MOTHER (*re-entering*). Here's the Kool-Aid and the beans.   100

JOHNNY. Ma, I got an announcement to make. Will you please sit down?

MOTHER. What is it?

FATHER (*to* The Brother). Give your chair to your mother.

BROTHER. What about my tamale?

MOTHER. Let him eat his dinner.   105

FATHER (*to* The Brother). Get up!

JOHNNY. Sit down, Mom.

MOTHER. What is it, son? (*She sits down.*)

DEATH. Funny little games people play, ha? The mother asks, but she already knows what her son is going to say. So does the father. And even
little brother. They are all thinking: "He is going to say: Cecilia and I
are getting married!"

JOHNNY. Cecilia and I are getting married!   *110*

MOTHER. Oh, son!

FATHER. You don't say!

BROTHER. Really?

MOTHER. When, son?

JOHNNY. When I get back from Vietnam.   *115*

DEATH. Suddenly a thought is crossing everybody's mind: "What if he doesn't come back?" But they shove it aside.

MOTHER. Oh, darling! (*She hugs* Cecilia.)

FATHER. Congratulations, son. (*He hugs* Johnny.)

MOTHER (*hugging* Johnny). My boy! (*She cries.*)

JOHNNY. Hey, mom, wait a minute. Save that for tomorrow. That's   *120* enough, ma.

FATHER. Daughter. (*He hugs* Cecilia *properly.*)

BROTHER. Heh, Johnny, why don't I go to Vietnam and you stay here for the wedding? I'm not afraid to die.

MOTHER. What makes you say that, child?

BROTHER. It just came out.

FATHER. You've let out too much already, don't you think?   *125*

BROTHER. I didn't mean it! (The Brother *exits.*)

JOHNNY. It was an accident, pa.

MOTHER. You're right; it was an accident. Please, sweetheart, let's eat in peace, ha? Juan leaves tomorrow.

DEATH. The rest of the meal goes by without any incidents. They discuss the wedding, the tamales, and the weather. Then it's time to go to the party.

FATHER. Is it true there's going to be a party?   *130*

JOHNNY. Just a small dance, over at Sapo's house.

MOTHER. Which Sapo, son?

JOHNNY. Sapo, my friend.

FATHER. Don't get drunk, okay?

JOHNNY. Oh, come on, dad, Cecilia will be with me.   *135*

FATHER. Did you ask her parents for permission?

JOHNNY. Yes, sir. She's got to be home by eleven.

FATHER. Okay. (Johnny *and* Cecilia *rise.*)

CECILIA. Thank you for the dinner, ma'am.

MOTHER. You're very welcome.   *140*

CECILIA. The tamales were really good.

JOHNNY. Yes, ma, they were terrific.

MOTHER. Is that right, son? You liked them?

JOHNNY. They were great. (*He hugs her.*) Thanks, eh?

MOTHER. What do you mean thanks? You're my son. Go then, it's get-   *145* ting late.

FATHER. Do you want to take the truck, son?

JOHNNY. No thanks, pa. I already have Cecilia's car.

CECILIA. Not mine. My parents' car. They loaned it to us for the dance.

FATHER. It seems like you made a good impression, eh?

CECILIA. He sure did. They say he's more responsible now that he's in the *150* service.

DEATH (*to audience*). Did you hear that? Listen to her again.

CECILIA (*repeats sentence, exactly as before*). They say he's more responsible now that he's in the service.

DEATH. That's what I like to hear!

FATHER. That's good. Then all you have to do is go ask for Cecilia's hand, right, sweetheart?

MOTHER. God willing. *155*

JOHNNY. We're going, then.

CECILIA. Good night.

FATHER. Good night.

MOTHER. Be careful on the road, children.

JOHNNY. Don't worry, mom. Be back later. *160*

CECILIA. Bye!

[JOHNNY *and* CECILIA *exit.* THE MOTHER *stands at the door.*]

FATHER (*sitting down again*). Well, old lady, little Johnny has become a man. The years fly by, don't they?

DEATH. The old man is thinking about the Korean War. Johnny was born about that time. He wishes he had some advice, some hints, to pass on to him about war. But he never went to Korea. The draft skipped him, and somehow, he never got around to enlisting. (The Mother *turns around.*)

MOTHER (*She sees* Death). Oh, my God! (*Exit*)

DEATH (*ducking down*). Damn, I think she saw me. *165*

FATHER. What's wrong with you? (The Mother *is standing frozen, looking toward the spot where* Death *was standing.*) Answer me, what's up? (*Pause*) Speak to me! What am I, invisible?

MOTHER (*solemnly*). I just saw Death.

FATHER. Death? You're crazy.

MOTHER. It's true. As soon as Juan left, I turned around and there was Death, standing—smiling! (The Father *moves away from the spot inadvertently.*) Oh, Blessed Virgin Mary, what if something happens to Juan.

FATHER. Don't say that! Don't you know it's bad luck? *170*

[*They exit.* DEATH *re-enters.*]

[*The Greyhound Bus Depot.*]

DEATH. The next day, Johnny goes to the Greyhound Bus Depot. His mother, his father, and his girlfriend go with him to say goodbye. The Bus Depot is full of soldiers and sailors and old men. Here and there, a drunkard is passed out on the benches. Then there's the announce-

ments: THE LOS ANGELES BUS IS NOW RECEIVING PASSEN-
GERS AT GATE TWO, FOR KINGSBURG, TULARE, DELANO,
BAKERSFIELD AND LOS ANGELES, CONNECTIONS IN L.A.
FOR POINTS EAST AND SOUTH.

[JOHNNY, FATHER, MOTHER, *and* CECILIA *enter.* CECILIA *clings to*
JOHNNY.]

FATHER. It's been several years since I last set foot at the station.
MOTHER. Do you have your ticket, son?
JOHNNY. Oh, no, I have to buy it.
CECILIA. I'll go with you.   *175*
FATHER. Do you have money, son?
JOHNNY. Yes, pa, I have it.

[JOHNNY *and* CECILIA *walk over to* DEATH.]

JOHNNY. One ticket, please.
DEATH. Where to?
JOHNNY. Vietnam. I mean, Oakland.   *180*
DEATH. Round trip or one way?
JOHNNY. One way.
DEATH. Right. One way. (*Applies more makeup.*)

[JOHNNY *gets his ticket and he and* CECILIA *start back toward his parents.* JOHNNY *stops abruptly and glances back at* DEATH, *who has already
shifted positions.*]

CECILIA. What's wrong?
JOHNNY. Nothing. (*They join the parents.*)   *185*
DEATH. For half an hour then, they exchange small talk and trivialities, re-
    peating some of the things that have been said several times before.
    Cecilia promises Johnny she will be true to him and wait until he re-
    turns. Then it's time to go: THE OAKLAND-VIETNAM EXPRESS
    IS NOW RECEIVING PASSENGERS AT GATE NUMBER FOUR.
    ALL ABOARD PLEASE.
JOHNNY. That's my bus.
MOTHER. Oh, son.
FATHER. Take good care of yourself then, okay, son?
CECILIA. I love you, Johnny. (*She embraces him.*)   *190*
DEATH. THE OAKLAND-VIETNAM EXPRESS IS IN THE FI-
    NAL BOARDING STAGES. PASSENGERS WITH TICKETS
    ALL ABOARD PLEASE. AND THANKS FOR GOING GREY-
    HOUND.
JOHNNY. I'm leaving, now.

[*Embraces all around, weeping, last goodbyes, etc.* JOHNNY *exits. Then parents exit.* THE MOTHER *and* CECILIA *are crying.*]

DEATH (*sings*). *Goodbye, Goodbye*
                Star of my nights
                A soldier said in front of a window
                I'm leaving, I'm leaving
                But don't cry, my angel
                For tomorrow I'll be back . . .

So Johnny left for Vietnam, never to return. He didn't want to go and yet he did. It never crossed his mind to refuse. How can he refuse the government of the United States? How could he refuse his family? Besides, who wants to go to prison? And there was the chance he'd come back alive . . . wounded maybe, but alive. So he took a chance—and lost. But before he died he saw many things in Vietnam; he had his eyes opened. He wrote his mother about them.

[JOHNNY *and* THE MOTHER *enter at opposite sides of the stage.* JOHNNY *is in full battle gear. His face is now a skull.*]

JOHNNY. Dear mom.
MOTHER. Dear son.   *195*
JOHNNY. I am writing this letter.
MOTHER. I received your letter.
JOHNNY. To tell you I'm okay.
MOTHER. And I thank the heavens you're all right.
JOHNNY. How's everybody over there?   *200*
MOTHER. Here, we're all doing fine, thank God.
JOHNNY. Ma, there's a lot happening here that I didn't know about before. I don't know if I'm allowed to write about it, but I'm going to try. Yesterday we attacked a small village near some rice paddies. We had orders to kill everybody because they were supposed to be V–C's, communists. We entered the small village and my buddies started shooting. I saw one of them kill an old man and an old lady. My sergeant killed a small boy about seven years old, then he shot his mother or some woman that came running up crying. Blood was everywhere. I don't remember what happened after that but my sergeant ordered me to start shooting. I think I did. May God forgive me for what I did, but I never wanted to come over here. They say we have to do it to defend our country.
MOTHER. Son what you are writing to us makes me sad. I talked to your father and he also got very worried, but he says that's what war is like. He reminds you that you're fighting communists. I have a candle lit and everyday I ask God to take good care of you wherever you are and that he return you to our arms healthy and in one piece.
JOHNNY. Ma, I had a dream the other night. I dreamed I was breaking into one of the hooches, that's what we call the Vietnamese's houses.

I went in firing my M-16 because I knew that the village was controlled by the gooks. I killed three of them right away, but when I looked down it was my pa, my little brother and you, mother. I don't know how much more I can stand. Please tell Sapo and all the dudes how it's like over here. Don't let them . . .

[DEATH *fires a gun, shooting* JOHNNY *in the head. He falls.* THE MOTHER *screams without looking at* JOHNNY.]

DEATH. Johnny was killed in action November 1965 at Chu Lai. His body   *205* lay in the field for two days and then it was taken to the beach and placed in a freezer, a converted portable food locker. Two weeks later he was shipped home for burial.

[DEATH *straightens out* JOHNNY'S *body. Takes his helmet, rifle, etc.* THE FATHER, THE MOTHER, THE BROTHER, *and* CECILIA *file past and gather around the body. Taps plays.*]

The Responsive Reader

1. Death plays a major role in Mexican folklore and custom. What is the role of Death in this play? What is the role of the soldier's family?
2. Does this play make a political statement about the war? Where and how?
3. In your judgment, would this play appeal primarily to Mexican Americans, or does it have universal appeal?
4. How do you relate to the humor in this play? What are its targets? How does it affect the tone of the play?

Talking, Listening, Writing

5. Are the people in this play too passive in their acceptance of what is in store for them?
6. Have people in our society become jaded about the arguments of anti-war or pacifist groups? What would you say to a group of people to make them pay renewed attention to warnings about war? What would you answer if someone approached you with a plea to join an antiwar group?
7. Have you lost someone close to you as the result of war, illness, accident? Write a tribute to the person.

Collaborative Projects

8. Valdez's text is well suited for a mini-production designed to bring the play to life for an audience and help them get into the spirit of the play. (One class production changed the GI in the Valdez play to a young woman and the war to the "Desert Storm" war against Iraq.) You and your classmates may want to organize a group project to stage your own reenactment of the Valdez play.

THE BOY DIED IN MY ALLEY

Gwendolyn Brooks

Gwendolyn Brooks wrote eloquent, challenging poems expressing her loyalty to people trapped in a web of poverty and racism. She populated the imaginary community of Bronzeville with a haunting array of the human beings behind the stereotypes and statistics. Her widely known poem "We Real Cool" has been called an anthem for doomed youth—who act "cool" and defiant as a defensive armor, who have dropped out and find themselves in the slow lane to a dead end. Brooks grew up in a home filled with poetry, story, and song. "No child abuse, no prostitution, no mafia membership," she later said about her close-knit, loving family. She came to Chicago from Kansas and was honored as poet laureate of the state of Illinois. She was the first African American woman to receive a Pulitzer Prize for poetry. Brooks spent much time working with young people in colleges and schools and promoting workshops and awards for young poets.

Thought Starters: How do people in a community learn of incidents of violence in their neighborhood? Who are the witnesses? Who are the messengers? Who are the observers? What are their feelings and reactions?

Without my having known.   *1*
Policeman said, next morning,
"Apparently died Alone."
"You heard a shot?" Policeman said.
Shots I hear and Shots I hear.   *5*
I never see the dead.

The Shot that killed him yes I heard
as I heard the Thousand shots before;
careening tinnily down the nights
across my years and arteries.   *10*

Policeman pounded on my door.
"Who is it?" "POLICE!" Policeman yelled.
"A boy was dying in your alley.
A boy is dead, and in your alley.
And have you known this Boy before?"   *15*

I have known this Boy before.
I have known this Boy before, who
ornaments my alley.
I never saw his face at all.   *20*

I never saw his futurefall.
But I have known this Boy.

I have always heard him deal with death.
I have always heard the shout, the volley.
I have closed my heart-ears late and early.
And I have killed him ever.   *25*

I joined the Wild and killed him
with knowledgeable unknowing.
I saw where he was going.
I saw him Crossed. And seeing,
I did not take him down.   *30*

He cried not only "Father!"
but "Mother!
Sister!
Brother!"
The cry climbed up the alley.   *35*

It went up to the wind.
It hung upon the heaven
for a long
stretch-strain of Moment.

The red floor of my alley   *40*
is a special speech to me.

The Responsive Reader

1. We usually learn about deadly violence from our newspapers or television news. How does it change our perspective that we learn about the murder in this poem from the police officer yelling and pounding on the door? How does the poet feel about the police officer? Is he just a harbinger of bad tidings—a messenger bringing bad news? Is he just "doing his job?" What is his role in the poem?
2. Did the poet or the person speaking in the poem know the dead boy, or didn't she? If the poet "never saw his face at all," how can she say, "I have known this Boy before"?
3. How did the poet see the boy "Crossed"? What makes her say "I did not take him down"? How is the religious analogy or allusion carried through into the last words that the poet hears the boy cry out in her mind?
4. How can the poet say "I have killed him ever"? How can a person be both "knowledgeable" and "unknowing"?
5. Is there any hint or suspicion in the poem of who actually killed the boy? Is it strange that there is no speculation about an actual suspect? Why do you think the poet never asks the question?

6. How would you sum up the "special speech" that the blood-stained floor of the alley has for the poet?

Talking, Listening, Writing

7. Why does so much of what we respond to in this poem come to us as sounds—sounds heard, remembered, or imagined? How does the poet use language to make sure we hear the sounds with our mind's ear? What are striking examples?
8. Are you one of the people who hear the shots but "never see the dead"? Have you closed your own "heart-ears late and early"?
9. Brooks once said, "I am absolutely free of what any white critic might say" about her poetry—because it would be amazing if a white person could enter into the reality of the experience of African Americans in this country. Do you think a reader would have to be African American or a member of a minority group to understand this poem and respond fully to its message? Why or why not?

Collaborative Projects

10. In one of her poems, Brooks wrote: "Art hurts. Art urges voyages— / and it is easier to stay at home / the nice beer at the ready." Working with a group, you may want to organize a poetry reading to honor Gwendolyn Brooks and her work.

BEYOND THE FINGER POINTING
Fred Barbash

After a shootout at a Colorado high school, a columnist for the Washington Post *said that "handgun shootings are a bloody way of life across America." On April 20, 1999, Hitler's birthday, two students at Columbine High School who wore black trenchcoats and exchanged Nazi salutes gunned down thirteen students and one teacher, killing themselves and maiming other students for life. Their weapons included handguns and a sawed-off shotgun. One of the dead was an African American student whom the killers singled out using a racist epithet and whose parents had complained without effect about an earlier death threat aimed at their son. In a video that had been seen by others, the two students had staged a homicidal fantasy, killing fellow students. Like other shootouts, the event produced a feeding frenzy on the part of the media and a temporary clamor for gun control. The leadership of the National Rifle Association took the stand that "it's not a gun control problem; it's a culture control problem." The author of the following article is the business editor of the* Washington Post. *He was the newspaper's London correspondent from 1994 to 1997. Barbash tries to take his readers beyond the immediate aftermath of the Columbine incident when, in the words of another writer for the* Washington Post, *"commentators, politicians, and all manner of experts were on television attacking their favorite scapegoats." Barbash tries to put the Columbine tragedy in a larger context.*

Thought Starters: Would you describe the high school or high schools you attended as a "safe environment"? Why or why not?

In March 1996, a demented gun enthusiast wielding four perfectly   *1*
legal weapons walked into a primary school in Dunblane, Scotland, and mowed down a teacher and 16 children, ages 5 and 6, before killing himself. I arrived at the school a few hours later to cover the story and left the town after several wrenching days thinking about my own children and whether there was any possibility that the British would seize the moment to attack their gun problem, lest they wind up like the United States.

To my amazement, the shootings did provoke a serious nation-wide deliberation, which included public hearings before a government-appointed commission about the way the perpetrator got his guns, the warning signs that might have been heeded but weren't, and the effectiveness of existing gun laws. The commission also considered the extent to which any new and restrictive legislation might affect the thousands of target shooters and gun clubs (including one composed of members of the

House of Commons) and whether a change in the law could be structured to preserve their sport while also protecting the public.

The testimony at the hearings replayed in excruciatingly slow motion the methodical slaughter of the Dunblane children, which regalvanized the public's anger. By the time legislation reached the floor of the Commons, the politicians knew they were being watched closely by their constituents, who were mobilized by lasting rage and by a grass-roots organization called Snowdrop. Over the considerable opposition of Britain's gun clubs and shooting enthusiasts—which have been an important force and an established part of British tradition—the Parliament soon enacted a ban on private possession of all large-caliber handguns. That was the work of a Conservative government. In June 1997, the newly elected Labor government tightened what was already one of the world's tightest gun laws by banning all handguns, regardless of caliber.

It was a "national conversation," something we often talk about here in the United States but rarely have—and have never really had on the subject of guns. The closest we've come to one was after the 1981 shooting of President Reagan and his press secretary, James Brady, a reaction that ultimately produced the 1993 Brady Act requiring federal background checks on gun purchasers.

So when a 14-year-old opened fire on his West Paducah, Ky., high   5
school classmates in December 1997, killing three and wounding five, I thought that this would move us beyond the paralyzed and polarized debate that now characterizes our discussion about the right to keep and bear arms. It didn't happen. I thought the same thing after the shootings in Jonesboro, Ark., where two middle schoolers killed four girls and a teacher and wounded 10 others in March 1998. Then came Edinboro, Pa., (April 1998, one dead) and Springfield, Ore. (May 1998, two killed, more than 20 hurt). Four in six months, and still there was no reaction to compare with what I saw in Britain after Dunblane. The American response was more of the same—incantations from the extremes; silence from the middle, and prayers and pieties from the top.

Perhaps the massacre at Columbine High School in Littleton, Colo., will be the one that rouses us. We'll see. The first signs have been discouraging.

The president, in his public comments immediately after the shootings in Colorado, said that something should be done. But for the life of him, he couldn't bring himself to mention anything specific. "Well, I think on this case it's very, very important that we have the facts, in so far as we can find them out. You know, we had the conference here last fall. The attorney general and the secretary of Education prepared the handbook for all the schools that we asked to be widely used. And we do have, from bitter and sad experience, a great cadre of very good, effective grief counselors. . . . I think after a little time has passed, we need to have a candid assessment about what more we can do to try to prevent these things from happening."

His wording—"after a little time has passed"—suggests that it would somehow be reckless or in bad taste to discuss remedies in our current state of grief. However, the administration signaled that it understood that something beyond prayers was called for. It announced that it would send Congress a series of gun control measures, including one aimed at adults who, through negligence, allow guns to fall into the hands of children. Hillary Rodham Clinton spoke out as well and Attorney General Janet Reno said, "We've got to get the guns out of the hands of young people"—which sounds good until you think about it. (Why only young people? The Dunblane massacre was the work of an adult.)

Meanwhile, the so-called gun "lobby"—the shorthand by which the media often describe the National Rifle Association and its supporters— conveyed that it understood the potentially explosive nature of this moment perhaps better than the president. Colorado sponsors of legislation to permit the carrying of concealed weapons and limit the ability of municipalities to restrict guns were busy withdrawing their bills. "Nobody's going to be able to discuss it rationally," Bill Dietrick, an NRA lobbyist in Colorado, told the Denver Post.

On the same day, the NRA itself said that it was canceling most of the   *10* events planned for its annual convention (which just happened to be set for Denver) to "show our profound sympathy and respect for the families and communities in the Denver area in their time of great loss."

I have no reason to doubt the NRA's sympathy. But I suspect what it really respects is the power that comes from an enraged populace, particularly from those who heretofore have remained uninvolved.

Acting While Enraged has moved this nation mightily in the past. A novel, "Uncle Tom's Cabin," galvanized abolitionist sentiment in the North before the Civil War. Another novel, Upton Sinclair's "The Jungle" (1906), helped give us our food safety laws. A horrible fire at the Triangle Shirtwaist Factory in 1911, in which 146 mostly immigrant female workers died because they had no way out, inspired the enactment of workplace health and safety laws. The Selma-to-Montgomery march helped inspire the civil rights revolution. Footage of men in barbed-wire camps moved us to involvement in Bosnia. Descriptions of small children laboring overseas to make our expensive running shoes is changing industrial practice. The list is as long as our history.

I sense great shock over these repeated outbreaks of violence at schools. But I do not yet sense outrage. Is it that school shootings are somehow seen as isolated acts with little or nothing in common? Or by accepting, as I certainly do, that there is a strong cultural aspect to such violence, do we somehow foreclose discussion of remedies that might only get at part of the problem rather than the whole?

We will, some experts tell us, never be able to fully explain the reasons for acts as heinous as those at Columbine High School. I accept that. But it's not the American way to conclude that nothing, therefore, can be done to stop those inclined to such violence.

Similar arguments against a proposed course of action—it won't solve   15
the whole problem, it might not work at all, the criminals will just ignore it—have been made against almost every piece of important social legislation in U.S. history. They've been made and generally rejected on the theory that in the absence of all the answers, we should go with the ones we have.

Why the stalemate? We let ourselves off too easily by blaming "the gun lobby." The gun lobby is powerful only insofar as the rest of America stays out of the debate. This is the classic situation of the funded and boisterous minority wielding outsized power thanks to the quiescence of everyone else.

The Second Amendment argument—at least in its current form—is a political one, deployed as a conversation stopper. Whatever the actual meaning of the Second Amendment to the Constitution ("A well regulated Militia, being necessary to the security of a free State, the right of the people to keep and bear Arms, shall not be infringed."), it is no bar to a vigorous debate over the pros and cons of banishing assault weapons or automatic weapons or semi-automatic weapons or any other high-powered weaponry. Because the Supreme Court has never defined how this flintlock-era part of the Bill of Rights applies to individual ownership of weapons of massive destruction, I (and more importantly, most legal scholars) see no constitutional obstacle to legislation.

Might those Americans who genuinely believe in a constitutional right to bear arms accept a revision of the amendment to suit the era of automatic weapons? By now, I suspect, most Americans believe that violence in the schools and in the country generally is both a gun problem and a culture problem. More importantly, I believe that most Americans would say that addressing the availability of high-powered guns somehow precludes tackling cultural issues. And it would be my estimate that most Americans, rather than regarding a gun control initiative as bad taste at this point or as disrespectful to the families of Littleton, would consider it part of an appropriate response to the deaths in Colorado.

The problem so far is that "most Americans" have been disinclined to join this controversy, as was the case with most Britons until the Dunblane killings. In my view, the greatest insult to the friends and families in Dunblane, West Paducah, Jonesboro, Edinboro, Springfield, Littleton and indeed to ourselves, would be silence.

The Responsive Reader

1. Do you think the Dunblane and the Columbine shootings can be usefully compared? What is similar, and what is different? Are the two

countries too different to make the comparison useful, or is there a similar lesson to be learned from both events?

2. Barbasch is critical of both the general public and the political leadership of the country. What does he fault them for? What does he say about the role of the gun lobby? What is his attitude toward the NRA?

3. What examples does Barbasch cite of other issues in our history where aroused public opinion brought about important changes in attitudes and legislation? Which of these to you seem most and which least relevant or convincing?

4. After he became president of the NRA, Charlton Heston said that the Second Amendment was the "most vital" of all the amendments and "more essential" than the First Amendment. Often disagreements about the amendment focus on its reference to a militia. Why does the reference matter? How does Barbasch seem to go beyond familiar arguments?

Talking, Listening, Writing

5. President Clinton has said that he went hunting as a boy and that he understands the gun culture of his Southern home state. What has been your experience with or observation of the "gun culture"? Can you contribute anything to the current dialogue about gun control from your experience?

6. NRA spokespersons stress the failure of society to enforce laws aimed at controlling gun-toting criminals or felons. Would more stringent controls on criminals have affected the incidents Barbasch discusses?

7. Media critics charge that the media exploit the sensational thrill of violent events like the Columbine shootings but do not follow up by showing the true cost in human suffering. Check media coverage of the Columbine event: How much follow-up coverage has there been of the shattered lives of the victims' families or of the years-long odyssey of wounded and maimed shooting victims?

8. To do something about murderous drunken-driving accidents after proms or graduation parties, some schools require that all students attending such events arrive by bus rather than private car. Do you think schools and parents could develop any similar initiatives, programs, or precautions to help stem gun violence in schools? (As a parent, would you be fatalistic about gun violence in the schools?)

Find It on the Web

For background on current gun-control initiatives and recent developments on the gun-control issue, one student researcher went to websites like the ones described below:

- The official homepage of the National Rifle Association (www.nra.org) guides the researcher to speeches by prominent NRA officials (like Charlton Heston), videos, and archives providing facts, statistics, and information about gun-related legislation.

- The website for the Anti-Gun Coalition of America (www.agca.com) provides information on people, organizations, and businesses that favor strong anti-gun legislation. It provides helpful links to other sites.

- While the NRA has moved toward possible compromise on issues like gun safety training, the Gun Owners group (www.gunownersca.com) is known as one of the more uncompromising pro-gun groups, sometimes called the Marine Corps of the pro-gun movement. Following up the Gun Owners logo may lead the researcher to "fact sheets" and other publications by the Gun Owners Foundation Online.

FORUM: *Tough on Crime*

The fear of crime became a major theme in American politics. In the attack ads that political candidates use to make an opponent look bad, the charge of being "soft on crime" plays a major role. An incumbent is blamed when a convicted killer is paroled and kills again. Legislators are blamed when a child molester returns to a community without warnings going to parents. Law-and-order candidates promise voters to put career criminals in jail and "throw the key away." A columnist said about one tough-on-crime governor that for a convict on death row to ask the governor for clemency was like "asking a shrub to recite Shakespeare."

Are tough sentences serving as a deterrent to crime? Do they express society's thirst for retribution or vengeance? Are they counterproductive, producing large numbers of embittered antisocial ex-offenders with no hope of reintegrating into society?

THE BROKEN WINDOW THEORY

Nathan Glazer

With crime rates in the United States unparalleled by rates in other developed countries, law enforcement in this country has come in for much public scrutiny. One section of public opinion accuses police and crime-fighting agencies of being too permissive—too lax in dealing with drug dealers, muggings, violent behavior at sports events, and molestation of citizens using public transport. Another section of public opinion accuses police of being too aggressive and insensitive, with many incidents of harassment of or police brutality toward members of minority groups. A major drop in official crime rates was at first greeted with skepticism by experienced observers of the crime scene. Were citizens accepting petty crime as a fact of life, no longer reporting it because they expected little assistance from the police? Did city authorities downplay crime statistics in order not to scare away businesses or tourists? Nathan Glazer is a widely published journalist who wrote the following article for the "Hard Questions" column of the New Republic.

Thought Starters: Is crime a concern in your neighborhood or on your campus? What kind of crime is most common or most serious? What crime prevention initiatives have you observed? What steps have you taken to protect yourself?

Good news is always welcome, but it is also somewhat unsettling   *1*
when one has no idea why the news is good. New York City [. . .] recorded less than 1,000 murders in a year for the first time in over two decades, as part of the persisting and sharp drop in crime. Reported crime has fallen more than 43 percent in the city in [. . .] four years, and it has been noted that New York City alone, with 3 percent of the American population, accounts for a large part of the national plunge in crime. And, while New Yorkers may not fear murder on a day-to-day basis, something they do constantly fear—car theft—[showed] an equally astonishing drop, from 147,000 in 1990 to 60,000.

There has also been a decline in infant deaths in New York City to fewer than 1,000. [. . .] Though not as sharp as the drop in crime, the infant mortality rate fell from 21.6 per 1,000 births in 1970 to about 8 in 1996. It takes a long time for social policy analysts to examine all the figures and to accurately explain them. At the moment, even the experts appear to be guessing. One authority quoted in *The New York Times* attributed the reduction in crime to three forces: the decline of crack, the economic upturn and more aggressive policing strategies. One of the causes—the [economy]—seems dubious: there has been little correlation between crime and economic surges (or recessions) in the past. Moreover, there [wasn't] much of an economic upturn in New York City for the unskilled and less educated who contribute most to crime; indeed, the city's unemployment rates have remained persistently high, much higher than the national average.

The other two explanations—the decline of crack and more aggressive policing—seem more convincing to me. And they underscore a fundamental divide in how we explain changes in social statistics: Are they due to some [. . .] change in society and individual behavior, or is there some change in government that directly affects how people behave?

Certainly government will take the credit for these welcome results. The strongest thing going for Mayor Rudolph W. Giuliani [was] the remarkable decline in crime during his tenure. But does government really deserve the credit? And, if so, what change in government caused the transformation?

George Kelling, now a criminologist at Rutgers University, has been 5 the leading advocate of the "broken windows" theory, named after a 1982 article he wrote with the political scientist James Q. Wilson. Kelling argues that when the environment deteriorates because the police ignore relatively minor transgressions of civility and decent public behavior, not only do these transgressions increase, but more serious crimes do as well. Get the police out of the police cars, he says. Let them walk the beat again, talk to the people in the community, stop kids from breaking windows even in abandoned buildings, pay some attention to the mild transgressions rather than focus exclusively on the worst. His views have been persuasive. There has been a shift nationwide to more community policing. It is certainly an attractive theory. Even if it does not reduce serious crime, it contributes to a better environment.

But there have been other changes in policing and crime control that make it difficult to pinpoint one cause for the lower crime rates. According to *The New York Times,* in one neighborhood that has seen such a decline, "Federal, state, and local law enforcement agencies are working to drive out drug dealers with aggressive policing tactics." In another New York neighborhood, a pilot program has consolidated the various divisions of the police—housing, narcotics and others—under the control of a locally based commander, making it easier to coordinate investigations and capture drug peddlers.

And there are other potential causes for the abrupt decline in crime. A TV program, reporting on an equally sharp drop in teenage murders in Boston, claims the fall is due to more aggressive control of teenagers on probation as probation officers work more closely with the police. A story in *The American Lawyer* attributes much of the reduction in New York City's murder rate to an aggressive young prosecutor using the Federal Racketeering Control Law to put away gang leaders for longer prison terms, and indeed, in the areas where the gang leaders have been prosecuted and incarcerated, there has been a sharp drop in homicides.

But there have also been other changes, owing nothing to government. More people now protect their cars against theft with wheel locks and car alarms (which unfortunately contribute to the din of the city). And more people install better door and window locks. Here people are acting on their own, regardless of what government does or doesn't do.

The steady fall in the infant mortality rate has received less attention in the press. But there do not appear to be any major new government interventions that might be responsible for it. Most programs directed at expectant mothers and infants have existed for twenty to thirty years, and in the last decade we have heard more about efforts to cut these programs than expand them. So we are back to the same question: Is government doing something right, or are more people simply doing something right?

We have become more skeptical about what government can do, but these positive changes, at least in crime, suggest that we have perhaps become too skeptical. The issue is not simply that government is doing something, but what it does and how it does it. Yet the changes we are seeing go beyond any governmental action. I do not think any expert would have predicted that the various reforms in policing and prosecuting would cause the recent plunge in crime. Nor do I think any expert looking at social conditions and government programs in New York City in 1980 could have predicted that the infant mortality rate would fall by 50 percent.

Perhaps government has been working less on social theory and more on resolving urgent problems through direct action. For example, New York City was afflicted for many years by the infamous squeegee men, who manned every major automobile entry into the city, cleaning windshields, often forcibly, in exchange for a tip. If upon taking office Mayor Giuliani had consulted sociologists, few would have predicted that having police simply get rid of the squeegee men would have much impact. But that is what the mayor did—and, strangely enough, the squeegee men did not return; nor was there any discernible increase in some other form of uncivil behavior or street extortion. So government can become more sensible even as it becomes smaller. But these statistics suggest that we are seeing changes in people's behavior that cannot simply be explained by what government is doing.

The Responsive Reader

1. What statistics does Glazer cite to support the widely believed conclusion that New York City did indeed experience a major drop in crime in the nineties? What areas of city life or what branches of crime were affected? What makes the statistics "astonishing"?

2. What is the "broken windows" theory? How did it change law enforcement and police practices? How much credit does Glazer give to this explanation for the decline in crime in New York City in the 1990s?

What changes in citizens' behavior and attitudes may have played a role? How are statistics for infant mortality related to the issue of crime rates?

Talking, Listening, Writing

3. Do you think that police should devote more time and effort to the so-called quality-of-life issues—preventing vandalism, fare-beating on public transportation, and other petty crimes? Why or why not? Do you agree with Glazer that such police work "contributes to a better environment"? Or do you think police work should focus on more serious violations of the law?

4. Official crime rates dropped nationwide in the 1990s, but local news broadcasts around the country have continued to devote a large percentage of their air time to coverage of local crime. If you watch television news, do you see much crime coverage? Do you think that news broadcasts about crimes make people more alert and careful? Or do you think they make viewers feel less secure by covering crime? Why or why not? What kind of crimes seem to get the most attention?

Collaborative Projects

5. Have charges of overly aggressive or insensitive police work been an issue in your area or community? Working with a group, you may want to track newspaper coverage of citizens' complaints, reports of police commissions, or other indicators of problems related to law enforcement practices or police tactics. What groups or organizations play a role in police-related controversies? Is there a pattern or common thread in the charges or the issues raised? What has been the outcome in key cases?

NO INDICTMENT
IN SHOPLIFTER'S DEATH

Emery P. Dalesio

A recurrent feature of the daily news is the story of citizens who take the law into their own hands. Homeowners shoot intruders. Off-duty police officers or firefighters gun down offenders fleeing the scene of a crime. Battered women kill abusive husbands. How do the media cover such incidents? How does the justice system deal with such incidents? The following news item is an Associated Press report that identifies the reporter, following the trend toward less use of anonymous, unsigned press reports both in newspapers and in newsmagazines. The report provides a mix of factual detail, witnesses' testimony, official commentary, sidelights, and human-interest detail. Do you as

*the reader come to understand what happened in this example of a violent in-
cident? Do you feel in a position to judge the behavior of the various participants in the drama?*

———————

Thought Starters: Disillusioned citizens have lost faith in the ability of
the police to prevent violent crime or bring an offender to justice. Are you
one of these disillusioned Americans? If not, what would you say to them?

———————

RALEIGH, N.C.—Jason Cort grabbed $130 from the Food Lion   *1*
cash register and ran out into the warm May night. A supermarket employee took off after him.

Cort, the troubled product of a well-to-do suburban family, wasn't
fast enough. Prosecutors say the store employee caught the 23-year-old
Cort and beat him to death with a tree limb.

The thrashing ended the hard-luck life of a young man who had
struggled with depression, a learning disability, alcohol and cocaine.

But the final chapter was written Monday, when a grand jury refused
to indict the store employee, college student Daniel Abram Rodbourn, on
manslaughter charges.

"It's telling the public that in an attempt to recover property, you can   *5*
kill somebody," said Cort's father, Steven Cort. He and his wife, Cheryl,
said they believe the grand jury was swayed against their son because crack
was found in his body.

"In my opinion, the minute they asked, 'Was he on drugs?' the curtain went down and Jason was on trial," Mrs. Cort said.

Cort was a skinny, learning-disabled kid who was so indecisive he
would ask his mother what to order off a restaurant menu. He grew herbs
and cooked with his mother, a neuromuscular therapist. He would scold her
if she tossed their cat off her lap, worried that the drop would hurt the pet.

"He was too sensitive for this world," said his father, a chemical engineer and entrepreneur. "I think that made him easy prey."

Rodbourn, a 25-year-old senior at North Carolina State University
majoring in zoology, could not be reached for comment. Neither he nor
his parents have listed telephone numbers, and an entry in the university's
student directory was outdated. Prosecutors did not know if he had hired
a lawyer.

Cort's parents had enrolled him in a private school that specialized in   *10*
learning-disabled students to help him graduate from high school. He was
hospitalized with depression in his teens and sent to live with a grandparent
so he could break off ties to friends who supplied him with drugs.

Finally, in January, he graduated from a hairstyling academy. His
parents celebrated with a ski trip to Aspen, Colo. A photo of Cort kicking

back in an armchair, his snowboarding boots crossed, sits on a glass table-top in a sun room of their home in Cary, a Raleigh suburb.

Trying to stay away from his former drug buddies meant Cort had few friends. He would turn over his pay from a hair salon to his mother, trying to beat the temptation of drugs. But his parents suspect someone talked him into buying a fix and robbing the Food Lion on May 9.

"Jason was not a leader. He was a follower," Steven Cort said. "He was an easy mark because of his sensitivity and his depression."

Police told Cort's parents that Cort broke away from two Food Lion customers who tried to stop him at the door. A woman manager of the supermarket told Rodbourn, "Go get him," according to police.

Rodbourn caught up with Cort, the two fought, and the 140-pound,   *15* 5-foot-10 Cort broke free, police told the family. Rodbourn overtook him again and beat him, prosecutors said.

Steven Cort said police told him Rodbourn beat his son with a 2-inch-thick, 5-foot-long tree branch. He said police told him one witness reported his son was struck at least 10 times. A second witness said Cort was hit at least twice as he lay on the ground. He suffered a broken skull, his parents said.

Police thought Cort was drunk and had only minor injuries. He was taken to a hospital to sober up, but lost consciousness. He was taken off life support on May 13.

A Food Lion spokeswoman refused to discuss the case or the store's policy on pursuing thieves.

Assistant District Attorney Howard Cummings said he thought there was enough evidence to indict Rodbourn. "The message is you get what you deserve, but I don't want to pass judgment on anybody," he told The News & Observer.

District Attorney Colon Willoughby said the grand jury's decision ef-   *20* fectively ends any attempt to prosecute. He said his office has a policy of not presenting a case to a new grand jury without fresh evidence.

The Corts said they never wanted prison but would have advocated community service if Rodbourn had been tried and convicted.

"Drugs ruined my family," Mrs. Cort said. "You cocoon them the best you can and then you have to set them free, and that's the scary part."

The Responsive Reader

1. In filling in friends or classmates on this news story, how would you answer questions that reporters often address as they deal with violent incidents? For instance, what was the role of home environment or of social background? Did drugs play a role—and if so, how? Did prejudice play a role? What was the role of police? What was the role of bystanders?

2. In the daily newspaper, cases like this one often appear among other routine accounts of life in our violent society. Do you think this was an unusual case—one of a kind? a kind of freak happening? a combination of unusual circumstances? Or are there elements in this case that are common in violent incidents or perhaps even typical?

3. How unbiased, or objective, is this news report? How much is fact, and how much is explanation or interpretation? Does the report point the finger or place blame? Does it steer the reader's sympathies? How?

Talking, Listening, Writing

4. If you had been serving on the grand jury, would you have voted to return no indictment? Why or why not? What in this case would have done most to influence your decision? What least?

5. Would you call this a case of vigilantism? What is your definition of a vigilante? What do you know about the history of vigilantism in this country? Have you seen evidence of a trend toward vigilantism in our society? What is your thinking on the subject?

Collaborative Projects

6. A widely publicized court case may become a cause célèbre, stirring up passions and being endlessly discussed and analyzed. Often it becomes a test case—putting the loyalties and biases of police officers, jurors, judges, and newspaper readers to the test. Have you followed such a case recently or in recent years? You may want to team up with classmates to prepare an account of it, exploring what it shows about our society or our justice system or our popular culture.

EMOTIONS CLOUDING RATIONAL DECISIONS

Steven Musil

College campuses are no longer refuges from a violent outside world. Emergency phones and escort services are an attempt to provide some minimal security after spates of rapes in dorms or assaults in parking lots. Students working a few blocks from college campuses witness shootouts in fast-food restaurants or convenience stores. Steven Musil was an editor for a student newspaper when he wrote the following editorial about the loss of a friend. He writes as a witness—someone who took in and cared about something that for many newspaper readers was just a statistic. Musil asks a central question that for many remains unresolved: In a case like this, how do we make the punishment fit the crime? How do we respond to the cry for retribution or for vengeance?

Thought Starters: Do you thinkof your school or campus as a safe place? Are you aware of safety precautions? Do you take precautions yourself?

"An eye for an eye and the whole world goes blind."

—Gandhi

The following is an open letter to a lost friend.

Dear Dennis,

It has been two-and-a-half years since we last spoke. I'm sorry that I   *1* haven't written to you before but I wasn't sure where to send this. I haven't seen you since two days before your funeral and I'm sure you must have many questions. First off, you probably know by now that Tony was your killer. Last week, a jury found him guilty and sentenced him to life in prison without the possibility of parole.

All the articles in the newspaper got me thinking about the whole mess again. I watched some of the trial downtown and a couple days ago I visited your memorial in front of Chili's. It has been hard to forget lately.

Many of us who were working at Chili's at the time of the murder were hoping for the death sentence. We wanted to see him die in the gas chamber for what he did to you. Some of us even felt sorry for him before we realized that he murdered you. The autopsy reported that you were shot once in the back of the head with a sawed-off .22-caliber rifle and then twice in the face after you fell to the floor.

The coroner said that you probably didn't know what was happening and you died instantly without suffering. Is that true? The sheriff found the rifle and about $1,600 in cash in his apartment on the day of your funeral. I was one of the last to be told.

The jury "let him off" because he had "no prior convictions of vio-   *5* lent crimes or anything of that sort," according to the jury foreman.

Everyone at Chili's liked you Dennis. Even Tony. He testified that he was in a confused, cocaine-induced trance and needed the money to cover some debts. He said that he knew he would have to kill whoever was in the restaurant at the time. You weren't even scheduled to work that day, but were doing another manager a favor. I'm thankful no one else was there.

It just seemed so unfair. You were so young. So nice, so gentle. I regret the hard time we gave you at the Fourth of July party the night before. Do you remember? We were kidding you because you were the only married manager without children. The night before you died you said that it was time to have a child.

They closed the store for a couple of days for the investigation and to clean up. With all the extra time, some of the cooks decided to go camping, stay together. We had a real hard time dealing with it so we just took off. We ended up on a beach south of Santa Cruz. We bought a couple cases of beer, built a bonfire and toasted your memory all night until the sun came up the next day.

That night we made a pact to visit the campsite every year in your honor. A year later, I was the only one that returned. Many of those people don't work at Chili's anymore and are hard to get a hold of. I'm sure they haven't forgotten you.

It touched some people so that they revised their personal stance on capital punishment. After your murder there were people stating that they had rethought the issue and now supported the death penalty, gun control, and assorted other related causes. I admit that I too made my gun control decision based on the emotional aftershock. I'm not sure if someone can make a rational decision of such importance based on an emotionally traumatic event.

Anyway, I don't have a lot of room to write to you. I have to tell you that I'm putting this behind me and you probably won't hear from me again. Know that we haven't forgotten you just because we are going on with our lives. Somehow I think you would have wanted it that way. Take care of yourself.

Your friend,
Steven

The Responsive Reader

1. What are the bare facts in this case? What are allegations, theories, or excuses?
2. What does this "letter to a lost friend" accomplish? What did it do for the writer? What does it do for the reader?

Talking, Listening, Writing

3. Who or what is to blame? What, if anything, can be done to help prevent a similar tragedy? Does this editorial make you rethink your position regarding "death penalty, gun control, and assorted other related causes"?
4. Musil says, "I'm not sure if someone can make a rational decision . . . based on an emotionally traumatic event." Don't we have a right to be emotional about events like the one that is the occasion for this editorial? Shouldn't we be emotional? What would a "rational" reaction be to what happened in this case?
5. A tired joke has it that when the students at one college were asked whether they were concerned about apathy concerning social issues, 87% responded: "I don't care." Do you think students of your generation or on your campus are guilty of apathy?
6. Write your personal response to the author of this "letter to a lost friend."

A THREAT TO JUSTICE
Families to Amend Three Strikes

The following text is from leaflets passed out in front of a county jail by members of prisoners' families. They claimed that a three-strikes law that had been advertised as getting repeat offenders off the streets was in fact putting many nonviolent offenders away for life, destroying not only their lives but the lives of their families. A long list of supporting organizations included the Los Angeles Times Editorial Board, the Bakersfield chapter of the American Legion, the American Civil Liberties Union, the California Association of Black Lawyers, the Archdiocese of Los Angeles, the National Lawyers Guild, la Gente de Aztlan, and Amnesty International.

Thought Starters: Suppose you are passing outside a court of law or local jail. Relatives of inmates approach you with leaflets and ask you to sign a petition. The governor has just vetoed changes to a three-strikes law that is putting family members away for life. Many of the family members whose pictures you are shown are in jail for nonviolent crimes. What would you say to the petitioners? Would you sign? Why or why not?

TAXPAYERS HAVE BECOME VICTIMS OF THREE STRIKES

Nonviolent offenders are being locked up in maximum housing units costing the taxpayer $27,000 per inmate per year. There are approximately 165,000 inmates in California prisons. A prison housing 4,000 inmates costs $300 million to build and $100 million a year to run. Three Strikes will add tens of thousands of prisoners to the state system. The state has built 19 prisons and only two universities in the last ten years. Prisons go up while schools fall down. Three Strikes does not make our street safer. It is about a prison industry complex. We need prevention, not detention. Let the time fit the crime. Put our money back into our education, environmental, social, elderly, youth, and other community programs.

SOCIETY HAS BECOME A VICTIM OF THREE STRIKES

80% of law enforcement time and money is spent prosecuting minor offenders, not violent criminals. The Justice Policy Institute states that "states that have not enacted harsher prison sentences for repeated felons have actually experienced a greater drop in crime than states that do have such laws." California has one of the highest incarceration rates in the world. Prisons are big business and people are the commodity.

FAMILIES HAVE BECOME VICTIMS OF THREE STRIKES

The Three Strikes Law has led to unduly harsh sentences for people with no history of violence, or people who have been convicted of relatively minor crimes. People with drug addictions are being "rehabilitated" with life sentences. Thousands of families have been affected. Many families have lost their families, friends, jobs, homes, and now live in poverty, again at the taxpayer's expense.

CONSIDER THIS 70–80% of Second and Third Strike convictions involve NONVIOLENT or NONSERIOUS OFFENSES. Nonviolent crimes and minor offenses (property crimes) such as possession of less than a gram of cocaine, forgery, or stealing a pair of jeans, result in a Strike. Multiple counts during one act count for multiple Strikes. The law is being retroactively applied, meaning crimes committed back in the 60s or 70s can count as Strikes. The Three Strikes Law is applied to juvenile crimes—going back to 16 years of age.

Our organization started in Orange County in 1996. It was started *5* by family members and friends of people who have been sentenced under the Three Strikes Law. We do not provide legal services. However, we keep current on any legal changes in the law. Our goal is to get Three Strikes back on the ballot, AMENDED. We believe the voters of California did not understand the Proposition they voted for. Three Strikes was publicized as aimed at violent offenders. However, 70–80% of offenders sentenced under the Three Strikes Law are NOT violent offenders. In fact, you do not have to commit a violent crime to go to prison for the rest of your life.

This law is an injustice to every person in California. Martin Luther King Jr. said, "an injustice anywhere is a threat to justice everywhere."

The Responsive Reader

1. How would questions like the following affect the way you react to the petition: How important to you is the distinction between "violent" and "nonviolent" crimes? Should new sentencing laws be retroactively applied to offenses dating back many years? Should they be applied to juvenile crimes from age sixteen?
2. Is cost to the taxpayer of lifelong incarceration a major consideration for you? Why or why not?

Talking, Listening, Writing

3. Teachers come to jails without pay to teach courses for inmates. After one of her students had been arrested, one teacher visited the prison late at night to bring a midterm exam for the student to take in case he was

released and had a chance to rejoin the class. Do you think this kind of personal initiative does any good? Why or why not?

4. How do you explain the gap between the legislators and the range of organizations supporting the families' initiative?

Writing to Persuade

Persuasion is the art of changing the reader's mind—and changing the reader's ways. A persuasive writer does not just want readers to say, "This is good to know," or "I sympathize with your problem," or "I have had the same experience myself." Much persuasive writing tries to influence behavior. It instigates action—a sale, a contribution, a vote. However, much persuasive writing also aims at a change of attitude—a different attitude toward women in the workplace, a raised consciousness about sexual harassment, or a more active concern about homophobia among gay-bashing young males.

TRIGGERING   Persuasive writing often has a special urgency. It serves a personal need or agenda. People who are concerned or aggrieved feel they need to make their voices heard so that something will be done.

- *Much persuasive writing asks us to help correct specific abuses.* When a family member or close friend has been killed by a drunk driver, people may want to transform their impotent rage into corrective action. They may join an organization pressuring legislators for stiffer penalties and tougher enforcement. They may join in letter-writing campaigns, writing letters to newspapers, local officials, or their representatives in Congress.

- *Much persuasive writing enlists our support for the good cause.* For people who live in a crime-ridden, drug-infested society, issues like gun control are not academic questions. People write about issues like gun control, prison reform, or AIDS counseling because they want us to care.

- *Much persuasive writing aims at a change of heart.* Writers may plead with their readers when they see their group or society at large taking a wrong turn. They plead for a return to traditional values, or an end to the degradation of our natural environment, or compassion for the down and out.

- *Much persuasive writing is advocacy.* It asks us to help defend people accused or to support an official or candidate. It aims at clearing someone's name or bringing the guilty to justice.

GATHERING What kind of material will sway your readers? If you respect their intelligence, you will make sure you know relevant facts, understand arguments pro and con, and respect the right of others to disagree. However, although your writing will have to be intellectually respectable, it will also have to *move* your readers. It will have to arouse their concern; it will have to activate their loyalties or sympathy. It will have to break through the crust of apathy. Look at the kinds of materials that persuasive writers use to reach and influence their intended audience:

- *Persuasive writers establish their authority.* You will have to show your involvement and commitment. You will have to show you know enough about the subject; you have earned the right to speak up. As with other kinds of papers, you may want to start by taking stock of your own relevant experiences, memories, thoughts, and feelings. Suppose you want to plead for heightened awareness of rape as a major social issue in our society. The following might be your **cluster** charting associations that the term *rape* brings to mind:

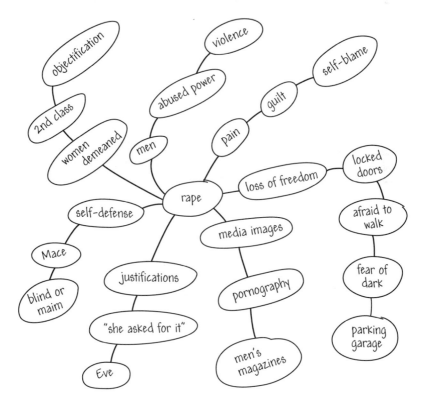

What kind of paper might this cluster generate? What major points would it touch on?

- *Persuasive writers dramatize the issue.* They may start with a dramatic incident that will shake up the blasé reader. Even frightening statistics may remain impersonal and colorless; they cannot compete with the impact of a real-life story like the following:

> I remember being awakened at about four o'clock in the morning. My parents told me they were leaving for the hospital—my brother-in-law had been shot. He had been at a small all-night store that night buying some milk. A quarrel started in the store. As he stepped out to avoid the whole scene, a car pulled up with three men inside. One of the men in the car shot him, putting a bullet through his head. Art is now partially paralyzed in his left leg and arm, and he has restricted speech and vision.
>
> Because there is little or no restriction on the purchase or use of guns, innocent people are killed or maimed every day. . . .

- *Persuasive writers appeal to shared values.* They compile examples and statistics that will arouse the indignation or activate the loyalties of the reader. Look at the following skeleton of a paper attacking the huge damage awards assessed against businesses and individuals accused of negligence. What are the standards or values that the writer appeals to in each successive section of the paper?

> ### Are You Insured?
>
> Courts are going out of their way to do away with traditional standards of fairness and shared responsibility. Increasingly, courts are disallowing the traditional defense of contributory negligence. One case involved a man who strapped a refrigerator on his back and ran a stunt footrace. One of the straps failed, and he collected $1 million from the strap manufacturer.
>
> Little attention is paid to the limited financial resources of small businesses or of individuals. The costs of litigation and the enormous damage awards are driving small companies to the wall. . . .
>
> The effects on the pharmaceutical industry are especially harmful. Liability for rare side effects is driving many manufacturers out of the vaccine market, even in cases where medical opinion agrees that the good the vaccines do far outweighs the possible harm. Vaccines (such as those for diphtheria and tetanus) for children are steadily climbing in price. . . .
>
> Who benefits from the inflation of damage awards? The big winners (in case you had any doubts) are the lawyers. A Rand study found that a typical court case costs $380,000, of which $125,000 went to the defense lawyers, $114,000 to the plaintiff's lawyers, and $141,000 in net compensation to the plaintiff.

- *Persuasive writers often use a key example to clinch an argument.* They discuss a test case in graphic detail. A reader who is already predisposed to think of tests as culturally biased is likely to remember a striking example like the following:

> Consider this question from a standardized group IQ test. "No garden is without its _____." The desired answer is one of these five: "sun-rain-tool-work-weeds." A child who happens to know the expression will recognize the missing word (weeds) and complete the sentence "correctly." If he doesn't have that piece of information, he'll have to figure out the answer. He might explain to a tester, "It isn't 'tools' because I once planted a garden with my hands." But there is no tester to tell. He might continue, "I don't know how to choose between sun and rain, so I won't use either one." Again there's no tester to hear his reasoning. "So it's either 'work' or 'weeds.'" Another pause. "Well, if a gardener worked hard, maybe he wouldn't have any weeds—but, if he doesn't work at all, he won't have any garden!" Triumphantly, the clever, logical, analytical young mind has selected—the wrong answer!
>
> When a computer grades that test, "work" will simply be marked wrong, and no one will be there to explain the thought process to the computer. Nor will anyone point out the differences between the child who has personal experience with gardens and the child whose closest contact may be the city park, ten blocks away from his fire escape.—*Arlene Silberman, "The Tests That Cheat Our Children,"* McCall's

▪ *Persuasive writers exploit the weaknesses of the opposition.* They look for contradictions. They look for a contrast between public pronouncements and actual practice. The author of the following excerpt took aim at an ironic discrepancy he saw between enlightened humanitarian ideals and personal behavior:

> Among trendy young professionals in our major cities, there is no stigma attached to using cocaine. In particular, the hip lawyers, doctors, movie stars, and so on who use the drug are not deterred, or even bothered much, by the mere fact that it happens to be illegal. But perhaps they will be receptive to a more fashionable approach. After all, many cocaine consumers are the same sort of people who will boycott lettuce or grapes because farm workers are underpaid, or a cosmetic because the company tortures rabbits, or tuna to protest the killing of dolphins. . . .
>
> Murder is as much a part of cocaine culture as tiny silver spoons and rolled-up hundred-dollar bills. There is seldom a major coke bust that doesn't also turn up an arsenal of automatic weapons. In a recent year in Miami, the cocaine capital of the Northern Hemisphere, a quarter of the city's 614 murders were committed with machine guns.—*David Owen, "Boycott Cocaine,"* Harper's

SHAPING A basic strategy in much persuasive writing—as in advertising and propaganda—is insistence. Often a writer will pile on graphic examples, keeping after the reader. Sooner or later, even a reluctant reader may begin to say: "I see what you mean. I didn't realize things were this bad or the needs this great."

To make your plea as effective as possible, try to spell out the heart of your message in pointed, memorable language:

Of all the drug problems afflicting our society, heroin is the most deadly. Once addicted, the user needs cash to feed the habit. The males steal and rob. The women become shoplifters and prostitutes.

Remember that much effective persuasion builds to a climax. The writer leads up to a high point or saves an especially telling example for last. A paper pleading for allowing the terminally ill to "go in peace" took up in turn the traditions of the medical profession and the cases of a hypothetical comatose patient, a brain-dead accident victim, and a patient with terminal cancer. But the paper saved for the end the case of a person close to the student writer:

My grandmother asked what I would do when it came time for her to die. I told her I would weep for her and be very sad, but I would remember how she lived. For me, this means that I could not let her linger in a life in between with machines and tubes. I must respect her wishes concerning how she wants to die. She must be able to go in peace the way she plans, not the way a doctor plans. She chose the way she lived, and with my help she will choose the way she dies.

REVISING Pleas written in the heat of passion or indictments written in the first flush of anger are best allowed to cool a day or two. Remember that a strong plea may seem shrill and biased when sent out unedited. When revising a persuasive paper, consider advice like the following:

■ *Focus your enthusiasm or channel your anger.* Do not scatter your shots. Do not flail out indiscriminately at miscellaneous abuses or multiple villains. Make sure your paper does not read like a mere inventory of grievances. Concentrate on worthy targets, and do them justice.

■ *Do not make weighty charges lightly.* Use strong words like *corruption* or *deceit* only after due deliberation and when you are sure of your target. Accusations made without the necessary backup often backfire.

■ *Reconsider strongly charged language.* When we are passionately committed to a cause, we naturally use emotional language. But consider that wildly enthusiastic language can seem immature or overdone. Abusive language can weaken your cause when it alienates fair-minded readers. Revise any labels that might be considered condescending or offensive.

■ *Revise ad hominem attacks.* In other words, be wary of using arguments directed "against the person." Broad hints about an opponent's divorce, troubled private life, or medical history may gain an advantage, but they may also alienate fair-minded people. Do without remarks about a person's baldness, obesity, accent, or limp.

How persuasive is the following sample paper? How much depends on the audience? What is the overall pattern or strategy adopted by the writer? Does anything in the paper have a special effect on you?

Justice

Three years ago I signed up to be a Big Sister to an eight-year-old girl through the Big Brothers/Big Sisters agency of the county. When the caseworker matched me with Sonia she warned me that Sonia's mother had decreed two topics as taboo for Sonia: sex and her father. I could somewhat understand the mother's prudery about sex, although I disagreed with it. But I was surprised and intrigued when the caseworker told me that Sonia's father was in a state prison, sentenced to death. I pitied the girl, wondering how she felt about having a father who brought her shame.

Sonia has rarely mentioned sex, so that part of the agreement was easy to keep. However, although I never brought up the subject of her father, I discussed how she felt about him whenever she wanted to discuss him. After about three months of seeing each other, Sonia told me that she had been to the movie *Pinocchio* as a very little girl but she didn't remember it. She explained that she had fallen asleep in the car and her father had carried her into the theater, held her as she slept through the movie, and carried her out again. I was astonished that she had a warm memory of trusting a man who had raped and brutally killed two teenage girls. Then she said that she liked visiting him in jail because she and her brothers got to eat a lot at the prison. I didn't discourage her from talking; I was discovering that she loved her father and was not ashamed of him.

Not only does Sonia love her father, but she has the same need to idealize him as all children need to admire their parents. I remember being moved once when she startled me as we were driving downtown by pointing to a tall building and exclaiming, "There's my daddy's cell." I was confused, so I asked her to explain. She told me that he wasn't there at that time but he had spent some time in jail in the city and she remembered visiting him there. She had pointed with pride to a building she associated with her father, just as another child might say excitedly, "There's my daddy's office." I realized that her father, a vicious killer, was loved and needed. If capital punishment is reinstated in the state, she will lose her father and she will have to sift through an immense burden of conflicting feelings—grief, anger, shame, confusion. His death would help no one. His victims are already dead and his death can't bring them back. Perhaps their relatives want justice, but his death is not justice. It would simply be vengeance. By killing him, we can't bring back the innocent; we can only hurt more innocent people.

I have always been opposed to capital punishment. I believe that, as a society, our role is to care for and protect each other. When one of our members hurts others, we remove him or her from the rest. But killing that person as punishment seems to be sinking to a low level of ethics. Policies of vengeance and "an eye for an eye" morality serve only to escalate violence. We forbid people to kill each other, yet as a legal institution, society dictates that killing is acceptable only when it deems it necessary, as in times of war and as punishment for crimes. I believe that if, as a society, we refuse to accept violence among ourselves and refuse to punish the violent with death, we are carrying out a commitment to peace and nonviolence.

Sonia has two pictures hanging in her bedroom that her father painted for her while imprisoned. One is of an Indian girl and the other of an eagle flying above a canyon. Sonia has told me that her father has painted a mural at the prison, as well. Perhaps she idealizes him in her ignorance; most people are guilty of idealizing imperfect people. Yet Sonia will be faced with the much harder job of reconciling her love for her father with the reality that he is a criminal. Most children only have to realize that their caretakers aren't strong, all-knowing, and perfect. To increase this child's pain for the sake of saving tax dollars or of satisfying the understandable, but impossible to achieve, needs for revenge that some people have, would be tragic. Allowing Sonia's father to live would save his family more pain, and it would allow our society to rise above ethics based on violence and revenge.

Topics for Persuasion Papers (A Sampling)

1. Write a fund-raising letter to help support a cause to which you are committed.
2. Write to students at your former high school about the negative effects or dangers of forming cliques or of ostracizing or putting down individuals or groups.
3. Do you have strong feelings about the "right to die"? Present your position, trying to persuade those who might disagree.
4. Do you feel strongly about an issue like child abuse, domestic violence, rape prevention, or the treatment of rape victims? Write a paper designed to arouse readers who in your opinion are too unconcerned or uncommitted on the issue.
5. What would you say to young people who have gang affiliations or who might get involved in youth gangs?
6. Write a letter to officials in which you call for stricter supervision of, or more official support for, the local police.
7. Can you persuade skeptical readers that talk about family values is more than election year rhetoric?
8. Are we as a society becoming too callous about the poor, the homeless, or the sick? How would you appeal to your reader's conscience?
9. What needs to be done to lessen violence in our communities? Try to persuade a skeptical or disillusioned reader.
10. Should parents do more to supervise or restrict their children's television viewing?

11

ECOLOGY
Saving the Planet

There is power in an antelope, but not in a goat or in a sheep, which
holds still while you butcher it, which will eat your newspaper if you
let it. There was a great power in a wolf, even in a coyote. You have
made him into a freak—a toy poodle, a Pekingese, a lap dog.

—*John (Fire) Lame Deer*

We all live downstream.

—*bumper sticker*

A central goal of Western culture has been to tame and control nature. Progress meant advances in freeing humanity from hunger and disease.
It meant release from back-breaking toil in the fields to wrest meager crops
from the earth. Without technology, one of its defenders has said, a human
being would be a naked ape—at the mercy of droughts, floods, blights, and
epidemics. Cities would cease to exist, with bands of survivors roaming the
countryside and plundering and scrounging for food.

In recent times, however, many voices have expressed second thoughts
about the blessings of our technological civilization. Our technology, our
modern lifestyle, has increasingly isolated us from contact with the natural
world. Air-conditioned buildings isolate us from the changing winds and
the fresh air. We walk on asphalt and concrete rather than on sand or grass.
We fly over prairies and rivers and mountains with the windows closed,
watching a Hollywood movie. The toxic by-products of our technological
civilization are poisoning the rivers, the oceans, the air.

Many have turned to other cultural traditions to search for a different sense of the relationship between humanity and nature. Other cultures
have envisioned a more organic relation between human civilization and
the natural world. They have or had a better sense of the interdependence
of creatures. Some cultures have taught human beings to look at all living
things with reverence. Their myths or religious traditions kept people in
touch with their roots in the natural world.

In recent years, an active ecological movement has tried to reverse the
trend toward the heedless exploitation and destruction of our natural environment. Environmental activists have tried to block floating factories that
were decimating fish populations and to stop logging companies that were
clear-cutting ancient forests. Politicians and self-styled "hard-nosed" business leaders have begun to reckon with those agitating to preserve the
wilderness or crusading for clean water and clean air.

Is it true that Western industrial civilization is at war with nature and
is bound to destroy our natural environment? Is it possible for people in the
modern world to live in harmony with nature?

ALLIGATOR COUNTRY: THE EYES OF NIGHT

Amy Blackmarr

> In recent years, there has been a movement to protect the last wild large predators in North America. In fact, there has been a movement to reintroduce grizzly bears, wolves, and coyotes into areas from which they had been driven years ago. On the opposing side, in the words of the author of a letter-to-the-editor responding to the following article, there are "people who move out to the country, encounter their wild neighbors, and have them removed or exterminated."

Thought Starters: A tourist taking a walk around a small lagoon at a motel in Florida may see a sign that says: CAUTION—ALLIGATORS. How would you react if you saw such a sign?

Nestled among the pines on the way to the swamp, about two miles from my cabin, lies the alligator pond. My neighbor Donnie started calling the place the alligator pond [. . .] because every time he flew over it he saw alligators in the water and on the banks.

But I had never seen one there. In fact, in all my years around the swamps of south Georgia until I moved to the cabin, I had never seen an alligator. So I was surprised one late-summer afternoon when, standing on the bank with my mongrel Max and German shepherd Queenie, I saw an alligator floating near the shore.

At first I didn't realize what it was. Its snout was out of the water, but only enough to resemble a big turtle head. But the more I looked at it, the more of it I saw, and I raced inside to call my neighbor Gene. He drove his wife Alice and their daughter and her fiancé over in the truck to have a look.

The sun was almost gone, and the rose-colored evening air was alive with mosquitoes, which made it hard to concentrate. My hands were sweating from the heat and Pop's old binoculars were foggy. Nevertheless, none of us had any doubt that it was an alligator we were squinting at, and an alligator that was squinting back at us. Maybe it was because of the dogs standing on the banks or maybe the alligator wanted one of us, but during the half hour the five of us passed around the binoculars and talked nervously about what to do, she brought her whole six feet up to within two shovel lengths of where we were standing. And there she floated—waiting, perhaps, for one of us to walk into the water or for everybody to just leave so she could go back to her turtle supper. That was fine by me. We had too many turtles in the pond, anyway. They ate the fish. So turtles, frogs, snakes—whatever that alligator wanted she was welcome to, as long as it wasn't dog legs, the neighbors, or me.

The next day I called the fish and game people. They would send out 5 a couple of trappers, the ranger said, but I'd have to wait until they could work me into their schedule.

"Alligators is partial to little gray dogs," the ranger said after I described Max. "Don't nobody know why. You say you got a dog pen? Well, I seen a gator climb a six-foot fence to get a dog one time. Gators is crazy when they're hungry. Don't you go near the water, now. Particularly not at night.

"No," I said. As if I would.

"See, a gator hunts at night," he went on. "How you can tell if you got one is, if you shine a flashlight at him, his eyes'll light up like taillights."

Like the eyes of a jack-o'-lantern is what he should have said. I could spot them all the way across the pond while, safe behind the screen door, I scanned the water with the flashlight. Slow as an old snapping turtle, that alligator would cruise around the pond in the dark, her eyes glowing just above the water as she watched the banks. She was magnificent, a neon-eyed monster straight out of a Stephen King novel.

"See, what a gator does is, he waits until a dog or something comes 10 right up to the edge of the water—then he goes after him," the ranger had explained. "Then he stuffs him under a log and waits for him to rot."

I locked Max and Queenie in the house at night and in the dog pen during the day, hoping the pond's too many turtles would keep the alligator from climbing the fence for a bite of little gray dog.

Around 10 o'clock one night several weeks later, the two trappers showed up with a bag full of rotting rattlesnakes in the back of a pickup. They'd use the snakes to bait the trap, they said, in case they couldn't catch her.

Catch her? I thought. Right.

And to my horror, they set off on the pond in a bass boat with nothing but their wits, their considerable brawn, their flashlight, and two long poles with nooses attached to the end—but not, thank heaven, with a boatload of ripe alligator bait.

For two hours, they chased the alligator around the pond. They'd 15 creep up behind her, and she would speed off to the opposite shore. They'd reach out a pole, and she'd dive under. Finally, around midnight, they paddled back to the bank, where I was sitting on the tailgate of their truck, watching. One of them reached for the bait.

"Gonna have to set the trap," he said. "We'll come back and check it in a few days."

Away they went across the water with their fragrant rattlesnakes.

After a while, I heard them coming back. They had almost made it to shore when they spotted the alligator. She had come up onto the bank near the truck and was lying not that far from where my legs were dangling.

The next thing I knew, one of the trappers had slipped a noose around her snout and was standing in thigh-deep water, wrestling with her as she thrashed. The other trapper grabbed her tail, and soon her jaws were taped shut and her legs were taped behind her back and she was immobilized. And then she was riding off in the back of the pickup.

If it hadn't been for the dogs, I would have liked to keep that alliga-   *20* tor. It was interesting, having an alligator in the pond. But then I wouldn't have the blue herons or the ducks or the otter, and maybe not the kingfishers, and certainly not the turtles. Probably not too many snakes. The fishing wouldn't be as good, either—or as safe.

But I've often wondered what happened to the alligator who found refuge in our pond for a while—if those trappers sold her to a farm for 10 dollars a foot or if she's in some Florida cypress pond under a rickety wooden bridge, where Yankee tourists pay a dollar to watch her sleep. Could be somebody's sitting on a south Georgia alligator wallet right now, or carrying a south Georgia alligator handbag, or wearing a pair of south Georgia alligator shoes. But that old proverb about walking a mile in another man's moccasins takes on a certain irony there.

To be honest, people don't seem to have much sympathy for the alligator. It's kind of an ugly duckling, and the fact that it eats whatever live bodies happen to enter the water doesn't endear it to the guardians of children and little gray dogs. But despite a menacing reputation, the alligator can have a singular kind of appeal—a power, a mystery, and a magical kind of charm as she glides around a pond on a summer night, piercing the darkness with her jack-o'-lantern eyes, looking for her supper.

The Responsive Reader

1. Blackmarr says that "people don't seem to have much sympathy for the alligator." How would you sum up her own attitude toward the one she encountered? Where in the article does she make you take a good direct look at the animal? What thoughts and emotions does it call up in her mind? Do you think you would have shared them or reacted differently?

2. How would you describe the attitude of the ranger? Why does Blackmarr quote the fish and game ranger directly and at length? Were you astonished by the attitude and procedures of the trappers?

Talking, Listening, Writing

3. Have you ever encountered a potentially dangerous animal in the wild? What were the circumstances? How did you react? What were your feelings at the time and afterward?

4. One correspondent in favor of saving the remaining mountain lions, bears, and alligators said that the same people who are trying to exterminate them would want to protect the elephants that are rampaging through the farms of villagers in Africa. Americans watch *National Geographic* specials about saving the lions of Africa and the endangered tigers of Asia. Do you think many Americans apply a double standard to the challenge of saving remaining wildlife?

5. Do you think predators should be allowed to survive in clearly limited areas such as national parks? Do you think they should survive only in zoos? Do you think predators should be allowed to coexist with humans outside areas such as national parks?

Collaborative Projects

6. Working with a group, investigate the pros and cons of plans to reintroduce predators such as wolves in parts of the United States. What are the arguments in favor? Who are the advocates or supporters of the initiatives? What are the arguments of opponents? What is the position of environmentalists, ranchers, hikers, campers, or local residents?

THE LAST OF THE WILD SALMON
Marie de Santis

> *We tend to be armchair ecologists who know the threatened wildlife of our planet mostly from television specials. The author of the following article knows the life of the oceans and rivers from close personal observation. De Santis worked for eight years as a commercial fisherwoman and the captain of her own boat. She told her story of the lure of the sea and of the hard work and dangers faced by those who make a living from the sea in her book* Neptune's Apprentice *(1984). In the following excerpt from her book* California Currents *(1985), she pays tribute to the wild salmon who are endangered by the destruction of their spawning grounds and the obstacles that dams and polluted or diverted rivers present to their age-old journey upstream. She hated to see the wild salmon replaced by artificially bred fish "no more suited to the stream than a poodle is to the woods." She addressed her book to those who "wish to continue living in a world with real animals" and who want future generations to "see more than the broken spirits of the animals of the zoo."*

Thought Starters: What animal would you choose as the best symbol of the threatened life on our endangered planet?

In a stream so shallow that its full body is no longer submerged in the water, the salmon twists on its side to get a better grip with its tail. Its gillplate is torn, big hunks of skin hang off its sides from collisions with rocks, there are deep gouges in its body, and all around for miles to go there is only the cruelty of more jagged rocks and less and less water to sustain the swim. Surely the animal is dying!

And then the salmon leaps like an arrow shot from a bow; some urge and will and passion ignores the animal body and focuses on the stream.

Of all the extremes of adaptation to the ocean's awful toll on the young, none is more mythic in proportion than the salmon's mighty journey to the mountain streams: a journey that brings life to meet death at a point on a perfect circle, a return through miles of narrowing waters to the exact gravel-bedded streamlet of its birth. A journey to spawning and death, so clear in its resemblance to the migrations of the sperm to the egg as to entwine their meanings in a single reflection.

On every continent of the northern hemisphere, from the temperate zone to the arctic, there is hardly a river that hasn't teemed with the salmon's spawn: the Thames, the Rhine, the rivers of France and Spain, Kamchatka and Siberia, Japan (which alone has more than 200 salmon rivers) and the arctic streams of Greenland. From the Aleutians to Monterey Bay, through the broadest byways to the most rugged and narrow gorge, the salmon have made their way home. There are many journeys for which the salmon endure more than 1000 miles.

As soon as the ice melts on the Yukon, the king salmon enter the river's mouth, and for a month, the fish swim against the current, 50 miles a day for a total of 1500. And like every other salmon on its run, the king salmon fasts completely along the way. In other rivers, salmon scale vertical rocks up to 60 feet high, against hurtling waterfalls.

The salmon gets to spawn once in life, and maybe that's reason enough. The salmon's instinct to return to the place of its birth is so unmodifiable and of such purity as to have inspired hundreds of spiritual rites in as many societies of human beings.

The salmon arrives battered and starved, with a mate chosen along the way, and never has passion seemed less likely from two more wretched-looking beings. But, there in the gravel of the streamlet, the female fans out a nest with the sweep of her powerful tail and the male fends off intruders. The nest done, the two fish lie next to each other suspended in the water over the nest; their bodies quiver with intense vibrations, and simultaneously they throw the eggs and the sperm. Compared with the millions of eggs thrown by a cod in a stream, the salmon need throw only 2000 to 5000. Despite the predators and other hazards of the stream, these cold mountain waters are a sanctuary compared with the sea. For the next two or three days, the pair continue nesting and spawning until all the eggs are laid. Then the salmon, whose journey has spanned the ocean and the stream, lies by the nest and dies.

Soon the banks of the streams are stacked with ragged carcasses, and the animals of the woods come down for a feast. The stream lies quiet in the winter's deepening cold. But within a month two black eyes appear through the skin of each egg. And two weeks later, the water is again alive with the pulsing of millions of small fish feeling the first clumsy kicks of their tails. The fingerlings stay for a while, growing on the insects and larvae that have been nurtured by the forest. Then, one day, they realize what that tail is for and begin their descent to the sea, a journey mapped in their genes by the parents they left behind.

The young salmon arrive in the estuary facing the sea, where they linger again and learn to feed on shrimp, small crustaceans and other creatures of the brine. Here, also, their bodies complete an upheaval of internal and external changes that allow them to move on to the saltier sea. These adaptations require such extraordinary body transformations that when the same events occur on the stage of evolution they take millions and millions of years. In the life of the salmon, the changes take place in only a matter of months. One of life's most prohibitive barriers—that between fresh and salt water—is crossed, and the salmon swim back and forth, in and out of the sea, trying it on for size.

Then one day, the youngsters do not return. The stream is only a dis-   *10*
tant memory drifting further and further back in the wake of time, only different—a memory that will resurrect and demand that its path be retraced.

So accessible is the salmon's life in the stream that more is known
about the reproduction of this fish than any other ocean animal. With the
ease of placing cameras underwater, there isn't any aspect of this dramatic
cycle that hasn't been captured in full color in some of the most spectacular
film footage ever made.

But once the salmon enters the sea, the story of its life is a secret
as deep and dark as the farthest reaches of the ocean it roams. The human
eye with its most sophisticated aids, from satellite to sonar, has never caught
more than a glance of the salmon at sea. Extensive tagging programs have
been carried out, but they tell us little more than that the salmon is likely
to be found anywhere within thousands of miles of its origins, and even this
is only a sliver of the picture because the tags are recovered only when the
salmon is caught by fishermen, who work solely within the narrow coastal
zone. Along with a few other pelagic fishes, like the tuna, that claim vast
stretches of sea for their pasture, the salmon's life remains one of the most
mysterious on earth.

The Responsive Reader

1. What makes the stage of the salmon's life cycle that she describes at the
   beginning the symbolic high point for the author?
2. What are the major stages of the salmon's life journey? What are key
   events or striking details at each stage?

Talking, Listening, Writing

3. For you, does the salmon's life cycle make a good symbolic representation of life on this planet? Why or why not?
4. What plant or animal with an especially rich or varied life cycle have you
   studied or do you know well? Trace it in rich authentic detail, emphasizing major stages.
5. Do people, institutions, or ideas have life cycles similar to those de Santis observed in the natural world? Focus on one central example, and
   bring it to life for your reader.

Collaborative Projects

6. How successful is the struggle to restore life to lakes and streams poisoned by pollution? What have been notable successes and notable failures? What in particular is the current status of attempts to save the wild
   salmon? For a possible research project, work with a group to collect and
   collate data from authoritative sources.

HEARTS OF OAK

John Vidal

The environmentalist movement knows no frontiers. Green parties in the United States and in other parts of the world are united in a common cause. Greenpeace volunteers have risked their lives to stop nuclear tests scheduled by the French government in the South Pacific. They have tried to block the operations of Japanese fishing fleets trapping dolphin along with tuna. German ecologists fight pitched battles with police over bulldozers that destroy green spaces in the way of airport expansion or over the transport of radioactive materials to contested storage sites. For many ecologists, saving the forests has become a powerful rallying cry. One of the photographs accompanying the following article showed a protester trapped at the top of a tall birch tree, treed like a raccoon, while a hardhat with a chainsaw was making his way up the trunk of the tree, cutting away the branches as he went along. The protesters were trying to block the cutting down of trees to make way for a bypass through a historic stretch of British countryside. In spite of their efforts, more than 10,000 trees were felled, and 788 people were arrested. Protesters were making plans for Phase Two when actual construction work on the road was scheduled to start. They were planning mass trespassing and "pixie work"—the British term for monkey-wrenching.

Thought Starters: Have you ever protested against anything? Have you ever joined in an organized protest? What was the issue? What was the result?

It's a bone-chilling midnight in late March, and the only way I can climb the 150-foot Corsican pine tree in Reddings Copse is to "prusik"— to grapple my way up a long rope using two loops of string barely thicker than shoelaces as moveable handholds. I move, fist over fist, toward a square of candlelight showing through a trapdoor 100 feet above me, gingerly bypassing the coils of barbed wire and a precarious bucket of urine. One last heave and I'm in the lowest tree house, a shelter built of old pallets, doors, and beams and hung with hooks, chains, ropes, locks, handcuffs— for people to grab on to when the bailiffs arrive. Here, way above where birds nest, there's no sight of ground.

Thirty feet above us in this, the highest tree for miles around, is a second tree house, and at the very tip of the pine a defiant Union Jack and a rainbow pennant fly from a ladder. From here you can see most of the southern English county of Berkshire. In the dawn mists it's a landscape out of King Arthur: rickety little wooden bridges, old water meadows, oak copses, a slow river. Running through it all is a nine-mile-long,

hundred-yard-wide scar of mud and broken trees—the route of the Newbury bypass.

The plan to carve a four-lane highway through this quintessential English landscape has enraged conservationists and the young. Tree house occupations have been an accepted mode of environmental dissent in Britain
since a 1994 road protest in London. What's different at Newbury is the
sheer size of the action: The first protester started living in the trees more
than six months ago and now there are scores of camps, with hundreds of
people in tree houses or in "benders" made of bent hazelwood and plastic
sheeting on the frozen ground. Some tree houses, like "the Mothership" at
the Kennet River camp, stretch across nine or ten trees and have separate
kitchens and sleeping areas. Others are no more than "twigloos," fragile
nests for one or two people in the highest branches.

This protest is as passionate and sometimes as dangerous as any war or
genocide I've covered in 12 years with *The Guardian* of London. The police have warned that they will arrest us on sight if we're found in the trees;
attorneys say we risk prison and a criminal record; and the guards say—off
the record—that they'll injure us if they can. Worse, one false step on the
ice at 100 feet and we will plummet to our deaths.

Tonight this pine will sleep about 15 people. The last defenders will   5
arrive at about 3 a.m. Then we'll drape ourselves around the trunk and
huddle next to each other in blankets and sleeping bags donated by well-
wishers. A small woodstove will burn, and there will be little sleep as the
wind gets up and a light snow drifts in to melt in clouds of breath.

The route of the bypass, which goes within half a mile of the sites of
two 17th-century English Civil War battles—the First and Second Battles
of Newbury—was picked years ago when the environment wasn't as high
on the British political agenda. Now the European Union is supporting the
bypass as the last link in a motorway chain that will run from the south of
France to Scotland. But it goes through what are supposed to be two of the
best-protected nature sites in Britain (protected by the national government, which can rescind the protection when it purchases the land, as it did
here) and through land given in trust to the nation. There has been no environmental impact survey. The scheme has united Britain's disparate environmental groups, archaeologists, climbers, walkers, and civil libertarians.
The busy market town of Newbury is divided.

But the actual protesters at the site—300 self-styled "eco-warriors"
in more than 30 camps along the route—are not your typical middle-class
environmentalists. Many in the trees tonight are misfits who live on the
margins of the British economy. Greg, who oils his dreadlocks with the sap
of fallen pine trees, is an air force officer training dropout. Howie is a neo-
tribal nomad by choice. Balin, a local man, has spent 16 days and nights
slung heroically under a tripod made of scaffolding bars. There's also a former art dealer, a philosophy student, a poet, an EU political officer. Local

villagers provide the ground support for the camps, opening their homes to the protesters and bringing food and drink. Much of the protest is playful. Bagpipes, flutes, and drums resound. Protesters have dressed up (and been arrested) in cow costumes. One man covers himself in oil so the police can't grab hold of him.

It is first light and the battle has begun. Through the mists emerge 100 policemen and 300 guards, escorting a giant cherrypicker that can reach 200 feet. They are followed by three giant front-end loaders, one carrying fire in its bucket. "It's like Verdi," says one man. "More like a siege," cries another. "They've brought their own damn hell torch."

The protesters screech like Amazonian howler monkeys, raining insults down on their adversaries. "We'd rather die than live like you!" shouts one woman. Within an hour climbers have cut the rope and wire walkways that run between the tree houses. There have been hand to hand fights in five nearby oak trees. Twelve people have been bundled onto mechanical platforms, brought down, and arrested.

Now it's our turn. Greg cuts the only rope down the tree as a state- 10
ment that no one will descend willingly. Mick from Liverpool is at the top of the tree bellowing oaths. "This land is ours," he cries. "Ours," repeats the echo.

The platform of the cherrypicker approaches. The workers test the lower tree house defenses, approaching from below, then from above, clipping the barbed wire and lopping the lower branches as they go. Jim shoves a mop at the chain saw operator to jam up his machine. Rachel hurls paint. Ralph is out on a branch with no safety harness, daring the bailiffs to remove him.

The cherrypicker moves closer, cutting through a hail of rice and flour. The workers begin to saw through the branches that the tree house is roped to. A terrible *crack* shudders the whole tree. There are screams of protest. Now they are cutting within six, within three feet of us. The noise is deafening. Fear mounts.

The battle lasts all morning. Suddenly the platform soars upward, to the top of the tree. The bailiffs detach and carry off the rainbow flag and the Union Jack. Then they leave us in peace.

The protesters have won a round: A bulldozer has accidentally pushed a small oak tree onto the largest machine and damaged it. The guards and police march off with their machinery, and the action moves on to the next camp, where eight trees are occupied. By nightfall 20 more people will have been brought down, arrested, and ordered to keep well away from the battleground. (Miraculously, there have only been two serious injuries in more than two months' high drama.)

The pine stands, its lower branches shorn, its defenses down. The 15
bailiffs say they will be back for us tomorrow. The tree people put the kettle

on and bring out the drums. "Every cup of tea is a victory," says Howie. "This is the start of the eco-wars," says Cat. The party will last through the night.

The Responsive Reader

1. Environmental awareness has become a cliché, with many people and organizations at least paying lip service. What makes the protesters described in this article different? What kind of people are they? What for you was startling or provocative about their methods or their behavior?
2. References to the Union Jack and to the historic battle sites remind readers that this confrontation is taking place in Britain and not the United States. Do you think the same thing could have happened more or less the same way in the United States? Why or why not?

Talking, Listening, Writing

3. In reading about events like this protest, or seeing photographs or television coverage, many readers have a gut reaction impelling them to take sides with one group or the other. Do you find yourself taking sides? Why and how?
4. For many people in the western United States, a powerful symbol of our threatened natural heritage is the giant redwood trees (*Sequoia sempervirens*) that reach a height of 360 feet. Many of those still standing were already growing at the time of the birth of Christ. In an ominous note, *Merriam Webster's Collegiate Dictionary* (tenth edition) calls the redwood a "commercially important" timber tree, and for years ecologists and nature lovers have done battle with the logging interests to save the remaining stands of original growth. Do you think you would have joined in the efforts to save the redwood trees?

Collaborative Projects

5. An article in *Time* magazine concluded that "green sentiment is again a powerful political force." Working with a group, you may want to investigate a test case like the controversies over logging in the Headwaters redwood groves in California or in Alaska's Tongass National Forest or over clear-cutting in the north woods of Maine. What is involved in the struggle of environmental organizations, corporate interests, and political alliances "over the future of huge tracts of forest land that lie before the logger's axe"?

CALIFORNIA CONDOR'S COMEBACK

Jane Kay

> *Part of the price Americans paid for the settlement of the American continent was the extinction or near extinction of the fantastic wildlife that flourished here before the arrival of the Europeans. The vanished flocks of passenger pigeons were estimated to number in the millions. Huge herds of buffalo had roamed the prairies, and their extinction took with them the livelihood and the lifestyle of the Native Americans of the plains. Early American naturalists painted huge swarms of flamingos circling in the skies and nesting in the swamps. In the final decades of the twentieth century, environmentalists, naturalists, and researchers mounted a dedicated effort to save remaining endangered wildlife from extinction. Special efforts concentrated on saving the big birds: the bald eagle, the crane, the condor. The author of the following news report is an environment writer for a leading West Coast newspaper.*

Thought Starters: What is the special fascination that birds have for bird watchers and ornithologists? What do you know about Audubon and the Audubon Society? What kinds of birds do you know by name and by sight? Do any have a special meaning for you?

When eminent naturalist Roger Tory Peterson published the third 1 edition of "Western Birds" a dozen years ago, he grimly noted that the 40 surviving California condors in the world lived in zoos.

Scientists had captured the last wild condors as part of an unprecedented attempt to save an endangered species. They would breed them, hatch the eggs and raise the young in cages. The goal: Return the largest flying birds in North America to nature.

Today, 10 years after biologists freed the first of those captive condors, no one is claiming that the giant scavenger is exactly flourishing. But after years of setbacks and missteps, the signs are encouraging.

Condors are increasing in numbers, surviving to maturity in the wild and acting more like real wild condors. There are 183 California condors alive today. Fifty-eight live free—33 in California and 25 in Arizona and Utah—and the remaining 125 are in breeding programs.

A huge leap forward came last year when three condors laid eggs in 5 the wild, the first in 15 years.

Condor biologists are upbeat about the bird's prospects.

"This magnificent bird was on the brink of extinction. And now people can see condors in the wild," said Bruce Palmer, California condor recovery coordinator for the U.S. Fish and Wildlife Service.

"A bird like this can never be remade. When they soar over your head, you can hear the wind through their feathers. It sends shivers up my spine," Palmer said.

Just as the peregrine falcon's removal from the federal endangered species list inspired other programs to save species, the condor is giving impetus to efforts to save the whooping crane, the bald eagle and the wolves.

The condor dates back hundreds of thousands of years. In the Pleistocene era, it fed on carrion of mammoths and later elk, antelope, seals and whales. As those mammals declined in numbers, the condor turned to cattle and sheep carcasses.   *10*

In prehistoric times, the condor lived as far south as Florida and along the Eastern Seaboard to New York. On the West Coast, it ranged from British Columbia to Baja California. In recent times, the condor lived in coastal mountains from California to Oregon and in the Sierra Nevada. It scavenged in grasslands, forests and canyons.

No one could miss the giant birds, with their 9½-foot wingspans. Their distinctive, naked red-orange heads, spiked with feathers and rimmed by black ruffs, change color with mood. Their black wings are lined with white.

The population dropped with the arrival of modern settlers, who hunted the birds. During the Gold Rush, miners stored gold dust in their quills. The condors also died from eating poisoned rodents and coyotes and carrion peppered with lead bullet fragments. They got tangled in power lines and soaked in oil spills.

By the 1940s, they bred only in the Sierra and the coastal range of California from Los Angeles to Monterey. They were sighted in Arizona.

Fearing the end of the species, the U.S. government listed condors   *15* among the first animals to win special protections for endangered species. After years of debate, the scheme was devised to preserve the species by breeding them in captivity. And in 1987, resource managers caught the last 27 condors and put them in the San Diego and Los Angeles zoos.

From the earliest days, the program faced emotional opposition. At the crux of the debate was whether humans should intervene to save a species that some experts believed was heading toward the evolutionary abyss no matter what was done.

The late conservationist David Brower stood against capturing the condors, saying it was a greater evil than letting the species "disappear with dignity."

Some critics questioned the wisdom of spending millions of dollars on the condor—the figure stands at $40 million so far, two-thirds from private donations—when it might be better spent on other endangered species.

Others debated the philosophies for managing the birds and for ensuring that their habitats were safe.

But the federal program forged ahead, and on Jan. 14, 1992, scientists   *20*
released the first pair of captive condors in Los Padres National Forest, 50
miles northwest of Los Angeles. The young female, Xewe, was shot at and
survived. But her partner, Chocuyens, was found dead nine months after
release, poisoned by ethylene glycol, possibly from antifreeze.

Since then, of the 128 birds released, 45 died from various causes, 25
have been returned to captivity and 58 remain free.

The releases have occurred every year in three locales: in Los Padres,
north of Ventura; near the Vermilion Cliffs, 30 miles north of Grand
Canyon National Park; and within the Ventana Wilderness in Big Sur.

Life is hard for wild condors raised in captivity. Although caretakers
try to minimize human contact, condors are a naturally inquisitive species
and often seek out populated areas where they can get into trouble. Many
have had to be recaptured for their own protection. In recent years, breeders have placed them with parents or mentor birds for socialization.

But the biggest cause of death is lead poisoning, affecting 20 or more
birds.

A big break came in March. After 15 years without a single egg in the   *25*
wild, a condor released in the Grand Canyon laid an egg hidden away in a
cave, just as its ancestors had done. The egg was cracked, quite common
among inexperienced birds, scientists said.

In June, north of Ventura, two females each laid an egg in the same
cave. They were taking turns sitting on one of the two eggs. "We figured
these eggs were never going to make it on their own," said Fish and Wildlife
biologist Greg Austin.

The team rappelled down and grabbed both the eggs, replacing them
with one dummy egg. One of their eggs was dead, but one was alive. They
rushed the live one to the Los Angeles Zoo, where it hatched. Austin and
others took an egg about to hatch from the zoo back to the nest. Two
days later, it hatched. Three days later, the hatchling was found dead outside the cave.

"We really wouldn't expect for them to be successful in their first
breeding attempt ever," Austin said. "The way we look at it, it's a benefit
to those birds. We don't think they know what to do until they see it. They
live for so long, they're going to figure it out."

Harvard evolutionary biologist Edward O. Wilson, in his new book,
"The Future of Life," says "11th-hour rescues from obliteration," such as
the work done for the condor, "have confirmed the generally innate resilience of endangered species.

"Given protection and uncontaminated food, the combined group   *30*
flourished," Wilson wrote. "For at least a while longer—and we most
prayerfully hope, for thousands of years to come—the California condor is
again a free-living species."

The Responsive Reader

1. What factual information does this article give you about the condor and its history? How would you describe the bird and its existence in the wild?
2. What do you learn about the aspects of human civilization that threatened the survival of the birds? What do you learn about the dangers they still encounter from humans today?
3. What was the situation at the beginning of the rescue efforts? What is the rationale for the current rescue effort—how is it supposed to work? How is it working out? What would you include in an interim report? How does the writer sum up the prospects for eventual success?
4. This article includes much factual information about the rescue initiatives. Where does the excitement, the fascination, or the enthusiasm that motivates those involved shine through? Do you think you could share in it? Why or why not?

Talking, Listening, Writing

5. Do you think the estimated $40 million spent on the effort to save the condors is well spent? Why or why not? Do you think the money should have been spent on more urgent needs? Do you think the condors should have been allowed to die "with dignity"?

Collaborative Projects

6. Working with a group, you may want to compile a status report on efforts to protect or bring back another species of the endangered big birds, such as the bald eagles or the sandhill cranes.

THE MONKEY WARS

Deborah Blum

> *Do animals have rights? Do they have the right to be protected against ex-termination, against wretched conditions, or against torture in medical experi-ments? The animal rights movement has led many to rethink their relationship with the animal world. It has led to crusades to rehabilitate and protect animals of the wild like the wolf and the coyote. Animal rights activists have challenged the unnatural conditions under which chickens and calves, for instance, are raised for food. They have made zookeepers reexamine the unnatural condi-tions under which animals are confined. In particular, the animal rights move-ment has focused attention on the suffering and destruction of animals in medical and military research. In the words of one activist, "A rabbit's right not to have oven cleaner poured into its eye is inherent. It exists whether the state recognizes it or not." Deborah Blum is a science writer who was trained at the University of Wisconsin and went to California to write first for* The Fresno Bee *and then for* The Sacramento Bee. *She first became interested in the ethics of animal experiments when apes used for laboratory experiments contracted the Ebola virus, which has proved deadly to patients and medical personnel in Africa. Her "Monkey Wars" series of articles won her the Pulitzer Prize.*

Thought Starters: Do animal trainers and pet owners have the right to do with animals as they please? Should we be concerned about how chick-ens or calves are raised to be butchered? Are zoos inhumane?

On the days when he's scheduled to kill, Allen Merritt summons up   1
his ghosts.

They come to him from the shadows of a 20-year-old memory. Eleven human babies, from his first year out of medical school. All born prematurely. All lost within one week when their lungs failed.

"We were virtually helpless," said Merritt, now head of the neonatal intensive care unit at the University of California-Davis Medical Center.

"There's nothing worse than being a new physician and standing there watching babies die. It's a strong motivator to make things different."

On this cool morning, he needs that memory. The experiment he's   5
doing is deceptively simple: a test of a new chemical to help premature babies breathe. But it's no clinical arrangement of glass tubes. He's trying the drug on two tiny rhesus monkeys, each weighing barely one-third of a pound. At the end of the experiment, he plans to cut their lungs apart, to see how it worked.

Even his ghosts don't make that easy. Nestled in a towel on a surgical table, eyes shut, hands curled, the monkeys look unnervingly human. "The link between people and monkeys is very close," Merritt said. "Much closer than some people would like to think. There's a real sense of sadness, that we can only get the information we need if we kill them."

Once, there was no such need to justify. Once, American researchers could go through 200,000 monkeys a year, without question. Now, the numbers are less—perhaps 20,000 monkeys will die every year, out of an estimated 40,000 used in experiments. But the pressures are greater.

These days, it seems that if researchers plan one little study—slicing the toes off squirrel monkeys, siphoning blood from rhesus macaques, hiding baby monkeys from their mothers—they face not just questions, but picket signs, lawsuits and death threats phoned in at night.

The middle ground in the war over research with monkeys and apes has become so narrow as to be nearly invisible. And even that is eroding.

Intelligent, agile, fast, but not fast enough, these non-human primates   10
are rapidly being driven from the planet, lost to heavy trapping and vanishing rain forests. Of 63 primate species in Asia—where most research monkeys come from—only one is not listed as vulnerable.

Primate researchers believe they are making the hard choice, using non-human primates for medical research because they must, because no other animal so closely mirrors the human body and brain. During the 1950s, American scientists did kill hundreds of thousands of monkeys for polio research, using the animals' organs to grow virus, dissecting their brains to track the spread of the infection. But out of those experiments came a polio vaccine. Using monkeys, scientists have created vaccines for measles, learned to fight leprosy, developed anti-rejection drugs that make organ transplants possible.

Outside the well-guarded laboratory wall, that choice can seem less obvious. Animal rights advocates draw a dark description of research. They point out that AIDS researchers have used endangered chimpanzees, without, so far, managing to help people dying of the disease. Further, conservationists fear that the research is introducing dangerous infection into the country's chimpanzee breeding program, badly needed to help counter the loss of wild animals.

"They're guzzling up money and animals, and for what?" asked Shirley McGreal, head of the non-profit International Primate Protection League. "Why not use those resources in helping sick people, why infect healthy animals?"

Her argument is that of animal advocates across the country—that scientists are sacrificing our genetic next-of-kin for their own curiosity, dubious medical gains and countless tax dollars.

No one is sure exactly how much money scientists spend experiment-   15
ing on monkeys, although the National Institutes of Health alone allocates almost $40 million annually to its primate research programs, including one

in Davis. Overall, more than half of NIH's research grants—approaching $5 billion—involve at least some animal research.

Rats and mice are the most abundant, some 15 million are used in experiments every year. But primates are the most expensive; monkeys cost a basic $1,000, chimpanzees start at $50,000.

For people such as McGreal, these are animals in a very wrong place. McGreal's long-term goal for monkeys is simple: out of the laboratory, back into what remains of the rain forests.

"I used to think that we could persuade those people to understand what we do," said Frederick King, director of the Yerkes Regional Primate Research Center in Atlanta. "But it's impossible. And that's why I no longer describe this as a battle. I describe it as a war."

The rift is so sharp that it is beginning to reshape science itself.

"Science has organized," marveled Alex Pacheco, founder of the country's most powerful animal rights group, People for Ethical Treatment of Animals. "Researchers are out-lobbying us and outspending us. They've become so aggressive that it puts new pressure on us. We're going to have to fight tougher too."

In the past year, researchers have made it clear just how much they dislike the role of victim. If Pacheco wants to call scientists "sadistic bastards"—which he does frequently—then Fred King is more than ready to counter with his description of PETA: "Fanatic, fringe, one of the most despicable organizations in the country."

But beyond name-calling, the research community is realizing its political power. Its lobbyists are pushing for laws that would heavily penalize protesters who interfere with research projects. And this year, to the fury of animal rights groups, primate researchers were able to win a special exemption from the public record laws, shielding their plans for captive monkey care.

For researchers, the attention focused on them is an almost dizzying turn-about. Not so long ago, they could have hung their monkey care plans as banners across streets and no one would have read them.

"When I first started, 20 years ago, monkeys were $25 each," said Roy Henrickson, chief of lab animal care at the University of California, Berkeley. "You'd use one once and you'd throw it away. I'd talk to lab vets who were under pressure about dogs and I'd say, I'm sure glad I'm in non-human primates. Nobody cares about them."

He can date the change precisely, back to 1981, the year Pacheco went undercover in the laboratory of Edward Taub. Taub was a specialist in nerve damage, working in Silver Springs, Md. To explore the effects of ruined nerves, he took 17 rhesus monkeys and sliced apart nerves close to the spinal column, crippling their limbs. Then he studied the way they coped with the damage.

Pacheco left the laboratory with an enduring mistrust of scientists and an armload of inflammatory photographs: monkeys wrenched into vises, packed into filthy cages. Monkeys who, with no feeling in their hands, had gnawed their fingers to the bone. Some of the wounds were oozing with infection, darkening with gangrene.

Many believe those battered monkeys were the fuse, lighting the current, combative cycle of animal rights. In the fury over the Silver Springs monkeys, Pacheco was able to build People for Ethical Treatment of Animals into a national force, and across the country, the movement gained power. Today, membership in animal advocacy groups tops 12 million; the 30 largest organizations report a combined annual income approaching $70 million.

And primate researchers have suddenly found themselves under scrutiny of the most hostile kind.

There are experiments, such as Allen Merritt's work to salvage premature infants, that the critics will sometimes reluctantly accept. The compound that Merritt is testing on young monkeys is a kind of lubricant for the lungs, a slippery ooze that coats the tissues within, allowing them to flex as air comes in and out.

Without the ooze—called surfactant—the tissues don't stretch. They rip. The problem for premature babies is that the body doesn't develop surfactant until late in fetal development, some 35 weeks into a pregnancy. Although artificial surfactants are now available, Merritt doesn't believe they're good enough. Two-thirds of the tiniest premature babies, weighing less than a pound at birth, still die as their lungs shred. He's trying to improve the medicine.   30

"There could be a scientific defense for doing that, even though it's extremely cruel," said Elliot Katz, head of In Defense of Animals, a national animal rights group, headquartered in San Rafael.

But Katz finds most of the work indefensible. He can rapidly cite examples of a different sort: a U.S. Air Force experiment, which involved draining 40 percent of the blood from rhesus macaques and then spinning them on a centrifuge, to simulate injured astronauts; a New York University study of addiction in which monkeys were strapped into metal boxes and forced to inhale concentrated cocaine fumes.

Last year, animal advocates rallied against a proposed study at the Seattle center, a plan to take 13 baby rhesus macaques from their mothers and try to drive them crazy through isolation, keeping them caged away from their mothers and without company. The scientists acknowledged that they might drive the monkeys to self-mutilation; rhesus macaques do badly in isolation, rocking, pulling out their hair, sometimes tearing their skin open.

This year, protesters have been holding candlelight vigils outside the home of a researcher at a Maryland military facility, the Uniformed Services University of the Health Sciences. That project involves cutting the toes from kittens and young squirrel monkeys and then, after they've wobbled into adjustment, killing them to look at their brains.

In both cases, there are scientific explanations. The Washington scientists wanted to analyze the chemistry of a troubled brain, saying that it could   35 benefit people with mental illness. The Maryland researchers are brain-mapping, drafting a careful picture of how the mind reorganizes itself to cope with crippling injury.

But these are not—and may never be—explanations acceptable to those crusading for animal rights. "This is just an example of someone doing something horrible to animals because he can get paid for it," said Laurie Raymond, of Seattle's Progressive Animal Welfare Society, which campaigned against the baby monkey experiment and takes credit for the fact that it failed to get federal funding.

Researchers are tired of telling the public about their work, documenting it in public records—and having that very openness used against them. The Washington protesters learned about the baby monkey experiment through a meeting of the university's animal care committee—which is public. The Maryland work came to light through a listing of military funded research—which is public.

When the U.S. Department of Agriculture, which inspects research facilities annually, complained about the housekeeping at the Tulane Regional Primate Research Center in Louisiana, the director wrote the agency a furious letter. Didn't administrators realize that the report was public—and made scientists look bad?

"The point I am making is that USDA, without intending to do so, is playing into the hands of the animal rights/anti-vivisectionists whose stated goal is to abolish animal research," wrote center head Peter Gerone, arguing that the complaints could have been handled privately. "If you are trying to placate the animal rights activists by nitpicking inspections . . . you will only serve to do us irreparable harm."

When Arnold Arluke, a sociologist at Boston's Northeastern University, spent six years studying lab workers and drafted a report saying that some actually felt guilty about killing animals, he found himself suddenly under pressure. "I was told putting that information out would be like giving ammunition to the enemy," he said. 40

He titled his first talk "Guilt Among Animal Researchers." The manager of the laboratory where he spoke changed "guilt" to stress. When he published that in a journal, the editors thought that stress was too controversial. They changed the title to "Uneasiness Among Lab Workers." When he gave another talk at a pharmaceutical company, he was told uneasiness was too strong. They changed the title to "How to Deal with Your Feelings." Arluke figures his next talk will be untitled.

"People in animal research don't even want to tell others what they do," he said. "One woman I talked to was standing in line at a grocery store, and when she told the person next to her what she did, the woman started yelling at her: 'You should be ashamed of yourself.'"

And when new lab animal care rules were published this year, it was clear that researchers were no longer willing to freely hand over every record of operation.

The new regulations resulted from congressional changes in 1985 to the Animal Welfare Act. They included a special provision for the care of laboratory primates; legislators wanted scientists to recognize that these were sociable, intelligent animals.

The provision—perhaps the most controversial in the entire act— 45
was called "psychological well-being of primates." When the USDA began drafting rules, in response to the new law, it received a record 35,000 letters of comment. And 14,000 consisted of a written shouting match over how to make primates happy. It took six years before the agency could come up with rules that the research community could accept.

Originally, the USDA proposed firm standards: Laboratories would have to give monkeys bigger cages, let them share space, provide them with puzzles and toys from a list.

Researchers argued that was unreasonable: Every monkey species was different, the rigid standards might satisfy one animal and make another miserable. Now, each institution is asked to do what it thinks best for its monkeys; USDA inspectors will be free to study, criticize and ask for changes in those plans.

But animal rights groups will not. Research lobbyists persuaded the USDA to bypass the federal Freedom of Information Act; the president of the American Society of Primatologists told the agency that making the plans public would be like giving a road map to terrorists. Under the new rules, the plans will be kept at the individual institutions rather than filed with the federal government, as has been standard practice. That makes them institutional property—exempted from any requests for federal records.

Tom Wolfle, director of the Institute for Laboratory Animal Resources in Washington, D.C., the federal government's chief advisory division on animal issues, said the research community simply needed some clear space. "The idea was to prevent unreasonable criticism by uninformed people," he said.

Advocacy groups have sued the government over the new rules, say- 50
ing they unlawfully shut the public out of research that it pays for. "In the end, they just handed everything back to the researchers and said, here, it's all yours," said Christine Stevens, an executive with the non-profit Animal Welfare Institute.

Stevens, daughter of a Michigan physiology researcher, finds this the ultimate contradiction, as well as "foolish and short-sighted." She thinks that science, of all professions, should be one of open ideas.

On this point, she has some unlikely allies. Frederick King, of Yerkes, no friend to the animal rights movement, is also unhappy with the research community's tendency to withdraw. "I don't know about the law," he said. "But our plans for taking care of our primates will be open.

"We are using taxpayers' money. In my judgment, we have an obligation to tell the public what we're about. And the fact that we haven't done that, I think, is one of the greatest mistakes over the last half-century, hell, the last century, that scientists have made."

Against that conflict, Allen Merritt's decision to make public an experiment in which he kills monkeys was not an easy one. His wife worried that anti-research fanatics would stalk their home. His supervisors worried that animal lovers would be alienated; one administrator even called the Davis primate center, suggesting that Merritt's work should not be publicly linked to the medical school's pediatrics department.

But Merritt, like King, believes that his profession will only lose if   55
it remains hidden from the public. "People need to understand what we're doing. If I were to take a new drug first to a nursery, and unforeseen complications occurred, and a baby died—who would accept that?"

So, on a breezy morning, he opens the way to the final test of lung-lubricating surfactants that he will do this year, a 24-hour-countdown for two baby monkeys. Those hours are critical to whether these drugs work. If human premature babies last from their first morning to the next one, their survival odds soar.

The tiny monkeys—one male, one female—taken by C-section, are hurried into an intensive care unit, dried and warmed with a blow drier, put onto folded towels, hooked up to ventilators, heart monitors, intravenous drip lines. During the experiment, they will never be conscious, never open their eyes.

"OK, let's treat," Merritt says. His technician gently lifts the tube from the ventilator, which carries oxygen into the monkey's lungs. A white mist of surfactant fills the tube, spraying into the lungs. And then, through the night, the medical team watches and waits.

The next morning, they decide to kill the female early. An intravenous line going into her leg is starting to cause bleeding problems. The monkey is twitching a little in her unconsciousness, as if in pain. Merritt sees no point in dragging her through the experiment's official end.

But the male keeps breathing. As the sun brightens to midday, the sci-   60
entists inject a lethal dose of anesthesia. Still, the monkey's chest keeps moving, up and down, up and down with the push of the ventilator. But, behind him, the heart monitor shows only a straight green line.

For a few seconds, before they shut the machines down and begin the lung dissection, Allen Merritt stands quietly by the small dead monkey, marshaling the ghosts of the babies he couldn't save, a long time ago.

The Responsive Reader

1. How does the opening anecdote raise the central issue in Blum's article? How does her story about the researcher and the two tiny monkeys bring the central dilemma into focus? Does she seem biased against the researcher? Why or why not?

2. Like other current crusades—antismoking, antiabortion—the campaign against animal experiments has often been intensely emotional. What do you learn about the polarization of opinion on the issue? Do you feel you can understand the point of view of both sides? Is there any middle ground?

3. Horror stories about tortured animals have played a major role in the crusade against animal experiments. What role do they play in this article? Do they sway your reaction one way or the other?

4. How much room does Blum give to the economics of animal research? How big are the stakes? How much room does Blum give to scientific explanations? How much would a layperson need to know to understand the scientific arguments involved?

5. To judge from this article, what has been the role of the government in this controversy?

Talking, Listening, Writing

6. Where do you stand on the issue of animal experiments? Would you approve of baboons or other apes being maimed and killed in the search for the answer to a killer virus? Would you approve of monkeys being mutilated in the search for therapies for traumatic injuries? Would you approve of trying out more effective new military weapons on animal targets?

Collaborative Projects

7. Working with a group, you may want to search computer indexes for current media coverage of topics like animal experiments, primate research, or medical research and animal rights. What have been recent developments? What is the current state of the controversy?

DREAMS OF THE ANIMALS

Margaret Atwood

The environmental movement and the Green parties of Europe have rekindled our sense of kinship with the animal kingdom of which we are a part. Animal rights activists have protested the wretched unnatural conditions of the caged animals in traditional zoos. They started crusades to save animals once marked for extinction as predators or vermin. Margaret Atwood may be the Canadian author best known by American readers. She published several volumes of poetry, and she has written about survival in harsh natural surroundings as a central theme in Canadian literature. Her novel The Handmaiden's Tale *was made into a chilling future fiction movie envisioning an anti-Utopian, dystopian society of the future in which sexism has run amok.*

Thought Starters: Do you like zoos? Do you like circuses? Do you like dog shows? Why do activists object to them?

Mostly the animals dream   1
of other animals   each
according to its kind

       (though certain mice and small rodents
       have nightmares of a huge pink   5
       shape with five claws descending)

:moles dream of darkness and delicate
mole smells

frogs dream of green and golden
frogs   10

sparkling like wet suns
among the lilies

red and black
striped fish, their eyes open
have red and black striped   15
dreams   defense, attack, meaningful
patterns

birds dream of territories
enclosed by singing.

Sometimes the animals dream of evil   20
in the form of soap and metal

but mostly the animals dream
of other animals.

There are exceptions:

the silver fox in the roadside zoo   *25*
dreams of digging out
and of baby foxes, their necks bitten

the caged armadillo
near the train   *30*
station, which runs
all day in figure eights
its piglet feet pattering,
no longer dreams
but is insane when waking;

the iguana   *35*
in the petshop window on St. Catherine Street
crested, royal-eyed, ruling
its kingdom of water-dish and sawdust

dreams of sawdust

The Responsive Reader

1. In the first half of the poem, why did Atwood choose the animals she includes? Why didn't she choose stereotypically beautiful, graceful, or cuddly animals to enlist the sympathies of the reader? Which of these animals would you usually find ugly or repulsive? (How do you feel about frogs, moles, or rodents?) How does the poet take you into the animals' world? How does she change or go counter to the usual associations the animals bring to mind?
2. What is the key difference between the animals in the wild and the animals we see in the second half of the poem? What are striking or telling contrasts? The poem does not editorialize or spell out the poet's message. What for you is the message carried by the images the poem calls up in the reader's mind?
3. What is the difference between the evil or nightmarish threats the animals encounter in the wild and the evil represented by humans? Is there a difference?

Talking, Listening, Writing

4. What do you know about initiatives to create more natural habitats for zoo animals? Have you visited or heard about enlightened modern model zoos? Do you think they would meet the objections of activists criticizing the traditional zoo mentality?

5. Pet owners, animal trainers, and other people working with animals are often accused of reading human or near-human thoughts and emotions into what they observe in animals. They see evidence of loyalty, fear of abandonment, anger, hostility, confusion, and other familiar human mental states. Are they going too far in projecting human thoughts and feelings onto animals? Have you been around animals enough to form an opinion on this question?

6. A whimsical cartoonist turned the tables on zoo visitors by imagining a people zoo where visiting animals could gawk at different specimens of the human species. You may want to write about an imaginary visit to a people zoo as a representative of the animal world.

Collaborative Projects

7. Look at the website of a group such as People for the Ethical Treatment of Animals (PETA). What are their beliefs about animal rights? Do you agree with some or all of their positions? Can you find statements by animal trainers or zoo officials who present a different view?

FORUM: *Betting on the Future*

It took hundreds of millions of years to produce the life that now inhabits the earth.

Rachel Carson

Concerned scientists and political activists warn us that humanity has developed the know-how to poison our planet or to kill all life on it several times over. Believers in progress had long celebrated science and technology as the means of liberating humanity from its ancient scourges: backbreaking toil, the threat of mass starvation, and uncontrolled diseases decimating humankind. However, science, long advertised as the fairy godmother of comfort and prosperity, has come to be seen by many as a mixed blessing, with our modern industrial lifestyle threatening to pollute our environment and make it uninhabitable for future generations. Ordinary citizens and newspaper readers often find themselves caught between two camps: Environmentalists see themselves as watchdogs and whistleblowers and warn of ecological disaster. Conservatives advertise themselves as voices of realism and common sense and label the other side doomsayers and alarmists. Do you temperamentally incline to one side or the other?

DON'T SAY IT'S GLOBAL WARMING

Molly Ivins

Molly Ivins is a nationally syndicated columnist for the Fort Worth Star-Telegram. *She serves as a gadfly to politicians, both in Texas and on the larger national stage, who put business interests first and the interests of consumers and ordinary voters last. She especially has been a thorn in the side of corporate public relations people who put a high-minded, public-spirited spin on initiatives designed to protect the bottom line—the inflated salaries of corporate executives and increased "shareholder value." Ivins wrote the following column during a year when unprecedented prolonged heat and drought was devastating the American Southwest. The death toll and record-breaking heat wave made many take a second look at the theory of global warming: Emissions of "greenhouse" gases resulting from our highly industrialized modern lifestyle are heating up the planet's atmosphere. Catastrophic climatic changes will turn large now-fertile areas into deserts. The melting of the polar ice caps will swamp coastal cities. An international treaty signed in Kyoto, Japan, set goals for changing the behavior of both industrialized and developing nations.*

Thought Starters: Global warming and the destruction of the ozone layer became highly charged political issues. How much do you know about the scientific issues underlying the controversy? Can you fill in your classmates on what is involved?

AUSTIN, Texas—As Texas endures the slow, agonizing death of our 1 entire agricultural sector by drought, a check of our media and political leaders shows we are also suffering from a bizarre silence on a topic that could be described as "the cause that dare not speak its name."

Local newspapers have responded heroically to the heat wave that has now killed more than 120 Texans, unleashing a torrent of efforts to help those most in peril. The one topic they have not addressed is: Why is this happening?

Of the few articles on the subject, all are limited to the answer "El Niño," which is half right. According to climatologists, this is an El Niño drought: El Niño shifted the jet stream just enough to hold the high that normally sits over the Rockies in the summertime east over Texas, so we are not getting the clouds and cooling that normally give us some relief.

But the other half of the answer, global warming, has gotten little or no attention.

A recent Dallas Morning News article gives the flavor of what little coverage global warming has gotten: "What did skies over Texas and a Washington debate about global warming share this week? An unusual amount of hot air, say experts on both meteorology and politics." Heh-heh.

The media are doing so poorly on this issue that it's an embarrassment   *5* to the profession, and we are being hoist partly by the petard of our infamous "objectivity." We continue to report global warming as though it were a "debate" among scientists. It is not.

What we mistake for a "debate" is actually a public relations campaign by the American Petroleum Institute, which has recruited and funded a few scientists who question the entire phenomenon. They, in turn, are given equal weight by the media, as though they were precisely as objective as the 2,500 scientists who work with the United Nations' Intergovernmental Panel on Climate Change.

According to USA Today, when 14 energy industry lobbyists gathered in April to work out the details of a $6 million lobbying plan on global warming, they targeted Congress, the news media, the public and . . . schoolchildren. "Informing teacher/students about uncertainties in climate science will begin to erect a barrier against further efforts to impose Kyoto-like measures in the future," says a memo obtained by the National Environmental Trust.

The notion that the IPCC is some group of fear-mongering enviros is easily disproved by study of any of its cautious work or the testimony of its chairman, Robert T. Watson. On the other hand, the API's notorious PR campaign is designed, in the words of its own strategy documents, to "reposition global warming as theory rather than fact."

In addition, a number of conservative think tanks have been churning out dubious studies allegedly proving that doing much of anything about global warming will cost each and every citizen a small fortune and "radically" affect all our lives. These studies have been given solemn coverage by the press.

Among the most important developments this year is the formation   *10* of a coalition of major companies—including Sun Co., 3M, British Petroleum, Lockheed, Maytag, United Technologies, Boeing, etc.—that not only accept climate change as a serious threat but also believe that action is necessary and can be taken without economic damage.

Meanwhile, the Republican Party of Texas has adopted the flat statement: "We oppose the theory of global warming and the Kyoto Agreement." That certainly takes care of that, as far as Texas Republicans are concerned.

The Responsive Reader

1. Many newspaper readers came to think of the global warming issue as a topic of controversy or a debate. Ivins claims the controversy is not a "debate." What is her point? What evidence does she have to back up her claim?
2. How does the "bottom line" enter into the controversy about global warming?
3. Ivins pins her charges and assertions to an array of carefully selected quotes, both pro and con. What sources does she use in this column, and how does she use them?

Talking, Listening, Writing

4. Ivins is sarcastic about the "objectivity" of the media. Why or how?
5. Do you consider Ivins herself objective or biased? She is the kind of assertive, aggressive writer who attracts loyal fans while alienating other readers. With which camp do you tend to identify? Why?
6. According to Ivins, a public relations campaign is aimed at making teachers and students think of global warming "as theory rather than fact." What is the point of insisting that scientific theories be identified as theories?

Find It on the Web

How familiar are you with the ideas of environmentalists? What do you know about Greenpeace and the Green parties of other countries? Green parties or politically organized environmentalists are on the march in Europe and are beginning to play a role in state-level politics in the United States. You may want to look for articles on the Green parties of Europe in publications like the British *Guardian* or the *Economist*.

SAVING NATURE, BUT ONLY FOR MAN

Charles Krauthammer

Charles Krauthammer is a conservative columnist who is a frequent contributor to Time. *As the 500th anniversary of Columbus's voyage to the New World was approaching, Krauthammer published a* Time *essay titled "Hail Columbus, Dead White Male." As is his custom, he skewered what he con-*

siders the intellectual fashions of the "politically correct" American left: He at-tacked the "sentimental" glorification of the natives by writers "singing of the saintedness of the Indians in their pre-Columbian Eden, a land of virtue, em-pathy, ecological harmony." In the Time *essay that follows, Krauthammer raises the familiar question of the economic cost of our current commitment to ecology and urges the setting of priorities.*

Thought Starters: Has the environmental movement made a difference? Has it created a backlash?

Environmental sensitivity is now as required an attitude in polite so-ciety as is, say, belief in democracy or aversion to polyester. But now that everyone from Ted Turner to George Bush, Dow to Exxon has professed love for Mother Earth, how are we to choose among the dozens of conflict-ing proposals, restrictions, projects, regulations and laws advanced in the name of the environment? Clearly not everything with an environmental claim is worth doing. How to choose?

There is a simple way. First, distinguish between environmental lux-uries and environmental necessities. Luxuries are those things it would be nice to have if costless. Necessities are those things we must have regardless. Then apply a rule. Call it the fundamental axiom of sane environmentalism: Combatting ecological change that directly threatens the health and safety of people is an environmental necessity. All else is luxury.

For example: preserving the atmosphere—stopping ozone depletion and the greenhouse effect—is an environmental necessity. In April scien-tists reported that ozone damage is far worse than previously thought. Ozone depletion not only causes skin cancer and eye cataracts, it also de-stroys plankton, the beginning of the food chain atop which we humans sit.

The reality of the greenhouse effect is more speculative, though its possible consequences are far deadlier: melting ice caps, flooded coastlines, disrupted climate, parched plains and, ultimately, empty breadbaskets. The American Midwest feeds the world. Are we prepared to see Iowa acquire New Mexico's desert climate? And Siberia acquire Iowa's?

Ozone depletion and the greenhouse effect are human disasters. They happen to occur in the environment. But they are urgent because they di-rectly threaten man. A sane environmentalism, the only kind of environ-mentalism that will win universal public support, begins by unashamedly declaring that nature is here to serve man. A sane environmentalism is entirely anthropocentric: it enjoins man to preserve nature, but on the grounds of self-preservation.

A sane environmentalism does not sentimentalize the earth. It does not ask people to sacrifice in the name of other creatures. After all, it is hard enough to ask people to sacrifice in the name of other humans. (Think of the chronic public resistance to foreign aid and welfare.) Ask hardworking voters to sacrifice in the name of the snail darter, and, if they are feeling polite, they will give you a shrug.

Of course, this anthropocentrism runs against the grain of a contemporary environmentalism that indulges in earth worship to the point of idolatry. One scientific theory—Gaia theory—actually claims that Earth is a living organism. This kind of environmentalism likes to consider itself spiritual. It is nothing more than sentimental. It takes, for example, a highly selective view of the benignity of nature. My nature worship stops with the April twister that came through Kansas or the May cyclone that killed more than 125,000 Bengalis and left 10 million (!) homeless.

A nonsentimental environmentalism is one founded on Protagoras' maxim that "Man is the measure of all things." Such a principle helps us through the thicket of environmental argument. Take the current debate raging over oil drilling in a corner of the Alaska National Wildlife Refuge. Environmentalists, mobilizing against a bill working its way through the U.S. Congress to permit such exploration, argue that Americans should be conserving energy instead of drilling for it. This is a false either/or proposition. The U.S. does need a sizable energy tax to reduce consumption. But it needs more production too. Government estimates indicate a nearly fifty-fifty chance that under the ANWR lies one of the five largest oil fields ever discovered in America.

The U.S. has just come through a war fought in part over oil. Energy dependence costs Americans not just dollars but lives. It is a bizarre sentimentalism that would deny oil that is peacefully attainable because it risks disrupting the calving grounds of Arctic caribou.

I like the caribou as much as the next man. And I would be rather *10* sorry if their mating patterns are disturbed. But you can't have everything. And if the choice is between the welfare of caribou and reducing an oil dependency that gets people killed in wars, I choose man over caribou every time.

Similarly the spotted owl in Oregon. I am no enemy of the owl. If it could be preserved at no or little cost, I would agree: the variety of nature is a good, a high aesthetic good. But it is no more than that. And sometimes aesthetic goods have to be sacrificed to the more fundamental ones. If the cost of preserving the spotted owl is the loss of livelihood for 30,000 logging families, I choose family over owl.

The important distinction is between those environmental goods that are fundamental and those that are merely aesthetic. Nature is our ward. It is not our master. It is to be respected and even cultivated. But it is man's world. And when man has to choose between his well-being and that of nature, nature will have to accommodate.

Man should accommodate only when his fate and that of nature are inextricably bound up. The most urgent accommodation must be made when the very integrity of man's habitat—e.g., atmospheric ozone—is threatened. When the threat to man is of a lesser order (say, the pollutants from coal- and oil-fired generators that cause death from disease but not fatal damage to the ecosystem), a more modulated accommodation that balances economic against health concerns is in order. But in either case the principle is the same: protect the environment—because it is man's environment.

The sentimental environmentalists will call this saving nature with a totally wrong frame of mind. Exactly. A sane—a humanistic—environmentalism does it not for nature's sake but for our own.

The Responsive Reader

1. What is the essence of Krauthammer's "sane environmentalism"? What are the test cases that help him expound his thesis? (What does he mean by "anthropocentrism"?)
2. What is Krauthammer's basic philosophical difference with what he calls "sentimental" environmentalism?

Talking, Listening, Writing

3. Prepare an oral presentation or write an essay to support or rebut Krauthammer's position. Support your point of view with detailed examples or cases in point.

FEEDING TEN BILLION PEOPLE

Mark Sagoff

In the seventies and eighties, warning voices said that the population explosion was straining the ability of the planet to feed the human race. We were burning up irreplaceable natural resources at a disastrous rate, in the process polluting the earth, the air, the rivers, and the oceans. We were heedlessly using up the limited resources of Spaceship Earth. The nineties saw a strong countermovement attacking pessimistic environmentalists as alarmists and naysayers. In the debate between the ecological doomsayers and the ecological pollyannas, Mark Sagoff is on the side of the optimists. He cites experts who claim that known reserves of oil and natural gas will last seventy to a hundred years. In the future, theoretically feasible drilling technology could tap geothermal energy—the heat of the earth's core—in amounts far exceeding our needs. Tidal energy and solar power are other largely untapped nonpolluting natural resources. In the following section from a larger article, Sagoff sets out to refute the theory that catastrophic food shortages will result if the planet's population continues to grow at projected rates.

Thought Starters: Have you encountered warnings about overpopulation and ecological catastrophe? Where or in what context? What was your reaction?

The United Nations projects that the global population, currently 5.7 billion, will peak at about 10 billion in the next century and then stabilize or even decline. Can the earth feed that many people? Even if food crops increase sufficiently, other renewable resources, including many fisheries and forests, are already under pressure. Should we expect fish stocks to collapse or forests to disappear?

The world already produces enough cereals and oilseeds to feed 10 billion people a vegetarian diet adequate in protein and calories. If, however, the idea is to feed 10 billion people not healthful vegetarian diets but the kind of meat-laden meals that Americans eat, the production of grains and oilseeds may have to triple—primarily to feed livestock. Is anything like this kind of productivity in the cards?

Maybe. From 1961 to 1994 global production of food doubled. Global output of grain rose from about 630 million tons in 1950 to about 1.8 billion tons in 1992, largely as a result of greater yields. Developing countries from 1974 to 1994 increased wheat yields per acre by almost 100 percent, corn yields by 72 percent, and rice yields by 52 percent. "The generation of farmers on the land in 1950 was the first in history to double the production of food," the Worldwatch Institute has reported. "By 1984, they had outstripped population growth enough to raise per capita grain output an unprecedented 40 percent." From a two-year period ending in 1981 to a two-year period ending in 1990 the real prices of basic foods fell 38 percent on world markets, according to a 1992 United Nations report. Prices for food have continually decreased since the end of the eighteenth century, when Thomas Malthus argued that rapid population growth must lead to mass starvation by exceeding the carrying capacity of the earth.

Farmers worldwide could double the acreage in production, but this should not be necessary. Better seeds, more irrigation, multi-cropping, and additional use of fertilizer could greatly increase agricultural yields in the developing world, which are now generally only half those in the industrialized countries. It is biologically possible to raise yields of rice to about seven tons per acre—about four times the current average in the developing world. Super strains of cassava, a potato-like root crop eaten by millions of Africans, promise to increase yields tenfold. American farmers can also do better. In a good year, such as 1994, Iowa corn growers average about 3.5 tons per acre, but farmers more than double that yield in National Corn Growers Association competitions.

In drier parts of the world the scarcity of fresh water presents the greatest challenge to agriculture. But the problem is regional, not global.

Fortunately, as Lester Brown, of the Worldwatch Institute, points out, "there are vast opportunities for increasing water efficiency" in arid regions, ranging from installing better water-delivery systems to planting drought-resistant crops. He adds, "Scientists can help push back the physical frontiers of cropping by developing varieties that are more drought resistant, salt tolerant, and early maturing. The payoff on the first two could be particularly high."

As if in response, Novartis Seeds has announced a program to develop water-efficient and salt-tolerant crops, including genetically engineered varieties of wheat. Researchers in Mexico have announced the development of drought-resistant corn that can boost yields by a third. Biotechnologists are converting annual crops into perennial ones, eliminating the need for yearly planting. They also hope to enable cereal crops to fix their own nitrogen, as legumes do, minimizing the need for fertilizer (genetically engineered nitrogen-fixing bacteria have already been test-marketed to farmers). Commercial varieties of crops such as corn, tomatoes, and potatoes which have been genetically engineered to be resistant to pests and diseases have been approved for field testing in the United States; several are now being sold and planted. A new breed of rice, 25 percent more productive than any currently in use, suggests that the Gene Revolution can take over where the Green Revolution left off. Biotechnology, as the historian Paul Kennedy has written, introduces "an entirely new stage in humankind's attempts to produce more crops and plants."

Biotechnology cannot, however, address the major causes of famine: poverty, trade barriers, corruption, mismanagement, ethnic antagonism, anarchy, war, and male-dominated societies that deprive women of food. Local land depletion, itself a consequence of poverty and institutional failure, is also a factor. Those who are too poor to use sound farming practices are compelled to overexploit the resources on which they depend. As the economist Partha Dasgupta has written, "Population growth, poverty and degradation of local resources often fuel one another." The amount of food in world trade is constrained less by the resource base than by the maldistribution of wealth.

Analysts who believe that the world is running out of resources often argue that famines occur not as a result of political or economic conditions but because there are "too many people." Unfortunately, as the economist Amartya Sen has pointed out, public officials who think in Malthusian terms assume that when absolute levels of food supplies are adequate, famine will not occur. This conviction diverts attention from the actual causes of famine, which has occurred in places where food output kept pace with population growth but people were too destitute to buy it.

We would have run out of food long ago had we tried to supply ourselves entirely by hunting and gathering. Likewise, if we depend on nature's gifts, we will exhaust many of the world's important fisheries. Fortunately, we are learning to cultivate fish as we do other crops. Genetic engineers have designed fish for better flavor and color as well as for faster growth, improved disease resistance, and other traits. Two farmed species—silver carp and grass carp—already rank among the ten most-consumed fish worldwide. A specialty bred tilapia, known as the "aquatic chicken," takes six months to grow to a harvestable size of about one and a half pounds.

Aquaculture produced more than 16 million tons of fish in 1993; capacity has expanded over the past decade at an annual rate of 10 percent by quantity and 14 percent by value. In 1993 fish farms produced 22 percent of all food fish consumed in the world and 90 percent of all oysters sold. The World Bank reports that aquaculture could provide 40 percent of all fish consumed and more than half the value of fish harvested within the next fifteen years.

Salmon ranching and farming provide examples of the growing efficiency of aquacultural production. Norwegian salmon farms alone produce 400 million pounds a year. A biotech firm in Waltham, Massachusetts, has applied for government approval to commercialize salmon genetically engineered to grow four to six times as fast as their naturally occurring cousins. As a 1994 article in *Sierra* magazine noted, "There is so much salmon currently available that the supply exceeds demand, and prices to fishermen have fallen dramatically."

For those who lament the decline of natural fisheries and the human communities that grew up with them, the successes of aquaculture may offer no consolation. In the Pacific Northwest, for example, overfishing in combination with dams and habitat destruction has reduced the wild salmon population by 80 percent. Wild salmon—but not their bio-engineered aquacultural cousins—contribute to the cultural identity and sense of place of the Northwest. When wild salmon disappear, so will some of the region's history, character, and pride. What is true of wild salmon is also true of whales, dolphins, and other magnificent creatures—as they lose their economic importance, their aesthetic and moral worth becomes all the more evident. Economic considerations pull in one direction, moral considerations in the other. This conflict colors all our battles over the environment.

The transition from hunting and gathering to farming, which is changing the fishing industry, has taken place more slowly in forestry. Still there is no sign of a timber famine. In the United States forests now provide the largest harvests in history, and there is more forested U.S. area today than there was in 1920. Bill McKibben has observed . . . that the eastern United States, which loggers and farmers in the eighteenth and nineteenth centuries nearly denuded of trees, has become reforested during this century (see "An Explosion of Green," April, 1995, *Atlantic*). One reason is that farms reverted to woods. Another is that machinery replaced animals; each draft animal required two or three cleared acres for pasture.

Natural reforestation is likely to continue as biotechnology makes areas used for logging more productive. According to Roger Sedjo, a respected forestry expert, advances in tree farming, if implemented widely, would permit the world to meet its entire demand for industrial wood using just 200 million acres of plantations—an area equal to only five percent of current forest land. As less land is required for commercial tree production, more natural forests may be protected—as they should be, for aesthetic, ethical, and spiritual reasons.

The expansion of fish and tree farming confirms the belief held by   15
Peter Drucker and other management experts that our economy depends far more on the progress of technology than on the exploitation of nature. Although raw materials will always be necessary, knowledge has become the essential factor in the production of goods and services. "Where there is effective management," Drucker has written, "that is, application of knowledge to knowledge, we can always obtain the other resources." If we assume, along with Drucker and others, that resource scarcities do not exist or are easily averted, it is hard to see how economic theory, which after all concerns scarcity, provides the conceptual basis for valuing the environment. The reasons to preserve nature are ethical more often than they are economic.

The Responsive Reader

1. At the beginning, what are the key questions Sagoff asks about the ability of the planet to feed the multiplying human race? Where at the end does he finally give a definitive answer to these questions? What is it?
2. Sagoff charts the history of increases in food production in recent decades, using the formidable array of statistics that is his trademark. What are key numbers? Where do they come from, and what do they show?
3. What are key data in Sagoff's optimistic account of future possibilities and prospects? What are major developments pointing toward an "entirely new stage" in food production? What is aquaculture?
4. Deforestation and logging of old-growth forests have long been targets of environmental activists. What account does Sagoff give of tree farming? Do you think it will defuse the controversies about the destruction of the world's forests?
5. In talking about the specter of famine, Sagoff shifts the emphasis away from limited natural resources in order to focus on other sources of scarcity and starvation. What are they? How much do you know about them?

Talking, Listening, Writing

6. What is new to you in Sagoff's arguments? What is familiar? Does he change your mind on any important issues?
7. Sagoff says that the reasons for protecting nature are moral or aesthetic rather than economic. Ethical, aesthetic, and spiritual considerations will have to provide the conceptual basis for valuing the environment. What does he mean? How would this emphasis change current attitudes about the environment?

8. Have you ever been concerned about hungry fellow Americans? Have you ever been concerned about world hunger? Do you know of any promising initiatives to combat hunger and malnutrition?

9. If you tend to agree with people like Sagoff, you may want to write an open letter to activists who predict ecological catastrophe. If you tend to disagree with Sagoff, you may want to write an open letter responding to his arguments.

Find It on the Web

Recent years have seen many studies evaluating for a general audience current studies of population growth and of the ability of the planet to feed its burgeoning human population. An example bringing together much detailed information from authoritative sources was Bill McKibben, "The Future of Population: A Special Moment in History" (*Atlantic* May 1998). McKibben is the author of several books about the environment, including *The End of Nature* (1989) and *Hope, Human and Wild* (1995). Working with a group, you may want to track more recent statistics on population growth or world hunger.

The Investigative Paper

Many writing classes now feature investigative papers—shorter, informal research papers—as an alternative to the full-length, formal library paper. Such investigative papers can help bridge the gap between the short, informal, weekly or biweekly paper and a full-fledged, documented research paper—which checks out a whole range of available material and gives full publishing information for readers who may want to verify your sources. Emphasis in the shorter investigative paper can be on the basic research skills—treating the paper first of all as a writing project, with the emphasis on tracking down, evaluating, and bringing together reliable information and informed opinion.

Honest writing results from a process of investigation. The writer has gone through a process of fact-gathering, of checking things out. In some kinds of writing, the emphasis on investigation, on finding out, is especially strong. Journalists serving as watchdogs on big government or big business are not satisfied with press releases or campaign handouts. They aim at getting out the real story. They dig and probe; they believe in the public's right to know. Historians and biographers try to unearth the truth behind official pronouncements. They try to get at the real human being behind the idealized public figure that has become a national monument. Students of current issues try to find out what is behind the buzzwords—"the white backlash," "victimology," "the men's movement," "Ebonics," "mainstreaming the disabled."

TRIGGERING Investigative writing is triggered when someone says: "There is more to this than meets the eye. The truth is worth ferreting out." Situations like the following might set you to work as an investigative writer:

- A watchdog group charges that local industry continues to discharge toxic materials into local waterways in violation of state and federal law. Spokespersons for concerned companies state that their firms are in compliance with applicable legislation. What is the truth?

- A political figure talks to an audience of developers about costly restrictions on logging, mandated to preserve the habitat of an endangered species. He claims that environmentalist legislation restricting logging has added between three thousand and five thousand dollars to the cost of the homes they are building. How much of this is true? What is the economic cost of protecting endangered species? Who is in a position to make informed estimates?

- What was behind the huge media flap about Ebonics, or "Black English"? Who were the leading critics, and what were their arguments? What did language scholars and teachers say? How did leaders in the African American community line up in the controversy?

- What progress has been made toward making insurers cover mental illnesses as illnesses? What is the story of recent legislative battles? Who carried the ball? Who fought the initiatives? What was the final result?

GATHERING   As an investigative writer, you may find yourself playing detective. For instance, the headlines about extending insurance coverage to people with mental illnesses may turn out to be mostly media hype. You may have to check out what disillusioned original supporters of the legislation actually said. You may have to check out what spokespersons for groups like the Mental Health Alliance said. In the final legislation, what were the compromises and the ifs and buts buried in the fine print? Here are some hints for the apprentice sleuth:

- *Check out relevant background.* Read up on the subject. Here are a student writer's notes on some promising sources for a paper on the "men's movement":

Review of Robert Bly's book *Iron John* in *Fremont News.*
Bly has focused attention on the complicated nature of what it means to be masculine and on recent changes in male identity. The "men's movement" is part of a larger trend toward redefining gender roles and reexamining male and female sexuality.

Jack Balswick, *The Inexpressive Male.*
The book explains why men are "inexpressive" and unable to communicate their feelings as women do. It offers suggestions on how men can overcome their fear of intimacy.

John Gray, *Men Are from Mars, Women Are from Venus.*
Gray writes about how to make a relationship between a man and a woman work by recognizing distinct characteristics of the male and the female.

Mark Simpson, *Male Impersonators: Men Performing Masculinity.*
Simpson explores the whole concept of masculinity, touching on topics like body building, skinheads, and pornography. He says that the men's movement is sought out by both straight and gay men who feel alienated from a macho culture.

■ *Listen to the people involved.* Listen to the stories of people whose lives have been affected. Establish them as authorities. When you investigate current efforts to weaken tough drunk-driving laws, you might introduce one of your key sources as follows:

> Three years ago a 23-year-old man, with a blood alcohol nearly three times the 0.10 legal limit, crashed head-on into a car carrying Jackie Masso, her husband Patrick, her daughter Patty, and a friend at 4:30 in the afternoon. Today Jackie Masso faces two to three more operations on her legs. Her husband must get his lungs pumped about three times a year because of congestive heart failure, and her 21-year-old daughter, after having her crushed nose broken and reset two times, faces yet more plastic surgery.
>
> Masso got MADD. She and her husband are copresidents of the local chapter of Mothers Against Drunk Driving, which has 400–600 paying members and 1,000 on a mailing list.
>
> Masso said she has noticed something in the many courtrooms where she has sat with families who have had a son or daughter killed or badly injured. She has noticed that the drunken drivers with multiple offenses always tend to blame their car, the weather, or the other driver—but never themselves.
>
> "I've never heard a drunken driver say he's sorry," she said.

■ *Pay attention to insiders' information.* Pay close attention when your sources cite internal memos and informal letters rather than official press releases. Listen carefully to people recalling informal conversations rather than public relations handouts prepared for a public meeting.

■ *Pay special attention to candid interviews.* Listen when people who feel misrepresented or slighted try to tell their side of the story.

SHAPING Many investigative papers start by documenting a public misunderstanding, a questionable official version, or misleading media stereotypes. Typically, the writer's assumption is that there is another side to the story. The paper will thus often play off an unauthorized, unofficial version against the established or familiar view. It may then sift testimony for and against the "revisionist" hypothesis. Finally, the paper may try to present a balanced conclusion.

Often an investigative paper will try to reenact the excitement of the search, of the hunt. It may create an air of mystery by first hints of something misrepresented or amiss. It may build suspense as the paper examines additional clues. It may lead up to a climax where a clinching admission or discovery provides the high point.

The following might be a working outline for an investigative paper:

the official version

first hints: discrepancies in official accounts

clues leading to an alternative version of events

a clinching discovery

a belated revision of the official account

REVISING The feedback you receive for your paper from peer reviewers or from your instructor will vary. The following is an exceptionally complete **running commentary** by an instructor on a paper investigating health insurance for mental illness. To judge from this commentary, what were the strengths of the paper? What needed work?

1. Introduction: Your startling opening statistics should wake up the apathetic reader. However, they need to be attributed to somebody. Who said this? What is the credibility of the source?

2. Thesis: The point that a "huge step" has been taken toward equal treatment of physical and "mental" illness, in spite of the last-ditch resistance of the insurance companies, comes through loud and clear. (The rest of your paper follows up your thesis extremely well.)

3. Backup of thesis: Explanation of the traditional "stigma" attached to mental illness and contrasting medical definitions of mental illness really back up your thesis. Good sources here. (But I would leave out the dictionary definition, which seems routine and has no real punch.)

4. Organization: The key point that mental illness is "treatable" leads naturally to a look at current new medications. But you seem to take a detour when talking about the drugs. Make it clearer that you basically *endorse* the new developments but that you are also sounding a warning that the drug-happy American public might expect too much from "miracle drugs"?

5. The part of your paper examining the restriction and denial of medical treatment as the result of a for-profit health care system is very strong. You make excellent use of a local authority at your own college. You explain well the economics of the shift from fee-for-service to managed care. Some of your readers might need more explanation of what "managed care" is all about?

6. The personal connection: Your stories about people you know about personally add much to your paper. As one of your peer reviewers says, "The suicide stories are very shaking and dramatic."

7. The section on the legislative battles to ensure insurance coverage for mental illness seems exceptionally informative and well-balanced, with well-deserved credit to advocates like Senator Domenici. However, you do a good job of showing how the fine print makes the apparent victory for his side just a limited first step. (Perhaps you should also identify by name some of the people who fought the legislation—so that voters who care about health issues can remember.)

8. Conclusion: Good circling back to the story of your friend's brother. Good and memorable punchline. Good work.

Some cautions and suggestions tend to come up again and again in readers' comments on investigative papers. Revision gives you a chance to rewrite your paper to sidestep familiar pitfalls:

- *Check the credibility of your sources.* Be wary of what is clearly biased or partisan testimony. Readers may not be impressed by a flack's defense of agency policy, a fired employee's disgruntled remarks, or a CEO's lauding the integrity of the company's balance sheet.

- *Guard against charges of having slanted the evidence.* If you filter out all doubt or disagreement, your readers will start reading your tract as one-sided propaganda. Many will discount it accordingly. Take on and try to rebut major objections that are likely to arise in your readers' minds. For instance, make sure you cite both management and workers when investigating a labor dispute.

- *Give facts and credible testimony a chance to speak for themselves.* There is a strong temptation to call evildoers the names they deserve. Some writers keep up a steady drumfire of labels like *inexcusable, self-interested, incompetent, maniacal, capricious, greedy for profits,* and *using political ploys.* Save weighty words and serious charges for places where you have clearly earned the right to use them. Support them by careful presentation of evidence.

- *Watch out for innuendo.* Innuendos, or insinuations, are damaging charges that are never openly made but only hinted at—and therefore not really supported or defended. ("Politician X attended the same fund-raiser as alleged mobster Y." Yes? What are you hinting or implying?)

A PAPER FOR PEER REVIEW The following is a paper investigating the "men's movement"—ridiculed by some but taken seriously by others. How and how well does the paper bring the issue into focus? How or how well does the student writer establish her authority? How would you chart the organizing strategy of the paper? What use does the student writer make of key sources? How informative is the paper? Is more than one side heard? How do you react to the paper?

Walk like a Man, Talk like a Man?

Another thing I learned—if you cry the audience won't. A man can cry for his horse, for his dog, for another man, but he cannot cry for a woman. A strange thing. He can cry at the death of a friend or pet. But where he's supposed to be boss, with his children or wife, something like that, he better hold 'em back and let them cry.
—John Wayne

Feminism and the women's movement have focused on defining the woman's role and helping women's advancement in the community. Adrienne Rich, a noted feminist poet, has said: "This drive of self-knowledge, for women, is more than a search for identity: it is part of our refusal of the self-destructiveness of male dominated society." This emphasis on and attention to women has allowed them to discover their role and self-identity in the family, the workplace, as well as the community at large.

However, with all the focus on what it means to be a woman in society, the new question that arises is, "What does it mean to be a man today?" Are men feeling lost and confused as to what their own role in our culture ought to be? In recent years, masculinity or the male sex role in society has become a popular topic of discussion. Books on masculinity—*Be a Man; The Limits of Masculinity; Men Are from Mars, Women Are from Venus*—have climbed the best-seller lists. Television talk shows have dealt with what the ideal male should be. Gatherings have been held for men to discuss what it means to be a man today. The Men's Movement, parallel to the Women's Liberation Movement, was established in order to deal with this new problem facing young males.

The conflict seems to be that young men do not have good and influential role models in our present society because there is such an ambiguity when it comes to defining this idea of the "ideal" male. Robert Bly, an award-winning poet and author of *Iron John,* says, "It is clear that the images of adult manhood given by the popular culture are worn out; a man can no longer depend on them." Should men maintain the tough, stone-hearted, protector image of the past, or should they follow the current trend of openly expressing their feelings and being in touch with their nurturing, feminine side?

Jack Balswick, author of *The Inexpressive Male,* writes that men have traditionally been defined as "independent, task-oriented, aggressive, and inexpressive—meaning they do not verbally express their feelings." The inability to express one's feelings openly or freely is most commonly associated with men of past generations. Alan Buczynski, author of *Iron Bonding,* states, "The notion prevails that men's emotional communication skills are less advanced than those of chimpanzees—that we can no more communicate with one another than can earthworms." Balswick says that men are "ill-suited for roles that call for a high degree of nurturant caring." Because of this lack of nurturant caring, whether it be with children, parents, or significant others, men are not mentally equipped to share their emotional burdens without feeling a sense of alienation or ridicule. One of my father's good male friends summarizes the problem by saying, "When I was growing up, if you were too open with your feelings and emotions, people thought you were weird or effeminate."

A closely related traditional trait of men is that they are hostile and aggressive by nature. According to Karen Huffman, author and researcher of *Psychology in Action,* "one of the clearest and most consistent findings in gender studies is greater physical aggressivenes in males." From an early age, boys are given toy weapons and are more interested in mock fighting and rough-and-tumble play. Typical role models in film and television—John Wayne, Arnold Schwarzenegger, Sylvester Stallone—help young and impressionable males acquire these idiosyncrasies. How many action films have you seen where the hero breaks down emotionally and has a cathartic moment, in which he discusses his fears and insecurities? Instead, these men are portrayed as vigilantes and heroes, who ultimately take the law into their own hands.

In a Clint Eastwood blockbuster, the hero, known as the "meanest sonofabitch in the West," had left his violent past behind but had to decide whether or not to put on his gun belt and seek revenge for the rape of a prostitute. When I saw this film, the audience, mostly men, cheered when the protagonist decided to be the gunslinging hero. As Mark Simpson, author of *Male Imper-*

sonators, sees it, when he "becomes a killer again, he becomes a man." These macho-male role models tend to acquire the beautiful female as well, both on screen and off.

These qualities of the tough and aggressive man are learned through cognitive growth and identification with the same-sex parent. According to Freud's social-learning theory, boys learn how to be masculine by watching and imitating the social behavior of their father or any male that is a dominant figure in their lives. Professor Manita, from the college psychology department, supports Freud's theory by saying, "Young boys are taught that they need to be either aggressive or submissive based upon observing their same-sex parent." Balswick maintains that this theory is also one of the main explanations for male inexpressiveness. He says, "The gist is that males are not rewarded, and are even punished, for expressions of emotion or any other behaviors that could be considered feminine."

School is another social institution that can powerfully influence young men's attitudes toward traditional masculinity. For example, in Andrew Tolson's book *The Limits of Masculinity,* he talks about the all-male boarding school that he attended as a young boy. He says, "The school transmitted, as a sanctioned part of their experience, a notion of 'manhood,' which remained the ideological reference point for the training of 'gentlemen.'" This notion of manhood was enshrined in the school's ten commandments, which was an instructional bible for these young boys to follow. The following are some of these commandments:

> Without big muscles, strong will, and proper collars there is no salvation.
>
> I must play games with all my heart, with all my soul and with all my strength.
>
> Enthusiasm, except for games, is in bad taste.
>
> I must show no emotion and not kiss my mother in public.

With all this in mind, it would be easy to conclude that "men are from Mars and women are from Venus." However, these traditional dividing lines are increasingly becoming blurred. Bly states it best when he says that "by the time a man is thirty-five he knows that the images of the right man, the tough man, the true man which he received in high school do not work in life." One reason is that women now find it more socially acceptable, politically correct, as well as sexually appealing for men to deny their brutish and aggressive tendencies and follow the archetype of the "sensitive" male. By sensitive male, I mean that he must be in touch with his nurturing feminine side, which allows him to express his emotions and insecurities. According to a survey published in the February '96 edition of *Young and Modern* magazine, 85% of the women polled preferred to date a sensitive male rather than a stud. Part of the explanation behind this may be that our current culture deems that communication is the essential element to any successful relationship.

Are we saying that men should now forget about the past role models and traditional notions of manhood that were once deemed acceptable and follow the archetype of the modern sensitive male?

Freud once observed that the concept of masculinity is among the most confused that occurs in science. The point he was most tenacious about was that despite traditional assumptions about masculinity, it never exists in a pure state. He went on to say that "layers of emotion coexist and contradict each other. Each personality is a shade-filled, complex structure, not a transparent unit." Freud believed that men had both masculine and feminine qualities from a biological and psychological standpoint. Carl Jung was another psychoanalyst who argued that an imperative task of gender development was integrating the man's masculine and feminine characteristics to produce a fully functioning person.

If men are innately given both feminine and masculine traits, one can only imagine how challenging it must be to try to find a balance between them. This has been a central question for the men's movement. Its main goal is to address the current crisis in masculinity through workshops and consciousness-raising groups. Robert Bly, who became the "self-styled spiritual" leader of the men's movement with his book *Iron John*, argues that young men today have gone too far in expressing their feminine side. He says, "They are too eager to please women, with the result that they are out of touch with the 'deep masculine,' the 'warrior' who is an essential part of the psyche." He goes on to say:

> There's something wonderful about this development—I mean the practice of men welcoming their own "feminine" consciousness and nurturing it—this is important—and yet I have the sense that there is something wrong. The male in the past twenty years has become more free. He's a nice boy who pleases not only his mother but also the young woman he is living with. But many of these men are not happy. You quickly notice the lack of energy in them. They are life-preserving but not exactly life-giving.
>
> Here we have a finely tuned young man, ecologically superior to his father, sympathetic to the whole harmony of the universe, yet he himself has little vitality to offer.

How far does Bly want young men to go back toward the "violently non-feminine behavior of maladjusted males," in the words of Mark Simpson, author of *Male Impersonators?* In order to escape the fate of the feminized male, must they "employ the threat of violence and show the sword"? According to Simpson, "Tens of thousands of American males have attended weekends in the forest based around [Bly's] Wild Man masculinity and the need to counteract the 'feminization' of modern men."

In an ideal world, I would say that men should be secure in both their masculine and feminine traits in order to maintain a sense of balance and truly find happiness in their lives. However, we have seen that this sentiment is a lot easier said than actually carried out. Instead, I feel that it would be more realistic to say that men should stay true to whichever side (whether it be their masculine or feminine traits) they feel instinctively comfortable with, despite current redefining of the sex roles. In society, it is only natural for differences to exist, and this is not necessarily an unfavorable attribute. In fact, differences are good and should be looked upon from a positive perspective.

Topics for Investigative Papers (A Sampling)

1. Is there hope for lakes and rivers in your area or state, or are they badly polluted? Are there any success stories for cleanup efforts?
2. Are toxic dumps a danger in your community or state? Who is responsible? What action is being taken?
3. Who is concerned about the academic performance of college athletes? Is it true that many don't graduate? What is being done about it?
4. Why do insurance companies treat physical and mental illnesses differently? What's behind the current movement to have insurers cover people with mental illnesses? How successful has it been?
5. What was at the center of the Ebonics, or Black English, controversy? Was it a local issue or one that has been an issue in other places? What explains the large outpouring of criticism? What do language scholars and teachers say?
6. Who employs illegal aliens? In your area, are there sweatshops, migrant camps, illegal nannies or cleaning women?
7. Are there employment barriers for minorities or for women in local police and fire departments? Who or what is responsible?
8. In your community or larger area, are there objections to practices like police profiling? Are they justified? Are they exaggerated? How are they dealt with, and by whom?
9. What is the record of the U.S. government concerning efforts to safeguard the variety of living species?
10. Are people who warn against ecological catastrophes alarmists? Focus on one widely debated threat: acid rain, water shortages for urban areas in the West, global warming, runaway population growth in underdeveloped countries.

12

TOMORROWS
The Shape
of the Future

I guess so many things are happening today that we're too busy to do anything but look, talk, and think about all of it. We don't have time to remember the past, and we don't have the energy to imagine the future.

—*Andy Warhol*

Since the time of the Greek philosopher Plato 2,500 years ago, writers projecting our common future have written utopias. Literally, a utopia is a place that exists "nowhere"—only in our dreams. Often these utopias were imaginary commonwealths where human beings had outgrown their tendencies toward selfishness, conflict, and war. They had learned to live in harmony, to share the wealth, to marry sagely and raise their children without traumas. They had learned to follow wise leaders—or to do without leaders altogether.

However, gradually apprehension and disillusionment seeped in: Writers wrote *dys*topias—the opposite of books projecting an ideal future state. Dystopias took readers to nightmare worlds where people were faceless nobodies in beehive societies. All pleasure or satisfaction came from artificial stimulants. Books were likely to be banned, and their owners persecuted. Big Brother (or the big master computer) did the thinking for everybody. A ghastly newspeak channeled everyone's language into officially approved ways to talk.

Aldous Huxley's novel *Brave New World* (1932) was read by millions of readers as one of the first great modern dystopias—in which the perennial human dream of a perfect utopian future had been turned inside out. His society of the future was populated by happy zombies manipulated by the all-pervasive media. Giving up on the utopian dream of a society in which all are created equal, Huxley's *Brave New World* featured an elaborate caste structure with the alphas at the top and the epsilons at the bottom. Stoned on a synthetic happiness drug, the people at the lower levels of the social heap accepted their lot.

How optimistic or pessimistic are Americans today about the trends shaping the society of the future? What kind of world are we leaving for the next generation?

NEW SPLASH IN VEGAS

Jon Carroll

For many foreign visitors, Las Vegas, like the Grand Canyon, is uniquely American. For culture critics both here and abroad, Las Vegas is an outstanding symbol of American popular culture—brash, vulgar, irresistible, and imitated everywhere around the globe. In a society that has a strong Puritan history and frowns on gambling, smoking, alcohol, and other frivolous entertainment, Vegas offers a 24-hour oasis of gambling, greed, glitz, and glamour. It attracts millions to a location in the Nevada desert where mostly tumbleweed and lizards naturally grow. It has become a byword for vulgar excess—where everything is fake on a grandiose scale: a hotel casino that is an imitation of the New York City scene, complete with Statue of Liberty; a project for an imitation Paris scene, complete with an imitation Eiffel Tower. The columnist who wrote the following article attended the opening of one the splashiest imitations yet—a huge $1.6 billion hotel casino pretending to take gamblers to the Italian Renaissance in the city of Florence in Tuscany, long considered a high point of traditional European culture.

Thought Starters: One headline for the following article read "Pricey Faux Italian Resort Opens in Las Vegas." *Faux* is the French word and *ersatz* is the German word for a cheap substitute. How do you feel about imitation leather, ersatz crabmeat, faux fur, or hotels that are recreations of European castles?

In the Conservatory, the harpist sat precariously in the middle of the   *1*
pond and played a brutally truncated version of "The Four Seasons" by Vivaldi. Behind her rose a two-story cornucopia disgorging oversized plastic pumpkins, Indian corn and sundry squashes. In front of her, separated by a yard of rust-colored chrysanthemums, stood a man in a John Deere baseball cap and a T-shirt that read, "The Only Exercise I Get Is Pushing My Luck."

"Bravo," he said hoarsely. The harpist nodded graciously, one corner of her peach-colored gown trailing in the penny-speckled water.

Welcome to Bellagio, another major entry in the cognitive dissonance sweepstakes, a $1.6 billion, 3,000-room Las Vegas resort/casino that opened this weekend in a blaze of celebrity.

Michael Jordan was there, and Clint Eastwood, and Warren Beatty, and Willie Brown, and many older men with younger women. At one point, after a private dinner for more than 1,000, the celebrities paraded through the casino accompanied by Cirque du Soleil performers in white face and long red coats, sort of like Cossack mimes. There were fanfares of trumpets as they walked.

Some patrons lined up and applauded. Others stared at dice tumbling against the sideboards of the crap tables. George Hamilton looked confused. 5

Last night, almost finished with Bellagio's rolling series of "openings" (one for the town, one for the high rollers, one for the celebrities, one for the media), Alan Feldman, vice president for public relations, exulted: "Considering how far we stuck our necks out, how much we promised, this has come off surprisingly well."

Commented visitor Lee Cheong of Los Angeles, "It's a nice place to gamble. I think maybe they're letting everybody win right now."

Bellagio ain't cheap. Room prices range from $159 to $459 per night; suites from $375 to $1,400. The hotel-casino is designed to look like a Tuscan village surrounding a lake, although it doesn't. Its campanile comes complete with Jumbotron. The lake is 900 feet long, and fountains—1,400 nozzles, 27 million gallons of water—periodically rise out of it, exploding like fireworks and dancing like fireflies, all in synchronization to music as diverse as "Luck, Be a Lady Tonight" sung by Frank Sinatra, and Aaron Copland's "Hoedown," known locally as the theme from the Beef Council ads.

Not numbered among the selections is "I'll Go With You," the mock-aria that evokes impossible romance in the Bellagio TV spots. It is sung by Andrea Bocelli, the blind Italian tenor who will perform at Bellagio's first New Year's Eve celebration.

Last week, Steve Wynn, the mogul behind Bellagio, was thoroughly soaked during a ceremonial opening of the fountains. The local papers took discreet pleasure in the drenching of the rain king, the man who will save Vegas unless he's wrong. 10

The fountains are a true democratic spectacle, deeply pleasurable, the apotheosis of dreams that have existed since humans first played in bathtubs. It literally stops traffic—each night, the music is mixed with sounds of car horns as cruisers pause to enjoy the water spectacular. Bellagio is right on the Strip, next to Caesars Palace and across the street from the still-unopened Paris, where the base of the half-scale Eiffel Tower squats dark and ominous.

The most publicized attraction at the hotel is the Bellagio Gallery of Fine Art, two small rooms plus a gift shop. It's a sort of one-stop-shopping, sprint-through-art-history experience, with two Van Goghs (including a swell "Entrance to a Quarry") and two Warhols and one of each of Manet, Renoir, Degas, Cézanne, Monet (that darned garden), Picasso (there are more of him in the Picasso restaurant downstairs), Kline, Pollock (a wonderful "Frieze"), Lichtenstein, Jasper Johns and six other usual suspects.

The entrance fee is $10 per person, which, pro-rated on a per-painting basis, makes the Bellagio Gallery of Fine Art the most expensive museum in the world.

The gallery is the most visible symbol of Vegas' emerging commercial aesthetic. The first phase, which culminated in the exquisite excess of Caesars Palace, capitalized on gangster chic—booze, broads and boxing.

Also, there were real gangsters. 15

The second period acknowledged changing demographics. All of a sudden Vegas was a theme park, a place for the whole family, a wonderland of old movies and fantasy castles and, in a burst of vernacular energy still unmatched, the completely loony New York, New York, where Mom and Dad and the kiddies could wander in disoriented bliss as a roller-coaster spun around the Statue of Liberty's torch.

But Boomers are older now, and their nests are empty or their fledglings have achieved their surly years. They want something distinctly adult, something sophisticated and elegant, some place where they can take their parents rather than their children. Pavarotti! Acres of flowers! A lobby so lovely you want to move in! A curving driveway lined with olive trees! A complex of swimming pools defined by rows of pencil-shaped cypresses, like something the Medicis would have created had only the Renaissance included Jacuzzis.

Is that what the fickle public wants? Maybe. That's the theory.

There's a certain kind of grand hubris to it all, a festival of water in the desert. The earlier phases acknowledged the local ecology—the hotels were called the Sands, the Sahara, the Dunes. Bellagio rises on the site of old Dunes, a $1.6 billion poem about water. It's either deeply troubling or distinctly hopeful—in Las Vegas, all glasses are both half full and half empty.

Bellagio is a huge gamble for Wynn, who also owns the Mirage and 20 Treasure Island. It is hoped that the new hotel—billed as the world's most expensive—will revive Las Vegas as a destination city. Published reports indicate that the city's visitor count, which in recent years had increased by more than 10 percent per year, has been slowing, and is up only 1.2 percent so far this year.

Gambling experts quoted in the Las Vegas Business Press, a local trade publication, fret about Bellagio's lack of signage. Most casinos have huge electronic signs over banks of slot machines promising double winnings or extra games; the Bellagio casino floor, by contrast, is almost sedate.

Wynn has a reputation as a conservative in the arcane world of glitz; he's betting that patrons will appreciate a relatively serene gambling experience. Vegas old-timers, who never went broke betting on more glitter, are not so sure.

There are 24 public guest elevators at the Bellagio hotel, Steve Wynn's new $1.6 billion resort-casino that is bringing fine art, fine food and fine flowers (10,000 mums! And they all want you to wear a sweater because it might get chilly later!) to Las Vegas.

These elevators are arranged in four banks of six, each set serving a different group of floors. They are wonderfully efficient; the hotel has 3,000 rooms, and yet your correspondent has never waited longer than 30 seconds for the sliding doors to open.

The elevators feed into a small anteroom that in turn leads to a grand   *25* hallway. Turn left, there's the casino; turn right, the pool. The key point: There's only one exit from the anteroom to the rest of the hotel.

The complication: Saturday night was celebrity night at the Bellagio. There was a huge banquet to benefit the prevention of a disease. After the banquet, the celebrities marched from the grand ballroom to the theater to see the premiere performance of "Q," the new Cirque de Soleil extravaganza.

The celebrities were accompanied by Cirque performers in white wigs, long red robes and whiteface. Trumpets flourishing marked their every footstep. Pages strode before them carrying the Bellagio logo, a "B" with surrounding curlicues.

It looked like the parade of athletes at some Olympic ceremony restricted to countries beginning with the letter B, their representatives chosen on the basis of net worth.

Bellagio management had decided, with singular lack of foresight, that as the celebrities strolled, the hallway could not be occupied by regular people. Red-coated security guards linked arms and prevented egress from the elevator room. "You'll have to wait 20 minutes," a man with a handheld radio said.

"Sod off, you bugger," said a man in a black T-shirt. He appeared to   *30* be British. He displayed certain social attitudes commonly associated with soccer hooligans. He appeared to be drunk. He appeared to have allies.

Caging up paying guests to prevent them from sharing the same airspace as famous people would appear to be a bad strategy. On the other hand, the law of Vegas is ruthless, and this glimpse of the iron fist under the velvet glove may have had pedagogical value.

The drama: The trumpets trumpeted, the celebrities strolled. As they reached the elevator bays, they were booed roundly. This startled the celebrities, who assumed that a Las Vegas casino was friendly territory. "Let us out," one woman called plaintively to Sidney Poitier, who smiled vaguely, as though he'd been asked for spare change.

Meanwhile, the elevator doors kept opening. More and more people spilled into the narrow anteroom. The people at the front pressed forward. The security guards pressed back. A hydraulic emergency was developing.

"I can't breathe," said a woman pressed against the red back of a security guard. The guard said nothing. "You stupid wanker," said the British man to Clint Eastwood. Clint Eastwood waved cheerfully.

A man not previously heard from, a short man in a white golf shirt,   *35* finally cracked. "This is it, I can't take anymore." He began pushing with an energy unmoderated by social constraint. The red line bent and then broke. Perhaps two dozen trapped patrons suddenly spilled into the celebrity parade.

The soccer hooligan came face to face with one of the white-wigged escorts. "Who are you supposed to be then?" he asked. "George Bloody Washington?"

Your correspondent blinked in the sudden openness of the hall. Like a released prisoner, he was uncertain what to do with his newfound freedom. A short man in a dinner jacket, perhaps a movie executive, grasped your correspondent by the shoulders. He said loudly: "I want you to stay calm."

"I am calm."

The man relaxed. "That's very sensible," he said. "You've done the right thing." One by one, our band of 20 inappropriate guests made its way toward the casino, against the flow of celebrities. It passed Michael Jordan, who was surrounded by men wearing curly phone cords in their ears. Your correspondent made no sudden movements.

When it got to the end of the hall, the group encountered a wall 40 of people behind a red rope. They were lined up to look at the celebrities. They were restrained by guards. One of them said, "No one in or out."

"But we're not celebrities," one straggler said, the plaintive cry of the ordinary human suddenly thrust into the limelight. "That makes no difference to me," said the guard, choosing the wrong time to assert his democratic principles.

Finally, a narrow path was cleared. The group snaked through it, reaching the comparative calm of the craps tables. "That was good sport," said the hooligan.

The Responsive Reader

1. Carroll traces several stages in the evolution of Vegas as a mecca of American popular culture. What were the two earlier stages? Does his description of them ring true or remind you of what you have seen and read?

2. For you, what are some key data or key details in Carroll's account of the current third phase? What do they show about the direction in which American popular culture is headed? For you, is there a keynote or a dominant impression that sums up for you much of what is described here?

3. What is the role of celebrities in this account? What light does it shine on the role of celebrities in our culture? Which of the names do you recognize? What is their claim to fame? Do any of them mean anything to you personally?

Talking, Listening, Writing

4. The popular culture of the casinos and the high culture of art museums used to be at opposite ends of the cultural spectrum. How do they seem to meet or merge here—on what terms? for what reasons? with what

results? Which of the names from the world of art history that are being dropped here mean something to you?

5. If you had the money, would you stay in a place like the one described here? Why or why not?

Collaborative Projects

6. Nevada long had a quasi-monopoly on gambling. Why or how? What has been the story of legalizing gambling elsewhere—from Atlantic City to Indian reservations in California? You may want to team up with classmates to investigate the current status of gambling as a bellwether of American popular culture.

CANDID CAMERA: CORPORATE SNOOPING 101

Mark Frankel

> *"Big Brother is watching you": In the heyday of totalitarian governments, citizens learned to express their private opinions only in whispers and out of hearing of hidden microphones and government spies. Communist governments in Eastern Europe maintained a huge surveillance apparatus, listening in on telephone conversations, opening letters, and filing the reports of an army of informers. Americans had their own horror stories: a president who kept an "enemies list"; the FBI snooping on suspected subversives and on the Reverend Martin Luther King, Jr. Today, Americans are learning to look over their shoulders and to try to shield their private communications from a new kind of snoop: The Big Boss is using state-of-the-art technology to monitor employees' work habits, bathroom breaks, union activities, and private communications. Mark Frankel is a writer for* Newsweek International *in New York. He looks at surveillance techniques with the jaundiced eyes of a journalist— a member of a profession that has always been a premier target of those who read with the informer's eye and listen with the informer's ear.*

Thought Starters: Have you ever felt you were being watched? Have you ever felt the pressure to watch your language, your moves, or your contacts with other people? Have you ever felt someone was keeping track, keeping a file, or compiling a dossier?

I used to think professional snoops were all variations on Harry Caul, the paranoid, guilt-ridden wiretapper of Francis Ford Coppola's *The Conversation.* But W. T. "Ted" Sandin clearly loves his work. With the infectious enthusiasm of a high-school camera club faculty adviser, the middle-aged Sandin runs Video Systems Inc., one of the country's leading manufacturers and distributors of covert video surveillance hardware. At Surveillance Expo '95, which brought several hundred private investigators and corporate security specialists (plus a smattering of Armani-clad Middle Eastern and Latin American gentlemen too discreet to expose their affiliations) to the McLean Hilton in Virginia last summer, Sandin was among the top draws. About three dozen conferees paid $100 each to attend his seminar on how to spy on other people in the electronic age.

He did not disappoint. Reminding his scribbling pupils that "surveillance means only extension of the eye," Sandin spent four hours demonstrating a collection of eye-popping miniature video cameras, each seemingly tinier than the last. The smallest was a black-and-white TV camera barely larger than a piece of Bazooka bubble gum. Attached to a tiny transmitter powered by a common 9-volt battery, such minicams can be hidden almost anywhere in a typical office or factory, Sandin explained. Light switches, exit signs or room thermostats are just a few of the possibilities for camouflage. "Be creative," he exhorted us.

In the name of personal security, Americans have already learned to accept and ignore video cameras in the public spaces they routinely pass through: parking lots, elevators, bank lobbies and hotel stairways. (According to STAT RESOURCES, a Massachusetts research firm, an estimated $2.1 billion will be spent on closed-circuit video gear this year alone.) Now they may have to learn to accept them in the workplace as well. Propelled by concerns with worker productivity, industrial espionage, personal security, drugs on the job and skyrocketing insurance liability, corporate America is increasingly resorting to secret monitoring of its employees. An August 1994 report by the Geneva-based International Labor Organization concluded that "Monitoring and surveillance techniques available as a result of advances in technology make methods of control more pervasive than ever before and raise serious questions of human rights."

Consider a few recent cases. In Phoenix, Arizona, Freddy Craig, a longtime elementary school principal, stumbled upon a video camera hidden in the ceiling of his suburban school office—as well as one secreted in the school shower he often used after jogging. The cameras had been installed by the newly hired school district superintendent, who claimed that Craig was under investigation for unspecified "misconduct" with his students' parents. The charges proved groundless.

In Elmira, New York, a former McDonald's restaurant manager went   5
to court seeking $2 million from the burger chain, as well as the local franchise, for invasion of privacy. In addition to overseeing the deep fryer and griddle, the plaintiff, Michael Huffcut, had been conducting an extramarital affair with another McDonald's employee. Huffcut's suit charged that not only did his former restaurant supervisor obtain copies of the romantic messages the illicit lovers left for each other on their office voice mail, he also played the recordings for Huffcut's wife.

Several years ago, the Boston Sheraton Hotel installed a hidden camera in the employees' locker room in what management claimed was an effort to crack a drug ring—and what lawyers for the hotel workers describe as a heavy-handed attempt to discourage union activity.

The threat is not limited to videocams and voice mail. Service industries place millions of workers in front of computer terminals where their performance is easily monitored by remote. Desktop computers, fax machines, pagers, computer networks, cellular phones and e-mail have become as ubiquitous as styrofoam coffee cups in most offices. While employees have been introduced to these contraptions with soothing talk about "personal passwords" and "private files," workers' privacy is easily shredded. In one of the few surveys of corporate electronic privacy policies, conducted by *MacWorld* magazine in 1993, of 301 U.S. companies polled, more than one in five had searched their employees' computer files, voice mail, e-mail or other digital network communications. "Users naturally assume that, because they have private passwords, only they can enter their e-mail and private files, . . . but even the most insignificant network managers can override passwords and enter files," says Charles Pillar, who conducted the survey.

While researching this article, I struck up an e-mail correspondence with a New York–based high-tech surveillance specialist who told me about his work:

> For a cellular phone interception system, I charge $2,500 to $4,000. This allows the employer to monitor all employees' cellular phone conversations or simply to keep a log of the times and length of calls and any numbers called, etc. It is not actually necessary to listen in on the conversations; they can be logged into a computer. The employer can thus see who has been using these phones for personal use to make $2-a-minute personal calls to the kids. . . .
>
> I've been called to do phone interception work a lot, especially with telemarketer and service representative type workers where the boss monitors the line to make sure that the employees don't have a nasty tone with the customers. . . .
>
> For computer modem interception, I usually charge $3,000. It allows an employer to passively monitor a particular telephone line and intercept the modem data that's going through [it]. The employer can, in effect, see everything that the employee types into his computer and that appears on his screen.

Most American workers assume that their privacy on the job is ensured by constitutional safeguards. Unfortunately, they are wrong. While the Fourth Amendment protects citizens against unreasonable search and seizure by the state, it does not touch private employers, who are free to run their businesses—and spy on their employees—as they please. Current federal privacy laws are case studies in half-measures. While the 1986 Electronic Communications Act prohibits eavesdropping on telephones without a warrant or permission, it provides a loophole that permits companies to monitor employees' calls "for business purposes." And, while privacy laws vary widely from state to state, cutting-edge gizmos such as mini-video cameras are so new they slip between existing wiretap statutes and labor regulations.

Privacy advocates, labor unions and groups such as 9 to 5, the work-   10
ing women's lobby, have long sought national standards that would regulate workplace surveillance. In the last Congress, Senator Paul Simon and Representative Pat Williams introduced such legislation, the Privacy for Consumers and Workers Act. But the U.S. Chamber of Commerce and the

National Association of Manufacturers (NAM) opposed the bill fiercely, and it died in committee. Privacy advocates have all but given up on trying to pass a meaningful piece of legislation this session.

Until Congress puts on the brakes, video cameras and other means of workplace surveillance will only get cooler, and more insidious. Back at the Surveillance Expo, Ted Sandin proudly demonstrated the latest thing: body video. Wearing a tiny camera hidden in a pair of plastic sunglasses, he strutted about the stage. In the audience, we watched, mesmerized, as an image of ourselves jiggled on a nearby video monitor. Sandin promised that as marvelous as this micro-gadgetry seemed, even niftier stuff was coming down the pike. After all, he reminded us, "This is a consumer-driven marketplace."

The Responsive Reader

1. What was "eye-popping" for the author about state-of-the-art surveillance technology? What for you were some of the most striking examples of sophisticated gadgetry?
2. Is there a common thread in Frankel's case histories of aggrieved parties? Does the right to privacy seem to apply equally to all of them? (*Is* there a right to privacy?)
3. What are the motives of employers employing surveillance technology? Which of their aims or justifications seem most important to you? Which methods or procedures seem to you most defensible?
4. To judge from this article, who tries to protect employees' and private citizens' rights, and why? Who fights them? (Do you find yourself taking sides? With whom or against whom?)

Talking, Listening, Writing

5. Many of our constitutional safeguards were developed to protect Americans against a tyrannical government. Do Americans tend to be paranoid about an intrusive government but naive and helpless when it comes to exploitation or manipulation by private interests? Do Americans tend to be more wary of big government than of big business?
6. What do you know about consumer groups, consumer advocacy, or other attempts to provide a counterweight to the economic and political power of corporations?

Collaborative Projects

7. Working with a group, you may want to investigate recent legislation or lawsuits involving the right to privacy.

FEDERAL FOOLISHNESS AND MARIJUANA

Jerome P. Kassirer

"Death with Dignity" became a watchword in the nineties. Surveys revealed that large numbers of terminal patients were kept alive by a depersonalized medical technology, often in severe pain, and against their own express wishes, against the wishes of family, and against the better judgment of nursing staff most directly involved with dying patients. As part of the movement to honor the rights and needs of dying patients, states started to pass laws allowing the medical use of marijuana to alleviate the extreme retching nausea or severe discomfort many terminal patients are subjected to as the result of chemotherapy or other medical interventions. Ample legal precedent exists: In two world wars, morphine was used to alleviate the hellish pain suffered by severely wounded veterans. The Virginia legislature passed a law in 1979 allowing doctors to prescribe marijuana to treat glaucoma and to help cancer patients cope with the side effects of chemotherapy. Nevertheless, politicians afraid of being labeled soft on drugs started a campaign to criminalize the patients and compassionate doctors or family. In the following editorial, the editor-in-chief of the New England Journal of Medicine, *the most prestigious medical journal in the country, published since 1812 by the Massachusetts Medical Society, weighs in on the subject of medical marijuana. In the words of a newspaper editor, the* Journal's *"editorials and commentaries by medical specialists have long played a major role in debates over health policy controversies." Dr. Kassirer is a kidney specialist formerly on the faculty at Tufts University Medical Center in Boston.*

Thought Starters: From your reading or firsthand observation, what do you know about living wills, hospices, or Dr. Kevorkian?

The advanced stages of many illnesses and their treatments are often accompanied by intractable nausea, vomiting or pain. Thousands of patients with cancer, AIDS and other diseases report they have obtained striking relief from these devastating symptoms by smoking marijuana. The alleviation of distress can be so striking that some patients and their families have been willing to risk a jail term to obtain or grow the marijuana.

Despite the desperation of these patients, within weeks after voters in Arizona and California approved propositions allowing physicians in their states to prescribe marijuana for medical indications, federal officials, including the president, the secretary of health and human services, and the attorney general sprang into action. At a news conference, Health and Human Services Secretary Donna E. Shalala gave an organ recital of the parts of the body that she asserted could be harmed by marijuana and warned of the evils of its spreading use. Attorney General Janet Reno announced that physicians in any state who prescribed the drug could lose the privilege of writing prescriptions, be excluded from Medicare and Medicaid reimbursement, and even be prosecuted for a federal crime. General Barry R. McCaffrey, director of the Office of National Drug Control Policy, reiterated his agency's position that marijuana is a dangerous drug and implied that voters in Arizona and California had been duped into voting for these propositions. He indicated that it is always possible to study the effects of any drug, including marijuana, but that the use of marijuana by seriously ill patients would require, at the least, scientifically valid research.

I believe that a federal policy that prohibits physicians from alleviating suffering by prescribing marijuana for seriously ill patients is misguided, heavy-handed and inhumane. Marijuana may have long-term adverse effects and its use may presage serious addictions, but neither long-term side effects nor addiction is a relevant issue for such patients. It is also hypocritical to forbid physicians to prescribe marijuana while permitting them to use morphine and meperidine to relieve extreme dyspnea (difficulty breathing) and pain. With both these drugs, the difference between the dose that relieves symptoms and the dose that hastens death is very narrow; by contrast, there is no risk of death from smoking marijuana. To demand evidence of therapeutic efficacy is equally hypocritical. The noxious sensations that patients experience are extremely difficult to quantify in controlled experiments. What really counts for a therapy with this kind of safety margin is whether a seriously ill patient feels relief as a result of the intervention, not whether a controlled trial "proves" its efficacy.

Paradoxically, dronabinol, a drug that contains one of the active ingredients in marijuana (tetrahydrocannabinol), has been available by prescription for more than a decade. But it is difficult to titrate the therapeutic dose of this drug, and it is not widely prescribed. By contrast, smoking marijuana produces a rapid increase in the blood level of the active ingredients and is thus more likely to be therapeutic. Needless to say, new drugs such as those that inhibit the nausea associated with chemotherapy may well be more beneficial than smoking marijuana, but their comparative efficacy has never been studied.

Whatever their reasons, federal officials are out of step with the public. Dozens of states have passed laws that ease restrictions on the prescribing of marijuana by physicians, and polls consistently show that the public favors the use of marijuana for such purposes. Federal authorities should rescind their prohibition of the medicinal use of marijuana for seriously ill patients and allow physicians to decide which patients to treat. The government should change marijuana's status from that of a Schedule I drug (considered to be potentially addictive and with no current medical use) and regulate it accordingly. To ensure its proper distribution and use, the government could declare itself the only agency sanctioned to provide the marijuana. I believe that such a change in policy would have no adverse effects. The argument that it would be a signal to the young that "marijuana is OK" is, I believe, specious.

This proposal is not new. In 1986, after years of legal wrangling, the Drug Enforcement Administration (DEA) held extensive hearings on the transfer of marijuana to Schedule II. In 1988, the DEA's own administrative-law judge concluded: "It would be unreasonable, arbitrary, and capricious for DEA to continue to stand between those sufferers and the benefits of this substance in light of the evidence in this record." Nonetheless, the DEA overruled the judge's order to transfer marijuana to Schedule II, and in 1992, it issued a final rejection of all requests for reclassification.

Some physicians will have the courage to challenge the continued proscription of marijuana for the sick. Eventually, their actions will force the courts to adjudicate between the rights of those at death's door and the absolute power of bureaucrats whose decisions are based more on reflexive ideology and political correctness than on compassion.

The Responsive Reader

1. What are the key points in Kassirer's support for his thesis that "a federal policy that prohibits physicians from alleviating suffering by prescribing marijuana for seriously ill patients is misguided, heavyhanded and inhumane"? What is the problem with asking for more research? What is the problem with drugs providing alternative therapy? What are the key arguments in favor of using marijuana?
2. What, according to Kassirer, is the history of the "legal wrangling" over the issue?
3. As Kassirer sees it, what does the future hold? How does he sum up the choice that will confront the courts, politicians, and voters?

Talking, Listening, Writing

4. Do you think controversies like the ones about medical marijuana or assisted suicide tend to polarize the public along predictable liberal vs. conservative lines? Why or why not?
5. What would you say in a letter to the editor in response to Kassirer's editorial?
6. Would you risk a jail term to relieve the insufferable pain of a dying patient?

Collaborative Projects

7. Kübler-Ross was among the pioneers objecting to doctors playing God and using a runaway medical technology in indefinitely prolonging the death agonies of patients. Working with a group, you may want to investigate current thinking and current controversies on the subject of death with dignity.

THE LAST ABORTION

Elinor Burkett

> In the nineties, abortion became a major battleground between the political right and left. The pro-life movement championed the sanctity of human life, defining life as beginning at conception. The pro-choice movement in turn defended a woman's right to choose when to have a child, when to start a family and plan her life on her own terms, with a mate of her own choice and without interference from the government. News reports focused on escalating violence directed at abortion clinics and abortion providers—bombings, killings of abortion doctors and their escorts, killings of receptionists, and intimidation of women trying to enter clinics. Predominantly male legislators worked to deny Medicaid or Medicare payments for abortions to poor women or to block funding for United Nations programs favoring birth control and abortion rights. In the meantime, a new abortion pill, first developed in France and making it unnecessary for women to run the gauntlet of antiabortion protesters, was getting attention in the media.

Thought Starters: Where have you encountered or been exposed to pro-life rhetoric or pro-life arguments? Where have you encountered or been exposed to pro-choice rhetoric or pro-choice arguments? Do you care one way or the other? Why or why not?

Abortion has squeezed the life out of women's politics, and the only way women will regain their political space is for abortion to disappear as a political issue.

Technological advances have long bolstered the cause of anti-abortion advocates, turning fetuses from anonymous creatures into living beings that are photographed, recorded, and loved. Now parents watch sonograms of their children months before birth, making it more difficult for them—and the public—to dismiss fetuses as subhuman parasites.

But the tables are turning, as medical advances allow women to know about their pregnancies days after conception and change the very nature of the act of abortion. For more than two decades, abortion has been a public act involving physicians and clinics and insurance carriers, which is precisely what has given the anti-abortion movement its power.

Imagine, then, an America in which abortion truly becomes a private act. No one would be able to calculate how many pregnancies are terminated each year, and there would be no clinics to be targeted for protests or bombings. No one would keep a list of abortion doctors because there would be no way of knowing which doctors they were. No one could wave lurid photographs of aborted fully formed fetuses because fetuses would be aborted before they bore any resemblance to human life. Can the abortion wars survive a brave new world of nonsurgical abortion?

It seems unlikely—and America is on the cusp of just such a reality.   *5* Recent medical advances have revolutionized American women's options for dealing with unwanted pregnancies. Worried about a missed period, a woman no longer has to wait to see her doctor; she can buy an early pregnancy test at her local pharmacy. Unhappy with the results of her test, she doesn't have to brave the protesters at local abortion clinics—if she is lucky enough to have such a clinic in her area. She can go to her own gynecologist and undergo a chemical abortion, a procedure ob-gyns are far more willing to perform than surgical abortions.

Doctors are supposed to report abortions to the Centers for Disease Control, so the government can continue to track the rate of abortion. But if they use the latest abortion procedure—a combination of methotrexate and misoprostol—rather than RU-486 and misoprostol, there is no danger of noncompliance, since no one tracks why a physician writes a specific prescription.

Methotrexate has been on the market for almost half a century as an anti-tumor agent and treatment for arthritis, lupus, and psoriasis, and misoprostol is widely prescribed for patients with ulcers. Fanatics can't root through a doctor's medical waste for telltale signs of an abortion induced by modern chemistry—which must be performed within the first six weeks of pregnancy. The only evidence is a tiny speck that looks like a blood clot. The cost is the price of two prescriptions plus the physician's fee for two office visits.

The anti-abortion crowd hasn't yet figured out how to fight this new breed of abortion, which lacks the images—aborted fetuses with recognizable features, the inherent violence of surgery—that have ignited them. Operation Rescue has sent threatening faxes to and picketed the offices of chemical abortion researchers but has found no other clear targets for its wrath. Leaders of more mainstream anti-abortion groups recognize that photographs of minuscule blood clots are unlikely to whip up their followers and that few people are likely to relate to fetuses when they are so underdeveloped that they still look like they have gills. They have begun to switch from calling abortion murder to bemoaning its physical and psychological dangers to women.

These more mainstream abortion opponents have twisted shaky research that might suggest a slight link between abortion and cervical cancer into alarmist headlines. They've warned women about the dangers of hemorrhage and infection from chemically induced abortions, although both are infrequent. When all else fails, they raise the specter of long-term, and still undiscovered, negative side effects from abortions.

"I'm very concerned that the women of this country are going to   *10* find . . . in five or ten years that we've opened a Pandora's box as far as complications and damage to women," says Dr. Donna Harrison, a Michigan ob-gyn, though she and her allies offer nothing tangible on which to base the warning.

While over the past two decades technology has undercut the positions of both the pro- and anti-choice forces, the most recent changes, in fact, open a window of opportunity for a truce in the abortion wars—if either side is willing to take advantage of it.

At the moment, all that separates the entrenched enemies is the will to educate women about responsible sexual activity and 10 short days: the 10 days between conception—thus far defined as the moment when a sperm fertilizes an egg—and pregnancy, which is the moment when the fertilized egg finishes its hazardous passage through the fallopian tubes to become implanted in the lining of the uterus—a journey about one zygote in four never completes.

Without implantation, there is no pregnancy, which is how an IUD works: It makes the uterine lining inhospitable to implantation. Stopping implantation through use of the latest medical technology thwarts pregnancy before it occurs. The technology is what physicians call emergency contraception, and it remains a well-kept secret. The most common method is two to four oral contraceptives (depending on the brand and strength) taken within 72 hours of unprotected intercourse, followed 12 hours later by another equal dosage. Researchers suggest that even the first, single dose might be almost as effective.

Is this abortion? It's clearly not termination, because a pregnancy never occurs. Indeed, the fertilized egg hasn't yet survived its greatest hazard—successful implantation. The most steadfast literalists might argue that this is nonetheless murder, since it occurs after conception. But then those same steadfast literalists also would have to wage war against IUDs. And can the pro-life crowd really argue with a procedure that could dramatically decrease the number of true abortions performed in the nation?

No truce is possible, however, without the cooperation of the pro-choice troops, who would need to put as much time, money, and energy into teaching women about morning-after pills as they've devoted to protecting surgical abortions. But with an opportunity to guarantee women control over their reproductive lives, how could they not? Is it so much to say to women: Look, if you have unprotected sex and don't want to become pregnant, pop some birth control pills and you won't have to worry? Can't we ask grown women to show that modicum of responsibility?

Such a truce is a fantasy, of course—not because the technology does not exist, and not because it poses a significant threat to the belief systems of either side. Neither side really seems to want an end to the abortion wars, which have gone on so long that both sides have lost the ability to envision peace. Resolution seems to have become less important than scoring a win, or at least ensuring that the other side suffers a loss. The stakes are, or have been defined as, too high—morally, politically, and financially.

15

Pro-choice forces have drawn a line in the sand and dared society to prove its contempt for women by crossing it, thus holding up the existence of unlimited surgical abortion services as the measure of women's liberation. A wealthy and powerful industry of abortion providers—one of the few lobbying groups in the nation to successfully convince the population that its interests are entirely selfless—has reinforced that position. Conservatives have responded by holding up America's abortion policy as the measure of the nation's commitment to life, a position reinforced by a movement that understands full well that abortion, more than any other issue, swells the ranks of conservative activism and thus fuels the engine of the conservative agenda.

The Responsive Reader

1. To judge from this article, what are the medical or scientific facts about new "morning-after" abortion pills? How do they work? What are their limitations? How are they different from other current options for terminating a pregnancy?
2. Will the availability of the new procedures put an end to the "abortion wars"? According to Burkett, how are the new developments affecting the conflict between antiabortion and proabortion forces? How are they changing the strategy of abortion foes?

Talking, Listening, Writing

3. In the often violent confrontation between antiabortion and proabortion forces, where does this author stand? Does she take sides? Would you call her biased, or would you call her objective?
4. Burkett claims that "abortion, more than any other issue, swells the ranks of conservative activism." If this is true, why do you think abortion became such a key issue for political conservatives?
5. In mergers between secular, or nonreligious, health organizations and health organizations run by religious groups, the nonreligious, nonsectarian organizations have had to agree to stop performing abortions, tubal ligations, and vasectomies and to stop contraceptive counseling. Do you think health providers should be allowed to deny services of this kind?

Collaborative Projects

6. What is the record of antiabortion activity or antiabortion violence in your area or your community? What coverage has there been in local papers or local media? What has been the role of the police or the courts? What have been the overall effects? What does the future hold?

Find It on the Web

You may want to explore the treatment of the politics and ethics of health care in authoritative journals read by professionals and scientists including, among others, the *New England Journal of Medicine, JAMA* (*Journal of the American Medical Association*), and *Nature* (a science journal published in Britain).

Do these journals have websites? Are they available online? Are recent copies available in your college library? You may want to look for material dealing with an issue like death with dignity, chemical abortion, health care for profit, or the use of DNA in paternity cases.

VIOLENCE AS FUN

Randall Sullivan

> *Randall Sullivan is a* Rolling Stone *reporter who set out to study the pattern of mayhem in the nation's schools that he said had "wounded the national psyche." Some incidents stood out in Sullivan's report: In Jonesboro, Arkansas, a thirteen-year-old boy and an eleven-year-old boy stole an arsenal including several high-powered hunting rifles and a clutch of handguns from a grandfather's house and ambushed schoolmates, killing four sixth-grade girls and a teacher and wounding ten other children. In Oregon, a boy who had been suspended for bringing a loaded pistol to school returned with a rifle to kill and maim classmates. A sixteen-year-old boy in Alaska stabbed his mother to death and used a gun to kill a girl who had broken up with him, killing another student as well and wounding eight more. Sullivan claims that in our culture we tend to confuse cause and effect. He discounts the predictable reactions of both the political right and the political left: The conservative right called for brutal punishment for kids with no sense of the lifelong consequences of their acts. The liberal left clamored for a clamping down on high-tech murder weapons sold with fewer controls than weak beer. In the following excerpt from a much longer two-part article, Sullivan zeros in on one of the true causes of the epidemic of "violent youth" underage killers.*

Thought Starters: Why do you think there is so much killing on TV? Do you get a thrill from seeing people killed on TV? Who does?

When medicine fails to deliver, we turn to softer sciences. The American Psychological Association, in its "Violence and Youth" report, identifies four contributing factors that propel juveniles toward violence: (1) early involvement with drugs and alcohol; (2) easy access to weapons, especially handguns; (3) association with anti-social, deviant peer groups; and (4) pervasive exposure to violence in the media.

While the first three of these probably pertain to many but certainly not every kid in the country, the fourth indicator cited in the APA report is more problematic. The media's influence on young people is arguably the most corrosive of all the factors cited and by far the most difficult to contain.

After the shootings in Springfield, columnists for the Portland and Eugene newspapers trotted out the now-familiar numbers: the 8,000 on-screen murders that the average American child will witness before finishing elementary school; the 106 deaths in *Rambo 3* and the 264 in *Die Hard 2*, et cetera. But it isn't the amount of violence in films, it's the quality of it:

the way onscreen killing is presented, the way it's at once glamorized and trivialized. No intelligent person believes that the overwhelmingly graphic depictions of violent death in *Saving Private Ryan* are going to inspire maniacs to any age to rush out and start slaughtering people. There's a considerable body of anecdotal evidence, however, to support the belief that movies like *Natural Born Killers* have influenced any number of young killers. Barry Loukaitis had told a friend, for example, that it would be "cool" to go on a murder spree like the one in Oliver Stone's movie.

"We have movie role models showing violence as fun, and video games where you kill and get rewarded for killing," observes Sissela Bok, author of a book (*Mayhem: Violence as Public Entertainment*) on the effects of violence in the media. Also, "A lot of violent movies blur the lines between good guys and the bad guys, and make a hero of anyone who fights," points out Harvard Medical Center's Alvin Poussaint. Even more troubling, Poussaint adds, is that "children now say in a proud voice that the violence doesn't upset them, as if that's part of growing up."

Television is the medium that reaches into more young lives than any   5 other, and perhaps the most compelling indictment of TV's role in the perpetuation of violence comes from a scholar who has only recently begun to address the subject directly. In 1996, Lt. Col. Dave Grossman, a former U.S. Army Ranger and psychology professor at West Point, published a book titled *On Killing: The Psychological Cost of Learning to Kill in War and Society,* which challenges conventional assumptions about how men behave in war and deal with taking another human's life. Before the advent of long-range weapons, Grossman explains, "battles were basically big shoving matches. These guys would face each other, threatening and shouting, pushing and cursing, until one side got afraid, turned and ran." Human beings, like every other species, have a natural resistance to killing their own, Grossman maintains, citing studies of Civil War battlefields that suggest no more than fifteen to twenty percent of soldiers were firing their rifles at the enemy. It was a pattern that held, Grossman says, until the start of World War II, when "the top brass of the U.S. Army decided, 'We have to change that.'"

The military increased the capacity of American soldiers to kill by instituting a four-part conditioning program. First, recruits were "traumatized and brutalized" in boot camp. "They were told, 'We live in a violent world, and the only way to adapt is to become violent,'" Grossman explains. Second, soldiers were taught to laugh and cheer in response to violence. The third "and probably most significant" change the military made was to replace the fixed bull's-eye targets on its marksmanship ranges with human silhouettes. "This was to get the recruits to aim and shoot without thinking," Grossman says. "It became a purely reflexive response." Finally, the recruits were given "warrior role models"—their drill instructors— who convinced them that killing the enemy was a noble act.

The success of the military's new conditioning program was beyond the expectations of even those who designed it: By the time of the Vietnam

War, the "fire rate" of U.S. soldiers had increased from twenty to ninety-five percent.

Only after his book came out, Grossman recalls, did he begin to realize that "this process I had described is exactly what we're doing to our children through the mediums we use to entertain them."

The effect of video games struck him first, after he agreed to testify for the defense at the trial of a South Carolina teenager who had shot a store clerk between the eyes while six cameras recorded the killing: "They asked why he shot this man, and all he could say was, 'It was an accident.' I realized it was true, that I was looking at a new breed of criminal in this country who has been conditioned to kill from a very early age. I started to watch kids playing point-and-shoot video games and realized that for a dollar or two they were getting the same training, at a much younger age, as we give Army recruits and police officers.

"Then I started to look at television and I realized that it was providing steps one, two and four of the conditioning process. It traumatizes and brutalizes kids with images of violence. Only this isn't an eighteen-year-old just off the bus but a two-year-old whose brain is not cognitively developed enough to distinguish fantasy from reality.

"TV not only teaches kids to laugh and cheer in response to violence, it also teaches them to associate it with their favorite candy bar or soft drink. And it's certainly giving them lots of role models who kill the bad guys."

The recent slight drop in the U.S. murder rate has been largely illusory, Grossman says. People tend to forget that crime is committed mostly by the young and that we have a rapidly aging population. Also, since 1970, the number of U.S. citizens who are behind bars has increased fourfold. "Medical technology is the main reason you can't use the murder rate as a measure of violent crime," Grossman explains. "If we still had 1940s medical techniques, the murder rate in New York City would be ten times what it is today. If you want to look at a category of crime, you have to look at aggravated assaults. And since 1957, when exposure to television first began to reach its saturation point, the per-capita rate of aggravated assault in this country has increased sevenfold."

It's not just here, Grossman adds: TV came a little later to Canada, but in the last twenty-five years the aggravated-assault rate in that country has increased fivefold. In Australia and New Zealand, the rate has gone up fivefold, as well, and in just fifteen years.

"What we know—and it's been proven beyond dispute—is that television is a greater factor in this increased degree of violence in our society than all other factors combined," Grossman says. "And that includes broken homes and abuse and neglect and all those sorts of things. The data linking TV viewing to violent behavior is three times better than the data linking tobacco and cancer."

Grossman scoffs at those who say the data are inconclusive. "Of all the studies that have been done, just under a thousand have found evidence of

10

15

a link between TV violence and real violence. Just eighteen have found no link, and twelve of these were funded by the TV industry."

Grossman was summoned by the federal government to Westside Middle School in Jonesboro barely an hour after the shootings there to counsel the school's teachers. When word of his presence got out, just about every newsmagazine in the country contacted him to appear on camera. "As soon as they heard where I was coming from, they didn't want me anymore," he recalls. "Not if I was going to say TV was the problem."

"I met only one TV producer who would be honest with me," Grossman continues. "This was a guy from CBS who had just come back from Bosnia. He sat with me in my living room, and I could tell he was really embarrassed to tell me they couldn't use me. Finally he admitted, 'Look, our own in-house people have told us what you're saying. We know it's true. I can tell you this: My own two-year-old daughter will never see TV until she's old enough to read.'"

"Apparently," Grossman adds, "he doesn't care what he does to somebody else's two-year-old daughter."

Grossman isn't advocating censorship, he hastens to explain: "What I'm asking for is education. The networks should run ads that tell people to keep their kids away from television until the age of at least five or six, until they've learned to read."

Given the power of television as an industry, it would appear that *20* Grossman has picked a fight he cannot win. But he's found a group of unlikely allies in a national organization of trial lawyers who are preparing to file product-liability lawsuits against the TV networks, much like the ones that have been filed against the tobacco companies. "Now, I'd be the first to say we have too many lawyers in this country and that they're like sharks swimming around in a barrel," Grossman admits. "But they're also the only hope we have of reaching the networks, because they can hit them where they feel it: in the wallet."

The Responsive Reader

1. In discussing the impact of movie violence on young people, what does Sullivan mean when he says "it isn't the amount of violence in films" but the "quality of it"? How is killing on the screen "at once glamorized and trivialized"?
2. What sources does Sullivan draw on to support his position? What use does he make of them? How authoritative do they seem—what are their credentials?
3. How is bombarding young viewers with media violence similar to training young Americans for combat? Do you think the analogy between military training and the TV exposure of young Americans is valid? Why or why not?

Talking, Listening, Writing

4. Chronicling the apparent epidemic of killings of students by students, Sullivan described them as "multiple-victim school shootings by white teenagers in rural communities or small towns." What is the point of describing them in this fashion?

5. Do you think there should be criminal penalties for adults who let children get their hands on loaded firearms?

6. The father of a student who had helped subdue one of the juvenile gunmen appeared at a news conference with an NRA cap and said, "I'm pro-guns. This event doesn't change how I feel about it." What, if anything, would you say to him?

Collaborative Projects

7. Are you concerned about the barrage of gunplay on TV, blunting the moral sensibilities of impressionable young Americans and possibly creating amoral young killers? You may want to prepare a draft of a letter to a network president for peer review or peer critique by your classmates.

LIFE AND DEATH AMONG THE XEROX PEOPLE

Olga Cabral

The nineteenth-century gospel of progress promised a better future when the march of technology would free humanity from backbreaking toil and banish the specter of famine. Spectacular advances in transportation and communication bridged huge distances. During the twentieth century, skeptical voices began to voice second thoughts, warning of the negative side effects and unintended consequences of technological advances. They protested the congestion and pollution caused by the public's love affair with the automobile. They warned of nuclear disaster. A new generation of office workers found themselves working in the dehumanized modern office envisioned in the following poem. Olga Cabral was born in Port of Spain in Trinidad. After coming to New York, she ran an art gallery, and she published juvenile fiction and several collections of poetry. She has written haunting, provocative poems on subjects like world hunger: "black child / brown child dying / on the naked roadsides / of HUNGER."

Thought Starters: For how much of your ordinary day do you listen to synthesized voices, push buttons to communicate, or otherwise interact with automated or robotized devices? Do you miss the human contact that the new systems and devices have replaced, or do you welcome the convenience or efficiency of dealing with machines and automated systems?

It was the wrong office
    but I went in
not a soul knew me
    but they said: Sit Down
they showed me corridors of paper
    and said: Begin Here

They wheeled in a machine
    a miniature electric chair
sparks flew from the earplugs
    antennas sprang from my nostrils
they switched on the current
    the machine said: Marry Me

I had forgotten my numbers
    they said it could be serious

they showed me the paper cutter   *15*
    it sliced like a guillotine
my head fell bloodlessly
    into the waste basket

I mined my way through stockrooms
    I wrote urgent xxxxxxxxxx's every day
to faces flat as paper   *20*
    the telephones feared nothing human
the windows were mirages
    permanently nailed shut

They handed me a skin
    and said: Wear This   *25*
it was somebody else's life
    it didn't quite fit
so I left it lying there . . .
    that was a queer cemetery.   *30*

The Responsive Reader

1. Cabral's poem takes us out of the real world to the nightmare world of
   a bad dream. However, bad dreams often exaggerate or distort elements
   from the real world. What details from the real world of office work
   surface in this poem in a spooky, frightening form? For example, have
   you ever felt that you were being equipped with earplugs and antennas?
   In what kind of building would you feel that "the windows were mirages / permanently nailed shut"? What would make a user feel married
   to a piece of equipment or a machine?
2. The poet starts by saying that "it was the wrong office" and "not a soul
   knew me." She says toward the end, "it was somebody else's life." Have
   you ever experienced similar feelings at work, in school, or in another
   situation? How do people cope with such feelings of alienation?

Talking, Listening, Writing

3. Critics charge that current methods of supervision and monitoring have
   contributed to the depersonalizing and dehumanizing of office work.
   One student wrote, "Productivity was the paramount concern of the
   company; each and every second was counted, monitored, and evalu-
   ated by the master computer." Have you experienced or observed current corporate methods of scheduling and monitoring? How did you react or adjust?
4. Luddites are critics of modern technology who envision a simpler,
   less stress-ridden life with less reliance on machines and gadgets and
   less planned obsolescence. They tell horror stories of two voice-mail

answering services conversing with each other or of student research papers ordered from an automated service and then read and graded by another automated service commissioned by the instructor. Have you seen evidence of the yearning for a simpler, more natural life less dependent on technology and leap-frogging technological progress? Where? With what effect or results?

5. Defenders of technological progress are fond of saying that there is no way to turn back the clock. One columnist published an article, "In Praise of Asphalt Nation," in defense of the automobile, which is often attacked as a source of congestion and pollution and urban sprawl. You may want to write a journal entry or paper titled "In Defense of . . . ," defending an example or a symbol of technological progress or the high-tech world that is currently under attack.

6. What is ergonomics? What is repetitive motion syndrome or repetitive stress syndrome? Working conditions in the computerized workplace have given rise to new kinds of stress and injury that become the subject of protests or litigation. Working with a group, investigate current complaints, suggested remedies, or recent or proposed legislation.

FORUM: *Terror Invades America*

Several generations of Americans had known war only through news reports and from the images on the television and movie screen. Horrendous civilian casualties, saturation bombings, ethnic cleansing, and genocide took place, to borrow the title of a Hemingway story, "in another country." Vietnam veterans who had seen war at first hand complained that the people at home did not really want to hear their story.

On September 11, 2001, for the first time since the Civil War, war came to the American homeland. As millions watched in horror, first one of the twin towers of the World Trade Center in lower Manhattan started belching flame and smoke after being hit by a hijacked American passenger plane. Then a second plane hit the second tower. Eventually both towers collapsed, burying over 3,000 people—workers and customers of the many national and international firms sharing the buildings. On an ordinary working day, as many as 50,000 people came to the trade center, and only a miracle of coordinated evacuation procedures allowed many people to reach safety. The dead included a large number of police officers and firefighters who had rushed to the disaster scene. A third plane, also hijacked by Muslim fundamentalists, crashed into the Pentagon, with hundreds of additional casualties. A fourth hijacked plane crashed in Pennsylvania, killing all aboard, after heroic passengers took on the terrorists.

The terrorist attack had not come without warning. An earlier attempt to blow up the World Trade Center using a car bomb had done limited damage, and the case against the terrorists implicated was still wending its way through the legal system. Horrendous bombings of two American embassies in Africa, staged by the same fundamentalist network that planned the September 11 attack, had killed and maimed hundreds of local workers and bystanders. Worried flight instructors had tried to warn the authorities about Middle Eastern nationals wanting to learn how to fly but not how to land a large commercial plane. However, these warnings were dimissed or misdirected, never reaching the FBI or the CIA or the Pentagon.

Earlier in 2001, the chair of a Harvard University institute studying international relations and the "Clash of Cultures" had congratulated Americans on the "vigilance" that he said had prevented further attacks from the terrorists. After September 11, political leaders and media voices said that what we had seen was America's "loss of innocence" and that "things would never be the same."

MANHATTAN DISPATCH

David Grann

New York City is the financial and cultural capital of the United States, and with its surrounding suburban areas it is the heart of American publishing. Many editors and journalists lived and worked within a few dozen blocks of the twin towers targeted in the September 11 attack. Many lost or knew people who lost cherished friends or relatives in the attack. Grann is one of several contributors to New Republic *magazine who lived and worked in Manhattan or across the bridges in Brooklyn. He is writing as an eyewitness— someone who can say: "I was there." He tells us what he saw, heard, and felt—before the flood of explanations, interpretations, accusations, and calls to arms the event would loosen.*

Thought Starters: Where were you on September 11? How did you learn of the attacks? Do you remember what eyewitnesses saw or said? What went through your mind as you watched the images or listened to the voices?

By the time I reached the roof of my apartment building on 21st *1*
Street, one of the towers was already gone. All you could see was a plume of smoke. An elderly tenant, who lives in the penthouse, was leaning over her railing, blinking at it.

"Some fool flew right into it," she said.

The doorman, Miguel, pulled out a Polaroid camera and took a snapshot. "I saw the plane come right in and hit it," he told me. "It was too low."

We stood there for a while not sure what to do. More and more people came up. One tenant said he saw the first plane flying so low he thought it was going to land on the street; a woman, whom I occasionally exchange glances with in the elevator, said we were "under siege" by terrorists. Then the second tower came down. Everyone waited for a thunderous crash—one man even crouched behind the wall—but there was not a sound except for the wail of sirens and the tenant in apartment 5A, who said, "This is war."

After a while I got back into the elevator with Miguel. His Polaroid *5*
had just come into focus and you could see, through smoke, one of the towers still standing. "You'll never see that again," he said.

The police had blocked off our street with an armored car. On the roof of the police station next door I could see snipers, poking their rifles through crevices, even though there didn't seem to be anything to point them at. By then all the roads and subways were closed off and, though I had gathered up my reporter pads and recorder, I had no way of getting anywhere. On my way upstairs again, I bumped into a volunteer police officer in 16D who was rushing to the scene; though I had never spoken to him before, I asked him if I could tag along. "I'll get you as close as I can," he said.

We got in his car and switched on the siren. Uncertain how to get there, we turned down one road, then another, until we wound up on Second Avenue, where the police had created an emergency lane. We were swept into a long line of ambulances and fire engines, many with men hanging off the sides, or piled on the tops, heading toward the smoke now spreading over the lower half of Manhattan. As we progressed downtown, past the Second Avenue Deli at 10th Street and through the East Village, we could see more and more people coming toward us, a mass of humanity. They moved in a steady, almost orderly march. Occasionally we slowed to let a bunch pass. "Look at that man," said the cop driving me. A figure in an impeccable suit and tie was crossing in front of us. He looked as if he had just stepped out of a board meeting, except that he was blackened by ashes from head to toe. Some people had taken off their shirts and wrapped them around their mouths to protect them from the smoke, even as they carried their brief cases or cell phones. One person carried an umbrella.

By Lafayette Street the police had created an armed perimeter around the entire area and we parked by the subway station. Volunteer EMTs and doctors had gathered, but no more victims were arriving, and the stretchers lay on the sidewalk. As we passed through the first of several police barriers, the cop with me flashed his badge. He was a short, stocky fellow with a boyish face. He said he volunteered as an officer in Long Island, but that he "had never seen anything like this before."

As we moved deeper inside the perimeter, the sun seemed to disappear. The smoke stung our eyes and a fireman gave us surgical masks to help us breathe; on the ground, a thick layer of soot covered everything. On one of the cars someone had written in the ashes with his finger TRIAGE HERE, with an arrow pointing into a building, now abandoned. The smaller streets, leading to the World Trade Center, were empty save for firemen. At one point we came across a car, still idling, left in the middle of the road. We also saw a deserted fruit stand. Finally there was an opening in the row of buildings through which we could see, only 100 or so yards away, where the tower once stood, nothing but a mass of rubble.

Police cars and ambulances that had arrived for what they believed was *10* the beginning of the rescue now sat cracked in half, their interiors still in flames. Several workers tried to put them out, their hoses stirring up the soot so that the few people in the vicinity rushed backward. A policeman removed a gas mask and said into a radio, "Haven't been able to find John. I'm still looking for John. We're still looking for John."

"I can't find my company," another fireman said.

There were no wounded visible, nor even the sound of a human cry. A man came by on a bicycle carrying a bucket filled with bottles of Evian water and little boxes of Visine, which he passed out. Several firemen took the bottles of water, sipped from them, and then poured them over their heads. We stood there for a long time, watching, and then an older man stumbled out of the smoke. He didn't seem to know where he was. There were no intact ambulances in the area, and he wandered toward a car that was on fire. "I better help him," my cop said. He took the man's arm and led him down the street. I asked him where he had come from, but he didn't seem to know. "I have MS," he said. We led him toward the perimeter, where other officers then carried him away.

When we walked back toward the rubble, I noticed something on the sidewalk. It had been cordoned off by yellow tape, as if part of a crime scene, but the tape had broken, which is why I hadn't noticed it before. Inside the area was a thick, metallic object about the size of a desk. "It's the fuckin' engine from one of the planes," a police officer told us. The cop and I stared at it for a while. "It must have cut through there," he said, pointing at the sky, "and landed all the way over here."

Not far behind it was a building with the door blown out, and we went inside for shelter. It was a real estate agency for luxury suites. There was an art deco painting on the wall and travel magazines strewn in the lobby. A camera was sitting on the front desk, along with other valuables, and a piece of half-eaten fudge. A message taped to the wall said MAKE SOFIA'S JOB EASIER.

The phones were working, and the cop and I both tried to call our families. I could hear him on the phone talking to his dad and then to his girlfriend. Afterward he asked me if my wife was OK, and when I told him she was, he seemed genuinely pleased. Another fireman came in and tried to call home as well, when suddenly someone yelled, "Building coming down, clear out," and there was a rush of people outside, firemen and police running past, and the three of us tried to get out. I slipped and fell on the wet floor, then got back up and ran after the cop. There was the sound of an explosion behind us, but the building didn't come down.

Neither of us had much interest in watching the fire burn any longer, and there didn't seem to be anybody to help. So we started to walk uptown, our clothes and hair by now covered in soot. All around us, on the ground or fluttering in the air, were thousands of pieces of paper. They had been blown out of the World Trade Center and were still swirling. I began to catch them in my hands, occasionally bending to pick some up. One said, "World Trade Center Master Options List Report: OPPENHEIMERFUNDS Inc. . . . Building 2WTC . . . Floor 30." Another paper, typed partly in Chinese, said "American TCC International Group, Inc., One World Trade Center, Suite 4763."

There were e-mails ("thanks for your voice message today") and desk calendars and Post-it notes. I tried to stuff them in my pockets, but I

15

couldn't get them all. The cop saw me and began to catch them too. By the time we got to the car we had such a large mound I had to put some in the back. I wasn't sure what to do with them, but when I got home I sat down and began to read. Most were too charred, but I could make out small clues, about some man named Andrew in suite 101 who received a FedEx package from Stamford on August 6 and another man, named Philip, who worked at Kidder Peabody and sent a package, also on August 6, to General Electric for $8.83. There was part of a novel with the initials "S.P." written on the inside flap; the reader had underlined a passage that said: "There was one thing she was sure of. She was going to become an editor." There was a man named David who wrote long e-mails with phrases like "segment specific retention/winback" and "deliverables were reprioritized," and a woman who had sent an e-mail that said only, "I'll see you at two. Love S." After reading through them, I put them in a neat pile and stored them in a box in the back of a closet. Then I went back upstairs to join the other tenants who had gathered on the roof to watch the empty sky.

The Responsive Reader

1. Grann takes his readers as close to Ground Zero as they are likely to get. He gives them snapshots and surreal images of the disaster scene, of witnesses, of rescuers, and of survivors. What images and impressions are likely to stay in your mind? Do they add up to any dominating or powerful general impression? Is there a connecting thread? What was different from what Grann might have expected? What is different from what you might have expected?
2. Grann weaves in glimpses or reminders of the lives and working days destroyed by the disaster. What form do they take? What kind of silent testimony do they provide? What effect do they have on you as the reader?
3. Grann's account stays close to the unedited raw data of what he took in at the time and on the scene. The media, putting their spin on the news, soon started to look for tales of heroism. Would you call Grann and the people he encountered heroes? Why or why not? What do you learn about ordinary people caught up in a horrifying disaster from his account?

Talking, Listening, Writing

4. A foreign consular official based in Manhattan commented on the overpowering wave of patriotism that swept over the city and the American nation in the wake of the September 11 attack. What forms did it take? What explains it? Do you think it will have a lasting effect on how Americans think about themselves and others? Why or why not?

BROOKLYN DISPATCH: UNDER THE BRIDGE

Paul Berman

> *In the first days after the September 11 events, government officials and media people began to warn against scapegoating obvious targets: Muslim Americans, Arab Americans, or anyone looking vaguely dark-complexioned and Middle Eastern. In World War I, popular anger and resentment had turned against German Americans. In World War II, it had turned against Japanese Americans. Berman is one of many voices telling Americans that militant Islamic fundamentalism is a radical movement that does not represent the whole Muslim religion or the Muslim world. Berman is the author of* A Tale of Two Utopias; The Political Journey of the Generation of 1968.

Thought Starters: Xenophobia, or hatred of foreigners, if often the ugly underbelly of a revival of patriotic fervor. At first hand or in the media, have you seen evidence of anti-Arab or anti-Muslim sentiment and prejudice?

I am writing seven or eight hours after the attack, and, through my   1
study window in Brooklyn, I see black plumes still billowing from lower
Manhattan. In the morning, from my rooftop, I watched the first flames en-
circle the twin towers and the black cloud float over the harbor. The smoke
seemed oddly speckled with glinting white spots, which I at first thought
might have been gulls. But they were papers sucked out of the burning
buildings. Some of the specks were also, I later learned, human body parts.
A silvery necklace as wide as a building seemed to drop from one of the
burning towers. I thought it might have been part of the façade, tearing
away. It was not the façade. The smoke cleared for a brief second, and the
tower was gone. Below me, on Brooklyn's Atlantic Avenue, fire engines began to scream, trying to push their way through traffic into Manhattan.

By late morning huge parades of people from Manhattan had begun
to make their way on foot across the bridges into Brooklyn and were dragging themselves along Atlantic Avenue, some of them still wearing masks
over their mouths and noses, a white soot on their clothes and shoes. I went
out into the street. Lower Atlantic Avenue has been a largely Arab district
for some 70 years, filled with storefronts adorned with Arabic letters and
names. Here and there among the crowd, people were hurling curses at
Arabs and at foreigners. A round-faced man declaimed, "Don't let any more
of these foreign Arabs come into this country no more! They hate us!" I
stopped at a store where I know a clerk from Morocco. He has told me he
admires the moderate and tolerant views of the late king of Morocco and
of the new, young king. Now the clerk was standing taciturn behind the

counter, his face compressed. Outside, the round-faced man was shouting, "We gotta get rid of all these foreigners!"

At Smith Street a woman who said she worked near the World Trade Center stood on the sidewalk, dust on her clothes; she, too, spoke against the Arabs. "This is where all these hateful people live!" she said, gesturing up Atlantic Avenue. I asked her what she had seen. She said she had seen people hurl themselves to the ground from very high floors of the World Trade Center. "Where is Bush?" she said, exploding in anger. "Where was the Army?" She had seen a terrified old man on the Brooklyn Bridge, unable to walk any further because of his panic, clutching a pole.

I walked to the Brooklyn Bridge and tried to cross into Manhattan, but I was turned away by the police. I tried to cross on the Manhattan Bridge, and I got part of the way over the river before I was turned back again. So I joined the endless stream of people going the other way, into Brooklyn—the vast and varied crowd that resembled a crowd in almost no other place on Earth, faces that were African, Asian, Latin, European—the whole of mankind. A Hasid sped by on a roller scooter. Near Long Island University, the sidewalks were filled with students passing out water, as if to the runners in a marathon.

It was a gratifying scene of communal solidarity. But on Fulton Street, as I headed back to my home, I saw that the storekeepers had pulled down their metal shutters and the street was empty. A cop told me that looters had begun to run up and down Fulton Street. In exchange for that information, I told him a rumor I had heard from one of his colleagues on the Manhattan Bridge: that large numbers of cops could not be accounted for and were probably buried under the twin towers. "Don't tell me that," he said.

The Responsive Reader

1. What are striking or hard-to-forget sights or details from Berman's eyewitness account? How does it compare with or what does it add to Grann's testimony?
2. How serious or widespread do you think are the antiforeign sentiments Berman records? Where does he see compensating signs of "communal solidarity"? What would you say to the people Berman heard expressing anti-Arab or antiforeign sentiments?
3. Why do you think Berman makes a point of the diversity of the "vast and varied crowd" he saw "that resembled a crowd in almost no other place on Earth"?

Talking, Listening, Writing

4. In Berman's account, the mass of humanity streaming across the bridges in flight from the flaming holocaust of lower Manhattan becomes a symbol for the martyred civilian populations who are the victims of war. In

the current spate of war movies, how much focus is there on the civilian victims of war?

Collaborative Projects

5. According to some recent estimates, civilian casualties in recent wars have far exceeded military losses. Working with a group, you may want to investigate the huge increase in civilian losses in World War II, the Korean War, or the Vietnam War.

AMERICA'S WEALTH DRAWS HATRED

Ken Garcia

In the first hours and days after the horror of the attack on the twin towers, many ordinary Americans used words like senseless, crazy, *and* unimaginable *to describe what they had seen on the ground or on the screen. However, the rhetoric of the administration and the media soon started using the vocabulary of a moral crusade against unspeakable evil. The forces of truth and justice would be mobilized and would prevail. When Americans started to listen to the instigators of the attackers, they in turn heard voices proclaiming a holy war against evil, calling divine justice down on America as the agent of Satan. When columnists like Ken Garcia tried to probe the reasons for the fanatical sense of righteousness and divine sanction of the suicide hijackers and for their murderous hatred of America, they were called unpatriotic and accused of making excuses for the enemy.*

Thought Starters: What did you know about Islam and the Muslim world before the September 11 attack? Had you heard the term *Islamic fundamentalism?* Had you paid attention to earlier attacks directed against Americans or American interests? Had you heard voices of warning? What did you think of them at the time?

If you walk around the financial districts of San Francisco, Seattle, Los Angeles or Chicago, it might be easier to see why outsiders or religious fundamentalists living in $20 tents might view the nation as blatantly prosperous, greedy, self-centered and uncaring. Despite the record prosperity in recent years, America gives less to help the world's poorest countries than other industrialized nations. But we spend most generously on ourselves— with the determined view that we have rightfully earned it.

That does not make us heroes to the world outside our borders. Americans are generally, some might say happily, oblivious of our country's image to the rest of the world. Our leaders may be quick to portray suicidal zealots as madmen and extremists, but it doesn't explain why there may be thousands of people ready to do harm to the United States for what is often viewed as its general excess.

In fact, there are millions of people around the world who despise our country for its wealth, its power, its military might, its crass commercialism, its often hypocritical moral views and its seeming detachment from so many of the world's problems. The United States is frequently viewed as isolated, pompous, hostile and self-serving—and that's among our allies.

So how could it be that a country like Afghanistan would get locked into our gun sights—a nation that we aided in its struggle against an oppressive Soviet regime, a nation whose soldiers we helped train, including one very high profile commander named bin Laden?

It helps if you know that Afghanistan is dirt poor, beset by famine, depleted by drought, fraught with political turmoil and run by a group that sees holy war as its sole spiritual alternative. No one will ever accuse the leaders of the Taliban of being overly moved by acts of reason. But the Taliban's apparent willingness to take on the globe's reigning superpower over their unblinking resolve to aid the world's best known terrorist at least provides a glimpse into the level of hate America inspires in some countries— places that in the coming months we may get to know frighteningly well.   5

It's hard to gain perspective when you spend each day in the heart and luxury of America's executive suites.

The Responsive Reader

1. Americans have traditionally thought of themselves as a generous people, with a tradition of goodwill toward others. Have you encountered or seen evidence of anti-American feeling or resentment—at home or abroad? What seemed to motivate it? Have you heard people voice grievances, accusations, or hate?

2. Have you seen evidence firsthand of the American worship of "excess" that might make others see the nation as "blatantly prosperous, greedy, self-centered and uncaring"? In what areas of American life? Do you see yourself surrounded by "crass commercialism"?

3. Critics of the luxury enjoyed by a privileged class of top managers and the wealthy and of the callous disregard of those struggling in poverty used to be brushed off as malcontents. As a columnist for the *San Francisco Chronicle* before its takeover by the Hearst corporation, Garcia castigated a new brand of top managers who secured fantastic bonuses by reducing loyal employees to temporary status and stripping them of their benefits and who finally walked away with "obscene" payouts after selling their institution "down the river." Do you think Americans will be inclined to be more critical of blatant greed and ostentatious display after the events of September 11? Why or why not?

Talking, Listening, Writing

4. Do you think critics of the nation's blatant prosperity and untrammeled pursuit of material wealth are unpatriotic?

Collaborative Projects

5. Americans are often accused of isolating themselves from the rest of the world and ignoring the resentments and revindications of others. Working with a group, you may want to interview foreign students on your campus to study their attitudes toward America.

PRIME TARGET IS WOMEN

Ellen Goodman

> *Afghanistan, bordered by Iran, Pakistan, and the former Soviet republic of Uzbekistan, was early identified as the home base—the host country and sanctuary—of the religious fundamentalist network that had planned the September 11 attacks on the World Trade Center as part of a jihad, or holy war, against the infidel West. Afghanistan had been devastated and impoverished by many years of superpower politics and civil war. The fundamentalist Taliban had emerged victorious from the struggle against the Soviet occupation and had instituted a rigid regime of religious austerity and repression. The decision of the Western powers to strike at the Taliban helped focus attention on the disfranchisement and oppression of the women of Afghanistan under a fundamentalist regime. Before the military action against the Taliban regime, an organization of Afghan women had smuggled out of the country videos documenting the oppression of Afghan women—the floggings, stonings, and shootings in a former sports stadium converted to a killing ground. Ellen Goodman, star columnist for the* Boston Globe, *has long been a widely admired commentator on current issues.*

Thought Starters: Before the media spotlight on Afghanistan and the Taliban regime, were you aware of or concerned with repressive treatment or disfranchisement of women in other countries? Were people you know aware or concerned? Why or why not?

From time to time, you see one cross the screen. A spectral heap of *1* humanity covered from head to toe.

You've been told that there is a woman under the burka, but there is no way to know. There is, after all, no public face on the women of Afghanistan. Nor is there any public voice. Laughing out loud is illegal. Singing is a crime.

From the very beginning, when the Taliban victory was welcomed by some as a promise of stability, this was the prime target of their campaign against unbelievers, against modern life and against the "West." The fundamental enemy of their fundamentalism took the female form.

The victims of their harshest internal terrorism were women, forbidden to work, banned from school, beaten for an exposed ankle, stoned for a lark. The female half of the population was placed under virtual house arrest, or if you prefer, slavery.

Now we see the Islamic fundamentalist attitudes toward women in new forms. In the will that one terrorist left behind ordering that "women are to be neither present at the funeral nor appear themselves sometime later at my grave." In the promise that "martyrs" in this jihad will secure a place in heaven—with 72 virgins to serve them.   5

Is "misogyny" too weak a word?

For more than a century, arguments about tradition and change have taken place over women's bodies and women's rights. It has happened in Afghanistan since the 1920s, when the reformist Afghan King Amanullah called upon the queen to remove her veil before a meeting of tribal elders, helping unite a rebellion against him. It has happened there since the 1980s when educated Afghan women were demonized as Soviet stooges.

But it's not just Afghanistan and not just Islam that have seen women as the symbol of life spinning out of control. Lynn Freedman, a public health professor at Columbia, talks about a "family resemblance" between fundamentalisms. All of them.

If fundamentalism, she says, "can be seen as, in part, a reaction to a sense of dislocation and a sense that their own culture is under siege, often women become the symbol of that. Women out of control are a symbol of their own situation out of control."

Indeed, in every text and every tradition, from Baptist to Buddhist, we can pick and choose references to support women's equality or to prove their inferiority.   10

Right now there is, of course, nothing to rival the regime or the repression in Afghanistan. An Afghan women's rights group operating out of Pakistan puts it best on its Web site, *www.rawa.org:* "Thank you for visiting the home page of the most oppressed women in the world." It is a sorry, but accurate, distinction.

So today, America is finally staking out women's rights as part of the moral high ground in the struggle against terrorism. But internationally, we still tiptoe around the subject of subjugation.

In the first shaky weeks of this war, we are making friends with the enemy of our enemy. The Northern Alliance may allow its women to go to school and to shop in public, if they have permission. But need it be said that these men are to the Taliban as the benign slaveholder is to the vicious slaveholder?

From the day that terrorist planes hit their targets, and Americans asked why, the president answered: They hate freedom. He has said more than once that we are in a struggle for freedom.

Now, catching a glimpse of the dehumanized shapes crossing the TV 15 screen, we know that freedom includes the women who form a mute and invisible backdrop to their own history.

The Responsive Reader

1. How much do you know about the restrictions that Goodman briefly reminds her readers of—restrictions on singing, laughing, music, women in the workplace, women appearing in public, and women showing their faces or any part of their bodies? Did you become aware of striking or especially disturbing examples of repressive practices or attitudes?
2. How does Goodman explain the psychological dynamics or cultural roots of the fundamentalists' misogyny? What is the connection between hatred of Western culture and negative attitudes toward women?
3. What news reports or other evidence have you seen of Afghan women cautiously returning to the world of work—as doctors, teachers, journalists, and members of other occupations? Why does Goodman adopt a "wait-and-see" attitude toward the emancipation or liberation of Afghan women?

Talking, Listening, Writing

4. Do you think Americans have the right to lecture people from other cultures about traditional or deeply rooted cultural practices? Do you agree that "internationally," the United States should cease to "tiptoe" around the subject of women's subjugation and women's rights?
5. What evidence have you seen that there is a "family resemblance" in the attitudes toward women shared by fundamentalists of other religions?

Collaborative Projects

6. Goodman says that "in every text and every tradition" there is a range of evidence supporting claims of women's equality or inferiority. Feminist scholars have reexamined traditional assumptions about the role of women in the early Christian church. Is there a range of different positions on women's rights and the role of women in a religious tradition you know well or with which you have special ties? For instance, is there a range of different views among Christian denominations, among branches of Judaism, or among moderate and traditionalist representatives of Islam? Working with a group, you may want to investigate current controversies and their historical roots. Choose one major religious tradition with which you have special ties or in which you have a special interest.

BABI YAR IN MANHATTAN

Yevgeny Yevtushenko

> *Yevgeny Yevtushenko became known in the West as a Russian poet who defied the party line of the Soviet Union at a time of Cold War propaganda. His poem* Babi Yar *paid tribute to the "tens of thousands of Jews, together with some Russians and Ukrainians" who had been killed in World War II in a Nazi massacre near the Ukrainian city of Kiev. In a country with a history of anti-Semitism, Soviet historians and media treatment of the Great Patriotic War against Nazi Germany had focused on the suffering and heroic resistance of the Russian people and downplayed the agony of Russian and Polish Jews who had been the special target of the Nazi campaign of genocide. Teaching young American students, Yevtushenko is in a special position to put the events of September 11 "in a larger context." He says that his American students "have never seen war on their land, only in the cinema." What is he trying to tell them?*

Thought Starters: Have you seen movies or documentaries—American, Russian, German, French—that made real the suffering of civilian populations in World War II? What do you know about the suffering and casualty rates of civilian populations in the Korean war or the Vietnam war?

Tatyana Samoilova is running up the staircase, wrapped in smoke from   *1*
the fire following a German bombing, jumping over the pulsating hoses. A
fireman with a blackened face, looking like a coal miner, tries to stop her,
but she slips from his hands and pushes open the door of the apartment,
where she had left her parents . . .

The floor has vanished. After the threshold, an abyss—only a half-
burned lampshade is swaying, and from the ticking ancient wall clock, a
small mechanical bird is sounding a farewell "cuckoo." Only a week before
the terrorist attacks in New York and Washington, my young students in
Oklahoma, at the University of Tulsa, were watching this bombing of Russia on the screen as I showed them the famous 1957 Russian film *The Cranes
Are Flying.* (This film symbolized "the thaw" in Russia and won many international prizes.) The students were watching, holding their breath, some
of them with tears in their eyes.

I was shocked when one girl wrote in her paper that she was glad my
course helped her discover so much kindness in the Russian people "despite
the fact that Russia during WWII fought together with the Germans against
America." To be honest, I was no less bitterly surprised in my homeland
when some Russian teenagers answered in a questionnaire that they didn't

know who Yuri Gagarin was. Sometimes in teaching cinema and poetry, it seems that I also teach history.

I was glad that *The Cranes Are Flying,* together with the beloved Italian film *The Bicycle Thief,* was so highly appreciated by my American students. But one wrote that it was very bad, even for a completely desperate unemployed man, to steal a bicycle in the presence of his little son. "Why didn't the father of the boy, instead of stealing, buy a new bicycle?" the student asked. How happy they are, I thought. They have always been able to buy new bicycles, and they have never seen a war on their land, only in the cinema.

But now war has come to their land. Empires with borders on the map are less dangerous than ones without geographical and moral borders. A new Air Empire of global terrorism unexpectedly turned the sharp noses of American planes against American skyscrapers. The scriptwriters and producers of this war created it in full Hollywood style, like a grandiose world show with visual and sound effects, and they didn't need to direct tens of thousands of involuntary "extras" to show horror in their eyes. But these scriptwriters miscalculated something. They didn't understand that non-ketchup blood in their real-life thriller could not make enthusiastic fans, except among the brainwashed. This tragedy in the United States happened, to the month, on the sixtieth anniversary of the Nazi massacre at Babi Yar—the ravine near the city of Kiev where they killed tens of thousands of Jews, together with some Russians and Ukrainians. (It is also the fortieth anniversary of my poem "Babi Yar" and nearly that of Shostakovich's Symphony No. 13, based on my poetry.) But even in my worst nightmare, I did not imagine a new Babi Yar in the heart of Manhattan. Today, Russia is crying together with America—I haven't seen anything like it since President John Kennedy was killed. I hope that these common tears can wash away everything that still divides us.

Planes stuffed with innocent victims, including children, ripped through more than skyscrapers. They ripped through the greatest books: the Bible, the Koran, Dante, Shakespeare, Goethe, Hugo, Dostoyevsky, Whitman. Many of the world's museums, dedicated to World War II, warn us of the potential catastrophe of culture by exhibiting books pierced by bullets. But where could we show skyscrapers pierced by planes? These planes were exploded inside us, and their fragments forever will wander under our skin. For a very long time, in our dreams we will see people jumping from inflamed floors to the asphalt. One of them, falling down, with his own body killed a would-be savior. For a very long time in our delirium, we will listen for signals of cellular phones under the ruins, even after all the debris has been trucked away. Something inside us has become ruined forever.

Thank God if it is only the ruins of our superiority over others. Thank God if it is only the ruins of our self-confidence, our boasting, our criminal carelessness. But God save us if it is to be the ruins of our kindness, on which we'll dance savagely with an evil vindictiveness that is always blind and always punishes those who are not really guilty.

To defend civilization we can act only in a civilized way. Otherwise we will look like those morally uncivilized, cruelly unreasonable fellow earthlings, transformed into aliens by fanaticism and desperation, who instead of sharing the grief of so many American mothers, triumphantly showed, with their fingers, before the TV cameras, the letter "V." Poor creatures, they don't understand that the cursed sunny morning of that Black Tuesday was also the darkest day for themselves.

The slogan "Terror Against Terror" is dangerous, because our wish to catch criminals as soon as possible, to point our finger at the first suspect, could lead to unforgivable mistakes. Using more and more terror as our only response, we'll have less and less pity, compassion and kindness inside us. I am *not* talking about pity toward the terrorists—they don't deserve it. It would be stupid to consider the walls of our houses hospitably inviting cheeks out of a mistaken Christian impulse—"If they strike one wall, turn to them the other." But, it will be terrible if instead of burning down terror we burn down our souls with our white-hot hatred, and become indistinguishable from those we fight against. [. . .]

If we want to finish terrorism, we must not become terrorists to all   10 others who are simply different. We must not stoop down to the level of complete suspicion of other political views and religious beliefs. Tough policy toward terrorism must not become a police conglomerate of the richest countries against the Third or Fourth World of pariahs. As long as there is hunger and poverty on our planet, there will also be desperation and terrorism. If you hide a bomb in a pocket with many holes, there are many chances that it will slip out.

Are the professional politicians of the world ready to solve such problems? Don't some of them waste too much time on election rallies? Don't they, too quickly after being elected, immediately begin to prepare for the next election or for a comfortable retirement? Don't they pay too much attention to their own security at the expense of the security of those who elected them?

A 23-year-old student of mine in Tulsa, Christopher Fitzwater, wrote: "Our 'cold wars' turn into wars against people instead of an ideology. People are basically all the same: our similarities far outweigh our differences. It takes politics, money and other intangible things to tear us apart. It is a pity that they do it so well." And another student, 24-year-old Ahmad Al-Kaabi, from United Arab Emirates, counsels that when it comes to aggression, we learn from nature: "In a world where humans stupidly fight to kill millions, cranes fly together in harmony and look for better choices."

We can be sure of the future if it belongs to such young people. Unfortunately, in too many countries, the young and talented squeamishly avoid politics, thinking it an unwashable, dirty kitchen, and they dive into business, into technology, into university teaching, sarcastically criticizing their governments. But politics, like all the rest of nature, won't tolerate a vacuum. As a result, those with negative energy and skill in its use are able to jump into politics and rule those more intelligent and honest than they.

The Responsive Reader

1. Why do you think Yevtushenko starts with a scene from a famous Russian war movie that he showed to his American students? (Do you think his students were exceptionally ignorant of twentieth-century history?) The Italian movie he also showed seems to be on an entirely different subject. How does he relate it to the central issue or issues of his article?
2. How were the September 11 events in some ways like a "grandiose" Hollywood production? (How were they in some ways more spectacular, suspenseful, and heart stopping than the most sensational Hollywood spectacle?) How were they at the same time very different from the Hollywood treatment of violence as entertainment? What are some key scenes and key details Yevtushenko calls back to mind?
3. How does Yevtushenko try to stop us from answering terror with terror? How does he try to stop us from responding to hate with hate? Have you seen evidence of the "always blind" vindictiveness he deplores? What specific reactions and policies does he warn against?
4. At the end of this abridged version of a longer article, the poet lectures today's young people about their attitude toward politics. What is his message? What is his warning? Do you think you and others of your generation are likely to heed it? Why or why not?

Talking, Listening, Writing

5. Do you agree with the Tulsa student who said, "People are basically all the same"? What evidence have you seen for or against the proposition that "our similarities far outweigh our differences"?
6. Faruq Achikzad, a United Nations official who has worked in the United Arab Emirates, in Pakistan, and in Afghanistan, said in an article titled "Afghanistan after the Taliban" that while the United States is combating international terrorism "it is imperative to identify its root causes" and try to deal with them. What do you think Americans have learned about the root causes of the terror attacks directed at the United States and other countries of the West?

The Documented Paper

When you bring together the best current information and thinking on a subject, you may be asked to provide full **documentation.** When you work on a documented paper, you keep a complete record of where you found your material—so that the reader can retrace your steps. Documentation is for readers who do not just accept your say-so. They want to be able to check things out for themselves. They want to decide whether you have drawn on reliable and up-to-date sources.

You document your sources for readers who may want to verify or challenge your evidence. You give the answers to questions like the following:

- PERIODICAL SOURCE If a quotation came from a magazine article, what was the full name of the author, the exact title of the article or selection, and the exact title of the publication? What was the date of the issue and the page number? What were the inclusive page numbers for a whole article? For a technical or professional journal, was there a special volume number (for a yearly set of issues) or a number for a specific issue? If you are quoting a newspaper story, is the journalist or columnist identified? What was the edition—for instance, morning or evening, national or regional? What was the section of the paper?

- BOOK SOURCE In what book did you find the material or the information? Did it have one author or several authors? Who published it— where and when? Was the book assembled, edited, or translated by someone other than the author or authors? Was it an updated or revised edition? On what page (or pages) did this passage occur?

- ONLINE SOURCE If you found the material online, how much information do you have about its source—for instance, authorship, institutional affiliation, continued availability? Who created or maintained a website you visited? What is the **Internet address** (URL) that will lead the reader to the online source?

- NONPRINT SOURCE Input from nonprint sources may include material from interviews, radio and television programs, or lectures. Do you have the name and the date if you interviewed or consulted an expert, eyewitness, or insider? Can you give the names of the director, sponsor, or key participants for material from a television program or series? Do you have the name of the speaker, sponsor, and occasion for part of a lecture series?

As a researcher today you have almost instant access to a wealth of information and informed opinion.

• Computerized library catalogs facilitate access to the full range of holdings of college libraries. Budget cuts for library acquisitions and library hours are counterbalanced at least in part by interlibrary loans and ambitious new library projects in public-spirited communities. Your library may be linked with other libraries nationally and internationally, so that you may be able to compensate for gaps in your library's resources.

• The Internet puts at your fingertips background information, informed opinion, and current controversy on a vast range of current issues and concerns. You may be using material from sources first published in hard copy and also available online, as well as material originally published online. You may use material on CD-ROM or material downloaded from a wide range of Internet sources.

• Reference books like the *Encyclopaedia Britannica* and the *Encarta* encyclopedia are now available online or on CD-ROM, allowing you to call up an article by typing in a key word or a string of key words—or allowing you to type in a question and click for the answer. Amazingly expert and well-written articles have multiple links to further information and background for a full range of subtopics. Specialized databases for every major academic field or area of knowledge guide you to expert technical or scholarly sources.

EVALUATING YOUR SOURCES You will need to convince your readers that you have consulted authoritative, reliable sources. What are the credentials of an author you are quoting? What is the author's credibility?

Evaluating Your Sources: A Checklist

When sifting through and evaluating promising sources, ask questions like the following:

✓ *Is the source an authority on the subject?* What is the author's track record? Does the author draw on firsthand investigation? Has the author written or lectured on the subject? Is the author associated with a prestige institution or influential organization? Is the author quoted or consulted by others?

Evaluating Your Sources: A Checklist

✓ *Is the work a thorough study of the subject?* Does it recognize previous work in the field? Does it look in depth at case histories, relevant experiments, or key examples? Does it carefully examine statistics?

✓ *Does the author turn to primary sources?* Reliable authorities often settle important questions by tracking **primary sources.** They may consult legal documents, diaries and letters, or transcripts of speeches. They may turn to interviews with eye witnesses, reports on experiments, or detailed statistical studies.

✓ *Is the source up-to-date?* Does it recognize recent research or new facts? If it was first published ten or fifteen years ago, has the author updated the findings—in a later study or in a revised edition?

✓ *Is the source impartial, or is it biased?* What are the commitments or loyalties of the authors? Are you going to make allowance for a probusiness slant in material from the U.S. Chamber of Commerce? Are you going to make allowance for a prolabor stance in material from the AFL-CIO or other labor organization? How credible is research on the health hazards of smoking if it was funded by a tobacco company?

✓ *For an online source, can you verify authorship and status?* Where did it come from? How reliable or authentic is it? Has it been shortened, adapted, pirated, circulated anonymously? How long is it likely to be available?

SEARCHING FOR ARTICLES You will often turn for material to publications ranging from daily newspapers and weekly newsmagazines to popular science magazines and to scientific and technical journals. Periodicals may appear on a weekly, monthly, or quarterly basis.

- You may turn to leading newspapers like the *New York Times, Washington Post, Wall Street Journal, Christian Science Monitor,* or *Los Angeles Times* for authoritative news coverage but also for background studies, book reviews, or editorial opinion. Ranging from the conservative to progressive, newsmagazines and journals of opinion include *U.S. News & World Report, Time, Newsweek, Harper's, Atlantic, Commentary, New Republic, Mother Jones, Nation,* and *Ms.* magazine. Magazines like *Wired* and *MicroTimes* print much material of special interest to students of computer science and electronic communication.

- You may turn to experts, scholars, or scientists writing for the general public in publications like *Science, Scientific American, Psychology Today, Discover* magazine, and *National Geographic.*

■ You may be drawing on material in scientific, technical, or scholarly journals in areas like psychology, sociology, medicine, history, or art. For instance, for a study of trends in juvenile crime you may find relevant source material in a journal called *Crime and Delinquency.* For a paper on the implications of current brain research, your sources might include articles in journals with titles like *New Scientist, Brain, Neurology, New England Journal of Medicine, Nature,* or *British Journal of Educational Psychology.*

Computerized databases like INFOTRAC give you an instant list of articles from hundreds of periodical publications. (Remember to check years covered—INFOTRAC, for instance, started comprehensive indexing only in 1991.) By typing in key words or **retrieval codes,** you can call up lists of sources on subjects like child abuse, wage parity, and illegal immigration. You can call up book reviews, articles by or about a person, and information about an institution or company.

When you are researching progress toward gender equity in college sports, for instance, the computer will call up articles whose titles include the words you have typed in as key words or as possible subject headings. Very general headings may generate huge numbers of possible articles, so try combinations that will help you zero in on relevant material:

women and athletics

women and sports

sports equity

women's physical education

women and college sports

funding for college sports

gender equality (equity) in sports

Remember advice like the following from a fellow student:

If you don't find what you are looking for under one heading, try another. Writing about careers for women, you may find some of what you want under "Women—Employment." But if you are resourceful enough, you may find a real bonanza under headings like "Women—television industry," "Women judges," and "Women lawyers."

Other large umbrella systems can lead you to specialized databases in areas like sociology, government policy, medical research, and education. These databases will guide you to articles published by experts and professionals. For instance, for a paper on how schools are dealing with challenges to bilingual education, you may turn to a specialized education database. You will be able to tap into a statistics database providing access to relevant government statistics.

A student researcher obtained a range of leads like the following from the newspaper index that is part of INFOTRAC when looking for newspaper coverage of women's progress toward equity in sports. Look at the format:

- After the title, this database often includes a brief parenthetical note on the focus or key point of the article.
- It then tracks the exact location of the item: publication, volume number, section and page, column (with length of article in column inches).
- It then gives the author's name and possible subject headings under which the item may be catalogued.

Database:	National Newspaper Index
Subject:	sports for women

The girls against the boys; women have played pro ball before. But never against men. Is this exploitation, or feminism . . . or both?
(Coors Silver Bullets; the first women's professional baseball team)

The Washington Post, April 24, 1994 v117 pF1 col 3 (82 col in).

Author: Laura Blumenfeld

Subjects: Baseball (Professional) - Analysis
Women athletes - Competitions

Features: illustration; photograph

AN: 15207085

Often source information includes an **abstract**—a summary of the findings or ideas developed in an article. The following printout from a sports-centered database includes an abstract that could help you decide whether the source is worth following up:

SilverPlatter 3.11   SPORT Discus 1975 - June 1994

SPORT Discus 1975 - June 1994 usage is subject to the terms and conditions of the Subscription and Licensing Agreement and the applicable Copyright and intellectual property protection as dictated by the appropriate laws of your country and/or by International Convention.

TI: Sport and the maintenance of masculine hegemony

AU: Bryson, -L

JN: Womens-studies-international-forum-(Elmsford,-N.Y.); 10(4), 1987, 349-360 Refs:37

PY: <u>1987</u>

AB: Discusses two fundamental dimensions of the support that sport provides for masculine hegemony: 1) it links maleness with highly valued and visible skills, and 2) it links maleness with the positively sanctioned use of aggression/force/<u>violence</u>. Examines four social processes through which <u>women</u> are effectively marginalized in their sport participation - definition, direct control, ignoring, and trivialization - using examples from the sports scene in Australia. Concludes that <u>women</u> need to challenge the definition of sport, take control of women's sports, persistently provide information and reject attempts to ignore women's sport, and attack the trivialization of <u>women</u> in sport.

AN: 213623

For articles published before the 1990s, you may have to search the multivolume print indexes in your library. The *Readers' Guide to Periodical Literature* indexes magazines for the general reader, from *Time* and *Newsweek* to *Working Woman, Science Digest,* and *Technology Review.* Other guides to periodicals for the general reader include *Applied Science and Technology Index, Biological and Agricultural Index, Business Periodicals Index, Humanities Index,* and *Social Sciences Index.*

As you track down promising sources, start a card file or computer file recording complete data for each item: author, complete title of articles, name of periodical, date, and page numbers. (Where appropriate, record the section of a newspaper or the volume number of a magazine.) Include brief **annotations** as a reminder. A source record annotated by you might look like this:

---

periodical   Guterson, David.   "Moneyball! On the Relentless

room   Promotion of Pro Sports." <u>Harper's</u> magazine

               Sept. 1994: 37-46

The author is a contributing editor of <u>Harper's</u> magazine. "I was not always so disgusted with sport; I was not always an aging crank," Guterson pleads before launching into a litany of the excesses of today's sports.

SEARCHING FOR BOOKS Data given on traditional index cards and on computer listings are similar, although they may be laid out differently. When you have heard of a promising book, you can look for it under the author's name or under the title. For instance, you would look under *Thurow* or under *Head to Head* for Lester Thurow's *Head to Head: The Coming Economic Battle among Japan, Europe, and America.* However, when still looking for useful sources, you will check under subject headings. For instance, if you had not heard of Thurow's book you might be looking for books with a similar focus under subject headings like ECONOMIC FORECASTING, GLOBAL ECONOMY, INTERNATIONAL ECONOMIC RELATIONS, U.S. ECONOMIC POLICY, JAPAN—ECONOMIC POLICY, or TRADE WARS—U.S. AND JAPAN.

Computer entries may look like the following **author card.** The **call number** will direct you or a librarian to the right section and the right shelf in the library.

Call #:	LB 2343.32 F54 1991
Author:	Figler, Stephen K.
Title:	Going the distance: the college athlete's guide to excellence on the field and in the classroom / by Stephen K. Figler. Princeton, N.J.: Peterson's Guides, 1991. xi, 208 p.: illus; 23 cm.
Notes:	Includes bibliography: pp. 203-208.
Subjects:	College student orientation -- United States College athletes -- United States.
Add Author:	Figler, Howard E.

As with articles, you will want to prepare **source cards** or source entries giving complete publishing data for your record of promising sources:

HQ 1426 W565	Wolf, Naomi. <u>Fire with Fire: The New Female Power and How It Will Change the 21st Century</u>. New York: Random House, 1993.

CONSULTING REFERENCE WORKS Reference works, ranging from multivolume sets to compact manuals, provide detailed authoritative information on specialized subjects. Many are now available online. You will find specialized reference works in a guide like Eugene P. Sheehy's *Guide to Reference Books,* published by the American Library Association. Here is a sampling of reference works that are often consulted:

- *The New Encyclopaedia Britannica* (now an American publication), updated each year by the *Britannica Book of the Year*
- The *Encyclopedia Americana,* with its annual supplement, the *Americana Annual*
- The Microsoft *Encarta Encyclopedia*
- *Who's Who in America,* a biographical dictionary with capsule biographies of outstanding living men and women
- *Who's Who of American Women*
- *The Dictionary of American Biography (DAB)*
- *American Universities and Colleges* and *American Junior Colleges*
- *The McGraw-Hill Encyclopedia of Science and Technology,* kept up-to-date by the *McGraw-Hill Yearbook of Science and Technology*
- *The Encyclopedia of Computer Science and Technology*
- The *Dictionary of American History* by J. T. Adams (in six volumes)
- The *International Encyclopedia of the Social Sciences*

TAKING NOTES To record the materials for a documented research paper or library paper, you may use computer entries. You can then transfer typed quotations and the like directly to the body of your paper, without the need for retyping. (Some writers still use traditional handwritten note cards, which they can reshuffle and organize in the order in which they will use them in their first draft.) You may also make use of newspaper clippings and photocopies of whole articles or key pages, with key passages highlighted for future use.

To ensure maximum usefulness of your notes, remember:

- *Start each note with a tag or descriptor.* Show where the material tentatively fits into your paper. Use headings like the following:

AZTECS—sacrificial rites

AZTECS—light-skinned gods

INCAS—tribal wars

- *Try to limit each entry to closely related information.* If you limit each entry to one key point, you can easily move the entry around and feed it into your project at the right spot—without having to break up an entry ranging over different points.

- *Mark all direct quotations with quotation marks.* Distinguish clearly between direct quotation (material quoted exactly word for word) and paraphrase (where you put less important material in your own words, often in condensed form).

- *Make sure each note shows the exact source.* Include all publishing information you will need later: full names, titles and subtitles, publishers or publications, as well as dates and places. Keep track of exact page numbers: the specific page or pages for a quotation, but also the *complete* page numbers for an article.

Here are sample entries from a computer file. The student writer is investigating new perspectives on the rise in juvenile crime, recording essential input:

- statistics documenting the rise in youth crime
- definition of a key concept (youth gangs redefined)
- comments on the failure of conventional approaches

JUVENILE CRIME—STATS

In 1981, youths were charged with 53,240 violent crimes. Ten years later, the figure was 104,137.

Federal Bureau of Justice

JUVENILE JUSTICE

Trying juvenile offenders as adults and locking them up for long periods of time "looks tough but is shortsighted." Institutions for adult criminals are useless when it comes to crime prevention or rehabilitation. "Juveniles in adult institutions are five times more likely to be sexually assaulted, twice as likely to be beaten by staff, and 50 percent more likely to be attacked with a weapon than youths in a juvenile facility." "Three different studies conducted over a ten-year period . . . show significantly higher recidivism rates for youths tried in adult courts compared to those tried in juvenile courts."

Michael E. Saucier, national chair of the Coalition for Juvenile Justice, speech before Congress March 1994—check issue of *Congressional Record*

REDEFINING GANGS

"Despite conventional thinking, gangs are not anarchies. They can be highly structured, with codes of honor and discipline. For many members, the gang serves as family, as the only place where they can find fellowship, respect, a place to belong. You often hear the word *love* among gang members. Sometimes the gang is the only place where they can find it." (p. 58)

"Sociopathic behavior exists within the framework of a sociopathic society. Under these circumstances, gangs are not a problem; they are a solution, particularly for communities lacking economic, social, and political options." (p. 58)

Luis J. Rodriguez, "Rekindling the Warrior," *Utne Reader* July/August 1994, pp. 58–59.

The author of a successful library paper was asked what advice she would give to students working on similar research assignments. She wrote down the following "Survival Tips":

• If possible, keep all source material until you have finished the paper. Often, you will not realize until later that you want to quote a particular phrase or use a set of statistics. If you have thrown out the article or returned the book to the library, you have a problem.

• Do not channel your search too narrowly. For instance, I was looking for material on women's progress toward parity in sports. I at first hesitated to check a book on violence in sports, because it had no chapter on women. But the book later helped me make an essential point about violence in traditional male sports.

• Allow as much time as possible for ideas to cook. Start your project early instead of waiting until the last hectic weeks or days.

• Talk to people about your paper. Try out your ideas on different kinds of potential audiences.

ORGANIZING YOUR MATERIAL What is going to be your focus? What will be the point of your paper as a whole? What will be your organizing strategy? How will you lay out your material in an order that will make sense to your readers?

Early in your project, develop a rough **working outline**—fitting the material you are collecting into a tentative overall scheme. From the beginning, look for questions or points that come up again and again. The student who investigated juvenile crime found much evidence of a trend toward treating juvenile criminals as adults. These might be some early notes:

—juveniles tried in adult courts and sent to adult jails

—liberal judges and politicians accused of being soft on crime

—strong trend toward harsher sentences

—growing impatience with and lack of sympathy for the young criminal

—disillusionment with programs for rehabilitation or with trying to give young people in trouble a second chance.

—news reports with titles like "Teen Gets Life Term" and "Tougher Treatment for Juveniles"

The student's first scratch outline might have looked like this:

SCRATCH OUTLINE: current get-tough mentality
                          sensationalizing juvenile crime
                          failure of "liberal" approaches
                          trying juveniles as adults

At this stage, the material pointed to a general conclusion like the following:

TRIAL THESIS: As the public gets more impatient with crime, juvenile offend-
                     ers are among the prime targets of harsher treatment.

Trying not to get caught up in the pessimism reflected in many of his sources, the student writer made an effort to look at the other side. Are there advocates of more emphasis on prevention and rehabilitation? He tracked down newspaper articles about priests, teachers, or counselors trying to keep young people out of jail or out of gangs. He looked at articles with titles like "Jails or Jobs?" and "Alternatives to Hard Time." He interviewed members of the college faculty who were known for their interest in troubled adolescents. This might have been his revised and expanded working outline:

WORKING OUTLINE:
    conservative current climate
       current get-tough mentality
       sensationalizing juvenile crime
       perceived failure of liberal approaches
    getting tough on juveniles
       trying juveniles as adults
       harsh sentencing
    searching for alternatives
       emphasis on prevention (education, job training)
       emphasis on rehabilitation (counseling, work camps)

The new, more positive, emphasis would be reflected in an adjusted thesis:

ADJUSTED THESIS: Although juvenile offenders are among the prime targets of a "get-tough" approach to crime, the search continues for approaches stressing prevention and rehabilitation.

In developing a draft following such a working outline, you pull out, adapt, or combine material from your notes. An effective paper weaves material from your notes into your text to support your key points. For any point you make, imagine a reader who asks: "What made you think so?"

USING YOUR SOURCES How do you work material from written and oral sources into your paper? Experienced writers aim at the right mix of word-for-word quotation and paraphrase. In **direct quotation,** you copy material verbatim—word for word. You put the author's exact words in quotation marks. (You signal all omissions—by spaced periods and square brackets; you signal your own added comments—by square brackets). In a **paraphrase,** you use *in*direct quotation. You put the author's ideas and information into your own words (no quotation marks). Often words like *that, why,* or *how* introduce indirect quotations:

DIRECT: The candidate for mayor said, "If elected, I promise to make the homeless people on our city streets my top priority."

INDIRECT: The candidate for mayor promised *that if elected she would make the homeless on the city's streets her top priority.*

You will often use direct quotation for a key idea, a central thesis, or an important charge or claim. Use a sentence or more of direct quotation to highlight a strong personal statement. Quote at first hand a controversial idea that might make a reader say: "Are you sure this is what the person said?"

DIRECT QUOTATION:
Advocates of recovery groups claim that almost everyone is in some sense a victim—mostly, of abusive parents. "What we are hearing from the experts," John Bradshaw told an interviewer, "is that approximately 96 percent of the families in this country are dysfunctional to one degree or another."

When you paraphrase, you put what someone said or wrote into your own words. Paraphrase gives you greater flexibility than direct quotation. You can shorten a long passage, highlighting key points. You can clarify technical information by translating it into accessible language. Note that even in an extended paraphrase, you may include short quoted phrases for an authentic touch.

ALL PARAPHRASE:

Sandra Benares, producer-director of documentaries, discussed the dilemmas of reproducing the language of the past in documentaries dealing with racial themes. For Mark Twain's *Huckleberry Finn,* Huck's friend and fellow run-away, an escaped slave, is, in the language of the time, N—— Jim. Mark Twain did not mean the use of the N-word to brand Huck as a racist. Should a scriptwriter or director therefore leave the word out?

PARAPHRASE WITH PARTIAL QUOTE:

As David Rieff says in an article on the recovery movement in *Harper's,* Americans have always felt that they can make themselves over to become something new. The great American tales are about busting loose. Their heroes find a way "of shucking off the bonds of family and tradition," striking out for new territories in order to achieve a new identity.

Study the way experienced writers *introduce* material from their sources. Who said this and where? In addition to the basic "Author X said . . . ," draw on the full range of other **credit tags,** or introductory phrases. Here are some examples. (Note that after a tag like "He says" or "the author states," a colon may replace the more usual comma before a long or formal quotation.)

CREDIT TAGS:

According to Susan Faludi, author of *Backlash,* the dialogue in these women's films "probes the economic and social inequities of traditional wedlock."

To quote psychologist Hilda Ignes, "Neurosis is the condition where an individual's emotional elevators go to top floor when least desired."

As Judith Guest says in *The Mythic Family,* "I have often been asked why it is that I only write about dysfunctional families. The answer that comes to mind is, what other kinds are there?"

In the words of an editor at *Ms.* magazine, "we women often dance gingerly around the kind of blokey lingo that men have built their reputations on."

David Rieff concludes: "It is a measure of the continued economic success of the United States that so many of its citizens could be so buffered from the real harshness of the world that they can spend their time anatomizing their own feelings."

Often you will want to include **credentials** of a source in your credit tag. What makes the quoted person an authority or worth listening to? What are the person's credentials?

AUTHOR CREDENTIALS:

Ann Smith, director of a Pennsylvania family service clinic, wrote *Grandchildren of Alcoholics* to "bring this group of people out of hiding and into recovery."

Eric Alterman, an outspoken columnist for *Nation* magazine, accused the editors of a rival publication of having helped to "launch the careers of a bevy of hawkish writers who have carried the talent for malevolent invective with them like a communicable disease."

How do you weave your quoted material into your text? At some points in your paper, you may be using input from a *single source,* pulling from your notes the most important or relevant parts. Here is a sample paragraph, drawing extensively on an article by a *New York Times* reporter.

PARAGRAPH DRAWING ON ONE SOURCE:
Individuals who work closely with juvenile criminals often support the idea of providing guidance and discipline. Being in close contact with young offenders, they come to know their motives and their needs. For instance, **Justice Michael A. Corriero is a member of the New York State Supreme Court in Manhattan** who tries to balance the need for punishment or deterrence with concern for the future life of the young offender. As Jan Hoffman of the *New York Times* reports, "**Judge Corriero** provides juvenile offenders hope for rehabilitation." **Corriero** gives juveniles the chance to earn a lighter sentence by placing them in "community-based intensive supervisory programs." **In the judge's view,** juveniles should not receive permanent felony conviction records—criminals convicted in adult courts have permanent records—since the juvenile "can't get a job with a felony conviction." And if the juvenile cannot contribute to society, **Judge Corriero asks,** "Have we really protected society?" ("Punishing Youths" B1).

Just as often, you will be pulling together related material from *several sources* to support a point. You will bring together or correlate input from a range of source material. The following sample paragraph does a good job of integrating material from three different sources:

PARAGRAPH DRAWING ON SEVERAL SOURCES:
The justice system is generally moving toward trying juvenile offenders in adult courts. Marvin Owens of Virginia Beach, Virginia, was sentenced to life imprisonment by **Circuit Judge Robert B. Cromwell Jr.** after a jury convicted Marvin of capital murder in the "execution-style slayings of his grandmother, a half-brother, and two cousins" ("Teen Gets Life" B7). Kevin Stanford was seventeen years old when he murdered Baerbel Poor in Jefferson County, Kentucky. After he had been transferred from juvenile court to adult court, the jury convicted Stanford of murder and sentenced him to death. When his case was appealed to the Supreme Court, **Justice Scalia,** in announcing the majority opinion, said that sentencing juvenile offenders to death did not violate the Eighth Amendment (*Stanford v. Kentucky* 316). **A survey of 250 judges conducted by Penn and Schoen Associates** and published in the *National Law Journal* found that "40 percent of the judges said the minimum age for facing murder charges should be 14 or 15, while 17 percent said it should be even lower, 12 or 13. The judges generally agreed that the criminal justice system should deal with young criminals more in the way it deals with adults" ("Tougher Treatment" A16).

Make sparing use of **block quotations** (four lines or more indented an inch or ten spaces, *no* quote marks). Save such block quotations for special occasions. For instance, give an author a chance to state a key position with important ifs and buts or to record mixed feelings on a tricky subject:

BLOCK QUOTATION:
　　Feminists have found it difficult to find affectionate or friendly terms that do not smack of traditional male condescension, like calling someone "sweetheart" or "honey." Kate Rounds, an editor at *Ms.* magazine, talks about the difficulty of finding "a more chummy way to communicate" and a more friendly term than the formal *woman:*

　　　　On a recent visit to a college campus, I was terrified by a big sign reading, "Women are not 'guys'!" For some time, I'd been using "guys" instead of "women," knowing I was offending the feminist language police. So I knew I'd have to watch my mouth during this visit. (96)

DOCUMENTING YOUR SOURCES—MLA STYLE

In writing a documented paper, you pay special attention to matters of format and style. Documentation styles vary from one area of study to another. Different areas of the curriculum use slightly different systems of coding information about sources.

- For papers in the humanities (English, philosophy), you will usually follow the documentation style of the Modern Language Association, outlined in the *MLA Handbook for Writers of Research Papers* (5th edition, 1999).

- For papers in the social sciences—sociology, psychology, education—you will usually follow the APA style, outlined in the *Publication Manual of the American Psychological Association* (5th edition, 2001).

- For papers in the sciences, you may be required to follow the style of the Council of Biology Editors (CBE), the American Institute of Physics (AIP), or the American Chemical Society (ACS).

- For technical writing, consult a reference like the *Microsoft Manual of Style for Technical Publications* (2nd edition, 1998).

Here are the basic features of the MLA style:

In the paper itself, use **parenthetical documentation:** Give exact page references in parentheses. You may also include quick identification of sources as needed. Then, at the end of your paper, provide an alphabetical list called **Works Cited.** Here you give complete information about your sources. Study the way parentheses, quotation marks, underlining, colons, and other punctuation features are used in sample passages and sample entries.

- Underline or italicize the titles of books and other complete publications: <u>The Color Purple</u> or *The Color Purple*. Underlining tells a printer typesetting the material to italicize the underlined part. Your instructor may tell you whether to use underlining or italics in your paper. Use italics for desktop publication or for camera-ready copy that goes directly to printing or photocopying.

- Put in quotation marks the titles of poems, articles, and other pieces that are *part* of a publication: "A Woman by Any Other Name" (the title of a magazine article); "Stopping by Woods" (a poem that is part of a larger collection).

- For online sources, put the **URL** or Internet address between angled brackets. Include the date you accessed the source—put the access date after the publication date. Try to have the whole URL on the same line, or break only after a period or a slash. Remember that URLs are like telephone numbers—they work only if every digit is exactly right. Here is an entry for an item from a news service online:

> "Murders down in New York, Los Angeles." <u>CNN online</u>. 29 Dec. 1997. 7 Jan. 1998 <http://cnn.com/us/9712/29/urban.homicides/html>

Samples of Parenthetical Documentation

Generally you should name author and publication in your running text. This way you make it clear who said what and who contributed what. You will then usually have to give only page numbers in parentheses. However, look at some of the other possibilities:

- simple page reference when you have identified the source:

> Octavio Paz has called the meeting of the Indian and the Spaniard the key to the Mexican national character (138).

- author's name and page reference when you have *not* identified the source:

> A prominent Latin American writer has called the meeting of the Indian and the Spaniard the key to the Mexican national character (Paz 138).

- more than one author:

> Tests and more tests have often been a substitute for adequate funding for our schools (Hirsenrath and Briggers 198).

- abbreviated title added when you quote more than one source by same author:

> Lin, who has called the homeless problem the result of "social engineering in reverse" ("Homeless" 34), examines current statistics in an indictment of official neglect (<u>On the Street</u> 78-81).

- a source you found quoted by someone else:

> Steinbeck said he admired "strong, independent, self-reliant women" (qtd. in Barnes 201).

■ a reference to preface or other introductory material, with page numbers given in lowercase roman numerals:

In his preface to <u>The Great Mother</u>, Neumann refers to the "onesidedly patriarchal development of the male intellectual consciousness" (xliii).

Note: References to the Bible typically cite chapter and verse instead of page numbers (Luke 2.1); references to a Shakespeare play usually cite act, scene, and line (<u>Hamlet</u> 3.2.73–76). After block quotations, a parenthetical page reference *follows* a final period or other terminal mark. (See sample paper for examples.)

Model Entries for Works Cited—MLA

Preparing your final list of Works Cited tests your ability to follow a required format. Notice features that set the MLA documentation style apart from style required for other areas of study. Indent the *second line* of an entry half an inch or five spaces. Leave only *one space* after periods marking off chunks of information. Abbreviate the *names of months* with more than four letters. Abbreviate the names of publishers: *Harcourt* for Harcourt Brace; *Oxford UP* for Oxford University Press.

A Checklist for Documentation: Works Cited—MLA Style

The following are distinctive features of the MLA documentation style:

✓ first line of entry flush left, next line or lines indented

✓ author's last name first (Faludi, Susan)

✓ full first names when used by authors—not just initials

✓ quotation marks for article or other *part* of a publication ("The Raven")

✓ underlining (or italics) for *complete* publication (<u>Researching Online</u>)

✓ normal use of capitals as in other titles (<u>The Grapes of Wrath</u>)

✓ no articles (*The, A,* or *An*) before names of publications (<u>New York Times</u>)

✓ months abbreviated if more than four letters (Jan., Mar., Sept.)

✓ names of publishers shortened (Harcourt for Harcourt Brace Inc.)

✓ complete page numbers for articles (do *not* use *p.* or *pp.*)

✓ Internet address or URL in angled brackets (<. . .>)

A. ENTRIES FOR PERIODICALS—newspapers, magazines, journals

    1 NEWSPAPER ARTICLE For a signed newspaper article, include the name of the author, with the last name first. Put the the title of the article in quotation marks. Underline or italicize the name of the newspaper. Give the date and page numbers. You may also need to specify the section of the newspaper or a special edition—late ed. or West Coast ed.

Buonaconti, Michael. "New Rules for Illegal Immigrants." <u>Valley Times</u> 12 Feb.
    2002: C6-7.
Bialek, Carla. "Trade and a Yin-yanging Yen." <u>New York Times</u> 22 Mar. 1994,
    late ed.: A4.

    2 UNSIGNED ARTICLE Start with the title of the article. List it alphabetically by the first word of the title (not counting *The, A,* and *An*).

"City Lights Bookstore Becomes Landmark." <u>San Francisco Chronicle</u> 29 June
    2001: A22.

    3 MAGAZINE ARTICLE Include author (last name first), title of article, and name of publication. Give the date with complete page numbers. The + sign shows that an article is continued later in the same issue.

Danto, Arthur C. "Age of Innocence." <u>Nation</u> 7 Jan. 2002: 47-50.
Foote, Stephanie. "Our Bodies, Our Lives, Our Right to Decide." <u>Humanist</u>
    July/Aug. 1992: 2-8+.

    4 ARTICLE WITH SUBTITLE Include the subtitle after a colon.

Cox, Craig. "Corporate Playland: Mexico City's Adventure in Marketing to
    Niños and Niñas." <u>Utne Reader</u> Mar./Apr. 2001: 30.

    5 ARTICLE WITH SEVERAL AUTHORS Put last name first for only the first author listed. For more than three authors, you may decide to list all coauthors if the names seem important. Or you may decide to use *et al.* (no italics), for "and others."

McChesney, Robert W., and John Nichols. "Getting Serious about Media
    Reform." <u>Nation</u> 7 Jan. 2002: 11-17.
Martz, Larry, et al. "A Tide of Drug Killings." <u>Newsweek</u> 16 Jan. 1989:
    44-45.

    6 ARTICLE WITH VOLUME NUMBER Include the volume number for a scholarly or technical periodical with continuous page numbering through a set of several issues—usually the issues for one year.

Steele, Shelby. "White Guilt." <u>American Scholar</u> 59 (1990): 497-506.

7 ARTICLE WITH VOLUME AND ISSUE For a professional journal with separate page numbering for each issue of the same volume, give both the volume number and the number of the issue:

Winks, Robin W. "The Sinister Oriental Thriller: Fiction and the Asian Scene." Journal of Popular Culture 19.2 (1985): 49-61.

8 SIGNED AND UNSIGNED EDITORIAL List a signed editorial under the editor's name. List an unsigned editorial under the first word of the title (not counting *The, A,* and *An*). Identify the entry as an editorial.

Kramer, Janet. "Focus on Magnet Schools." Editorial. Oakland News 12 Mar. 2000: C3.
"Spotlight on Democracy." Editorial. San Francisco Chronicle 3 Jan. 2001: A20.

9 LETTER TO THE EDITOR Give the name of the letter writer and the title of the letter if available. Identify the entry as a letter.

Cardona, Teresa. "The Mirage of Racial Harmony." Letter. San Jose Mercury News 12 Oct. 1999: C3.

10 BOOK REVIEW Start an unsigned review with the abbreviation *Rev.,* for "review." For a signed review, include the reviewer's name and also any title for the review.

Rev., of The Penguin Book of Women Poets, ed. Carol Cosman, Joan Keefe, and Kathleen Weaver. Arts and Books Forum May 1990: 17-19.
Lemann, Nicholas. "Lost in Post-Reality." Rev. of Life the Movie: How Entertainment Conquered Reality by Neal Gabler. Atlantic Jan. 1999: 97-101.

11 QUOTED MATERIAL IN TITLE If a title is enclosed in double quotation marks, use single quotation marks for quoted material within the title.

Will, George. "'Soft Money' Sheltered by Bill of Rights." Washington Post 3 Jan. 2001: 28.

B. ENTRIES FOR BOOKS
12 STANDARD ENTRY FOR A BOOK Include basic publishing data: place of publication, publisher's name, and year. Use shortened or abbreviated names of publishers: *Prentice* for Prentice Hall, Inc., *Princeton UP* for Princeton University Press):

Tan, Amy. The Kitchen God's Wife. New York: Putnam's, 1991.

13 BOOK WITH SUBTITLE Add subtitle after a colon.

Kozol, Jonathan. <u>Amazing Grace: The Lives of Children and the Conscience of a Nation</u>. New York: Crown, 1995.

14 COAUTHORED BOOK For a coauthored article or book put the last name first for the first author only. For more than three authors, you may decide to use *et al.* (no italics), for "and others." However, you may decide to list all coauthors of an important work.

Fischer, Claude S., et al. <u>Inequality by Design: Cracking the Bell Curve Myth</u>. Princeton: Princeton UP, 1996.

Fischer, Claude S., Michael Hout, Martín Sánchez Jankowski, Samuel R. Lucas, Ann Swidler, and Kim Voss. <u>Inequality by Design: Cracking the Bell Curve Myth</u>. Princeton: Princeton UP, 1996.

15 WORKS BY SAME AUTHOR For an additional entry by the same author, substitute three hyphens for the author's name:

Steinem, Gloria. <u>Outrageous Acts and Everyday Rebellions</u>. New York: Holt, 1983.

---<u>Revolution from Within: A Book of Self-Esteem</u>. Boston: Little Brown, 1992.

16 EDITED BOOK Name the editor (or editors) of material edited or collected by someone other than the author or authors. Use the abbreviation *ed.* or *eds.* For work by a single author, put an editor's name after the title.

Shockley, Ann Allen, ed. <u>Afro-American Women Writers 1746-1933: An Anthology and Critical Guide</u>. Boston: G. K. Hall, 1988.

Barrett, Eileen, and Mary Cullinan, eds. <u>American Women Writers: Diverse Voices in Prose since 1845</u>. New York: St. Martin's, 1992.

Dickinson, Emily. <u>The Complete Poems of Emily Dickinson</u>. Ed. Thoma H. Johnson. Boston: Little, Brown, 1978.

17 TRANSLATED BOOK Name the translator for material translated from another language:

Freire, Paulo. <u>Pedagogy of the Oppressed</u>. Trans. Myra Bergman Ramos. New York: Seabury, 1970.

18 NEW OR REVISED EDITION Add *2nd ed.* or *Rev. ed.* for a later edition of a book:

Guth, Hans P., and Gabriele L. Rico, eds. <u>Discovering Literature: Stories, Poems, Plays</u>. 3rd ed. Upper Saddle River, NJ: Prentice, 2003.

19 SPECIAL IMPRINT Identify a special imprint or special line of books of a publisher, like the Vintage Books published by Random House.

Acosta, Oscar Zeta. <u>The Revolt of the Cockroach People</u>. New York: Vintage-
    Random, 1989.

20 PART OF A COLLECTION Include complete page numbers for an article, poem, or other selection that is part of a *collection,* or anthology:

Gutierrez, Irene. "A New Consciousness." <u>New Voices of the Southwest</u>. Ed.
    Laura Fuentes. Santa Fe: Horizon, 1992. 123-34.

When you list several articles from the same collection, you may choose to list the whole collection as a separate entry in your Works Cited. You then also list the individual selections. You **cross-reference** them to the whole collection, giving simply the editor's name but also showing the complete page numbers. Items like the following would appear in appropriate alphabetical order in your Works Cited:

Aufderheide, Patricia, ed. <u>Beyond PC: Toward a Politics of Understanding</u>.
    St. Paul, MN: Graywolf, 1992.
Boyte, Harry C. "The Politics of Innocence." Aufderheide 177-79.
D'Souza, Dinesh. "The Visigoths in Tweed." Aufderheide 11-22.

21 WORK IN SEVERAL VOLUMES Specify the volume if you have used only one. If you have used more than one, list the whole multivolume work.

Woolf, Virginia. <u>The Diary of Virginia Woolf</u>. Ed. Anne Olivier Bell. New York:
    Harcourt, 1977. Vol. 1.
Churchill, Winston S. <u>The Age of Revolution</u>. New York: Dodd, 1957. Vol. 3 of
    <u>A History of the English-Speaking Peoples</u>. 4 vols. 1956-58.
Trevelyan, G. M. <u>History of England</u>. 3rd ed. 3 vols. Garden City: Anchor-
    Doubleday, 1952.

22 INTRODUCTORY MATERIAL If you quote from introductory material written by someone other than the author, start with the contributor's name and add a label like *Introduction, Preface, Foreword.* Include complete page numbers for the introductory material. These may be given as lowercase roman numerals. In the second sample entry, the roman numerals stand for 21–57.

Bellow, Saul. Foreword. <u>The Closing of the American Mind</u>. By Allan Bloom.
    New York: Simon, 1987. 11-18.
DeMott, Robert. Introduction. <u>The Grapes of Wrath</u>. By John Steinbeck. Ed.
    Robert DeMott. New York: Viking, 1989. xxi-lvii.

23 ENCYCLOPEDIA ENTRY For entries appearing in alphabetical order in the best-known encyclopedias, omit the publisher's name and page number. However, because of frequent updates or revisions, you may have to specify the edition.

"Aging." Encyclopaedia Britannica: Macropaedia. 1993 ed.

24 INSTITUTIONAL PUBLICATION Studies and reports often list an organization, commission, or institution as the author.

Task Force for Science Education. Closing the Gender Gap in Science. Houston: Doublefield, 2002.

25 PAMPHLET OR BROCHURE Informal locally published material may not identify authors or give full publishing information. Give as much information as is available. Use *n.d.* for "no date of publication."

Foothills Walking Club. Saving the Green Spaces. Fremont, CA, n.d.

26 REISSUED BOOK If an older book is being reissued unchanged, include the date of the original publication. If new material has been added (for instance, a new introduction), include that information.

Wharton, Edith. The House of Mirth. 1905. Introd. Cynthia Griffin Wolf. New York: Penguin, 1986.

27 PUBLISHED CORRESPONDENCE When you quote from a specific letter, show author, recipient, and date.

Hemingway, Ernest. "To Lillian Ross." 28 July 1948. Ernest Hemingway: Selected Letters, 1917-1961. Ed. Carlos Baker. New York: Scribner's, 1981. 646-49.

28 BIBLE OR LITERARY CLASSIC Specify which of the many different Bible translations or editions of a Shakespeare play you have used. Put the editor's name first if you want to highlight the editor's contribution.

The Holy Bible. Revised Standard Version. 2nd ed. Nashville: Nelson, 1971.
Hubler, Edward, ed. The Tragedy of Hamlet. By William Shakespeare. New York: NAL, 1963.

29 TITLE WITHIN A TITLE An underlined (italicized) book title may include the name of another book. Shift back to roman (not underlined) for the title-within-a-title:

McNulty, Irene. An Unauthorized Guide to Joyce's Ulysses. Chicago: Wishbone, 1997.

C. ENTRIES FOR ELECTRONIC SOURCES—Online, CD-ROM, e-mail

Guidelines for documenting electronic sources are being updated as new technology evolves and as users find new ways to make it serve their purposes. For most of your entries, start with as much of the usual publishing information as is available—including authors, titles, and dates. This way a reader may be able to locate the material even if a net address has changed or the material is no longer available online.

- Include the **posting date** or the date the material was last updated. Follow it with the **access date**—the date you visited the source or site. The access date can tell your reader how recently the material was available.

- For material from the Net, include the **Internet address**—the **URL** (uniform resource locator). Put it between angled brackets. Typically, the electronic address will start with the access mode, usually < **http://. . .** >. (Other access modes include *telnet* and *ftp*.) The address will then go on to the relevant path and specific file names (often beginning with **www.,** for the World Wide Web). If you can, have the whole URL on the same line. If that is not possible, have a break only after a period or slash. Doublecheck to make sure that dots, slashes, colons, capitals, and spacing are exactly right. Do not add hyphens, spaces, or final periods.

- For material from other electronic sources, specify the **medium,** such as CD-ROM, diskette, or magnetic tape.

30 NEWS SERVICE ONLINE Include both publication date and access date:

Dellio, Michael. "A Wheelchair for the World." <u>Wired News</u> 27 July 2000. 10 Jan. 2002. <http://www.wired.com/news/technology/0,1282,37795-2,00.html>

31 NEWSPAPER ONLINE Include authors and original page numbers if available. The contents of major newspapers are often archived and kept available.

"Giuliani Vows an Even Shinier Polish on Big Apple." <u>Washington Post online</u> 2 Jan. 1998. A19+. 7 Jan. 2001. <http://search.washingtonpost.com/wpsrv/Wplate/1998-01/02/1211-010298-idx.html>
Coates, Steve. "A Dead Language Comes to Life on the Internet." <u>New York Times on the Web</u> 28 Oct. 1996. 7 Jan. 2001. <http://www.nytimes.com/web/doscroot/library/cyber/week/1028Latin.html>

32 NEWS DIGEST ONLINE Include reporters' names if available:

Aldinger, Charles. "U.S. Panel Urges Separate Military Barracks." <u>Time</u> 16 Dec. 1997. 2 Feb. 2002 <http://pathfinder.com/news/latest/RB/1997Dec16/150.html>

33 ONLINE PUBLICATION ONLY Increasingly you will find material published only online, with no corresponding print publication:

People for Ethical Treatment of Animals. "Let's Visit Animal Research Laboratories." 16 Sept. 1995. 13 Oct. 1999. <http://www.envirolink.org/arrs/peta/labvisit/office.html>

34 ONLINE AND PRINT PUBLICATION Increasingly you will find books available both in print versions and online.

Barsky, Robert F. Noam Chomsky: A Life of Dissent. Cambridge: MIT P, 1997. 8 May 1999. <http://mitpress.mit.edu/chomsky/>

35 WEBSITE OF ORGANIZATION Many organizations and special interest groups maintain websites, often with numerous links to material on special related topics.

Serra Club of Bethlehem, Pennsylvania. Blessed Junípero Serra. Updated 1 Dec. 2000. 23 Jan. 2002.

36 REFERENCE BOOK ONLINE If you can, give the version number and date.

Britannica Online. Vers. 97.1.1. Mar. 1997. Encyclopaedia Britannica. 7 Apr. 1998. <http://www.eb.com/>

37 CD-ROM Give the name of the producer of the CD-ROM and production date if available. Since databases on CD-ROM are often updated, give the date of the version you used if available.

Morring, Frank, Jr. "Russian Hardware Allows Earlier Space Station Experiments." Aviation Week and Space Technology 16 (May 1994): 57. InfoTrac: General Periodicals Index. CD-ROM. Information Access. Aug. 1994.

38 PERSONAL E-MAIL Give dates for e-mail to you or to others.

Shillings, Emily. E-mail to the author. 14 Feb. 2003.
Bruno, Philip. "Re: Uninsured." E-mail to Susan McNeil. 12 Aug. 2002.

D. NONPRINT SOURCES—interviews, letters, talks, media sources
39 PERSONAL INTERVIEW Keep track of dates for interviews and other oral sources.

Canderas, Sylvia. Personal interview. 29 Oct. 1999.
Bouvier, Jacqueline. Telephone interview. 2 Feb. 2003.

40 PUBLISHED INTERVIEW Give the names of persons interviewed and persons doing the interviewing. Label the material as an interview.

Asimov, Isaac. Interview. <u>Scientists Talk about Science</u>. By Anne Harrison and
    Webster Freid. Los Angeles: Acme, 1987. 94-101.

41 PERSONAL LETTER For a letter to you, name the letter writer and label the material as a letter. Give the date.

McElroy, Sophia. Letter to the author. 12 Apr. 2002.

42 SPEECH OR LECTURE Identify the speaker and give an appropriate label (Lecture, Keynote speech) along with such data as the occasion, the sponsor, the location, and the date. If you know the title of the talk, include it in quotation marks.

Kernan, Dorothy. Keynote speech. Opening General Sess. New World Forum,
    Dallas. 8 June 1995.
Vindavi, Jean. "Trash Journalism and a Misinformed Public." Valley Lecture
    Series, Santa Clara. 14 Oct. 2002.

43 PRINTED SPEECH If you are quoting from a print version of a speech, add full publishing data to the information about place, sponsor, and date. Use *rpt.* for "reprinted."

Malkowski, Vladimir. "Dissent and the End of the Soviet Empire." Public Af-
    fairs Forum, Albuquerque. 23 Aug. 1998. Rpt. <u>West Coast Review</u> Spring
    1999: 76-82.

44 TELEVISION OR RADIO PROGRAM Underline (italicize) the title of a program. For an episode in a series, put the title of the specific episode in quotation marks, followed by the name of the series (with no italics or quotation marks). Identify network or station, and include location and date. Pull a name out in front to highlight a person's contribution.

<u>The Poisoned Planet</u>. Narr. Jean Laidlaw. Writ. and prod. Pat Verstrom. WXRV,
    Seattle. 12 Feb. 1996.
Marlowe, Carl. "The Early Stravinsky." The Great Composers. KPFA, Berkeley.
    9 Mar. 2001.

SAMPLE SEARCH AND SAMPLE PAPER— MLA STYLE

The following materials take you through major phases in a research paper project. You will be able to study first a writer's detailed notes with source information and then a paper that might result. Remember that as you write on the computer, the major phases of the writing process tend to blend and merge. As you build up your file of research notes, you will already be sorting them out and may see a tentative outline of your paper take shape. As you feed material into your file, you may already be adapting it—introducing it, interpreting it—for use in your finished paper.

Choosing a Topic

Much research and argument have gone into the rewriting of American history—reexamining traditional textbook perspectives. Some current controversies in this area can lead the researcher to a wealth of both conventional print sources and more recent material from the Internet. Here are some sample topics under the general heading of "REVISIONISM: Rewriting American History."

Tentative Topics: COLUMBUS—Discovering America or Spearheading the European Invasion

JUNIPERO SERRA: Saint or Instrument of Colonization

PRESENTISM: Judging Slavery by Today's Standards or the Standards of the Past

POLEMICS OF THE CULTURE WARS: Propaganda or Reality

Choice of Sample Topic: JUNIPERO SERRA: Updating the Controversy

(Phase One) TRIGGERING—Raising the Issue

The following might be a student's **journal entry** or notes for a **planning report:**

The role of Father Junipero Serra in developing the California missions is highly controversial. Father Junipero Serra is considered a saint by some, but to others he was a man who used brutal force to advance a religion that was trying to survive in a new world. In 1934, Serra was proposed for sainthood and accomplished the first step of sainthood by becoming "venerable." On September 2, 1988, John Paul II beatified Serra after the miraculous cure of a nun with lupus. There is still controversy to this day whether Father Serra should be considered a saint. Proponents of Father Serra would say that it was a very different time and his harshness toward the Indians was accepted during those days. Opponents like Edward Castillo, a professor at Sonoma State University, would conclude that Serra enslaved the Indians in these missions and resorted to harsh punishment when they disobeyed him.

(Phase Two) Gathering—Taking Notes

The following is a sampling of notes with a mix of summarized background information, extensive direct quotation, and paraphrase.

1 TRADITIONAL OFFICIALLY APPROVED HISTORY:

The online edition of the *Catholic Encyclopedia,* with a 1999 copyright, accessed in January 2002, uses an entry on Junipero Serra first prepared by Zephryn Engelhardt for publication in 1912. The entry praises Serra's "extraordinary fortitude," his "insatiable zeal, love of mortification, self-denial," and his executive abilities. The extensive entry devotes maybe half a dozen lines to the Native Americans at Serra's missions, with no comment on their treatment or their fate.

QUOTATIONS:

At the Sierra Gordo Indian Missions, Serra "learned the language of the Pame Indians and translated the catechism into their language."

In San Diego, he "founded the first of the twenty-one California missions which accomplished the conversions of all the natives on the coast as far as Sonoma in the north."

"He confirmed 5309 persons, who, with but few exceptions, were Indians converted during the fourteen years from 1770."

SOURCE:

Engelhardt, Zephryn. "Junipero Serra." The Catholic Encyclopedia Online Edition. 1999. 23 Jan. 2002. <http://www.newadvent.org./csthen/ 13730bhtm>

2 CURRENT WEBSITES ATTESTING TO CONTINUED VENERATION OF SERRA:

Several of these are home pages of churches named after Serra, one as recently as 1988.

Blessed Junipero Serra. Serra Club of Bethlehem, Pennsylvania. Updated 1 Dec. 2000. 23 Jan. 2002. <http://www.catholic-church.org/serra-beth/ serra-4.htm>

Blessed Junipero Serra Catholic Church. Updated Jan. 2002. 23 Jan. 2002. <http://www.fatherserra.org/>

Padre Serra Parish-Camarillo, CA. 23 Jan. 2002. <http://www.padreserra.org/ index.htm>

3 CURRENT BALANCING OF PRO AND CON:

The PBS (Public Broadcasting System) website *New Perspectives on the West* includes a biographical entry on Junipero Serra—"a virtual icon of the colonial era whose statue stands in San Francisco's Golden Gate Park and in the U.S. Capital." This entry explains the role of Serra in the conflict between Jesuits and Franciscans over control of the missionary efforts. When Pope John Paul II in 1987 beatified Serra, this was the second of three steps necessary for the Church's awarding of formal sainthood. The entry sums up both the charges against Serra triggered by the papal initiative and the arguments in his defense.

> Many Indians and academics condemned this decision, pointing to the harsh conditions of mission life and Serra's own justification of beatings. (In 1780, Serra wrote: "that spiritual fathers should punish their sons, the Indians, with blows appears to be as old as the conquest of [the Americas]; so general in fact that the saints do not seem to be any exception to the rule.") Defenders of Serra cited the context of his times, his enormous personal sacrifices and religious zeal, and his opposition to punitive military expeditions against the Indians as exonerating factors.

In the judgment of the author of the PBS entry, for the Native Americans of today's California "the missions and their Franciscan administrators were part and parcel of an enormously destructive colonization process." Giving population loss figures actually lower than other estimates, the author says:

> The Spanish, largely through disease, were responsible for a population decline from about 300,000 Indians in 1769 to about 200,000 by 1821. The strenuous work regime and high population density within the missions themselves also caused high death rates among the mission Indians. By law, all baptized Indians subjected themselves completely to the authority of the Franciscans; they could be whipped, shackled or imprisoned for disobedience, and hunted down if they fled the mission grounds.

A quote from one of Serra's fellow friars complains that the Native Americans "live well free but as soon as we reduce them to a Christian and community life . . . they fatten, sicken, and die."

SOURCE:

PBS (Public Broadcasting System). "Junipero Serra." <u>New Perspectives on the West.</u> 2001. 23 Jan. 2002. <http://www.pbs.org/weta/thewest/people/s_z/serra.htm>

4 REEXAMINING THE MISSIONARY EFFORT:

In a long article weighing both sides of the Serra controversy, Bob Emmers, who identifies himself as a journalist, takes readers from the Serra Chapel at the San Juan Capistrano mission, with the heavy silver of its altar from the Mexican mines conquered by Cortez, to the cemetery for 3,000 mission converts "who died of disease, gunshot, accident, overwork, old age." Emmers says, "here also lies buried a culture." He cites estimates that during the mission period the Native American population of California declined from 300,000 to 100,000 or even 30,000. The Spanish mission records frequently mention "fugitives"—people who tried to escape from the mission system.

- Edward Castillo, a California State University professor and descendant of the Coahulla and Lusieño tribes, is quoted as saying that the missions were not death camps, "but they were labor camps. In a lot of ways the system was similar to the slave plantation system in the South." Castillo says that the Native American culture of California was not a simple one. Their view of the cosmos was rich, their society was complex in its beliefs and traditions, and their economic system ensured that even the poorest had access to resources. The coming of the Spanish destroyed all that. Castillo says:

> You cannot excuse Father Serra. He had spent 10 years in Sierra Gorda, so he knew wherever the Spanish went, there would be death. He was not a demon, but he endorsed and administered a system that restrained people and executed people. He was in charge of the machinery. He saw sacrifice as necessary and believed that lives were less important than souls.

- The current chief of the Juaneño tribe, David Belardes, is quoted as saying:

> For his time, Father Serra thought he was doing his best according to his beliefs. He thought he was doing his best for us. But it was not good. There were killings. Villages were burned. Families were split apart. It was like a plantation system, and the Native Americans were like serfs.

SOURCE:

Emmers, Bob. "Apologize for This: Mission Founder Junipero Serra brought Death and Destruction to California's Natives." OC Weekly. 17-23 March 2000. <http://www.ocweekly.com/inl/00/28/news-emmers.shtml>

5 DEFENSE AGAINST CRITICISM:

In reponse to protesters' charges, defenders of the church position accused "activists" of spreading "a complete misrepresentation of the truth and the reality of this time period."

> Many activists have claimed Serra to have been a very unholy man who beat and tortured Indians. But there has never been one piece of historical documentation to prove any of their claims. . . . Expert, unbiased historians, after piecing through all the historical documentation and other evidence, have confirmed no abuses or mistreatment have occurred by Serra. But it is sad that the historical facts of Serra's life and the California Mission system today are still tainted by wild opinion and speculation of activists without any attempt to substantiate their claims.

■ *Defenders of Serra stress the benefits of the mission system to the Native Americans:* The missionaries helped to improve the lives of the natives by introducing new and more reliable food--the agricultural system of raising crops and livestock. Mission land was supposed to be handed over to the natives "when they were comfortably acculturated to society and Christianity."

■ *Abuses are blamed on the Spanish soldiers.* "The Indians certainly faced terrible hardship adjusting to this new way of life," but the military (with whom Serra often feuded) were to blame: "They mainly suffered from abusive soldiers who were responsible for the spreading of diseases, such as pox and syphilis, and the mistreatment of Indians."

■ *We must see the harshness of the system relative to its time.* "It is true when one looks at it from an anthropological view, the mission system seems harsh. But we must remember we are looking at it through a twentieth century viewpoint." We need to take into account "the societal norms towards unknown civilizations of the time . . . , what the Natives most likely would have endured without a mission system," and that the missionaries saw themselves as responsible for the "care of the souls of the Natives for their salvation." Then we can see that "the reasoning of Serra was for the benefit of the Indians." As for the punishment of those resisting conversion or trying to escape, "the claims by anti-Serra activists of Indian whippings were really comparable to a slap on the wrist (which was a common punishment in Spain)."

■ *The goal of saving souls was paramount:* "The reality is that the Indians now had a reliable food source. . . , learned new trades, which later would become useful; and, most importantly from the Catholic viewpoint, their souls were saved (which was the only known way of achieving salvation from the Catholic perspective of that time)."

SOURCE:

Grisin, Brian. "Junipero Serra and the California Missions." 2001. 23 Jan. 2002. <http://www.geocities.com/Paris/Cathedral/3300>

(Phase Three) Organizing—Developing a Working Outline

Organizing a substantial body of material becomes a major challenge. By grouping material from sources under major headings, a writer will already be setting up categories that may later become major sections of a paper. The first working outline for the Junipero Serra paper may still have reflected roughly the order in which the writer discovered promising material:

First Working Outline:
- officially approved history
- evidence of current veneration of Serra
- balancing pro and con
- charges against Serra
- refutation of charges

A revised and adjusted outline might keep the defenders of Serra from having the last word. It might highlight criticism of Serra from his own time. It might allow the paper to conclude with a careful sizing up of the controversy by today's descendants of the Native American tribes that became part of the mission system:

Second Working Outline:
- overview of the controversy
- background for Serra's life and work
- criticism of Serra from his own time
- defense of Serra from church sources
- testimony from descendants of the California tribes

(Phase Four) Drafting and Revising

Writers use different strategies to develop a first complete draft of a paper. In filling in a working outline with material from notes, some start at the beginning and push ahead section by section. Others may develop the most important or most nearly-ready-to-go sections first and then fill in less crucial parts of the paper. In drafting the first complete version of a paper, the writer must keep important needs in mind:

- to bring the central issue or key question into focus
- to set directions, making readers see and keep in view the overall plan

- to establish and show the connections between major sections of material
- to introduce and show the relevance of quotations and other supporting evidence
- to maintain the right mix of selected source material, interpretation or explanation, and evaluation or comment

Some common revision strategies will prove especially helpful in revising a paper that has brought together a mass of information and quotation.

Checklist for Revision

✓ *Strengthen the overall framework.* Do not allow the reader to feel lost as facts, quotations, and details pile up. Can you make sure that the four or five major stages of your paper will stand out clearly? Or that the major steps in your argument will be easy to follow?

✓ *Strengthen transitions.* Highlight connections between one part of the paper and the next. Insert a logical link like *however, on the other hand,* or *finally* at a strategic point to clarify the connection between two ideas.

✓ *Revise for clear attribution.* Who said what? Who furnished statistics or background information? Repeat the name of a quoted author if a *he* or *she* might point to the wrong person.

✓ *Integrate undigested chunk quotations.* Check for a good mix of direct quotation, paraphrase for less important points, and summary of background information. If you have too many block quotations, break them up. Work partial quotations into your own text for a smoother flow.

✓ *Do a final check of documentation style.* Teachers and editors of research-based writing are sticklers for detail. Follow instructions for formatting the paper: running heads, indentation, spacing. Use capitals, colons, parentheses, quotation marks, and the like exactly as the style guide for your class or for your publication says.

(Phase Five) The Documented Paper—MLA

The following finished student research paper observes the MLA guidelines for documentation. Study this paper as a model for the format of your own paper. No separate title page is necessary unless your instructor requires it. Use double spacing throughout, including in block quotations and Works Cited (no quadruple spacing after title or before and after paragraphs). Running heads (*Richards 1* and so forth) start flush right at the top of page one and continue through the Works Cited page. The extra-wide indentation for a block quotation is roughly one inch or ten typewriter spaces on the left—no extra space on the right.

Writers and readers of documented papers may lose sight of the larger purposes of a writing project as they grapple with the technicalities of research and documentation. As you study the following sample paper, pay attention to the larger questions of purpose, content, strategy, and use of evidence:

Sample Questions for Peer Review

✓ What did the student writer set out to do?

✓ Who would make a good audience for this paper?

✓ What organizing strategy did the writer work out for the paper?

✓ Where did the writer turn for material?

✓ What use did the writer make of material from the sources?

✓ How clear or helpful are attribution and documentation of the sources?

✓ How balanced or persuasive are the conclusions?

Richards 1 running head
flush right

Pat Richards

Professor Guth double spacing
throughout

English 2

15 March 2002

A Flawed Saint?

"Just as the Christian Jesus said, 'Forgive them, for they quotes within
quote

know not what they do,' we pray, 'Forgive them, Great Spirit, for

they know not what they do.'" These words were spoken by An-

thony Miranda, a Costanoan Native American in the basilica of

the Carmel Mission in California after its founder, Father Junipero

Serra, was being proposed for sainthood in Rome. His words drew

"shocked gasps and stares at what many of the worshipers con-

sidered a sacrilege." A man in the back of the basilica loudly

called out, "Why don't you take your pagan rites and get out of

this church?" The group of twenty Native Americans carrying cer-

emonial rattles, feathers, and abalone shells filled with burning

sage retreated to the church cemetery. They assembled at the

foot of a crude wooden cross that marks the graves of "2,364 author and page
number in
parentheses

Christian Indians and 14 Spaniards," buried there between 1771

and 1833 (O'Neill 17).

When Pope John Paul II in 1987 beatified Serra, this was the

second of three steps necessary for the Church's awarding of for-

mal sainthood. Serra has been called "California's founding fa-

partial quotes ther" and "the most overlooked man in American history" in one

of the leading religious magazines in the United States (Fay,

Gomez, and Wynn 71). In its entry on Junipero Serra, the PBS

Richards 2

(Public Broadcasting System) website <u>New Perspectives on the West</u> calls Serra "a virtual icon of the colonial era whose statue stands in San Francisco's Golden Gate Park and in the U.S. Capital." Current websites attest to the continued veneration of the Franciscan friar, including the home page of the Serra Club of Bethlehem, Pennsylvania. Several of these are home pages of churches named after Serra (one as recently as 1988), such as the Blessed Junipero Serra Catholic church or the church of the Padre Serra Parish in Camarillo, California. It has been said that Serra's devotion to his missionary work "was an inspiration to those who followed in his footsteps" (Krell and Johnson 310). After he died, we are told, his parishioners "flocked to the church where his body lay, bearing bouquets of flowers and weeping inconsolably" (Fink 48).

online references

However, Serra has also been accused of enslaving and torturing his converts, sending out search parties to hunt down the "fugitives" who escaped from his churches, and committing genocide. His proposed canonization (raising him to official recognition as a saint) provoked a storm of criticism from the American Indian Historical Society. According to an article in <u>U.S. News & World Report,</u> "records are replete with documentation of whippings and other harsh treatment" of the indigenous people under his jurisdiction ("Question" 24). Can both parties to this controversy be speaking of the same person?

quote marks for shortened title of unsigned article

According to Augusta Fink's <u>Monterey: The Presence of the Past,</u> Father Serra was born Miguel Joseph Serra in the humble town of Petra on the island of Majorca, Spain, in 1713. In 1749, he

Richards 3

realized his dream of becoming a missionary when he was sent to

Mexico to help convert the Native Americans to Christianity. Dur-

ing the next twenty years, he founded and guided a mission

among the Pame tribe in northern Mexico and often preached in

inclusive page
numbers for
summary of
information

Mexico City (4-8). At the Sierra Gordo Indian Missions, Serra

"learned the language of the Pame Indians and translated the

catechism into their language." In San Diego, he "founded the

first of the twenty-one California missions which accomplished

the conversions of all the natives on the coast as far as Sonoma in

the north" (Engelhardt). According to an article in Life magazine,

Serra arrived in California in 1769. "Unlike the Spanish military

and many of the clergy, he immediately made friends with the lo-

cal tribes." Serra died "cradled in the arms of some of his 6,000

Christian converts." According to the author of the article, "Serra

has been the unofficial state 'saint' for generations" (Fay, Gomez,

and Wynn 68-71).

Much recent work has painted a less saintly picture of the

credentials of
oral source

Spanish priest. Alma Villanueva, a professor at the University of

California at Santa Cruz, spoke to me of "mass graves" of Indians

unearthed near several of the California missions and used the

term *genocide*. In the book The Missions of California: A Legacy

of Genocide, the American Indian Historical Society has circulated

the same charges. The book provides numerous documented re-

ports of the indigenous inhabitants being subjected to "forced

conversion," "forced labor," and "physical punishment." It in-

cludes an account of an early settler who wrote, "For the slightest things they receive heavy floggings, are shackled and put in stocks, and treated with so much cruelty that they are kept whole days without a drink of water" (Costo and Costo 69).

In his book, <u>The Ohlone Way: Indian Life in the San Francisco-Monterey Bay Area</u>, Malcolm Margolin quotes the explorer La Perouse, who compared the missions in Father Serra's charge to slave colonies he had seen in Santo Domingo:

> We declare with pain that the resemblance [to the Santo Domingo slave colonies] is so exact that we saw both the men and the women loaded with irons, while others had a log of wood on their legs. . . . Corporal punishment is inflicted on the Indians of both sexes who neglect their pious exercises. (162)

double indent for block quote with bracketed addition and ellipsis for omission

Margolin quotes a visitor to the mission at Santa Clara about the confinement of young unmarried women by the padres "to assure the chastity of their wards":

> We were struck by the appearance of a large quadrangular building, which, having no windows on the outside, resembled a prison for state criminals. . . . The dungeons are opened two or three times a day, but only to allow the prisoners to pass to and from the church. I have occasionally seen the poor girls rushing out eagerly to breathe the fresh air and driven immediately into the church like a flock of sheep, by an old ragged Spaniard with a stick. After mass, they are in the same manner hurried back into their prisons. (161)

page numbers only in parentheses

Richards 5

A quote from one of Serra's fellow friars complains that the Native Americans "live well free but as soon as we reduce them to a Christian and community life . . . they fatten, sicken, and die" (PBS).

In response to protesters' charges, defenders of the church position have accused activists of spreading "wild opinion and speculation" and "a complete misrepresentation of the truth and the reality of this time period." In a detailed defense of Serra, Brian Grisin says, "there has never been one piece of historical documentation to prove any of their claims. . . . Expert, unbiased historians, after piecing through all the historical documentation and other evidence, have confirmed no abuses or mistreatment

online source

have occurred by Serra." The online edition of the <u>Catholic Encyclopedia</u>, with a 1999 copyright, continues to use an entry on Junipero Serra first prepared by Zephryn Engelhardt for publication in 1912. The entry praises Serra's "extraordinary fortitude," his "insatiable zeal, love of mortification, self-denial," and his executive abilities. The extensive entry devotes half a dozen lines to the Native Americans at Serra's missions, with no comment on their treatment or their fate.

In a carefully argued rebuttal to the protesters' charges, Grisin stresses the benefits of the mission system to the Native Americans: The missionaries helped to improve the lives of the natives by introducing new and more reliable food—the agricultural system of raising crops and livestock. The natives "learned new trades, which later would become useful." Abuses are

Richards 6

blamed on the Spanish soldiers: "The Indians certainly faced terrible hardship adjusting to this new way of life," but the military were to blame: "They mainly suffered from abusive soldiers who were responsible for the spreading of diseases, such as pox and syphilis, and the mistreatment of Indians."

We must see the harshness of the system relative to its time. "It is true when one looks at it from an anthropological view, the mission system seems harsh. But we must remember we are looking at it through a twentieth century viewpoint." We need to take into account "the societal norms towards unknown civilizations of the time" and "what the Natives most likely would have endured without a mission system." The missionaries saw themselves as responsible for the "care of the souls of the Natives for their salvation." Then we can see that "the reasoning of Serra was for the benefit of the Indians." As for the punishment of those resisting conversion or trying to escape, "the claims by anti-Serra activists of Indian whippings were really comparable to a slap on the wrist (which was a common punishment in Spain)."

mix of quotation and paraphrase

The goal of saving the souls of the natives was paramount: "most importantly from the Catholic viewpoint, their souls were saved (which was the only known way of achieving salvation from the Catholic perspective of that time)."

Those defending Father Serra tend to play down or belittle the hardships suffered by those in his care. Fink's book reports that the last few years of Serra's life were "difficult ones." There were "few new converts and many runaways among the Indians,

Richards 7

and a series of plagues, which were probably smallpox, had decimated the small Christianized group that remained" (48). Margolin says that "300 or more Indians out of a thousand might die
during a severe epidemic year" (163).

To judge Father Serra's role in these events, we need to remember how badly the Spaniards and the Native Americans misunderstood each other. They represented two vastly different cultures. In the words of another book about the California missions,

> The California Indian has often been criticized be-
> cause he lived a life of slothfulness, not stirring him-
> self to raise crops, herd flocks, or practice other disci-
> plined forms of food production characteristic of more
> advanced cultures. . . . Ironically, the civilized
> Spaniards, who looked down upon the childlike Indians,
> suffered famines after they first settled in the same envi-
> ronment when their imported foodstuffs failed to arrive
> on time. (Krell and Johnson 50)

author and page
number after
period ending
block quotation

Serra probably never doubted the rightness of his actions.
As Fink points out, the Native Americans "resisted conversion to
the Christian faith, which required complete separation from the
pagan community. Children presented for baptism had to live at
the mission under the supervision of the padres" (43). It must be
noted, however, that not even his countrymen always took his
side. Governor Neve "refused to round up Indian fugitives from
the missions, who, Serra felt, had broken the contract they made
at baptism" (48).

Richards 8

The historical evidence makes one thing clear: Serra's methods were overzealous by twentieth-century standards. Some would argue that he was overzealous by anyone's and any time's standards. When we are faced with documented accounts of what happened to many indigenous inhabitants under his authority, it is hard to consider Father Serra worthy of being made a saint. In the words of Jack Norton, a Native American professor at Humboldt State University, a candidate for sainthood "should epitomize virtue and kindness" (qtd. in "Question" 24).

quoted at
second hand

Richards 9

Works Cited

first line of each entry flush left, additional lines indented

Blessed Junipero Serra Catholic Church. Updated Jan. 2002.

    23 Jan. 2002. <http://www.fatherserra.org/>

URL of online source

Costo, Rupert, and Jeanette H. Costo, eds. The Missions of Cali-

    fornia: A Legacy of Genocide. San Francisco: Indian Histori-

    cal, 1987.

Donohue, John W. "California's Founding Father." America

    11 May 1985: 306.

Engelhardt, Zephryn. "Junipero Serra." The Catholic Encyclope-

    dia Online Edition. 1999. 23 Jan. 2002. <http://www.

    newadvent.org./csthen/13730bhtm>

Fay, Martha, Linda Gomez, and Wilton Wynn. "So You Want to Be

several authors

    a Saint." *Life* Sept. 1987: 68-71.

Fink, Augusta. Monterey: The Presence of the Past. San Fran-

    cisco: Chronicle Publishing, 1972.

Grisin, Brian. "Junipero Serra and the California Missions." 2001.

    23 Jan. 2002. <http://www.geocities.com/Paris/Cathedral/

    3300>

Krell, Dorothy, and Paul C. Johnson, eds. The California Missions:

    A Pictorial History. Menlo Park, CA: Lane, 1979.

Margolin, Malcolm. The Ohlone Way: Indian Life in the San

    Francisco-Monterey Bay Area. Berkeley: Heyday, 1978.

O'Neill, Ann W. "Confrontation at the Mission." San Jose Mercury

    News 26 Sept. 1987: B17-19.

inclusive page numbers

Padre Serra Parish-Camarillo, CA. 23 Jan. 2002. <http://www.

    padreserra.org/index.htm>

Richards 10

PBS (Public Broadcasting System). "Junipero Serra." <u>New Per-</u>

<u>spectives on the West</u>. 2001. 23 Jan. 2002. <http://

www.pbs.org/weta/thewest/people/s_z/serra.htm>

"A Question of Faith in California." <u>U.S. News & World Report</u> 11

May 1987: 24.

Serra Club of Bethlehem, Pennsylvania. <u>Blessed Junípero Serra</u>.

Updated 1 Dec. 2000. 23 Jan. 2002. <http://www.

catholic-church.org/serra-beth/serra-4.htm>

Villanueva, Alma. Personal interview. 2 Feb. 2002.   nonprint source

DOCUMENTING YOUR SOURCES—APA STYLE

Many publications in the social sciences follow the APA style of documentation, outlined in the *Publication Manual of the American Psychological Association* (5th edition, 2001). You may be asked to follow this style in areas like psychology, linguistics, or education and also business, social work, nursing, and justice administration.

- For brief identification of sources in the text of a paper, the APA format uses the **author-and-date** method. When using this style, include the year or date of publication after the author's name (Ortiz, 2002). Do not repeat the author's name between parentheses if you have already mentioned it in your text (2002).

- The APA style often gives a source and the publication date of research without a page reference. Interested readers are expected to become familiar with the relevant research literature and consider its findings in context. However, give an exact page reference with all direct quotation.

- For scholarly work, the APA prefers reliance on material from **refereed** professional publications. In refereed journals, the material has been reviewed and approved for publication by outside experts.

- The APA discourages the use of Internet material that may be available only for a limited time. Some material from online publications and also from special interest groups or newsgroups is preserved in web **archives.** You can access content from back issues of many major newspapers and other periodicals in their archives.

The *APA-Style Helper 3.0* on CD-ROM is designed to help you format source information in the APA style. Check for updated information and current releases at http://www.apastyle.org/stylehelper.

Samples of Parenthetical Documentation

Study the following sample citations. Note distinctive features like the use of commas, the abbreviations *p.* and *pp.* for "page" and "pages," and the symbol & (the ampersand) for "and."

1 AUTHOR AND DATE ONLY:

Anorexia nervosa is a condition of extreme weight loss that results when young women compulsively starve themselves (Grayfield, 1993).

2 DATE ONLY—author's name in your own text:

Tobin discusses new integrated treatment approaches to eating disorders, using effective clinical screening protocols that help patients and care managers plan treatment (2001).

3 PAGE REFERENCE—for direct quotation or specific reference:

Anorexia nervosa is "not really true loss of appetite" but "a condition of emaciation resulting from self-inflicted starvation" (Huebner, 1982, p. 143).

4 WORK BY SEVERAL AUTHORS Name the several authors—up to six coauthors. Then add *et al.* (for "and others") instead of additional names. Name only the first of the authors and then put *et al.* in any later references.

Commercials tout crash diets that promise young women beauty and success. (Mendoza, Phillips, & Watson, 2002).

The harmful effects of crash diets and appetite suppressants have been well documented (Dawson et al., 1999).

5 SAME AUTHOR For several publications in the same year, use *a, b, c,* and so on, in order of publication:

Kravitz and her research team have conducted experiments with results that challenge conventional treatment methods. (1999, 2000a, 2000b).

6 REFERENCE TO SEVERAL SOURCES List in alphabetical order, divided by semicolons:

Official statistics have tended to underreport or underestimate the true extent of homelessness (Joel, 1999; Kramer & Swenson, 2001).

7 UNKNOWN OR UNLISTED AUTHOR Identify source by shortened title:

Jury selection became the subject of study for self-styled "experts" ("Psyching Out Prospective Jurors," 1999).

8 INSTITUTIONAL AUTHORSHIP In general, use **acronyms** (made up from initial letters) or abbreviations only in second or subsequent citation:

Many promising drugs or "silver bullets" proved to have disastrous side effects (National Institute of Mental Health [NIMH], 1999).

Research into the biochemistry of the brain has led to genuine breakthroughs in the treatment of emotional disorders (NIMH, 2000).

9 PERSONAL COMMUNICATIONS In the text of your paper, identify letters, memos, e-mail, and telephone interviews as personal communications. Include the date. Because they cannot be consulted or verified by the reader, omit personal communications in your References.

Police officers often feel that the media put a negative spin on reports of police work (Victor Gonzalez, personal communication, March 13, 2000).

Sample Entries for References Directory

Use the heading "References" for your final alphabetical list of works quoted or consulted. Note the distinctive **author-and-date** sequence, with author identification followed by the date in parentheses:

Stefan, L. B. (1991). *Youth and the law: Getting tough on juvenile crime.* Boston: Benchmark Books.

■ Indent *first* line of each entry one-half inch (or five typewriter spaces). Start with the last name of the author, followed by *initials* (not full first names). Then put the date in parentheses. For dates of newspapers or periodicals, do not abbreviate months (1996, September 21).

■ Use *lowercase* letters in titles, except for words you would normally capitalize in your text. Do not put titles of articles in quotation marks. Italicize the name of a complete publication—newspaper, magazine, book. Use the full names of publishers, omitting tags like *Inc.* and *Co.*: Cambridge: Harvard University Press. Use *p.* and *pp.* for "page" and pages."

A Checklist for Documentation: References—APA Style

The following are distinctive features of the APA documentation style:

✓ Start an entry in your References flush left; then indent next line or lines.

✓ For first names and middle names, use initials only.

✓ Put publication date in parentheses after authors' names.

✓ Use no quotation marks for titles of articles.

✓ Italicize titles of books and other whole publications.

✓ Use lowercase letters within titles.

✓ Show both date posted and date retrieved for Internet material.

✓ Use accurate URL or retrieval path for Internet sources.

A. PRINT SOURCES

1 STANDARD ENTRY FOR AN ARTICLE Put the last name of the author first, followed by initials only (no first or middle names). Put the date in parentheses—do not abbreviate months: (2002, February 19). Do not

put titles of articles in quotation marks. After the first word of the title or sub-title, use lowercase letters except for words you would normally capitalize in your text. Italicize the name of the newspaper or magazine, and use normal capitalization for words in titles of publications. Keep the article *The* in the names of publications like *The Wall Street Journal* and *The New York Times.*

Include complete page numbers, using *p.* and *pp.* for "page" and "pages." If appropriate, specify the edition of the newspaper—early or late, east or west: *The Wall Street Journal,* eastern ed., p. A3.

Muschamp, H. (2001, May 6). Fitting into history's fabric. *The New York Times,* p. AR44.

Losos, J. B. (2001, March). Evolution: A lizard's tale. *Scientific American,* pp. 86-91.

Note: If page numbers for the article are not continuous, use a comma to separate the numbers: pp. 7, 9–10.

Miller, G. (1969, December). On turning psychology over to the unwashed. *Psychology Today,* pp. 53-54, 66-74.

2 STANDARD ENTRY FOR A BOOK Use initials only instead of an author's first name and middle name: Nader, R. Capitalize only the first word of the title or subtitle, but capitalize proper names that are part of a title as you would in ordinary prose: *A life of Eleanor Roosevelt.* Use the full names of publishers, omitting only tags like *Inc.* and *Co.*: Cambridge, MA: Harvard University Press.

Chomsky, N. (1994). *Secrets, lies and democracy.* Chicago, Odonian.

3 ARTICLE OR BOOK WITH SUBTITLE Use a colon to separate the title and subtitle.

Martin, R. (2002, February). Meltdown: Big steel in the borderless economy. *Wired,* pp. 88-93.

Kozol, J. (1995). *Amazing grace: The lives of children and the conscience of a nation.* New York: Crown Publishers.

4 ARTICLE OR BOOK BY SEVERAL AUTHORS List the names of up to six coauthors, last names first. Put the "and" sign, or ampersand (&), before the last author's name. After six authors, put *et al.* (not italicized, for "and others") instead of additional authors' names.

Smith, D. V., & Margolske, R. F. (2001, March). Making sense of taste. *Scientific American,* pp. 32-39.

Minuchin, S., Rosman, B., & Baker, L. (1978). *Psychosomatic families: Anorexia nervosa in context.* Cambridge, MA: Harvard University Press.

Boyer, P. S., Clark, C. E., Hawley, S. M., Kett, J. F., Salisbury, N., Sitkoff, H., & Woloch, N. (1995). *The enduring vision: A history of the American people.* Lexington: D.C.: Heath.

Hale, P., Makgoba, M. W., Merson, M. H., Quinn, T., Richman, D. D., Vella, S., et al. (2001). Success hinges on support for treatment. *Nature, 412,* 272.

5 UNSIGNED OR ANONYMOUS PUBLICATION Start with the title and alphabetize by the first word of the title, not counting *The, A,* or *An.*

Assessing the damage. (2002, February 21). *Economist,* pp. 78-79.

6 JOURNAL ARTICLE WITH VOLUME NUMBER Italicize the volume number for a professional journal, with complete page numbers following a comma: *6,* 152–169. Do not use *p.* or *pp.* after a volume number.

Harrison, R. G. (2001). Diverse origins of biodiversity. *Nature, 411,* 636–663.

7 VOLUME NUMBER AND ISSUE If needed, include both the volume number and the number of the issue. Put the issue number in parentheses between the volume number and the page numbers: *6*(3), 152–169. The issue number may be needed if page numbers are not continuous for the whole volume.

Steinhausen, H., & Glenville, K. (1983). Follow-up studies of anorexia nervosa: A review of research findings. *Psychological Medicine: Abstracts in English, 13*(2), 239-245.

8 SIGNED OR UNSIGNED EDITORIAL After the title, add the label *Editorial* in square brackets. If the editorial is unsigned, begin with the title.

Epstein, R. (2001, July/August). Physiologist Laura: She's not a psychologist, and we don't want her [Editorial]. *Psychology Today,* p. 5.
What is sacred? [Editorial]. (1995, November/December). *Mother Jones,* pp. 3-6.

9 LETTER TO THE EDITOR Add the label after the title, in square brackets.

Lafont, L. (2002, January 6). Retirement plans at risk [Letter to the editor]. *The Los Angeles Times,* part II: 8.

10 BOOK REVIEW Start with the author and title of a book review and include the title of the book reviewed in square brackets:

Sheaffer, R. (1995, November). Truth abducted [Review of the book *Close encounters of the fourth kind: Alien abduction, UFOs, and the conference at MIT*]. *Scientific American, 273*(5), 102-103.

11 LATER EDITION OF A BOOK Include *2nd ed.* for second edition, for instance, or *rev. ed.* for revised edition:

Zettl, H. (2000). *Television production handbook* (7th ed.). Belmont, CA: Wadsworth.

Rosenthal, R. (1987). *Meta-analytic procedures for social research* (Rev. ed.). Newbury Park, CA: Sage.

12 TRANSLATED BOOK Put the translator's name (or translators' names) followed by *Trans.* after the title.

Freire, P. (1970). *Pedagogy of the oppressed* (M. B. Ramos, Trans.). New York: Seabury Press.

13 SAME AUTHOR Repeat the author's name with each title. Put works in chronological order.

Bruch, H. (1973). *Eating disorders: Obesity, anorexia nervosa, and the person within.* New York: Basic Books.

Bruch, H. (1978). *The golden cage: The enigma of anorexia nervosa.* Cambridge, MA: Harvard University Press.

14 EDITED BOOK For a book with an editor's name, put the abbreviation for *editors* (*Ed.* or *Eds.*) in parentheses.

Hartman, F. (Ed.). (1973). *World in crisis: Readings in international relations* (4th ed.). New York: Macmillan.

Popkewitz, T. S., & Tabachnick, B. R. (Eds.). (1981). *The study of schooling: Field based methodologies in educational research and evaluation.* New York: Praeger.

15 ONE OF SEVERAL VOLUMES Include the volume number for one of several volumes:

Gianini, F. P. (2001). *History of the missions* (Vol. 2). Las Vegas: Nevada Publications.

16 PART OF A BOOK For a part of a book, use the appropriate label—such as *Preface, Introduction,* or *Afterword.*

Aufderheide, P. (1992). Preface. In P. Aufderheide (Ed.), *Beyond PC: Toward a politics of understanding* (pp. 1-4). Saint Paul, MN: Graywolf Press.

17 PART OF A COLLECTION For part of a collection or anthology, identify both the article or other short item and the collection of which it is a part. If you cite several articles from the same collection, give full publishing information each time.

Borges, J. L. (1972). A new refutation of time. In S. Sears & G. W. Lord (Eds.), *The discontinuous universe: Selected writings in contemporary consciousness* (pp. 208-223). New York: Basic Books.

18 INSTITUTIONAL AUTHORSHIP For institutional authorship, list the organization as the author.

American Psychological Association. (1982). *Ethical principles in the conduct of research with human participants.* Washington, DC: Author.

19 ENCYCLOPEDIA ENTRY List an unsigned entry in an encyclopedia or other reference work under the first word of the entry. If the author of an entry is identified, include the name.

Russia. (1994). In *The new encyclopedia Britannica* (15th ed. Vol. 10, pp. 253-255). Chicago: Encyclopedia Britannica.

20 MONOGRAPH IN A SERIES A monograph is a research study focused on a single topic. If it is published as part of a series of related studies, identify the series and include the serial number if applicable. Monographs may be published as supplements or special editions of a professional journal. Use *Monograph* in square brackets to show that a study is bound with an issue of the journal.

Harris, P. L., & Kavanaugh, R. D. (1993). Young children's understanding of pretense. *Monographs of the Society for Research in Child Development, 58* (1, Serial No. 231).

LaRue, S. (1999). Stress disorders and the ergonomics of the workplace [Monograph]. *Journal of Applied Psychology, 84,* 152-171.

21 UNPUBLISHED RESEARCH Identify locations of unpublished doctoral studies and the like. Identify locations of abstracts—short, pointed summaries.

Minoza, F. (1998). *Photography as social criticism.* Unpublished doctoral dissertation, University of Michigan, Ann Arbor.

Javorsky, L. (1999). Icons and the Russian tradition (Doctoral dissertation, Stanford University, 1999). *Dissertation Abstracts International, 60,* 232.

B. ELECTRONIC SOURCES

Like other documentation styles, the APA style has evolved in response to developments in electronic communication. In research guides and Internet guidelines, you may encounter earlier variations and adaptations of the APA format. The following model entries are based on the 2001 APA *Publication Manual* (5th edition, 2001).

22 STANDARD INTERNET SOURCE Include as much standard publishing information as is available. Specify the retrieval date and give the full URL—the retrieval path leading to the specific document. Make sure to copy exactly colons, slashes, and double slashes without adding spaces and with no final period.

Holmes, K. (1999). *Use all your smarts: Multiple intelligences for diverse library learners.* Retrieved August 22, 2001, from http://www.lesley.edu/faculty/kholmes/presentations/M1.html

23 INSTITUTIONAL SOURCE Start by identifying the organization or institution.

New City School. (2000). *Multiple intelligences table.* Retrieved August 19, 2001, from http://www.newcityschool.org/table.html

24 NEWSPAPER OR NEWSMAGAZINE SOURCE For material from a newspaper or newsmagazine online, you may need only the host name. The host name www.nytimes.com will take readers to *The New York Times* online. Date and title will then take them to the specific item.

Brennan, C. (2001, March 11). Our obsolete voting system. *The New York Times.* Retrieved August 18, 2001, from http://www.nytimes.com

25 ARTICLE FROM INTERNET JOURNAL Include both the publication date and the retrieval date. Include the volume number if applicable. Material published directly on the Internet will often not have conventional page numbers—if available give the number of the article, chapter, or section instead.

Frederickson, B. L. (2000, March 7). Cultivating positive emotions to optimize health and well-being. *Prevention & Treatment, 3,* Article 0001a. Retrieved November 20, 2001, from http://journals.apa.org/prevention/volume 3/pre003000a.html

26 ELECTRONIC COPY FROM DATABASE If you have retrieved a copy of a print publication from an electronic database, direct your readers to the database.

Berman, Z. (1997). New challenges to personality profiles. *Journal of Applied Psychology, 82,* 328-338. Retrieved January 4, 2000, from PsycARTICLES database.

27 REPORT FROM GOVERNMENT DATABASE You may be drawing on government reports or agency statistics traceable through the GPO Government Printing Office database.

U.S. General Accounting Office. (1997, February). *Telemedicine: Federal strategy is needed to guide investments* (Publication No. GAO/NSAID/HEHS-96-97). Retrieved September 15, 2000, from General Accounting Office Reports Online via GPO Access: http://www.access.gpo.gov/su_docs/aces/aces160.shtml?/gao/index.html

28 MESSAGE TO NEWSGROUP OR DISCUSSION GROUP Include the author's name if available. Give the date the message was posted. Give the subject (the subject line, or "thread") of the message. Add the number of the message in square brackets if applicable.

Simones, R. (2001, February 6). Mapping the memory centers [Msg 3]. Message posted to news://sci.psychology.consciousness

29 INFORMATION SERVICE If a document is available from an information service like the National Technical Information Service (NTIS) or the Educational Resources Information Center (ERIC), identify the service and give the item number.

Kurth, R. J., & Stromberg, L. J. (1984). *Using word processing in composition instruction.* (ERIC Document Reproduction Service No. ED251850)

30 CD-ROM Label the medium in square brackets: [CD-ROM]. Include source and retrieval number or similar information.

Bernanos, S. (2001). *The world of business writing* [CD-ROM]. VocEd File: Item 432122.

C. NONPRINT MEDIA
31 AUDIO SPEECH OR PROGRAM Indicate the role of speakers or performers. Label the medium in square brackets.

Sirven, K. (Speaker). (1999). *Sharing our planet* Cassette Recording No. 34-09. Portland, OR: Western Wildlife Association.

32 TELEVISION PROGRAM Identify the producer if available. Label the medium in square brackets.

Crystal, L. (Executive Producer). (1993, October 4). *The MacNeil/Lehrer news hour* [Television broadcast]. New York and Washington, DC: Public Broadcasting Service.

33 RADIO PROGRAM Identify the director or important participants.

Vitale, K. (Interviewer). (1996, May 6). Interview with C. Lobos. *Behind the news* [Radio broadcast]. Washington, DC: Public Broadcasting Service.

34 MOTION PICTURE Start with the name of the producer or director. Include the name of the scriptwriter if important and available.

Fellini, F. (Writer/Director), & Zapponi, B. (Writer). (1972). *Roma* [Motion picture]. Italy: Italo-Francese-Ultra Film. (Available from MGM-UA Home Video)

35 MUSIC RECORDING Start with the composer or songwriter if available. The note "(n.d.)" shows that date of composition or copyright was not available. Name the recording artist in square brackets. Name both the individual piece and the album or CD if applicable. Specify the medium: [CD], [DVD], [Record], [Cassette].

Dorsey, T. A. (n.d.). Walk over God's heaven [Recorded by Mahalia Jackson]. On *Mahalia Jackson: Gospels, spirituals & hymns* [CD]. New York: Columbia. (1991)

36 ART WORK Include title and location.

Martinez, F. (2001). *The serpent god* [Art work]. San Jose, CA: Institute of Mexican American Art.

37 PERSONAL COMMUNICATION Personal communications include personal letters, telephone interviews, and e-mail messages. Identify the source and date in your parenthetical citation in your text, for instance: (M. Mario, personal communication, May 2, 2003). However, omit personal communications from your References. They are not a matter of public record and cannot be accessed and checked by your reader.

SAMPLE RESEARCH PAPER PAGES—APA STYLE

Formatting the Research Paper: APA Style

- Follow any special instructions from your instructor or editor concerning use of a **title page** or inclusion of a **formal outline.**

- Use the title, usually a shortened version, instead of your name as **running heads:** *Slave Revolts* instead of *Slave Revolts in the Caribbean.*

- **Double-space** all materials, including block quotations.

- Use normal **5-space** indentation for whole block quotations (40 or more words).

- Start a new page for your **References**—your final complete source list.

- Your instructor may require you to include an **abstract** on a separate page at the beginning (with the heading *Abstract*). An abstract is a brief summary of the paper (perhaps 150–250 words), showing its focus and major findings.

The following pages are the opening pages of a research paper formatted in the APA style. The sample pages are followed by the complete References list. Note the use of **running heads** using a shortened title—not the student writer's name. Note the use of the **author-date style** both in the brief parenthetical references in the text and in the detailed References at the end. Note the use of specific page references for direct quotations.

running head
using shortened
title

James Perry

Professor Guth

English 176

21 November 2001

Child Criminals in Adult Courts--a Crime in Itself?

In August 1993, at a day camp in Savona, New York, Eric

Smith, a 13-year-old, brutally murdered a 4-year-old. Eric grabbed

the younger boy in a headlock, smashed his head three times

with a rock, stuffed a napkin and a plastic bag in his mouth, and

pummeled his body with a rock. Eric's trial began on August 1 in

Bath, New York. Despite his young age, he was tried as an adult

because of the severity of his crime and also because of a law al-

lowing children as young as thirteen to be tried as adults when

author and date
with page
number

accused of murder (Nordheimer, 1994, p. B5).

Eric's case was an early indication of frightening trends in

America--an increase in the severity of juvenile crime, and a de-

crease in the age at which children commit crimes. His trial also

heralded a continuing trend in American juvenile justice--children

are being tried in adult courts in more cases and at younger ages.

Experts, elected representatives, and the general public have

been grappling with the issue of how to deal with juvenile crime,

and treating youths as adults became a popular solution. Many is-

sues are relevant in the debate over whether to try children as

adults--how major a problem is juvenile crime; is being harsh

with juvenile criminals in the best interest of the defendants

Child Criminals 2

and in society's best interest, in terms of rehabilitating criminals, deterring and reducing crime, and justice; is treating child criminals as adults the most effective and most cost-efficient way of dealing with them; and so on.

The alternative to treating juveniles as adults is a more rehabilitative approach--some experts advocate more preventive efforts, as opposed to more punishment-oriented programs such

preview of the argument

as trying youths in adult courtrooms. In this paper, I intend to show the causes for the growing sentiment toward trying youths as adults. Then I intend to argue that while juvenile crime is a problem, it may not be the epidemic that it has been made out to be, and that although it is necessary to be firm in dealing with juvenile criminals, the best way to deal with them may not necessarily be through adult courts and strictly "getting tough." A summary of recent research available online from the American Civil Liberties Union is titled "Defusing the Myth: Prosecuting Children as Adults Doesn't Work to Decrease Crime." The authors claim that transferring children from juvenile courts to adult criminal courts does not decrease the number of repeat offenses and may in fact be counterproductive (ACLU, 2000).

In a way, the American justice system seems to be coming full circle. The nation's first juvenile court was established in 1899 in Cook County, Illinois, as a way to deal with young offenders in a more rehabilitative style, as opposed to the harsher justice found in adult courts (Andrews, 1994.) However, by the

author and date in parentheses

1960's, the public had become more concerned about juvenile

Child Criminals 3

crime, as the youth population was growing and becoming more violent. Americans began to question the principles and effectiveness of the current juvenile justice system and argued in favor of harsher, firmer alternatives. The 1966 U. S. Supreme Court case *Kent vs. United States* established guidelines for the transfer of young offenders to adult courts. The youths' threat to the safety of the public and amenability to treatments within the juvenile justice system were to be considered (Houghtalin & Mays, 1991). Since this time, more and more laws have been proposed and implemented to make it easier, and in some cases mandatory, for youths to be sent to adult courts for certain crimes, both violent and nonviolent. The public seems to want young criminals to be held responsible for their crimes and to be punished, and they believe that this can best be done in adult courts, where child criminals presumably will face harsher sentencing, often including time in adult prisons.

Measures to treat juvenile offenders as adults have been proposed and supported for several reasons. While some experts advocate and have implemented more preventive measures, these are difficult to implement and would have more of a long-term effect, leaving Americans wondering "what we are supposed to do in the meantime" (Methvin, 1994, p. 95). Bob Herbert argued that attempts to rehabilitate young offenders and treat them lightly are "well-intentioned" but "out of touch with the increasingly violent reality of juvenile crime" (1994, p. E15). Other measures had failed to reduce juvenile crime; for instance, gun control laws

quoted phrases

Child Criminals 4

were not believed to have a significant effect on violent crime by
youths, since they tend to obtain the guns through illegal means
anyway (Witkin, 1991, p. 28). Although experts disagreed as to
the extent and seriousness of current juvenile crime, the public
felt that juvenile crime is a major problem, and they supported
measures to deal with it. In the words of a Maryland assistant
public defender, the public's focus on juvenile crime created the
"political climate" that supported antijuvenile crime measures
(Stepp, 1994, p. A12).

Many officials within the justice system believed that some
young criminals should be treated as adults and tried in adult
courts. A study published in August 1994 showed that many
judges in the juvenile justice system thought that "the criminal
justice system should deal with young criminals more in the way
it deals with adults." For instance, two out of five judges sur-
veyed thought child offenders should be eligible to receive the
death penalty in some situations, and a majority felt that the minimum age for facing murder charges should be lowered ("Tougher

short title for
unsigned article

Treatment," 1994, p. A16). Former administrator of the Office of
Juvenile Justice and Delinquency Prevention Ira Schwartz found
that "juvenile court judges and youth probation workers are
among the staunchest supporters of jailing for juveniles" (1989,
p. 18).

Many legislators, and a large portion of the general public,
shared the sentiments of these justice authorities. Maryland delegate Joseph F. Vallario Jr. said that "if [youths] want to do adult-

bracketed
addition

type crimes, we're going to treat them like adults" (Stepp, 1994, p. A12). Another Maryland delegate, Ulysses Curie, wrote that because of the increasing violence and youth of juvenile offenders, "the juvenile system must be changed to respond to this reality" by treating youths more like adults (1994, p. C8).

Both Democrats and Republicans supported measures to treat young criminals more like adults; both of the Maryland delegates quoted above were Democrats, and a major part of the Republicans' "Contract with America" was the "Taking Back Our Streets Act," which supported harsher punishment of crime ("Youth and Crime," 1995, p. 18). In recent years, many states have added legislation that lowered the ages at which youths can be tried as adults for certain crimes, added new crimes to those for which a juvenile may or must be tried as an adult, implemented mandatory sentencing for children convicted of certain crimes, and so on. For instance, Louisiana added attempted murder and aggravated battery to the list of offenses for which a juvenile may be tried as an adult.

A rare dissenting opinion was registered by Supreme Court Justice Brennan in *Stanford v. Kentucky* (1992). Citing an earlier court opinion, he said:

> The reason why juveniles are not trusted with the privileges and responsibilities of an adult also explains why their irresponsible conduct is not as morally reprehensible as that of an adult. Adolescents are more vulnerable, more impulsive, and less self-disciplined than adults.

normal indent for
block quotation

Child Criminals 6

References

American Civil Liberties Union. (2000, August 11). *Defusing the myth: Prosecuting children as adults doesn't work to de-crease crime.* Retrieved September 18, 2001, from http://www.aclu.org/congress/kids.htm

Andrews, J. H. (1994, March 7). Criminals, but still children. *The Christian Science Monitor,* p. 17.

Armstrong, S. (1994, March 7). Colorado tries more carrot and less stick in punishing juvenile crime. *The Christian Science Monitor,* pp. 1, 4.

Bayh, B. (1989). Foreword. In I. M. Schwartz, *(In)justice for juveniles: Rethinking the best interests of the child* (pp. xi-xiii). Lexington: Heath-Lexington.

Curie, U. (1994, February 6). Reality requires tougher responses to juvenile crime. *The Washington Post,* p. C8.

Fiagone, C. (1995, February 13). Jacksonville's tough answer to problem of youth crimes. *The Christian Science Monitor,* pp. 1, 14.

Herbert, B. (1994, July 24). Little criminals, big crimes. *The New York Times,* late ed., p. E15.

Houghtalin, M., & Mays, G. L. (1991). Criminal dispositions of New Mexico juveniles transferred to adult court. *Crime and Delinquency 37,* 398-407.

Kotlowitz, A. (1994, February 13). Their crimes don't make them adults. *The New York Times Magazine,* pp. 40-41.

Methvin, E. H. (1994, April). Behind Florida's tourist murders. *Reader's Digest,* pp. 92-96.

(annotations: lowercase in titles; online source; date in parentheses)

Child Criminals 7

National Center for Policy Analysis. (1997, May 16). *The federal government and juvenile crime.* Retrieved September 18, 2001, from http://www.public-policy.org./~nepa/ba/ ba229.html

Nordheimer, J. (1994, August 2). Murder trial begins for teenager. *The New York Times,* late ed., p. B5.

Renner, M. (1999). Ending violent conflict. In World Watch Institute, *State of the world.* New York: W. W. Norton.

Stanford v. Kentucky, 106 U.S. 339 (1992).

Stepp, L. S. (1994, October 15). The crackdown on juvenile crime-- Do stricter laws deter youths? *The Washington Post,* pp. A1, A12.

Tougher treatment urged for juveniles. (1994, August 2). *The New York Times,* late ed., p. A16.

Witkin, G. (1991, April 8). Kids who kill. *U.S. News and World Report,* pp. 26-32.

Youth and crime [Editorial]. (1995, January 10). *The Christian Science Monitor,* p. 18.

A GLOSSARY OF TERMS

abstraction A general idea (often *very* general) that "draws us away" from the level of specific data or observations; large abstractions are concepts like justice, dignity, and freedom

ad hominem Getting personal in an argument; distracting from the merit of ideas by attacking the person, character, or private life of an opponent (Latin for "directed at the person")

allusion A brief mention that brings a whole story or set of associations to the reader's mind

analogy A close comparison, traced into several related details, often used to explain the new in terms of the familiar

analysis Explaining a complex phenomenon by identifying its major parts, stages, or causes

bandwagon Trying to sway people by claiming that the great majority is on the speaker's or writer's side (and that he or she must therefore be right)

brainstorming Freely calling up memories, data, or associations relevant to a topic, without at first editing or sorting them out

cause and effect The logical connection between actions and their consequences, making us focus on reasons and results

claim What we assert in an argument and then need to support with evidence or examples

classification The setting up of categories that help us sort out a mass of data

cliché A tired, overused expression that may have been clever or colorful at one time but has long since lost its edge

cluster A network or web of ideas centered in a key term or stimulus word, from which various strands of ideas and associations branch out

comparison Tracing connections to demonstrate similarities and contrast differences

connotation The attitudes, emotions, or associations a word carries beyond its basic factual meaning (or denotation)

context What comes before and after a word or a statement and helps give it its full meaning; the setting or situation that helps explain what something means

data Facts, observations, or statistics that provide the input for reasoning or interpretation

deduction The kind of reasoning that applies general principles to specific situations

definition Staking out the exact meaning of a possibly vague, ambiguous, or abused term

dialectic The kind of reasoning that makes ideas emerge from the play of pro and con; ideally, dialectic proceeds from thesis (statement) to antithesis (counterstatement) and from there to synthesis (a balanced conclusion)

discovery frames Sets of questions that help a writer explore a topic

doublespeak A verbal smokescreen designed to cover up unpleasant facts (such as calling an airplane crash "unscheduled contact with the ground")

draft A possibly unfinished or tentative version of a piece of writing, subject to revision

fallacy A common pattern of faulty logic, leading to wrong conclusions

figurative language Language using imaginative comparisons, such as calling someone a gadfly (metaphor) or punctual as a clock (simile)

hasty generalization Generalizing from a limited sample, such as labeling a brand of cars defective because two that you know about were defective

image Something we can vividly visualize; something that appeals vividly to our senses

763

induction The generalizing kind of reasoning that finds the connecting thread or common pattern in a set of data

inference The logical jump from facts or observations to what we interpret them to mean

innuendo A damaging hint stopping short of an outright charge that could be challenged and refuted

jargon Pretentious, overblown pseudoscientific or unnecessarily technical language

metaphor An imaginative comparison that treats one thing as if it were another, without using a signal such as *like* or *as* ("he *surfed* to the speaker's table on a *wave* of applause")

narrator In fiction, the person—real or imaginary—telling the story

paraphrase Putting a statement or passage into one's own words

peer review Feedback given to a writer by classmates or fellow writers

persona The identity assumed or the public role played by a writer in a piece of writing (the persona may be different from the writer's private personality)

post hoc fallacy Short for *post hoc ergo propter hoc,* Latin for "it happened after this; therefore it's because of this"; blaming something on a highly visible recent event rather than on true long-range causes (there was an earthquake after a nuclear test; therefore the test triggered the earthquake)

premise A basic shared assumption on which an argument is built

rationalization A creditable, reasonable-sounding explanation that clears us of blame

redundancy Unintentional duplication that makes for dense, lumpy prose: "The problem will *eventually* resolve itself *in due time*"

rhetoric The practice or the study of effective strategies for speech and writing (sometimes used negatively to mean empty or deceptive use of language)

simile An imaginative comparison signaled by such words as *like* or *as* ("the library had bare solid walls *like* a *prison*")

slanting Presenting only evidence or testimony that favors your own side

syllogism A formal deductive argument that moves from the major premise ("mammals need air to breathe") through the minor premise ("whales are mammals") to a logical conclusion ("whales need air to breathe")

thesis The central idea or unifying assertion that a paper as a whole supports; the claim a paper stakes out and defends

transition A link showing the logical connection between one sentence or paragraph and the next

valid Logically correct (but logically correct reasoning may lead to untrue conclusions if based on faulty premises)

CREDITS

Amoja Three Rivers, "Cultural Etiquette: A Guide" in *Ms.* Magazine, September/October 1991. Copyright © 1991 Ms. Used with permission.

Roger Angell, "Return of the Cliché Expert." Copyright © 1996 Roger Angell. Originally published in *The New Yorker.* All rights reserved. Reprinted by permission.

Maya Angelou, "Phenomenal Woman" from *And Still I Rise.* Copyright © 1978 by Maya Angelou. Used by permission of Random House, Inc.

Arthur Ashe, "A Black Athlete Looks at Education" from *The New York Times,* February 6, 1977. Copyright © 1977 by the New York Times Co. Reprinted by permission.

Nanette Asimov, "Fewer Teen Girls Enrolling in Technology Classes" from *San Francisco Chronicle,* October 14, 1998. Copyright © 1998 by the San Francisco Chronicle. Used with permission.

Margaret Atwood, "Dreams of the Animals" from *Selected Poems* 1965-1975 by Margaret Atwood. Copyright © 1976 by Margaret Atwood. Reprinted by permission of Houghton Mifflin Company. All rights reserved.

Toni Cade Bambara, "The Lesson" from *Gorilla, My Love.* Copyright © 1972 by Toni Cade Bambara. Used by permission of Random House, Inc.

Fred Barbash, "Beyond the Finger Pointing" from *The Washington Post,* Sunday, April 25, 1999. Copyright © 1999 The Washington Post Writers Group. Reprinted with permission.

Elizabeth Bell, "Teaching Tolerance Before Hate Takes Root," *San Francisco Chronicle,* March 13, 2001. Copyright © 2001 Elizabeth Bell. Reprinted by permission of the San Francisco Chronicle, Inc.

William J. Bennett, "Love, Marriage, and the Law." Copyright © 1996 William Bennett. Originally appeared in the *Wall Street Journal.* Used with permission.

Paul Berman, "Under the Bridge" from *A Tale of Two Utopias: The Political Journey of the Generation of 1968* by Paul Berman. Copyright © 1996 Paul Berman. Reprinted by permission of W.W. Norton, Inc.

David Bernstein, "Mixed Like Me," in *Next: Young American Writers on the New Generation,* Eric Liu, editor. Copyright © 1994 by David Bernstein. Reprinted by permission of the author and W.W. Norton & Company, Inc.

Nell Bernstein, "Learning to Love" from *Mother Jones,* 1995. Copyright © 1995 Foundation for National Progress. Used with permission.

Elizabeth Birch, "A Day to Leave the Closet" originally appeared in the *San Jose Mercury News,* September 27, 1998. Copyright © 1998 Human Rights Campaign Foundation. Reprinted by permission of Elizabeth Birch, Executive Director, Human Rights Campaign.

Amy Blackmar, "Alligator Country: The Eyes of Night" from *Going to Ground.* Copyright © 1997 Viking Penguin.

Deborah Blum, "The Monkey Wars" from *The Sacramento Bee,* 1992. Copyright © 2002 The Sacramento Bee. Used with permission.

INDEX OF AUTHORS AND TITLES